# HANNIBAL AND SCIPIO

The second Punic war between Carthage and Rome began in 218 BCE and ended in 202 with the dramatic defeat at the battle of Zama of Carthage's commander Hannibal by his adversary, the Roman Scipio. The two men were born about a decade apart but died in the same year, 183, following brilliant but ultimately unhappy careers. In this absorbing joint biography, celebrated historian Simon Hornblower reveals how the trajectory of each general illuminates his counterpart. Their individual journeys help us comprehend the momentous historical period which they shared, and which in distinct but interconnected ways they helped to shape. Hornblower interweaves his central military and political narrative with lively treatments of high politics, religious motivations and manipulations, overseas commands, hellenization, and his subjects' ancient and modern reception. This gripping portrait of an epic rivalry will delight readers of biography and military history and scholars and students of antiquity alike.

SIMON HORNBLOWER, FBA, is a former senior research fellow in Classical Studies at All Souls College, Oxford, and was previously (from 2006 to 2010) Professor of Classics and Grote Professor of Ancient History at University College London. Over the past fifty years he has written, edited, or co-edited twenty-five books, including *Commentary on Thucydides* (3 volumes, Oxford, 1991–2008), *Herodotus: Histories Book V* and *Book VI* (Cambridge, 2013 and 2017) and, most recently, *Livy: Ab urbe condita Book XXII* (Cambridge, 2020) and *Lykophron: Alexandra* (Oxford World's Classics, 2022).

'A prominent ancient historian of the Classical Greek period like Simon Hornblower does not entertain the idea of writing an intertwined history of two equally prominent figures from the Roman Republic and Ancient Carthage unless he intends to enjoy the ride. Despite the fact that Hannibal and Scipio were seen together only once, producing an intertwined narrative of their lives is wholly sensible – and no sustained attempt to do so has yet been made. The author has built his project into a magnificent piece of scholarship.'

*Toni Ñaco del Hoyo, ICREA Research Professor, University of Girona*

'The parallel lives of two of antiquity's greatest commanders, as told by one of today's greatest classicists. Assuming the role of a modern-day Plutarch, Hornblower delves into the families, formative years, military exploits, political struggles, and fraught twilight years of these colossal adversaries.'

*Michael J. Taylor, Professor of History, University of Albany*

Fresco painting of Hannibal and Scipio confronting each other, by Luigi Ademollo (1812), in the Museo Civico of Lucignano, province of Arezzo, Italy. Reproduced by permission of the Comune of Lucignano.

# HANNIBAL AND SCIPIO

*Parallel Lives*

SIMON HORNBLOWER

CAMBRIDGE
UNIVERSITY PRESS

Shaftesbury Road, Cambridge CB2 8EA, United Kingdom

One Liberty Plaza, 20th Floor, New York, NY 10006, USA

477 Williamstown Road, Port Melbourne, VIC 3207, Australia

314–321, 3rd Floor, Plot 3, Splendor Forum, Jasola District Centre, New Delhi – 110025, India

103 Penang Road, #05–06/07, Visioncrest Commercial, Singapore 238467

Cambridge University Press is part of Cambridge University Press & Assessment, a department of the University of Cambridge.

We share the University's mission to contribute to society through the pursuit of education, learning and research at the highest international levels of excellence.

www.cambridge.org
Information on this title: www.cambridge.org/9781009453356

DOI: 10.1017/9781009453318

© Simon Hornblower 2024

This publication is in copyright. Subject to statutory exception and to the provisions of relevant collective licensing agreements, no reproduction of any part may take place without the written permission of Cambridge University Press & Assessment.

When citing this work, please include a reference to the DOI 10.1017/9781009453318

First published 2024

*A catalogue record for this publication is available from the British Library.*

*A Cataloging-in-Publication data record for this book is available from the Library of Congress*

ISBN 978-1-009-45335-6 Hardback

Cambridge University Press & Assessment has no responsibility for the persistence or accuracy of URLs for external or third-party internet websites referred to in this publication and does not guarantee that any content on such websites is, or will remain, accurate or appropriate.

*To the memory of Peter Brunt*
*(23 June 1917 – 5 November 2005)*

# Contents

| | |
|---|---|
| *List of Maps* | *page* xiv |
| *Preface and Acknowledgements* | xv |
| *Notes for the Reader* | xviii |
| *Family Tree 1 Hannibal* | xix |
| *Family Tree 2 Scipio* | xx |
| *Timeline* | xxi |
| *List of Abbreviations* | xxiii |

Prologue — 1
- 0.1 Introduction — 1
- 0.2 Ancient and Renaissance Explorations of the Parallels — 3
- 0.3 Modern Explorations of the Parallels — 5
- 0.4 Alan Bullock — 6
- 0.5 Roman and Carthaginian Imperialism — 7
- 0.6 The 'Past Presumptive' Tense — 7

1 Hannibal and Scipio on Themselves — 9
- 1.1 Introduction — 9
- 1.2 Hannibal's Record: A Guess — 11
- 1.3 Scipio's Epitaph or *Elogium* — 13
- 1.4 How Much Did Hannibal's Bronze Tablet Say? — 16
- 1.5 'In Their Own Words?' The Limits of the Evidence — 20
- 1.6 What Did Hannibal and Scipio Look Like? — 24
- Appendix 1.1 Sources; Speeches — 28
- Appendix 1.2 Plutarch's Lost *Lives* of Scipio — 31
- Appendix 1.3 The 'Roving Anecdote' — 34

2 Origins: Hannibal: 247–221, Birth to Aged 26 Years, Scipio: 235–218, Birth to Aged 17 Years — 41
- 2.1 Introduction — 41
- 2.2 Names — 45
- 2.3 What Did 'Barca' Signify? — 47
- 2.4 Childhood and Early Youth: Hannibal — 50

|       | 2.5 Family, Childhood, and Early Youth: Scipio | 53 |
|---|---|---|
|       | 2.6 The 230s and 220s: Hannibal and His Carthage | 59 |
|       | 2.7 The 230s and 220s: Roman Events in Scipio's Youth | 70 |
|       | Appendix 2.1 Objections to a New Theory about the Name Barca | 72 |

## 3 Hannibal Victorious, 221–216: Aged 26–31 Years — 79
- 3.1 Hannibal as Commander in Iberia — 79
- 3.2 Saguntum and the Causes of the War with Rome — 80
- 3.3 War Declared; Hannibal Leaves for Italy — 83
- 3.4 Across the Alps and into North Italy — 85
- 3.5 The Battles at the Ticinus and Trebia, 218 — 88
- 3.6 The Battle at Lake Trasimene, 217 — 90
- 3.7 The Battle of Cannae, 216 — 96
- 3.8 After Cannae — 105
- Appendix 3.1 Hannibal Increasingly Isolated? — 107
- Appendix 3.2 How Many Maharbals? — 111

## 4 Scipio 216–205: Aged 19–30 Years — 113
- 4.1 The Aedileship — 113
- 4.2 Scipio's Father and Uncle in Iberia, 218–211 — 114
- 4.3 Young Scipio Appointed to the Iberian Command, 210 (Aged 25) — 117
- 4.4 New Carthage and Neptune, 209 — 119
- 4.5 The Battles of Baecula (208) and Ilipa (206) — 123
- 4.6 Scipio's Foundation of Italica (206): A Hadrianic Myth — 128
- 4.7 Home in 206 to the Consulship for 205, but Not Yet a Triumph — 135

## 5 Hannibal Frustrated in Italy, 216–208: Aged 31–39 — 137
- 5.1 Downs and Ups in Campania — 137
- 5.2 Hannibal's Treaty with Philip V of Macedon, 215 — 141
- 5.3 Syracuse — 145
- 5.4 Tarentum — 148
- 5.5 Capua — 149
- 5.6 Conclusion — 152

## 6 Overseas Commands: Freedoms and Perils — 155
- 6.1 Introduction — 155
- 6.2 How Much Communication with the Authorities at Home? — 155
- 6.3 Peripheral Imperialism: Decision-Making by the Man on the Spot — 158
- 6.4 A Case Study: Italian Locri, 215–204 — 163

## 7 Politics and Factions at Carthage and Rome — 172
- 7.1 Introduction: Carthage — 172
- 7.2 Rome — 173
- 7.3 The Political Aspect to the 'Trials of the Scipios' — 180

## Contents

**8 The Tipping Point: The Battle at the Metaurus or Sena, 207, Hannibal Aged 40**    182
     8.1 Introduction    182
     8.2 The Political and Religious Prelude at Rome    183
     8.3 The Campaign and Battle    186
     8.4 Reception: The Poets    193
     8.5 Conclusion    195
     Appendix 8.1 Livius Salinator: Both *Decemuir* and Consul?    196
     Appendix 8.2 The Metaurus Vow and Other Vows before or during Battles    197
     Appendix 8.3 Salinator's Triumph – or Nero's Also?    201
     Appendix 8.4 The Name of the Battle: Cicero in the *Brutus*, and Other Writers    202

**9 Hannibal and Scipio Meet and Fight at Last: Zama, 202, Aged 45 and 33**    207
     9.1 Scipio in Africa: Battle of the Great Plains    207
     9.2 Hannibal Leaves Italy    212
     9.3 Futile Diplomacy: Hannibal and Scipio Meet and Talk at Last    214
     9.4 The Battle of Zama    218
     9.5 After Zama    220

**10 The Religion of Hannibal and Scipio**    222
     10.1 Introduction: Rituals, Divination, Sacrifice, Oaths    222
     10.2 Priesthoods    230
     10.3 The Hannibalic Legend    232
     10.4 The Scipionic Legend (i): Supernatural Birth    235
     10.5 The Scipionic Legend (ii): New Carthage and Neptune    239
     10.6 Dreams and Epiphanies    240
     10.7 Conclusion    242

**11 Scipio Triumphant, 202–193: Aged 33–42**    244
     11.1 Introduction    244
     11.2 Scipio's Triumph, 201    245
     11.3 Scipio and Flamininus    248
     11.4 Censor and *Princeps Senatus*, 199    251
     11.5 Scipio's Interventions, or Lack of Them, in the 190s    253
     11.6 The Visit to the East: Did Scipio and Hannibal Meet and Talk?    259

**12 Hannibal as Political Reformer at Carthage, 196: Aged 51**    266
     12.1 Introduction: The Contrast with Scipio    266
     12.2 Hannibal as Reformer    267

**13 Hannibal, Scipio, and the Greek World**    274
     13.1 Introduction    274
     13.2 Scipio at Syracuse; Scipio and Greek Culture    275
     13.3 Hannibal at Capua; Hannibal and Greekness    279

|   |   |   |
|---|---|---|
| 13.4 | Greekness at Rome and Carthage in the Time of Hannibal and Scipio | 283 |
| 13.5 | City Foundations in Iberia: The Barcids | 291 |
| 13.6 | Conclusion | 295 |
|   | Appendix 13.1 Hannibal and 'Learning Greek *Litterae*' | 296 |

## 14  Hannibal Flees to Antiochus III; His Intrigues; 195–193: Aged 52–54 — 298

| 14.1 | Introduction | 298 |
|---|---|---|
| 14.2 | The Flight from Carthaginian Territory: How Did He Manage It? | 299 |

## 15  Hannibal and Scipio as Military Advisers in the Late 190s: The Road to Magnesia, 190: Aged 57 and 45 — 303

| 15.1 | Introduction: The Seleucids | 303 |
|---|---|---|
| 15.2 | Antiochus in the Mid-190s | 307 |
| 15.3 | The Ariston Affair | 310 |
| 15.4 | Hannibal's Childhood Oath Again | 314 |
| 15.5 | The Roman Decision for War | 316 |
| 15.6 | The War until Magnesia | 320 |
| 15.7 | Hannibal as Adviser: Conclusions | 327 |
| 15.8 | Scipio as Adviser | 328 |
| 15.9 | Conclusion: Two Advisers Compared | 334 |
| 15.10 | Magnesia | 335 |

## 16  Hannibal and Scipio: The Military Comparison — 337

| 16.1 | Introduction | 337 |
|---|---|---|
| 16.2 | First Rule: Stay Alive! | 339 |
| 16.3 | Family Inheritance | 344 |
| 16.4 | The Creation of a New Sort of Army: Hannibal? | 346 |
| 16.5 | The Creation of a New Sort of Army: Scipio | 349 |
| 16.6 | Logistics | 351 |
| 16.7 | Weaponry | 356 |
| 16.8 | Battle Tactics | 357 |
| 16.9 | Punic Deception – or Roman? | 358 |
| 16.10 | Other Sorts of Fighting | 360 |
| 16.11 | The Political Dimension: 'Hearts and Minds' | 362 |
| 16.12 | Man Management | 366 |
| 16.13 | Conclusion | 367 |

## 17  Hannibal's Years of Wandering, 190–183: Aged 57–64 — 369

| 17.1 | Introduction | 369 |
|---|---|---|
| 17.2 | First Stop Crete | 370 |
| 17.3 | Second Stop Armenia | 373 |
| 17.4 | Third Stop Bithynia | 374 |

|     |      |                                                                                |     |
| --- | ---- | ------------------------------------------------------------------------------ | --- |
|     | 17.5 | Hannibal and City Foundations in Asia Minor                                    | 377 |
|     | 17.6 | Fourth and Final Stop a Bithynian Country Estate: Hannibal's Death, 183        | 379 |
|     | 17.7 | Hannibal's Grave                                                               | 382 |
| 18  | The Downfall and Death of Scipio, 187–183: Aged 48–52                          || 384 |
|     | 18.1 | Introduction                                                                   | 384 |
|     | 18.2 | The Attacks of 187                                                             | 388 |
|     | 18.3 | The Attack on Publius Alone in 184                                             | 391 |
|     | 18.4 | A Campanian Villa: Scipio's Death, 183                                         | 392 |
| 19  | Afterlives                                                                            || 395 |
|     | 19.1 | 'Hannibal's Legacy' in Italy                                                   | 395 |
|     | 19.2 | Hannibal's Dream: The Devastation of Italy                                     | 398 |
|     | 19.3 | Manpower and the Land                                                          | 401 |
|     | 19.4 | Hannibal's Legacy at Carthage                                                  | 405 |
|     | 19.5 | Hannibal's Literary Legacy                                                     | 406 |
|     | 19.6 | Scipio's Legacy                                                                | 415 |
| 20  | Conclusion: Parallel Lives                                                            || 427 |

*References*     436
*Index*     466

# Maps

1 Iberia in the time of Hannibal and Scipio *page* 40
2 Italy and Sicily 78
3 North Africa 206
4 Greece and the east Mediterranean 272–3

*Preface and Acknowledgements*

This book is a joint scholarly biography of two of the greatest generals of the ancient world, the Carthaginian Hannibal and his eventual opponent and victor the Roman Scipio Africanus. But although they were 'generals', the scope and interest of their careers goes far beyond the purely military. And by the forbidding word 'scholarly', I mean only that it has plentiful footnotes and provides full references to ancient evidence and to modern discussions. But all Greek and Latin is translated (as are most of the quotations from works in modern foreign languages), and technical terms are defined and briefly explained at their first occurrence.[1] So I hope that it will be accessible to non-specialists. On the other hand, this is not a pair of popular biographies. There are, in several languages, many such individual biographies of both Hannibal and Scipio, which are not listed here or in the References.[2]

In summer 2022, Denis Feeney read and much improved the whole book by his perceptive comments, large and small, on an earlier and shorter draft. I am much indebted to him for this generous help. But the usual exculpatory clause applies.

Then three expert referees commissioned by Michael Sharp at Cambridge University Press saved me from much error and omission. Their very full reports drew my attention to much modern scholarship I had missed (or underestimated). I am grateful to all the referees; and also to Michael for identifying them, and persuading them to do the job so promptly; and generally for his support and encouragement throughout. I also thank Katie Idle at Cambridge University Press for cheerful and efficient work at the production stage, Liz Davey, calmly helpful content manager, and Kathleen Fearn for excellent, vigilant, and thoughtful copy-editing.

---

[1] Roman institutional terms are defined at their first appearance. Known Carthaginian terms are very few (the literary sources usually render them by what they take to be their Greek or Latin equivalents) and are explained in the course of Chapter 2.

[2] But see the end of Chapter 19, 'Afterlives'.

In autumn 2020, after John Briscoe and I published our Cambridge 'green and yellow' edition of and commentary on book 22 of Livy, Michael asked if either of us would now be interested in writing biographies of either Hannibal or Scipio. We both said no, but I countered with a suggestion of a parallel pair of biographies on the Bullock model, aimed at both non-specialist and academic readers. Michael reacted positively and encouraged me to have a go.

Chris Pelling helped me over those parts of Chapters 11 and 17 for which Plutarch's *Life* of Titus Quinctius Flamininus is important evidence: Plutarch there narrated both Scipio's alleged meeting with Hannibal at Ephesus in 193, and Hannibal's death ten years later. Chris not only read a draft of Chapter 17 but also very kindly scanned and sent me the entire original typescript English versions of his Italian introductions to and commentaries on the *Lives* of Philopoemen and Flamininus (Pelling 1997, a scarce book in this country) before I was eventually able to acquire a copy of my own from Italy.

The late Jim Adams, among many email conversations, supplied me with valuable thoughts on the meaning of *litterae* in connection with Hannibal's education in Greek, a topic discussed in Appendix 13.1 where I quote one of his emails. Stephen Colvin and Alan Griffiths helped me with the meaning and interpretation of 'those around someone', οἱ περί τινα (p. 111), and Benet Salway with the name Hannibalianus (p. 414). In connection with the Iberian place name Gracchuris, David Levene kindly supplied me with his then-forthcoming commentary on *Periocha* 41 of Livy (see now Levene 2023). Fiona McHardy generously sent me a copy of her excellent forthcoming chapter on the symbolism of battlefield mutilation and decapitation and allowed me to cite it as forthcoming. I had heard and watched, via Zoom, her lecture on the topic at Trinity College Dublin (12 May 2023), because of its relevance to the posthumous decapitation of Hasdrubal after the Metaurus battle and the consul Nero's insulting use of it (Livy 27.51.11; see p. 191). In August 2022, Lily Herd, Assistant Editor at the *TLS*, supplied me with a copy of the anonymous December 1965 review of Toynbee's *Hannibal's Legacy* and helped me to identify its author as A. H. M. Jones. Thanks to all of them.

I learned much from John Briscoe about Livy's Latin during our collaboration on our 'green and yellow' book 22, and I thank him for this. At Oxford, for many years I taught Roman history of the period covered by the present book to some very able undergraduate pupils, whom I remember with affection and gratitude. I then came back to

Livy and Hannibal circuitously, via work after 2010 on the historically minded poet Lycophron, who in my opinion shows some obliquely expressed awareness of Hannibal. Finally, Esther Eidinow helped me in various ways throughout the writing and preparation of the book, and I am deeply grateful.

For permission to use the photographs on the cover, and for providing them, I express warm thanks to the authorities, in particular Omar Nappini, at the Museo civico at Lucignano, Tuscany. For this choice of illustration, see Notes for the Reader.

# Notes for the Reader

When Carthaginian names are followed by a number, as for example 'Hanno (18)', the bracketed reference is to the numbering in Geus 1994, a prosopography of all Carthaginians down to 146 BCE attested in literary sources. But this will not be done mechanically and invariably. *Digital prosopography of the Roman Republic* (*DPRR*) numbers for Roman individuals are usually given at first mention, very occasionally more often. For priests and priesthoods, I have used the English translation of Jörg Rüpke's *Fasti sacerdotum* (Rüpke 2008), half of which consists of alphabetized biographies.

I have cited *OCD* by the fourth edition of 2012. There is a fifth and purely online edition with new or revised entries, general editor Tim Whitmarsh, but this is (slowly) ongoing and far from complete at the time of writing. Most of the entries I have looked for during the writing of this book have not yet been written, revised, or replaced since 2012.

Finally, a note about the dust jacket. I would have liked to have illustrated the book with reliable ancient portraits of both Hannibal and Scipio. This can be more or less plausibly done for Scipio, but not for Hannibal. (See p. 27.) I have therefore abandoned the search for veracity and have used instead an early nineteenth-century fresco depicting the pair, from the Italian town of Lucignano. It was drawn to my attention by Denis Feeney, who saw it *in situ* in 2023.

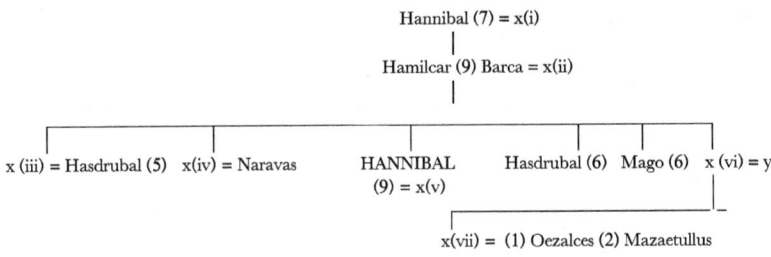

Family Tree 1: Hannibal

## Notes

1 The bracketed numbers after the named Carthaginians (all male) are those of the excellent Carthaginian prosopography of Geus 1994. For his Barcid genealogical tree see p. 267, 'Stammtafel II'. But I do not agree with all his findings, and his tree includes individuals whose existence his own text rejects (e.g. he gives Hamilcar (10) as an additional brother of HANNIBAL (9) and fourth son of Hamilcar (9), but with an asterisk to mark uncertainty; see Chapter 2 p. 50 n. 58).
2 'x' = woman whose name is unknown, y = an unknown man
3 For Hamilcar's father Hannibal (7), see Nepos, *Hamilcar* 1.1.
4 For HANNIBAL's siblings, see in detail Chapter 2 p. 50. The order of births given above is conjectural, except for that of his brothers.
5 For x (iii), see Livy 21.2.4 with p. 50 n. 61, rejecting Diod. 25.12, who says his wife was Spanish. This Hasdrubal is the non-Barcid who succeeded Hamilcar in the Spanish command. Geus 1994: 77 and 188 makes Mago (9) a son of this marriage, but this is conjectural. He was certainly a Barcid relative of HANNIBAL: Livy 23.41.2.
6 For x (iv), see Polybius 1.78.8–9.
7 For x (v), HANNIBAL's Iberian wife, see Livy 24.41.7. The tradition (Silius Italicus) that her name was Imilce, and that she had a son by HANNIBAL, is not accepted in the present book. See p. 43.
8 For x (vi), a daughter of Hamilcar (9), see Livy 29.29.12. Geus' tree (and see 1994: 77–8 and 121 n. 691) differs because of his belief (see §10) that Hanno (22) was a nephew of HANNIBAL and that this Hanno's sister married Oezalces.
9 For x (vii), granddaughter of Hamilcar (9), and daughter of x (vi) and an unknown father, see §8 and p. 50.
10 The tree at Geus 1994: 267 includes, as Hamilcar (9)'s second daughter, a wife of a Bomilcar and mother of Hannibal (11), Maharbal (3), and Hanno (22). But this is based on Appian's description of a Hanno at Cannae (*Hannibalike* 20.90, 216 BCE) as Hannibal's 'nephew', in an unreliable military context; see Chapter 3 p. 102 n. 148.

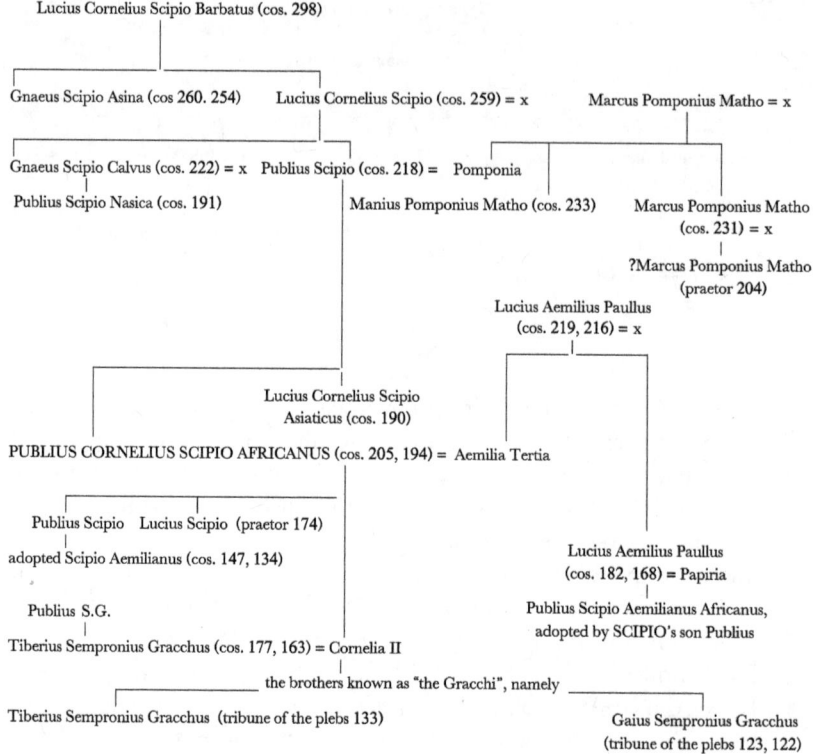

Family Tree 2 Scipio

## Notes

1. References to the *Digital prosopography of the Roman Republic* (*DPRR*) are not included here but will usually be provided at the first mention of the individual, many at the start of Chapter 2. SCIPIO, the subject of this book, is *DPRR* CORN 0878.
2. Individuals and marriage relationships not mentioned in the present book are not included.
3. 'cos.' means consul
4. 'x' means a woman whose identity is unknown; '=x' means married to an unknown woman
5. It is not certain whether Marcus Pomponius Matho the praetor of 204 was son of Manius or Marcus, hence '?'.
6. The theory that Aemilia and SCIPIO AFRICANUS had another son, Gnaeus, is highly unlikely and not accepted in this book. See p. 58 n. 113.
7. For the paternity of Cornelia's husband Ti. Sempronius Gracchus, see p. 146 n. 53.

# *Timeline*

|         | Hannibal                            | Both                            | Scipio                              |
|---------|-------------------------------------|---------------------------------|-------------------------------------|
| 264–241 |                                     | First Punic war                 |                                     |
| 247     | born                                |                                 |                                     |
| 235     |                                     |                                 | born                                |
| 233     |                                     |                                 | brother Lucius born                 |
| 229     | death of father Hamilcar            |                                 |                                     |
| 221     | takes command in Iberia             |                                 |                                     |
| 219     | captures Saguntum                   |                                 |                                     |
| 218–201 |                                     | Second Punic war                |                                     |
| 218     | crosses Alps, wins at Ticinus, Trebia |                               | saves father at Ticinus             |
| 217     | wins at Trasimene                   |                                 | marries Aemilia                     |
| 216     | wins at Cannae                      |                                 | military tribune at Cannae          |
| 215     | treaty with Philip V                |                                 | ?Salian priest (till death)         |
| 213     |                                     |                                 | curule aedile                       |
| 212     | captures Tarentum                   |                                 |                                     |
| 211     | marches on Rome                     |                                 | father and uncle killed in Iberia   |
| 210     |                                     |                                 | takes command in Iberia             |
| 209     | loses Tarentum                      |                                 | captures New Carthage               |
| 208     |                                     |                                 | wins at Baecula                     |
| 207     | brother Hasdrubal killed at Metaurus |                                | |
| 206     |                                     |                                 | wins at Ilipa                       |
| 205     |                                     |                                 | first consulship                    |
| 204     |                                     |                                 | crosses to Africa                   |
| 203     | leaves Italy for Africa             |                                 | wins at Great Plains                |
| 202     |                                     | Scipio defeats Hannibal at Zama |                                     |
| 201     |                                     |                                 | celebrates triumph at Rome          |
| 199     |                                     |                                 | censor, *princeps senatus*          |

xxi

(*cont.*)

|  | Hannibal | Both | Scipio |
| --- | --- | --- | --- |
| 197 |  | Flamininus defeats Philip V at Cynoscephalae |  |
| 196 | *sufete* at Carthage; his reforms (and earlier years?) | | |
| 195 | flees Carthage; to Antiochus III |  |  |
| 194 |  |  | second consulship |
| 193 |  | ?Hannibal and Scipio talk at Ephesus | to Carthage and East |
| 191–190 |  | Rome at war with Antiochus |  |
| 190 | defeated at sea | Lucius Scipio wins battle of Magnesia | adviser to Lucius |
| 189–183 | to Crete, Armenia, Bithynia |  |  |
| 187 |  |  | suffers first forensic attacks |
| 184 |  |  | more forensic attacks |
| 183 | dies by poison in Bithynia |  | dies at Liternum (Campania) |
|  |  | (149–146 Third Punic war) |  |

# *Abbreviations*

Ancient sources are usually abbreviated as in *OCD*⁴, except that Pol. = Polybius, Th.= Thucydides, and the titles of Cicero's works are given in full and have been translated into English; similarly, I have translated most other titles of works by other authors, so Aurelius Victor, *On famous men*, not *de uiris illustribus*. The elder Pliny's work is abbreviated as *NH* for *Natural history* (not *HN* for *Naturalis historia*).

| | |
|---|---|
| *ACGC* | C. Kraay, *Archaic and Classical Greek coinage*, London, 1976 |
| *AE* | *Année Épigraphique* |
| *Anth. Pal.* | Palatine anthology (of Greek epigrams): Loeb edition, Cambridge, MA, 5 vols. (W. R. Paton, *The Greek anthology*, 1916–18; revision by M. Tueller in progress, 2014–), or ed. H. Beckby (*Anthologia Graeca*, 2nd ed., Munich, 1967–8) |
| Austin | M. M. Austin, *The Hellenistic world from Alexander to the Roman conquest: a selection of ancient sources in translation*, 2nd ed., Cambridge, 2006 |
| *Barr.* | R. Talbert (ed.), *Barrington atlas of the Classical world*, Princeton, 2000; see also the two-volume map-by-map Directory (same date and publisher) |
| Beckby | see under *Anth. Pal.* |
| Bill. | M. Billerbeck, *Stephani Byzantii* Ethnica, 5 vols., Berlin and New York, 2008–17 |
| *BNJ* | I. Worthington (ed.), *Brill's new Jacoby*, online edition, 2006– |
| BW | T. Büttner-Wobtst, *Polybii historiae*, 5 vols., Leipzig, 1893–1905 (Teubner ed.) |
| *CA* | J. U. Powell, *Collectanea Alexandrina*, Oxford, 1925 |
| *CAH*² | *Cambridge ancient history*, 2nd ed., Cambridge The following vols. are cited: D. M. Lewis, J. Boardman, S. Hornblower, and M. Ostwald (eds.), Vol. VI, *The fourth century* BC, 1994; |

F. W. Walbank, A. E. Astin, M. W. Frederiksen, R. M. Ogilvie, and A. Drummond (eds.), Vol. VII.2, *The rise of Rome to 220 BC*, 1989; A. E. Astin, F. W. Walbank, M. W. Frederiksen, and R. M. Ogilvie (eds.), Vol. VIII, *Rome and the Mediterranean to 133 BC*, 1989; J. A. Crook, A. Lintott, and E. Rawson (eds.), Vol. IX, *The last age of the Roman Republic, 146–43 BC*, 1994

CGL      J. Diggle (ed.), *The Cambridge Greek lexicon*, Cambridge, 2021

CHGRW      P. Sabin, H. Van Wees, and M. Whitby (eds.), *The Cambridge history of Greek and Roman warfare*. Vol. 1, *Greece, the Hellenistic world, and the rise of Rome*, Cambridge, 2007

CIL      *Corpus inscriptionum Latinarum*

CIS      *Corpus inscriptionum Semiticarum*, Paris, 1881–1950

CPI      A. Bowman, C. Crowther, S. Hornblower, R. Mairs, and K. Savvopoulos (eds.), *Corpus of Ptolemaic inscriptions*, 3 vols., Oxford, 2021–

CPJ 4      N. Hacham and T. Ilan (eds.), *Corpus papyrorum Judaicarum*, vol. 4, Berlin, 2020

CT      S. Hornblower, *Commentary on Thucydides*, 3 vols., Oxford, 1991–2008

DPRR      *Digital prosopography of the Roman Republic*, based at King's College London, AHRC-funded project led by H. Mouritsen and M. Robb, 2018– (https://romanrepublic.ac.uk)

FLP      E. Courtney, *The fragmentary Latin poets*, Oxford, 1993 (with extensive addenda to 2003 paperback edition at pp. 499–536)

FGrHist      F. Jacoby, *Die Fragmente der griechischen Historiker*, 15 vols., Leiden, 1953–8

FRHist      T. Cornell and others, *The fragments of the Roman historians*, 3 vols., Oxford, 2013 (cited by non-Roman numberings throughout, '3: 123' not 'III: 123')

HCP      F. W. Walbank, *Historical commentary on Polybius*, 3 vols., Oxford, 1956, 1967, 1979

HE      A. S. F. Gow and D. L. Page, *Hellenistic epigrams*, Cambridge, 1965

$HN^2$      B. V. Head, *Historia numorum: a manual of Greek numismatics*, Oxford, 1911

| | |
|---|---|
| *HN Italy* | N. K. Rutter (principal ed.), *Historia numorum: Italy*, London, 2001 |
| *HRR* | H. Peter, *Historicorum Romanorum reliquiae*, 2 vols., Leipzig, 1870, 1906; $1^2$, Leipzig, 1914 |
| *IACP* | see References under Hansen and Nielsen 2004 |
| *IC* | M. Guarducci, *Inscriptiones Creticae*, 4 vols., Rome, 1935–50 |
| *ICO* | M. G. Amadasi Guzzo, *Le iscrizioni fenicie e puniche delle colonie in Occidente*, Studia semitica 28, Rome, 1967 |
| *IG* | *Inscriptiones graecae* |
| *ILLRP* | A. Degrassi, *Inscriptiones Latinae liberae rei publicae*, 2 vols., $1^2$ 1965, 2, 1963 (2nd ed.), Florence |
| *ILS* | H. Dessau, *Inscriptiones latinae selectae*, 3 vols., Berlin, 1892–1916 |
| *Inscr. Ital.* | *Inscriptiones Italiae* |
| *LGPN* | P. M. Fraser, E. Matthews, and others, *A lexicon of Greek personal names*, 5 vols. in 8 fascicles so far, Oxford, 1987–2018 |
| Lightfoot | J. Lightfoot, *Hellenistic collection: Philitas, Alexander of Aetolia, Hermesianax, Euphorion, Parthenius*, Loeb edition, Cambridge, MA, 2009 |
| LSJ | H. G. Liddell and R. Scott, *Greek–English Lexicon*, 9th ed., Oxford, 1940 |
| ML | R. Meiggs and D. Lewis, *Greek historical inscriptions to the end of the fifth century* BC, Oxford, 1969 |
| *MRR* | T. R. S. Broughton, *Magistrates of the Roman Republic*, 3 vols., New York (vols. 1 and 2) and Atlanta, GA (vol. 3), 1950–86 |
| *OCD*[4] | S. Hornblower, A. Spawforth, and E. Eidinow (eds.), *The Oxford Classical dictionary*, 4th ed., Oxford, 2012 |
| OCT | Oxford Classical Text |
| *OLD* | P. G. W. Clare (ed.), *Oxford Latin dictionary*, Oxford, 1982 |
| O/ R | R. Osborne and P. J. Rhodes, *Greek historical inscriptions 478–404 bc*, Oxford, 2017 |
| *PA* | J. Kirchner, *Prosopographia Attica*, 2 vols., Berlin, 1901–3 |
| Pf. | R. Pfeiffer, *Callimachus*, Oxford, 1949–51 |
| *PLRE*[1] | A. H. M. Jones, J. R. Martindale, and J. Morris, *Prosopography of the later Roman Empire*, vol. 1, Cambridge, 1971 |
| Polybios-Lexikon | A. Mauersberger, revised by C.-F. Collatz, G. Glockmann, M. Gützlaf, and H. Helms, *Polybios-Lexikon*, 3 vols. in 8 |

| | |
|---|---|
| | fascicles, Berlin, 1998–2006 (cited by non-Roman numberings throughout, '3.2: col. 1234' not 'III.2: col. 1234') |
| *R.-E.* | A. Pauly and G. Wissowa (eds.), *Real-Encylopädie der klassischen Altertumswissenschaft*, 83 vols., Stuttgart, 1894–1980 |
| R/O | P. J. Rhodes and R. Osborne, *Greek historical inscriptions 404–323 BC*, Oxford, 2003 |
| Rose | (Aristotle fragments) V. Rose, *Aristotelis fragmenta*, Leipzig, 1886 |
| Sandbach | (Plutarch fragments) See References under Sandbach 1969 |
| *SEG* | *Supplementum epigraphicum graecum*, 1923– |
| Shuckburgh | E. S. Shuckburgh, *The Histories of Polybius: Translated from the text of F. Hultsch*, 2 vols., London, 1889 |
| Sk. | See References under Skutsch 1985 |
| *Suppl. Hell.* | H. Lloyd-Jones and P. J. Parsons, *Supplementum Hellenisticum*, Berlin, 1983 |
| *SVT* | H. Bengtson, H. Schmitt, and R. M. Errington, *Die Staatsverträge des Altertums*, vols. 2–4 (there was no vol. 1), Munich, $1975^2$, 1969, 2020 |
| *Syll.*$^3$ | W. Dittenberger, *Sylloge inscriptionum graecarum*, 3rd ed. (revised by others), Leipzig, 1915–24 |
| *TLL* | *Thesaurus linguae latinae*, Leipzig–Stuttgart–Berlin, 1900– |
| Walbank and Habicht | F. W. Walbank and C. Habicht, revision of W. Paton's Loeb edition of Polybius, 6 vols., Cambridge, MA, 2010–12 |
| W/M | W. Weissenborn and H. J. Müller (eds.), *Livius ab urbe condita*, 10 vols. in various editions, Berlin, 1880–1924, and reprints |

# *Prologue*

## 0.1 Introduction

In the late first century CE, Plutarch wrote paired *Parallel lives* of Greek and Roman individuals, all of them men, except that the later chapters of his (*Mark*) *Antony* are about the life or rather death of Cleopatra. But the model for the present project is not so much Plutarch's biographies as Alan Bullock's 1,158-page late-life masterpiece *Hitler and Stalin. Parallel lives*, which treats its two subjects in alternate narrative and analytical chapters.[1] His method was chosen so as to bring out the differences between his subjects as well as the similarities.[2] I hope to do the same in this joint biography.[3] Naturally, I also hope that examination of each career will illuminate the other and will contribute to the understanding of the momentous historical period which the two men shared, and which in their distinct but interconnected ways they helped to shape. More about Bullock and his book later.

Twenty years ago, I published a mainly literary monograph comparing two fifth-century BCE Greek authors who may or may not have met each other, Thucydides and Pindar.[4] This juxtaposition raised some eyebrows, but I was not the first to offer it, because the acute ancient critic Dionysius of Halicarnassus put them side by side as the two main exponents of what he called the 'severe style'.[5] I now try to do something approximately similar for two later figures, the Carthaginian Hannibal and the Roman Scipio, but this time as a mainly historical undertaking. But that distinction between literary and historical is far too simple: the evidence for the

---

[1] Bullock 1993.   [2] Bullock 1993: xxii.
[3] This prologue includes no theoretical defence of the sometimes disparaged and patronized genre of biography. Syme 1958: 91, writing in his own person, claimed that 'biography offers the easy approach to history'. I have not found this to be so.
[4] Hornblower 2004.   [5] *On the arrangement of words*, ch. 22.

lives of Hannibal and Scipio is after all mainly literary, and some of the salient parallels between them are in effect literary devices.[6] The evidence available to Bullock was not only vastly different in quantity from the evidence about Hannibal and Scipio, but also in nature (he was able to exploit archives, documents, statistics, first-hand memoirs, and works by other modern biographers).

Nobody should be surprised at the juxtaposition of two of the greatest military commanders of any period of history, who met on the north African battlefield of Zama in 202 BCE, where Scipio effectively ended the second Punic war by defeating Hannibal, who had invaded Italy from Iberia in 218.[7] Before the battle, they met and parleyed formally, as representatives of their two powers. (This certainly historical meeting means they were unlike Hitler and Stalin, who never met, not even during the two years of the Molotov–Ribbentrop pact of 1939–41.)[8] They were close contemporaries, twelve years apart in age. Hannibal was born in 247.[9] Scipio was born in either 236 or 235.[10] Of these, 235 is here preferred, although certainty is not possible.[11] Twelve years after Zama, in 190, the Romans under one of their two consuls for the year, Scipio's brother

---

[6] For the ancient sources used in the present book, see Appendix 1.1.

[7] For the three wars between Carthage and Rome, I retain the traditional 'second Punic war' (and 'first' and 'third' ditto) for convenience, and not by way of privileging a Roman perspective. For the Carthaginians, they were presumably the 'Roman wars'. Toynbee 1965 wrote of the 'Romano-Carthaginian double war of 262–201', an accurate but clumsy locution, at which several of his reviewers rightly protested. For the dates, see Timeline.

[8] Hitler nevertheless keenly studied photographs of the meeting between the two foreign ministers, so as to satisfy himself that Stalin's ear lobes were not joined to his head, which he believed, in accordance with some crackpot genetic or physiognomic theory, would be evidence that he was Jewish: Bullock 1993: 668–9. The lobes were separate and 'Aryan'.

[9] The famous Hannibal is Geus no. (9); see Family Tree 1 n. 1 for Geus numbers. In 202, just after his defeat at Zama, Hannibal says he had left Carthage at age nine and returned after thirty-six years (Livy 30.37.9, cf. 30.35.10 and 35.19.4; in the corresponding passage at Pol. 15.19.3, he is made to say he had returned at age 'over forty-five'). So his return to Africa was in 203, aged forty-four, to Carthage itself in 202, and he was born in 247. The best discussion is at Seibert 1993a: 7 n. 2, rejecting some other ancient passages.

[10] Scipio is *DPRR* CORN0878. The most reliable indications of his age are (i) Pol. 10.3.4, he was seventeen when he saved his father at the battle of the Ticinus (10–15 October 218), which would make his birth year 236 if born after mid-October, or 235 if his eighteenth birthday was before mid-October; (ii) Pol. 10.6.10: Scipio was twenty-seven in 209 when he was about to march to New Carthage in Iberia, but this must mean 'in his twenty-seventh year' i.e. he was twenty-six, in view of (i). See also (iii) Livy 26.18.7, Scipio was 'about twenty-four' when he offered himself for the Iberian command in 211 (but this was really in 210). The fullest and best modern discussion is Sumner 1973: 35–6.

[11] A birthday in the first three-quarters of the year might seem preferable to one in the last quarter on grounds of simple statistical probability (see previous n.). But against that is the danger that the sources may have exaggerated Scipio's precocity, cf. *HCP* 2: 199: 'his age at the Ticinus can have been reduced for effect'. It is slightly easier to believe he was military tribune at Cannae (2016) at age twenty than at nineteen. But that is far from conclusive, and nineteen is here preferred.

Lucius, fought and defeated the huge army of the Seleucid king Antiochus III at Magnesia in Asia Minor. In the run-up to this campaign, Scipio and the exiled Hannibal each acted as military and political adviser to one of the opposing commanders, a further striking parallel. Even more remarkably, Antiochus benefitted from the advice not only of Hannibal in the period before Magnesia, but also of Scipio, at two private meetings with the king's emissaries on the eve of the battle. But for different reasons, neither Hannibal nor Scipio was actually present at the battle itself.

They died in the same year, 183. In the second century BCE, the Greek historian Polybius, our most important surviving source, noticed this synchronism and provided obituarial notices for both men in the year of their death, and for a third death of that year, his personal hero the Greek leader Philopoemen, on whom he had already published a separate but now lost monograph.[12] The last years of both Hannibal and Scipio were sad. Both were brought down by their domestic enemies. Hannibal, a hunted exile in Asia Minor, was forced to take poison; Scipio died in a kind of internal self-imposed exile. But the parallels are more numerous and go deeper than any of this, as I hope the chapters of this book will show.[13] In particular, both men fought far from home for many years and maintained armies without easy or frequent communication with their home authorities. These overseas commands had consequences for decision-making in their respective fatherlands.

## 0.2 Ancient and Renaissance Explorations of the Parallels

Plutarch wrote no *Life* of Hannibal or of any other 'barbarian' except the fourth-century BCE Persian king Artaxerxes II.[14] He did, however, write two *Lives* of closely related Romans called Scipio, both now lost. One of them was

---

[12] See 23.12–14 of his main historical work. These three obituaries survive only in extracts. At 9.24–6, he gave another valuable character sketch of Hannibal.

[13] For a list of parallels, large and small, see the index under 'parallels between Hannibal and Scipio'.

[14] Hannibal features importantly in his *Lives* of the Romans Fabius, Marcellus, and Flamininus, and – more unexpectedly – of Lucullus (see p. 373–4 for Hannibal in Armenia in the 180s). There are briefer allusions in other *Lives*; see Ziegler and Gärtner 1980 (the index vol. of the Teubner ed. of Plutarch's *Lives*): 31, esp. the long list of incidental mentions at the end of the Ἀννίβας entry, prefaced by 'cf.'. Plutarch would also have had much to say about Hannibal in whichever of the two lost Scipio *Lives* was devoted to Africanus; frag. 2 (a self-reference at *Pyrrhus* 8.5) shows that one of these included a famous anecdote about how Scipio talked to Hannibal at Ephesus in 193 (p. 33 n. 105). Hannibal also features occasionally in Plutarch's non-biographical collection of writings, the *Moralia*, e.g. for not being good at public speaking, δημηγορεῖν (812e), cf. Mossman 2018: 78 (and 75 for other mentions of Hannibal in Plutarch). But we will see in the present book that Hannibal is, rightly or wrongly, given some eloquent speeches in the ancient literary tradition.

free-standing (that is, it had no Greek pair), the other was in the *Parallel lives* series, paired with that of the fourth-century BCE Theban commander Epaminondas. The best scholarly opinion is divided as to whether the paired Scipio was Africanus, the Roman subject of the present book, or his grandson by adoption Scipio Aemilianus. For the problem, see Appendix 1.2. Either way, it is clear that Plutarch did write a *Life* of Africanus somewhere. The idea that Hannibal and Scipio Africanus might be paired in Plutarchan fashion is an obvious and attractive one, so the humanist Donato Acciaiuoli in 1470 took the next logical step and wrote (in Latin) such a pair of *Lives*, which were added to the multi-authored translation of the *Lives* printed by G. A. Campano. In a spirit far different from the kindly Plutarch, Niccolò Machiavelli in *The Prince* (1513) praised Hannibal for his cruelty and deplored Scipio's leniency.[15] Plutarch's paired *Lives* are of Greeks and Romans, and the inclusion of Hannibal in the series would to that extent have been an anomaly – unless, that is, we were to accept a recent theory according to which Hannibal's family took their surname Barcas from the Greek city Barke in Cyrenaica to the east of Carthage, which would make Hannibal into a sort of Greek. But this theory will be rejected later.[16] Most of Plutarch's Greek and Roman pairs are widely separated in time, but Philopoemen and Flamininus were close contemporaries, as were Scipio Africanus and Hannibal.

Polybius' three adjacent obituaries, although apparently brief, were serious and perceptive. In the second century CE, the Greek satirist Lucian again brought Hannibal and Scipio together, in his twelfth *Dialogue of the dead* (sections 380–9 in the modern referencing convention). Alexander the Great also took part in this fantasy debate, and the president was the mythical judge of the underworld, Minos. Hannibal is made to claim that he did all he did without calling himself son of the Egyptian god Ammon or narrating in details his mother's dreams (382). In other words, he was unlike Alexander – or Scipio. Hannibal is also tendentiously made by Lucian to speak of himself as an 'untutored barbarian'.

---

[15] Ziegler 1949: 316; see Mossman 2018. Acciaiuoli's Scipio is certainly Africanus. Another Renaissance scholar, Simon Goulart, wrote a Plutarchan *Epaminondas*; see Mossman 2018: 82–3. Machiavelli's comparison between Hannibal and Scipio: *The Prince* ch. 17 (= Bondanella 2005: 58–9). Cf. Lintott 1999: 237. Ancient literary insistence on Hannibal's cruelty was a cliché: see p. 408. Scipio's (relative) leniency was sometimes misplaced: see Chapter 6.4 for the Pleminius affair, which Machiavelli acutely gave as his example.

[16] On Hall 2020, see Appendix 2.1.

## 0.3 Modern Explorations of the Parallels

Andreola Rossi in 2004 published an excellent article with the title 'Parallel lives: Hannibal and Scipio in Livy's third Decade' (that is, books 21–30 of his history, in effect a monograph on the Roman war against Hannibal).[17] Professor Rossi has kindly allowed me to use what is in effect her title.[18]

Rossi, whose focus is a particular long section of Livy, is far from being the only modern author to have examined Hannibal and Scipio side by side. There are for example Meyer 1923 (essay by an outstanding ancient historian on 'Hannibal und Scipio' in a multi-authored volume on 'Meister der Politik', great politicians in history, not just ancient) and Christ 1970 (a brief contribution to a similar large-scale edited work). Fisher 2016 (*Hannibal and Scipio*), is a short, readable, popular monograph in the 'Pocket Giants' series. For his concluding assessment, see the end of my own concluding Chapter 20. Two other recent works call for more extended discussion.

Brizzi 2007a is a joint book-length treatment of Hannibal and Scipio, worth a mention because the author is a distinguished expert on Hannibal.[19] It is a confusing hybrid between scholarly work and popular novel.[20] Part 1, 'Scipio on the eve of Zama' begins 'Publius did not sleep much that night' (7); part 2 begins in exactly parallel fashion 'Hannibal did not sleep much that night'; and so on. That creates the expectation of a historical novel. And there are many other such touches of pure invention. For example, 'Publius [Scipio] saw his doctor that morning' (there is no evidence for this or for the doctor) prepares us in lively fictional fashion for his death. The author admits that he has allowed himself such liberties, *licenze*, elsewhere in the book.[21] But how is the innocent reader to tell what is invented and what is not?

---

[17] Rossi 2004. This (a ten-book unit) is a specifically Livian sense of 'Decade', so I capitalize it, to distinguish it from the word's usual sense of a ten-year period, and I do the same for 'Pentads', units of five books. See also Mineo 2009 on Livy's presentation of the parallels between Hannibal and Scipio.

[18] Livy's narrative of the second Punic war has stimulated other explorations of parallels between individuals. Strunk 2021 argues that Livy intended to suggest a parallel between Hannibal and his political opponent Hanno on the one hand, and Caesar and the Younger Cato on the other.

[19] Halfway through writing my own book, I bought a copy of Brizzi 2007a online, attracted by book title and name of author (I could find no review in any language). Until it arrived, I wondered if I had been wasting my time, and the author had already done in Italian what I had set out to do in English.

[20] The same author's 'Moi Hannibal . . .' (Brizzi 2007b) is a readable full-length 'autobiography' of its subject and is naturally a blend of fact and imagination.

[21] Brizzi 2007a: 179, 337, and 381. The invented doctor is even given a name, 'Philocles'. At 380, it is conceded that the name is imaginary, but the idea of a Greek doctor at Rome in that period is claimed to be plausible, *verosimile*. So too Hannibal's son (who on the better view is a late poetic fiction, see p. 43) is called 'Hamilcar', after his grandfather: 180, 336, an invention admitted and defended in the Note (382). Only a pertinacious reader of the main text could be expected to track down this sort of thing in the Note. There is a place for imaginative or partially imaginative

Moore 2020, a more conventional book, examines the ways in which Polybius presents Hannibal and Scipio as learning from experience: Moore concludes that in Polybius' opinion (1) they both do, but (2) in the end, the comparison is to Scipio's advantage. At one point, Moore says that his interest is not in the views of Hannibal himself but in Polybius' characterization of him.[22] In practice, he finds it understandably hard to keep these apart.[23] It is a weakness of Moore's book that he examines only Polybius' own surviving text, not the many portions of Livy which draw closely on Polybius.[24] He has nothing, for example about the final chapters of Livy book 33, the events at Carthage in 195 BCE which led to Hannibal's flight.

## 0.4 Alan Bullock

Alan Bullock (1914–2004, Lord Bullock from 1976) studied classics and ancient history as an undergraduate at Wadham College, Oxford from 1933 to 1936 – he had the good fortune to be taught Greek history by H. T. Wade-Gery and Roman by Ronald Syme – before switching to a second degree in modern history (1936–8).[25] He was awarded first-class honours in both degree courses. He was well aware that in his 1993 book he was following in the footsteps of Plutarch. But he also makes clear in the preface to that book that the more important ancient influences on him were Aristotle and Thucydides on tyranny and tyrants. His first and best-known book had been *Hitler, a study in tyranny*.[26]

I have imitated Bullock's layout by providing alternating treatments of my two 'parallel lives' (I will use that expression to denote the two human subjects of my book), covering their careers at different phases of their lives, but interspersed with thematic chapters. Like Bullock, I have given the respective ages of the two lives in the chapter titles. By coincidence, one of my lives, Hannibal, was about a decade older than the other, Scipio, just as Stalin was ten years older than Hitler. But Stalin outlived Hitler by eight years, whereas Hannibal and Scipio died in the same year, 183 BCE.

---

reconstruction in a work of history (see pp. 10, 22, and 373 for examples in the present book), but it should be flagged clearly in the text for what it is.

[22] Moore 2020: 63 n. 21

[23] On his treatment (at 41–4) of Hannibal's inscribed monument recording his own achievements, see p. 19 n. 50.

[24] Moore 2020: 58 seems to imply that we know little of Polybius' treatment of Hannibal's development after book 3 because of the fragmentary state of the text of Polybius thereafter. But this called for discussion of the extent of Livy's use of non-extant Polybius for the rest of the Hannibalic War, Livy books 23–30. Thereafter (books 31–45), heavy use of Polybius by Livy is not in doubt.

[25] For Bullock's own biography, see Dickson and Harris 2008.   [26] Bullock 1952.

## 0.5 Roman and Carthaginian Imperialism

The nature of Roman imperialism has been warmly debated in the past four decades or so (much more than Carthaginian).[27] The present book is offered as a comparative biographical study – albeit a discursive one – and not primarily intended as a contribution to the debate. But I ought to state a position. Rather than allowing it to emerge gradually during the course of the book, I do so here. I prefer the modern view that the Romans in the period covered by this book were unusually, even uniquely militaristic, aggressive, and belligerent. This is not to deny that other Hellenistic states behaved in militaristic and belligerent ways (the 'anarchy' thesis). In particular, I do not think that Carthage, where support for Hannibal in his Italian years was less than whole-hearted, was militaristic to anything like the same degree as Rome – certainly not before the middle of the third century BCE.[28] To condemn Roman imperialism is nothing new. 'The hero of the third century was the Semite who defended the liberty of his country – Hannibal.' That was Momigliano, summarizing the position of De Sanctis, in unexpected language.[29]

## 0.6 The 'Past Presumptive' Tense

Peter Thonemann had nothing to do with the writing of this book and has read no word of it. But I am grateful to him for his implied warning about what he wittily called the 'past presumptive' tense,[30] a warning conveyed in his *TLS* review (Thonemann 2018) of a book about Vercingetorix (headed in the online version 'the trouble of writing a biography based on almost

---

[27] For which see Chapter 3, Section 3.6.
[28] Erskine 2010, Smith and Yarrow 2012a, and Burton 2019 provide useful reviews of the debate. Nobody nowadays seriously regards Roman imperialism as defensive, except in the sense implied by Brunt's famous comparison of Roman reactions to the possibility of a threat as those of 'a nervous tiger, disturbed when feeding' (1990b: 307 (originally 1978)). The view to which I still subscribe is that of Harris 1979 and 1984; also briefly 2016: 42, where he approves what I said in 2007 at *CHGRW*: 30, 38–9. Gruen 1984 was mainly concerned with the east Mediterranean and argued that the Greeks themselves were responsible for inviting Roman intervention. Rich 1993 and 2001: 63 regarded both Harris 1979 and his targets as offering too monocausal an explanation. Eckstein 2006 was more theoretical and wider-ranging geographically than Eckstein 2008, which was confined to the Greek east (he was a pupil of Gruen). Eckstein, scornfully dismissed by Harris 2016: 42, argued in terms of 'anarchy', ceaseless struggle between equally belligerent powers. (Against Eckstein's 'one-sided' use of 'Realist' theory, see Tröster 2009.) Taylor 2020a likewise devotes as much attention to the military strengths of Rome's enemies as to Rome's. Burton 2011 argues that Roman decision-makers respected ideals of friendship seriously in their foreign policy.
[29] Momigliano 1994: 67. 'Condemn' is Momigliano's word, not mine.
[30] Not the same as another recent coinage, the 'plupast' of Grethlein and Krebs 2012. That term is applied when a historian refers to events which happened earlier than the historian's own narrative.

nothing'). He made fun of formulations such as 'the family of Vercingetorix would have owned', 'Vercingetorix would have come to know', and so on. I expect there are too many assertions in the past presumptive in the present book, but at least I am conscious of the danger, in a period for which the sources, although voluminous and chatty (I think especially of Livy), have frustrating limits. When on holiday in Orkney in summer 2022, I visited the excavated Neolithic village at Skara Brae, and I was impressed by the honest method explicitly adopted in the nearby museum and exhibition. In the explanatory panels, the many conjectural assertions were printed in italics (language, religion, social and political arrangements), incontrovertible facts in normal font. On that system, some of the present book would have to be printed in italics, but at least we are a lot better off than for the Neolithic period.

CHAPTER I

# *Hannibal and Scipio on Themselves*

## 1.1 Introduction

Famous modern generals and politicians write their memoirs, sometimes with help from ghostwriters; and their biographies are written by other people.[1] There are some rough ancient equivalents to military memoir-writing: the best-known surviving examples are Xenophon's lengthy and heavily autobiographical *Anabasis* (the 'march up country') and Julius Caesar's accounts of his campaigns.[2] Both men used the third person singular about themselves, and both had self-exculpatory motives for writing. Biographies existed in the ancient world.[3] The same Xenophon wrote an encomiastic sketch, with biographical elements, of his friend the Spartan king Agesilaus. Neither Scipio nor Hannibal wrote memoirs in the modern sense, or even in the limited, campaign-focussed way that Xenophon and Caesar did; and biographers did not tackle their lives until much later. So if we want a sense of how Hannibal and Scipio might have presented themselves and their careers, we must improvise and use our imaginations.

The present book begins, it may be thought, back to front, with two partly imaginary inscriptions which purport to celebrate retrospectively much of the career of Hannibal, and all the career of Scipio. Hannibal's will be based on a genuine surviving and at one time inscribed document, which does not survive complete as an inscription, but which was partially summarized by our two main surviving sources, Polybius in Greek and

---

[1] This chapter anticipates facts and discussions to be provided later in the book, and in this chapter itself; to keep the text and footnotes as uncluttered as possible, I give very few detailed forward references.
[2] There are other attested but lost examples, as we shall see later in this chapter. See Section 1.4, p. 19.
[3] Momigliano 1971 (50–1 on the *Agesilaus*).

Livy in Latin. They were primarily interested in the military statistics which it supplied.

Scipio's is an entirely imaginary creation by me, but it lists known facts in the simple succinct manner of such Roman commemorations. I hope these two items will serve as an introduction to most of the themes of the book, and to many Roman constitutional terms, and will provide a narrative outline. Both, even Scipio's, are incomplete: they cover only the successes of each man, not the unhappy years before their deaths in 183 BCE. That is because we know that Hannibal's record stopped in 205 when he inscribed it; and Scipio's fictitious contemporary epitaph can naturally be assumed to have contained nothing explicitly negative.[4] This chapter will end by asking how far our two parallel lives speak to us in their own words and will discuss the limitations of our evidence, including the difficulty of knowing what the two men looked like.

I have provided modern BCE dates in the two 'documents', for the convenience of readers. Republican Roman epitaphs did not give dates; if they had done, they would have been in the form 'in the consulships of x and y': there were two consuls a year, and they were the highest Roman 'magistracy'. The Romans went on dating in this way until Justinian in the sixth century CE.[5]

Hannibal's bilingual tablet (Punic and Greek) is much likelier to have been dated than Scipio's. The Punic half would have done so in one of two ways: either to 'the 195th [or whatever exact year] from the [creation of the] office of *sufete*', an annual eponymous Carthaginian magistracy instituted around 600 BCE; there are earlier inscribed precedents for this formula. Or he may have dated it by the *sufete* of the particular year in which he inscribed the text.[6] Not only the Romans, but many Greek cities and therefore Greek historians also dated in this way. The Greek version might – again, if it had dates at all – have used the more international 'Olympiads', the dating system by the Olympic festival in Greece, held in midsummer every four years and believed in antiquity to have begun in 776, so that 220/219 is the 'first year of the 140th Olympiad'.[7] This usefully international system was devised by the important Greek historian

---

[4] There survives a very brief genuine, but much later inscribed, *elogium* of Scipio: p. 13.
[5] Bickerman 1980: 69. 'Republican' as a dating term means the period between about 500 BCE, when the Romans got rid of their kings, until the start of the principate of Augustus, conventionally 31 BCE – that is, of the Roman Empire in the chronological sense. Rome had an empire with a small 'e' long before that, in fact from the mid-third century BCE.
[6] For the first method, see Huss 1985: 460 (cf. Hoyos 2006: 11). For the second, see Huss 1985: 473 and n. 58. For *sufetes*, see further p. 12, cf. 64.
[7] As at Pol. 3.16.7.

Timaeus, who came originally from the Sicilian city Tauromenium, but who worked in Athens in about 300 BCE and was a pioneer of Greek scholarly interest in Rome and Italy. His writings were probably known to Hannibal's Greek tutor, the historian Sosylus of Sparta.

## 1.2 Hannibal's Record: A Guess

Here is a guess at what the complete version of Hannibal's autobiographical record might have looked like:

> I, Hannibal Barca, general of the Carthaginians and son of the general Hamilcar, inscribed this record in Italy at the sanctuary of Juno Lacinia near Croton in the year 205, on an altar built and dedicated by myself. I write it in both Punic and Greek, but not in Latin, the language of the Romans.
>
> In the year 219, I captured the Roman allied city Saguntum in Iberia.[8] In the next year, I went to Gades, where I discharged my earlier vows to my protector Hercules and made new ones for the campaigning ahead. I then marched north from our Iberian capital New Carthage, and at the Ebro river I received promises of success from Jupiter.[9]
>
> Here are the numbers of my forces, so that posterity may know what careful dispositions I made for Iberia and Carthage, and with what small forces I defied the Romans for thirteen years. I sent home to Africa 13,580 infantry, 870 Balearic slingers, and 1,200 cavalry, some for the protection of Carthage, others to be distributed through Africa. I sent recruiting officers to the cities of Africa with orders for the provision of 4,000 picked men to act as a garrison and hostages at Carthage. I left Iberia in the charge of my brother Hasdrubal and gave him 11,850 African infantry, 300 Ligurians, 500 from the Balearics, 450 Libyphoenicians, about 800 Numidians and Mauri, and 300 Ilergetai from Iberia, together with 20 elephants. I also gave him a fleet of fifty quinqueremes, two quadriremes, and five triremes. Thirty-two of the quinqueremes and the five triremes were provided with equipment and crews. I left Iberia with only 90,000 infantry and 12,000 cavalry and 37 elephants.
>
> I crossed the Pyrenees and Alps, leaving my subordinate officer Hanno 10,000 infantry and 1,000 cavalry to control the region, and entered Italy.[10] My army defeated the Romans four times in two years, at Ticinus and Trebia (218), Trasimene (217), and Cannae (216). Each battle was greater than the last.

---

[8] In this book, I usually prefer 'Iberia' (which includes modern Portugal) and 'Iberian' to the modern 'Spain' and 'Spanish'. Some modern authorities use both indifferently, e.g. Taylor 2020a: 69–70. When referring to the names of the Roman province(s), I say *Hispania(e)*.

[9] These three cities are modern Sagunto, Cartagena, and Cadiz.

[10] Geus 1994: 120, 'Hanno (21)'.

Hannibal's inscription and monument were placed at the sanctuary of Juno 'Lacinia' near the south Italian town of Croton.[11] They have been seen, perhaps rightly, as belonging to a near eastern tradition of recording achievements: there are examples from Tyre, the Phoenician city which was held to have colonized Carthage.[12] But there was a Greek tradition too.

Hannibal in his Italian years was not a civil magistrate.[13] 'General' is how he would have designated himself. The highest magistracy at Carthage was that of *sufete*, of which there were two every year (or at any rate two eponymous ones); Hannibal was elected to that office after his defeat at Zama and return to Carthage. But despite its superficial resemblance to the Roman consulate, the office of *sufete* did not in this period combine military and civil roles.[14]

The Punic version of the tablet will certainly have called Juno, Greek Hera, by the name of her approximate Carthaginian equivalent Tanit.[15] At Rome, Juno was thought to have favoured the Carthaginians against the Romans until the Metaurus battle in 207: there is poetic evidence for her grand reconciliation with Rome in that year.[16] But in 215, Hannibal has evidently not lost hope of her favour. Hercules is (approximately) both Greek Herakles and Carthaginian Melqart. In tradition or myth, Hannibal had a special relationship with and imitated Hercules.[17]

As for the end, Hannibal was buried in Bithynia, where he took poison. His tomb has never been found but was alleged to have borne the simple

---

[11] Lacinia is a cult epithet of Juno, derived from the Lacinian promontory (*Barr.* map 46 F3). Jaeger 2006 studies the object and its text as part of the larger narrative theme she identifies: the recurrence of the temple of Juno Lacinia in Livy's history.

[12] Near eastern: Meister 1990: 121–2 (exchange between T. Schmitt and K. Meister regarding Meister 1990: 87); for Tyre, Schmitt cites Brizzi 1983; compare Jaeger 2006: 393 n. 10.

[13] In English public life, a magistrate is a kind of judge. But in the study of ancient Greek and Roman history, it is used in a much wider sense: a state official, appointed by election or lot, who might have military and financial as well as legal duties.

[14] See Aristotle, *Politics* 1273a29–30 and 37 (calling the *sufetes* 'kings', βασιλεῖς, and distinguishing them from the generals, στρατηγοί); Warmington 1966: 144–5; Huss 1985: 458–61 (*sufetes*), 478 (generals); Picard 1994: 375 (*sufetes* 'had no military competence' in the time of Agathocles, about 300). Much earlier, Hanno (3), author of a naval voyage along the west coast of Africa, was both general and *sufete*. Aristotle (*Politics* 1273b8) criticized the accumulation of offices at Carthage, but the fundamental civil–military distinction seems to have been maintained in Hannibal's time, and Aristotle's assertion is problematic (Saunders 1995: 165; note his p. 163 on this Aristotle passage: 'the constitutional procedures are desperately hard to fathom'). See further p. 64.

[15] Groag 1929: 11 n. 2.

[16] See p. 193 and n. 13, citing Ennius at Goldberg and Manuwald 2018a: 240–1, Book VIII t[estimonium] 2, as elucidated by Badian 1972 and Feeney 2016 and 2021.

[17] A final detail about the inscription: Hannibal's list must have said how many elephants he took with him from Iberia (he specifies how many he left with Hasdrubal); but this has dropped out. The total is given, for a slightly later stage of the journey, by Appian, *Hannibalic War* 4/13, cf. Scullard 1974a: 155. For Hannibal's elephants (mostly African, a few Indian), see p. 26.

Latin metrical inscription – a half-hexameter – 'here lies Hannibal', *Hannibal hic situs est*.[18] A curious tradition grew up about Hannibal's grave in the Severan period, third century CE. The poet Ennius wrote an epigram for Scipio, which began with the same formula:

> here he lies, to whom nobody, neither citizen nor foreigner, was able to render recompense for his efforts in proportion to his deeds.[19]

It may have continued

> from the sun rising over the marches of Maeotis (the sea of Azov), there is nobody who can become equal in deeds, *factis*.[20]

The parallel with Hannibal's epitaph is temptingly neat, but the opening funerary formula is common and need not show specific knowledge of Ennius on Scipio.[21] Ennius wrote another epitaph on Scipio, but this one purported to be spoken by Scipio himself and claimed divine status.

## 1.3 Scipio's Epitaph or *Elogium*

Livy makes Scipio's brother Lucius complain that no eulogy of Publius was spoken at the *Rostra* (the speaker's platform at Rome) after his death, but this is unreliable, part of a section in which Livy largely followed the confused account by a poor authority, Valerius Antias, of the attacks on the Scipio brothers in the 180s.[22] A real inscribed *elogium* of Scipio does exist. It is however not contemporary but dates from the time of the emperor Augustus (27 BCE–14 CE). It is only a very short fragment, the surviving words of which merely record the four magistracies he held. It runs as follows, but the words inside square brackets are restored:

---

[18] Not Hannibal's own work: his own inscription pointedly did not use Latin.
[19] Hannibal's Severan grave and Latin epitaph: p. 383. Ennius' epigram: *Hic est ille situs, cui nemo ciuis neque hostis/quiuit pro factis reddere opis pretium*: Goldberg and Manuwald 2018b: 230–1, epigrams 1a–b; combined from Cicero, *On laws* 2.57 (first four words) and Seneca the Younger, *Letters* 108.33; Scaliger was the first to combine them (brilliantly); hence the complete version of Vahlen 1928: 215 (epigram no. III), as cited by Jaeger 1997: 161. Cf. Henderson 2004: 102.
[20] *A sole exoriente supra Maeotis paludes/nemo est qui factis aequiparare queat*: Goldberg and Manuwald 2018b: 234–5, epigram 3a, from Cicero's *Tusculan disputations* 5.49 (cf. Vahlen 1928: 216, epigram no. IV). Henderson 2004, writing before Goldberg and Manuwald, follows those who take 1a–b and 3a together, but there is no certainty. Would Ennius have repeated the word *factis*?
[21] With the Ennius line, Henderson 2004 ingeniously compares *Vatia* (a personal name) *hic situs est* at Seneca (first century CE), *Letter* 55.4 and suggests that Seneca had Ennius in mind.
[22] Livy 38.54.9 with Briscoe 2008: 192.

> [Publius Cornelius, son of Publius,] Scipio Africanus; twice consul; censor; curule aedile; trib[une of the soldiers].[23]

This does not get us far. Here is my much fuller but mostly imaginary epitaph, as it might have looked when inscribed soon after Scipio's death:

> Publius Cornelius Scipio, son of Publius, grandson of Lucius, of the tribe Cornelia.[24] Consul twice (205, 194), censor (199), aedile (213), military tribune (216), Salian priest (215).[25] As a private citizen aged twenty-five, he was granted *imperium* to wage war in Iberia (210), after the deaths in battle of his father Publius and his uncle Gnaeus.[26] Such a grant was without precedent. In Iberia, he captured New Carthage with divine help (209) and defeated Carthaginian generals at Baecula (208) and Ilipa (206). In Africa, as proconsul, he defeated the Numidian chief Syphax (203) and the Carthaginian general Hannibal (202).[27] For these achievements, he was awarded a triumph and the honorary surname (cognomen) Africanus.[28]

---

[23] *Inscr. Ital.* 13.3.89: [*P(ublius) Cornelius P(ubli) f(ilius)*] / *Scipio Africanus* / *co(n)s(ul) bis censor* / *aedilis curulis* / *trib(unus) mil(itum)*. Two censors were elected at intervals of five years; their main duties were compiling the list of citizens (*census*) and revising membership of the senate. See further p. 251. Curule aediles looked after the city of Rome; military tribunes were the most senior-ranking officers in a legion. See Suolahti 1955: 57–187. They were usually expected to have at least five years of military experience (Suolahti 1955: 52; Keppie 1998: 39–40), but this cannot always have been true of those who (like nineteen-year-old Scipio himself at Cannae, p. 106) were sons of senators. The other sort of tribune was the tribune of the people: non-military but important. In the present book 'tribune' on its own means 'tribune of the people'.

[24] 'Tribes' were subdivisions of the Roman citizen body. By Scipio's time, there were thirty-five.

[25] The Salian priesthood (of Mars) imposed restrictions of movement on the holder. The date of Scipio's election is uncertain. He is first attested as Salian priest in 190 (see pp. 331 and 230 for the historical context and for the functions of the twelve Salii). But in the Augustan period, holders had to have a living father and mother (Wissowa 1912: 491 n. 9 and Rüpke 2008: 8, both citing Dion. Hal. 2.71.4). Rüpke 2008: 81 and 642 no. 1372 assumes that this rule already existed in Scipio's time, so that his election must pre-date his father's violent death in 211. He therefore dates the election to 215 but thinks even 216 possible. Such early dates would mean Scipio was Salian priest during all his years of energetic campaigning in Iberia. But we do not hear that this ever posed religious obstacles for him. That is surprising. (In any case, it was probably open to him to resign on election to the consulate for 205, so it was not a lifetime job: Rüpke 2008: 8 and – on Scipio – 642 n. 5, with slightly different emphasis.) The alternative is to deny that the rule about both living parents was in operation two centuries earlier (was it part of a pseudo-antiquarian 'revival' designed to attract the young and so rejuvenate the order?) and to date Scipio's election to some year after his return at the end of 206.

[26] *Imperium* was supreme power at Rome, especially but not only command in war.

[27] A proconsul was typically an ex-consul whose military authority, *imperium*, was extended by *prorogatio* after his year of office. For *prorogatio* (which began in 210 BCE), see Bellomo 2019: 195–202, and *OCD*⁴ *pro consule, pro praetore* (E. B[adian], A. W. L[intott]). Modern Eng. 'prorogue' (suspend, discontinue, a session of the UK parliament, as was attempted illegally in 2019) has a distinct – and virtually opposite! – meaning.

[28] 'Triumph' at ancient Rome had a specific meaning, a general's procession to the temple of Jupiter to celebrate a victory. Entitlement to a triumph was not automatic and was often fiercely contested: it had to be voted by people and senate. Mommsen 1887–8: 1.126–36 is still fundamental for the facts and conventions; see also Itgenshorst 2005 (esp. on sources); Östenberg 2009 (esp. on visual evidence); Bastien 2007; Beard 2007; Krasser, Pausch, and Petrovic 2007; and, for Livy's accounts

## Scipio's Epitaph *or* Elogium

As censor, he and his colleague appointed him chief senator, *princeps senatus*.²⁹ As legate, he accompanied his brother Lucius Cornelius Scipio in his victorious campaign against the Syrian king Antiochus at Magnesia (190).³⁰ He died at Liternum in Campania (183).

My fictitious epitaph of Scipio contains one colourful detail which is unlikely to have featured in the original (or at least cannot be paralleled from the handful of known elite epitaphs of the period): the claim that he captured New Carthage *with divine help*. But Scipio would certainly have mentioned his tenure of the Salian priesthood. This imposed certain restrictions on its holder and helps to explain why Scipio played no actual military as opposed to advisory role in the battle of Magnesia at which his brother Lucius defeated Antiochus.

As I have composed it, Scipio's epitaph does not actually name his decisive battle against Hannibal as Zama. That is because that name was not attached to it until late in the first century BCE, when it was so called by the Latin biographer Cornelius Nepos. In the same way, the almost equally decisive 'battle of the Metaurus river' in 207 owes its usual modern name to the poet Horace, who wrote his Pindaric celebration of the battle even later than Nepos. In the 40s BCE, Cicero had casually called it 'the battle at Sena', after the town Senigallia nearby (the full ancient name was Sena Gallica).³¹

Of these two texts, the first is essentially historical, but with, I will argue, legitimate additions. The second is an entirely fictitious composition by me, but the facts are as there given, and the type of epitaph conforms to the third-person style of Roman elite epitaphs of the period.³² In particular, there survive numerous contemporary epitaphs of the Scipio family from their family tomb at Rome, but not one for the great Africanus, although there was a statue to him there. He was surely buried at his Liternum villa.³³

---

of contested triumphs (but ranging more widely than that), Pittenger 2008. 'Triumph' in *OCD*⁴ (E. B[adian]) is a good concise account but cites only Beard of these recent works.

²⁹ *Princeps senatus*: this was not a magistracy but entailed various roles, duties, and privileges. See Chapter 11.4. The Roman senate, a wealthy and aristocratic body, consisted of about 300 former magistrates and was the chief authority in Roman public life; it supervised military, political, and religious business. Its prestige was at its greatest in the war against Hannibal, at least after 216, when it had catastrophically underestimated Hannibal.

³⁰ This (military adviser) was one of several distinct senses of *legatus*.

³¹ Nepos, *Hann.* 6.3; Horace, *Odes* 4.4.38; Cicero, *Brutus* 73. See Appendix 8.4.

³² The emperor Augustus adopted the first-person style for his *Res gestae* or record of achievements, written by himself in his seventies (he lived 63 BCE to 14 CE). The version probably 'represents a draft of 2 BC', but he likely worked on it from as early as 23 BCE: see Brunt and Moore 1967: 6. Cf. Cooley 2009.

³³ Livy 38.56 with Briscoe 2008: 197–8. For the tomb of the Scipios at Rome, see Coarelli 2015.

It is inconceivable that he was buried without an epitaph in one of these sites.[34] That is why I have provided him with one. Some of the surviving epitaphs of office-holding Romans of the Republican period were near-contemporary, others (like Scipio's own genuine *elogium*, already quoted) were inscribed in the time of Augustus or later but may have drawn on orally preserved family traditions. There is no fixed set of formulae: some early epitaphs are in verse, most in prose. I have drawn eclectically on the sort of text, especially the Scipionic family epitaphs, which can be found in the standard modern collections.[35]

## 1.4 How Much Did Hannibal's Bronze Tablet Say?

It is certain, from the two main historians of the period, one Greek, one Latin, that Hannibal, during what for him was the otherwise inactive summer of 205 BCE, inscribed a bilingual inscription at the temple of Juno Lacinia in south Italy.[36] The Latin historian Livy was derivative from the Greek Polybius (about 200–118 BCE). In the middle of the second century, Polybius wrote that he was proud to have read and used what he called 'a bronze tablet on which Hannibal himself had made out these lists' of his forces.[37] The Roman Livy (about 59 BCE–17 CE) drew heavily on Polybius for his Latin narrative of the Roman war against Hannibal (218–201 BCE) and of the following years. At the beginning of Hannibal's invasion of Italy, under the year 218, book 21, Livy provided – with no mention of his source, not Polybius nor an intermediary nor the inscription – almost exactly the same factual material about troop numbers as Polybius did under the same year in his book 3. Livy then described Hannibal's erection of the altar itself in book 28, in his narrative of the much later year in which the object was inscribed, that is, in summer 205; but unlike Polybius, he makes no claim to have seen it himself.[38] It is usually and rightly assumed that Livy's source in his first passage, book 21,

---

[34] Val. Max. (5.3.2b) says his tomb 'in involuntary exile', i.e. at Liternum, was inscribed 'ungrateful fatherland, you do not even have my bones', *ingrata patria, ne ossa quidem mea habes*. (Cf. De Sanctis 1969: 582 n. 277; Henderson 2004: 100.) This, the only evidence, may be spun out of Livy 38.53.8, on which see Briscoe 2008: 189, rejecting Walsh's suggestion (1993: 187) that the line might be from Ennius (*ossa . . . habes* is the first half of a hexameter).

[35] *ILS* nos. 1–17 and 43–68, or *ILLRP* 309–19 (but the latter does not include epitaphs of Republican individuals, where these were written and inscribed in later times).

[36] On the bilingualism of the tablet, see Adams 2003: 207 n. 1.

[37] Pol. 3.33.5–18 (forces which he designated for the protection of Iberia and Africa; claim to autopsy at §18); 3.56.3–6 (forces which he took to Italy).

[38] Livy 21.21.9–23.6 and 28.46.16.

was Polybius' book 3. For much of his third 'Decade' – books 21–30, the Hannibalic War narrative – Livy probably used Polybius directly rather than through a Latin intermediary such as Coelius Antipater, who wrote a monograph on the Roman war against Hannibal.[39]

There is an important and interesting divergence between Polybius book 3 and Livy's second passage, the one in book 28. Livy there calls Hannibal's monument in the temple of Juno Lacinia 'a huge tablet, written in Punic and Greek, recording his *res gestae*', his achievements.[40] This is clearly the same physical object that Polybius saw, but Livy's language ('achievements') implies a much fuller and more ambitious document than the description in Polybius book 3. Which of these two authorities is right? Normal principles of source-criticism teach us to prefer the original source to the derivative; so Polybius ought to be preferable to Livy, and a mere list of forces preferable to a record of *res gestae*. If so, perhaps Livy wanted a grand finale to his book 28 and therefore elaborated the more modest description which Polybius had given in his book 3. That is certainly possible.[41]

But it is not necessary or desirable, for several reasons. First, it is surely improbable that the bronze tablet began, with no introduction or explanation at all, 'This is a list of the forces which Hannibal left behind or took with him'. Why, on that assumption, should Hannibal have been content with anything so meagre, and what did he expect his readers to make of his intentions in writing it down?

Second, the interesting detail about the tablet's bilingualism serves no obvious literary purpose and did not feature in Polybius book 3. Livy surely did not invent it. He got it from somewhere. Why not Polybius? Perhaps through a Latin intermediary, but that would not affect the present argument.

Third, Polybius in book 3 may after all contain a tiny hint that the inscription consisted of more than a mere list. He says that he considered it

---

[39] For Livy's 'Decades', see p. 5.

[40] But Livy does not here use the actual word *monumentum*. This weakens the idea (Jaeger 2006: 391–3, approved by Levene 2010: 29 n. 68) that in his description of Hannibal's altar and tablet, Livy had in mind his own history, conceived as a sort of monument, as in his main Preface to the whole work, at §10. A better approach might be looked for in the expression *res gestae*, which occurs both in the Preface (§3) and at 28.46.16. It would also have called to mind Augustus' inscribed *Res gestae*. But Livy probably did not know of this latter inscription when he wrote his third Decade.

[41] Hornblower 2018: 72 n. 150, but also citing Tränkle 1977: 224 n. 123 for the suggestion that Livy used Coelius Antipater at 28.46.16, and that Coelius in turn drew on Polybius. I now prefer to believe (with what I take to be the implication of Tränkle's view) that a Greek equivalent of the words *res gestae* did indeed feature in Polybius, but in book 13 (see p. 18) not in his book 3. It is, however, not necessary to bring Coelius into it.

'an absolutely first-rate authority *at least as regards matters of this sort*', that is, about numbers of forces, where the qualification 'at least' can be plausibly read as implying that it contained other material also.[42] That might refer to a more personal, autobiographical record.

Finally, the argument from principles of source criticism is mistaken. Polybius' account of the war against Hannibal is complete only until the catastrophic Roman defeat at the battle of Cannae in 216; after that, we have only extracts, sometimes substantial but often not, covering the remaining fifteen years. The surviving text of Polybius' narrative of Hannibal's last years in Italy is particularly gappy. In one of the missing sections of book 13, where he covered events of 205–204, Polybius could perfectly well have given a fuller account of Hannibal's altar, and of the contents and character of the inscription, than he had done in book 3.[43] From that book 13, there survive only three very short geographical fragments, all of them about places in south Italy.[44] But that is enough to indicate that this was where Polybius covered Hannibal's operations near Croton in those two years. To be sure, he had called the inscription a list of forces under the year 218 (in book 3), because that was his narrow purpose in citing it at that moment (and in any case see my third point, on the possible implication of 'at least'). I therefore conjecture that Livy used Polybius for both 218 and 205, and that I am entitled to attempt a reconstruction of the non-statistical contents of the tablet.[45] An autobiographical element should be no surprise. But it had better not be too boastful, for reasons we must now consider.

The real surprise is that an inscription put up by a defeated and much-feared Carthaginian general should still have been on site and intact for Polybius to inspect, half a century later. How to explain this? In the years after Zama, upper-class Romans (but not Scipio himself) pursued

---

[42] Pol. 3.33.18, περί γε τῶν τοιούτων ἀξιόπιστον. Jaeger 2006: 394 acutely draws attention to the little word γε, 'at least'. It may (unless the first four words of Greek are mere verbiage) imply a reservation on Polybius' part about the credibility of what Jaeger calls the 'rest of the record'. But she does not speculate as to the nature of the 'rest'. The Loeb translation (Paton, rev. Habicht and Walbank) ignores περί γε τῶν τοιούτων entirely; Shuckburgh has 'for such facts', which is better but not enough. No comment in *HCP*.

[43] Jaeger 2006: 395 thinks Livy's placing of the inscription at the end of book 28 is deliberate artistry (my words), but rightly adds at n. 19 'This is not to rule out Polybius possibly reusing the inscription in the chronologically "correct" position' (i.e. in 205).

[44] 13.10.1–3, all from the epitome of Stephanus of Byzantium's *Ethnica*, a late but valuable work giving geographical information ascribed by name to earlier authorities, many of them now lost for the most part.

[45] A referee suggests that the 'periplus' of Hanno (3) (an account of a voyage along the coast of west Africa, see p. 12 n. 14 and p. 61) might be a good parallel for something more like a narrative.

Hannibal relentlessly until he was driven to suicide in 183, but then they began to regard him with retrospective respect.[46] This is natural enough: the greater the defeated enemy, the greater their own achievement. True; but lower down the social scale, and especially in communities which had suffered from the presence of his army, the fear and hostility are likely to have persisted. It was shrewd of Hannibal to insure the tablet against destruction by housing it in a sacred place.[47] But piety has its limits, and perhaps the choice of languages, that is, the equally shrewd avoidance of Latin, helped to save it from defacement or other vandalism at the hands of passing Roman squaddies.[48] Croton, like many of the cities of south Italy, was an ancient Greek city-foundation, although refounded as a colony by the Romans in the 190s. Greek was thus a natural choice for the area. To write in Punic, not Latin, the 'language of power', was patriotic assertion.[49]

If the reconstruction offered here is on the right lines, the tablet was, on a modest scale, a work of history.[50] Hannibal has indeed been categorized in modern reference works as a 'fragmentary Greek historian'.[51] But that inclusion is only for a letter in Greek, probably some sort of anti-Roman warning, sent to the Rhodians, and – we are told – describing the achievements, the *res gestae*, of Gnaeus Manlius Vulso, the Roman commander in Asia Minor in 189. None of the actual text of this letter survives.[52] Hannibal's inscription of his own *res gestae*, however succinct and brief, would have been at least as good a candidate for inclusion: we know of several autobiographical memoirs, most of them by military or political leaders.[53]

---

[46] Cf. Hoyos 2003: 4. For later admiration of Hannibal at Rome, see pp. 413–4.

[47] So Groag 1929: 11 n. 3. The story of Hannibal's later slaughter of Italians in the very same temple (30.20.6) should not be believed: p. 167, cf. 213.

[48] A referee compares the plastering over of the Oscan dedication to Lucius Mummius at Pompeii, probably by Sullan colonists. For Mummius, destroyer of Corinth, see *DPRR* MUMM1495, and for the inscription itself, see Taylor 2020: 53 and n. 89.

[49] For Latin as a 'language of power', see Adams 2003: 545.

[50] Moore 2020: 41–4, esp. 43 n. 25 sees Hannibal's monument as an example of attention to *akribeia*, (historiographical) 'accuracy' in a Greek tradition, on the part of Hannibal as well as of Pol. himself. Moore treats this as an early stage in Hannibal's development towards maturity. But although his prudent preparations took place at the start of the war, his act of record came at its end. So they are evidence for two distinct stages of Hannibal's personal development, as Moore 2020: 44 finally acknowledges.

[51] He is no. 181 in both *FGrHist* and *BNJ*, where see the commentary by D. Roller, who remarks that 'it is hardly unexpected that [Hannibal] would have some publications, and that they would be in Greek'. But he does not mention the tablet, still less promote it to the status of a 'fragment'.

[52] See Briscoe and Hornblower 2020: 3 n. 13; Marek 2023: 98. The source is Nepos, *Hann.* 13.2. For Vulso, see *DPRR* MANL1103.

[53] *FGrHist* nos. 227–38. See Meister 1990, stressing (89) the variety of the genre. Certainly it is a potentially capacious and extendable category. Why should Solon's self-justifying political poetry not have qualified?

There is a parallel between Hannibal and Scipio at the historiographical level: Scipio has also been categorized as a 'historian'. The evidence consists (like that for Hannibal) of just one item, and it too is a letter. It was sent to King Philip V of Macedon and is mentioned by Polybius; but it is doubtful whether the letter was a work of history, or whether Scipio was a historian.[54] As for history-writing proper, Cicero says that no product of Scipio's leisure hours was 'committed to writing', *mandata litteris*, although this may mean no more than nothing survived to his day.[55] So of our two parallel lives, Hannibal has the better claim to the title of 'Greek historian'.

Hannibal's inscribed record was an autobiography only in a partial sense: he lived for another twenty-two years after 205. Scipio's imaginary epitaph covers his complete life, with an implied closural allusion to his 'internal exile' at his country estate at Liternum in Campania, to which he haughtily withdrew after his political enemies had brought him low by the 'trials of the Scipios', for which the Latin name is 'Scipiones': the plurals there refer to the forensic attacks on both Publius Scipio and his brother Lucius. That completeness is part of the definition of epitaphs and obituaries.

## 1.5 'In Their Own Words?' The Limits of the Evidence

The biographer of modern, early modern, or even medieval and a very few ancient individuals can expect to be able to draw on the subject's own words. Speeches and writings by both Hitler and Stalin are plentiful (but unlike Hitler, Stalin was no orator) as indeed they are for Archbishop Laud in the seventeenth century, and even for Demosthenes and Cicero.[56] The biographer of Hannibal and Scipio has a much harder job. To be sure, Polybius, Livy, and the fragmentary historians and poets put many elaborate speeches into the mouths of both of our parallel lives, but these are almost without exception inventions, at the level of detail. This tradition goes back to the earliest surviving Greek historians, Herodotus and Thucydides in the fifth century BCE, and indeed before them to Homer, who did not need to worry about authenticity and makes his mythical Trojans speak perfect Greek. Polybius sometimes gives speeches which Livy does not bother to transmit, such as Hannibal's conventional speech

---

[54] No. 232 (= Pol. 10.9.3) in both *FGrHist* and *BNJ*, where see again H. Beck's commentary (notably sceptical). Meister 1990: 87 accepts Jacoby's view. By contrast, Scipio's like-named son Publius was a real historian.
[55] *On duties* 3.4.   [56] Laud: Trevor-Roper 1940 (biography).

of encouragement to his troops before Cannae.⁵⁷ Conversely, Polybius knew that there was a debate in the Roman senate after Cannae about whether to ransom their prisoners but does not mention that the ransom proposal was opposed by Titus Manlius Torquatus, to whom Livy gives a long, savage, and successful speech.⁵⁸ The most plausible candidates for authentic utterances by Hannibal are the shortest, such as his alleged piece of pithy black humour during the battle of Cannae itself. After he had heard that the consul Aemilius Paullus had ordered his cavalrymen to dismount, he remarked: 'I would have preferred him to have handed them over to me in chains.' If this was indeed said, it would presumably have been in Punic and then translated by somebody. This joke at the expense of an enemy's mistake curiously resembles a remark of Scipio in 204 BCE during the preliminary campaigning in Africa before Hannibal's departure from Italy the next year: on both occasions, the leader encourages his men by observing that the enemy's behaviour is highly convenient from his own and their points of view. The Carthaginian commander in 204 was called Hanno (28) son of Hamilcar, and he billeted his cavalry in the town of Salaeca. Scipio commented 'Cavalry under roofs in summer! May there be more of them, so long as they have a commander of that sort!' Again, this is likely to have been remembered by those who heard it.⁵⁹

But this is a meagre harvest. So the bronze tablet copied by Polybius and used by Livy has unique value as containing, at least in the section which records his military and naval forces, Hannibal's own undoubted words. Hannibal's treaty with Philip V of Macedon in 215 is preserved by Polybius and is probably 'a Greek translation produced in Hannibal's chancellery'.⁶⁰ The document as preserved must reflect Hannibal's wishes, if not his actual words as dictated in some Italian tent.⁶¹ But there must also have been input from Philip and his 'chancellery'. Otherwise there is, of alleged compositions by Hannibal, an interesting but obviously inauthentic Greek letter preserved on papyrus. It pretends to be addressed by 'Hannibal king of the Carthaginians' to the Athenians after Cannae and mentions the Wooden Horse built by Epeios, by which Troy was captured. This, it has been speculated, might be an anti-Roman production from the

---

⁵⁷ 3.111.  ⁵⁸ Pol. 6.58, Livy 22.60.5–27; *DPRR* MANL0787.
⁵⁹ Livy 22.49.3 and 29.34.7. For Paullus, see *DPRR* AEMI0826.
⁶⁰ Pol. 7.9; *HCP* 2: 42. 'Chancellery' is an imposing word for the staff of a general in camp.
⁶¹ Hoyos 2003: 213 calls it 'the nearest equivalent we can come to anything composed by Hannibal himself'. For the treaty, see Chapter 5.2.

later 180s, comparable to the verse 'Sibylline oracles' and other apocalyptic literature of the period.[62]

We have seen that Scipio's real epitaph does not survive, and even if it did, it might be only the words of his family.[63] But famous people do occasionally stipulate exactly what they want said on their graves, just as they often plan their own funerals. What is not said can be as revealing as what is. Thomas Jefferson's grave monument at Monticello does not say that he was president of the United States, but only that he was the author of the Declaration of Independence and of the statute of Virginia for religious freedom, and Father of the University of Virginia. Such silences are eloquent.[64] Jefferson's epitaph, at least, is known to reflect the exact wishes of the person commemorated. Since our epitaph for Scipio is anyway imaginary, let us go even further. We might imagine Publius on his deathbed in his rural exile, dictating to Lucius the wording of his epitaph, and refusing his brother's invitation to say anything about Rome's ingratitude in his final years except by noting the tomb's location at Liternum, not in the grand family vault at Rome. Readers of the epitaph would have taken the point.

So far so speculative. We do, however, have three Greek inscriptions which contain Scipio's own words – in Greek. The first is very short: the inventory record of a dedication at Delos, the Aegean island sacred to Apollo, of a golden laurel crown, probably in 194 BCE. The inventory says that the object bore the inscription 'Publius Cornelius Scipio to Apollo Delios'.[65] The other two are longer. One is a joint letter by Publius and his brother Lucius to the council and people of Heraclea under Latmos in Caria (south-west Asia Minor), in 190 BCE after the Roman victory over Antiochus III at Magnesia 'by Mount Sipylos', *ad Sipylum*: '[Lucius Cornelius Scipio], consul of the Romans, [and Publius Scipio his broth]er, to the council and [people] of Heraclea [greetings].' The letter goes on to claim that 'we are favourably disposed to all Greeks', and to issue a grant

---

[62] Hamburg papyrus no. 129; Seibert 1993a: 525 n. 24 and 1993b: 5–6 with n. 18; Momigliano 1975: 40–1. For Sibylline oracles and other such anti-Roman verse literature, see Hornblower 2018 ch. 5, and add *CPJ* 4 no. 614, hexameter Sibylline oracle reconstructed from newly published fragments.

[63] Ennius wrote a verse epitaph purporting to be spoken by Scipio himself from beyond the grave and claiming divine status (the surviving part ends 'to me alone the greatest gate of heaven lies open'). Goldberg and Manuwald 2018b: 235–7, epigrams 3b.

[64] It would be nice, in this connection, to cite Aeschylus' funerary epigram (*FGE* 476–9), which boasts that he fought the Persians at Marathon (490 BCE), but not that he wrote plays. But it is a pseudo-epitaph, composed centuries later than its subject.

[65] *Inscriptions de Délos* no. 442 line 102. It is disputed whether Scipio visited the island in person, but that is immaterial for the present purpose. 'Delios' means 'of Delos'.

of freedom. The attribution to the Scipios is virtually certain; in particular, the last two letters of the Greek word 'brother' can be read. The other inscribed letter is much more fragmentary, but it does contain the whole of the Greek word 'brother' and was also evidently sent by the Scipios. It was addressed to the council and people of Colophon in coastal Ionia (central western Asia Minor, north of Caria) and concerns the inviolability, *asulia*, of the nearby sanctuary of Apollo of Claros, a prestigious oracular site. The brothers confirmed this valued status.[66] It is uncertain how far the brothers actually composed the detail of these Greek letters.

In addition to these two letters preserved on stone, there are several literary mentions or summaries of letters sent by the Scipio brothers in or about 190.[67] Memnon, the historian of another Heraclea (on the Black Sea), says that the Scipio brothers each sent a letter to Memnon's home city, and he briefly gives their gist.[68] And from Polybius we learn of letters they sent simultaneously to Aemilius Regillus, commander of the Roman fleet (this one in Latin, naturally), and to King Eumenes of Pergamum updating each of them on the diplomatic and military situation; and of another, and more interesting, letter, to King Prusias of Bithynia.[69] Polybius summarizes this: the Scipios urge the wobbling Prusias to take the Roman side, on the grounds that the Romans had regularly left kings in place and even increased their dominions.[70] Two of the royal examples cited are very minor Spanish chieftains called Andobales and Colichas, of whom however Publius Scipio had first-hand experience. The letter, which exaggerates Roman generosity, almost amounts to a piece of indirect speech and should perhaps be regarded as such, that is, as fictitious at the level of detail. After all, those obscure Iberian chieftains had already featured in Polybius' own narrative and were in any case not very good examples in view of what happened to them later.[71] That is, Polybius may

---

[66] See pp. 162–3. Sherk 1969 nos. 35 (tr. Sherk 1984: no. 14, Austin no. 202, and Ma 1999: 366–7 no. 45), Heraclea under Mount Latmos; and 36 (tr. Ma 1999: 368 no. 46), Colophon; cf. also (for the *asulia*) Rigsby 1996: 352–3 no. 173 (no tr.). For the historical context of the Colophon letter, see now Jones 2019: 142–4.
[67] For Publius Scipio's letter to Philip V of Macedon, see p. 20 n. 54.
[68] *FGrHist* and 434 Memnon 18.6–9 (Heraclea in the Black Sea). Not yet in *BNJ*.
[69] Regillus (*DPRR* AEMI1175) and Eumenes: Pol. 21.8.1. Prusias: 21.11.3–12, compare Livy 37.25. For once in this period, we can compare Pol.'s original with Livy's adaptation, for which see Tränkle 1977: 105; Briscoe 1981: 327–8; Pausch 2011: 186 and n. 345.
[70] See Rawson 1991 [1975]: 174 and n. 23, part of an excellent discussion of the ambiguities of Roman attitudes to kings and kingship.
[71] Briscoe 1981: 328, n. on Livy 37.25.9, explaining why Livy's version did not list the kings. Prusias, far away in Bithynia, would not have heard of the Iberian chieftains, but Polybius' and Livy's readers would have done.

have done what Thucydides explicitly admitted to doing: he provided the Scipios with arguments rhetorically appropriate to the 'general purport' of what his researches told him was actually said. In that sense, their letter to Prusias would be as much a literary creation by the historian as was the sick Nicias' lengthy letter home to the authorities in Athens, wretchedly asking for recall from his command in Sicily in view of his painful disease of the kidneys.[72]

It may be objected, and reasonably too, that these various letters by the Scipios are official documents expressing and implementing the precise wishes and decisions of the Roman senate, so do not represent the thought and language of the Scipios themselves. But that raises the large question of policymaking on the spot, 'peripheral imperialism'.[73] In any case, detailed application of general senatorial wishes can hardly have been referred home every time from distant Asia Minor. Of the brothers, Lucius was the consul, but Publius' glittering record and far greater experience made him the dominant partner. The words are surely his.

So much for contemporary evidence for what was actually said or written by Hannibal and Scipio. Most of the remainder of this book will necessarily draw on the traditions about our two lives, as transmitted by literary authorities, most of them writing much later than the events they described. They all wrote in either Greek or Latin. No Carthaginian history written in Punic survives, if there ever was one. The position resembles the fifth- and fourth-century BCE 'Persian wars' of the Greeks against the Persians, of which no Persian written account exists.[74]

## 1.6 What Did Hannibal and Scipio Look Like?

Finally, a biography of a modern, early modern, or even medieval individual would naturally be expected to reproduce at least one photograph or painting of its subject. Regrettably, it is (in my perhaps too sceptical opinion) not possible to do this with confidence for Scipio, still less for Hannibal. We shall see that more or less speculative attempts have been made to identify coin images as their portraits, but none of these actually bear their names.

Literary sources help a little. Back in the fifth century BCE, Thucydides almost never told us what anybody looked like, except in medical contexts. But this extreme of austerity was exceptional even in his own century, and

---

[72] Th. 1.22.1 and 7.11–12.   [73] Fieldhouse 1981: 23 for the nineteenth century. See p. 158.
[74] See further Appendix 1.1.

## What Did Hannibal and Scipio Look Like?   25

by the Hellenistic period, historians were very happy to provide that sort of personal detail.[75] If Plutarch's *Scipio* had survived, we would certainly have been told something about his appearance, to judge from the opening of his *Life* of Flamininus, and many other of his *Lives*. Plutarch wrote several decades later than the elder Pliny, according to whose *Natural history* Scipio was the first Roman to shave daily, so this detail comes from some other, lost and probably Hellenistic, writer.[76] It may be related to that part of the 'Scipionic legend' which saw him as another Alexander, who differed from his father Philip II in being clean-shaven and was so represented in art. In this, he was followed by most Hellenistic rulers, but not the bearded Philip V and Perseus of Macedon, or the Seleucid kings Achaeus (a usurper, uncle of Antiochus III) and Demetrius II.[77] Scipio's absence of beard might be historical if he himself encouraged the 'legend', as is likely.

In the surviving literary sources, Scipio's personal appearance is always focalized through the effect he had on others.[78] Polybius' introductory character sketch says nothing about this.[79] His imposing and magnificent physical presence in the bloom of his youth, including his 'flowing hair', *promissa caesaries*, made a strongly favourable impression on the Numidian prince Masinissa; conversely, his adoption of Greek cloak and boots in the gymnasium at Syracuse attracted Roman soldierly disapproval.[80] We do know what he looked like – quite a spectacle – in his ceremonial, archaic, paramilitary dress as a Salian priest for the twice-yearly dance and hymn to Mars; the outfit and panoply included tall caps, robes with scarlet stripes and purple borders, and a figure-of-eight shield.[81] Otherwise, there exist what are thought to be contemporary and later portrait coins of Scipio, and a gold ring from Capua, and if the identifications are sound, these may crudely approximate to the reality.[82] One of the alleged contemporary coin

---

[75] Hornblower 2016.
[76] Pliny *NH* 7.211, cf. Scullard 1930: 36 n. 1. Pliny here calls him just 'Africanus'; this is more likely to be the subject of the present book than his adoptive grandson Aemilianus, who was also called 'Africanus'.
[77] Smith 1988: 46 and n. 2.
[78] By contrast, Livy's authorial character sketch of Scipio's consular colleague of 205, the *pontifex maximus* (head of the main priestly college) Publius Licinius Crassus, includes good looks among his admirable qualities (30.1.5, under the year 203).
[79] 10.2.
[80] Livy 28.35.5–7 and 29.19.11–12. The Syracuse episode has implications for Scipio's attitude to Greek culture: p. 275.
[81] Dion. Hal. 2.70–1; Scullard 1981: 85.
[82] Vollenweider 1974: 57–64, esp. 57 and taf[el] (i.e. fig.) 37 for the gold ring; Toynbee 1978: 18–19. It is a fine portrait of someone, now in the Naples Museum. It is signed by 'Herakleidas', and probably dates from the late third or early second century. Scullard 1970: 249–50 cites Val. Max. 3.5.1 for a ring worn by Scipio's son Lucius 'carved with the head of Africanus'. A coin of the moneyer in 112 or 111

candidates is an issue from Canusium, where Scipio rallied the survivors of the disaster at Cannae; but this theory is now authoritatively dismissed as 'unsubstantiated'.[83] A bust in Copenhagen is plausibly argued to be a portrait of Scipio, rather than of Sulla (early first century BCE), as had been thought.[84] Certainly, the men depicted on all these objects are clean-shaven.

As for Hannibal, his appearance is (even) more elusive, and we do not even know for sure if he was bearded or not. Livy's character sketch at the start of the war narrative says he wore the same clothes as his troops, but this does not get us very far and is anyway one of a series of stock attributes of the self-denying good commander; the influence of Sallust can be detected here. Only the opening three paragraphs have any claim to be about Hannibal the individual.[85]

When writing this book, I have been asked, 'was Hannibal Black?', to use modern racial categories and terminology. He was after all born in (north) Africa.[86] The answer must be no, in the absence of detailed knowledge of his ancestry. Carthage was an implant by a colonizing power. As we have seen, it was thought of as founded from Phoenician Tyre, and the colonial connection was still close enough for Hannibal to head for Tyre as his first stop in his flight eastwards in 195. Hannibal may not have looked much different from Phoenicians (Tyrians), or even from the Asia Minor Greeks who gave him refuge in his years of wandering after that. The literary sources do not suggest otherwise. We might however have an idea of what one part of his army as a whole looked like. A remarkable Etruscan coin has been thought to suggest that Hannibal used a Black mahout (whose head is depicted on the obverse) to ride and control at least one of his elephants (a definitely Indian elephant is depicted on the reverse: Hannibal did have a few Indian ones).[87] It is true that

---

Gnaeus Cornelius Blasio (*DPRR* CORN3529) is sometimes thought to recall Scipio, but the grounds are so weak that I ignore this.

[83] Vollenweider 1974: 58–9 and taf. 38.1; Toynbee 1978: 1. Unsubstantiated: *HN Italy:* 78 no. 660.
[84] Coarelli 2002, followed by Wallace-Hadrill 2008: 221–2 with photo at fig. 5.3, also Bendala Galán 2015b: 45, with photo at 44.
[85] Livy 21.4.2–10.
[86] Hannibal has in recent years been claimed as Black or part-Black; see Sailor 2002 (a reference I owe to Denis Feeney), discussing a plan to make a movie about Hannibal starring the Black actor Denzel Washington. It seems not to have got off the ground.
[87] Most of Hannibal's elephants were African, of the north African 'Forest' type, *Loxodonta cyclotis*, much smaller than the African 'Bush' elephant, *Loxodonta africana*; the Carthaginians were good at training 'Forest' elephants for battle, but because of their small size it was not possible to fit them with towers, at least on the battlefield: see Charles 2008. Hannibal had, however, some Indian ones, and these were the best he had; they were acquired from Hellenistic kings. Cf. p. 87 for the Indian elephant called Surus. For Hannibal's elephants generally, see Scullard 1974a: 146–77.

## What Did Hannibal and Scipio Look Like?      27

Hannibal's army was generally more linguistically and ethnically diverse than that of Scipio or any other Roman commander of the time. But there are other possible contexts for the coin, such as the invasion of Pyrrhus, or the exploits of the family of the Metelli in the first Punic war.[88] The coin remains mysterious, the human head more so than the elephant, and any connection with Hannibal is speculative.

There is a splendid, famous, and often reproduced bust in the Naples Museum.[89] But it is a Renaissance work of no evidential value.[90] Portrait coins from Iberian mints (especially New Carthage) were at one time believed to depict Hannibal, Hamilcar, and Hasdrubal in the guise of the god Melqart/Herakles. (Those claimed for Hannibal are clean-shaven.)[91] But here are two expert and opposite views. The first is from 1956: 'the heads, with their strongly marked features and close-curling hair, show so much of the African Semite that one may suspect the engraver of having individual models in mind'. That is, these are claimed as portraits of Barcid family members. The second is from 2021, after quoting the first: 'this type of racialized reading of antiquity here and elsewhere must be acknowledged as such and rejected'.[92] I agree with the second quotation and conclude that the attempt to detect Hannibal's features on any of these coins must be abandoned.

Livy's main but meagre description of Hannibal's appearance is, like Scipio's, focalized through contemporary observers: he was thought to have inherited his father Hamilcar's vigorous eyes and energetic facial expression.[93] He had only one of those eyes after 218, as a result of ophthalmia incurred during his crossing of the Alps. He therefore belongs to an intriguing and surprisingly large category of 'one-eyed men against Rome'.[94] We also hear that he wore different-coloured wigs and changes of clothes as a precaution against assassins.[95] In the first century CE, there

---

[88] Snowden 1970: 130–1 and the Italian coins illustrated at 70–1 plate 41; Scullard 1974a: 172–3 and plate XXII b; Baglione 1976 plate XXVII no. 1; *HN Italy*: 26 no. 69, photo at plate 2. For the various possibilities, see Harris 1971: 140 and esp. Baglione 1976: 156–67. *HN Italy* merely refers to Baglione. Hannibal's diverse army: Pol. 1.67 and Livy 30.33.8.
[89] See e.g. Hoyos 2003 plate 1 and the dust-jackets of Barceló 2004 in the 2012 reprinting (also at p. 176) and Brizzi 2011a.
[90] Seibert 1993b: 43. It is bearded. Hoyos' caption says 'identification not certain' (an understatement), but he uses it all the same.
[91] Seibert 1993b: 42–3, 'Porträts', but without discussing the beard problem.
[92] Robinson 1956: 39, a very influential passage; Yarrow 2021: 119, caption to fig. 3.6.
[93] Livy 21.4.2.   [94] Africa 1970; see further p. 87 and n, 56 for the 'one-eyed' theme.
[95] Pol. 3.78.1–4 (217 BCE), cf. Livy 22.1.3 with Briscoe and Hornblower 2020: 144. These wigs were thought of as an example of 'Punic deceit'. Pol. adds that he changed his clothes frequently for the same reason. For 'Wagner' chief Prigozhin's wigs, see p. 91 n. 79.

were still three statues of Hannibal on display at Rome: like Cleopatra, he continued to fascinate the Romans. But no actual descriptions of these survive.[96]

Parallel lines never meet, by definition. But parallel lives can surely be allowed to do so. Hannibal and Scipio each knew what the other looked like, because they met in person at least once, first before Zama, and perhaps again at Ephesus in 193.[97] In addition, the young Scipio as military tribune could just conceivably have glimpsed Hannibal in the distance on the battlefield of Cannae, and again in 211, when Hannibal rode right up to the walls of Rome and allegedly threw his spear over them.[98]

## Appendix 1.1  Sources; Speeches

I have not provided a separate chapter on the sources, which are mostly literary. What follows is a very brief sketch.[99] The first point to be made, and made emphatically, is that in terms of literary source material there is no parallel between Hannibal and Scipio, in that no written Carthaginian history of the period survives, if there ever was one, and no historically minded contemporary Carthaginian poetry like that of Ennius in Latin or Lycophron in Greek (the latter's date is however disputed).[100] The literary sources for the lives and actions of both our parallel lives are all in either Greek or Latin. Some indirect input from the Carthaginian side in the surviving histories was provided by members of Hannibal's entourage, notably his friend and teacher Sosylus of Sparta and Silenus of Caleacte. Both these wrote in Greek.[101]

Before turning to the literary sources in detail, I address other types of evidence. For Greek inscriptions, where English translations are available, I have for preference cited according to these: see Abbreviations or References under Austin, O/R, R/O, and Sherk 1984. For collections of untranslated Greek inscriptions, see again Abbreviations, especially *IC, IG,*

---

[96] Pliny *NH* 34.32; Smith 1988: 78. Cleopatra comparison: see pp. 414, 434.   [97] See pp. 261–5.
[98] The confrontation at Cannae between Hannibal and young Scipio in Silius Italicus (9.412–13) is poetic fiction. The spear-throw: Plin. *NH* 34.32 with p. 150.
[99] For more detail, especially about the sources for the war between Hannibal and the Romans, the second Punic war, see Briscoe and Hornblower 2020: 8–13.
[100] Huss 1985: 505 said that historiography was at home in Carthage, but the evidence he cited was very meagre: mostly fragmentary or lost.
[101] See Briscoe and Hornblower 2020: 10 (Silenus used by Coelius). Sosylus and Silenus are *FGrHist* and *BNJ* nos. 176 and 175. For other, very fragmentary or nameless, Greek writers about Hannibal, see *FGrHist* 178 (Eumachus of Naples), 179 (Xenophon, not the famous one), and 180 (generalizing references by Pol.); cf. *HCP* 1: 42, n. on Pol. 1.3.2, and 2: 39, n. on 7.7.1. It is a pity so little is known about the Neapolitan Eumachus, given Hannibal's important failure at Naples (p. 139).

*SEG*, and *Syll.*³ (vol. IV of *SVT* has German translations); *CIL*, *ILS*, and *ILLRP* for Latin; *CIS* (with Latin translations); also *ICO* (with Italian translations) for Punic inscriptions from Malta, Sicily, Sardinia, and Spain, including Ibiza. Punic inscriptions from Carthage have been exploited by economic and religious historians, but no narrative or biography can be constructed out of them.[102] I claim no specialist expertise in archaeology or numismatics but have drawn gratefully on much recent work.[103] The first volume (2001) of a new edition of *Historia numorum* (ed. 2, 1911), the standard edition of the coins of the entire Greek world, covers the Greek coins of Italy only, but it includes issues from cities and areas under Carthaginian control during Hannibal's occupation of the south.[104]

The main (partly) surviving literary sources are Polybius and Livy.[105] Polybius was a near-contemporary of some of the events described in the present book; he talked to prominent Romans and visited sites himself. For the antecedents and early stages of the war, he drew, not mindlessly, on an important history by Quintus Fabius Pictor, written in Greek; but this work probably did not go much if at all beyond Trasimene in 217.[106] Livy used Polybius heavily but supplemented him with material from other, mainly Latin, writers, and from his own invention.[107] Neither author survives anything like complete, although we have plenty of both: the

---

[102] For exploitation of Punic inscriptions by Pilkington 2019, see p. 209 n. 79. He helpfully provides his own English translations for all those he quotes.

[103] For Iberian archaeology, see esp. Bendala Galán 2015a (edited collection); for the Hellenistic West, esp. Sicily and north Africa, Prag and Quinn 2013 (edited collection); for the Punic and Phoenician Mediterranean generally, López-Ruiz and Doak 2019 (edited handbook), and add, for Carthage, Pilkington 2019. In this book, Italian archaeology is cited most often in Chapter 19, sections 1–3, discussing Hannibal's legacy in Italy.

[104] *HN Italy*: see esp. 161–3 nos. 2013–32, 'Carthaginians in south west Italy'. The old edition: *HN*². On how to use the evidence of coins, see esp. Yarrow 2013 and 2021.

[105] See p. 16. There are multi-volume Loeb editions (Greek or Latin and facing English translation) of Polybius and Livy. The old Polybius Loebs have all been revised recently: see Abbreviations under Walbank and Habicht. The Livy volumes are in process of revision. For Walbank's commentary on Polybius, see Abbreviations under *HCP*. For large-scale modern commentaries on Livy, see References under Ogilvie, Oakley, and Briscoe, but such commentaries on books 21–30 are still lacking in English; but see Feraco 2017 (book 27) and Beltramini 2020 (book 26), in Italian. For book 22 (Trasimene and Cannae narrative), see Briscoe and Hornblower 2020.

[106] *FRHist* no. 1. Briscoe and Hornblower 2020: 10, 13, and 14 n. 21.

[107] For the 'fragments' (quotations in later writers) of these, and commentaries on them, see *FRHist*. This translates all ancient material, including testimonia (ancient information about rather than by those historians), but regrettably provides no commentary on the testimonia. The fragments of the Greek historians were collected and commented on by Jacoby in *FGrHist*. For translations and new commentaries, see *BNJ* (online). It retains Jacoby's numbering of historians, 'testimonia', and fragments. Most of the Latin historians with whom we are concerned used a year-by-year arrangement, and so are called 'annalists'. But 'annalistic' is also often used by extension among modern scholars as a term of disparagement of writers of this sort who are thought to be mendacious.

untranslated Greek text of Polybius fills four modern volumes, the Latin of Livy fills six.

Plutarch's *Lives* and voluminous other works are discussed elsewhere.[108] One brief but valuable ancient biography of Hannibal survives, the generally admiring Latin *Life* by Cornelius Nepos (about 110–24 BCE).[109] Several works by the Greek Appian of Egyptian Alexandria (second century CE) give useful additional material; Polybius was his main source for the period covered by the present book.[110] The Greek writer Polyaenus, also in the second century CE, recorded ten stratagems in his main chapter on Hannibal, not all of which are attested elsewhere.[111] In Latin, Sextus Julius Frontinus' collection of stratagems (late first century CE) is also valuable.[112] Valerius Maximus, writing in Latin in the time of the emperor Tiberius (14–37 CE), preserved a number of anecdotes which illustrate both the good and bad qualities of individuals unsystematically.[113] The learned Latin miscellanist Aulus Gellius (second century CE) will be drawn on frequently.[114] Diodorus Siculus ('of Sicily') has valuable material in book 25 about the Carthaginians in Iberia, and his books 11–21 are the main source for the wars between Carthage and the rulers of Greek Sicily. Other writers will be cited from time to time, above all the priceless Latin military handbook 'epitome of military matters', *Epitoma rei militaris*, by the late military writer Vegetius in about 400 CE; and Justin's epitome of Trogus.[115] I refer to the author of *On famous men* as (Sextus) Aurelius Victor, although it is not thought to be a genuine work of his. It too is in Latin.

The Latin poet Ennius, a contemporary and admirer of Scipio, will often be cited in this book, but his works survive only in fragments.[116]

---

[108] See p. 3 n. 14 and Appendix 1.3. There are Loeb and Teubner editions of all Plutarch's writings.

[109] Text: Marshall 1977 (Teubner ed.; no Loeb). On Nepos, Stocks 2014: 25–7; Lobur 2021; Ginelli 2021: 1–54 (general introduction).

[110] The Loeb Appian has been valuably revised by B. McGing. What McGing calls the *African book* is in the present work called the *Libyan history*, abbrev. *Lib*. Some modern scholars refer to it as the *Punic history* (abbrev. *Pun*.). Other relevant books of Appian are the *Hannibalic (Hann.)*, *Iberian*, and *Syrian* (Seleucid) *histories*.

[111] 6.38. There is another at 7.48. Krentz and Wheeler 1994 provide a reprinted Greek text and their own facing translation, on a kind of Loeb model.

[112] Loeb edition: Bennett and McElwain 1925.

[113] Teubner ed. (no Loeb): Kempf 1888. See Stocks 2014: 29–32, Briscoe 2019: 1–14.

[114] See Holford-Strevens 2003. Loeb ed.: J. C. Rolfe (1924); OCT: P. K. Marshall (1990).

[115] Full name Flavius Publius Vegetius Renatus. See Milner 1996: translation, with introduction and notes; no Latin text, for which see Reeve 2004 (OCT). Vegetius drew on a variety of earlier Latin writers. Justin: Seel 1972 (Teubner Latin text); Yardley 2003. See further p. 170 n. 77.

[116] See now Goldberg and Manuwald 2018a and 2018b (Loeb editions); for Ennius' historical poem the *Annals*, they build on Skutsch 1985. For the poet Lycophron, whose date is disputed but who may also have been a contemporary of Hannibal and Scipio, see most recently Hornblower 2022 (tr. and commentary).

From the first century CE, Silius Italicus' *Punica* is a seventeen-book Latin verse epic about Hannibal's war against Rome. It is a special case, a problematic mix of history and fantasy.[117]

Four maps are here provided.[118] Map references in footnotes are to the *Barrington Atlas* (*Barr.*). Such references presuppose the detailed map-by-map references to the ancient evidence, and modern arguments for identifications, which are provided in the *Barrington map-by-map Directory*, to which reference will not be routinely made.

\*\*\*

Finally, speeches in literary sources will often be cited or quoted, and this needs justification, given that ancient prose historians often invented speeches, as Homer had done.[119] Some speeches are 'indirect' ('x said that . . . ', followed by a report), some are 'direct' (conventionally enclosed in quotation marks in modern European languages). Indirect speech is as much speech as direct but can be used to feed in authorial comment.[120] Polybius did not go in for large-scale invention, except in pre-battle harangues. Where Livy's speeches can be compared with their Polybian originals, he can be shown to have often amplified and embellished. In particular, he includes many *exempla*, historical examples; these are likely to be additions. Some of Livy's speeches are attempts at characterization and allow a viewpoint other than that of the authorial voice; they may even conflict outright with the narrative. Both Polybius and Livy use speeches to illustrate policy.

## Appendix 1.2  Plutarch's Lost *Lives* of Scipio

Plutarch wrote two now lost *Lives* of Romans called Scipio Africanus.[121] One of them was free-standing (no pair), the other paired with that of the fourth-century BCE Greek (Theban) commander Epaminondas, also lost.[122]

---

[117] Loeb ed.: Duff 1934. See Stocks 2014; cf. also Marks 2005 and 2008, Augoustakis and Fucecchi 2022.

[118] They are based on the following maps in *CAH* VIII (new ed.): 1 and 4 (Iberia, except that Baecula has been moved to reflect recent discoveries, see p. 123), 2 (Italy and Sicily), 9 (north Africa), 11 (Greece and the east Mediterranean).

[119] On speeches in Livy and Polybius, see Briscoe and Hornblower 2020: 50–6, the essential points of which are here summarized. See also Pausch 2011: 157–89.

[120] On indirect speech, see Laird 1999: 144–8; *CT*: 33 (for Hdt. and Th.); Briscoe and Hornblower 2020: 50 n. 128 and 273, n. on Livy 22.40.1–3.

[121] I thank Chris Pelling for valuable email exchanges about the subject-matter of this appendix, but he has not read it and should not be held responsible for anything said.

[122] Other free-standing examples are the surviving lives of Artaxerxes, Aratus, Galba, and Otho, and the lost lives of e.g. Pindar, Augustus, and Tiberius.

We owe this information to a list of Plutarch's works, known (incorrectly) as the 'Lamprias catalogue' because his son Lamprias was said to have compiled such a list.[123] But both Scipio Africanus and his adoptive grandson Aemilianus (the eventual destroyer of African Carthage in 146 BCE) were entitled to call themselves 'Africanus' and were so called in antiquity; we use the different names for convenience, to keep them apart, and that will be done in this appendix.

It is inconceivable that Plutarch wrote two biographies of Aemilianus but not one of Africanus, Rome's greatest general ever. It follows that he did somewhere in his oeuvre write a biography of Africanus, so the matter could perhaps be left there for present purposes. But the possibility of a pairing between Africanus and Epaminondas is of interest for how Scipio was viewed, and the possibility will be alluded to sometimes in the present book. The problem has been much discussed, but there is no consensus.[124]

Even if the Lamprias catalogue did not exist, we would know that Plutarch wrote a biography of at least one of the two Scipios we are interested in. There are three 'fragments' embedded in Plutarch's other *Lives*; that is, passages where he cross-refers to what he said in those lost biographies of a Scipio or more than one. One is clearly about Africanus, the other two about Aemilianus.[125] But that does not solve the problem, 'where did the references come from?', because Plutarch could have talked about Africanus in a *Life* of Aemilianus and vice versa. Nor should we forget the free-standing *Life*, which Plutarch could have referred to vaguely and without making that clear.

Here are the arguments for assigning the paired Scipio *Life* to Africanus. (The slightly differing formulae used in the three Plutarch fragments, to denote either the biography in question or the individual written about, have also sometimes been used to try

---

[123] For text, translation, and discussion, see Sandbach 1969: 3–29. See also Ziegler 1949: cols. 60–6.
[124] Here is a selection of modern views. In favour of Africanus: Sandbach 1969: 74 (citing earlier work); Russell 1972: 113 n. 26; Ziegler 1949: 258; Georgiadou 1997: 6–8. Of Aemilianus: Pelling 2002: 373.
[125] No. 2 Sandbach is the story that Scipio (Africanus) met Hannibal at Ephesus in 193; see Chapter 11.6. (The story is also recounted in the *Flamininus*, but without a cross-reference.) The cross-reference is at *Pyrrhus* 8.5, ὡς ἐν τοῖς περὶ Σκιπίωνος γέγραπται, literally 'as has been written in the work about Scipio' or 'as in what has been written about Scipio'. Almost exactly the same formula is used at *Gaius Gracchus* 10.5 (frag. 4 Sandbach): after naming 'Scipio Africanus' (i.e. Aemilianus) in full, he says ὡς ἐν τοῖς περὶ Σκιπίωνος γέγραπται, 'as has been written in the work about him', or 'as in what has been written about him'. But in frag. 3 (*Tiberius Gracchus* 21.9), he says explicitly περὶ μὲν οὖν τούτων ἐν τῷ Σκιπίωνος βίῳ τὰ καθ' ἕκαστα γέγραπται, 'about this it has been written in detail in the *Life* of Scipio'. This too is clearly, to judge from the context, Aemilianus, who has just been referred to (§7) as 'Scipio Africanus' in full, as in the *Gaius Gracchus*.

## Appendix 1.2

to determine which Scipio was meant, but they are unconvincing, and I ignore arguments based on them.)[126]

(1) Africanus was by far the greater commander, whose decisive victory over Hannibal at Zama in 202 was comparable to Epaminondas' decisive victory over the Spartans at Leuctra in 371. No such victory could be claimed for Aemilianus.

(2) Both Africanus and Epaminondas were put on trial by their ungrateful fellow-countrymen. Plutarch himself made this comparison explicitly elsewhere.[127] Appian made it too, and is thought by some to have taken it from Plutarch's *Parallel life*.[128] But this is not agreed.[129] Cicero mentions in the same breath Epaminondas, Hannibal, the *Maximi*, and the *Africani* (i.e. Aemilianus and the older Africanus), but the plural means that this does not help with our problem.[130]

(3) The Thebans Pelopidas and Epaminondas were close colleagues and friends. Plutarch, himself a Boeotian, devoted a *Life* to each of these great Boeotians who fought against the Spartans. The *Pelopidas* is paired with the (Marcus Claudius) *Marcellus*, an outstanding Roman general killed in action during a battle against Hannibal, just as Pelopidas was killed in battle.[131] There would be a neat symmetry if the Roman *Lives* corresponding to the Theban ones were of two great generals who, unlike the 'Delayer' Fabius, so called from his strategy of non-confrontation, fought aggressively against Hannibal: Marcellus and Scipio Africanus (it was said that Romans called Fabius their shield and Marcellus their sword).[132] They were not friends as were the two Thebans, but the death of Pelopidas in battle in 364 left Epaminondas as the sole commander capable of defeating the Spartans, until his own death at the battle of Mantinea in 362. Similarly, Marcellus' death left Africanus as the only serious challenger to Hannibal, although Mantinea was not a decisive victory as was Zama.

And now for Aemilianus. There is only one main reason, but it is a strong one:

---

[126] Ziegler 1949: cols. 249–50; Sandbach 1969: 74.
[127] *Moralia* (the collection of his various works other than the biographies) 540d–541a.
[128] *Syr.* 40–1/205–18; Ziegler 1949: col. 249; Russell 1972: 113 n. 26.
[129] For doubts see Brodersen 1991: 217, who thinks Appian could have got it from a collection of rhetorical examples.
[130] *On the orator* 1.210.   [131] *DPRR* CLAU0908. For this man see pp. 95 n. 100; 141.
[132] Fabius is *DPRR* FABI0712. 'Sword and shield': Plut. *Marc.* 9.7, quoting the first-century BCE philosophical historian Posidonius (*FGrHist* 87 F42a); cf. Plut. *Fab.* 19.4. With the double metaphor Kidd 1988: 901 compares Livy 3.53.9.

(1) Epaminondas was an intellectual (indeed a trained philosopher), as was Aemilianus but not Africanus, despite the story of Africanus' book-reading at Syracuse in the run-up to Zama.

Most of those scholars who have written about this problem admit to uncertainty and lack of confidence. On balance, I prefer to conclude, also unconfidently, that Africanus was paired with Epaminondas, but even if he was not, we have seen that Plutarch did write a biography of Africanus.

## Appendix 1.3   The 'Roving Anecdote'

Hannibal was a charismatic figure, with whom Greek and Latin authors were fascinated. Many anecdotes were told about him, and to a slightly lesser degree about Scipio. How, if at all, can we know which were true? It would be a dull and two-dimensional history which contained no anecdotes about individuals, and there are plenty of them in Polybius as well as in Livy. Naturally, Plutarch in his biographies (and the *Moralia*) illustrated character by means of anecdotes.[133] Other literary sources collected brief anecdotes about Hannibal and Scipio, indeed the two men are favourite pegs. Some are clearly derived from what survives of the large-scale historians, some are not; some are shared between two or more collections. But how are we to decide whether and in what sense they are believable and usable? Among mainstream ancient historians, Arrian was rare in giving thought to the problem, and he announced in the Preface to his *Anabasis* of Alexander that he would be largely following the accounts of Ptolemy I (king of Egypt) and Aristobulus; and he gives his reasons for trusting them. But he then explains that he has added material from other writers where this is worth recording, and not unbelievable; he will refer to these 'only as things said', *hōs legomena monon*.[134] This appendix tries to lay down some principles for using anecdotes.

One type of anecdote will be mentioned several times in the present book. It will be called the 'roving anecdote'. There is no canonical definition of this purely modern expression, but I propose to use it where the same essential story is told by different sources (or perhaps the same

---

[133] For the *Moralia*, see p. 3 n. 14.
[134] Polybius (23.14.12) provides a precedent but should not be over-translated. After giving some illustrations of Scipio's character from the 180s when he was under attack by his enemies (see Chapter 18), he says, in the translations of both Shuckburgh and the revised Loeb edition of Walbank and Habicht, that he has related 'these anecdotes' for the sake of the good reputation of the dead and to encourage their successors to perform noble deeds. But the Greek for 'these anecdotes' is just ταῦτα, 'these things'.

## Appendix 1.3

forgetful source!) *about different agents*.[135] The last element of that definition is important: sometimes the same action or conversation is recorded about Hannibal by different writers, but the envisaged situation or interlocutor may be different. Some illustrative examples in the chapters which follow are as follows; none of them are true roving anecdotes, although they pose similar problems of veracity:

(i) A scornful remark about military divination is attributed to Hannibal. But in one source Hannibal says it to King Prusias I of Bithynia, and in another to the Seleucid king Antiochus III.[136] This is not 'roving' because it is about Hannibal both times.

(ii) A bizarre naval stratagem by which pots of venomous snakes are hurled at the enemy is said by one source to have been actually carried out by Hannibal when helping Prusias in a sea-battle; but in another source he merely demonstrates it, but to Antiochus not Prusias.[137] These variations do not inspire confidence in the strict historicity of either story, but they are not 'roving anecdotes' in the strong sense here proposed. The snakes story would be a genuine roving anecdote only if the unnamed 'Carthaginian' agent in a similar story told by Galen were someone other than Hannibal, and that is possible but perhaps not very probable.[138]

(iii) A famous story is told by several writers about a conversation between Scipio and the exiled Hannibal. The details vary, and Plutarch even manages to tell it, perhaps through faulty memory, with a significant difference in two of his different surviving *Lives*. This is not a roving anecdote: it always has those same two men as the principals and would make no sense if spoken by anyone else but those two. See pp. 261–5.

(iv) Cicero tells a story about how the exiled Hannibal in the later 190s attended a long and annoying lecture about generalship at Ephesus, delivered by a named and independently attested Aristotelian philosopher called Phormio.[139] A roughly similar story about Hannibal is reported by Stobaeus, an omnivorous collector of extracts from Classical authors.[140] Often he gives his source, but not for this one.

---

[135] The obvious candidate for this sub-category is Plutarch, whose writings were voluminous. In different *Lives*, he gives radically different versions of Hannibal's meeting with Scipio at Ephesus, but that is not a roving anecdote as here defined, because it concerns the same people each time.

[136] Cic. *On divination* 2.52 and Val. Max. 3.7. ext. 6 (to Prusias); Plut. *On exile* 66 (to Antiochus). See p. 227 n. 34.

[137] Nepos, *Hann*. 10 (Prusias); Frontinus *Stratagems* 4.7.10 (Antiochus). See p. 376.

[138] Galen vol. XIV Kühn p. 231. See p. 376 n. 35.   [139] *On the orator* 2.75–6.

[140] *On generals* IV 13 no. 58, p. 368 Wachsmuth and Hense; II: 399 Gaisford. Cf. Brink 1941.

'About Hannibal: when he heard a Stoic philosopher maintaining that only the wise man is a true general he laughed, thinking that it is impossible for someone without experience acquired through deeds to have knowledge of such matters.' It would be bad method to use Stobaeus to argue that Cicero's Phormio story is a mere roving anecdote, for two reasons: first, in Stobaeus it is told about Hannibal as principal figure, not about someone else altogether, as in a true 'roving anecdote'. Second, there are too many differences, for example the philosopher is a Stoic; we are told something about his doctrine; and there is nothing about Hannibal being an exile. We should choose between the versions, and Cicero's more circumstantial version is here accepted. See further p. 37–8 for more members of the category of stories to which both these belong. The Phormio story is not (unlike the pots of snakes) intrinsically incredible, so we are entitled to argue that Cicero's is the likelier version of a plausible story – which may, however, be no more than a fiction which made use of a known philosopher to illustrate Hannibal's outlook towards amateurs. If, hypothetically, the identical story, which has a definite anti-Greek tinge, had been told about, say, Cato the elder attending a lecture by Carneades, it would be a true roving anecdote, and the purpose of its re-application to Cato as main agent would be to illustrate an attitude to Hellenism rather than to generalship and who is competent to talk about it.[141] I return later to this group of stories with the theme battle-hardened-general-despises-amateur-theorists. Some are candidates for 'roving'.

Here by contrast are two well-known and genuinely roving anecdotes which, despite their status as such, have been legitimately used by modern historians of the Roman Empire and Greek religion respectively. Cassius Dio says that a woman approached the Roman emperor Hadrian and asked for his attention, but he told her he had no time. She said, 'then do not be a king'. The story is quoted by Fergus Millar on the first page of his *Emperor in the Roman World*.[142] But as Millar himself acknowledged, almost the same story was told about both Philip II of Macedon and Demetrius the Besieger.[143] He nevertheless used the story to illustrate how emperors, like Hellenistic kings, were expected to dispense justice.

The Spartan Lysander remarked that 'I cheat boys with knuckle-bones, men with oaths'.[144] But this cynical attitude to perjury is also attributed to

---

[141] Cato: *DPRR* PORC0907.   [142] Cassius Dio 71.32.1; Millar 1977: 1 and n. 3.
[143] Plut. *Moralia* 179 c–d and *Demetr.* 42.7.   [144] Plut. *Lys.* 8.4–5

## Appendix 1.3

Philip II of Macedon and to Dionysius I of Syracuse. Robert Parker used Lysander's remark to illustrate how 'merry rogues exploited the institution [of oaths] at every period', and like Millar he acknowledged that the story was told of others as well as of the individual he mentions in first place.[145]

Neither Millar nor Parker was concerned to characterize Hadrian and Lysander biographically. They were using the roving anecdotes cautiously, to illustrate particular ancient attitudes. That is the most that can be done with roving anecdotes, and it is not nothing.

So what if any roving anecdotes are about Hannibal? An attractive candidate might seem to be stratagems, where they are also attributed to some other person, perhaps far distant in time and/or space.[146] For example, Hannibal on Crete is said to have put a layer of gold on top of vessels filled with stones; this recalls a trick played (with slightly different motives) by a man in Herodotus.[147]

Again, Hannibal tied flaming twigs to the horns of cattle to simulate troops with torches and was so able to make a getaway. But this looks rather like a stratagem recommended by the Greek writer Aeneas the Tactician in the fourth century BCE.[148] Had someone on Hannibal's staff read this handbook?

Finally, a story which is about Hannibal indirectly but whose main agent is Scipio.[149] When Scipio was in Africa for the final campaign, some of Hannibal's spies were captured and brought to him. Instead of torturing them or interrogating them about Hannibal's forces, he had them shown round his army, gave them dinner, and sent them on their way. Hannibal was so impressed by this that it made him eager to meet Scipio in person.[150] Xerxes had done much the same with some Greek spies in 480 BCE.[151] And the consul Publius Valerius Laevinus in 289 BCE is said to have treated Pyrrhus' spies in the same way.[152] Walbank thinks that the Scipio anecdote may be true despite the models, because Scipio 'may have known and utilized these earlier stories'.[153] One can often say something of the sort.

Now let us return to Hannibal stories in the same category as that of his reaction to Phormio the philosopher. There is a further complication, and this does raise again the question of the 'roving anecdote'. We saw that Hannibal is

---

[145] Parker 1983: 186–7 and n. 237.
[146] For an undatable Carthaginian stratagem attributed both to a Maharbal (by Frontinus) and to a Himilco (by Polyaenus) and thus a roving anecdote in the full sense, see p. 112.
[147] See p. 371.
[148] Pol. 3.93–4, Livy 22.17, with p. 99. A referee suggests that there is a further similarity, with the biblical Samson's 300 foxes with firebrands attached to their tails (Judges 15.3–5), and that this might be a piece of Semitic folklore.
[149] Pol. 15.5.   [150] Pol. 15.5; Livy 30.29.2–3, Val. Max. 3.7.1c.   [151] Hdt. 7.146.
[152] Dion. Hal. 19.11.   [153] HCP 2: 450, citing other authors for Laevinus and Pyrrhus.

alleged to have disapproved of the Stoic who said that only the wise man can be a general. But two pages later, Stobaeus, this time evidently using Plutarch, but without citing him, says that some king or general called (probably) Eudamidas heard a philosopher claim that only a wise man can be a general.[154] Eudamidas commented that this sentiment was admirable, but the speaker had not heard the bugle sounding around him (Plutarch's version). Now there are two known Spartan kings called Eudamidas, one dated to about 330–294 BCE, the other to 294 (?)–244 BCE.[155] There was also a Spartan commander (not a king, and not very famous like Brasidas) called Eudamidas in the 380s.[156] If we could trust the detail (in Stobaeus, not Plutarch) that the philosopher in question was a Stoic, the later of the two kings called Eudamidas would be historically preferable in view of the history of Stoicism. But this detail is attached to Hannibal, not to Eudamidas. The best conclusion is that here we really do have a 'roving anecdote', told about two distinct individuals, and accordingly both anecdotes are highly suspect as evidence for the biography of Hannibal or indeed Eudamidas. They are usable only as indicating Greek military attitudes to theory as opposed to practice: compare our conclusion about Millar and Parker.

Finally, there is a special category of anecdote, and a special sort of complication, which concerns Scipio in particular.[157] 'Roving' is not quite the word for it, but there are similarities with that category. A number of doings and sayings are attributed to 'Scipio Africanus', but this could be either the Scipio who is the subject of the present book, or else Scipio Aemilianus, who was also called Scipio Africanus. Occasionally there are good reasons for preferring the one Scipio over the other. There is an example in Frontinus' book of stratagems: Scipio 'Africanus' answers some critics by saying that his mother gave birth to a commander not a warrior, and there are good reasons for identifying this speaker as Aemilianus (it suits his Numantine campaign in Iberia).[158] But that is rare good fortune, and sometimes such an anecdote suits

---

[154] Stobaeus IV. 13, no. 65, p. 370 Wachsmuth and Hense; 2: 400 Gaisford. Plutarch *Moralia* 192B, from the *Remarks by Kings and Generals*. One manuscript of Stobaeus has Eudaimonidas, an attested name (at Sparta and Messenia), but far rarer than Eudamidas or the dialect equivalent Eudemides. Decisive, however, is the absence of a known king or general anywhere called Eudaimonidas.

[155] *LGPN* IIIA: 162, Εὐδαμίδας nos. 9 and 11; Bradford 1977: 161–2, nos. 1 and 2. I adopt Bradford's dates.

[156] Xen. *Hell.* 5.2.24; Poralla 1913: 54 no. 295. Successive Teubner editions of the *Moralia* identify this man as Plutarch's Eudamidas, but one of the kings is likelier.

[157] But not only Scipio. See text for the problem – which Eudamidas?

[158] Front. *Strat.* 4.7.4; Astin 1967: 263 no. 44 (see next n.). For the opposition commander/warrior see Chapter 16.2 (on the need for generals to stay alive).

either man (or neither).[159] In around 400 CE, Vegetius included two specific references to 'Scipio Africanus', both of which are evidently about Aemilianus because Iberian Numantia explicitly features in them.[160] Historically, Aemilianus not Africanus is associated with military activity against Numantia. That is therefore also likely to be true of a third passage of Vegetius which approvingly attributes to an unspecified 'Scipio' a maxim to the effect that you should always give a fleeing enemy an escape route.[161] It is true that this might be thought superficially reminiscent of Africanus, who allowed Hasdrubal Barca to escape after Baecula, but that was an obvious and regrettable mistake. Frontinus reports the same maxim in a chapter on 'advice' and attributes it to 'Scipio Africanus', but again he probably – as in the 'mother' story – means Aemilianus.[162]

This appendix should not be taken as implying that roving anecdotes were peculiar to the ancient world. But perhaps the favoured categories differ. It may be that jokes are to the modern world what stratagems (also a source of entertainment) were to the ancient.[163]

To sum up: genuinely roving anecdotes are usable only as illustrations of attitudes and perceptions, not as specific evidence about any one of the different individuals about whom they are told. Anecdotes of other sorts, including sayings, must be judged according to the criteria for believability that apply to any contested piece of historical narrative. Could this as a matter of simple fact have happened or been uttered at the time and place alleged? Is it anachronistic or plausible in its supposed context? Is it in character as displayed elsewhere? Does it help to explain other credible events, or other courses of action followed by the individual in question? The test must if possible go deeper than 'do I want to believe it?'.

---

[159] Astin 1967: 248–69, appendix 11, *dicta Scipionis*, lists sixty-eight utterances attributed to Aemilianus (some preserved by more than one author, listed as e.g. no. 41a, b, c) but concedes that some could be about the older Scipio, e.g. nos. 5, 66; and presumably that might be true of others in his *incerta* ('uncertain') section at the end, nos. 55–68. But at no. 62, alleged quotation by the emperor Pius, 'Scipio' is surely Aemilianus.

[160] 1.15.5 and 3.10.19–20. In addition, there are several passages in Vegetius where Scipio Africanus the elder is probably in the author's mind as the unnamed deviser or employer of particular stratagems or tactics. The same is true of Hannibal.

[161] 3.21.3.

[162] Front. *Strat.* 4.7.16. Astin 1967: 268 nos. 65a (Frontinus) and 65b (Vegetius) attributes both of them confidently to Aemilianus. Milner 1996: 107 n. 5 cites Frontinus but does not discuss the problem, 'which Scipio?'. For another dictum of 'Scipio Africanus' in Frontinus where the speaker is certainly Aemilianus, see Astin 1967: 260, no. 35b, cf. 35a.

[163] For example, this story of an earnest undergraduate's question to a famous professor is told at Oxford about Gilbert Murray and at Cambridge about Henry Sidgwick: Q: 'Are you interested in incest, professor?' A: 'Only in a general sort of way.'

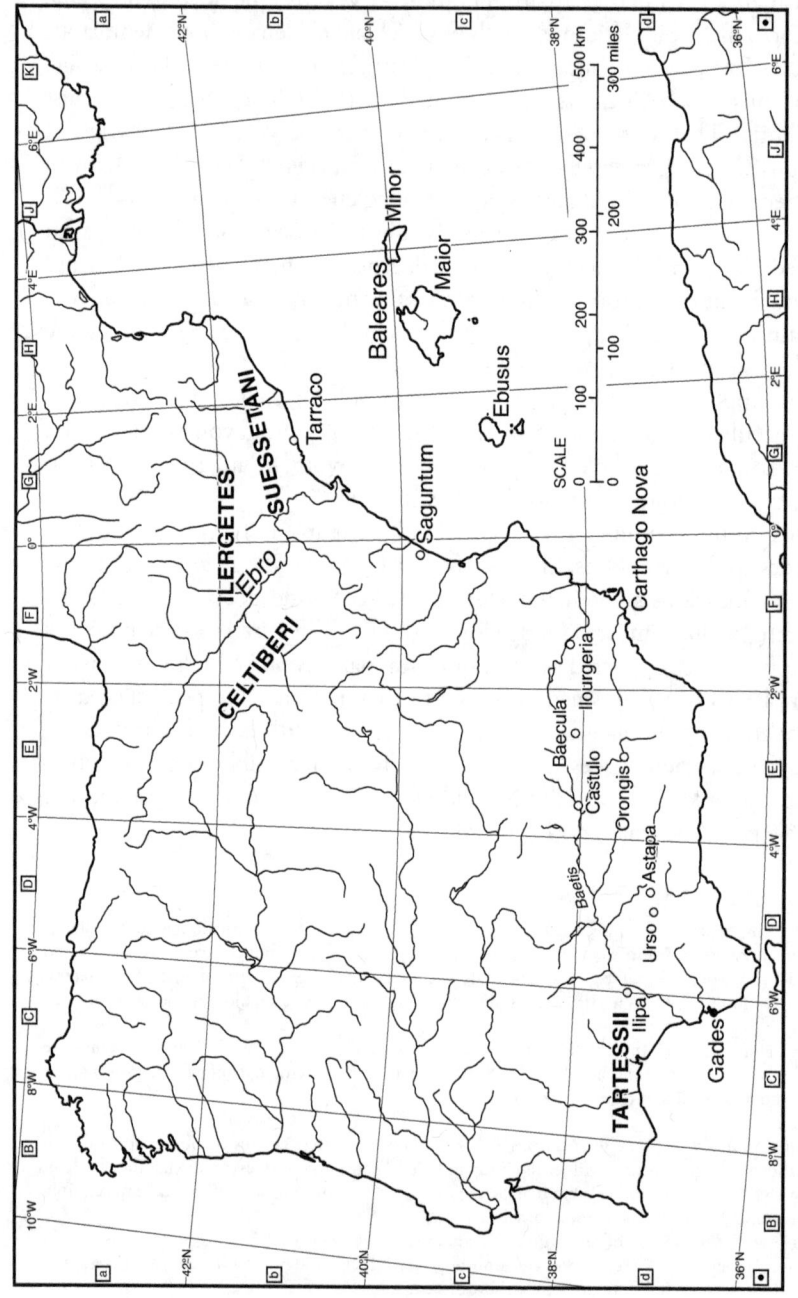

Map 1 Iberia in the time of Hannibal and Scipio

CHAPTER 2

# *Origins*
## *Hannibal: 247–221, Birth to Aged 26 Years, Scipio: 235–218, Birth to Aged 17 Years*

### 2.1 Introduction

Hannibal, the older by more than a decade of our two parallel lives, must come first in the individual discussions in this chapter, and usually also throughout this book.[1] As often with otherwise well-documented individuals from the ancient world, we know only half of Hannibal's parentage: his mother has left no trace on the record, so we can only guess what part she played in his early upbringing. His father was a famous general, Hamilcar (9) Barca, and his younger brothers were Hasdrubal (6) and Mago (6): see Family Tree 1, which also gives his – to us nameless – sisters. Hamilcar's father was another Hannibal (7), so the boy was presumably named after his paternal grandfather, a common ancient and modern habit.[2]

Roman upper-class mothers were more visible than Carthaginian, even when their names have not been handed down. Roman women were assigned their father's family name.[3] Astonishingly, daughters were all given the same single name, so that modern reference works distinguish Scipio's as 'Cornelia I' and 'Cornelia II'.[4] (How this worked domestically is a puzzle.) Scipio's own mother was a Pomponia, from a good consular family with close ties to the Aemilii and the Cornelii Scipiones.[5] Her brothers Manius and Marcus Pomponius Matho were consuls in 233 and

---

[1] Hannibal was born in 247, Scipio in 235: see p. 2. For Hannibal's early life, see Nepos, *Hannibal* and Livy 21.1-4. Modern reconstructions: Seibert 1993a: 7–50; Geus 1994: 76–82; Hoyos 2003: 52–3.
[2] Nepos, *Hamilcar* 1.1, the only source. See Geus 1994: 73–4, 'Hannibal (7)'. Ancient naming habit: Th. 6.54.6, Dem. 43.74.
[3] See Section 2.2 for the function of the 'gentilician' Roman *nomen*.
[4] They are *DPRR* CORN3946 (no. 1, mother of the Gracchi) and CORN4228 (no. 11, married to Scipio Nasica Corculum, CORN1396). We do sometimes hear of women with extra names such as *Tertia*, 'Third', placed after or before the family name, like Scipio's wife Aemilia Tertia (*DPRR* AEMI3945; called Tertia Aemilia at Val. Max. 6.7.1), but it is not quite certain that these indicate order of birth.
[5] Silus Italicus 13.615; *DPRR* POMP4246.

231 respectively.⁶ It is sad to reflect that one line in a largely fanciful first-century CE poet, Silius Italicus, is the sole authority we 'have to thank', as Münzer rightly and graciously put it, for the name of Scipio's mother.⁷ After all, it is not as if Republican Romans and their historians were constrained by Classical Athenian conventions about not naming 'respectable' women.

Pomponia may have had something of a reputation for abnormal piety: she visited various temples and sacrificed to the gods about her son Lucius' candidature for the aedileship.⁸ This is related by Polybius, who does not however bother to name her.⁹ She features, again anonymously except for Silius, in stories about Scipio's miraculous birth. It is in this semi-mythical context that we are further told that she had long been childless and had despaired of having children.¹⁰ In this respect, her story resembles that of the biblical Hannah, who eventually gave birth to Samuel although hitherto 'the LORD had shut up her womb', or of Elizabeth, mother at a miraculously advanced age of John the Baptist.¹¹ The context in Silius is Scipio's visit to the underworld, where Pomponia explains to her son how she was really impregnated by Jupiter in the shape of a large serpent.¹² The basic 'fact' of the encounter with the mother's ghost reprises the exchange between Odysseus and Anticlea in Homer's *Odyssey*.¹³ But the mother informing her son of his supernatural paternity is more like Herodotus' account of the Spartan king Demaratus' interrogation of his mother.¹⁴ The nearer model for the whole section of Silius is book 6 of Virgil's *Aeneid*. Münzer took all this in his stride; some modern authorities

---

⁶ *DPRR* POMP0791 (Manius) and 0853 (Marcus). See Family Tree 2; Münzer 1920: 161–3, with a small tree at 162 (cf. 102 for a larger tree of the Cornelii Scipiones) [1999: 150–2 with 418 n. 182, cf. 99]. The tree at *R.-E.* IV (1900): cols. 1429–30 was presumably also by Münzer, who wrote the *R.-E.* entries on Aemilianus and Africanus' brother Lucius (Münzer 1900a and 1900b), but not the entry on Africanus himself, for which see Henze 1900; cf. now Etcheto 2012: 162–5 no. 12 and *DPRR* CORN 0878. For the connections between the Pomponii and the Scipiones, Münzer 1920: 162 n. 1 [1999: 418 n. 182]. Scipio partly owed it to his cousin the praetor Marcus Pomponius Matho (*DPRR* POMP1010) that his reputation did not suffer worse than it did during the shocking Pleminius affair (204 BCE), for which see pp. 163–71.
⁷ Münzer 1920: 162, 'Ferner danken wir' [1999: 151, 'we owe, moreover'].
⁸ For this office, see pp. 14, 113.    ⁹ Pol. 10.4.4.    ¹⁰ Aulus Gellius 6.1.1–4.
¹¹ Hannah: 1 Samuel 1.2–20. Elizabeth: Luke 1.5–25. For the Hannah narrative as a 'type-scene', see Alter 2011: 103–9, esp. 108. For 'type-scenes', a concept taken from Homeric studies, see generally Alter 2011: 55–77. Despite 'biblical' in this excellent book's title, it is confined to the Old Testament, so Elizabeth does not feature.
¹² Silius 13.642–3. Silius and Pliny the Elder (*NH* 7.47) make Scipio's mother die giving birth to Publius Scipio, but this is impossible in view of his younger full brother Lucius. See Walbank, *HCP* 2: 200 (Pliny makes the birth 'Caesarian', to suggest a similarity with Julius Caesar's family).
¹³ *Od.* 11.152–224. See e.g. Marks 2005: 197 n. 65.    ¹⁴ Hdt. 6.68–9.

give the name of Scipio's mother as an incidental fact, but not its source and context.[15]

But if we accept the name Pomponia on Silius' say-so, it might be argued that by parity of reasoning we have no right to reject Imilce as the name of Hannibal's Iberian wife, a detail which is also owed solely to Silius.[16] But the name Imilce is, in the more obviously recognizable Punic form Himilce, suspiciously Carthaginian rather than Iberian (but not quite impossible given the extent of Carthaginian colonization in Iberia).[17] So the argument from parity is unsound. There were still members of the Pomponian *gens* around at Rome in the first century CE, and their family traditions are much more likely to have been kept alive, and accessible to the author of a quasi-historical epic, than Hannibal's. Silius' *Punica* is a mix of the historical and fantastic – as we have just seen, Pomponia herself is made to converse with Scipio in the underworld – and we are perfectly justified in placing different personal names on different sides of the divide. Of the two female names, Pomponia but not Imilce will be accepted here.[18] The more important point is that a Republican Roman noble such as Scipio, brought up in narrower attitudes, would not have married an Iberian girl, as Hannibal did, and as his brother-in-law Hasdrubal may have done; but see Family Tree 1 n.5. (There is a parallel between Hannibal's multi-racial and multilingual recruitment of troops and foreign mercenaries, and Roman preference for citizen and allied manpower.[19]) Hannibal's wife was, then, historical, but the existence of a son fathered by Hannibal is very doubtful. Silius is the only source for this and for the stories about him, one of them wildly implausible.[20]

Scipio's wife was an Aemilia, from a family which had been prominent since the first half of the third century.[21] She was sister of the consul Lucius Aemilius Paullus, who as consul fell at Cannae in 216; the daughter of Scipio and Aemilia was a Cornelia (II), so named

---

[15] So e.g. Scullard 1973 [1951]: 36 and 1970: 28.
[16] 3.97; for the undoubted fact of the Iberian marriage, see Livy 24.41.7.
[17] So, correctly, Bruère 1952: 224 n. 1 (but he stops short of denying the historicity of the name). Huss 1985: 281 n. 103 gets round this difficulty by the speculation that young Mrs Hannibal took a new name on marriage.
[18] Stocks 2014: 96 n. 50 thinks the name was Silius' own invention. Geus 1994: 172–3 (and 267 Stammtafel 11) accepts the reliability of the name, but see Ameling 1997: 244, who would have preferred to see her in Geus' mythical and literary section (but the wife as opposed to her name is historical).
[19] As a referee suggests. For Hannibal's ethnically mixed army, see p. 27 n. 88 and cf. p. 346.
[20] For these stories, see p. 52.
[21] Scullard 1973 [1951]: 35–6. See Etcheto 2012: 165–6, no. 12; *DPRR* AEMI3495, and for Paullus see p. 21 n. 59. On the date of the marriage, see p. 58 and n. 112.

in conformity with the rule noted earlier. Cornelia was the mother of two famous tribunes of the people in 133 and 123 BCE: the 'Gracchi', Tiberius and Gaius Sempronius Gracchus. She had married another Tiberius Sempronius Gracchus, who had an outstandingly successful military and diplomatic career in Iberia during the 170s; he was consul in 177 and again in 163. In her widowhood, she is said to have turned down a grander suitor, King Ptolemy of Egypt.[22] Inscribed much later, her terse funerary *elogium* runs 'Cornelia. Daughter of Africanus. Of the Gracchi'.[23] The word 'mother', *mater*, is missing at the end, not because the inscription is incomplete, in the sense of broken or damaged at that point, but for the splendid reason that the relationship was so famous that it went without saying. It was she who inherited the parental drive and distinction, rather than her brothers, whose achievements were modest: the physically weak Publius was an orator and historian.[24] Lucius got to the praetorship in 174 but no further.[25] He was expelled from the senate by the censors elected in that year.[26]

Scipio's father Publius and his uncle Gnaeus fought in Iberia and were killed there in separate but almost simultaneous engagements in 211. Their careers, and the extraordinary circumstances in which they were succeeded by the young Publius Scipio as a private citizen, who thereby displaced the more experienced Gaius Claudius Nero, will be treated in a later chapter (4).[27] For the moment, the important point is that Scipio and Hannibal were both sons and successors of soldiers who had – until their unhappy and premature ends – campaigned with distinction in Iberia, as Scipio's son-in-law Tiberius Gracchus would go on to do half a century later. Iberia was the making of many Roman careers in this period, including that of Scipio's nemesis Marcus Porcius Cato the Elder, or 'the Censor'. Scipio's phenomenally successful overseas career in Iberia looks forward to the careers of less constitutionally minded and more ambitious individuals in later times.

---

[22] Plut. *Gracch.* 1.7. Probably Ptolemy VI Philometor. He visited Rome in 164 (Pol. 33.11) and might have met her then, but the marriage proposal must have come later.
[23] *ILS* 68, of the time of Augustus. See Hölkeskamp 2018: 445 and n. 88. For her famous portrait statue, see Plin. *NH* 34.31.
[24] Cic. *Brutus* 77; *FRHist* 3 and *FGrHist* 811 (a history in Greek).
[25] See *DPRR* CORN1331. For his capture and return to Scipio by Antiochus III, see p. 331. A praetor was a military commander, second in importance and status only to the consuls. There were four from 228 and six from 198. See Brennon 2000.
[26] Livy 41.27.2; Val. Max. 3.5.1.   [27] See Chapter 4.3. He is *DPRR* CLAU0908.

## 2.2 Names

Prosopography, the study of family ties and regional origins, relies on naming habits; that is, on 'onomastic' evidence, some of it epigraphic, derived from inscriptions. None of this onomastic variety is true of Carthaginian personal names, which are mostly single except when expanded by nicknames or by-names, so that the scope for accurate Carthaginian prosopography is more limited than for Roman.[28] Hamilcar, Himilco, Hannibal, Hasdrubal, Mago: these personal names, and a very few others such as Hanno, recur again and again in Carthaginian history. Just in the index of names at the end of Briscoe's 2006 Oxford Classical Text of Livy books 21–5, there are five Hasdrubals, three Hamilcars, Magos, and Hannos, and two Hannibals.[29] Sorting out such one-word homonyms is difficult. Sometimes the literary sources do provide extra designations for Carthaginians.[30] An example is Hasdrubal 'the bald', which is comparable to the Roman 'Calvus', which has the same meaning and as it happens was the additional *cognomen* of Scipio's uncle Gnaeus Cornelius Scipio; but the sense or status of such by-names can be a puzzle. There is also an obscure but sinister Hannibal (10) the 'single-combat-man'.[31] Among prominent Carthaginians, 'Mago the so-called Samnite' was probably some sort of nickname, not an indication of Italian origin, from the region Samnium.[32] And how should we visualize Hanno 'the Mullet', a sort of fish?[33] Sometimes, such additional names may possibly be inherited surnames: Hannibal's own extra name 'Barkas' or 'Barca' surely belongs in this category.[34] But if so, the precise rules or conventions for transmission escape us. For the social historian, this is a frustrating contrast with the vast and mostly epigraphically attested

---

[28] But for a prosopography of Carthaginians attested in literary sources down to 146, see Geus 1994.
[29] In Geus 1994, which covers Carthage from the beginnings to 146 BCE, there are in the historical persons section sixteen Hasdrubals, eighteen Hamilcars, sixteen Magos, thirty-three Hannos, and thirteen Hannibals.
[30] On such additional Carthaginian names, see the good discussion by Geus 1994: 217–26, 'Die karthagischen Doppel-und Beinamen', calling them memorably (217) 'a spot of colour in the onomastic desert'.
[31] Geus 1994: 148–9, 'Hasdrubal (10) der Kahle'. Hannibal (10), the 'single-combat-man' (Μονομάχος), was supposedly a kind of 'double' of the famous Hannibal (9), and the real author of his 'cruelties'. The Greek word can mean 'gladiator', but that sense is not appropriate here. Was this double a protective device? Medieval kings had lookalikes in battle. Cf. Shakespeare, *Richard III* 5.4.11–12 (Richard at Bosworth field): 'I think there be six Richmonds in the field:/five have I slain today instead of him.' (The Earl of Richmond is about to become King Henry VII by killing Richard in single combat.)
[32] See Appendix 2.1.
[33] Appian, *Libyan history* 108/514; Geus 1994: 128–9, 'Hanno (31) der Fisch'.
[34] This has been challenged recently, but see Appendix 2.1.

repertoire of Greek or Latin personal names, which can often help to identify the regional origins of bearers, especially where the name is neither common nor rare, but area-specific. And both Greek and in formal contexts Latin names are coupled with a father's name or patronym (Romans sometimes added the paternal grandfather's name, flagged by *n.* for *nepos*, 'grandson' as well as *f.* for *filius*, 'son'). Only a very few Carthaginians are regularly denominated by their patronyms; an example is 'Hasdrubal son of Gisgo', whom Scipio defeated at Iberian Ilipa in 206.[35]

Athenians were further identified by one of the 139 local divisions or demes of Athens' territory Attica, so the great Pericles was son of Xanthippus from Cholargos, and Romans added the names of their 'tribes'. So Cicero, whose tribe was the Cornelia and who had the same *praenomen* Marcus as his father and grandfather, was M. Tullius M. f. M. n. Cor. Cicero. Republican Romans usually had three names (*tria nomina*) but used all three only in formal contexts.[36] These consisted of, first, a *praenomen* such as Gnaeus, Publius, or Lucius (but the choice of *praenomina* was small, and amazingly the Cornelii Scipiones confined themselves to just those three).[37] In second place, a family or 'gentilician' *nomen* such as Iulius/Julius or Cornelius, denoting membership of a *gens* or 'lineage' much larger than a single family unit. And often, third, a kind of extra surname or *cognomen* such as Caesar or Scipio (but the famous Gaius Marius had no *cognomen*). So we are explicitly told that Scipio's title 'Africanus', 'the African', was in fact a second *cognomen*, a tribute to his victory over Hannibal in north Africa.[38] His full name was therefore P. Cornelius P. f. L. n. Cor. Scipio Africanus, since his father was another Publius and his grandfather a Lucius.[39] In addition, Romans regularly – and for us helpfully – signified adoption by means of an extra element, the pre-adoption *nomen* with a standard new suffix. The most famous example is Octavian, who became the first emperor Augustus – a title, not a family name. He was born an Octavius but was adopted by Julius Caesar in his will, so strictly became Gaius Iulius Caesar Octavianus, although it is a mere modern convention to call him 'Octavian', a name which in its

---

[35] See Geus 1994: 143, 'Hasdrubal (8)' and 33 'Gisgo (5)'.
[36] On Roman names, see Salway 1994; Henderson 1997: 19–24 and (on the *tria nomina*) 136 n. 25.
[37] Oakley 2005b: 166 (who wonders what a Scipio family would have done in the event of a fourth son!). The Livii Salinatores even confined themselves to two. At the end of the Republican period, conventions about *praenomina* crumbled, so that we hear of *Paullus* and even *Imperator* in first position.
[38] Livy 30.45.6.
[39] Specific evidence for his tribe is lacking, but the Cor[nelia] was the tribe of his *gens*. See Taylor 1960: 307.

Latin form Octavianus he did not use. So Publius Cornelius Scipio Aemilianus Africanus, who destroyed Carthage in 146, was the son of a famous Lucius Aemilius Paullus, conqueror of Macedon in 168, and grandson of Scipio's father-in-law, the consul Lucius Aemilius Paullus, who fell at Cannae in 216. But he was adopted by Publius, the otherwise obscure son of the great Scipio Africanus, one of the two subjects of this book. Scipio Aemilianus possessed the extra *cognomen* 'Africanus', not only because he inherited it from his grandfather by adoption, but because he too defeated African Carthage in 146. (So he had three *cognomina*: Scipio, Aemilianus, Africanus.) His double right to the name Africanus is insisted on by the ghost of Scipio Africanus, whom Cicero imagines as addressing a prophetic speech to his like-named adoptive grandson in the 'Dream of Scipio'. This philosophical mini-treatise on the afterlife formed the closure to Cicero's *On the Republic*.[40]

## 2.3 What Did 'Barca' Signify?

Hamilcar is often referred to in the Greek literary sources with the extra name Barkas, or even as Barkas alone (Latin Barca).[41] Polybius treats this as a surname.[42] Modern authorities habitually refer to the whole family as the 'Barcids' or 'Barkids', as if by analogy with the Athenian Alcmeonids – or indeed with much later dynasties like the Abbasids (the 'Scipiadae' or Scipiones will be discussed shortly).[43] But this habit is misleading. In the first place, English 'Barcid' is a purely modern term, neither derived from, nor particularly close to, the only known Latin adjectives formed from Barca, which are 'Barcinus' (Livy) or 'Barcaeus' (Silius).[44] As for Greek, the only ancient literary source to use anything close to the word 'Barkid' is the late Greek historian Cassius Dio, and even this is spelt in a slightly different way.[45]

In the second place, the dynastic implications of the English word are far from certainly justified. It is true that Livy several times refers to the

---

[40] For the 'Dream', see more fully p. 417.
[41] In what follows, the spelling with 'c' or 'k' will be varied according to the language of the source used ('k' when the source is Greek). 'q' is an attempt to reproduce the Punic.
[42] 1.56.1 (with a different middle consonant. χ: Βαρχίδης, 'Barchides'). The explanatory Greek word he uses is ἐπικαλούμενος, literally 'called in addition'. Appian (*Hann.* 2/3) uses the corresponding noun ἐπίκλησις to say the same thing about Hamilcar. The noun is one of the regular Greek words for a divine epithet, but that does not imply cult for Hamilcar or his sons.
[43] Warmington 1966: 146; Huss 1985: 257–8 ('barqidisch', 'antibarqidisch', 'probarqidisch'); Hoyos 2008: 24; Stocks 2014: 38; and frequently Hall 2020. See also Norden 1927: 333.
[44] 10.554.    [45] Cassius Dio 11.10, Zonaras 8.10 (derived from Dio).

'Barcine faction' and once to the 'Barcine family', and he calls Hannibal's brother Hasdrubal *Barcinus*, but not as it happens Hannibal himself.⁴⁶ 'Barcine' should, however, probably not be regarded as an inherited family designation, but as more like an extra Roman *cognomen* of the 'Africanus' sort. Livy's *Barcinus* need mean no more than 'faction/family/son of Hamilcar Barkas'. (Hamilcar had no securely attested grandsons, so we do not know if Barkas continued to be applied to any generation beyond the sons.)⁴⁷ On this view, the closest parallel to *Barcini* in references to Scipio's family may, coincidentally, be the informal and poetic *Scipiadae*. This is a metrically convenient Greek-style lengthening: *Scipio* is in most metres an intractable long-short-long, a 'cretic' in the technical term.⁴⁸ But it does not refer to the family *gens* as a whole, which is that of the Cornelii. Instead, it was used in a more limited way, to denote either the two Scipio brothers, father and uncle of Africanus, who were killed in 211; or else the great Africanus himself and his grandson by adoption Aemilianus or Africanus. It is never used of another high-profile pair of Scipio brothers, Publius Africanus and Lucius, who collaborated in the defeat of Antiochus III in 190 and were the targets of the 'trials of the Scipios' in the 180s.

A pseudo-prophecy in Virgil celebrated the 'twin Scipiadae, two thunderbolts of war, Libya's disaster', *geminos, duo fulmina belli,/ Scipiadas, cladem Libyae*.⁴⁹ At first sight, this phrase, especially *geminos*, evokes the ill-fated brothers Publius and Gnaeus who died in Iberia in 211 (although these were a pair rather than actually twins); that at any rate is how the ancient Virgilian commentator Servius took the words. But *Scipiadae* can also be applied to the successful grandfather and his adoptive grandson because the poem immediately continues by calling the pair 'Libya's (i.e. Africa's) disaster'. This is most easily referred to the reasons for the shared *cognomen* Africanus, because Aemilianus sacked African Carthage in 146.⁵⁰ But Feeney has offered the brilliant polysemic suggestion that all four

---

⁴⁶ *Barcina factio*: 21.2.4, 9.4; 23.12.6; 34.61.11 (part of the story of Hannibal's agent Ariston at Carthage, for which see p. 310). *Barcina familia*: 23.13.6. Hasdrubal: 25.39.13.

⁴⁷ Geus 1994: 267, 'Stammtafel 11', includes several grandchildren of Hamilcar (9) Barca, but all are conjectural and are rejected in the present book: (i) Mago (9), a son of the non-Barcid Hasdrubal (5) and a daughter (name unknown) of Hamilcar. (ii) A very doubtfully historical son of the famous Hannibal (9) by his Iberian wife. (iii) Four children of Bomilcar (2) by another daughter of Hamilcar (9): a daughter and three sons, including Hanno (22), a nephew of Hannibal (9).

⁴⁸ Henderson 1997: 38 and 143 n. 53 is good on 'the Scipiadic fight with metrics', noting that Ovid daringly scanned Scipio as a dactyl, long-short-short: *Art of love* 3.410 (for this line see also p. 422). Silius gratefully followed Ovid: *Pun.* 9.413.

⁴⁹ See already Lucretius 3.1034, *Scipiadas, belli fulmen, Carthaginis horror*, with Henderson 2004: 103–4.

⁵⁰ Virgil, *Aeneid* 6.842–3 with Norden 1927: 333.

Scipios were simultaneously and perhaps deliberately meant.[51] By another curious coincidence, *Barca* and *Scipio* can mean the same thing, lightning or thunderbolt; this would certainly give extra point to Virgil's metaphor.[52]

The preceding discussion assumes the usual and, in my view, correct interpretation of Hannibal's family name. There is, however, a recent theory that the name might refer to the family's geographical origins from the Greek city Barce in Cyrenaica, but the reasoning is unsound.[53] Since the counter-arguments are technical and would be out of scale in the main text, I relegate detailed discussion to Appendix 2.1.

Hannibal and Hasdrubal both bore 'theophoric' (that is, god-derived) names, formed from the semitic god Baal, as did Adherbal and Hannibal's outspoken cavalry commander Maharbal.[54] 'Hamilcar' is formed from Melqart, patron god of Tyre, the mother-city of the colony of Carthage, and usually equated to the Greek Heracles and Latin Hercules. Greek names were frequently theophoric – unlike Republican Roman: even Roman *cognomina* invoked deities only very rarely.[55]

One way in which a royal or other prominent individual's name could live on in the ancient world, at least for a time, was by an eponymous city-foundation, or by a renaming of an existing city.[56] In the Greek world, the practice is even older than the many Alexandrias, cities supposedly founded by Alexander the Great: Philippi and Philippopolis were named by and for Alexander's father Philip II.[57] But neither Hamilcar nor Hannibal – nor indeed Scipio – chose this way of perpetuating their memories.

---

[51] And indeed a fifth, because Quintus Caecilius Metellus Scipio (*DPRR* CAEC2347) was defeated and killed fighting against Caesar's forces at Thapsus in Libya (46 BCE), so that he suffered rather than inflicted a Libyan *clades*; Feeney 2021: 1.109–10 and n. 74. Nisbet 1995: 414–30 protested generally against polysemic interpretations, but (a) his main target was too-clever critics of Horace's *Odes*, and he accepted (427) that Virgil went in for 'evocative spread of meaning'; (b) he was mainly objecting to over-ingenious meta-poetical approaches ('sailing' = writing epic poetry, and so on); (c) he did not call a halt to all searches for multiple meanings, and he offered or accepted some himself.

[52] Barkas: Huss 1985: 246 n. 230 ('Blitz'). Scipio: see again Norden 1927: 333 (noting the onomastic similarity between Barcids and Scipios; so too Henderson 1997: 142 n. 49). *OLD scipio* gives only the meanings rod, staff, cane, or baton, but see Norden for the possibility that the family was playing on one of the Greek words for 'thunderbolt', σκηπτός (*skeptos*) = κεραυνός (*keraunos*). (See also Feeney 2021 as in previous n.) Cf. the royally born Ptolemy 'the so-called Keraunos', 'Thunderbolt', early third century: Pol. 9.35.4.

[53] Hall 2020.    [54] For whom see esp. Livy 22.51.

[55] A notable exception, derived from Saturn, is Lucius Appuleius Saturninus (*DPRR* APPU1766), turbulent tribune of the people in 100 BCE.

[56] Renamed cities, in particular, were liable to revert after the death or disgrace of the eponymous individual; cf. the sequence St Petersburg, Petrograd, Leningrad, St Petersburg. See Fraser 2009: 324–76 for an annotated list of eponymous Hellenistic city-foundations, and Fraser 1996 for Alexander's foundations, arguing that many were named after him by Ptolemaic writers so as to reduce the Seleucid achievement (see p. 304 n. 7).

[57] And Thessalian Gomphoi (*IACP* no. 396) was renamed Philippi for a while.

## 2.4 Childhood and Early Youth: Hannibal

Hamilcar (9) had six certainly known children including the famous Hannibal (9): three sons, three daughters (see Family Tree 1).[58] Hannibal (9)'s younger brothers Hasdrubal (6) and Mago (6) will play important roles in the narrative which follows. His sisters are inevitably more elusive. Appian mentions a nephew of Hannibal (9) called Hanno who has been identified with an attested Hanno (22) son of Bomilcar (2).[59] Since we hear of no son of Hamilcar (9) called Bomilcar, the nephew would necessarily be son of a sister not brother of Hannibal (9).[60] But the context in Appian is unreliable, an account of Hannibal's senior dispositions at Cannae in 216 which differs from that of his usual source Polybius. So since the implication of the doubtful word 'nephew' is the only evidence for her existence, she is omitted from Family Tree 1. A firmly attested sister of Hannibal (9) married the non-Barcid Hasdrubal (5) who succeeded Hamilcar (9) in the Iberian command: he is explicitly called Hamilcar (9)'s son-in-law, *gener* (Diodorus, probably wrongly, says he married a Spanish woman).[61] A second sister was promised in marriage by Hamilcar (9) to a Numidian prince called Naravas, provided he remained loyal to Carthage.[62] A third sister features in another Numidian dynastic connection.[63] Her daughter, who was therefore Hannibal (9)'s niece, was widow of Oezalces, an uncle of the Masinissa who will play an important part in the present book. She was married off to a usurper called Mazaetullus in 204 BCE. We hear no more of her specifically, but Mazaetullus survived Masinissa's recovery of his ancestral throne and led an undisturbed life thereafter, so perhaps she did too.[64]

Stories about the childhoods of famous ancient people usually serve to make the point that adult qualities were already on display. As a boy, the future Cyrus the Great of Persia behaved like a king: elected leader by the other children, he punished another child severely for disobedience and

---

[58] In this paragraph, and elsewhere, in cases of confusing homonyms, I give the numbering of named Carthaginian individuals as in Geus 1994 but will not do this systematically throughout the book, so as to avoid making it indigestible. 'Hannibal' with no number is the famous bearer of the name, Geus' Hannibal (9). Doubtful traditions gave Hamilcar four sons not three. Val. Max. 9.3 ext. 2 gave the number four but no names. The late writer Ampelius (36.2) named the fourth as Hamilcar, but see Geus 1994: 58, 'Hamilcar (10)' with an asterisk implying a doubt as to his existence. Cf. Hoyos 2003: 21–2 and 223 (appendix, special note 1); and MacDonald 2015: xiii (family tree).

[59] Nephew: App. *Hann.* 20/90; son of Bomilcar: Pol. 3.42.6 and Livy 21.27.2.

[60] See Geus 1994: 18–19, 'Bomilcar (2)', esp. 18 n. 79, and 121, 'Hanno (22)'; also 267, 'Stammtafel 11'.

[61] Livy 21.2.4 (*gener*). Diod. 25.12, a muddle with Hannibal (9). Unless he was a widower?

[62] Pol. 1.78.8–9. For this man, who may be the *Nrwt* attested on a neo-Punic inscription, see Huss 1985: 260 n. 65 and Geus 1994: 77 n. 448.

[63] Livy 29.29.12. On the different arrangement in Geus 1994, see Family Tree 1.

[64] Livy 29.30.12–13.

reacted with defiance when reproved for this, at a time when that royal future was unknown to him or anyone else.[65] Such tales obviously invite suspicion, and we ought not to privilege any of them because we feel they have the 'stamp of authenticity'.[66] But one much-discussed story about the child Hannibal is in a special category, because in its original form it does not serve to introduce a biography but was allegedly recounted by Hannibal himself in his years of wandering, when the Seleucid king Antiochus III suspected him of pro-Roman sentiments. In order to reassure the king, he recalled how, when he was aged nine, his father Hamilcar sacrificed to Baal before setting out for Iberia and induced the boy to swear an oath, if he wished to accompany him, 'never to show good will towards the Romans'.[67] Livy tells it twice.[68] The first time is at the start of his Hannibalic war narrative, but without its Seleucid context, and with the brief vague formula 'the story goes that ... '. He also here gives a different form of the oath from Polybius: 'to be an enemy of the Roman people', *hostem fore populo Romano*.[69] The first version might be thought to imply that, despite his obviously anti-Roman gesture, the father nevertheless intended to forbid actual hostility.[70] The second time Livy narrates the oath story, he gives the full context – the conversation in exile with Antiochus – and this time an exact translation of Polybius' version of the oath, 'never to be a friend of the Roman people', *numquam amicum fore populi Romani*. Polybius' own narrative does not survive for this later episode. Evidently Livy saw no material difference between the two formulations; nor did Nepos, who stressed the enduring relationship with Rome more than the oath.[71] In any case, it can be agreed that the story in some form or other was 'probably true'.[72]

So the young Hannibal accompanied his father to Iberia, but nothing more is specifically recorded of him until he succeeded to the Iberian command after the death of his brother-in-law Hasdrubal, in 221. Livy reports, as we have seen, that the boy Hannibal on his arrival in Iberia was thought to resemble his father Hamilcar in striking physical

---

[65] For ancient Greek literary treatments of childhood, see Pelling 1990. Cyrus: Hdt. 1. 114–16.
[66] Badian commented wittily about this phrase: 'that useful mark, often appealed to by scholars, is (alas) usually discernible only to the author's inner eye' (1972: 159 n. 1).
[67] Pol. 3.11.4–7 ('never to εὐνοήσειν'), Nepos *Hannibal* 2. On Silius Italicus' much-elaborated version of the oath and its context (1.81–122), see Tupet 1980, arguing interestingly that Silius added a magical element derived from Virgil on Dido in *Aeneid* 4.
[68] Livy 21.1.4; and 35.19.3, under 193 BCE.  [69] Scullard, *CAH* 8: 22–3; Walsh 2003 [1985]: 21.
[70] Too much has been pedantically made of this stronger formulation. Walbank (*HCP* 1: 315) rightly treated Hamilcar's administering of the oath as a show of 'hatred' for Rome.
[71] *Hann.* 1.3 and 2.4–6.  [72] So, rightly, Lazenby 1978: 20.

appearance.⁷³ The same passage of Livy says that he was called on when any deed of bravery was needed, but by Hasdrubal, so that (if it is not worthless conventional praise) was several years after Hasdrubal had assumed the command in 229, by which time Hannibal was already eighteen.⁷⁴ There follows in Livy a famous anticipatory character sketch of the adult Hannibal, which however owes much to Sallust, and concludes with a rhetorically phrased allegation of Hannibal's extreme irreligiosity which is contradicted by Livy's own narrative.

The date at which Hannibal married his Iberian wife is unknown; our only reliable source, Livy, mentions the fact retrospectively under 214 BCE, when her powerful and famous native city Castulo went over to the Roman side.⁷⁵ But it is an obviously plausible assumption that the marriage predated his departure from Iberia to Italy. Livy uses the marriage only incidentally, so as to illustrate the closeness of Castulo's previous ties with Carthage; so we should not make too much of his silences about her (he does not name her or say whether the couple had any children). But we have seen that she is best left anonymous because Silius' name for her is not reliable. Silius goes much further than merely naming her: he tells us that she had a son by Hannibal, and that he sent his wife and their – always unnamed – son back to Carthage, after his capture of Iberian Saguntum in late 219.⁷⁶ The episode is splendidly worked up and is full of literary echoes of Greek and Latin predecessors, notably Homer and Lucan, but should not be taken as fact.

Even more implausible is Silius' second and equally elaborate treatment of the 'Hannibal's son' motif, situated before the battle of Trasimene in 217: Hanno (18) tries to have the son sacrificed!⁷⁷ Both stories should be rejected as history, and with them the existence of the son.⁷⁸ Even Silius stopped short of inventing a name for the son, as he had done for the mother: that would have violated the known facts too obviously, by making Hannibal's child seem more like a reality. Any such heir to the

---

⁷³ Livy 21.4. See p. 27.
⁷⁴ Livy (21.4.10) says Hannibal served under Hasdrubal for a 'triennium', i.e. three years from 224 to 221, age twenty-three to twenty-six. This probably means he was second-in-command for those three years. The alternative explanation, preferred by Walsh 2003: 128, is that this continues the 'fiction that Hannibal came to Iberia at Hasdrubal's instigation': this invented story imputed corrupt pederastic motives to Hamilcar and Hasdrubal, and perhaps a passive role to Hannibal himself. If rumour really associated Scipio with same-sex activity, that would be a curious parallel between young Hannibal and young Scipio, but the alleged evidence probably does not refer to Scipio at all. See p. 56.
⁷⁵ 2.41.7.   ⁷⁶ 3.62–162.   ⁷⁷ 4.763–822.
⁷⁸ So, rightly, Bruère 1952; Stocks 2014: 96–102. Geus 1994: 172–3 thinks that both episodes are unhistorical, but that the son's existence is entirely credible (172 n. 1008).

great man, and a continuator of the Barcid line, ought surely to have left some trace on the reliable record. But there is no such trace.

## 2.5 Family, Childhood, and Early Youth: Scipio

Scipio's family was 'patrician' in the technical sense; that is, the Cornelii belonged to a group of privileged aristocratic families, as opposed to the far more numerous 'plebeian' families.[79] The first certainly attested Cornelius Scipio (a Publius) held office at the start of the fourth century, as a military tribune with consular power in 395.[80] But the first to be buried in the family vault was Lucius Scipio Barbatus a century later (consul 298); his tomb with its famous inscribed *elogium* survives (see Family Tree 2, which starts with Barbatus).[81] It has been neatly said that the boast of the Scipiones was that 'the Punic Wars were family business from first to last'.[82] Two members of the family were awarded triumphs over Carthaginians in the first Punic war of 264–241: Barbatus' sons Lucius Scipio in 259, the year of his consulship, and Cn. Scipio Asina (consul 260 and 254) in 253. Of these, Lucius was father of two more brothers: Gnaeus Scipio Calvus (consul 222) and Publius (consul 218), who campaigned together in Iberia until killed in 211.[83] Publius' son was Scipio Africanus who defeated Hannibal at Zama: the two subjects of this book.[84] Scipio Aemilianus, a Cornelius Scipio by adoption, sacked Carthage in 146.[85]

The Scipio family did not look east until Africanus' brother Lucius Scipio Asiagenes defeated Antiochus III of Syria at Magnesia in 190. No earlier Scipio had shown any interest in the world on the other side of the Adriatic, to judge from the records of a patchily documented period; but there is no Livy or Polybius for this period, so we have to be careful about

---

[79] See *OCD*[4] 'patricians'. For the Cornelii Scipiones, see Etcheto 2012, with the full prosopographic catalogue of the family at 157–94. For a theory that the monumental arch on the way up to the Capitol, erected by Scipio Africanus in 190, celebrated the whole family of the Cornelii Scipiones, see p. 329, citing Hölkeskamp 2018 for the complex and competitive monument as an example of architectural and artistic 'intersignification'.

[80] *DPRR* CORN0376. A problematic 'Publius Cornelius Scipio' is said by Livy (5.19.2) to have been Master of the Horse to the dictator Camillus in 396. (For those offices, see p. 90 n. 71.) See Ogilvie 1965: 671–2 and *DPRR* CORN0373: he is more likely to have been a Publius Cornelius Maluginensis.

[81] *DPRR* CORN0628. On the early Cornelii Scipiones, see the excellent discussion at Oakley 2005b: 161–6 (long n. on Livy 10.11.10), and Etcheto 2012.

[82] Henderson 1997: 36.

[83] *DPRR* CORN0722 for Lucius, father of 0817 (Gnaeus) and 0832 (Publius); 0723 for Asina.

[84] See *MRR* I: 205–6, 210, 212, 232–3, 237–9, 245, 256, 255–6, 260, 264, 269, 274. See *DPRR* CORN0978 for Scipio Africanus, the subject of this book.

[85] *DPRR* CORN1504.

making negative assertions of this sort. But it was not a Scipio but a Quintus Ogulnius who in 292 led a commission to Epidaurus to bring the serpent of Asclepius to Rome.[86] Then in 273 a three-man deputation sent to the court of Ptolemy II Philadelphus of Egypt consisted of two Fabii and the same Ogulnius. The commanders against the Illyrians in 229 were the consuls Lucius Postumius Albinus and Gnaeus Fulvius Centumalus.[87] Earlier in the century, no Scipio is attested as active against the eastern invader Pyrrhus.

Both Scipio brothers, Publius Africanus and Lucius Asiagenes, feature in a not altogether accurate literary list of Roman victories, dating from the first century CE. The Elder Seneca, author of works on declamation and rhetoric, wrote: 'Scipio may boast of defeating Hannibal, Fabricius of Pyrrhus, another Scipio of Antiochus, Paullus of Perseus, Crassus of Spartacus, Pompey of Sertorius and Mithridates.'[88] The list is in chronological order, with one exception: Pyrrhus' defeat was at Beneventum in 275, three-quarters of a century before Zama, so should be in first place. But it seems that Hannibal and Scipio Africanus were too famous to be allowed to languish in second place. Or perhaps the author, who was not writing history, wanted for some stylistic reason to separate the two Scipio brothers. Seneca the Elder assigns defeats over Hannibal to Publius Scipio Africanus, and over Antiochus to his brother Lucius. But Publius was his brother's legate and adviser for the Magnesia campaign, just as Hannibal advised Antiochus. So in a way Publius features twice in the list, as victor in both west and east.

So much for the Cornelii Scipiones. On his mother's side, which should not be neglected, Africanus was descended from the Pomponii Mathones. This was a 'plebeian' family, whose distinction did not quite match that of the Cornelii Scipiones: the consulships in 233 and 231 of Pomponia's brothers Manius and Marcus were both the first and the last to be held by the family.[89] But Manius was voted a triumph for military operations in Sardinia. Marcus may, many years after his consulship, have been the praetor who in famously laconic words announced the defeat at Trasimene in 217.[90] He commanded in Gaul as pro-praetor in subsequent

---

[86] Livy 10.47.6–7; *DPRR* OGUL0632.   [87] *MRR* 1: 182, 197, 228.

[88] *Controversies* 7.2.7: *glorietur deuicto Hannibale Scipio, Pyrrho Fabricius, Antiocho alter Scipio, Perse Paulus, Spartaco Crassus, Sertorio et Mithridate Pompeius.* The jump of nearly a century to Crassus is odd. Why did the author not add Marius' defeat of Jugurtha? The inaccuracy is that Gaius Fabricius (*DPRR* FABR0675) did not defeat Pyrrhus. In 275, the year of the defeat, Fabricius as censor lacked *imperium*.

[89] Münzer 1920: 161 [1999: 150]; see p. 41 for these brothers.

[90] Livy 22.7.8. Praenomen unknown. In *DPRR* POMP0857 he is registered as son of either the consul of 231 (Manius) or that of 233 (Marcus), and as brother of a praetor in 204 (next n.).

years, but the identifications are uncertain.[91] This means that by the time the future Scipio Africanus reached the age of thirteen in 222, the year of his uncle Gnaeus' consulship, he had no fewer than three consular uncles, and his father was consul four years later.[92] These were the living male relatives among whom the boy grew up.[93] There was also the example provided by the *imagines* of earlier ancestors, the death-masks exhibited in the family *atrium* or entrance hall.[94]

From Scipio's infancy only one actual story is preserved. It is part of the 'Scipionic legend', that is, the complex of traditions which presented Scipio as possessed of semi-divine charisma, and which reprise familiar royal or biblical type-scenes.[95] See Chapter 10.4. Even 'infancy' is however not quite the right word, because the story concerns his conception as a result of his mother's intercourse with a huge snake. Livy, who records this as a mere belief, inevitably compares it to the myth of Alexander's conception as a result of a visit to Olympias by a large snake.[96]

We know little about the education in this period of Roman children of Scipio's class in general.[97] Nothing at all is known about Scipio's in particular. Actual schools, such as are attested for even small towns in Classical Greece, sometimes when disasters happened to them, are not heard of.[98] According to Plutarch, a freedman called Spurius Carvilius was the first to open a school at Rome, between 254 and 234 BCE, a *grammatodidaskaleion* ('school for letters'), which sounds like an elementary school.[99] But education was mostly undertaken within the family – as Plutarch also says. If a Greek 'pedagogue' was hired, that would have a bearing on Scipio's knowledge of Greek to some level. A young man would normally be attached to a family member for a kind of political and

---

[91] For the problem, *MRR* I: 246 n. 4; Briscoe and Hornblower 2020: 173, n. on Livy 22.7.8. Livy records that a later M. Pomponius Matho, *DPRR* POMP1010, probably another son of the consul of 231 (if 'another' is right, see previous n.), was sent to Delphi with gifts from Hasdrubal's booty at the Metaurus (28.45.12), and as praetor in 204 went to Sicily to investigate charges against his kinsman Scipio and his legate Pleminius (29.20.4).

[92] Scullard 1970: 164, discussing the factors which helped to advance Scipio's career, writes of 'the eminence of his father and uncle'. If the consulship is an indicator of eminence, as it surely is, this should be 'father and three uncles'.

[93] Manius Pomponius is not specifically heard of after his consulship of 233, but this does not mean he was dead by 222.

[94] Flower 1996.

[95] Walbank 1985: 121, citing Dio 16 frag. 57.39, Val. Max 1.2.2. Type-scenes: Alter 2011.

[96] Livy 26.19.6–9, Gell. 6.1.1–2. Alexander: Justin 9.5.9 and 11.11.3–6 with Hamilton 1969: 4–5.

[97] For much of what follows, see Rawson 1989: 431.

[98] Disasters to schools: Hdt. 6.27.2 (Chios), Th. 7.29.5 (Boeotian Mycalessus), Paus. 9.6–8 (Astypalaea).

[99] Plutarch, *Roman questions* 59, *Moralia* 278E with Rose 1924: 196 and (date) 194.

military apprenticeship. For Scipio, it is tempting to imagine that this role was filled by his father or one of his consular uncles. When asked by someone in later life, he is reported to have rated two rulers, Dionysius I and Agathocles, the highest of all; it is probably relevant that both of them had fought against Carthage.[100] This opinion could have been formed at any time, but factual knowledge of their doings might go back to his formative years.

Two generations after Scipio, his adoptive grandson Scipio Aemilianus preferred hunting to the usual ways in which young men of his class spent their time, 'on legal cases and formal greetings'; and his biological father Aemilius Paullus brought up his sons not only on traditional Roman lines but also on the Greek pattern, exposing them not only to Greek scholars and rhetoricians, but also to sculptors and painters.[101] Cultural change was, however, rapid in the intervening years, and it would be risky to read all this back into the 220s.

An anecdote known from a three-line comic fragment of the poet Naevius, quoted by Aulus Gellius, was taken by Gellius to refer to the sex life of the teenage Scipio.[102] It says that a man whose achievements were great and many, and who has unique pre-eminence 'in the world', *apud gentes*, was once hauled away by his father, wearing 'nothing but a Greek cloak', *cum pallio unod*, from his girlfriend – or possibly but much more surprisingly his boyfriend, adopting the variant masculine reading *amico* not the feminine *amica*.[103] Either way, the sexual partner is likely to have been an enslaved person.[104] This, if there is any truth at all in the identification with the younger Scipio (unlikely), would have to pre-date

---

[100] Pol. 15.35.6 for the anecdote.
[101] Pol. 38.29.8–9; Plut. *Aem.* 6.8, with Astin 1967: 14–15 and 26–7.
[102] *Etiam qui res magnas manu saepe gessit gloriose,/cuius facta uiua nunc uigent, qui apud gentes solus praestat,/eum suus pater cum pallio unod ab amica* [or *amico*, see n. 109] *abduxit*: Ribbeck 1888: 29, Naevius incertarum fabularum frag. 111, from Aulus Gellius 7.8.3–6. For Gellius, see p. 30.
[103] *FRHist* 3: 344 (J. W. Rich); Holford-Strevens 2003: 307–8 and nn. 4, 5, and 8, who shows that the older reading is *amico* (masculine), and that the feminine *amica* is a fifteenth-century conjecture. If so, the conjecture was a good one: despite Holford-Strevens n. 8, the context is Valerius Antias' perverse belief in Scipio's womanizing, not in his vague 'lack of sexual control' i.e. same-sex activity (more shocking in Roman eyes); and Gellius would not have thought that Antias took Naevius' lines as evidence for womanizing unless he, Gellius, read *amica*. If however *amico* is right – and the Greek *pallium* might favour that – it would tend against associating the line with Scipio at all. Scipio's Rome was not Alcibiades' Athens, and if (improbably) the Naevius lines were more than merely comic fantasy, such same-sex activity as they imply could have rendered Scipio criminally liable (Edwards 1993: 71), perhaps under the Republican *lex Scantinia*, if it was already on the statute book (its exact date is uncertain). Taylor 2022: 132 n. 17 prefers *amica* because (1) heterosexual plots are frequent in Greek New Comedy, and (2) *amica* is a more insulting term than *amicus*. For the *pallium* as a Greek article of clothing (equivalent of Greek ἱμάτιον), see *OLD pallium* (1)b.
[104] And therefore (if male) a suitable object of penetration.

*Family, Childhood, and Early Youth: Scipio* 57

the elder Publius Scipio's departure for Iberia in 217.[105] The Greek tunic motif will recur much later in the Scipio story, as part of a hostile tradition that he abandoned himself to luxury at Sicilian Syracuse in 204 BCE.[106]

The comic lines are probably worthless as evidence for young Scipio's actual behaviour. But the context in Gellius does raise the question of his sexual attitudes and actions in later life, which may be discussed here. One much-discussed incident happened in 209, after the capture of New Carthage in Iberia: some of Scipio's subordinates offered him a beautiful young Iberian woman, but he declined the 'gift', at least according to the better sources.[107] Tradition made the adult Scipio unusually restrained in sexual matters, the 'Continence of Scipio' celebrated in later ages.[108] Against this favourable view, it has been objected that Scipio's 'fondness for women' is corroborated by Polybius' word *philogunēs*, 'womanizer'.[109] Not so. This word comes from the introduction to his extended narrative of Scipio's restraint in handing the Iberian girl back intact to her father, perhaps in imitation of Alexander's treatment of the defeated Persian king Darius III's women.[110] The focalization is not Polybius' own, but that of the young Roman men, presumably soldiers, who brought the girl as a gift to Scipio, 'knowing', that he was *philogunēs*. Scipio is alleged to have told them that if he were a private individual, no gift would be more welcome, but since he was a general, it was the opposite of welcome. If Scipio really said anything like this, he was unpompously teaching the odious young men a lesson and making a point about the superior

---

[105] Gruen 1990: 96 and esp. 100–1. He says 'uncertainty abounds here' and calls it a 'stock comic scene' but is reluctant to discard it altogether ('the jibes of the poet might be apposite'), citing Scipio's 'reputation for his amatory adventures': not listed. Scullard 1970: 290 n. 178 says briefly that Naevius had 'ridiculed an amatory escapade of Africanus', implying both that Scipio was indeed the target and that the 'escapade' was historical. I leave aside Scullard's main concern there, the enmity between Naevius and the Metelli family, supposedly friends of Scipio at all times. Taylor 2022: 132 judges that 'the lines undoubtedly refer to Africanus'.

[106] See p. 275.

[107] Pol. 10.19.3–7 and Livy 26.50 (without the lecture to the soldiers but with the romantic detail that the young woman was engaged to be married to a Celtiberian called Allucius). The minority view: the evidence is complicated, and this footnote can be ignored by readers indifferent to the detail. Gellius (7.8.6) attributes to Valerius Antias (*FRHist* 25 F 29, with Eng. tr. of the whole Gellius passage, 7.8.3–6) both (a) the identification of the man in Naevius – n. 102 – with Scipio (Gellius was probably wrong about this), and (b) a generally low view of Scipio's morals, 'opposed to that of all other writers' (Gellius). Gellius claims that the episode in Naevius was the basis for Antias' contrary view that Scipio at New Carthage retained the girl for his sexual pleasure. But the literary connection (Naevius/Antias) is 'fanciful'; so Rich, *FRHist* 3: 344. That is surely right. It is important that the identification of Naevius' object of ridicule as Scipio derives from Gellius not Antias.

[108] Cf. Taylor 2022: 128 and n. 2 ('quite likely based on an actual incident'); 133–4.

[109] Literally 'woman-lover': Pol. 10.19.3 with *FRHist* 3: 344 (J. W. Rich); Holford-Strevens 2003: 307 n. 8.

[110] Rawson 1989: 433; see p. 423.

obligations of high military command. Critics in the twenty-first century would certainly have preferred him to have delivered a stronger rebuke, but his mistaken leniency towards the outrages committed at Locri by Quintus Pleminius shows that he did not find it easy to reprimand delinquent subordinates. And it is a dismal fact that women and girls were and often still are regarded as legitimate war booty for male gratification.[111]

Scipio was unusually young, perhaps still a teenager, when he married Aemilia; this early marriage marks him as belonging to an aristocratic family. The evidence is indirect: the probable birthdates of his sons Publius and Lucius (see Family Tree 2). If the older son Publius was born in about 216/15, his father Africanus would have been no more than nineteen. Publius' birthdate in turn depends on the better-documented career of his brother Lucius, who was certainly praetor in 174, and must have been at least thirty then, under the *lex Villia annalis* of 180. So he was born no later than 214, and Publius earlier still.[112] The couple, then, had four children: two daughters already mentioned, Cornelia I and II, and these two sons Publius and Lucius. Of the four, only Cornelia II, the mother of the Gracchi, was a person of any real consequence and distinction. A third son and fifth child Gnaeus, bearing the only other male praenomen used by the family, is cautiously listed in the new digital Roman Republican prosopography as praetor in 177, but such a child almost certainly never existed.[113]

---

[111] For Scipio's treatment of Sophoniba, see p. 423; Taylor 2022: 142. For the Pleminius affair see pp. 163–71. He is *DPRR* PLEM1026.

[112] See Rosenstein 2004: 82 (drawing on Saller 1994) for men more usually marrying in their mid- to late twenties, and for Scipio as an aristocratic exception. Scipio's age at marriage has to be calculated from the complicated and uncertain evidence about his sons, discussed exhaustively at Sumner 1973: 35–6, cf. Rosenstein 2004: 239 n. 106.

[113] The daughters: p. 41. Sumner 1973: 35 tentatively posited a third and youngest son Gnaeus as the praetor in 174 instead of Lucius, but this is usually and rightly rejected as an error at Val. Max. 4.5.3. See Briscoe 2012: 109, discussing Livy 41.27.2. *DPRR* CORN1331 rightly makes Lucius the praetor of 174, but hesitantly accepts (CORN1309, with many question marks) that the shadowy Gnaeus Cornelius Scipio of Livy 41.8.1 (supposedly one of five men elected praetor in 178 for 177) was a son of Africanus and Aemilia. This is repeated in the entries for 'his' parents (CORN0878 and AEMI3945). But there is no other evidence, and in view of the *lex annalis* (see text) he would need to have been born in at latest 217, which would push his parents' marriage back too early. *MRR* 1: 399 n. 1 and Briscoe 2012: 59 (cf. 1973: 182 on 32.7.15) identified this alleged praetor of 177 with Cn. Cornelius Scipio Hispallus (CORN1090) who had been praetor already in 179. The identity and parentage of the praetor of 177 must remain obscure, always assuming Livy is not in simple error: by a law of 181, there should have been only four praetors, so this Gnaeus is best eliminated.

Otherwise Scipio's life is a blank from his birth to the battle at the Ticinus river in 218, when at aged seventeen he is said to have saved the life of his father Publius the consul, evidently having received the usual tough military training for a member of his social class or he would not have been there at all. Since we know that Scipio's uncle Gnaeus had trained his temporary successor in Iberia, the energetic Marcius Septimius, in 'all the arts of war', it is hard to believe that he and the boy's father did not also train young Publius, their nephew and son, in the same arts.[114]

If the Ticinus incident indeed occurred, it was the first occasion on which Hannibal and the teenage Scipio were on the same field of combat, albeit in very different capacities. Scipio went on to serve aged nineteen as a military tribune at Cannae in 216, and Silius turned this unhistorically into a personal confrontation there between him and Hannibal.[115] To make sense of the adult careers of Hannibal and Scipio, it is necessary to run briefly over the events they either witnessed or heard about in their youth, and to sketch the Carthaginian, Iberian, and Roman backgrounds to their formative years.

## 2.6 The 230s and 220s: Hannibal and His Carthage

If Hannibal left Carthage aged nine, as the oath story implies, he was a stranger to his homeland for the next thirty-five years, and to his home city for thirty-six, because he did not leave Italy for north Africa until the autumn of 203 or set foot in Carthage itself until autumn 202. He left again, this time permanently, seven years later and was an exile for the next twelve years until his death in 183. This means that he spent only seventeen of his sixty-four years in Carthage or the vicinity (247–238 and 203–195) – just one year more than a quarter of his entire life – and the rest in Iberia, Italy, and the eastern Mediterranean. After his decisive defeat at Zama, he apologized to the senate at Carthage for his manhandling of a man called Gisgo (7), a foolish advocate of further resistance, pleading his own long unfamiliarity with civic life and laws.[116] This passage at the end of Livy's third Decade

---

[114] Ticinus: Pol. 10.3, explicitly attributing the story to the younger Scipio's friend Laelius. Another version had the father rescued by an enslaved person (*FRHist* 15 Coelius Antipater F 12 with Briscoe at 3: 247), probably part of an anti-Scipionic tradition. See Scullard 1930: 37 n. 1; *HCP* 2: 198–9. For the incident see also p. 341 (an emendation in Polybius would mean that thereafter he rarely took such risks). Marcius: Livy 25.37.3. For this man (*DPRR* MARC0943) see p. 116.
[115] 9.412–85. For Scipio as military tribune, see p. 14 n. 23.
[116] Livy 30.37.9, where Hannibal is made to give the figures of nine and thirty-six years. See p. 268 for the incident, and, for Hannibal's birthdate, p. 2.

closely recalls, surely deliberately, another at the start, where his enemy Hanno advised that the absent Hannibal should be kept at home in Carthage and made to live under the same laws and magistracies as everyone else.[117]

The Carthage into which Hannibal was born was settled from Phoenician Tyre in the eastern Mediterranean, now southern Lebanon.[118] The historian Timaeus, true to Greek notions of decisive, personally led acts of city-foundation, treated this as a single epochal event.[119] He dated it to 814 BCE, and the latest archaeological finds may indicate that this was more or less right.[120] But he dated the foundation of Rome to the same year, so was also making a symbolic point about the intertwined future destinies of the two cities.[121] He had in mind Dido's foundations of Carthage and Aeneas' of Rome.[122] So at present, the beginnings of Carthage are thought to be not much earlier than the first Greek overseas settlements in the west, as traditionally dated: Cumae in Italy, 750 BCE, and Naxos in Sicily, 734, both founded by Greeks from the island of Euboea. Many Mediterranean communities were feeling the pinch of population pressure at about the same period.

'Carthage', 'Qrthdst', means 'new city' in Punic (compare Greek Neapolis, modern Naples); so when Hannibal's brother-in-law Hasdrubal (5) founded a new Carthage on the south-east coast of the Iberian peninsula, he called it just 'Carthage', not 'new new city': Carthaginian frugality with names extended to places as well as to persons. It was the Romans who gave the Iberian city, Tyre's 'granddaughter' city, the name 'New Carthage', *noua Carthago*.

---

[117] 21.3.6. This opponent is Geus 1994: 117–18, Hanno (18) 'der Rab'.

[118] The fullest and most reliable modern history of Carthage is still Huss 1985, updated but not always improved on by many of the contributions to López-Riaz and Boak 2019. (The relevant chapters are too short and sketchy to be much help and sometimes contradict each other: cf. n. 120). Pilkington 2019 (on 'the Carthaginian empire' to 202 BCE) makes interesting use of inscriptions in Punic, but they are less informative than might have been hoped; and he does not pretend to cover all aspects of Carthaginian life.

[119] The model for this epochal approach was Thucydides 6.2–5 on the cities of Sicily.

[120] *FGrHist* and *BNJ* 556 F 40, supported by Dridi 2019: 142; but Aubet 2019: 28, apparently referring in the same edited volume to the same radiocarbon evidence, prefers ca. 775 BCE.

[121] Cf. Momigliano 1977: 54. The eventual conventional date for Rome's foundation was 753 BCE, but that was not arrived at until calculations by the learned polymath Varro in the first century BCE.

[122] Timaeus knew much of Dido's story (*FGrHist* and *BNJ* 566 F 82), but Virgil was probably the first to connect her with Aeneas and his westward journey from Troy; see Hornblower 2018: 120. Traditionally, the fall of Troy was centuries earlier than any acceptable date for the beginnings of both Carthage and Rome. Dido's Punic name was Elissa (Timaeus). See further Justin 18.4–6.

## The 230s and 220s: Hannibal and His Carthage

The position of the mother-city Carthage in modern Tunisia was splendidly suited to the naval commerce for which the city became celebrated.[123] Situated on a peninsular site, it faces out into the Gulf of Tunis on the east and is separated from the interior by lagoons on the west.[124] There were two connected harbours, military and commercial, and this double harbour was called the 'Cup'.[125] A narrow isthmus provided defensive insulation. This formidably strong natural layout resembles that of many a Greek colonial foundation, most notably Syracuse in eastern Sicily – supposedly founded a year after Naxos, in 733 – where the virtual island of Ortygia is joined to the mainland by the narrowest of causeways. Greek settlements sometimes began on actual offshore islands, which functioned as a bridgehead until the new arrivals 'dared to transfer their settlement to the mainland', as Livy put it about the Euboean Greeks who moved across from Pithekoussai, modern Ischia, to Cumae.[126] A Greek or Italian trader would have found many familiar sights at Carthage, and similarly a Carthaginian at Syracuse. From this harbour, Carthaginian sea-captains led exploratory expeditions in the sixth century south along the west coast of Africa (Hanno (3)) and north to the 'Tin islands' (Himilco (1)).[127]

The century and more of conflict between the Romans and Carthaginians from 261 to 146 BCE can obscure the long preceding period of 'Rome and Carthage at peace', to quote the title of a valuable monograph particularly concerned to establish Roman 'attitudes to, and borrowings from, Carthaginian religion', and Roman purchase of Africans as enslaved people.[128]

The Romans and Carthaginians exchanged several peaceful treaties in the centuries before hostilities began in 261: in about 508 or up to half a century later, 348, perhaps 343, 306 (a renewal), and 279.[129] But the pattern of friendly diplomacy is clear, as is the marked emphasis

---

[123] On the topography, see Huss 1985: 44–51 with map at 45. There is no map of Carthage in López-Ruiz and Doak 2019.
[124] Pol. 1.73, from autopsy: he was present when Scipio Aemilianus destroyed Carthage in 146.
[125] Κώθων: App. *Lib.* 95–6/447–55; 127/605; Huss 1985: 47; De Lisle 2019: 179 (some of the building works post-date 201).
[126] 8.22.6.  [127] See p. 93 n. 89.
[128] Palmer 1997: 11. On enslaved people, he is surely correct but sometimes forces the evidence. Livy 22.33.1–2 tells of the gruesome punishment of a Carthaginian spy captured early in the Hannibalic war, then separately of twenty-five enslaved men crucified for conspiracy. For Palmer (27), there 'can be little doubt' that these 'had the same origin' as the spy. Livy could have said this but does not. On the next page, Palmer is sure the spy 'headed' the plot.
[129] This is the modern consensus on difficult problems; the evidence of Polybius and Livy is hard to evaluate because they do not always record the same events under the same years as each other. See *SVT* nos. 121, 326, 438, 466; Huss 1985: 86–92 (dating the first treaty to the first half of the fifth century), 149–55, 204–6, 201–11; Palmer 1997: 15–30.

on trade.¹³⁰ One treaty of the set is specially significant because of its date: 306 was also the year to which a speaker in Polybius dated the beginning of the formal Roman friendship with another great Hellenistic sea-power and commercial centre: the east Aegean island of Rhodes.¹³¹ There is an unmistakable west–east symmetry between these two pieces of Mediterranean diplomacy by the Roman senate. In the late fourth century, the Romans were themselves making their first serious moves towards naval power.¹³² At that time, they shared with their new friends the Rhodians a concern to reduce Etruscan piracy.¹³³ Perhaps a shared anti-Etruscan motive applied to the Roman–Carthaginian alliance also, although ancient states needed the enslaved people provided by piracy (the Carthaginians certainly supplied already-enslaved people to Rome, or for future enslavement), so they tended to intervene only when piratical activity got badly out of hand from their point of view.

In the Classical period (the fifth and fourth centuries BCE), Carthaginian forces frequently clashed with Greek not Roman enemies, competing for control of Sicily. So at Himera in 480, the tyrant Gelon defeated an alliance led by Hamilcar (1), son of Hanno of Carthage and an unnamed Syracusan mother. An inscription shows that Gelon recorded his victory at Delphi, grandly representing himself as a mere private citizen.¹³⁴ The military outcome was reversed two generations later by Hamilcar's grandson Hannibal. And this sequence – battles, successes by both sides, followed by treaties – continued indecisively through the reigns of later Syracusan strong men: Dionysius I, died 367, and Agathocles, died 289.¹³⁵ It has, however, been noticed that 'Carthaginian aggression time and again faltered at the critical moment of success ... The chain of mishaps is decidedly suspicious.'¹³⁶ On this sceptical view, Carthaginian overseas imperialism in these centuries was for long

---

[130] This emphasis is the main theme of Palmer 1997: 15–30. Ameling 1993 sought to overturn the notion of Carthage as a maritime aristocratic trading state, but see Serrati 1999. Eckstein 2006: 163 also refuses to see the early Carthaginians as peaceful traders.
[131] Pol. 30.5.6. The implied date has been questioned and the passage 'emended' to push the friendship down a hundred years later, but see Hornblower 2018: 87 n. 20.
[132] Harris 2017a, esp. 15 and 20–1 for the Rhodian aspect.   [133] Bresson 2007.
[134] Hdt. 7.165–6; ML no. 28. Himera was a Greek outpost on the north coast of Sicily (Th. 6.62.2). Whittaker 1978: 65 rightly insisted that the Carthaginians were part of a coalition and warned against exaggerating the impact and importance of the Himera victory. Dridi 2019: 151 does not cite Whittaker (nor does anyone else in López-Ruiz and Boak 2019) but concludes 'the defeat probably had a strong effect on Carthage'.
[135] Huss 1985: 92–203 for the detail of these interminable campaigns. Much of it comes from Diodorus.
[136] See next n. Eckstein 2006: 160 rejects Whittaker's conclusions, arguing that what was lacking was sufficient power and a good enough commander. This does not easily fit his line that Carthage was no less militaristic than Rome or any other Mediterranean state.

## The 230s and 220s: Hannibal and His Carthage 63

desultory and unsystematic: they saw Iberia and Sicily as spheres of influence, not subject territories.[137] More recently it has been argued, using archaeological and mainly Semitic epigraphic evidence, that it is only the bias of the Greek and Latin sources that has concealed the origins of Carthaginian imperialism; it developed through the need for an sphere of domination in North Africa: trade with Athens led to the colonization of the Cape Bon peninsula, notably at Kerkouane.[138] These radical adjustments or outright rejections of the traditional picture, based as it was on Greek and Latin literary sources and little else, are attractive. But as soon as we leave those sources behind, evidence for the motives of individuals and groups becomes conjectural – or rather, more than usually conjectural: there is plenty of authorially inferred motivation in both Thucydides and Polybius. As far as their Mediterranean rivals went, for most of the time the decision-making Carthaginians appear to have wanted no more or less than a free hand for their seaborne commerce, so that their attitudes to their Greek, as to their Roman, rivals were similarly pacific in intention. But they were ready to respond to provocation from ambitious prestige-hungry Greek warlords.

Not that Carthage itself lacked for ambitious charismatic individuals. It is difficult to devise a constitution which will be safe from subversion or outright overthrow by such people, but Carthage came close. Luckily for modern historians, the philosopher Aristotle in the fourth century took an interest in Carthaginian arrangements from a comparative perspective; and Livy narrated, with valuable and apparently well-informed political detail, an episode from the mid-190s about Hannibal's reforming activity in the years after Zama (see Chapter 12).[139] Polybius in his book 6 compared the Roman constitution and military arrangements with the Carthaginian and concluded that the Carthaginian had been superior in the past, but at the time of the war with Hannibal the opposite was true.[140]

---

[137] See Whittaker 1978, esp. 68 for the two quotations in my text. He provides a convincingly long list of such 'mishaps'. His view that Carthaginian imperial institutions in Sicily and Sardinia did not pre-date the fourth century BCE is now shared by Pilkington 2019: 44. Quinn 2018: 87 also follows Whittaker; she argues (88–90), partly on the evidence of coinage, that after about 400 the Carthaginians, a 'rising imperial power', started to appeal to a common Phoenician identity previously lacking.

[138] The Athens–Carthage nexus is important for Pilkington's general thesis. Hard evidence is provided by the inscribed but very fragmentary Athenian decree about Carthage, O/R no. 189 (with tr.), 406 BCE, cf. Th. 6.15.2 and 88. 6. See Pilkington 2019: 152–3. Cape Bon: Pilkington 2019: xv, 102, 107, 117, 181. Kerkouane: *Barr.* map 32 H3.

[139] Aristotle, *Politics* 1272–3, a difficult section, on which see Saunders 1995: 161–6; Livy 33.45–9. Otherwise, there are scattered passages in Polybius, Justin, and Diodorus.

[140] Pol. 6.51-2. In ch. 52, he says that Carthage was superior by sea, but Rome by land, because of excessive Carthaginian dependence on mercenary troops.

The main safeguard at Carthage after the Archaic period was a separation of powers: supreme military command was vested in generals, but the top civil magistrates were the *sufetes* or *shofets* (sometimes erroneously called 'kings' in some Greek literary sources), of whom there were two.[141] This naturally prompted ancient analogies with the Roman consuls (and indeed the two Spartan kings), but there was a crucial difference: unlike a consul, the *sufete* had no military authority.[142] Alongside these annual appointments were a council of elders (*gerousia*) or senate of several hundred members (including a small inner council) and a panel of 104 judges, sometimes referred to as 'the Hundred'. A popular assembly exercised real decision-making powers in situations where *sufetes* and senate disagreed. But the set-up was oligarchic, not democratic in anything like the Classical Athenian sense. And it was certainly not monarchical.[143] Livy mentions what he calls a quaestor.[144]

The Carthaginian land army, commanded by these non-political generals, included, in the fourth century at least, a 'sacred band' of 2,500.[145] This picked citizen group sounds similar to the elite Theban corps who were defeated by Philip II of Macedon at Chaeronea (338). Otherwise, the Carthaginians relied heavily on forces supplied by their allies and dependent territories, and on mercenary soldiers. It was not only Hannibal's expeditionary force which was diverse in ethnic and linguistic composition. The excellence of Hannibal's cavalry in the second Punic war is at first sight hard to reconcile with Polybius' claim that the Carthaginians pay some slight attention to their cavalry. But this is actually intended positively, as the second half of a sentence which says that by contrast they entirely neglect their infantry (itself an exaggeration); and anyway Hannibal's cavalry consisted mainly of Iberians and Numidians.[146] The contribution of elephants to Hannibal's Italian campaigns and at Zama will be

---

[141] See p. 10.
[142] For the non-military *sufete* or *shofet*, see p. 12. Pilkington 2019: 125–31 argues (125) that the office was an instrument of Carthaginian imperial control (in North Africa). Not likely.
[143] It is unlikely (see p. 266 n. 3) that Polybius in a lost part of book 23 described Hannibal as 'seeking fame in a monarchical state', although he certainly said in that context that Scipio sought fame in an aristocratic, and Philopoemen in a democratic, state.
[144] 33.46.4, evidently a financial official, from the context and the Roman analogy. The Roman quaestorship, for which see Pina Polo and Díaz Fernández 2019, was the lowest regular magistracy. The precise total of quaestors then was probably more than the previous six. Sulla in 81 raised it to twenty.
[145] Diod. 14.80.4 and 20.10.6, perhaps also 20.29.5 'those stationed around the general'; Huss 1985: 476 and n. 3.
[146] Pol. 6.52.3; Huss 1985: 477.

discussed in the narrative chapters.[147] The fleet was manned by citizen Carthaginians.[148] Polybius regarded Carthage as navally superior to Rome, but that had ceased to be true by the second Punic war.[149]

We know almost no hard facts about Carthaginian law, as opposed to generalities about the city's legal institutions. It is not easy to find out more. The fullest and most reliable modern handbook on Carthaginian history and institutions closes its mainly narrative book of nearly 600 pages with valuable general sections on the constitution, government, military matters, economy, coinage, society, literature, art, and religion, but not law as such, as opposed to the make-up of legal bodies.[150] The same is true of the Carthaginian parts of the more recent Oxford handbook of the Phoenician and Punic Mediterranean.[151]

The 'magistrates' had general jurisdiction at Carthage, according to Aristotle, who insists that they tried cases of every sort without exception, unlike the other Greek states with which he compares Carthage; by 'magistrates', a vague word, he is probably talking about the 104 judges whom he has just mentioned.[152] This body is said by Justin to have been established in the fifth century as a check on returning generals, whose acts, their *res gestae*, were examined by the 'Hundred' (as Justin calls them). These judges had acquired dominance at Carthage by 196 BCE, when Hannibal sought to curb their powers.[153]

Largely thanks to these features, there was in Carthaginian history virtually no *stasis* (civil strife) according to Aristotle, and very few attested attempts at tyranny. In the sixth century, a general called Malchus seized Carthage after some conspicuously successful overseas campaigning but was soon overthrown and executed. In 308, another general, Bomilcar (1), tried and failed to stage a similar coup and was crucified.[154] There are other such stories, few of them specific or believable.[155] (Nor is any example of

---

[147] For the types of elephants available to Hannibal see p. 26 n. 87.   [148] Huss 1985: 479.
[149] 6.52.1–2.
[150] Huss 1985. On Carthaginian religion generally, see Huss 1985: 510–46, and for Hannibal's religion in particular Huss 1986.
[151] Lopez-Ruiz and Doak 2019.
[152] His word is ἀρχαί: *Politics* 1273a19–20 and 1275b12; see Huss 1985: 465, at the end of his chapter on the constitution ('Verfassung'). For the 104 judges, see 1272b 34–5. they are probably the same as Justin's Hundred.
[153] The identity of Aristotle's 104 with Justin's 'Hundred' (19.2.5) and Livy's 'order of judges', *iudicum ordo* (33.46), is probable but not certain; see Huss 1985: 464 n. 67. Livy (33.46.3) talks of their *impotens regnum*, where the adjective means their rule was 'uncontrollable', not 'powerless'.
[154] No *stasis*: Ar. *Pol.* 1272b32. Malchus: Justin 18.7, Diod. 20.43–4.
[155] Ar. *Pol.* 1307a says that a Hanno, either in the fifth century (Geus 1994: 105 and n. 611, 'Hanno (4)'), or perhaps in the fourth-century wars against Dionysius I of Syracuse (cf. Newman 1887–1902: 4.370–1), tried to make himself sole ruler at Carthage. He compares him to Pausanias the fifth-

crucifixion for defeated Carthaginian generals securely attested, whatever Romans liked to believe.)[156] But when Hannibal in 195 was forced to flee by his political enemies, the recorded accusation against him was not that he wanted to rule Carthage like a despot, but that he was in collusion with the Seleucid king Antiochus. And as we have seen, in a heated meeting soon after Zama, Hannibal apologized for uncivil behaviour. The story in Cassius Dio, that he was tried after Zama for not capturing Rome and for stealing Italian plunder, is unreliable.[157]

The equilibrium was not seriously disturbed until the events which precipitated the 'first Punic war' between Romans and Carthaginians. (The standard modern history of Carthage naturally calls it the first *Roman* war.)[158] Its probable cause was a change in Roman senatorial attitudes: as recently as 279, when the Greek king Pyrrhus of Epirus threatened Roman control of Italy, a Roman–Carthaginian treaty actually included a clause by which the Carthaginians undertook to supply Rome with naval help in case of need.[159] The Roman decision-makers were becoming more aggressive towards Carthage, and this altered stance goes far to explain their provocative readiness to accept a protective role towards the Mamertini (the name means 'sons of Mars the war-god'), a formidable army of mercenary soldiers from Italian Campania whose lawlessly violent operations in Sicily alarmed all who came into contact with them. On one plausible reconstruction of Roman behaviour and motives, the recently concluded subjugation of the Italian peninsula left the Roman warrior class in need of a new theatre for the military glory on which political success depended.[160] This attitude was not, however, a purely officer-class phenomenon. The senate was unhappy about the morality of helping the Mamertines and regarded the advantages of intervention to be of no more than equal weight with the moral considerations. So the decision was left to the people in (probably) the centuriate assembly, which voted with the consuls, who were promising booty.[161]

---

century Spartan Regent but does not say whether, like Pausanias, he was isolated and eliminated by the home authorities. Hannibal's brother-in law Hasdrubal (5) was alleged, improbably, to have planned to subvert the laws of Carthage (Pol. 3.8.2–4 from Fabius Pictor, *FRHist* 1 F 22).

[156] See p. 384.  [157] Dio book 17 frag. 86, from Zonaras 9.14. See p. 267.
[158] Huss 1985: 216. On modern expressions for the Punic war(s), see p. 2 n. 7.
[159] Pol. 3.25; *SVT* no. 466; Huss 1985: 210.
[160] Harris 1979: 182–90. For other general approaches to Roman imperialism, see p. 7.
[161] Pol. 1.11.1–3. For the centuriate and other assemblies, see p. 173. Tan 2013 plausibly suggests that the consul Appius made sure that the voters included many of his own mobilized soldiers. Burton 2011: 128–32 argues that the moral considerations were genuinely felt. Perhaps they were, by some senators. Pol.'s emphasis on booty probably derives from Fabius Pictor: Harris 1979: 186 n. 3.

The war's fluctuating course will not be narrated here in detail.[162] Only its final phase concerns us because it brought Hannibal's father Hamilcar (9) Barca to prominence. In 247, he arrived as the new naval commander and established himself at Heircte near modern Palermo; then he abandoned Heircte and recaptured the strong elevated city of Eryx at the far west of Sicily, a place of great religious importance for its temple of Venus/Aphrodite.[163] From here, he conducted guerilla operations until 242. But in that year the war ended at sea, by the total Carthaginian defeat off the Aegates islands near Sicily. The ensuing treaty ceded Sicily to the Romans in its entirety and imposed a massive indemnity on Carthage.[164] The Romans now had their first overseas province, although the word *prouincia* in the technical sense of an regionally conceived task assigned to a magistrate was slow to develop and is first attested many years later, about Iberia in 218.[165] This settlement and the accompanying impositions were harsh enough, but the eventual resumption of armed conflict could probably have been avoided if the Romans had not taken a further step which even Rome's admirer Polybius regarded as flagrant injustice: the annexation of Sardinia on a specious pretext.[166] The background was a prolonged and bloody post-war struggle in 241–238 by the Carthaginians to suppress a revolt of their own mercenaries, some of whom had occupied Sardinia. After the revolt had been savagely suppressed by Hamilcar and colleagues, the Carthaginians moved to expel the mercenaries from Sardinia; but the Romans used this as an excuse to seize the island. In 233, the consul Manius Pomponius Matho, Scipio's future kinsman by marriage, campaigned there and was awarded a triumph.[167] This is an indication that upper-class Romans wanted Sardinia as a fresh theatre in which to gain glory, and because it was a valuable source of grain and minerals. Neighbouring Corsica was invaded in the 230s and annexed by the early 220s.[168] But this may not be an entirely new

---

[162] The main ancient source is Polybius book 1. Modern treatments: Huss 1985: 216–51, Lazenby 1996a, and Hoyos 2011 (edited collection) part 2.
[163] For Eryx and Venus Erycina, 'of Eryx', see p. 96.   [164] Pol. 1.62.
[165] Richardson 1986: 4–10. Some would argue that the territorial sense developed later and was still not crystallized even after 197 when Iberia was split into two provinces, Hither and Further *Hispania*. See Díaz Fernández 2021b: 53–9.
[166] Pol. 3.15.10 and 30.4; Harris 1979: 190–3; Derow 2015: 140–1.   [167] *MRR* 1: 224.
[168] *MRR* 1: 222–6; Harris 1979: 192–3. The evidence is scattered and less satisfactory than for Sardinia, because it is non-Polybian.

development: Aristotle's pupil Theophrastus provides tantalizing evidence for a failed Roman attempt to colonize the island at an earlier, perhaps much earlier, date.[169] Sicily, Sardinia, Corsica: Rome had suddenly become a Mediterranean power. And in the other direction, two consular armies crossed the Adriatic in the first Illyrian war of 229, the first serious military intervention by the Romans in the eastern Mediterranean. On Delos in the Aegean, Italian traders were already active, like Bouzos of Canusium in Italian Apulia.[170] In all this, there was plenty of cause for Carthaginian anxiety – and anger.

Hamilcar was now allowed by the authorities to turn his attention to Iberia; this is the context of the oath about the Romans which he invited the nine-year-old Hannibal to swear before father and son set off from Carthage. Hamilcar subdued much of southern Iberian peninsula and founded a city, Leuke Akra, 'White Promontory', probably on the site of modern Alicante.[171] When in 231 a Roman deputation arrived and demanded to know what he was doing, he is said to have replied that he was raising the funds to pay off the war indemnity.[172]

Hamilcar's death in 229 is variously reported. Polybius gives no location and does not specify the enemy. He says quite vaguely that he died 'worthily of his great achievements, fighting against the most warlike and powerful enemies, acquitting himself boldly and bravely at the moment of danger'.[173] Polybius does not say or imply that he exposed himself recklessly, as did Marcellus in 208.[174] Diodorus has a lot more circumstantial detail, and a different take. He says Hamilcar was besieging Helice, perhaps modern Elche; but the king of the Oretani came to the city's relief. Hamilcar took to flight and was pursued by the king but managed to save his sons and friends by taking a different road; he plunged on horseback into a river (perhaps the Ebro) and died in the waters, under his horse. His sons Hannibal and son-in-law Hasdrubal escaped.[175] This narrative differs from that in Polybius.[176] It is hard to know how to choose

---

[169] See Theophrastus, *History of plants* 5.8.1 with Fraser 1994: 184–5.
[170] *IG* XI (4) 642 with Hornblower 2019, suggesting that he was the father of the female benefactor Busa who helped the Roman survivors of Cannae at Livy 22.52.7.
[171] Diod. 25.10.3. Richardson 1986: 17; De Lisle 2019: 174. [172] Cassius Dio 12 frag. 48.
[173] Pol. 2.1.8. The verb for 'fighting' is παρατασσόμενος; see *Polybios-Lexikon* 2.1: col. 122.
[174] The relevant Greek (previous n.) is χρώμενος τολμηρῶς καὶ παραβόλως ἑαυτῷ. The revised Loeb edition translates 'after freely exposing his person to danger on the field', but this is too specific. See *Polybios-Lexikon* 3.2 χράω: col. 1061.
[175] Diod. 25.10.4; see *HCP* I: 152 and Richardson 1986: 19 n. 30. On the Ebro, see next n.
[176] Walbank (*HCP* as in previous n.) says Polybius' account 'though anti-Barcine, is not inconsistent with [Pol.], who prefers to stress Hamilcar's death κατὰ τὸν τοῦ κινδύνου καιρόν', 'at the moment

between them. It would be rash to prefer Diodorus without knowing his source for this period and region. It has been called 'Roman annalistic writing of the worst sort'.[177] The conclusion has to be: we do not know exactly how Hamilcar died.[178]

Hamilcar was succeeded by his son-in-law Hasdrubal (5), who avenged his death by vigorous campaigning against the treacherous culprits. If Appian can be relied on, Hasdrubal appointed Hannibal his second-in-command.[179] Over the next years, Hasdrubal extended Carthaginian control still further over southern and central Iberia but used diplomacy as well as force, perhaps including his marriage to an Iberian wife, if this had a political aspect as it probably did.[180] This, if historical, anticipated Hannibal's marriage to his Iberian wife.

Hasdrubal, like Hamilcar, founded a city. It was on a spectacular, brilliantly chosen site facing the Mediterranean on the east coast of Iberia, and would play an important role in the Hannibalic War: New Carthage.[181] And it was Hasdrubal who agreed to the restrictions on Carthage of the 'Ebro treaty' of 226/5, the alleged breach of which by Hannibal was an immediate cause of that war with the Romans. At about the same time (the sequence is controversial), the Romans made an alliance with the coastal city of Saguntum; the implications of this for Roman relations with the Carthaginians were far from innocent. Hasdrubal was assassinated in 221 and succeeded by Hannibal, who had been in Iberia uninterruptedly since 238.[182]

We now leave Hannibal for the moment, to look at Roman affairs in the years when Scipio was growing up.

---

of danger'. He reports Diodorus as saying Hamilcar was drowned 'still fighting', but these words have no equivalent in Diod. 25.10. They may be based on 25.19 (= Johannes Tzetzes, *Chiliades* 1.27, lines 700–19), a longer and explicitly derivative version of what looks like 25.10, but Tzetzes in the *Chiliades* is famously inaccurate. Tzetzes is probably just embroidering Diodorus, and his specification of the famous 'Ebro' no more than a guess.

[177] Schwartz 1959: 73. This derogatory sense of 'annalistic' is no longer favoured.
[178] Appian gives yet another version of the death (result of an Iberian trick entailing wagons pulled by oxen and loaded with firewood). Here Walbank (*HCP* 2: 152) is right to say that it does not fit into Diod.'s account.
[179] Appian *Iberian history* 6/23 (ὑποστράτηγος); Huss 1985: 478 and n. 30; Wollner 1987: 105.
[180] Diod. 25.12, if this source can be trusted. See Family Tree 1, n. 5.
[181] Pol. 2.13.2 (cf. 10.10), Diod. 25.12. See Ramallo Asensio and Ros Sala 2015: 162–72.
[182] Livy (21.3.2) says Hasdrubal summoned Hannibal (from Carthage) by letter. This, from a speech at Carthage by the family's enemy Hanno (18), is accepted by Huss (1985: 278 with n. 79), but Hoyos (2003: 85) is right to reject it as part of a smear story about sexual relations between the two men. Livy himself makes Hannibal speak of his complete absence from his homeland before returning in 203.

## 2.7 The 230s and 220s: Roman Events in Scipio's Youth

Scipio was twelve years younger than Hannibal, so he played no active role in the events of the 230s and 220s. What follows can therefore be briefer than the previous section. It will merely outline the main events the boy *would have heard* discussed at home or among his peers, or even witnessed for himself.[183]

Roman history in these years is very hard to recover in detail because of the loss of Livy's books 11–20, his second Decade, apart from a small fragment of book 11 and brief later summaries of all the missing books, the *periochae*. Livy's third Decade (books 21–30), which covers the war with Hannibal, survives complete. We have the first two books of Polybius, but his history concentrated on foreign affairs. Some of his detailed narrative covers the first Punic war and its consequences for Carthage and Rome. The years 225–222 saw heavy Roman fighting against the Celts or Gauls by the consuls of those years; one of these was Gaius Flaminius (cos. 223), who was to die at Trasimene in his second consulship, 217.[184] The sources for 223 emphasize his disobedience to the senate and neglect of the auspices, just as in 217, the events of which may however have coloured the tradition retrospectively.[185] But his radical tribunate in 232 had already made him unpopular with the senatorial class.

Trouble with Gauls was nothing new. By contrast, two other wars were epoch-making in that they brought consular armies across the Adriatic for the first time: the so-called Illyrian Wars of 229 and 219, under the commands of two pairs of consuls: Albinus and Centumalus in 229 and Lucius Aemilius Paullus and Marcus Livius Salinator in 219.[186] In later consulships, the last-named pair went on to command armies in Italy against Carthage: Paullus fell defeated by Hannibal at Cannae in 216, and conversely Salinator defeated Hasdrubal at the Metaurus river in 207. The date at which the Roman senate began to interest itself politically in the lands to the east of the Adriatic has been much discussed, but the minimalist view

---

[183] The words in italics are, I confess, a good example of the 'past presumptive' tense, for which see p. 7, citing Thonemann.
[184] *MRR* 1: 230–3, esp. 232 for Flaminius, who is *DPRR* FLAM0793.
[185] For the auspices (*auspicia*), 'birdwatching', see *OCD*⁴ *auspicium*, and (on Flaminius in 217) Konrad 2022: 212–54. This Roman ritual, divinatory observation of the behaviour of birds, was held to provide divine validation (or not) of proposed action by magistrates.
[186] Pol. 2.11; *MRR* 1: 228 (with 227 for the incident which provoked the first war) and 236. For Paullus see p. 43 and Family Tree 2; Salinator is *DPRR* LIVI0827

## The 230s and 220s: Roman Events

(no serious interest before 201) should be rejected, partly because of epigraphic discoveries since 1921, above all an important inscription from (most likely 220s) Chios mentioning Romulus and Remus.[187] The first Illyrian war was always hard to dismiss as an anomaly.

This open military engagement with the Greek world was a novelty, but contacts of other kinds were long-standing. The Romans were admitted for the first time to the Isthmian festival and games near Corinth in 228; but Romans had visited Delphi, where the Pythian festival and games were held, at least as far back as an embassy sent in 394, admittedly not as athletes or charioteers.[188] But a celebration of the four-yearly Pythian festival and games fell in that same summer 394.[189] So it is very possible that the Roman delegation witnessed the event or at least the preparations for it. The Pythia and Isthmia were two of the four great festivals of the old Greek world, together with those at Olympia and Nemea. When the proconsul Titus Quinctius Flamininus proclaimed the freedom of the Greeks at the Isthmian festival of 196, he was using the same technique as Alexander the Great in his proclamation of the Exiles Decree at the Olympic festival of 324.[190] There was some equivocation here, to put it mildly: in the same year (228) that the Romans were first admitted to the Isthmian games in Greece, a Gaul *and a Greek* were buried alive at Rome, an expression of fear of external threats.[191] The patrician consul of the year was Quintus Fabius Maximus Verrucosus ('warty'), the 'Delayer'.[192] What were educated young Romans of the senatorial class expected to make of this? Scipio was seven at the time. He was probably brought up on stories of Carthaginian barbarities. The historicity of that most notorious of

---

[187] Minimalist view: Holleaux 1921; cf. p. 145 n. 48. But Derow and Forrest 2015 (revised version of a 1982 study): 262 (with n. 26, making clear this section was primarily the work of Forrest), drew attention to the anti-Macedonian character of Roman diplomacy in the years after 305: friendly contacts with Rhodes from 305, Egypt from 273, Aetolia from 263, and Pergamum from 211. On the date (disputed) of the Chios inscription, see Hornblower 2018: 87 with n. 20; 116–18.

[188] Isthmian games: Zonaras 8.19.7. Delphi in 394: Livy 5.28.1–5 with Ogilvie 1965: 689 (and 660–1 on 5.15.1). The tradition has been doubted (see e.g. Hoffmann 1934: 129–31) but is rightly defended by Ogilvie.

[189] The start date of the Pythia was held to be 582.    [190] Diod. 17.109.1. Flamininus: p. 249.

[191] Orosius 4.13.3, Zonaras 8.19.9, Tzetzes, commentary on Lycoph. *Alexandra* 603–9; see Briscoe and Hornblower 2020: 310–11, n. on Livy 22.57.6 (which records a similar sacrifice after Cannae, on which Livy comments both that it was un-Roman but also that it had been done before, *iam ante*, in fact in 228). The motive: Eckstein 1982. At the same moment in 216, as Livy has just reported (22.57.5), Quintus Fabius Pictor was sent to Greece to consult the oracle at Delphi, an even more striking equivocation.

[192] *DPRR* FABI0712. The closest *MRR* (1: 228) gets to mentioning this horror is a bare citation of Tzetzes (previous n.) as evidence for Fabius' second consulship of 228; nor do the Isthmian games feature at all.

Carthaginian practices, child sacrifice, has been doubted by archaeologists and historians in the past, but it is now thought credible.[193] There is, however, no doubt about the parallel evidence for human sacrifice *at Rome* in Scipio's early lifetime.

In the uneasy interval between the first and second Punic wars, the western Mediterranean saw continued Roman military activity, which was surely a topic of conversation in the houses of senatorial families. It is obvious that vigorous Carthaginian operations in Iberia during the 220s, as already narrated, were closely watched: the Ebro treaty and Roman diplomacy with Saguntum. Roman control of Sicily and Sardinia was a direct and immediate consequence of the first war, but the gruelling annexation of Corsica was not fully achieved until the 220s. All this needed explaining to young men ambitious for military glory.

## Appendix 2.1  Objections to a New Theory about the Name Barca

This appendix considers and rejects the main thesis of Hill 2020, according to which the family of Hamilcar, and therefore also of his sons Hasdrubal and the great Hannibal, were fairly recent immigrants from the Greek or partly Greek city in Cyrenaica called Barke, as Herodotus calls it.[194] (The Hellenistic city was renamed Ptolemais.) The family were in fact, so the theory goes, *mixellenes*, 'mixed Greeks'. Hill has a lengthily developed theory to account for how the first relevant member of the family might have ended up in Carthage. In a nutshell: his explanation is that this was after military service under Ophellas in the late fourth century. He explains Mago the 'Samnite' in a similar sort of way. He denies, against the consensus, that Βάρκας means 'lightning' or 'thunderbolt' (like Scipio, on Norden's view of Virgil's *duo fulmina belli*).[195] But he maintains rather that is an *ethnic*, although Hill never actually uses that technical word for

---

[193] See p. 228.
[194] *Barr.* map 38 B1; Hdt. 4.160.1 (written as if introductory, but already mentioned at 3.91.2). He spells it in his usual Ionic Greek way, with final eta, Barkē, and this form prevailed in literary texts, as at Diod. 1.68.2, Strabo 17.3.21, Steph. Byz. (n. 201), and Claudius Ptolemy 4.4.11, although the local spelling in the West Greek dialect of Cyrenaica would have been Βάρκα with final long alpha, just as Cyrene was Κυράνα locally and for Pindar. This must be why Jacoby on *FGrHist* 270 (Menekles of Barke), Jones 1971: 350–5 and Applebaum 1979 spell the city 'Barka' without explaining why. But the spelling Βάρκα is not certainly attested on coins or in inscriptions from Barke itself. For the regular ethnic Πτολεμαιεῖς ἀπὸ Βάρκης ('citizens of Ptolemais from Barke') in papyri and inscriptions from elsewhere, see Cohen 2006: 393 and Fraser 2009: 363.
[195] See Hill 2020: 72, but at Cicero's speech *For Balbus* 34, which Hill cites, the preferable reading may be *lumina*, 'lights', not *fulmina*, 'thunderbolts': Reid 1908: 78. Norden's view: see p. 49.

an adjectival inherited indicator of local origin.[196] Modern cities have ethnics too, such as 'Londoner', 'Madrileño', or 'Sydneysider'. The thesis is bold, wide-ranging, and ingenious, but should be rejected.

(1) It would be astonishing if Hannibal were really a sort of Greek, and yet neither Polybius, whose life overlapped with Hannibal's, nor anyone else in all antiquity drew attention to the fact. Hill plays up Barke as a Phoenician city and plays down its Greekness.[197] But it had an Olympic victor in 460 BCE at a time when Greekness was still strictly policed as a criterion for entry.[198] There is also Herodotus' Greek foundation story for Barke; and Sophocles includes chariots from Barke in a deceptive but plausible chariot race narrated in detail.[199] It can however be freely admitted that there was probably a sizable Carthaginian element in the city's population, at any rate by the third century BCE. Hill well discusses such mixed groups as Libyphoenicians and so on.[200] This argument is not intended to exaggerate Barke's Greekness. Certainly, it was more of a *Libyan* city from the outset than was Cyrene, and its very name looks un-Greek.

(2) The standard ethnic of the city of Barke was Βαρκαῖος.[201] Polybius uses it of a man called Ammonius.[202] So he knew the correct usage perfectly well and would not have departed from it in so inexplicably anomalous a direction. Hill claims that 'the forms ὁ Βάρκας and Βαρκαῖος are nearly the same'.[203] Not so. Ancient grammarians studied ethnics intensely, and they formulated rules about them; Fraser (2009) analysed the plentiful but often difficult evidence. Place names like Thera or Barke – examples Fraser actually uses – regularly end in -αῖος.[204] Anyway, if Barkas were an ethnic it would be accented oxytone, that is with an acute accent on the last not first vowel: not Βάρκας but Βαρκάς like Ἀρκάς, 'Arkas', the regular ethnic of a person from Arcadia.

---

[196] Ethnics are not themselves 'toponyms' (substantival place names), as implied at Hill 2020: 76. They are adjectival, *derived from* toponyms. See Fraser 2009.
[197] Hill 2020: 79–82.
[198] Moretti 1957 no. 261 (Amesinas). Policing: cf. Hdt. 5.22, Alexander I of Macedon.
[199] Hdt. 4.160.1; Soph. *El.* 727, using the correct ethnic Βαρκαῖος.
[200] Libyphoenicians were part-African, part-Punic (Phoenician).
[201] Steph. Byz. Βάρκη, β 45 Bill. The 'ethnic' Βαρκαῖος was sometimes used as a personal name; for this general category of names; see Bechtel 1917: 536–46, also Fraser 2000 and 2009: 215–24. Bechtel's list includes Βαρκαῖος, father of a priestess Xanthippe at Ptolemaic Cyrene; for this and other examples see *LGPN* 1.
[202] 5.65.8.   [203] Hill 2020: 76, cf. 99.   [204] Fraser 2009: 63.

Stephanus of Byzantium's entry Βάρκη gives a couple of variant ethnics, but Βάρκας is not one of them.[205]

(3) Expressions for 'called' or 'so-called' (the verbal form ὁ ἐπικαλούμενος in Polybius, the noun ἐπίκλησιν in Appian) are used of Hamilcar's extra name Barkas; but that is not a formula used by Greek writers for true ethnics. Polybius uses ἐπικαλούμενος of Roman *cognomina*, after giving the *nomen* in first place, so he refers to 'Claudius called Nero'.[206] This use of the compound verb goes back to the Classical period: Xenophon uses it for the nicknames of the Athenian Theramenes as 'buskin' (i.e. political trimmer) and the Spartan Dercylidas as 'Sisyphus' ('wily', after the mythical character of that name).[207]

(4) Hill rightly stresses the relevance of certain other Carthaginians, most of them in Polybius, who are interestingly designated by what look like ethnics.[208] But in each case bar one, these Polybian names are, like Barkas, accompanied by one of the 'so-called' expressions, or variants.[209] Hill discusses 'Mago the Samnite' at some length.[210] But he does not note that Polybius actually calls him 'the *so-called* Samnite', ὁ Σαυνίτης *προσαγορευόμενος*, where the participle is equivalent in sense to ἐπικαλούμενος. So this is not a true ethnic or indicator of origin, but some kind of nickname.[211] Its bearer was an evidently Carthaginian officer and friend of Hannibal.[212] So too there is, in the first Punic war, a Hannibal 'the so-called Rhodian',

---

[205] Geus 1994: 220–1, on the meaning of 'Barca', rightly ignores the city in Cyrenaica.
[206] 18.10.8. He usually gets these right, but 'Cocles called Horatius' at 6.55.1 is the wrong way round.
[207] *Hellenica* 2.3.31 and 3.1.8.
[208] See Geus 1994: 224 for additional names of this topographical sort, but he does not use the term 'ethnics'.
[209] Another variant is ὁ καί, 'who was also', as at Diod. 25.8, 'Hamilcar who was also Barkas'. The most famous (but still imperfectly understood) example of this is 'Saul who was also Paul' at Acts 13.9, on which see Williams 2015 and Corsten 2019: 138.
[210] Pol. 9.25.4, the only reference anywhere to him as 'Samnite'. Hill 2020: 95–6, cf. 78 n. 77. He is Geus 1994: 'Mago (10) der Samnit'.
[211] Classical Athenian examples of ethnics as nicknames are Theramenes 'the Ceian', referring to the island of Ceos (Davies 1971: 228, no. 7234) and perhaps Lichas 'the Samian' (Hornblower 2011: 222). Geus 1994: 224 rightly rejects the idea that Mago (10) the Samnite's extra name was a victory name comparable to Roman *cognomina* like Africanus. He thinks such topographical names were genuine indicators of origin (i.e. ethnics) but does not discuss the difficulty of the 'so-called' type of formula.
[212] Walbank (*HCP* 2: 154) considers the possibility that Hamilcar 'who had the extra name the Samnite' (ᾧ Σαυνίτης ἐπώνυμον ἦν) at App. *Lib.* 68/305 and 70/318 (150 BCE) was Mago's grandson, in which case the by-name might, as he says, have been hereditary. Domestication of some unfamiliar Phoenician word (see again Walbank) is likelier. In the inventory of the paintings owned by Charles I of England, Pieter Bruegel the Elder is listed as 'old Peter Brewgill' (Ferris 2020: 170–2).

## Appendix 2.1

apparently named from the island of Rhodes, a powerful maritime state like Carthage.[213] Is it significant that his only appearance in history is for a *naval* exploit?

To this generalization about the addition of 'so-called', the sole exception in Polybius is 'Mago the Bruttian' (after Bruttium, a region in extreme south Italy) without 'so-called'.[214] But Walbank is probably right to call this too a 'nickname', applied for reasons beyond our recovery.[215] Genuine mixed Carthaginian-Italian parentage is however a possibility.[216] Hill rightly cites Herodotus' remarkable statement that the fifth-century BCE Carthaginian general Hamilcar (1) had a Syracusan mother.[217]

One possible explanation for such designations as 'the so-called Rhodian' is visits by the individual to the area in question. Carthaginians certainly moved around the Mediterranean in more peaceful times. In the mid-fourth century BCE, a Carthaginian called Nobas was awarded proxeny, an honorary diplomatic status, by the central Greek Boeotians.[218] One can imagine that back home in Carthage this might have earned him the hypothetical nickname 'Nobas the Boeotian'. Three Latin writers mention a diplomat Hamilcar (he went on a mission to Alexander the Great) with the apparent *cognomen* 'Rhodanus', which is most plausibly interpreted as 'from the city of Rhoda/Rhode', a north Iberian coastal foundation by Massilia (Marseille) in southern Gaul, a place whose ethnic was

---

[213] ὁ ἐπικαλούμενος Ῥόδιος, Pol. 1.46.4. See Geus 1994: 73, where however he is, despite Polybius, inexplicably listed as 'Hannibal (6) der Rhodaier' (which would mean 'from [Iberian] Rhoda', like Hamilcar (4); and cf. 224 for the additional name, treated as an indicator of origin, but without discussing 'the so-called'. At Pol. 1.46.10 and 59.8, this Hannibal is simply 'the Rhodian', without addition of 'so-called', but also without his name 'Hannibal'. This is understandable short-hand: Polybius would not have written 'the so-called Rhodian'.

[214] 36.5.1. Hannibal 'the Rhodaian' (previous n.) is another exception (he is not 'so-called'), but he is not in Polybius.

[215] HCP 3: 657.

[216] For this Mago, see Geus 1994: 191–2, 'Mago (15) der Bruttier', and 224, where he is among those individuals whose additional names are conjectured to be indicators of origin (i.e. ethnics). In fact, he is the *only* really plausible candidate for this category, since he is, uniquely, not designated the 'so-called Bruttian'.

[217] Hdt. 7.166; Geus 1994: 36–40; Hill 2020: 78. Terrenato 2019: 91 and n. 50 sees this as an indication that Syracusan and Carthaginian elites (a term he does not properly define, despite pp. 43–51 where it is equated with 'aristocracy') were building on 'existing links of intermarriage and friendship' as support for their 'mutually incompatible expansionist policies'. The general conclusion is paradoxical, and we know nothing about the background of this particular marriage. For the converse phenomenon, two Syracusan brothers with a Carthaginian mother, see Livy 24.6.2 (215 BCE, Hippocrates and Epicydes, cf. p. 146). On Terrenato 2019, see Harris 2021.

[218] R/O no. 43.

Ῥοδαῖος.²¹⁹ This extra name, if correctly transmitted, might refer to visits to Rhoda or even to Massilia in southern Gaul, a very plausible destination for a mobile Carthaginian.

(5) Hill proposes, against earlier translators, to take *Sarrana prisci Barcae de gente*, 'sprung from the Phoenician/Tyrian house of ancient Barcas', near the opening of Silius Italicus' epic as 'meaning the city in Cyrenaica rather than a [male] person named "old Barca"'.²²⁰ This is linguistically impossible.²²¹ The Latin *prisci* is here the masculine form of the genitive of the adjective *priscus*; but the name of the Greek city Βάρκη is feminine in Herodotus, and so is the equivalent Latin toponym *Barce*, as Silius himself knew.²²² So for Hill's theory to work as a matter of Latinity, it would be necessary to emend *prisci* to the feminine *priscae*, but Hill does not suggest this. On the correct translation of the line in Silius, it certainly does imply that Hamilcar was not the first of his family to be called Barcas, and that, as far as it goes and for what it is worth (which is not a lot), is support for the idea of a 'Barcid' dynasty. But Silius goes on to trace Hamilcar's family to Dido's father the mythical *Belus*, and he calls Barcas son of Belus, *Belides*.²²³ Historically, this is very dubious evidence. It seems to be an attempt to make Hannibal an actual blood relation of Dido, almost as if Silius is taking literally Dido's final prayer in Virgil for an avenger 'out of my bones', meaning the famous Hannibal (9).²²⁴

---

²¹⁹ Geus 1994: 42–3, 'Hamilcar (4) der Rhodaier' and (for the pseudo-ethnic) 221 n. 1297. The ancient evidence: Orosius 4.6.21, *Rhodanus*, Justin 21.6.1, *Rodanus*, Front. *Strat.* 1.2.3, *Rhodinus*. (Ennius, *Annals* 213 Sk., Goldberg and Manuwald 2018a: 218–20, evidently had the story, but he is not a source for the name 'Hannibal Rhodanus'.) None of the variants encourage us to take it as 'Rhodian', i.e. from the island of Rhodes (as by HCP 1:110, Skutsch 1985: 380). The standard ethnic for a man from Rhodes is Ῥόδιος, Latin *R(h)odius*, occasionally *Rhodiensis*. For the solution (Iberian R(h)oda, *Barr.* map 25 I 3), see Norden 1915: 87 n. 1 and Skutsch 1985: 380, citing Steph. Byz (p 40 Billerbeck) Ῥόδη for the ethnic Ῥοδαῖος. Since Geus accepts it, I do not understand why he calls Hannibal (6) 'der Rhodaier'.
²²⁰ *Punica* 1.72, about Hannibal's father Hamilcar. Hill 2020: 74.
²²¹ So also at the only other occurrence of the name *Barcas* (not *Barce*) in Silius, where *proles Barcae* must mean 'offspring of Barcas': 17.460, placed symmetrically at the end of the epic, to match the opening.
²²² See e.g. Hdt. 4.160.1; Silius *Punica* 3.251.
²²³ Sil. 1.72–5. Belus (like his son Barcas) has no separate entry in the 'mythical and literary persons' section of Geus 1994: 205–16, but for Belus see p. 208, under 'Dido'.
²²⁴ *Aen.* 4.625. Cf. Tupet 1980: 189. Virgil himself went some way in this direction by giving Dido's dead husband Sychaeus' nurse the name Barce (4.632; cf. Hornblower 2018: 120 n. 68, with acknowledgment to Denis Feeney). See p. 412. The Carthaginian Barce, wife of Spartan Xanthippus at Silius Italicus 4.356, is a different woman, but part of the same tendency. Both women are missing from the 'mythical and literary persons' section of Geus 1994: 205–16. They belonged at his p. 206.

I conclude that Hill's thesis should be rejected. It might be objected that '(so-)called Barkas' might still allude in a vague way to a Carthaginian who had some sort of connection with or fondness for the city Barke, without any implications about family origins. But then it is hard to see why Polybius and other Greek authors did not use the properly constructed ethnic, 'Hamilcar the so-called Barkaian', Ἀμίλκας ὁ Βαρκαῖος ἐπικαλούμενος, on the analogy with the so-called Rhodian or Samnite.

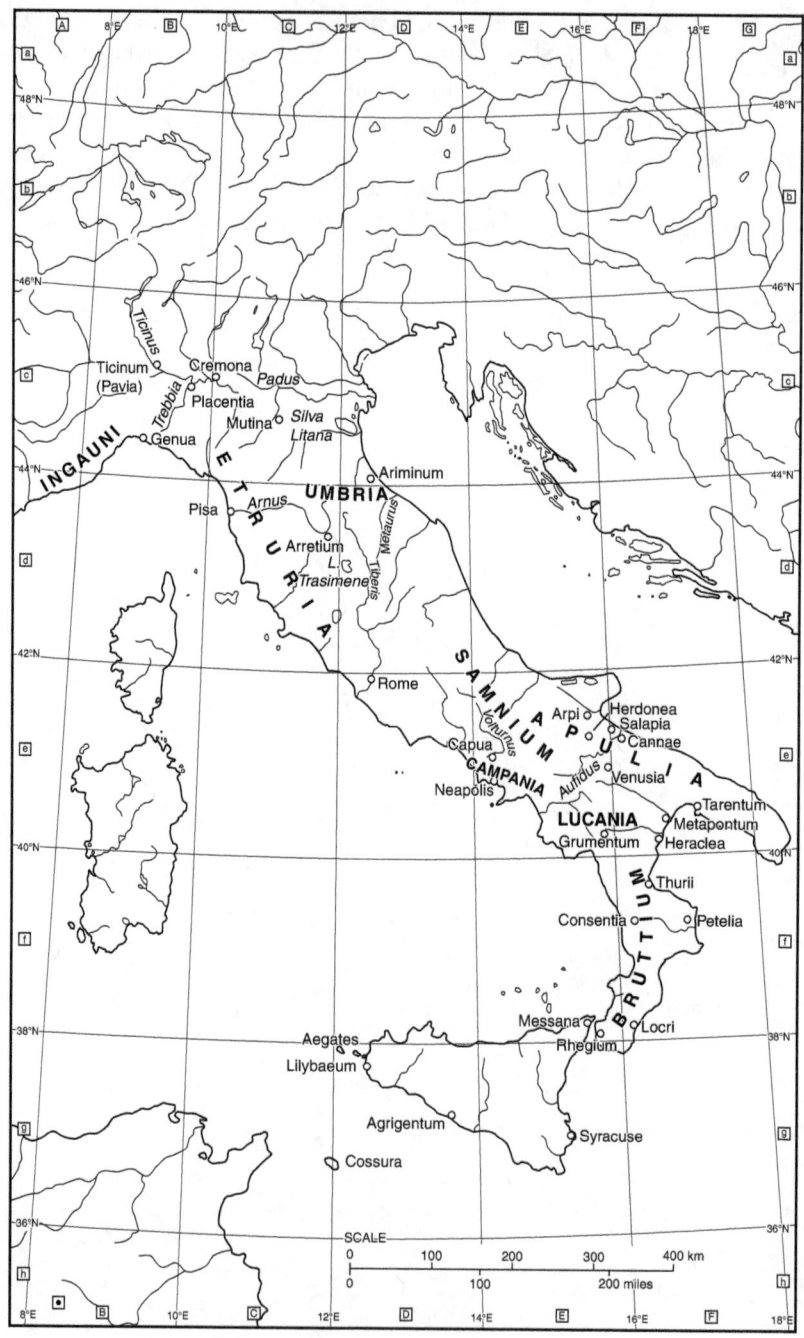

Map 2  Italy and Sicily

CHAPTER 3

# *Hannibal Victorious, 221–216*
## *Aged 26–31 Years*

### 3.1 Hannibal as Commander in Iberia

Scipio's appointment to the Iberian command aged twenty-six was phenomenally precocious by Roman standards. Hannibal was exactly the same 'young age', *aetate immatura* as Justin put it, when he was immediately and unanimously acclaimed supreme commander by the army in Iberia.[1] But civil ratification by the Carthaginian assembly at home was needed, as Polybius and Livy make clear.[2] And there may have been a further stage of ratification at Carthage: by the senate.[3] But the senatorial debate recorded by Livy at this point does not relate to the absent Hannibal's appointment as commander in 221. It relates to a much earlier time when the attractive boy Hannibal was still in Carthage and had been sent for by Hasdrubal for sexual motives, a slanderous fiction.[4]

Hannibal now (221–219) asserted himself militarily, vigorously attacking and subduing Iberian peoples to the north and west of New Carthage: the Orcades and their capital city Althaea (Polybius) or Cartala (Livy), the Vaccaei, and the Carpetani.[5] Cartala provided him with plentiful booty, a never-to-be overlooked factor in the financing of ancient warfare. His

---

[1] 29.1.7, after a list of young hereditary rulers who, by coincidence, acceded to their thrones in the same year 221, starting with Philip V of Macedon.
[2] Pol. 3.13.3–4, Livy 21.3.1 'the approval of the *plebs* followed'. Cf. Huss 1985: 279 and n. 87; 478; Hoyos 1994: 249–52.
[3] Livy's text of the relevant sentence is corrupt. See Briscoe's OCT. Some words may have dropped out to the effect that *the senate approved the army's choice* – so explicitly App., *Iberian history* 8.30 – and the people, the *plebs*, followed suit.
[4] Senatorial debate: Livy 21.3.2–6. Livy jumps several years back in time between 3.1 and 3.2 and returns to the interrupted sequence only at 5.1. So rightly W/M on 5.1.
[5] Livy 21.5–6; Pol. 3.13–14. For the city's name, see Livy 21.5.4; Pol. 3.13.5. *HCP* 1: 317 places it inland up the Guadiana River, but it may (Walsh 2003: 129) have been coastal, north of New Carthage. *Barr. map-by-map Directory* p. 452 lists it under 'unlocated toponyms'. The tribal regions: *Barr.* map 27 A2–3 (Olcades, with a query), 27 AB 1–2 (Carpetani), 24 G3 (Vaccaei).

victory against the third of these peoples, on the River Tagus at a site near modern Toledo, is the reader's first sight of him in action.[6] He stationed his forces on one side of the river and by deliberate inaction lured the enemy to attempt a crossing, whereupon he unloosed his forty elephants at them. The Carpetani withdrew; the Carthaginians now crossed successfully and easily routed the enemy. There is an element of cunning and subterfuge here, anticipating his tactics at the Trebia.[7] It is the kind of ploy which gave rise to the notion of 'Punic trickery', much favoured by Livy but already present in a small way in Polybius.[8]

## 3.2 Saguntum and the Causes of the War with Rome

Hannibal's next move was far more serious in its implications and consequences: an attack on the city of Saguntum in eastern Iberia, on an elevated site near the coast.[9] 'Livy's account of the origins of the Second Punic War is very dramatic – we shall never forget Saguntum's fall – but glides over the surface of things.' So wrote Momigliano, in an influential essay on the causes of ancient wars.[10] This was a way of saying that Livy failed to distinguish between the two types of cause defined by Thucydides and refined by Polybius. Thucydides thought that the true but unavowed cause (*prophasis*) of the Peloponnesian war was Spartan fear of the growth of Athenian power, but he then listed the immediate and publicly alleged reasons (*aitiai*) alleged on either side. Polybius, surely with Thucydides in mind, added a third tier of explanation, 'beginnings', *archai*.[11] And he further echoed the phraseology of Thucydides when he said that the Romans thought that Hasdrubal was making Carthaginian power in Iberia 'greater and more formidable'.[12] If we adopt this scheme – deep as opposed to surface causation – Livy can on Momigliano's view be said to have neglected the 'true but unavowed causes' in favour of the (mere) alleged reasons and beginnings.[13] Although Polybius was Livy's main source for the Hannibalic war, he does not, in the surviving books, adopt Polybius' view that its cause was

---

[6] Pol.'s account at 3.14 is simpler and clearer than Livy's at 21.5.     [7] Cf. Livy 21.54.4–9.
[8] 3.78.1 (describing Hannibal's wig disguises as a precaution against assassination). For *Punica fraus* as an important theme in Livy, see Briscoe and Hornblower 2020: 291 n. on 22.48.1, citing ancient passages and modern discussions.
[9] On the much-discussed problem of the origins of the second Punic or Hannibalic war, see esp. Rich 1996, concluding that Polybius was essentially right to explain the war in terms of the 'wrath of the Barcids'. See further p. 82 for the degree of Hannibal's personal responsibility.
[10] Momigliano 1966: 121.     [11] Th. 1.23.6; Pol. 3.6.6; cf. Hornblower 2011: 306.
[12] Pol. 2.13.3. But only the phraseology: at 3.8.1–9.2, Polybius rejects Fabius Pictor's view that Hasdrubal's ambition and love of power was a cause of the war. Cf. Moore 2020: 41 and n. 19.
[13] For ancient ideas about historical causation, see Pelling 2019 (not only about Herodotus).

the unjust Roman seizure of Sardinia from Carthage.[14] Modern analysis goes deeper still and suggests that the cause of the changed attitude towards Carthage was that the Roman officer class needed fresh outlets and theatres for aggression, now that control of peninsular Italy was secure.[15] The qualification 'in the surviving books' is, however, important: Livy's books 11–20, which made up the entire second Decade, are lost, but the brisk later summary (*periocha*) of Livy's book 20 – not the work of Livy himself – shows that he did report that the Romans 'suppressed rebellions' on the islands of Sardinia and Corsica.[16] This expresses a pro-Roman view, to be sure (Sardinia was really the locus of rebellion against *Carthage*). But it is just possible that Livy's original full narrative in book 20 was somewhere accompanied by anticipatory ('proleptic') comment on the deeper causal significance of these Roman actions. So Livy's superficiality may have been unfairly exaggerated by Momigliano. But his word 'dramatic' was right, as will appear. Other Iberian cities had fallen to Hannibal, but only Saguntum gets the full treatment in the sources. Why? Saguntum was special because it was a Roman ally, and Hannibal knew exactly what he was doing.[17] Two pieces of Roman diplomacy, both probably in the mid-220s, had made it clear that the Romans had interests in Iberia: in combination, these were provocations and made a collision with Carthage inevitable.[18] The first in time was the Roman alliance with Saguntum, a place thought of as connected to Rome by various ties of kinship. One of these ties was with similar-sounding Zacynthus, which was one of the 'Ionian islands' of the Adriatic Sea between Greece and Italy, and which had supposedly treated Rome's wandering mythical founder Aeneas kindly.[19]

The second piece of diplomacy, by which the Carthaginians undertook not to cross, that is go north of, the River Ebro under arms, was an implied

---

[14] 3.15.10 and 30.4.  [15] Harris 1979. For Sardinian and Corsican fighting, see next n.
[16] *Sardi et Corsi cum rebellassent, subacti sunt.* In *MRR* (1: 231–2), this is taken to refer to, and only to, (a) the original occupation of Sardinia by Tiberius Sempronius Gracchus, consul 238 (*DPRR* SEMP0761), cf. Pol. 1.88.8–12 (with *HCP* 1: 149–50: the right Livian date may be 237), and (b) the Corsican operations of Gaius Licinius Varus, consul 236, *DPRR* LICI0783. That fits the general order of narration in *periochae* 21 and 20. But *periocha* 20 may have condensed what in Livy were events of several years. Reduction of those two islands was neither quick nor easy. For example, Scipio's uncle Manius Pomponius was awarded a triumph for warfare on Corsica in 233 (*MRR* 1: 224).
[17] The precise relationship (formal or informal?) is uncertain. See Richardson 1986: 22 (cf. 29, where he calls Saguntum a Roman 'ally').
[18] On the causes of the war, a much-disputed topic, see (for the view here taken) Harris 1979: 200–5; Briscoe 1989: 44–5; Seibert (1993b): 117–20); Briscoe and Hornblower 2020: 3–4. See also Rich 1996 and Beck 2011 (over-confidently claiming at 234 that the 'wrath of the Barcids' can be 'dismissed from the academic discussion'). On Schwarte 1983, see Rich 1985.
[19] Coarelli 2001 (dating the alliance earlier than the 220s); Aranegui Gascó 2006: 73 (Hercules as symbol of the Rome–Saguntum link); Fragoulaki 2013: 260 on Dion. Hal. 1.50.3 (Aeneas).

renunciation by Rome of territory south of the river: see Map 1.[20] In itself, the second was not a *casus belli*, an act of provocation leading inevitably to war, but it was inconsistent with the first, because Saguntum was certainly south of the Ebro in reality (admittedly there is some confusion in the ancient sources about this).[21] So if the Carthaginians attacked Saguntum, the Romans would be bound to defend their allies.

When Hannibal looked certain to attack Saguntum, its citizens appealed to Rome for help. But Roman intervention was very slow to come – instead, the two consuls of the year were sent off to fight in Illyria across the Adriatic – and the siege began. A two-man Roman embassy arrived to warn Hannibal off; he forwarded it to Carthage, where in Livy's account the Barcids' family enemy Hanno (18) delivered an unsuccessful speech urging the repudiation of Hannibal. The long fierce siege continued, and Livy applies to it all his powers of narration.[22] He describes the desperate counter-walling of the defenders as the Carthaginian siege works inched their way towards the centre of the ever-diminishing city. Near the end, many of the survivors started a fire in the forum and threw in the city's gold and silver, and 'most of them jumped in themselves'. After the city fell, Hannibal is to have spared the sanctuary of Artemis 'motivated by piety', *religione inductus*.[23]

How far was Hannibal's attack on Saguntum the result of his own unauthorized initiative? This is part of a more general problem about overseas commands, affecting Scipio as well as Hannibal.[24] Livy says baldly, immediately after narrating Hannibal's appointment to the command, that he 'decided to make war on the Saguntines', *Saguntinis inferre bellum statuit*.[25] The early Roman diplomatic demand for the surrender of Hannibal himself (a suggestion endorsed by Hannibal's Carthaginian enemy Hanno (18)) and the inquiry by the later Roman ambassadors, whether Hannibal's attack on Saguntum was authorized or not, imply that the Romans were willing to regard the attack as his unauthorized initiative.[26] This would help to explain

---

[20] Pol. 2.13.7. Richardson 1986: 25 and n. 61 may well be right that this was not an actual clause of the treaty, but that was its implication. Eckstein 2012 upholds the view that the Romans made the concessions of the treaty through fear of the Gauls.

[21] Polybius usually gets this right. The main exception is 3.30.3, where he seems to say that Hannibal's attack on Saguntum broke the Ebro treaty, but he has probably failed to make it clear enough that he is here adopting a point of view ('focalization') not his own. See Richardson 1986: 22–4.

[22] That Hannibal struggled to take Saguntum by siege is relevant to his later decision not to besiege larger and better-protected Rome.

[23] Livy 21.11.11 and 14.2 (details of the siege). Artemis: Pliny, *NH* 16.216; Huss 1986: 224 and n. 8.

[24] See Chapter 6.    [25] Livy 21.5.1–2.

[26] So Rich 1996: 31, citing Silius (was it the madness of Hannibal that started the war or the Carthaginian senators?). Demand for Hannibal's surrender: Livy 21.6.8, cf. 21.10.13 (Hanno). Ambassadors' inquiry: 21.18.2–3.

their slowness. Certainly, several years after the war had been well and truly lost, Hannibal's enemies were happy to describe him as having been personally responsible for starting the war as well as for waging it.[27] But that easy Hannibal-blaming attitude was only to be expected.

On the other hand, Polybius says that Hannibal did send to Carthage for instructions about Saguntum, but frustratingly he does not record an official reply. Only Appian does so: he says the senators told him to take whatever action he saw fit. We can, if we like, welcome this as conveniently filling in a gap in the record.[28] But it is doubtful whether Appian had good independent evidence for that reply, given that Polybius was his usual source. It is possible to imagine why Hannibal's inquiry was not answered, if it was not: a divided and nervous senate might at this initial stage have preferred 'plausible deniability'. The tentative conclusion should be that the authorities at Carthage accepted a war which Hannibal's independent actions did much to bring about.

Hannibal's longer-term thinking is a matter for speculation. It was obvious that an attack on Saguntum meant war with the Romans. What did he hope to achieve and how? Had he already planned to invade Italy by crossing the Alps (that would have been very far-sighted), and if so, what did he expect would happen then, and what did he want? Not a 'war to destruction', a *Vernichtungskrieg*, as is clear from his refusal to attack Rome after his crushing victory at Cannae, and by the clause in his treaty with Philip V of Macedon (215) which envisaged Rome's survival after defeat.[29] Rather, he wanted to loosen or end Roman dominance in Italy, hence his differential treatment of Roman and Italian prisoners after the great battles, notably Trasimene in 207. Reasonable war aims would have been parity of esteem between Roma and Carthage and the restoration of Carthaginian naval and commercial ascendancy in the west Mediterranean.

## 3.3 War Declared; Hannibal Leaves for Italy

It was in late 219 that Saguntum (and with it plenty more booty) fell to Hannibal, after eight months of close conflict, and without an immediate Roman declaration of war in support of their friends, *amici*, the Saguntines.[30] But this declaration duly followed at the beginning of the new consular year,

---

[27] Livy 33.45.8, 195 BCE.
[28] Pol. 3.15.8 (cf. Hoyos 1994: 257); Appian, *Iberian history* 10/37. Filling a gap: *HCP* I: 323 ('he was probably authorized') and Lazenby 1978: 25, both citing Appian.
[29] See p. 143.   [30] Booty: Livy 21.15.1.

218; the delay does not indicate pacific Roman intentions.[31] The new consuls were Scipio's like-named father Publius, to whom by the lot was assigned the whole of *Hispania* (Iberia) as province, and Tiberius Sempronius Longus, who was initially allotted Sicily and Africa but was instructed in a letter from the senate to join his colleague in north Italy when the scale of the emergency became clear.[32] This was the first time that *Hispania* had been assigned as a province to anyone, and it continued to feature on the annual list of provinces for the rest of the Republican period.[33] Polybius drew the correct conclusion: the senate expected that the war would be fought in Iberia.[34] One of the praetors, Lucius Manlius Vulso, was sent to Cisalpine Gaul.[35]

A larger Roman deputation now left for Carthage, to put just one question: was Hannibal's attack on Saguntum officially authorized, carried out *publico consilio*? If the answer was yes, they were instructed to declare war. The five *legati* now sent were all senior figures in every sense, both elderly (*maiores natu*), and all but one of them former consuls. These included a Lucius Aemilius (probably Paullus), consul in 219 and 216, who was to die at Cannae; and Marcus Livius, probably Salinator, consul in 219 and again in 207 when with his colleague Gaius Claudius Nero he defeated Hannibal's brother Hasdrubal at the battle of the Metaurus.[36] The *legati* were led by a Fabius, probably not the famous Quintus Fabius Maximus the 'Delayer', but Marcus Fabius Buteo.[37] After listening to a wordy speech from an unnamed Carthaginian senator, Fabius merely gathered his toga and offered the choice of peace or war. A shout came in reply: 'Give whichever you like.' So he shook out his toga and said he gave war. The rhetorical Livy might have been suspected of inventing this memorably vivid moment and gesture, but no, it is in his source Polybius.[38]

---

[31] Burton 2011: 240–2 has to explain Roman slowness as evidence that their notions of 'friendship', *amicitia*, were 'inherently flexible'.

[32] Pol. 3.40.2; Livy 21.17.1 (initial lot); 21.51.5 (senatorial letter). In this period, the senate designated in advance (the verb is nominare) the areas of command for senior magistrates. Their precise areas were then decided by the lot (*sortir[*]). See W/M on 21.17.1; *OCD*[4] 'provincia/province'. Longus: *DPRR* SEMP0833.

[33] Richardson 1986: 1. [34] 3.14.3 with Richardson 1986: 31 and n. 3.

[35] Manlius: Livy 21.17.7; *MRR* I: 237–8. Manlius (*DPRR* MANL0836) got into difficulties with the Gallic Boii and had to be rescued by his fellow-praetor, Gaius Atilius Serranus (*DPRR* ATIL0835).

[36] Livy 21.18.1. For the identifications see *MRR*: I: 241 n. 8 (followed by *DPRR* AEMI0826 and LIVI0827), arguing against W/M's view that Paullus and Salinator were too young to be called *maiores natu* and would anyway have been detained in Rome by their trial for embezzlement (for this view see also Gruen 1990: 91 n. 50, citing *MRR* for Salinator's later career but not I: 241 n. 8). But this view of W/M was abandoned in the relevant vol. of the most recent ed. (1921, rev. Rossbach). As for the trial, *MRR* is right, citing Münzer 1926, that the embassy could have preceded the trial; so too W/M (1921) and by implication de Sanctis 1968: I and 465.

[37] *DPRR* FABI0762; cf. Scullard 1973: 42 and 274.

[38] 3.33.3–4, compare Livy 21.18.13–14. Polybius narrated another laconic ultimatum half a century later (168): Gaius Popilius Laenas in Egypt drew a circle in the sand with his staff, demanding a reply before Antiochus IV left the circle: 29.27.5. See p. 378 n. 43.

Hannibal now prepared to leave Iberia for Italy, after first visiting Gades and discharging his vows to Hercules/Melqart and making new ones.[39] It was now that he made the dispositions of forces which, many years later, he recorded in detail on the bronze tablet at the sanctuary of Juno or Hera Lacinia near Croton.[40] These included forces left behind in Iberia, and others for the protection of Carthage, as well as those which he took with him to Italy. Realizing that the cooperation of the Celts of Cisalpine Gaul would be crucial for the success of his planned invasion, he sent messengers there with 'unlimited promises'; the Celts' answers were encouraging.[41] He left his younger brother Hasdrubal (6) in charge of most of Carthaginian Iberia, and a little later Hanno (21) was assigned to the Iberian region adjoining the Pyrenees.[42] Hannibal never again saw his brother Hasdrubal alive.

## 3.4 Across the Alps and into North Italy

Hannibal crossed the Pyrenees and Alps into north Italy.[43] The passage over the Pyrenees should not be neglected in favour of the Alps, as it often has been, in both ancient and modern times. But Juvenal, in a highly selective list of Hannibal's achievements and vicissitudes, and despite his double treatment of the Alps, nevertheless found room to mention that 'he crossed the Pyrenees', *Pyrenaeum / transiit*.[44] But the main prose sources are not interested in the details of what must have been a tough passage through the Pyrenees: in their narratives, Polybius and Livy both dispose of it in just five words.[45] Instead, they prefer to explain at length how Hannibal led his army over the Rhône north of Massilia (Marseille) and to dwell on the logistical feat by which he got his thirty-seven elephants across, probably on rafts rather than making them swim; elephants are good swimmers, and if they drown, as can happen, it is probably from heart

---

[39] Livy 21.21.9: and see p. 233 for the dream-epiphany which he experienced on his way up the coast to the Ebro, 21.22.5–23.1.
[40] For the full details see p. 11.
[41] Pol. 3.34.1–4, with Walbank *HCP* 1: 365, rightly rejecting the suggestion (Hoffmann 1951) that he initially intended only to subdue northern Iberia but changed his mind on hearing of the Roman declaration of war. The suggestion is, however, accepted in the Loeb Polybius, revised by Walbank himself and Habicht in 2010 (vol. 2: 89 n. 90). Richardson 1986: 29 stresses the importance of the Gauls or Celts in Hannibal's thinking, given the weakness of the Carthaginian navy after 241.
[42] 3.35.5.
[43] On the focalization of the Alps narrative through Hannibal, see Pausch 2011: 142–56.
[44] In his *Satire* on the vanity of human wishes, 10.151–2; cf. 152–3 and 166–7 for the Alps.
[45] Pol. 3.35.7, Livy 21.24.1. In addition, Livy makes Hannibal, in indirect speech, encourage his troops before the Alpine crossing by reminding them that they had made their way through the Pyrenees past fierce tribes: 21.30.5 and 7. Cf. 23.45.3, Marcellus (more indirect speech).

failure.⁴⁶ Hannibal's elephants have always exerted fascination. On the last stages of his way to the Alps, Hannibal's forces had trouble with one group of the Allobroges tribe but routed them successfully, although his own troops suffered losses.⁴⁷

The consul for 218, Publius Scipio, who had sailed from Pisa to the Massilia region to take up his Iberian command, was completely taken by surprise by the speed of Hannibal's advance, and he narrowly failed to make contact with the enemy. Scipio then made the momentous decision to send his brother Gnaeus Scipio Calvus on to Iberia, while he himself sailed back to Italy.⁴⁸ He had no opportunity to consult the senate about this: the decision to persevere with Iberia was his alone, and it 'was to prove crucial both to the course of the war and to the history of Roman Spain'.⁴⁹ (And, we can add, to the career of his greater son.) Such independent decision-making on the spot was a recurrent feature of the overseas careers both of Hannibal and of Scipio Africanus.

Publius would not return to Iberia until 217.⁵⁰ Gnaeus, who had sailed from the Rhône mouth to Emporium, a Greek foundation near modern Barcelona, defeated and captured both Hanno (21), the Carthaginian commander of the region, and Andobales (or Indibilis), king of the Ilergetes. Then he went into winter quarters at Tarraco. He took with him large quantities of booty. Hasdrubal partially retrieved these reverses by a sudden attack on the over-complacent Roman crews, but the booty stayed in Roman hands.⁵¹ 'Go, you madman, rush through the savage Alps, so that you may please schoolboys, and become a subject for declamation.' So Juvenal. Despite the 'but all of them ended up in a coffin' sarcasm which is the message of the military-glory section of the poem, in the next line he places Hannibal's achievement by implication in the highest possible category:*unus Pellaeo iuueni non sufficit orbis*, 'one world is not enough for the boy from Pella'. That is, for Alexander

---

⁴⁶ Pol. 3.42.1–47.4 and Livy 21.26.6–29.7; Scullard 1974a: 156–8 (the elephants).
⁴⁷ Macdonald 2015: 95–6; Oakley 2019b analyses acutely in detail Livy's use of and changes to Polybius' narrative here (Pol. 3.50.1–51.13, Livy 21.32.6–33.1).
⁴⁸ Pol. 3.49.1–4. For Gnaeus Scipio, see p. 54.
⁴⁹ Pol 3.64.10; Livy 21.32.3 and 40.3–4 (Publius tells his men his brother is in Iberia 'under my auspices' but also 'in accordance with the wishes of the Roman senate and people'); see Richardson 1986: 33–5 with nn. 6 and 16; quotation in text from p. 35; independently, but with similarity of thought and expression, Eckstein 1987: 189 ('this may have been a crucial decision . . . the whole course of the war, and of Roman history, might then have been different', sc. if Scipio had acted differently. See also, in the same approving spirit, Lazenby 1978: 52). But Eckstein, unlike Richardson, says (Publius) Scipio sent his army on to Iberia 'because the senate had mandated it'. When exactly?
⁵⁰ See p. 115.
⁵¹ Pol. 3.76. Livy 21.60–1. For Emporium near Barcelona (*Barr.* map 25 I3, marking it 'Emporiae'), see Castanyer, Santos, and Tremoleda 2015: 109–11, and for similarly coastal Tarraco, modern Tarragona (*Barr.* map 25 G4), see Ruiz de Arbulo 2015.

*Across the Alps and into North Italy* 87

the Great. Hannibal's spectacular passage of the Alps with an army and elephants cried out for comparison with his protector Hercules, Greek Herakles, Carthaginian Melqart, who, in the Roman (not the earlier Greek) mythical tradition, had in one of his twelve Labours (the pursuit of the cattle of Geryon) crossed the Alps on his journey from Iberia to Italy and built a military road between the Alps and the sea.[52]

Hannibal's own exact route across the Alps is disputed to this day. He clearly left the Rhône to follow its tributary the Isère, but there agreement ends. The likeliest mountain pass must be one whose Italian end is closest to Turin, where he is first heard of in action after his descent.[53] That probably indicates that the best candidate for the pass is the Col de Clapier.[54] Astonishingly, all his elephants got through; but at Trasimene in 217 there was only one left, on which Hannibal himself rode. (The numerical attrition among the elephants was due to the bad spring weather and casualties from the fighting in north Italy.) It is possible that the single remaining creature was a one-tusked Indian beast called Surus, mentioned by Cato as the bravest in the Carthaginian battle-line.[55] Hannibal himself lost an eye at this time from the foul weather, so that the most formidable one-eyed enemy of Rome (there were others) now perhaps rode on a one-tusked elephant.[56] If so, when Juvenal wrote 'when the one-eyed leader was riding on a Gaetulian [African] beast', he did not know about the Indian Surus, or he forgot, or he simply did not care to be pedantically accurate.[57]

---

[52] Juvenal 10.166–7 and 168 ('one world . . . ', the family motto of James Bond). Hercules: Diod. 4.19.3–4; cf., for the 'road of Herakles' (the first Greek source to feature this), Ps.-Aristotle, *On marvellous things heard*, 85, which does not, however, mention the Alps, just as Diod. 4.19 does not mention Hannibal. Tarn 1948: 392–3 insisted, rightly, that Diodorus did not mean that Herakles' road *cut through* the Alps. Later Latin traditions specifically associated Herakles with the Alps (p. 71). The cattle of Geryon: one derivation of 'Italia' was from *italus*, a bull: *FGrHist* 566 Timaeus F 42.

[53] For the Taurini, who gave their name to the modern city, Pol. 3.60.8, Livy 21.38.5.

[54] Walbank 1985: 107–19 [orig. 1956]; for the Col de Clapier, Proctor 1971: 210–16; Lazenby 1978: 45–6 with plate IV; 302 map 3. But Hoyos in Yardley 2006: 620–30 at 626–9 prefers the Col de Montgenèvre further south. The Taurini: *Barr.* map 39 B3.

[55] Pol. 3.74.11. For the one elephant, see Scullard 1974a: 161; Briscoe and Hornblower 2020: 155, n. on Livy 22.2.10. For Surus, see Cato, *FRHist* 5 F 115 and Ennius *Annals* 540 Sk. (Goldberg and Manuwald 2018a: 396–7) with Scullard 1974a: 174–7; Charles 2008: 342 (but I am not sure why he says Scullard in 1974 had 'retreated from his earlier position', that is, from the identification of Surus with Hannibal's one elephant).

[56] Pol. 3.79.12, Livy 22.2.11; cf. p. 27. For other 'one-eyed men against Rome' (e.g. Sertorius and Civilis), see Africa 1970 and Moeller 1975. For the general theme of one-eyed commanders in history, see J. Hornblower 1981: 222–3 on Antigonus 'the One-eyed', citing Nelson and quoting Tolstoy on Field Marshall Kutuzov. One-eyed queen: Candace, successful against Roman armies in the time of Augustus: Strabo 17.1.54. For Philip II of Macedon, see p. 339.

[57] 10.158 with Scullard 1974a: 161.

When news reached Rome that Hannibal was already across the Alps with an army and had entered Italy, Publius Scipio's consular colleague Longus was recalled and led his army post-haste up Italy to Ariminum, modern Rimini. He had reached Lilybaeum in western Sicily on his way to take up his African command and had even found the time to cross from Sicily to Malta and take the island from the Carthaginians.[58]

### 3.5 The Battles at the Ticinus and Trebia, 218

In north Italy, Hannibal defeated the Romans in a mainly cavalry engagement at the River Ticinus.[59] That was followed by a larger battle at the River Trebia near Placentia (modern Piacenza), another tributary of the Padus (modern Po).[60] These are the first two of the four Roman defeats or disasters – Latin *clades* can mean either – in rapid succession and increasing order of magnitude; the others are Trasimene (217) and Cannae (216).[61]

Before the Ticinus, both Polybius and Livy report speeches of encouragement by Hannibal and Publius Scipio, although they position them in different orders.[62] Livy makes Scipio interestingly remark that Hannibal claimed to be a rival to Hercules as traveller. He gives Hannibal a denunciation of Roman imperialism absent from Polybius; this is thought to reflect the self-lacerating Roman historiography of Livy's own time; but the speech is generally magnificent and in effect an authorial tribute to Hannibal by its amplification of the Polybian original.[63] Hannibal had preceded his speech by staging a memorable object lesson (*paradeigma*): he brought forward some prisoners from the Alps in poor physical condition from ill use and invited them to fight each other like gladiators: the winners would win prizes of horses and military cloaks, the losers would die. They all volunteered. Hannibal now addressed his troops and told them they faced the same choice: 'conquest or death'.[64] The episode has some resemblance to Herodotus' story

---

[58] Pol. 3.61.9 and 68.13–14; Livy 21.50.11–51.7 (51.1–2 for Malta, on which see p. 289).

[59] Polybius says (3.65.9) that it was both a cavalry and infantry battle, but that was (as he says) because many of the riders dismounted during the battle. At 3.68.9, it is called a cavalry battle only.

[60] *Barr.* map 39 D3 and F3. See also the battle map at Connolly 1981: 169.

[61] Livy 22.31.10, relating to the period before Cannae, calls Trasimene the third *clades*, which implies that Ticinus was the first and Trebia the second. See Briscoe and Hornblower 2020: 245. For Trebia as a *clades*, see 21.57.1.

[62] Pol. 3.63 (Hannibal), 64 (Scipio); Livy 21.40–1 (Scipio), 43–4 (Hannibal).

[63] Livy 21.41.7 (Scipio on Hercules); 21.44.5 (Hannibal on Roman imperialism), with Walsh 2003 [1985]: 206; Adler 2011: 87–98; Burton 2019: 32. On the speech as a fine contribution to Hannibal's positive literary afterlife, see p. 409.

[64] Pol. 3.63.2, cf. Livy 21.43.5, *hic uincendum aut moriendum*; see also §2, 'that wasn't just a spectacle but an image of your own situation'.

of Cyrus the Great summoning the Persians and making them spend one day clearing thorny shrub-land and the next day feasting; he then asked them which day they preferred and got the obvious answer. He drew the conclusion: endure lives of hardship and slavery, or free yourselves from the Medes and have fun. If the similarity is admitted, it need not show knowledge of Herodotus on anyone's part, neither that of Greek-speaking Hannibal nor the sources. It might be that in real life, ancient generals sometimes found that such simple object lessons worked better than fancy rhetoric.[65]

In the battle at the Ticinus (mid-October 218), Hannibal's cavalry outperformed Scipio's, and this fundamental Roman weakness would not be fully redressed until Zama in 202.[66] The battle also illustrated Hannibal's 'favourite tactic' of pinning the enemy's centre while attacking his wings and rear.[67] Publius Scipio was wounded in the battle. Polybius and Livy says that the son saved his father's life, and Livy adds that this was to be the young man who would end the war and be called 'Africanus', a forward reference to the outcome of Zama in Africa.[68] The narrative anticipation – 'prolepsis', in the language of narratology – is notable: Livy will soon be narrating a string of Roman disasters, but at the same time he prepares the reader very early on and metahistorically for the change of fortune. At the very beginning of the third Decade, he had said that 'the *eventual victors* came closer to ruin than their opponents'.[69]

Scipio's wound meant that the newly arrived Longus played the leading Roman role before and during the ensuing battle at the Trebia, although Longus consulted his convalescent colleague, who in vain urged delay. This places the primary blame for the defeat at Longus' door. It is possible that the Trebia narrative of Polybius, who was a friend of Scipio Aemilianus, is a little biased against Longus, out of friendly loyalty to the Scipionic family.[70] This disagreement between the consuls introduces the important theme of the Roman commander who acts impetuously, often against the protests and warnings of a more cautious colleague. The theme is already present in

---

[65] Hdt. 1.125–6. Moore 2020: 53 notes that instead of relying on historical examples, as Publius Scipio had done, Hannibal gives his troops 'a more relevant model'.
[66] Pol. 3.65; Livy 21.46–7. Livy's account characteristically differs from Polybius' by opening with gloomy portents which had to be expiated: a wolf entered the camp, and a swarm of bees settled above the commander's tent.
[67] Lazenby 1978: 33.
[68] Pol. 10.3; Livy 21.46.7–8, rejecting at 46.10 a rival version which gave the credit to an unnamed Ligurian slave.
[69] 21.1.2; compare his portentous words about Scipio after Cannae as 'predestined leader', *fatalis dux*, of the war, 22.53.6 (p. 106).
[70] Pol. 3.70.1–8. See *HCP* 1: 404 (n. on §5); Lazenby 1978: 59 agrees but defends Longus' decision to try and knock Hannibal out before he could recruit more Celts.

Polybius but is much sharpened by Livy, especially in book 22, which narrates not only the main Roman disasters at Trasimene and Cannae but the intervening clashes between the two men who were chosen to cope with this leaderless emergency, Fabius the 'Delayer' as dictator and his Master of the Horse Minucius.[71] The Alexander-historians had played with the same motif of temperamental opposition between colleagues, but it is usually Alexander who overrules the cautious Parmenio and gets away with it by success. This sort of personality clash is not generally exploited so as to illustrate Hannibal's qualities, except that, in his verbal exchange with Maharbal after Cannae, he allows himself to be rebuked for failure to exploit his victory boldly and immediately.[72] So he is there presented as the cautious one.

Hannibal's tactics at the Trebia were clever and successful: an attack while the enemy were cold and breakfastless, and an ambush by Numidians under the command of his brother Mago (6).[73] He also made battle use of elephants for the only time before Zama. The invading Carthaginians had clearly won, but their victory was not a rout, because the vanguard of the Roman centre fought well, and they were able to retire to Placentia, where other survivors joined them.[74]

The next occasion on which the two consuls of a year together faced a Carthaginian invader in north Italy, after one of them had driven an army up through Italy at top speed, would have the opposite outcome: the decisive battle of the Metaurus in 207, won by Livius Salinator and Claudius Nero against Hannibal's other brother Hasdrubal.

### 3.6 The Battle at Lake Trasimene, 217

After Trasimene in the following year, the praetor Pomponius would memorably announce at Rome a defeat in a great battle.[75] It might have been better for the Romans if the disaster at Trebia had been announced with similar starkness, because that would have put the senate and future commanders more clearly on notice that the republic faced its most formidable invasion

---

[71] For Minucius, see *DPRR* MINU0820. 'Dictator' in this period, at least, has a very different meaning from the modern and negative word for an autocrat. A dictator was an entirely legitimate officer, appointed with supreme power for a short term in an emergency. See Wilson 2021. His second-in-command was called *magister equitum*, 'Master of the Horse'; see Wilson 2021: 211–35, concluding (235) that the dictatorship 'consisted of two men'. For the theme of rashness versus caution, persistently stressed in Livy book 22, see Briscoe and Hornblower 2020: 46–7. And compare Livy 21.53.8 on Longus (focalized through Hannibal).
[72] Livy 22.51; see p. 105.
[73] Pol. 3.69–75; Livy 21.53–6; Lazenby 1978: 55–8 and his map 5 for the likely battle site.
[74] Pol. 3.74.4–8. See Lazenby 1978: 58.   [75] See p. 96 for the words used.

since that of Pyrrhus more than half a century earlier.⁷⁶ As it was, Longus initially tried to conceal the defeat, although the truth soon percolated through, and the authorities took defensive steps: troops were sent to Sicily, Sardinia, and Tarentum; a fleet of sixty quinqueremes (warships) was prepared; Hiero II of Syracuse was asked for military help and sent it. The consuls-elect, Gaius Flaminius and Gnaeus Servilius Geminus, who would take up office in March 217, began energetically recruiting and forwarded supplies to their intended bases at Ariminum and Etruria.⁷⁷

Iberia needed no immediate attention. At any rate, we are told of no action taken.

Livy reports that during the painfully wet and freezing winter after the battle at the Trebia, Hannibal led two raids on Roman trading centres, *emporia*, in the Placentia region and was wounded in the first raid.⁷⁸ The wound may be historical: Polybius does not mention it but is silent about Hannibal's operations in this winter generally. He does say that he spent it in Cisalpine Gaul, and that it was during this winter that Hannibal started disguising himself with wigs of various colours and changes of clothes.⁷⁹ The wound, the loss of the eye, and the anxiety about assassination make the shrewd and decisive generalship in 217 and 216 the more impressive.

A more typical absence from Polybius of a topic narrated in massive detail by Livy at the end of his book 21 is the list of alarming prodigies and corresponding expiatory rituals. His assumed reader is thought of as knowing that these prefigure the Trasimene disaster where Flaminius fell. But, says Livy, the measures taken were largely effective at the time in allaying religious fears. No such cheerful formula closes his otherwise comparable list near the beginning of Livy's next book.⁸⁰ He is ramping up the tension. He also reports, as Polybius again does not, the related senatorial accusations of improper religious behaviour levelled against Flaminius; he was criticized for having entered his consulship at Ariminum instead of performing the required inaugural vows and sacrifices at Rome: 'they said he was at war not only with

---

⁷⁶ Trebia as *clades*: Livy 21.57.1.
⁷⁷ Pol. 3.75. For these two see *DPRR* FLAM0793, SERV0852. For quinqueremes, see p. 209 n. 12.
⁷⁸ Livy 21.57.8 (the wound). *Emporia* is a loanword from Greek ἐμπόρια, 'markets'. The common translations, 'supply/storage depots', are not quite right. One of them was at Victumalae (Livy 21.57.9). *Barr.* map 39 C3 puts it about 20 km north-west of Vercellae, but this is a long way from Placentia, so Livy may have got the name wrong. On the other hand, Strabo (5.1.12) says Vercellae and Victumalae were near each other, and both were near Placentia. See Walsh 2003: 209 (n. on 21.45.3).
⁷⁹ Winter in Gaul: Pol. 3.77.3. Wigs: Pol. 3.78.1–4; Livy 22.1.3. On 6 July 2023, CNN carried a video showing the results of a raid on the office of 'Wagner' military chief Yevgeny Prigozhin. Items found included a cache of different-coloured wigs 'presumably for disguise'.
⁸⁰ 21.62.11, contrast 22.1.8–20. 'Largely' is *magna ex parte*.

the senate but with the immortal gods', a splendid sentence.[81] This chapter of Livy explains, in a retrospective analysis which reprises or assumes some material presumably given fully in the lost book 20, the reasons why Flaminius had enemies in the senate: earlier in his career (232), he had as tribune passed or supported popular, anti-senatorial, legislation, a law about public land. But he was more than a populist: in his first consulship (223) he had won a victory against the Insubrian Gauls, although a hostile literary tradition criticized his tactics. Gaius Terentius Varro, the consul in 216 who lost the battle of Cannae, will be similarly presented as a demagogue. As Flaminius sacrificed a calf, the creature escaped and spattered the crowd with blood, and this was seen as a bad omen. This is a classic illustration of an important justificatory move in patriotic Roman history-writing: Roman defeats must be due to divine anger, incompetent generalship, or difficult terrain – anything but military inferiority.[82]

Flaminius marched his army from Ariminum across the Apennines into Etruria and encamped before Arretium (modern Arezzo), reinforced by troops he had taken over from Longus and Atilius.[83] Hannibal too marched, but in more difficult conditions, from Cisalpine Gaul to Etruria. Polybius describes admiringly the care with which he gathered information about the terrain ahead, and about Flaminius' movements, and his over-confident, demagogic, and crowd-pleasing character. He attaches a typically didactic lecture on the need for a good general to find out what sort of enemy he is up against.[84] Even allowing for the unusual hostility towards Flaminius of the sources, and the tendency of ancient historians to infer motive and states of mind from subsequent events and actions, the trap which Hannibal laid for Flaminius would have been impossible without the acquisition of first-rate intelligence.[85] His use of scouts, guides, spies, and informers meant he could even be described on one occasion as knowing as much about the situation on the Roman side as on his own.[86] We have no definite idea what maps or detailed

---

[81] 21.63.6.
[82] Livy 21.63.14. Cf. Oakley 2005a: 13–16, with modern references, part of a long n. on Livy 9.1.1–16.19. For Varro, see *DPRR* TERE0818.
[83] Livy 21.63.15. On the numbers of Roman legions, see Briscoe and Hornblower 2020: 81–4. The total before Trasimene was eleven, of which Flaminius in Etruria had two and his consular colleague Servilius at Ariminum another two.
[84] 3.79–80, esp. 80.3 for his advance assessment of Flaminius personally. Didactic chapter: 3.81.
[85] Unusual hostility: Rosenstein 1990: esp. 92–113 (but see Oakley 2005a: 15) argues plausibly that incompetent generalship was rarely used to explain defeats. A referee observes that Flaminius, as a 'new man' (first member of his family to reach the senate and consulship), did not have a well-positioned family to protect his reputation.
[86] See Livy 22.41.5 (authorial) with general discussion at Briscoe and Hornblower 2020: 238, n. on 22.28.1. See also, for Polybius, Miltsios 2013: 103–5.

itineraries, if any, he might have brought with him into the country he was invading.[87] But that is equally true of Aristotle's scientifically minded pupil Alexander, and of other ancient generals operating far from home.[88] The Carthaginians were a maritime people, and this is reflected in the scope of their attested geographical writings and guide books.[89] Carthaginians traded in Italy from early dates, and Aristotle mentions a treaty between Carthaginians and Etruscans.[90] An Etruscan-Phoenician bilingual inscription on a gold tablet from Pyrgi, a harbour of Caere in Etruria (about 500 BCE), was found in 1964 but may not be evidence of an enduring Carthaginian social presence, rather than of visiting Phoenicians from Cyprus or Sardinia.[91] A little to the north, there was a place called Punicum, 'the Punic one', which, it has been claimed, 'ought to be directly related to some sort of Carthaginian occupation on the Tyrrhenian [Etruscan] coast'. But it is attested only in the late itinerary known as the *Tabula Peutingeriana*, and the argument depends in part on fragile assumptions about the Pyrgi tablet.[92] It is uncertain how far these contacts could have been translated into precise geographical knowledge of the inland Etruscan region which Hannibal was now entering from the north, always assuming that before he left Iberia he had the time and opportunity to interrogate merchants and to plan an Italian itinerary in any detail. The implication of the surviving narratives is rather that he made his inquiries and decisions as he went along. Like a good chess player, he did not think too many moves ahead. As we have seen, his grand strategy was not to destroy Rome but to end Roman control of Italy; his immediate strategy was to exploit Roman mistakes, of which there were about to be plenty. Flaminius' intentions are harder to guess at: perhaps he hoped to trap

---

[87] But see good remarks at Fronda 2011: 255. Informal land itineraries existed: from the first century CE, four silver cups from Vicarello (near Lake Bracciano, about 40 km north-west of Rome), in the shape of milestones, are inscribed with a detailed itinerary from Iberian Gades (Cadiz) to Rome: *CIL* XI 3281–4. See Dilke 1985: 122–4 (with a drawing of one of the inscriptions at 123 fig. 25).

[88] Dilke 1985: 29.

[89] In the fifth century BCE, Hanno wrote a *periplous* or port-by-port guide to the west coast of Africa. In the sixth century, a sailor called Himilco narrated his voyage to Iberian Tartessus and the 'Tin Islands' (England and Ireland), but only a second-hand report survives. For both these two, see Hennig 1944: 87–107, Huss 1985: 75–85. For an English translation of Hanno, see now Roller 2021. Hannibal could have been aware of the Greek history of Timaeus, but that might not have been much help on topography.

[90] *Politics* 1380a.

[91] It is an inscribed dedication to Astarte by an unnamed Etruscan king. See *ICO*: 158–67, appendix no. 2; Adams 2003: 202–3 (with translation of the Phoenician) and n. 363. It is what Adams called an 'idiomatic bilingual' text, i.e. not a word-for-word rendering. Cf. Pilkington 2019: 32, also with translation. He thinks the visitors were Phoenician traders from Sardinian Tharros.

[92] Palmer 1997: 78–9; *Barr.* map 44 A1.

Hannibal between two consular armies, his own and that of Servilius at Ariminum.[93]

On the misty or foggy morning of 20 or 21 June 217, Flaminius marched by the northern shore of Lake Trasimene, along the narrow defile, and into a deadly ambush launched from above.[94] Polybius and Livy agree about the greater density of the fog at this lower level, but Livy makes much more of it than did his source and generally enhances the atmosphere of ghastliness and foreboding by comparison with Polybius.[95] In order to bring out its horrors for the Roman army – reduced visibility and communication – he borrows some of the techniques of Homeric and Thucydidean descriptions of night fighting.[96] Most of the three hours of fighting probably took place at the north-east of the lake between Magione inland and Torricella on the shore.[97] It was so intense that Livy claims that a massive earthquake went unnoticed by the combatants, the sort of 'marvel' so dear to Hellenistic historiography. Flaminius himself was killed by a Celt named by Livy as Ducarius, an authentically Celtic name; after that, morale and resistance crumbled.[98] Some of the Romans died in the lake, trying to swim in their armour.

On the Roman side there were 15,000 dead and 10,000 survivors; on the Carthaginian, there were 2,500 dead, but others died later of wounds. Hannibal overruled Maharbal's offer to spare the lives of all the prisoners. But he released the Italians among them, explaining that 'he had not come to fight against the Italians, but against the Romans for the freedom of the Italians', an important programmatic statement, whatever exactly he meant by 'freedom'.[99] He also tried 'very carefully', *magna cum cura*, to find Flaminius' body and give it burial, but he failed. (He was successful with the bodies of

---

[93] Lazenby 1978: 65. On Hannibal's movements and intentions before Trasimene, see Konrad 2022: 213–33.

[94] For the battle, see Pol. 3.82–4 and Livy 22.4–7 (Briscoe and Hornblower 2020: 161 for the date). Polybius uses the name 'Trasimene' once only, and then for the lake not the battle: 3.82.9, spelling it 'Tarsimenne'. In retrospective mentions, he always uses the roundabout formula 'the battle in Etruria'.

[95] See Briscoe and Hornblower 2020: 36–7 and (detailed commentary) 160–72. Van Gils and Kroon 2022, on fright and horror in Livy book 22, especially the Trasimene narrative, nowhere discuss how Livy reworked Polybius' account: they do not even mention Polybius.

[96] Cf. Homer, *Iliad* 11 (the *Doloneia*) and esp. Ajax's prayer to Zeus to lift the mist and 'kill me in the light since that is your wish' (17.646–7); Thucydides 7.42–6 (disastrous Athenian night attack on Epipolai in Sicily, 413).

[97] For the view of the battle and its topography taken here, see Briscoe and Hornblower 2020: 162–3.

[98] Earthquake: Livy 22.5.8. Ducarius: 22.6.3–4. Morale: Livy 22.6.5; compare the effect when Mago was wounded and fell almost lifeless: 30.18.13. The same happened to the Persians at Plataia in 479 (Hdt. 9.63, death of Mardonius); cf. West 2013: 149 and n. 35 on Greek epic: 'it is a typical motif that at the fall of the champion the troops turn to flight'. Epic no doubt reflected reality, so 'motif' need not imply fictionality.

[99] Pol. 3.85.4. After Cannae, when Hannibal similarly separated allied from Roman prisoners and gave the former more favourable treatment, Livy comments that he had done the same at the Trebia and Trasimene (22.58.2). But he had reported nothing of the sort after Trebia.

Paullus after Cannae, and then of Marcellus, just as Marcellus himself was said to have exercised *cura* over the burial of Archimedes, killed in ignorance at the fall of Syracuse.)[100] Livy will echo his own phrase at the end of his narrative of the battle at the Metaurus river in 207: the consul Claudius Nero flung Hasdrubal's head in front of Hannibal's camp. He had preserved it 'carefully', *cum cura*. Respect for the dead was a form of piety everywhere, certainly including Carthage, and in the ancient world disrespect was as offensive to the gods as it was to men.[101] Livy does not spell out the contrast between the pious Carthaginian general and the impious Roman consul; he lets the similarity of phrasing do that for him. So much for his own earlier rhetorical outburst about Hannibal's total irreligiosity.[102]

Young Publius Scipio, the other subject of the present book, was a military tribune the next year, at Cannae. Where was he in 217? He was certainly of military age. It is tempting to play the counterfactual game.[103] What if he had been serving under Flaminius at Trasimene? He would very likely have been killed. This would have made no difference to anything until 211. But who would have succeeded to the Iberian commands of his father and uncle after they fell in that year? Most probably Gaius Claudius Nero (praetor in 212, future consul in 207) would have been continued for several years: in reality, he commanded in Iberia as propraetor until relieved by young Scipio.[104] We would then have to think away Scipio's achievements at New Carthage, Baecula, and Ilipa, all due to exceptional military ability and to military reforms. Hasdrubal would have had no difficulty in joining Hannibal at some point. Nero would have been pinned down in Iberia, so there would have been no shared consular victory at the Metaurus. What would have happened after that would partly depend on whether in this hypothetical situation Marcellus, the only Roman general with the flair and aggressiveness to confront Hannibal with any hope of success, was killed

---

[100] Cf. also Livy 25.17.4–7: Hannibal (on one of three versions) burnt the corpse of Tiberius Gracchus (*DPRR* SEMP0866) on a ceremonial pyre. On another account, he sent Carthalo (6) to the Roman camp with Gracchus' already-severed head, but this was evidently not intended as disrespectful treatment. For decapitation, see p. 191. For Archimedes: Livy 25.31.10, cf. p. 148. For the career of Marcellus (*DPRR* CLAU0908), an outstanding but reckless general who captured Syracuse from the Carthaginians, see further p. 141 n. 26.

[101] 'Carefully': Livy 27.51.11. Carthage: Huss 1985: 528. At 529 with n. 159 and 1986: 231 he cites *Excerpts of Polyaenus* 14.20: Hannibal persuaded his men that those who die bravely in war soon return to life. Strictly, this would imply that he expected Flaminius, Paullus, Marcellus, and the others to make a comeback. The gods: Homer, *Iliad* 24.18–20, Apollo prevents Achilles' attempt to mutilate Hector's corpse (but Zeus had allowed this at 23.403–4). For Greece and Rome, see further Briscoe and Hornblower 2020: 61 and n. 139.

[102] 21.4.9.

[103] On counterfactuality and 'if . . . not' presentation, see Briscoe and Hornblower 2020: 48–50.

[104] *MRR*: I. 280; *DPRR* CLAU0908.

in 208, as in historical fact he was.¹⁰⁵ There would in any case have been no Zama, and the war could have gone for several years after 202. We will resume the counterfactual game when we reach Zama.¹⁰⁶

### 3.7 The Battle of Cannae, 216

'We have been defeated in a great battle' was the announcement of Trasimene by Scipio's cousin Pomponius the praetor, amid scenes of panic at Rome.¹⁰⁷ In this emergency, they appointed Fabius Maximus dictator and Marcus Minucius Rufus his Master of the Horse. Livy says that their duties included cutting down the bridges over the rivers – that is, the Tiber and Arno. His readers might have recalled his account of the semi-mythical episode when Horatius kept the Etruscans at bay while the bridge over the Tiber was frantically cut down behind him by the city's defenders.¹⁰⁸ Fabius told the senate that the defeat was due to Flaminius' neglect of the proper religious observances 'more than', *plus . . . quam*, to rashness and incompetence.¹⁰⁹ The formulation does not quite exclude human error. But elaborate religious measures were voted. These included the consultation of the Sibylline Books, which instructed the Romans to vow a temple to Venus Erycina, of Eryx in Sicily, and Fabius dedicated it two years later. Eryx at the far west of Sicily was in the Carthaginian sphere of influence, so that the Romans were propitiating a goddess believed to be friendly to Carthage under the name Astarte.¹¹⁰ At the same time, Eryx may already have been associated with the legend of the Trojan Aeneas' foundation of Rome.¹¹¹

The other consul Servilius sent reinforcements ahead of the battle, but they arrived too late and were crushed by Maharbal. The announcement of this fresh disaster reached Rome three days after that of Trasimene.

Hannibal meanwhile decided to 'refrain from' approaching Rome 'for the time being', although fully confident of success.¹¹² This interesting comment

---

¹⁰⁵ *DPRR* CLAU0810.  ¹⁰⁶ See p. 405.
¹⁰⁷ Pol. 3.85.8 (not naming Pomponius), Livy 22.7.8. For this Pomponius, see p. 54.
¹⁰⁸ Pol. 3.87.6–9; Livy 22.8.6–7. For the offices of dictator and Master of the Horse (explained here by Pol.), see p. 90 n. 71. Horatius: Livy 2.10, immortalized by Macaulay: 'Hew down the bridge, Sir Consul', etc.
¹⁰⁹ Livy 22.9.7.
¹¹⁰ Livy 22.9.9–10 with Briscoe and Hornblower 2020: 179–80. See Gruen 1990: 9–14, also 1993: 46–7; Palmer 1997: 53–72; Parker 2017: 61 and n. 107. For a Punic dedication to Astarte, see *ICO*: 53–5, Sicily no. 10, third to second century BCE.
¹¹¹ Virgil, *Aeneid* 5.759–60. Aeneas, Troy, and Rome: see p. 291.
¹¹² Pol. 3.86.8, κατὰ τὸ παρόν. Cf. Lazenby 1978: 66, 'whatever his reasons, Hannibal decided'. For ἀποδοκιμάζω (a favourite verb of Pol.) with simple infinitive not noun, see *Polybios-Lexikon* 1.1: col. 181, sense (2), with six other examples: *darauf verzichten, davon absehen* ('renounce', 'refrain from'). Translators (Loeb, Shuckburgh) say 'dismissed/rejected *the idea of*'; in English, the object

by Polybius was not picked up by Livy, who was more concerned with the immediate reactions at Rome to the defeat. Polybius' comment is an implied example of 'presentation by negation': it could mean (1) polemically, 'he did not, as some authorities wrongly claim, decide to approach' (perhaps unlikely); or (2) 'he did not, as you might have expected after such a victory'; or (3) 'he did not, as his advisers urged'. If (3) were right, the sequel to Trasimene would anticipate Cannae, after which Maharbal famously criticized Hannibal for knowing how to win, but not how to use a victory by marching on Rome straightaway.[113] But (2) is easier. On the present occasion at least, Hannibal was surely right: he had no siege equipment, and the city was very well fortified.[114] The other consul was still potentially in the field, although with diminished forces. More positively, Hannibal's best hope of winning over allies lay in the Greek south of Italy. But 'for the time being' leaves the possibility open for the future, and indeed Hannibal did on one later occasion move right up to the walls of Rome.[115]

Instead of approaching Rome, Hannibal moved his army through Umbria and Picenum across to the Adriatic side of Italy, perhaps with a small diversion to attack Spoletium, modern Spoleto.[116] He devastated the territory of the Praetuttii, Marrucini, and Frentani and entered Daunia (Apulia, see Map 2).

There now followed what has been called a 'game of cat-and-mouse', meaning pursuit and escape without capture or open confrontation.[117] This is a good description of the nervous interval between Trasimene and Cannae, but the animal roles are not always easy to assign. For the most part, Hannibal looks like the cat, attempting to lure the Roman mouse into the open and then pounce. That was not going to be easy. Two catastrophic defeats had taught the Romans, or at any rate the new dictator Fabius, that to confront Hannibal in the open field was, for the time being, folly.[118] Instead Fabius, now reinforced by Servilius' army from Ariminum, chose to track the enemy and ignore grumbling accusations of cowardice.

---

has to be supplied but may mislead if taken to mean that the 'idea' was suggested by advisers – although it may have been, see interpretation (3).

[113] Livy 22.51; see p. 105.
[114] The so-called Servian wall, built in 378 soon after the Gallic sack (Livy 6.32.1), was in good shape, and daunting. See Oakley 1997: 636 and fig. 13 at 637.
[115] See p. 150.
[116] Livy 22.9.1–2; *Barr.* map 42 D3. Not in Pol., and doubted by Lazenby 1978: 66, but defended by Briscoe and Hornblower 2020: 177. Pol. says he bathed his horses in old wine and 'likewise' cured his men's wounds, whatever exactly that means: 3.88.1–2.
[117] Lazenby 1978: 69.
[118] For 'Fabian strategy', see Erdkamp 1992, identifying some implausibilities in Livy's account.

Polybius says that the advantages of the Romans lay in 'an inexhaustible supply of provisions and men'. This acute remark could be extended to the entire second Punic war in Italy.[119]

Hannibal continued zigzagging over Italy; he now crossed the Apennines into Samnium, ravaged the territory of Beneventum, site of the Roman defeat of Pyrrhus in 275 BCE, and captured a city called Telesia.[120] His target was the 'Falernian field', the *ager Falernus*, part of the enormously fertile volcanic region of Campania, where he devastated the entire plain.[121] His aim, says Polybius, was either to force the Romans to fight or to convince the various peoples of Italy that the Romans were abandoning the open country to him; but so far no city revolted to him, such was the 'fear and respect', *kataplexis* and *kataxiosis*, in which the Romans were held.[122]

It was en route for Campania that Hannibal told his guide to direct him to 'Casinum', but his Latin pronunciation was so terrible that the guide took him to Casilinum near Capua instead.[123] The key sentence is difficult, but the gist is 'because Carthaginian speech was repugnant to the pronunciation of Latin names'.[124] The story has been doubted, partly because Casinum is thought to be too far north to be a plausible destination. But its main interest lies in its perceived linguistic implications. The guide was surely an Italian – after all, his function was to provide knowledge of the area – so the story implies that this primary Latin speaker had some knowledge of Punic.[125] But some of the conversation could have been in Latin. It has been claimed that Hannibal was wholly ignorant of Latin.[126] But that is improbable for so intelligent a man, even at this early stage of the campaign, and by the time he left Italy, Hannibal had surely picked up some Latin, even though his base for many years had been was in the Greek-speaking south. Interpreters are mentioned only occasionally in ancient sources generally.[127] Polybius is followed by Livy in saying that Hannibal and Scipio before Zama spoke through interpreters, and

---

[119] 3.89.9. Cf. Taylor 2020a: 73.
[120] Pol. 3.90.7–8; Livy 22.13.1. Telesia (*Barr.* map 44 G3) is Livy's name; Pol. calls it Venusia, but that city is far away in Daunia (Apulia). See Briscoe and Hornblower 2020: 195.
[121] Pol. 3.92.8.
[122] Pol. 3.90.12–14, an important passage for its wider implications. See p. 364. The compound Greek words have the same first element, producing an effect which is hard to reproduce in English. For these concepts and their importance for understanding Hannibal's eventual failure, see Briscoe and Hornblower 2020: 8 and n. 25; cf. p. 364.
[123] For the whole episode, see Livy 22.13.6–9 with Briscoe and Hornblower 2020: 196–7; not in Pol. See *Barr.* map 44 F3 (Casilinum) and E3 (Casinum, mod. Cassino, about 50 km north-west).
[124] For the many textual problems, see Briscoe 2018: 57–8.   [125] Adams 2003: 205–6.
[126] Rochette 1997: 158, part of a study of bilingualism in Hannibal's army.
[127] For earlier evidence for interpreters, see Briscoe and Hornblower 2020: 197.

this explicitness is unusual.[128] But interpreters must have been far more common than this in reality. On the present occasion, Hannibal is said to have had the guide flogged and crucified as an example to others. If so, he acted very unfairly, since the premise of the anecdote is that the mistake was due to his own trouble with place names. The whole story may have been designed (or invented) to illustrate Hannibal's cruelty.

On another and more famous occasion soon afterwards, Hannibal was the mouse who gave the cat Fabius the slip.[129] Hannibal's devastation of Campania was successful in that it generated frustration and mutinous discontent in Fabius' army, stoked by his disloyal Master of the Horse Minucius. An officer called Lucius Hostilius Mancinus ignored orders and got himself and his best cavalry killed.[130] But destroying Campanian crops was not the way for Hannibal to win the love of the local population, and anyway he now risked being cornered in the much less hospitable district he had now reached, the environs of a place called Callicula north of Teanum and Cales; so he needed to move on.[131] He was, however, being closely watched. He escaped at night by a stratagem: he tied flaming twigs to the horns of oxen and drove them up to the higher ground, so giving the impression that his numbers were greater than they really were and frightening the enemy by the hint of the supernatural. A trick of this sort had been recommended by the fourth-century Greek writer Aeneas the Tactician: give cattle some wine and then drive them towards the enemy camp wearing bells.[132] This might conceivably indicate specific knowledge of Aeneas' entertaining collection of stratagems on the part of Hannibal or a well-read member of his staff, but stories of the weaponizing of animals are so frequently attached to ancient commanders that the ruse may be of a type anecdotally familiar round campfires without the need for book-learning. Livy's account is more elaborate and fanciful than Polybius'. In

---

[128] Pol. 15.6.3, Livy 30.30.1; and for some code-switching by Aemilius Paullus in 168 BCE, see Livy 45.8.6 (with Adams 2003: 577), again surely from Polybius.

[129] Livy remarks that Hannibal realized that his own cunning methods were being turned against him: 22.16.5. The point is a good one, although the phrasing is borrowed from Sallust (*Jugurtha* 48.1).

[130] Livy 22.14–15; *DPRR* HOST4817, probably father of 1275. Several members of this unlucky family were prominent in the second century (Briscoe and Hornblower 2020: 203, n. on Livy 22.15.4), and this may explain Livy's decision to narrate the present minor episode at length.

[131] *Barr.* map 44 F3. But the exact location of Callicula, and the positions of the two sides, are uncertain. See the plausible sketch map at *HCP* 1: 428.

[132] Pol. 3.93–4, Livy 22.17. cf. Aen. Tact. 27.14. Appian, *Iber.* 5/19–21 (cf. Mayor 2022: 218) relates an oxen-and-fire stratagem allegedly carried out successfully by Iberian chiefs against Hannibal's father Hamilcar, who was killed in the resulting fighting. But (a) the details are different (in Appian, the oxen pull wagons filled with firewood, which is then set alight), and (b) the story is inconsistent with the other evidence for Hamilcar's death: *HCP* 2: 15. It is a sort of roving anecdote: Appendix 1.3.

particular, he says the cattle looked as if they were breathing fire. But this comparison does not work for flaming twigs tied to horns, and it looks like a purely literary reminiscence: the magical fire-breathing bulls used by Jason in Greek mythology.[133]

Annoyance at Rome with Fabius' policy of non-confrontation led to an unprecedented step: Minucius' *imperium* was made equal to that of Fabius.[134] But Minucius overreached himself. Elated by a minor military success, he had to be rescued by Fabius, and he made a sincere show of penitence, after which the two clasped hands in reconciliation.[135] Both Polybius and Livy assure us that Hannibal was well aware, from prisoners, deserters, and spies, of the rivalry between the two Roman generals.[136] His use of first-rate military intelligence is meant to be kept in mind by the reader through the whole period during which the armies were at close quarters.

Hannibal wintered (217–216) at Gereonium, a strictly unidentified site but probably a little south-west of Larinum in the country of the Frentani.[137] At Rome, bitterly contested elections, described at length by Livy, resulted in consulships for Gaius Terentius Varro and Lucius Aemilius Paullus, father-in-law of Scipio Africanus.[138] It is possible that the favourable portrait of Paullus in the sources, and their corresponding censure of Varro, can up to a point be explained by Polybius' friendship with Paullus' direct descendant Scipio Aemilianus. But if so, his partisanship is betrayed mildly: the high praise for Paullus is not authorial comment but focalized through Paullus' contemporary supporters. He is represented as trying to dissuade the inexperienced Varro, but any disagreement between them was about tactics, not about whether to fight at all.[139] The ultimate responsibility lay with the senate, which disastrously underestimated Hannibal, despite three defeats at his hands, and was determined on battle. In fairness, part of the reason for this was soundly logistical, the loss of Cannae itself to Hannibal as a large-scale magazine for grain storage.[140] As for Varro, Livy's snobbishly expressed

---

[133] Livy 22.17.5. For weaponized cattle, and Jason's bulls, see Briscoe and Hornblower 2020: 205–8. Cf. p. 37 n. 148 (Samson). See also Mayor 2022: 199.

[134] Livy 22.25.10, preferable to Pol.'s version (3.1.3.4), that Minucius was actually made co-dictator. See Briscoe and Hornblower 2020: 231. Wilson 2021: 373–4 nos. 73 and 74 believes that both were dictators.

[135] Livy 22.23–30; 30.6 for the hand clasps (not handshakes).    [136] Pol. 3.104.1, Livy 22.28.1.

[137] Pol. 3.100–2, Livy 22.23.9, cf. 18.7; *Barr.* map 44 G2.

[138] Livy 22.34–5. For these two, see already pp. 92 and 43, cf. 21.

[139] Pol. 110.2–3 and 8; 112.2; Briscoe and Hornblower 2020: 80.

[140] Pol. 3.107.7 and 108.1. Cf. Freedman 2022: 51 (about the French defeat by the North Vietnamese at Dien Bien Phu in 1954): 'the fundamental mistake, common to most military defeats, was to underestimate the enemy'. The Romans were complacent after many years of success. Cannae as lost granary: see p. 354 with 355 n. 93 on Pol. 3.107.2–7.

contempt for his humble origins, his trading connections – his father 'said to be' a butcher – and his demagogic methods is not taken from Polybius but recalls Cleon as depicted by Thucydides and Aristophanes.[141]

The consuls were given eight legions.[142] A legion was made up of between 4,200 and 5,000 infantry and 300 cavalry, to which allied forces must be added at roughly the same level, except that they supplied three times as many cavalry. At Cannae, Hannibal's army was outnumbered almost two to one in infantry (40,000 : 80,000). But he had cavalry superiority in both numbers (10,000 : 6,000) and quality, and this was the decisive arm. Finally, his troops were by now seasoned and well trained.

From Gereonium, Hannibal moved south-west across Daunia to Apulian Cannae, the 'place of reeds', where the Romans stored grain and other supplies collected from the region of Canusium, modern Canosa.[143] The River Aufidus (modern Ofanto) flows past the battle site; and although nowadays a sluggish stream, it is still reedy. Cannae was a hilltop settlement of great antiquity, overlooking the Aufidus plain. Hannibal took possession of the grain and supplies in the citadel of Cannae, and it was this news which led the senate to decide on battle and to send the consuls out to fight. Livy's claim that Hannibal was, immediately before Cannae, desperately short of supplies ('scarcely enough for ten more days') is a non-Polybian motif designed to accentuate the success of Fabian strategy and very unlikely to be true.[144]

For the battle which follows, and its aftermath, we have the full accounts of both Polybius and Livy.[145] But this is the last episode of the long opening section of narratives for which both of the two main ancient histories of the Hannibalic war survive complete and can be compared in detail. After the end of Polybius book 3, his text now has large gaps and has to be supplemented from Livy, who used him extensively but with additions, omissions, and occasional misunderstandings. For the most part, Polybius' reputation rightly stands higher than Livy's as a recorder of fact, and he was

---

[141] See esp. Livy 22.25.18–26.4. 'They say' (*ferunt*) at 22.25.19, about his father, does amount to an admission that this was mere gossip.

[142] Pol. 3.107.9 and 15. See Briscoe and Hornblower 2020: 81–4, 'Manpower' and 276 (Cannae numbers, for which see also Taylor 2020a: 60–1).

[143] Pol. 3.107.2–3. There is an excellent new museum housing recent archaeological finds and (at least in summer 2019) a small cinema showing a good computer-generated reconstruction of the battle.

[144] Livy 22.40.9 with Erdkamp 1992: 132 n. 7, Levene 2010: 197 n. 73; cf. Briscoe and Hornblower 2020: 277.

[145] Pol. 3.107–18; Livy 22.40–61. References of a more detailed sort will usually not be given. See Lazenby 1978: 75–86; Connolly 1981: 183–8; also Daly 2002, an attempt, influenced by Keegan 1976, to give the view from below, the ordinary soldiers' experience of the battle. For such 'face of battle' approaches, see p. 338. Oakley 2019a is a detailed comparison of Polybius and Livy, including a valuable day-by-day chronology of the prelude to the battle and the battle itself.

much closer in date to the events he describes; but on the battle of Cannae itself, Polybius is not invariably preferable. Livy's casualty figures are lower and more plausible, and he brings out the factor of physical exhaustion as Polybius did not.[146] Again, Polybius wrongly makes the ex-consul Marcus Atilius Regulus die at Cannae when in fact he was not present at the battle. He mixed him up with *Marcus* Minucius (Rufus), caught out by his own habit of calling Romans by their *praenomina* only. Regulus had been elected consul in 217 to replace Flaminius but returned to Rome before Cannae, pleading old age.[147]

Paullus' first and larger camp was on the left bank, but he then established a smaller one on the right bank. Hannibal's first camp was on the right bank near Cannae town, but he then moved across to pitch a second camp on the left bank, on the same side of the river as the main Roman camp. After sunrise on the day of the battle, Varro led his main forces across the river to the right bank, and Hannibal did the same, crossing in two places. The Roman army now faced south-west and the Carthaginian north-east. Hence, Polybius can say of the battle that the Roman right wing and the Carthaginian left wing were drawn up by the river. The battle was therefore fought on the right bank in a constrained space.

A minor victory, in which Livy saw the hand of fate, increased Roman confidence. Hannibal's excellent sources of intelligence kept him informed about this and about the tensions between the consuls.

On the Carthaginian side, Hasdrubal (9) commanded the left wing, Hannibal and his brother Mago the centre. Livy says Maharbal was the commander of the right wing, but Polybius says this was Hanno; Maharbal is generally more prominent in Livy than in Polybius.[148] The Roman left was commanded by Varro, the right by Paullus, and the centre by Servilius Geminus, Flaminius' consular colleague in 217.[149]

---

[146] Exhaustion: Livy 22.47.10 with Briscoe and Hornblower 2020: 290, cf. 286.

[147] Livy 22.40.6, cf. 22.25.6 with Briscoe and Hornblower 2020: 232–3 for Pol.'s error at 3.116.11. For Regulus, see *DPRR* ATIL0806 (wrongly saying he died a violent death in 216, but then correctly and inconsistently saying he was censor in 214).

[148] Livy 22.46.7; Pol. 3.114.7; see further p. 105 for Maharbal. Hasdrubal (9), Geus 1994: 148. Appian, *Hann.* 20/90 says Mago commanded the right, Hannibal's 'nephew Hanno' the left, and he himself the centre, while Maharbal held another 1,000 troops in reserve. Appian may have misrepresented Polybius. This nephew Hanno has been identified with 'Hanno the son of Bomilcar the *sufete*' at Pol. 3.42.6, cf. Livy 21.27.2: Geus 1994: 121, 'Hanno (22)'. If that were right, Bomilcar would have married one of Hamilcar Barca's daughters (so Hoyos 2003: 223 and MacDonald 2015: xiii). But Appian's 'nephew' claim may be plain wrong. See Family Tree 1, n. 8.

[149] Servilius' role in the battle is ignored by Pol. and Livy, but other sources gave him a heroic death. See Briscoe and Hornblower 2020: 287 on Ennius 268–86 Sk., Book VIII frag. 12 (Goldberg and Manuwald 2018a: 240–3, frag. 1), long speech by Servilius to a trusted friend) and App. *Hann.* 18–25/78–110.

## The Battle of Cannae, 216

The Roman plan was simple: to use their superior infantry numbers to destroy Hannibal's foot soldiers in the centre.[150] The outcome of the battle depended essentially on Hannibal's deliberate thrusting forward of this centre in a weak bulging crescent formation, a tactic resembling that of the weakened Greek centre at Marathon in 490 BCE.[151] The Roman centre crashed through this bulge, flattened it, and reversed it, but then they over-pursued, whereupon the fresh troops on both of the Carthaginian wings about-faced and attacked the now-exhausted Romans in the flanks. Meanwhile Hasdrubal had skilfully contrived to move his cavalry right round from the left wing so as to charge the Roman rear. Hannibal had anticipated this tactic at the Ticinus.[152] The Roman army was now surrounded and was virtually annihilated. The shock defeat was in large part due to two factors: the inflexibility of the formation adopted on this occasion and Roman inferiority in cavalry.[153] As for inflexibility, the traditional manipular legion was designed to be flexible, but at Cannae the maniples were stacked to an unusual depth, partly from space constraints between river and high ground, and partly because the troops and especially the officers were inexperienced.[154] Both of these weaknesses would over the next years be remedied by Scipio: the first by military reforms in Iberia, and the second by the diplomacy which enlisted Masinissa's Numidian cavalry in time for Scipio to defeat Hannibal at Zama in 202. The brilliance of Hannibal's victory, against an opponent numerically much superior in infantry, lay in exploiting these two weaknesses: by engineering an enveloping movement with which the exhausted Roman infantry could not cope, and by provoking a battle on flat terrain generally suited to cavalry.[155]

Polybius and Livy both rightly insist on Carthaginian cavalry superiority. Roman weakness in cavalry, already noticeable at the Ticinus, was not fully remedied until Zama, when – as just noted – the Numidian Masinissa's skilled and numerous horsemen gave Scipio a decisive

---

[150] It has been suggested that Hannibal had advance intelligence of the likely Roman dispositions, so as to enable him to plan his complicated tactics: *CHGRW*: 407 (P. Sabin). This is unverifiable but perfectly possible.

[151] Livy 22.47.5; cf. Daly 2002: 39, citing Hdt. 6.111–13, where however the Greek tactics were simpler and the Greek forces less variegated.

[152] Livy 22.48.5–6. Ticinus: Livy 21.46.7, with Lazenby 1978: 53. On the ruse of the pretended Numidian deserters at Livy 22.48.1–4 (it is not in Pol. and has been doubted), see Briscoe and Hornblower 2020: 290.

[153] There was also a tradition that Hannibal chose a position which would ensure that sun and dust would adversely affect the Romans. Vegetius' advice to the reader at 3.14.1 may have Hannibal at Cannae in mind; see Milner 1996: 93–4 n. 3 (add Polyaenus 6.38.4). But see Briscoe and Hornblower 2020: 288 on Livy 22.46.8–9, who acknowledged the alternative role of chance, perhaps so as to exculpate the Romans.

[154] See Daly 2002: 36–7.

[155] Although he would have preferred the left not the right bank, Pol. 3.112.2 with Lazenby 1978: 79, who gives Varro some credit for deciding to switch to the right bank.

advantage. But at Cannae the Romans did have the support of allied cavalry: Campanians, Sidicines, and Lucanians.[156]

Livy reports that the Roman casualties, who included the consul Aemilius Paullus, were allegedly a staggering 45,500. Polybius has 'about 70,000', and 10,000 prisoners. Polybius says that the Carthaginian losses were about 4,000 Celts, 1,500 Iberian and African troops, and 200 cavalry.[157] Paullus' last moments are recorded in moving detail by Livy, who describes how a military tribune, Gnaeus Cornelius Lentulus, found the badly wounded Paullus and urged him to escape, but Paullus refused and waited to be killed. This Lentulus will make a less attractive reappearance at the end of the war, when as consul in 201 he desperately hopes to be assigned Africa as his province, and so steal some of Scipio's glory.[158]

To the figures which Livy gives for Roman prisoners taken in the battle (3,000 infantry, 1,500 cavalry) must be added those taken in the two camps. Of these, 7,000 escaped to the smaller, 10,000 to the larger camp; 600 of these made their way to Canusium with a military tribune Publius Sempronius Tuditanus, and 4,200 later, so the total captured in the camps was 12,200 but not equally divided between the two. Polybius adds another 8,000: 10,000 men had been left in camp by Paullus before the battle, of whom 2,000 were killed by Hannibal. So the total of those taken in the camps was 20,200.[159]

The Romans who escaped to Canusium were fed and otherwise looked after, and on a lavish scale, by an Apulian woman called Busa, who was honoured by the senate for this generosity after the end of the war. She is an interesting figure, unusual among Livy's women for her independent property power. She is perhaps the daughter of a man called Bouzos of precisely Canusium who (as a Greek inscription shows) was honoured on the Aegean island of Delos – an important commercial hub – at about the right date and was no doubt one of the many Italian merchants attested

---

[156] Pol. 3.111.2 (Hannibal to his troops), Livy 22.44.4 (also focalized through Hannibal); 21.47.1 (Ticinus); 30.33.13 and p. 218–9 for Zama; Roman allies at Cannae: 22.42.4 and 11, cf. 22.13.2.

[157] Livy 22.49.15; elsewhere, e.g. in the speech at 22.59.5, and in other speeches, he rounds this up to 50,000; Pol. 3.117.3–4. This figure of 70,000 was perhaps reached (so *HCP* 1: 440) by subtracting the number of prisoners from the legionary total of 8 × (5,000 Romans + 5,000 allies = 10,000), excluding cavalry and ignoring survivors. But 'any estimate of casualties is likely to be unreliable' (*HCP*; similarly Brunt 1971a: 419; Lazenby 1978: 84); Livy is probably closer to the truth. De Ligt 2012: 139 and n. 7 accepts Livy's figures but thinks Pol.'s are a round figure for the total of those killed or captured. Taylor 2020a: 43 also prefers Livy. Carthaginian losses: Pol. 3.117.6.

[158] 22.49.6–12, cf. 30.40.7 (201); *DPRR* CORN2877.

[159] Livy 22.49.13–52.4; Pol. 3.117.7–11. For Tuditanus, who had a distinguished career ahead of him, see *DPRR* SEMP0882.

there epigraphically in the Hellenistic period. The Renaissance scholar-poet Boccaccio praised Busa's munificence.[160]

## 3.8 After Cannae

Two stories circulated about the immediate sequel to the battle. One of them was told to illustrate Hannibal's character, the other Scipio's: a neat parallel.

First Hannibal. Many ancient authors told versions of the story, including Cato in the 150s (the earliest surviving source for it, although fragmentary); but Polybius did not. In Livy's version – the most memorable – everyone else urged him to take a rest, but Maharbal said that in four days he could dine on the Capitol at Rome, and he himself would ride ahead with a cavalry contingent. Hannibal praised his enthusiasm but said he needed time to think about the idea, whereupon Maharbal told him 'you know how to win but not how to use a victory'.[161] The opening – 'everyone else . . . but so-and-so did/said something different' – is a focussing device found in Homer and Herodotus, but that does not invalidate it.[162] More troublesomely, there is a doubt about Maharbal's role or even presence at Cannae, but his presence in some capacity can hardly be seriously in doubt: where else would he have been? As to his role, the perceived problem is that whereas Livy said that Maharbal commanded the right wing at Cannae, Polybius gave it to Hanno.[163] But in a way, the identity of Hannibal's interlocutor does not matter: some such exchange could have taken place, and the importance of the story is as a kind of counterfactual speculation: what if Hannibal had marched on Rome straightaway? Livy makes this more or less explicit: it was thought that the day's delay saved 'the city and the empire', *urbi atque imperio*. But Hannibal's decision, as given by Livy rather than Cato, was right: Rome was not defenceless, and he was not equipped for a large-scale siege.[164] The destruction of Rome was not his aim, and the anecdote illustrates his realism – and tolerance of outspoken

---

[160] Livy 22.52.7 and 54.3–4; not in Pol. Bouzos: *IG* XI (4) 642. For the possible Delian connection (missed by P. Keegan 2021), Hornblower 2019, a prosopographic study. Boccaccio: *On famous women* ch. 69 with Briscoe and Hornblower 2020: 48 n. 115.
[161] Livy 22.51.1–4. For the sources and variants, see Klotz 1940: 147 and Cornell *FRHist* 3: 126–7, discussing *FRHist* 5 (Cato) frags. 78–9; also Briscoe and Hornblower 2020: 299. In Cato (who has the vivid dinner detail), Hannibal waits a day then *accepts* the plan, but the (unnamed) 'Master of the Horse' says 'too late' (*sero est*). This was improved by Livy or his source into the famous reply about not knowing how to use a victory.
[162] *Odyssey* 8.532–3, Hdt. 5.92.1.   [163] Livy 22.46.7; Pol. 3.114.7.
[164] Rome and the empire saved: 22.52.4. Lazenby 1996b reaffirms and expands on his earlier view (1978: 85–6) that Maharbal was wrong. Rome not defenceless: see p. 97.

criticism from a senior officer, whoever the officer really was. Near the end of the war, Hannibal is said to have regretted not marching on Rome straight after Cannae. But this is an implausible part of a rhetorically overdone passage in which Hannibal regrets, with groaning, gnashing of teeth, and so on, that he must obey orders and quit Italy.[165]

The still-teenaged Scipio was a military tribune at Cannae, a prestigious post for one so young; as the son of a senator, his military career was evidently accelerated. (The Augustan *elogium* confirms that he really was a military tribune.) After the battle, he stiffened the resolve of the survivors at Canusium.[166] Of the four military tribunes there, Scipio and Appius Claudius Pulcher had been elected commanders on the spot.[167] Some of them, led by Lucius Caecilius Metellus, planned to sail away from Italy to join one of the (Hellenistic) kings, presumably as mercenaries. Scipio, whom Livy calls 'the predestined leader, *fatalis dux*, of this war', would have none of this.[168] He drew his sword and held it over their heads as he swore never to abandon Italy or to allow anyone else to do so; then he made the others swear in the same terms, threatening to use his drawn sword against any who refused. They complied, 'as scared as if they were looking at the victorious Hannibal'. In this way, Livy neatly associates the two future opponents – and the two subjects of the present book. The whole story, which there is no reason to doubt despite its absence from Polybius, is given by Livy. The tribunate is an independently attested fact, but Livy's generous allocation of space to the oath story, wherever he found it, was his own choice. As at the Ticinus, he goes out of his way to 'remind' readers of Scipio's glorious but still far-distant future.

Hannibal offered to ransom the Roman prisoners, but the senate refused the pleas of the prisoners' representatives and of their distraught families. Livy's narrative of Cannae, and his book 22, ends with three elements: a long and heavily fictionalized version of the senatorial debate which ended with this

---

[165] Livy 30.20.8.
[166] Livy 22.53. There is nothing in the theory that a coin issue at Canusium carried a portrait of Scipio and commemorated this episode, see p. 26.
[167] For military tribunes see p. 14 n. 23 on the Augustan *elogium*. Usually, as we saw there, they were the most senior officers in a legion, and five years of military service was expected. But since Scipio was now only twenty, that can hardly have been true of him, assuming that the five-year convention already applied at this date. For Appius Claudius, consul in 212, killed in 211, see *DPRR* CLAU0858.
[168] 22.53.6. Livy had used these two portentous words about the early fourth-century dictator Marcus Furius Camillus, 5.19.2 (396 BCE). Interestingly, Livy there calls his Master of the Horse 'Publius Cornelius Scipio'. This man's *cognomen* was really not Scipio but Maluginensis (that is shown by the *Fasti*). To be sure, the Scipiones descended from that branch of the Cornelii (*MRR* 1: 88 n. 2); but to call him Scipio was tendentious (cf. Ogilvie 1965: 671–2) and is another foreshadowing of Africanus. In the crisis of the Gallic invasion, Camillus was said (Livy 5.52–3) to have resisted a proposal to abandon Rome and move to Veii, another anticipation of the present passage.

stern decision, then a (short) list of the Italian peoples who defected to Hannibal, and finally the astonishing vote of thanks to the surviving consul Varro for 'not despairing of the republic'. Polybius, by contrast, ends his book 3 with authorial praise of the constitution and wise decision-making which enabled the Romans to recover from the shattering of their military reputation so as to defeat the Carthaginians and make themselves masters of the world. Then he promises to provide an account of that constitution – but the Greek word *politeia* is broader, in effect 'way of life', including military arrangements. He keeps that promise in book 6, in whose final chapter he gives the decision not to ransom the Cannae prisoners – this had been ignored by him in his book 3 narrative – as the outstanding illustration of the 'perfection and strength of principle' of the Roman *politeia* as it was at that time.[169] His judgement was right: the senate's conduct of the war, which had begun so disastrously, was the high point of steady Roman senatorial government (although it should not be forgotten that it was the senate which had decided to fight at Cannae). The refusal to ransom their own men sent a firm message to Hannibal, and Polybius and Livy in their own different ways spell it out by looking to the eventual outcome: the Romans were able to survive the costliest military defeats and emerge victorious, thanks to the qualities of their political, military, and social system; but also because, despite their culture of competitive conformism, they were lucky enough to possess an individual of the calibre of the 'predestined leader' Scipio. If the whole war was the high point of senatorial direction of affairs, Cannae itself was the high point of Hannibal's success. But if in summer 216 he hoped for a delegation from Rome seeking peace on anything like his terms, he was to be disappointed. What would he do next? What could he do?

## Appendix 3.1  Hannibal Increasingly Isolated?

At one stage of the siege of Saguntum, Hannibal absented himself from the siege to fight elsewhere; this enables Livy to introduce Maharbal, who was left in temporary command and 'conducted himself so energetically', *impigre rem agente*, that nobody, we are told, noticed Hannibal's absence.[170] It is natural to assume that this lively character will be developed as an important adjutant and adviser, but that would not be quite right. On one occasion,

---

[169] Livy 22.58–61; Pol. 3.118, cf. 6.58.
[170] 21.12.1–3. Compare Thucydides' introduction of the audacious Brasidas at 2.25.3. It is here assumed that this Maharbal is identical with the Maharbal who is prominent in book 22. This has been doubted by Geus 1994, but see Appendix 3.2.

after Trasimene in 217, Hannibal seems actually to overrule him.[171] He is mentioned on two other occasions before Cannae, but only as receiving orders.[172] On a later and more famous occasion, Maharbal, who in Livy's version commanded the entire right wing at Cannae, is said to have rebuked Hannibal outspokenly for his refusal to follow up his victory by marching on Rome.[173] After that, he features only once more and very briefly but then disappears from the record.[174] Polybius mentions him anywhere only for his role immediately after Trasimene.[175] Neither Maharbal nor anyone else is said to have been appointed as permanent second-in-command, as Appian says Hannibal himself was so appointed by his brother-in-law Hasdrubal. At earlier periods of Carthaginian history, there is occasional evidence for joint commanders-in-chief.[176] But regular duality was a feature of the purely civil office of *sufete*.[177] In any case, Hannibal never seems to have shared his overriding field authority. He therefore did not enjoy, or perhaps was not hampered by, the need to cooperate and share his thinking with a single equal as a matter of course. Even the bitter political enemies Livius Salinator and Claudius Nero put aside their mutual hatreds so as to defeat Hasdrubal at the Metaurus during their shared consulship of 207. Conversely, failure of two commanders to cooperate might lead to defeat, as in 105 when the consul Gnaeus Mallius and his immediate predecessor the proconsul Quintus Servilius Caepio disastrously lost the battle of Arausio in Gaul against the Cimbri and Teutones.[178]

Polybius, in his sketch of Hannibal's character, attributed some of his bad actions to the influence of friends, but he does not specify satisfactorily, and the narratives of Polybius and Livy do not bear out the implications of excessive influence exerted by others. Generally, it is striking how seldom Hannibal is reported as consulting or listening to an adviser, colleague, seer, or

---

[171] 22.6.11–12 with Briscoe and Hornblower 2020: 170: Maharbal promised safe passage to Roman escapees after Trasimene (p. 94). They surrendered, but Hannibal ignored the guarantees and put them in chains. Pol. 3.85.2 makes the overruling explicit: Hannibal told the prisoners that Maharbal had no authority to make promises. Did Maharbal go along with this repudiation, i.e. was it an agreed trick? Wollner 1987:115 takes the story at face value.

[172] 21.45.2 and 4; 22.13.9.

[173] Cannae: 22.46.7. But since Pol. (3.114.7) says it was Hanno who commanded the right, Maharbal's entire role at Cannae has been doubted (cf. p. 105). See Briscoe and Hornblower 2020: 299. Rebuke: Livy 22.51, already discussed.

[174] Livy 23.18.4. This does at least show that he got away with his bold criticism earlier.

[175] 3.84.14, 85.2, and 86.4.

[176] See Wollner 1987: 71–2 (Hanno and Bomilcar against Agathocles, 310–309), 85–6 (first Punic war).

[177] Huss 1985: 460.

[178] *MRR* I: 555; *DPRR* SERV1629. Knowledge of such events may have coloured Livy's treatment of 207.

confidant of any sort or nationality, as opposed to guides and interpreters.[179] But this impression is partly due to the lack of intimate sources on the Carthaginian side, for there are a few exceptions which may give a truer picture, at least for the early years. Before the battle at the River Trebia in 218, Hannibal consulted his youngest brother Mago, and others of his military advisers, *synedroi*, and there is some other evidence for the existence of such a council of war.[180] As for other particular episodes, after Trasimene in 217 Hannibal consulted with Mago again, and with friends, about where and how to attack.[181] Then Plutarch reports a good-humoured and encouraging exchange with a senior officer called Gisgo before Cannae in 216. Gisgo said he was amazed at the enemy numbers, but Hannibal said 'Yes Gisgo, but you have overlooked something even more amazing: among all those many, there is not one called Gisgo': general laughter.[182] From the Trebia episode, it is natural to infer that Hannibal routinely talked everything through with his younger brothers Hasdrubal and Mago – tactics, strategy, policy – but there were no further opportunities for conversation with Hasdrubal after Hannibal himself left Iberia for Italy, or with Mago after the latter returned to Iberia in 215. Hannibal's consultation of the fellow-officers, also at the Trebia, is comparable to the behaviour of Scipio's father Publius, who soon after Saguntum consults as a matter of course with his military tribunes about

---

[179] Evil friends: see Pol. 9.26.1 (but there his friends are said to have been less important than his circumstances) and 10, cf. *HCP* 2: 151 on 9.22.10. The only individual friend mentioned at 9.22–6 is Hannibal (10) the single-combat man who advocated cannibalism. It is hard to take this anecdote seriously. See further p. 400 on Pol.'s view that Hannibal's cruelty was the result of bad friendships. Huss' military chapter (1985: 475–80) does not discuss advisers, but at 478 n. 29 he referred to work being done by his doctoral pupil Bernd Wollner on the competence of Carthaginian generals. See now Wollner 1987 (82–3 and 111 for military advisers). For seers, see p. 227: Hannibal acted as his own diviner.

[180] Pol. 3.71.5 (Trebia). On the special meaning of the noun here see *Polybios-Lexikon* 3.1: col. 329, σύνεδρος (a) (β), 'v. Karthagern, spez. *Mitglied des Kriegrates, Berater*' (i.e. Carthaginian member of a military council, adviser), citing also 3.20.8. There the revised Loeb ed. translates οἱ μετ' αὐτοῦ σύνεδροι, lit. 'the σύνεδροι with him' as 'the members of [Hannibal's] Council of war', who in Walbank's view (*HCP* 1: 334) were 'probably representatives of the Punic government'. He cites the treaty with Philip V at 7.9.1, γερουσιασταὶ Καρχηδονίων οἱ μετ' αὐτοῦ, 'Carthaginian senators present with [Hannibal]'. Wollner 1987: 111 agrees. After Scipio captured New Carthage in 209, the prisoners included what look like Carthaginian representatives of this sort: Pol. 10.18.1 with *HCP* 1: 218 and Wollner 1987: 127. Livy's account of the pre-Trebia council ends 'so the meeting of officers was adjourned', *ita praetorium missum*. For *praetorium* with this sense in a Roman context, cf. 26.15.6 and 30.5.2, *praetorio dimisso* (cf. *OLD* 1(b)). But Livy's narrative on its own is puzzling because he has so far mentioned orders to Mago only. He has perhaps rendered Pol. carelessly.

[181] Pol. 3.85.4, cf. Seibert 1993a: 156, 'Kriegsrat'. This was not picked up by Livy – a warning of the capriciousness of our sources.

[182] *Fabius* 15.2–3. Plutarch's Greek about Gisgo is εἰπόντος δέ τινος τῶν περὶ αὐτὸν ἀνδρὸς ἰσοτίμου, 'one of those around him, an Equal Ranker, said ... ', where ἰσότιμος cannot mean joint commander with Hannibal but must be a Hellenistic designation of high rank, perhaps shorthand for 'equal in rank (to First Friends or Kinsmen)', cf. Fraser 1972: 2.187 n. 73; *SEG* 45.2037. Gisgo may be Geus 1994: 35, 'Gisgo (6)', one of three envoys sent by Hannibal to Philip V of Macedon in 215: Livy 23.34.2.

where best to try to engage Hannibal.[183] But we do not hear of such pre-battle consultations by Hannibal anything like as often as by commanders on the Roman side; and perhaps back in Iberia, where there was no longer a commander of Hannibal's unique prestige, there may have been more consultation between Carthaginian commanders.[184] In particular, there is, where Hannibal is concerned, an appearance of change over time: all the evidence and examples we have considered are from the early years of the war, up to 215. The impression over the years in Italy is of Hannibal as an increasingly solitary figure by comparison with Scipio Africanus, who could rely on the well-attested Roman councils of war.[185] He also had, when absent from Rome and his network of relatives, his friend Gaius Laelius and latterly his own brother Lucius. (Laelius' like-named son was similarly close to Scipio Aemilianus and was with him at the destruction of Carthage.)[186]

One Polybian habit needs discussion. He often writes of 'those around, οἱ περί, so and-so', with the accusative of the person. When he writes of 'those around Hannibal', οἱ περὶ Ἀννίβαν, this occasionally means 'Hannibal and his officers or advisers' (so that these very few passages should be added to the evidence for such advisers); but more often it has the wider extension 'Hannibal and his troops/army', and similarly for other individuals whose names in the accusative are preceded by οἱ περί (in earlier or archaizing Greek οἱ ἀμφί): the phrase always denotes a *group* of some sort, such as a philosophical school or fellow-members of an embassy. It follows that – contrary to a myth which goes back at least as far as Eustathius in the twelfth century CE – 'those around x' is never a wordy Hellenistic prose periphrasis for 'x alone'. The myth was exploded in 1977 by the late Michel Dubuisson (1956–2008, a short life) in a fine 283-page Liège dissertation (for which he was awarded the licentiate at age twenty-one!), covering in acute detail every relevant writer from Homer to Anna Comnena, with the unexplained exception of Strabo, who has been the subject of subsequent attention by others. The point is important because relevant to Hannibal's degree of isolation, but I relegate detailed discussion to a footnote.[187]

---

[183] Pol. 3.41.8.
[184] Livy 27.20 (Iberia, 209) begins with Scipio's council of war. The chapter then records at greater length a discussion between Hasdrubal and the other Carthaginian commanders, among whom there may not have been a single supreme commander (Wollner 1987: 126). Later in book 27, Hasdrubal before the Metaurus is not said to consult anyone.
[185] For the plentiful evidence about such councils of war (*consilia*) see Briscoe and Hornblower 2020: 281–2, n. on *fere omnes* at Livy 22.43.8.
[186] They are *DPRR* LAEL0992 and 1524.
[187] Dubuisson 1977, available as a University Microfilm; I am grateful to Stephen Colvin for alerting me to it and sharing with me a copy of the pdf, and to him and Alan Griffiths for email discussions.

## Appendix 3.2  How Many Maharbals?

The name Maharbal is of a familiar theophoric type, formed from Baal. More than one Maharbal features in the literary sources. In this chapter, it has been assumed that the Maharbal whom Hannibal left in charge at Saguntum in Livy's book 21 is identical with the cavalry commander who is prominent in book 22, and who is celebrated for having outspokenly rebuked Hannibal because he refused to march on Rome after Cannae. In my view, Ehrenberg 1928 was right to identify these two as Maharbal (2). (We will deal with his Maharbal (1) in the next paragraph.) Geus, however, separates the Livy book 21 and book 22 Maharbals as his nos. (2) and (3). His reason is that the late historian Annaeus Florus gives the patronymic of the outspoken Maharbal as Bomilcar, whereas Livy in book 21 gives that of the Saguntum deputy as Himilco.[188] But Livy at his next mention of a Maharbal gives him no patronymic, presumably taking for granted that he has already introduced him properly in book 21.[189] As for Florus, it is reported that in one manuscript *momilcaris* was corrected to *bomilcaris*.[190] That could suggest that the patronymic was hard to read, and – whether or not this is so – we might consider emending the name to *Himilconis*. It has

---

Two Pol. passages where οἱ περὶ Ἀννίβαν seems to mean 'Hannibal and his officers/advisers' are 3.52.7 and 8.25.1 (so, plausibly, Dubuisson 1977: 82, but see 63, cf. 59, for the commoner sense 'Hannibal and his troops'). The 1998 *Polybios-Lexikon* entry περί (2.1: cols. 228–82; accusative uses 255–82) was by Gluckmann, see n. 2 of the unpaginated preface. He was evidently unaware of Dubuisson, and included (cols. 263–4) a rubric listing thirty-seven places where – he said – οἱ περὶ x, or x + 2, or + 3, others, 'very probably', *sehr wahrscheinlich*, meant the person(s) alone (but I count only thirty-six in the list). Of these, all nineteen single-person examples had already been explained away by Dubuisson (who nevertheless thought that in Pol. and other post-classical writers 'οἱ περὶ X *and* Y' can mean 'X and Y alone'; for the rationale see his p. 75. His particular examples of this double expression were challenged by Gorman 2003, who concluded (p. 144) that 'the periphrastic usage of οἱ περὶ τινα is completely foreign to the usage of Polybius'; he does not however address Dubuisson's subtle rationale.). Commentaries: the most relevant is *HCP* 1: 89 (n. on 1.30.2, μετὰ τῶν περὶ τὸν Ἀσδρούβαν): 'Polybian usage sanctions the simple translation "with Hasdrubal"'. See rather Dubuisson 1977: 69, 79–80. So the translations rejected by Walbank in *HCP* ('H. and his colleague', Shuckburgh; 'H. and his staff', Paton's Loeb, retained by Walbank and Habicht in their revision) are correct after all.

There is a complication: Dubuisson did not deal with Strabo. Radt, in 1980 and 1988, both reprinted in his *Kleine Schriften* (Harder, Regtuit, Stork, and Wakker 2002: 242–6 and 362–8) discussed Strabo's use of οἱ περί with accusative, but again without knowledge of Dubuisson 1977. He maintained that in general the construction can be used periphrastically and offered examples in Strabo. But none of these, either in Strabo or elsewhere, turn out to be decisive, and all can be explained on Dubuisson's principles. For a further exchange, see Gorman 2001 (the Polybian part of which is essentially repeated in Gorman 2003) and Radt 2002, by now aware of Dubuisson.

[188] Florus *Epitome* 1.22.19, *Poenum illum dixisse Maharbalem Bomilcaris ferunt* . . . 'it is reported that a well-known Carthaginian, Maharbal son of Bomilcar, said that . . .'. See Geus 1994: 194. For *illum* as 'well-known', see *OLD ille* 4.

[189] 22.6.11, the episode concerning the Trasimene prisoners, cf. p. 94.

[190] Rossbach 1886 (Teubner edition): 55.

even been conjectured that both of the words *Maharbalem Bomilcaris* should be deleted as an explanatory gloss; they are strictly unnecessary after *Poenum illum*.[191] Or Florus was plain wrong; he was after all mainly following or even epitomizing Livy (some manuscripts actually call his historical work an epitome of Livy), so his independent authority is limited. I conclude that Geus' view is to be rejected, and that there is only one Maharbal in Livy.

There is a further complication. Frontinus says that a Maharbal, who is given no patronymic, was sent by the Carthaginians against some rebel Africans, to whom he gave wine spiked with mandrake, *mandragora*.[192] But Frontinus does not say that this Maharbal was an officer of Hannibal. The stratagem, if historical at all, is undatable.[193] If Frontinus did have Hannibal's officer in mind, the supposed date of the incident is not likely to be the period of the second Punic war, because Maharbal is then attested only in Italy, and presumably came over with Hannibal from Iberia. Ehrenberg distinguished Frontinus' Maharbal as no. (1) and separated him from his no. (2).[194] Similarly, Geus lists Frontinus' Maharbal as no. (1), and separates him from his nos. (2) and (3).[195] So Ehrenberg, Huss, and Geus are all agreed that Frontinus' Maharbal is not to be identified with any Maharbal in Livy, and that is surely correct.

As for the mandrake trick, Ehrenberg observed that it is attributed by Polyaenus to a Himilco, perhaps the opponent of Dionysius I of Syracuse, *c.* 400.[196] So, this is a genuine 'roving anecdote': see Appendix 1.3.

To conclude: only one known Maharbal is known to have been active in the second Punic war and is not to be identified with Frontinus' Maharbal, who is doubtfully historical and undatable.

---

[191] See Klotz 1940: 147 n. 5, cf. Geus 1994: 194 n. 1148.
[192] Front. *Strat.* 2.5.12; cf. Mayor 2022: 169, misleading on the details.
[193] Ehrenberg 1928 called it 'historically worthless'. [194] Cf. also Huss 1985: 123 n. 116.
[195] Geus 1994: 193. [196] Polyaen. 5.10.1.

CHAPTER 4

# *Scipio 216–205*
# *Aged 19–30 Years*

## 4.1 The Aedileship

At the Ticinus (218), the seventeen-year-old Scipio rescued his father the consul; then (216) he served as a precocious nineteen-year-old military tribune at Cannae and rallied survivors at Canusium. In between, nothing connects him with either Trebia or Trasimene.

The next recorded episode concerns his candidature and election, in the tribal assembly, for the magistracy called the 'curule' aedileship of 213 BCE; in their year of office, the two curule aediles held the 'Roman games' on a lavish scale.[1] Livy says that the tribunes (of the people, the *tribuni plebis*) had tried to obstruct his candidature. But he said 'if all the Roman citizens, the *Quirites*, want to make me aedile, I am old enough'; the popular vote massively confirmed this. (The conventions about minimum age for magistracies were not legally fixed until 180 BCE.)[2] The superb – or arrogant – remark might seem implausible, a retrojection of his precocious appointment to the Iberian command three years later. But contempt for small-minded criticism was a trait which he displayed near the end of his life too, in the 'trials of the Scipios'.

Polybius, but not Livy, records the alleged role of his exceptionally pious mother Pomponia in this election, but without naming her. His story of her visits to temples and sacrifices on her son's behalf contains some impossible details, notably the implication that the date was 217 not 213,

---

[1] Livy 25.2.6–8; *MRR* I: 263, citing the Augustan *elogium* of Scipio (p. 14). Aediles looked after the city of Rome in various ways. There were two kinds; the other was the plebeian. For 'curule', see Briscoe and Hornblower 2020: 234–5, n. on *duabus aedilitatibus* at Livy 22.26.3. Curule aediles were entitled to use the official ivory chair, the *sella curulis* confined to senior ('curule') magistrates. The annual *ludi Romani*, held in the Circus Maximus, lasted three days at this period. See Oakley 1998: 770–1.
[2] For the *lex Villia annalis*, the work of the tribune Lucius Villius, see Livy 40.44.1; *MRR* I: 388.

and the opening assertion that his actually younger brother Lucius was the older, and that Pomponia was anxiously sacrificing on his not Publius' behalf. Publius told her that he had twice dreamed that both of them were elected; this duly happened, says Polybius, in another factual error. In fact, only Publius was elected of the two brothers; his colleague in 213 was Marcus Cornelius Cethegus, and Lucius had to wait until 195.[3] Polybius tells the story to illustrate Publius' clever and industrious character and the general belief that he was in communication with the gods.[4] It is not clear whether by 'clever' he means that Publius was supposed to have invented the dreams, or merely that he exploited them. Comparison between Polybius and Livy on this episode should make anyone think twice before assuming that Polybius is always to be preferred as a recorder of fact.[5]

## 4.2 Scipio's Father and Uncle in Iberia, 218–211

News of young Scipio's father and uncle, Publius and Gnaeus, reached Rome through their official dispatches to the senate from the Iberian war front.[6] It would be surprising if the brothers did not take advantage of the courier to write to their families as well as to the state authorities. Letters home from soldiers are well attested from the late Republic.

The Iberian situation which young Scipio faced in 210 can be understood only by tracing the activities of Publius and Gnaeus from 218 until the catastrophe which overwhelmed them almost simultaneously in 211. How far such tracing was possible for the young man himself is impossible to say without knowing how much detail their letters to Rome contained, or indeed how many such letters were sent and received.[7] Polybius says that young Scipio had 'from the very outset learned by careful inquiries at Rome' about the situation in Iberia.[8] We would like more detail about this,

---

[3] Pol. 10.4–5; *MRR* 1: 340. Cethegus (*DPRR* CORN0815) was censor 209 and consul 204. In 213, he was not only co-opted aedile but also as priest, *pontifex*: Rüpke 2008: 82 and 633 no. 1317, cf. 7 for the college of *pontifices*.

[4] Industriousness, φιλοπονία, is not obviously on display here. Pol. 32.8.4 on Eumenes II of Pergamon has the same combination, where the word for cleverness is ἀγχίνοια. 'Industrious' is appropriate there because the context is obituarial, whereas book 10 describes a brief episode in Scipio's life. φιλοτιμία, 'ambition', or φιλοδοξία, 'love of fame' (cf. 23.14.1, about Scipio himself), would make better sense here, but neither corruption is textually very likely. The gods: cf. Aulus Gellius 6.1.6.

[5] Livy is also preferable to Pol. on the Roman casualties at Cannae: p. 102, cf. 104.

[6] See e.g. Livy 23.29.17, cf. 48.4, probably the same letter: Richardson 1986: 43 n. 56.

[7] Scullard 1973: 66, discussing young Scipio's election to the Iberian command, remarked that 'for all that is known', he might have served in Iberia after Cannae. This cannot be disproved, but is unlikely. If he had had Iberian experience, that would have been an argument in mitigation of his youth and might have been expected to feature.

[8] 10.7.1.

but the fact, if it is a fact, is important. Nor is it easy for us to trace events, because the main sources' coverage of Iberian affairs is patchy until the younger Scipio arrives: Polybius' text is fragmentary after book 6; Livy is fuller but often lacks clarity, even when it is likely that he drew on lost parts of Polybius.

In 218, Publius took what we have seen was the momentous decision to send Gnaeus on to Iberia while he himself returned to northern Italy to fight Hannibal at the Ticinus and Trebia; and Gnaeus scored successes against Hanno.[9] But Publius rejoined Gnaeus in Iberia in 217.[10] The initial Roman expectation had been a war in Iberia, but Hannibal's speed altered that. The main task of the Roman brothers was now to prevent the two Carthaginian brothers from reuniting, an aim which the Carthaginian senate instructed Hasdrubal to achieve. This meant containing the younger brother, Hasdrubal (6) in Iberia. For several years they were successful in this, notably by defeating Hasdrubal heavily at the Ebro River in 215 or possibly 216.[11] Their other and related aim was to subdue or win over as many Iberian peoples as possible, so starving the Carthaginians of supplies and manpower. Already in 217, Publius had won local goodwill by returning some Iberian hostages to their families; a Carthaginian commander called Bostar had been tricked by his fellow-countryman Abelux into handing them over to the Romans.[12] The Ebro victory helped them to do this, so that they were able to operate successfully on the eastern coastal strip, although they could not recapture Saguntum until 212.[13] But their own army was in serious need of money for wages, clothing, and food, and they appealed to the senate on these lines. The senate accepted that these requests were reasonable, but the dire situation in Italy after Trasimene and Cannae meant that it had to borrow from the companies who supplied the Roman armies.[14] On the other hand, since the same letter brought the news of the victory over Hasdrubal Barca, it caused jubilation at Rome: it seemed to show that he would not be able

---

[9] See p. 86.  [10] Livy 22.22.1.
[11] Livy 23.26–9. The senate's instruction: Hasdrubal replied in writing, urging that he be allowed to stay in Iberia; the senate was unconvinced and made orders accordingly: 23.27.9–28.6. But his defeat at the Ebro meant that a march to Italy was out of the question for the time being. The senate's instructions were recalled later by two of the three local Carthaginian commanders at a council of war in 209 (Livy 27.20.6), where however there is no mention of any referral to the senate at that time. The commanders seem simply to have carried out their own far-reaching decisions (27.20.8). On this, see further p. 186.
[12] See Pol. 3.96.7; Livy 22.22 with Briscoe and Hornblower 2020: 218–22; Richardson 1986: 37; Geus 1994: 21–2, 'Bostar (4)'.
[13] Richardson 1986: 39–40.
[14] Livy 23.48–9 (48.4 for the letter, 49.1 for the companies, *societates*). On logistics, see p. 353.

to join Hannibal in Italy, a frightening prospect in 215; this hope turned out to be false, but not until 207, by which time Hannibal was much weakened; and anyway in that year Hasdrubal was defeated and killed at the Metaurus. This forward-looking implication is perhaps why Livy chose to record the letter.

In 212, the brothers decided to divide their forces, Publius taking two-thirds, and this led to utter disaster in 211. Publius established himself at Castulo at the head of the Baetis River.[15] From here he set out against Hannibal's youngest brother Mago and Hasdrubal son of Gisgo, who were supported by Numidian (north African) cavalry under Masinissa.[16] Hearing that the Iberian leader Andobales was on his way to reinforce the Carthaginians, Publius moved off to try and prevent him but was defeated and killed by the Numidians. His legate Tiberius Fonteius, left behind in the camp, survived. Meanwhile Gnaeus had been abandoned by his Celtiberian (part-Celtic part-Iberian) allies. With a much weakened force, he set out from the Tader to join Publius, but he too was defeated and killed.[17] His funeral mound, the *rogum Scipionis*, was still a landmark in the time of the Elder Pliny.[18]

The perilous Roman situation was saved by a hitherto-unknown figure, but a long-standing pupil of Gnaeus Scipio in 'all the arts of war', a man of equestrian rank and probably also a military tribune. He was Lucius Marcius Septimius, whom Livy introduces in language which exactly translates Xenophon's self-introduction in the *Anabasis* after the Greek generals had been treacherously killed: 'there was a man in the army called…'.[19] Like Xenophon in a similar vacuum of authority, Marcius

---

[15] For the locations of his and Gnaeus' winter quarters, see Appian, *Iberian history* 16/161. But he gives Gnaeus' as Orso, which is too far west, about 200 kilometres away from Publius, and he probably met his violent end on the River Tader, modern Segura: see Lazenby 1978: 130; Richardson 1986: 41 n. 47; McGing 2019: 161 n. 15. Castulo was the home city of Hannibal's wife: p. 52.

[16] Geus 1994: 181–8 'Mago (6)' and 143–8 'Hasdrubal (8)'.

[17] Livy 25.32–6; but probably based on a lost section of Polybius. The sententious 25.33.6 (Roman commanders should not trust foreign help) is unusual for Livy but very much in Polybius' manner: see Hoyos 2006: 663, n. on the passage. This is preferable to W/M's suggestion that Livy had a contemporary event in mind.

[18] *NH* 3.9 with Tipps 1991 (cf. p. 131). The exact site has not been located. For recent attempts, see the works cited by Bellón and others 2016: 75 n. 7.

[19] His introduction at Livy 25.37.2–3, followed by Val. Max. 8.15.11, calls him *eques Romanus*; Val. Max. elsewhere (2.7.15) says military tribune (he had forgotten this when he came to write book 8, see Briscoe 2019: 234). Marcius is rightly treated as both *eques* and military tribune by Nicolet 1974: 942–3 no. 222. *DPRR* MARC0943 lists him hesitantly as '*tribunus militum?*' (Because Cicero, *For Balbus* 34 called him a centurion, Suolahti 1955: 372 denied that he could have been an *eques*, but Cicero is here confused, see Briscoe, just cited) The military tribunate (p. 14) was a senior and prestigious post, but appropriate for a young man personally trained by Gnaeus Scipio. For Xenophon, see *Anab.* 3.1.4.

was elected commander by the surviving soldiers. He vigorously rallied them – Livy has him claiming in a lively speech of encouragement to have been visited in dreams by the dead Scipio brothers – and led a successful counter-attack on one, possibly two, Carthaginian camps.[20] But unlike Xenophon, Marcius was answerable to a strict government back home. The senate acknowledged that his achievements were splendid, *magnificae*; but many of its members felt displeasure at his styling himself *propraetor* in his dispatch to Rome; the prefix *pro* meant that he regarded himself as acting in place of an elected praetor. This may seem monstrous ingratitude in such a grave crisis; it was prompted by reluctance to endorse the bad precedent of a general being appointed by an army far from home. It was resolved to arrange without delay for the proper election of a successor to Publius Scipio; meanwhile, Marcius was written to by the senate, with pointed omission of the usurped and offending title.[21] An authentic *propraetor* Gaius Claudius Nero, one of the future consular commanders at the battle of the Metaurus, now arrived to supersede Marcius and Fonteius, and he managed to maintain a Roman military presence north of the Ebro.[22] He trapped Hasdrubal in a pass called the Black Stones, but the Carthaginian forces and their leader escaped under cover of negotiations.[23] The war was, however, about to be transformed, and not only in Iberia.

## 4.3 Young Scipio Appointed to the Iberian Command, 210 (Aged 25)

Nero had not done badly, but there was agreement at Rome on the need for a larger army and a fresh commander, although no agreement on who that should be. There followed two exceptional decisions; a senatorial invitation to the people to elect a proconsul for Iberia, and a popular vote to confer a 'proconsular military command', *imperium pro consule*, on young Scipio. This was exceptional in that he was a mere *privatus*, a private citizen who had not held a relevant magistracy, only an aedileship; this was the first time such an anomalous appointment was made. (That is, he was not a promagistrate in the traditional sense.) This, as we shall see, meant that he was not entitled to a triumph on his return from Iberia. Livy naturally

---

[20] Livy 25.37–9. For the dream, Livy 25.38.5–6 with Harris 2009: 176 and n. 312, observing that Marcius' obscurity means the story was probably contemporary; Briscoe and Hornblower 2020: 71.
[21] Livy 26.2.1–6. The pettiness continued: despite his achievements, Marcius did not become a senator, as observed by Suolahti 1955: 182 (cf. 126) and Nicolet 1974: 943.
[22] Lazenby 1978: 132.   [23] Livy 26.17.

stresses Scipio's own personal initiative and glamour, both of which appealed to the people.[24] But he must also have had powerful backers in the senate. Publius Licinius Crassus Dives, *pontifex maximus* since 212 and censor in 210, is one suggestion.[25] But there is no specific evidence for support by Crassus or by any other known political ally of Scipio's family. His father and uncle had won respect from many of the Iberian communities, and this was surely a factor: the senate could not afford to throw away the diplomacy of the two Cornelii brothers.[26] We might compare Thucydides on the appointment at strongly democratic Athens of Asopius son of the famous Phormio as commander in north-west Greece, 'because the Acarnanians had asked the Athenians to send out a son or relation of Phormio as commander'.[27] Some at Rome may have clung to the reassuring idea that the Punic wars were 'family business' for the Cornelii Scipiones, two of whom had held consulships in 260 and 259 during the first Punic war.[28] And it has been rightly said that 'with an aristocratic belief in heredity, the Roman governing class gave its favoured young men rapid promotion'.[29]

Scipio's military experience so far was small, and we have seen that his knowledge of Iberian affairs is overwhelmingly likely to have been second-hand, not based on service there. He did not however arrive alone, but with a more experienced colleague, the *propraetor* Marcus Junius Silanus; but even this man is not known ever to have served in Iberia.[30] It seems that the senators were not entirely happy with a sole command for young Scipio. When they landed at coastal Emporium on the Iberian side of the Pyrenees, they marched south to Tarraco, where Scipio tactfully and shrewdly congratulated his predecessor Marcius, who was understandably popular with the army.[31]

---

[24] Livy 26.18. For the importance of the people in the appointment see Scullard 1973: 54. On Scipio's exceptional appointment, see Scullard 1970: 31–2 ('an important stage in Rome's constitutional development') and 108. But see p. 434 n. 13.

[25] Scullard 1973: 67; cf. *MRR* I: 271 and 278; *DPRR* LICI0926. For his priesthood and religious activities, see Rüpke 2008: 82 and 768 no. 2235, cf. 7 for the *pontifex maximus* as permanent chairman of and spokesman for the priestly college. It is the traditional Latin title for the pope (abbrev. 'P. M.'), but the ancient Roman Republican equivalent had no such authority or standing. He could, for example, be overruled in the college.

[26] Christ 1970: 777.

[27] Th. 3.7, 428 BCE. This comparison is not offered so as to suggest actual Iberian lobbying at Rome: there was hardly time for that.

[28] Cf. Henderson 1997: 36. See p. 53.   [29] Nisbet 1995: 137, discussing Virgil's Ascanius.

[30] *DPRR* IUNI0925. As praetor (212) he is attested in Etruria: *MRR* I: 268.

[31] Livy 26.19–20; Scullard 1970: 39–40. For Emporium and Tarraco, see p. 86 n. 51.

## 4.4 New Carthage and Neptune, 209

There followed a spectacular success by Scipio.[32] He revealed his advance thinking many years later, probably in 190, in a letter to Philip V of Macedon. But the way in which Polybius cites this document, at the polemical close of his introduction to the relevant three chapters of narrative, makes it difficult to be sure exactly how much of the preceding detail, which includes plenty of characteristically confident assertions about what was in Scipio's mind, may go back to the letter.[33] Polybius' closing claim, explicitly citing the letter, is that 'it was with the calculations which I have expounded above that Scipio approached his Iberian campaign generally and his siege of New Carthage in particular'. It is reasonable to ascribe the important opening and more general sentences to Scipio himself: he is there said to have concluded that the cause of his father's death was twofold, the treachery of the Celtiberians and the division of the Roman armies (that is, by his father and uncle in 212).[34]

Scipio applied the second of these lessons immediately, by exploiting the identical mistake which had now been committed by the three Carthaginian commanders: risky division of forces. Polybius even says that they had quarrelled with each other.[35] Hannibal's brother Hasdrubal Barca was in central Iberia, at a site near modern Toledo; Hasdrubal son of Gisgo was near the mouth of the Tagus; and Hannibal's brother Mago was probably in the far south, near modern Gibraltar, 'none of them within less than ten days from New Carthage'.[36] That they remained so badly out of position through the winter indicates that they did not take young Scipio seriously. Scipio's decision in spring 209 to strike at New Carthage was both shrewd and daring: not only did its fine harbour provide crucial access to the Mediterranean, but it had huge symbolic importance because founded by Hannibal's brother-in-law Hasdrubal. Its capture would impress the Iberian leaders and so reduce the risk of the treachery which he had identified as the first cause of the disaster in 211. It would also provide large quantities of money and supplies.[37]

---

[32] For the capture of New Carthage, modern Cartagena, see Pol. 10.6–20; Scullard 1970: 39–67; Lazenby 1978: 134–40; Ramallo Asensio and Ros Sala 2015.
[33] Pol. 10.7–9, esp. 10.9.3 (citation). For attribution of motive in Polybius, see Miltsios 2013: 92–9, with reservations at 93 about the extent of 'inferred motivation'.
[34] Pol. 10.7.1–2. Lazenby 1978: 134 has no doubt that these points derive from the letter.
[35] 10.7.3, compare 10.6.5, speech of Scipio to his troops.
[36] Pol. 10.7.5. The Carthaginian commander at New Carthage was not Hannibal's brother but another Mago, Geus 1994: 190–1, 'Mago (12)'; cf. *HCP* 2: 213 on Pol. 10.12.2.
[37] It has been called 'a key element in the Carthaginian logistical infrastructure': *CHGRW*: 388 (J. P. Roth). Money: Pol. 10.8.3.

Scipio had shared his plan with no one except his friend Laelius, who was given command of the fleet.[38] He himself set off south at high speed with about 25,000 land troops and 2,500 cavalry.[39] Polybius had visited the city, and his account is generally accurate, but his compass bearings are wrong.[40] Scipio encamped at what Polybius calls the north side of the city, but for 'north' we must read 'east-north-east'.[41] The city was joined to the mainland by a narrow isthmus; to the north of it was a lagoon, and to the south a fine harbour which gave on to the Mediterranean. Scipio first tried a frontal attack from the east, which was repelled with losses on both sides; Scipio took part and supplied encouragement, protected by three shield-bearers.[42] He then turned his attention to the lagoon on the north. He had heard from fishermen that the water was shallow and mostly fordable, and that the level (sometimes?) receded in the evenings. This much would surely have been known to the Carthaginian defenders as well.[43] But the effect on the water of an unpredictable brisk north wind made it possible for Scipio to claim divine help, in effect an epiphany of Neptune, Greek Poseidon.[44] The Romans crossed the lagoon and took the city on its lightly defended north side. An epigram in the *Greek Anthology* by the first-century CE poet Antiphilus describes how 'Carthage' (he must be referring to *New* Carthage) was under attack, when a heron standing in the water and feeding at supper time betrayed the city to the enemy by thus showing that the water was shallow; hence the bird is always locally called 'the traitor'. This little aetiology has been ingeniously and convincingly associated with Scipio's siege of 209 BCE.[45]

---

[38] Pol. 10.9.4. For Laelius, see *DPRR* LAEL0092. He was one of Polybius' informants (Pol. 10.3.2).

[39] Pol. 10.9.6–7. At §7, he says that Scipio arrived on the seventh day, but this is incredible given that he and his land forces started out from Tarraco and the Ebro mouth: Livy 26.41.1–2. See *HCP* 2: 204–5.

[40] For his description of the city, see 10.9.8–10.13 with *HCP* 2: 205–11. For the topography of the Punic city, see Keay 2013: 312 fig. 10.7, cf. p. 69.

[41] Pol. 10.9.7 with *HCP* 2: 205–6.

[42] Pol. 10.13.1. For commanders taking such care of themselves, see p. 341.

[43] Livy 26.45.8 (the wind). The failure of the local commander Mago (12) to take precautions against the enemy's exploitation of a known and regular phenomenon has caused scholarly unease. Perhaps it was not entirely regular and predictable, or perhaps Mago simply could not spare the troops. See Scullard 1930: 70–1 and 75; Lazenby 1978: 136–7.

[44] Divine epiphanies need not be appearances by a god in human form, nor need they be visual rather than manifested via another sense. And they can be weather phenomena, as at Pol. 11.24.8–9 (rainstorm after Ilipa, cf. p. 127). In 204, Scipio sacrificed to Jupiter *and* Neptune on embarking for Africa, p. 239.

[45] *Anth. Pal.* 9.551 (=*GP* 841–8) as emended and elucidated by Griffiths 1970: 38–9, approved by Scullard 1970: 256, who had read the article in advance of publication. The manuscripts have Καλχηδών, 'Chalcedon'. Read Καρχηδών, 'Carthage'.

The Roman troops swarmed into the city and on Scipio's explicit orders treated the inhabitants with notable savagery: kill and spare nobody, according to the Roman way with a captured city.[46] But that was before Mago's final surrender, after which the prisoners were treated more humanely, and skilled enslaved people were led to hope for freedom.[47] An immense quantity of booty was taken and distributed among the soldiery in the Roman way, described at length by Polybius.[48] One of the two men who claimed to be the first to scale the walls was Sextus Digitius of Paestum in south Italy. We will meet him in a later chapter as an object of Scipio's patronage.[49]

The crossing of the lagoon formed an important part of the 'Scipio legend'. It encouraged comparisons between Scipio and Alexander, who in 334/3 had led his army by the sea near Phaselis in southern Asia Minor, thanks to a north wind which alone made the offshore route passable; it was thought that this was achieved 'not without divine intervention', and that the sea did Alexander 'obeisance', *proskunesis*.[50] Polybius says that when Scipio's troops 'raced through the shallow water, it seemed to the whole army that it was by divine foresight'.[51]

Scipio's capture of New Carthage has rightly been called 'one of the greatest military achievements of the period'.[52] Certainly, the political gains were immediate. Prominent Iberian leaders – Edeco, the variously spelt Andobales or Indibilis, Mandonius – now shifted their support towards Scipio, supposedly disenchanted with Carthaginian arrogance.[53] In spring 209, they prostrated themselves before Scipio and hailed him as

---

[46] Pol. 10.15.4–6; Pol. remarks that Romans in such situations sliced dogs and other creatures in half. On the moral implications for the assessment of Scipio of his treatment of the population of New Carthage, before and after the surrender, see p. 423.

[47] Mago's surrender and its result: Pol. 10.15.7–8. Scipio's treatment of the prisoners: 10.17.6–15. This is said to have created feelings of goodwill and trust, 17.15. For the skilled slaves, χειροτέχναι, at 17.9 and 15, see p. 424 n. 153.

[48] Pol. 10.15.7–17.6.   [49] Livy 26.48; see p. 278.

[50] Arrian, *Anabasis of Alexander* 1.26.1–2. Alexander's historian Callisthenes famously said of this occasion that the sea 'did him obeisance', προσκύνησις: *FGrHist* 124 F31. But see Plutarch *Alex*. 17.8: Alexander himself made no mention of an epiphany in letters about the episode (Brunt 1976: 106–7 n. 1).

[51] Pol. 10.14.11. For the 'legend', see Chapter 10.5.

[52] *CHGRW*: 373–4 (J. P. Roth): the capture 'involved a bold strategic move, as well as tactical skill and risk-taking'.

[53] Pol. 10.35.8. The word for arrogance is ἀγερωχία, used here only in what survives of Polybius, and a very rare formation from an adjective which went down in the world, having meant 'brave', 'noble', or 'proud' in Homer.

king, *basileus*.⁵⁴ On this occasion at least, he did not refuse the title, but that soon changed.

More important for the immediate future was the military training organized at New Carthage by Scipio, described in a full and detailed chapter of Polybius.⁵⁵ Weapons training and the manufacture of weapons feature prominently.⁵⁶ But the crucial sentence describes 'exercising and training outside the city for the infantry, and manoeuvres and rowing for the fleet'; this probably included formation drill, though Polybius is not specific about this.⁵⁷ All this needed time, about which we lack precise information.⁵⁸ But at the other end of the Mediterranean, the Achaean leader Philopoemen similarly trained up his army in preparation for his victory in southern Greece over the Spartan Machanidas at Mantinea in 207, and Polybius notes that he did so in less than eight months, as if the shortness of the period was remarkable.⁵⁹ Scipio's methods paid off most conspicuously at Ilipa in 206, where his complicated, rapidly executed outflanking manoeuvres would have been impossible without highly trained and disciplined troops capable of flexibility and coordination of what in Roman military history was a novel sort.

It was now that a beautiful young Iberian woman was offered to, but refused by, Scipio.⁶⁰ It is a minor illustration of the local diplomacy which is so constant a feature of the ancient narratives of this struggle between the invading powers for ascendancy in the peninsula: the Iberian (and African)

---

⁵⁴ Pol. 10.38.3. Polybius adds that 'those present', οἱ... παρόντες, approved. This must refer to Iberian not Roman bystanders. So, correctly, Aymard 1967b: 388. The word for 'prostrated' is προσκυνήσαντες. *Proskunesis* (for which see n. 50) notoriously meant different things in different ancient cultures, notably as between Greek and Persian. It featured in ancient accounts of Alexander's wish for deification, but that aspect is not obviously relevant here, despite the 'miracle' at New Carthage.

⁵⁵ 10.20.

⁵⁶ On the slashing 'Iberian sword', *gladius Hispaniensis* (Livy 31.34.4), perhaps introduced by Scipio at this time, see p. 350 n. 66. It was a ferocious weapon. Scipio certainly made his soldiers at New Carthage practise with wooden swords whose tips had buttons, to prevent bloodshed: Pol. 10.20.3; Carter 2006.

⁵⁷ 10.20.6, τῶν μὲν πεζικῶν στρατοπέδων κατὰ τοὺς πρὸ τῆς πόλεως τόπους χρωμένων ταῖς μελέταις καὶ ταῖς γυμνασίαις, τῶν δὲ ναυτικῶν δυναμέων κατὰ θάλατταν ταῖς ἀναπείραις καὶ ταῖς εἰρεσίαις. The Loeb ed. translates γυμνασίαις 'drilling', but this is too specific: Shuckburgh's 'training' is better, cf. *Polybios-Lexikon* 1.1: col. 405, *Exerzierübung*. (So it differs little from μελέταις.) But formation drill is well attested for the Republic: see Roselaar 2015 (esp. 40 n. 161 for New Carthage). Rosenstein 2004: 203–4 n. 20 is therefore right to assume that Scipio, here and at Syracuse, devoted much time to training his army in drill. See Livy 29.22.2 (with Roselaar 2015: 40) for the military display at Syracuse, designed to silence his critics: the verb there for infantry drill is *decurrentes*, *OLD decurro* 7. See also Roselaar 2015: 38, citing Vegetius 1.26 for combat exercises. See also Veg. 1.28.9, quoted at p. 351 n. 68.

⁵⁸ Pol. 10.20.1 says Scipio spent 'some time', χρόνον μέν τινα, at New Carthage in the way he proceeds to describe. Presumably training occupied the winter of 209–208.

⁵⁹ Pol. 11.10.9.   ⁶⁰ Pol. 10.19.3; Livy 26.50. See p. 57.

## The Battles of Baecula (208) and Ilipa (206) 123

leaders oscillate between the Roman and Carthaginian sides according to their successes or reverses. Only one of these leaders was to matter in the longer term: the young African prince Masinissa; he added his cavalry to Scipio's forces and enabled him to strike the decisive blow against Hannibal at Zama. Masinissa enters the story as a young man in 213, when he is cooperating with the Carthaginians.[61] In 212, he was still a Carthaginian ally.[62] The 'change', *mutatio*, came in 206, and the Roman alignment was cemented by a personal meeting, when Masinissa was struck with astonishment by Scipio's physical appearance and beauty (including his flowing hair), like the wonder felt by the Homeric Achilles when at last meeting 'godlike Priam'.[63]

Livy says that before returning to Tarraco, Scipio ordered the repair of the damaged walls of New Carthage. But otherwise, the history of the city under Roman control, when it was a famous centre for the mining of silver, must be largely reconstructed from archaeological evidence.[64]

### 4.5 The Battles of Baecula (208) and Ilipa (206)

The loss of New Carthage forced Hasdrubal Barca to seek a decision on the battlefield: if he won, he would restore Carthaginian ascendancy in the eyes of the Iberian tribal leaders; if he lost, he could try to slip out of Iberia to join his brother Hannibal in Italy – as later happened. That at any rate is what Polybius says, but he may be merely inferring motive from outcome, especially since the obvious third possibility is ignored: total failure and death.[65]

Thanks to outstanding archaeological research by a Spanish team, the site of the battlefield camps of Baecula has recently been identified successfully from the discovery of weapons, coins, and various kinds of *impedimenta* and the excavation of camp zones. For long it was thought to be close to modern Bailen, but it is now located further east, at Cerro de las Albahacas near Santo Tomé in the Upper Guadalquivir valley.[66] The battle

---

[61] Livy 24.49, but he delays a detailed excursus on Masinissa's rise to local prominence until 29.29–33.
[62] 25.34.2, where however Livy remarks proleptically that it was his friendship with Rome which would make him famous and powerful.
[63] Change: Livy 28.16.12. The later meeting: 28.35. Cf. Hom. *Il.* 24.483.
[64] Livy 26.51.9; Ramallo Asensio and Ros Sala 2015: 173–9.
[65] 10.37.1–5. Inferred motivation is common in the historians of antiquity from Herodotus onwards, and for this passage cf. Richardson 1986: 48: 'although it is hard to imagine where he [Pol.] can have found the information, it is likely enough'.
[66] See Bellón and others 2016. Their n. 1 lists their other, less accessible, publications of the new discoveries and conclusions, some in English, some in Spanish (among the latter note esp. Bellón Ruiz and others 2015: 183–92: includes excellent illustrations). The older view: *HCP* 2: 247; Scullard 1970: 257–8 n. 53; Lazenby 1978: 141. For the new position, see Map 1. At *Barr*. map 27 B3, the old

unfolded on high ground, and Scipio's tactics of a double envelopment owed something to Hannibal's at Cannae, which Scipio had witnessed eight years earlier.[67] But there were differences.[68] Scipio sent his light-armed troops against Hasdrubal's centre on the lower part of the hill; but he divided his main body of legionary troops into two contingents who ascended the hills on either side of the Carthaginian camp: one of these, under his own command, successfully attacked Hasdrubal's left flank and the other, under Laelius, attacked Hasdrubal's right. The Roman centre gained the plateau at the top, but Hasdrubal was able to withdraw about half or two-thirds of his forces. Back in Rome, Scipio was criticized later for this. One important result of the new identification of the site is to explain why it was so difficult for Scipio to pursue. The answer is that the Roman and Carthaginian camps were more than 5 km apart, and this distance would have meant at least a two-hour march for a consular army. This would have given Hasdrubal plenty of time to escape.[69]

Scipio was again hailed as king, *basileus*, by his Iberian admirers, who prostrated themselves once more, but this time he politely told them he preferred to be called 'general', for which Polybius' Greek is *strategos*. Livy's word here is *imperator*, from which our 'empire' and 'imperial' derive, and which later in Roman history acquired imperial connotations, but it did not possess them at this date: Livy makes Scipio say that his troops had already hailed him as *imperator*. This must have been immediately after Baecula. It is however the first such recorded acclamation and is not in Polybius. It seems that Livy was here using a source other than Polybius, but he may be right.[70]

As for the acclamation as 'king', Greek *basileus*, Latin *rex*, it caused Scipio on this occasion to give an explicit but subtly nuanced reply: he had had time to think about it since the earlier occasion.[71] He now said, according to Polybius, that he wanted both to be and to be called 'royal', 'kingly', *basilikos*, but he did not want either to be a king or to be called 'king' by anybody. Livy put it slightly differently: Scipio, after saying that

---

site is marked at bottom left of the box as 'Baecula?', and the new site is bottom right near modern 'S. Tome'.

[67] For the battle itself, the main literary sources are Pol. 10.37–40 and Livy 27.17–20. Cannae: Seibert 1993a: 372 suggests that Scipio's dispositions show that he had made a thorough study of Hannibal's battles.

[68] A referee observes that at Cannae, Hannibal relied on the Romans to plunge into the trap, but at Baecula Scipio counted on Hasdrubal to hold a position in front of the camp while Scipio launched enveloping assaults, bringing the trap to him.

[69] Bellón and others 2016: 77–8.    [70] Pol. 10.40.3–9; Livy 27.19.4; Aymard 1967b: 390–1.

[71] See esp. Aymard 1967b: 390–5 and Rawson 1991: 179–80.

for him the greatest title was *imperator*, continued that the royal name, *regium nomen*, was a great thing elsewhere but 'intolerable at Rome', *Romae intolerabile*. They might 'silently', *tacite*, think that he possessed a royal mind or character, *regalis animus*, but they must avoid the word – that is, that of 'king', *rex*. The main differences are, first, that Livy unlike Polybius, explicitly says the title 'king' is intolerable at Rome; and second, that in Livy Scipio permits the Iberian chiefs merely to think silently what in Polybius they can say openly: that is, that he has the character of a king.[72] It is futile to want to recover Scipio's exact words. Polybius is the first and best source, but Livy's additions and discrepancies, whether his own or not, are revealing about attitudes in his own first-century BCE time, the age of Julius Caesar, especially the application of the strong word 'intolerable' to *rex*. (The focalization of this piece of indirect speech is unclear: is it a concealed authorial opinion or Scipio's?) This was certainly one strand of Roman thinking and attitudes, especially after Caesar, but another always coexisted with it, a fascination with Hellenistic kingship and a pleasure in being regarded, individually and collectively, as the peers of kings.[73] It is important that, for Greeks and Macedonians, a *basileus* was neither always nor necessarily king of a particular area or people.[74] The most conspicuous example of a Hellenistic king without a kingdom was Antigonus Gonatas, son of Demetrius the Besieger, until in 277 'he became, at last, king of the Macedonians'.[75] So Scipio might ('tolerably'?) be thought of as king; but not of Rome or at Rome.

So Baecula was both a military and political victory, but not a complete one. Livy puts into the mouth of Fabius Maximus in 205 a speech attacking Scipio and his record. One of the charges is that '[you allowed Hasdrubal] to slip through your hands and so sent him away into Italy', *e manibus tuis in Italiam emisisti*; he continues 'but you will say, he was defeated by you', *uictum a te dices*. There is some truth in the criticism, even though the new identification of the site makes the battle's outcome more explicable. Scipio's modern admirers cannot deny that to this extent Baecula was a partial failure, retrieved only by a consular victory next year at the Metaurus which nobody could have foreseen, and in which Scipio played

---

[72] Aymard 1967b: 391.
[73] This is the theme of Rawson's 1975 study, 'Caesar's heritage: Hellenistic kings and their Roman equals', reprinted as Rawson 1991: 169–88. In about 189, a letter of the Scipio brothers to Prusias of Bithynia insisted on Roman favour towards kings: p. 23.
[74] Aymard 1967: 394 ('sans royaume et sans sujets') and Rawson 1991: 180.
[75] Tarn 1913: 166, and esp. 113 (on the years before 277): 'His kingdom, in fact, at this time was his army of mercenaries, and nothing else; and what he had really inherited [from his father Demetrius II] was a number of garrisons posted in different Greek cities.'

no part. Scipio did however send a force to the Pyrenees to keep watch on Hasdrubal.[76]

The decisive battle for Iberia was fought at Ilipa in 206. The site is disputed but is usually located under some hills north of Seville (Hispalis), close to modern Alcala del Rio (the 'rio' in that Spanish name is the River Guadalquivir/Baetis).[77] The Carthaginian authorities in Africa had sent out another Hanno to replace Hasdrubal Barca, and he recruited among the Iberian tribes; the other two commanders were Hasdrubal son of Gisgo, and Mago, now based at Gades.[78] But Hanno was soon defeated by Junius Silanus and taken prisoner; he was eventually transferred to Rome. It is likely that by early 206 Mago and this Hasdrubal had heard news of the defeat and death of Hasdrubal Barca at the hands of Livius Salinator and Claudius Nero on the Metaurus in 207. Hasdrubal son of Gisgo cannot initially have wanted a confrontation with Scipio, but the need to reinforce Hannibal was now pressing, and he evidently decided he had no choice.[79] So he and Mago left Gades and took up position at Ilipa. For some days the two armies faced each other with no decisive move by either side; this was often the pattern in ancient set-piece battles, such as that between Greeks and Persians at Plataia in 479, and between Scipio and the Carthaginians at the Great Plains in 203.[80] Scipio now carried out what a patriotic Roman historian would no doubt have been called two 'Punic deceptions' if they had been carried out by a Carthaginian. His first ploy was a last-minute change to his dispositions. Because Hasdrubal had regularly placed his best, that is, African, troops in the centre and his Iberian allies on the wings, Scipio did the same; that is, he put his Romans in the centre. But on the day of the battle, he arranged them the other way round, the strongest on the wings. The second 'deception' was to abandon his previous habit, which had been to copy Hasdrubal by bringing his

---

[76] Fabius: Livy 28.42.14–15. Pyrenees force: Pol. 10.40.11.
[77] The main ancient sources are Pol. 11.20–4 and Livy 28.12–16 (calling it Silpia, 12.14). It has however been argued that they make better sense if the battle site was on the Upper Baetis: see Hoyos 2002, against the traditional site further west (so e.g. Scullard 1970: 262–3 n. 63; at *Barr.* map 26 E4, that site is marked as 'Ilipa Magna'). But there can be no certainty without such archaeological evidence as has now fixed Baecula. Some of Hoyos' arguments are attractive. But the definitive repositioning of Baecula makes some difference to e.g. Hoyos 2002: 102; and it is not relevant that the battle is not named by the ancient sources (Hoyos 2002: 99): the same is true of Metaurus and Zama. So on Map 1, I have retained the traditional location for the battle site of Ilipa. (Hoyos' map at 113 marks more than one possible location, on his hypothesis.)
[78] Geus 1994: 126 'Hanno (26)'.
[79] For the rest of this section, 'Hasdrubal' means the son of Gisgo not Hannibal's brother Hasdrubal Barca: Hasdrubal (8) not (6) in Geus 1994.
[80] Hdt. 9.39; Pol. 14.8.2–4.

troops out late in the day; instead he ordered them out at crack of dawn – but making sure they had breakfasted first. The Carthaginians had to mobilize in a hurry; they therefore had to fight hungry and this, together with the intense heat of southern Iberia, meant that by noon they were in poor physical shape.[81] Now Scipio delivered the tactical master-stroke which was made possible only by the months of training at New Carthage. The Romans, 45,000 men in all, were outnumbered by the 54,500 Carthaginians, and Scipio needed to redress this imbalance.[82] He did so by a complicated manoeuvre described in detail by Polybius; Livy hardly tries to reproduce it. Briefly, the Roman left and right wings altered their formations by wheeling round in such a way as to outflank the enemy wings; he held back his centre, which was composed of possibly unreliable Iberian troops. This time, unlike at Baecula, there was only a temporary escape back to their camp for the Carthaginian centre (Hasdrubal could have done more with it to avert total defeat). 'If a god had not' helped them to safety by a cloudburst and heavy, persistent rain, in other words without some divine intervention, they would have been driven out of the camp.[83] As it was, Hasdrubal was able to retreat next day, but Scipio pursued him and his forces dwindled to nothing through desertions and casualties. Hasdrubal and Mago got away on shipboard.[84]

Scipio now made his first visit to Africa, so as to try to win over the Numidian prince Syphax: the importance of the Numidians to the eventual outcome of the war is hard to exaggerate, not least by their cavalry contributions.[85] By an astonishing coincidence, Hasdrubal (8), with seven triremes, had also made his way there, with the same aim in view, and he nearly captured Scipio, who had only two quinqueremes. But the Roman ships managed to reach the harbour, and Hasdrubal and Scipio found themselves sharing a couch at the royal dinner-table. Both Syphax and Hasdrubal were impressed by Scipio's personality and conversation – presumably there were interpreters – but Livy claims, perhaps

---

[81] Breakfast for Romans but not Carthaginians: Pol. 11.22.4 and 8; cf. Front. *Strat.* 2.1.1, where Hasdrubal the Carthaginian general is Gisgo not Barca. Roth 1999: 312 and n. 223 assigned both passages in error to Baecula. At p. 54 he correctly assigned Pol. 11.22.4 to Ilipa.

[82] Livy 28.12.13–14 (Carthaginian total); 28.12.13.5 and Pol. 11.20.8–9 (Roman, cf. Taylor 2020a: 56 n. 4). Pol.'s Carthaginian total is much too high (11.20.2, 70,000 infantry and 4,000 cavalry), although surprisingly accepted by Taylor 2020a: 93 and 171 with note a. See rather Scullard 1970: 88–9. Scipio's battle tactics do not need to be explained by so large a manpower deficiency.

[83] Pol. 11.24.8–9, εἰ μὲν οὖν μὴ θεός..., a nice use of the 'if... not' or counterfactual construction, to describe this epiphany, for which cf. p. 120 n. 44.

[84] Livy 28.16. Carthaginian casualties are unknown. Cf. Taylor 2020a: 65 ('heavy').

[85] For Numidia and Numidians in and before the second Punic war, see Taylor 2020a: 70–3.

anachronistically at this early stage, that Hasdrubal was in no doubt that Scipio had designs on the conquest of north Africa.[86]

Back in Iberia, a city called Ilourgeia had revolted from Rome; Scipio's troops stormed it, and on his direct orders they inflicted savage reprisals.[87] He showed equal ruthlessness when suppressing a mutiny in his camp on the River Sucro: no fewer than 35 of perhaps 8,000 mutineers were executed. The episode was an important one: the soldiers had genuine grievances (elided by the literary sources), and Scipio's violent suppression was achieved only by a deception of a more than 'Punic' sort, and a vow of games.[88] His last military operation in Iberia was the defeat of Andobales, who had changed allegiance again, in a battle on the River Ebro.[89]

### 4.6 Scipio's Foundation of Italica (206): A Hadrianic Myth

After the battles at Ilipa and on the Ebro, Scipio is said by a single ancient source to have settled wounded soldiers at Italica, in the south of Iberia, at modern Santiponce near Seville. What Appian says is this: 'he [Scipio] left a small force for them [the conquered Iberians] suitable for a peaceful situation, and settled his wounded in a city which he named Italica after Italy. This is the home city of Trajan and Hadrian, the later emperors.'[90]

I begin by providing in a nutshell the remarkable story of the modern debate about Italica. In the twentieth century, this passage of Appian was, with certain explicit or silent adjustments, confidently taken by historians of Rome to be good and usable evidence that Scipio in 206, after Ilipa, founded a new city for his veterans, not only the wounded, but also for some of the Indigenous population.[91] That would have been a 'first' in several ways, as we shall see. Gradually, unease began to set in, because of

---

[86] Livy 28.18.10–11; cf. Pol. 11.24a. It is possible that the conversations were conducted in Greek, but interpreters might still have been useful.

[87] Livy 28.19–20; for the name of the place, Pol. 11.24.10. See further p. 342 (Scipio in personal danger).

[88] Pol. 11.25–30; Livy 28.24–9. See Chrissanthos 1997; Machado 2021: 406. For a literary analysis of the differences between the end sections of the speeches put in Scipio's mouth by Pol. (11.29) and Livy (28.29.2–8) see Conway 1922: 8–9: Pol.'s aims to arouse fear, Livy's is warmer. Vow: p. 198 n. 79.

[89] Pol. 11.31–3; Livy 28.31–4. For a 'cattle trick' by Scipio before this battle, see p. 359 n. 112.

[90] *Iberian history* 38/153; *Barr.* map 26 D4. Modern studies: Caballos Rufino and León Alonso 1997; Caballos Rufino 2010; Rodriguez and Garcia 2015 (valuable study; despite its title, which translates as 'Italica: The foundation of Publius Cornelius Scipio Africanus in the heart of Punic Hispania', it puzzlingly concludes at 240 col. 2 that the precise 'paternity' story, i.e. Scipio as founder, was forged in the time of Trajan and Hadrian); Padilla Monge 2017: Jiménez Sancho 2021.

[91] I do not list all those many scholars, but here are two eminent ones: Syme 1964: 144 [1979: 620], in an otherwise sceptical article, wrote categorically that Italica was 'founded by Scipio in 206 BC', not even bothering to cite his source, Appian. De Sanctis did not mention Scipio's foundation of Italica in his Hannibalic war volume (1968, originally 1912), but did so at 1969 [originally 1923]: 470 and

the lack of supporting literary, epigraphic, numismatic, or archaeological evidence for what Appian was taken to be saying.[92] Finally, in 2017, there was a full-scale and (almost) complete demolition job, so that in 2021 it could be said with equal confidence that 'nowadays the most accepted opinion rejects a military foundation by Scipio'.[93] In what follows, I try to look at the problem afresh, with special attention to the literary aspect, which has not so far been examined thoroughly, in particular silences from ancient authors from whom explicitness might have been expected. I now return to the detail.

There had been a local, Turdetanian settlement on the site of the later Italica.[94] But that sort of colonially insensitive overlay was usual in the history of 'new' Greek and Hellenistic cities, including Naxos, which was the first Greek settlement on Sicily, and the most celebrated and successful of them all, Egyptian Alexandria. Italica had a long and prosperous future, especially but not only in the time of Hadrian (emperor 117–138 CE). In that period, the city was lavishly endowed with fine public buildings. Hadrian's predecessor Trajan was actually born there, as Hadrian was not: he was born in Rome and seems to have had an ambiguous relationship to Italica, which he did not visit as emperor.[95] Italica received municipal status under Caesar or Augustus and became Colonia Aelia Augusta Italica under Hadrian.

Appian specifies only 'the wounded', which is usually changed or expanded: most modern authorities think this not enough, so they tacitly change it to the wider term 'veterans'.[96] They reason that Italica must have been more than some kind of field hospital or infirmary for Roman and Italian soldiers.[97] And Appian's Greek compound verb for 'settled' hints at

---

n. 222, discussing the beginning of the Romanization of Iberia, citing Appian and *CIL* 11 199, for which see n. 112.

[92] Hesitations are implied in Galsterer 1997 and Keay 1997, as will be seen. But both nevertheless upheld and (Galsterer) defended the foundation story against possible objections.

[93] The demolition job: Padilla Monge 2017 (brief English abstract at 100). For the quotation in the text, see Jiménez Sancho 2021: 189, taken from the full English abstract (p. 194 for the Spanish version).

[94] Keay 1997: 24–5.

[95] See Syme 1964: 142–4 and 145 [=1979: 617–8 and 620–2]. See also Opper 2008 (book of the British Museum exhibition 'Hadrian, empire and conflict' in that year): 129 for the staggeringly lavish building programme at Italica. For Hadrian's holding of a traditional local office at Italica, see Dench 2005: 221.

[96] Scullard (1970: 104) went further: 'some of his Roman and Italian veterans, including the sick and wounded', where everything but the last word is conjecture. But Scullard's 'Italian' is plausible, given the city's name.

[97] Cf. Galsterer 1997: 51: Italica not a 'Feldlazarett'. Bouiron 2022: 541 assumes the wounded were from the fighting at Ilipa, but Appian does not say this, and it is too restricted.

an Indigenous Iberian element as well as the Romans and Italians.[98] The verb may be compatible with a new foundation, although this has been denied.[99]

If Appian meant that Scipio founded a new city called Italica – and if he was right – this would be important, even epoch-making, in several ways. It would be the first Roman settlement outside Italy generally, and the first overseas city founded by a Roman commander, perhaps without senatorial advance approval.[100] The position had vital strategic value, near the land route linking the Guadalquivir and Guadiana rivers, and it had easy access to the metals of the western Sierra Morena.[101] The name would show that it was intended for Italians – perhaps south Italian specifically – as well as Romans.[102] It would also be proof of Scipio's forbearance in not naming a city after himself, like a Hellenistic ruler.

In view of all this, it is mysterious that, at least until late antiquity, the only literary evidence for so important an event should be this single sentence in Appian's *Iberian history*. This singularity should not be passed over without an attempt at explanation.[103] It is surely surprising that Livy does not record the foundation by Scipio in his very full narrative of 206. His main source was Polybius, whose own narrative of 206 is incomplete, but not as fragmentary as it is for 205. We do have his account of the mutiny and Scipio's subsequent military operations, then his return in triumph to Rome, but there are certainly gaps, so theoretically the apparently unmentioned Italica could have fallen out in one of these.[104] In that case, however, why was it not picked up by Livy, who unlike us had access to Polybius' full text? The biographical aspect apart – he is naturally

---

[98] His word for 'settled' is συνῴκισε, 'he *joined* them in settlement' to the city, where the prefix σύν (or the dialect variant ξύν), 'with', implies that he added them to an existing population (no other group is mentioned). Cf. Galsterer 1997: 51.

[99] Padilla Monge 2017: 79. It is true that the verb has the city's future population as its object, so resembles Th. 1.15.2 (Theseus' synoecism of Attica) rather than Th. 1.24.2, 6.2.5, or 6.5.1 (where the verb's object is a jointly founded new city itself). It is not certain, however, whether Appian's Greek should be pressed so strictly.

[100] Galsterer 1997: 51.   [101] Keay 1997: 25; Galsterer 1997: 51–2.

[102] Cf. Brunt 1971a: 206: the name Italica 'suggests that settlers there were not exclusively Roman'. Galsterer 1997: 52 suggests that *south* Italians are meant, because of the original scope of the word 'Italia'.

[103] The only scholar I can find who addresses this detail of the problem is Galsterer (1997: 51). He says Livy's silence is not surprising because Italica had no special importance until the time of Trajan and Hadrian. But this underestimates Italica's standing in the Augustan period (cf. Keay 1997: 37). And Galsterer does not address Polybius' account of the year 206, which is missing but of which we have Livy's version. Is it to be supposed that Livy read about Scipio's Italica in Pol. but decided to ignore it? A suitable place for Livy to have mentioned it would have been at the start of 28.38.

[104] Pol. 11.25–33.

interested in everything done by Scipio – he must have been aware of and interested in Italica, a reasonably important place even in his own day. As for Appian himself, his *Iberian history* is clearly dependent on Polybius, but with variations and additions: he has just described the mutiny, with some non-Polybian details.

Two later Greek sources in particular might have mentioned the foundation by Scipio (as they do not) in the course of mentioning Italica (as they do). Strabo, writing in the time of Augustus, but perhaps drawing on the learned Artemidorus of Ephesus (about 100 BCE), merely said in a geographical enumeration that after Corduba (modern Cordoba) and Seville there are Italica and Ilipa. He says no word about Scipio, although in the previous chapter he said that Corduba was 'a foundation of Marcellus' (this is Marcus Claudius Marcellus, in his third consulship, 152 BCE). Stephanus of Byzantium, in his long entry on Italy, says in passing that 'there is a city Italike in Iberia'. Again no word about Scipio, although Stephanus often mentions founders; so (to take an example at random) he says that Thessalonica was a foundation of Cassander.[105] As for other writers, it was only to be expected that the geographer Claudius Ptolemy would merely list Italica in his usual dry way. But rather more than the city name might have been hoped for from the chattier Pliny the Elder, especially given that he has mentioned the funeral mound of (Gnaeus) Scipio, Scipio's uncle, just a few lines earlier.[106]

Since Appian does remind us that Italica was the home city of the emperors Trajan and Hadrian, and there is no supporting evidence for the Scipio story, it is beginning to look as if all Appian's detail about Italica, Scipio's role included, reflects invented tradition from close to Appian's own day.[107] So it is now time to look at the late antique source, such as it is. The *Historia Augusta*, a late biographical work of disputed date but not earlier than the fourth century CE, cites the emperor Hadrian himself for the statement that his ancestors 'settled at Italica in the time of the Scipios'.[108] This might be counted as independent evidence that Scipio

---

[105] Strabo 3.2.2 (Italica); cf. 3.2.1 (Corduba) with *MRR* 1: 453 and *DPRR* CLAU1318 (grandson of the conqueror of Syracuse, CLAU0810). Steph. Byz. ι 117 and θ 36 Bill. What we have is an epitome, but a detail about the famous Scipio would surely have attracted an epitomator.
[106] Ptol. 2.4.13; Pliny *NH* 3.11, cf. 3.9 for the funeral mound, on which see p. 116.
[107] Padilla Monge 2017: 98–9. Jiménez Sancho 2021: 189 and 194, without discussing the *Historia Augusta* passage specifically, similarly suggested that Hadrian had an interest in promoting a prestigious version of Italica's origins. For 'invented tradition', see Hobsbawm and Ranger 1983. Their collection has been so influential that it is hard to remember that the title phrase is a paradox.
[108] *FRHist* 97 F1 = *SHA Hadrian* 1.1. B. M. Levick (*FRHist* 3: 626), commenting on the fragment, says the implied date for the ancestors' settlement is 206 BCE, after Ilipa. For Hadrian's great-great-

Africanus founded it. Or it might support the theory that the tradition about Scipio as founder did not take firm shape until the second century CE. But if this is a genuine quotation from Hadrian, a claim to ancestral settlement in the time of the Scipios (presumably Africanus and Aemilianus, that is, sometime in the second century BCE?) falls far short of an endorsement of a tradition that Africanus founded Italica in 206.

If not Scipio, then who? And if not 206, then when? The early history of Italica, on the assumption that it began life as a settlement of Italians in 206, is elusive, to put it no more strongly. Livy's full text is missing after book 45, which ends in 167 BCE, so theoretically he could have mentioned it in a lost later book. But in that case it might have been hoped that something relevant would have survived in the indirect and derivative Livian tradition, most obviously in the *periochae*, one of which does mention Tiberius Gracchus' foundation of Iberian Graccuris (178 BCE).[109]

There are only two pieces of evidence for Italica's existence in the entire second century.[110] The first is again from Appian's *Iberian history*, a casual mention in the course of some military narrative (143 BCE). The Roman commander sends 'Gaius Marcius, an Iberian man from the city of Italica' on frequent missions against Viriathus, a local leader in Lusitania, modern Portugal.[111] The Iberian Marcius has a Roman name, perhaps the result of intermarriage in demographically diverse Italica?

The second piece of evidence is much less secure: a very brief, fragmentary, and disputed Latin inscription which has been restored so as to read '[Lucius Mumm]ius son of Lucius *as imp(erator)* dedicated [at the village of Ital]ica some spoils from his capture of Corinth' (146 BCE). But it is now thought that, even if the restorations are correct, this is not an original inscription of the middle of the second century BCE but a later invention, perpetrated in the same spirit as the invented tradition of Scipio's foundation.[112] Otherwise, the epigraphy of Italica is meagre before the

---

grandfather Aelius Marullinus from Italica (triumviral period, i.e. late 30s BCE), see Wiseman 1971: 21 and n. 3, 208 (list of senators) no. 5 (*DPRR* AELI3302). For the *Historia Augusta* itself (date, reliability or not), see *OCD*[4] (J. F. Ma[tthews]).

[109] *Periocha* 41; see p. 294. We do in fact have most of book 41, but the text has gaps.

[110] From the first century BCE, there are mentions at Orosius 5.23.10 (war against Sertorius) and (using the ethnic *Italicensis*) at Caesar, *Alexandrian war* 52.4 and *Iberian war* 25.4. See also p. 167 n. 62.

[111] 66/282: Γάιον Μάρκιον θαμινὰ ἐπιπέμποντος αὐτῷ, ἄνδρα Ἴβηρα ἐκ πόλεως Ἰταλικῆς. See De Sanctis 1964: 227 for the military context, but on the problematic identity of the Roman commander Quinctius (or Quintus), see *DPRR* QUIN1555. He has distracted scholarly attention from the no less interesting figure of Marcius, who is not in *DPRR* because he is not a Roman.

[112] As restored in *CIL* 11 1119 = *CIL* 1² 630 = *ILS* 21d, it reads [*L/Mumm*]*ius L. f. imp(erator)/ded. Corintho capta/*[*uico Ital*]*icensi*. (This Mummius, for whom see p. 19 n. 48, was Scipio Aemilianus'

early first century BCE, and the epigraphically attested Cornelii there are not necessarily derived from *Cornelius* Scipio Africanus: there were many branches of the *gens Cornelia*.[113]

Italica has been excavated, but since the place was inhabited and flourished for so many centuries, archaeology is of little help in understanding the earliest Roman phase.[114] An authoritative assessment is that 'little is known about Republican Corduba and even less about Italica (206 BC) prior to the mid first century'.[115] The discovery of early coins from Italica with Scipio's name and portrait on them would be very welcome, for many reasons.[116]

Broader considerations have been offered. They take the form of a denial that Scipio could have acted in the unprecedented ways which the traditional view implies: this was not, it is claimed, the Roman *modus operandi* at this period.[117] This is a risky and undesirable line of argument, seemingly intended to prove that Scipio *could not have* founded Italica, rather than that he did not; the second is a matter to be settled by the available evidence, which might increase and improve in the future. 'This period' was one of wartime crisis in which many precedents were broken: Scipio's own appointment to the vital Iberian command despite his youth and inexperience; the beginning of prorogation of senior office in about 210; and the frequent iteration (repetition) of consulships after the heavy senatorial losses at Cannae.[118]

Let us instead temporarily suppose that Appian somehow got hold of a correct but non-Polybian tradition. In order to understand what sort of place Scipio's Italica was, on this hypothesis, we must look at comparable foundations.

Hasdrubal (5)'s foundation of New Carthage is close in time. It had an essentially Punic layout, but in choice of location it resembled a Greek city-foundation of a recognizable type, situated as it was on a superb coastal

---

colleague as censor in 142: *MRR* I: 474.) A century ago, De Sanctis accepted it unquestioningly (see n. 91) as supporting evidence for Appian on Scipio's foundation of Italica. But Padilla Monge 2017: 90–7 argues at length that the inscription is much later than the second century BCE. Astin 1967: 114 and n. 3 accepted its authenticity, but it is not in Yarrow 2006b: 68–70, catalogue of the epigraphic evidence for Mummius' many dedications of spoils from Corinth.

[113] Padilla Monge 2017: 78 and 85.
[114] Keay 1997: 24 (cf. 28) calls the archaeological record for pre-Hadrianic Italica 'poor'.
[115] Keay 2013: 313, and see previous n. Simon Keay (1954–2021) was a distinguished expert on the archaeology and history of Iberia.
[116] For Italica's coins, see Chaves Tristan 2010, cf. Keay 1997: 37–8 (coins depicting the wolf which suckled Romulus and Remus); $HN^2$: 5 (Italica as later municipality). No Scipio coins so far, of any date.
[117] Jiménez Sancho 2021: 194 (cf. English abstract at 189). [118] For prorogation see p. 14 n. 17.

position, easily defensible on the landward side, and with access to a fertile interior to the north.[119] By contrast, on the hypothesis that Appian had somehow got hold of a usable tradition, the intended population of Scipio's inland Italica consisted of veterans (including the wounded), apparently added to an existing community of local people. So Italica was less similar to New Carthage than to one of the far eastern cities of Alexander which functioned as an outpost, planted as a garrison rather than as a self-governing *polis*. A well-attested example is Alexandria Eschate (the 'Furthest') in Sogdiana, probably modern Khojend, near the former Persian city Cyropolis, which it was intended to replace.[120] If Italica was indeed founded by Scipio in 206, it would have resembled this sort of distant settlement, begun to short order on one soldierly leader's initiative, more than it resembled Rome's senatorially organized, popularly ratified, and easily reached colonies in Italy.[121] That is not unthinkable. But it does not get rid of the evidential problem, the lack of supporting evidence for Appian.

A half-hearted suggested compromise solution is that, at most, Scipio in 206 temporarily deposited some of his wounded troops at a place which later acquired the name Italica.[122] But this is methodologically unsound. We cannot pick and choose from Appian's account like this, accepting that the care for the wounded but not the naming of the place was due to Scipio. New evidence might conceivably turn the invented tradition about Scipio and Italica into a real tradition or might reveal the identity and date of the actual founder. But for the moment the safest conclusion is that Appian's whole section on the founding of Italica should be discounted as a Hadrianic myth, and that the stages by which Italica became a city by 143 BCE (as shown by Appian's 'Marcius the Iberian from Italica' in that year) are not recoverable on present evidence. Scipio Africanus did not found it. If Scipio Aemilianus had done, by an easy confusion on Appian's part, we

---

[119] Punic layout: Keay 2013: 311 and 312 fig. 10.7.
[120] Arr. *Anab.* 4.4.1, stressing the military element: Greek mercenaries, any of the neighbouring 'barbarians' who shared in the settlement as volunteers, ὅστις τῶν προσοικούντων βαρβάρων ἐθελοντὴς μετέσχε τῆς ξυνοικήσεως, and Macedonians no longer fit for active service; the language about the second group is closely similar to Appian's about Italica (n. 98): συνῴκισε/ξυνοικήσεως. For Cyropolis, see Arr. *Anab.* 4.3.1–4. For Alexandria Eschate, including its probably intended supersession of Cyropolis, see Fraser 1996: 67, 151–61; Cohen 2013: 252–5.
[121] Scullard 1930: 157 even suggested Italica was founded as another example of Scipio's imitation of Alexander. But this idea must now be given up, and anyway at 1970: 240 (cf. 104) he preferred to distinguish between Italica and eponymous Hellenistic cities. This point remains valid, whoever founded Italica. For the Republican Roman system of colonies (citizen and Latin), see *OCD*[4] 'colonization, Roman'.
[122] Padilla Monge 2017: 99. Hence my '(*almost*) complete demolition job' (p. 129).

would surely have heard of it from some other source. But some other individual in the second century presumably did and was presumably a Roman, whether or not the senate took the initiative or ratified it after the event.

## 4.7 Home in 206 to the Consulship for 205, but Not Yet a Triumph

Scipio was now ready to return to Rome, 'bringing back a glorious triumph and a glorious victory to his fatherland', as Polybius puts it. But the word 'triumph' is here used figuratively: one did not 'bring home' a triumph in the technical Roman sense. The word is pointedly chosen: Scipio on this occasion was refused the actual triumph which he asked for.[123] (To qualify for a triumph, a commander must, among other conventional requirements, have fought under his own auspices as a magistrate or promagistrate, and Scipio in Spain was neither.) So there is no actual contradiction between our main sources, as has sometimes been wrongly assumed.[124]

Why did he ask for a triumph when he must have known the conventions? But these were not set in stone, and he may have hoped that they could be bent by the senators in his favour; in any case he had nothing to lose by an ostentatious assertion that his deeds deserved a triumph.[125] And in fact he conducted what has been called an 'Ersatz-Triumph', a substitute triumph, by entering the city on foot, carrying to the treasury 14,342 pounds of silver and a large quantity of coined silver.[126]

Although he was refused the triumph, he was elected consul for 205 when he would be thirty, and received Sicily as his province, with permission to cross to Africa 'if he judged it to be in the interests of the *res publica*'. He made preparations for an invasion of Carthaginian Africa, and here we leave him for the moment, apart from registering briefly one episode which was to have damaging consequences for his reputation, and which haunted him as late as the 180s.[127]

---

[123] Livy 28.38.4; but he eventually celebrated a triumph in 201. For the other conventions, some of them dubious, see p. 246, discussing 201.
[124] Pol. 11.33.7, κάλλιστον θρίαμβον καὶ καλλίστην νίκην τῇ πατρίδι κατάγων. This has been taken (*MRR* I: 209; Beard 2007: 78 and 352 n. 14) to mean he actually celebrated a triumph. But for θρίαμβος here see correctly *Polybios-Lexikon* 1.3: col. 1169 ('bildl[ich]' i.e. figurative); cf. Richardson 1975: 52, Pol. 'seems to be equating θρίαμβον with νίκην [victory]'. Appian (*Iber.* 38/156) misunderstood Polybius. If Appian really thought Scipio had celebrated a triumph in 206, why did he save his very full, and partly generalizing, description until that of 201?
[125] For these two good points, see Pittenger 2008: 124–5.
[126] Livy 28.38.5; Itgenshorst 2005: 163.    [127] Sicily: Livy 28.45.8, cf. 29.1.1. The 180s: 38.51.1.

While he was at Sicilian Messina, he crossed to the Italian mainland to take Locri back from the Carthaginians. Hannibal also moved to the neighbourhood of Locri to try to prevent this, so that Scipio and Hannibal came close to fighting each other on Italian soil, three years before they actually met on the battlefield of Zama. But Hannibal abandoned Locri when he realized the strength of the unexpected Roman presence. Scipio returned to Messina, leaving his legate Pleminius in charge at Locri. This choice of individual was a grave error, as we will see when we examine in more detail Pleminius' disgraceful behaviour and Scipio's misguided subsequent support for his subordinate.[128]

Of the Carthaginian commanders, Hanno had been taken prisoner. Hasdrubal (8) remained at Syphax's court until 203, not long before Zama: this lengthy stay must have been approved by the Carthaginian government, unless he had been exiled. Hannibal's brother Mago at Gades received instructions from Carthage to take his fleet to Italy; he was sent money along with his orders, and he violently extracted more money from the citizens of Gades. He sailed up the coast to New Carthage and made a misguided attempt on the city. When this failed, he returned to Gades but found himself shut out. He crossed to Majorca but received a ferociously hostile reception there too – he was repelled by slingers, a Balearic military speciality – so he established himself on Minorca instead. He spent the winter of 206–205 there but then crossed to north Italy and captured Genoa. Emissaries and reinforcements from Carthage reached him later in 205. His activities caused great concern at Rome; but in 203 he was defeated by the proconsul Lucius Cornelius Lentulus and the praetor Publius Quinctilius Varus. He was badly wounded, after which his troops turned to flight. He was visited by more emissaries by sea from Carthage, who ordered him to return to Africa and told him that a similar mission had gone to Hannibal with the same instruction. Mago almost certainly died on the sea journey back to Carthage. Hannibal was now the only survivor of the three Barca brothers. Livy gives him emotional speeches deploring the decision of the Carthaginian senate and regretting his own failure to attack Rome after Cannae; but this last detail is unlikely to be historical.[129]

---

[128] For all this see Livy 29.6–9 and p. 163. For Italian Locri, see *Barr*. map 46 D5; Redfield 2003.
[129] Gades to Majorca: Livy 28.36–7. Genoa: 28.46.7–8, and Fabius' speech at 28.42.13. Emissaries from Carthage: 29.4.6. Emotional Hannibal: 30.18–20.

CHAPTER 5

# *Hannibal Frustrated in Italy, 216–208*
## *Aged 31–39*

## 5.1 Downs and Ups in Campania

We have taken Scipio's story down to 205 and must now return to Hannibal. What would or could he do after Cannae in 216, once he had realized that there would be no Roman deputation asking for peace terms? The question is a very old one. His officer Maharbal asked it by implication when he vainly urged an immediate assault on Rome.[1] For both Hannibal and Scipio, assertions contained in lengthy recorded speeches are likely to be inventions by the author; on the whole, intentions must be inferred from actions, although short memorable utterances may have a greater claim on belief. The younger Scipio's presumable aims were simple: to end Carthaginian dominance in Iberia, and then to rid Rome and Italy of the invader by invading his African homeland. Hannibal's war aims are less obvious, but his different treatment of Roman and allied prisoners clearly shows that he wished to detach the cities and regions of Italy from their Roman masters. When he released allied prisoners without ransom after Cannae, he is quoted (as part of a very short reported speech) as saying that his war with the Romans was not *interneciuum*, 'to the death', but for *dignitas* and *imperium*, 'honour' and 'dominion'.[2] This is 'a fair statement of Hannibal's war aims', and perhaps it was indeed remembered by its hearers.[3] The prosaic implication of these grand words is that Hannibal wished to keep Carthage's sea-based mercantile empire intact and to

---

[1] Maharbal: Livy 22.51. Livy makes Hannibal's old enemy Hanno (18), after Hannibal's brother Mago (6) brought news of Cannae to Carthage, ask Mago in the senate if the Romans had sued for peace and received the negative answer he had obviously expected: 23.13.1. See Geus 1994: 118 and 182.

[2] See *OLD imperium* 5. The second Latin word here is sometimes translated 'empire' (e.g. by Fronda 2015: 216), but that is perhaps misleading at this date.

[3] Livy 22.58.3; quotation in text: Briscoe and Hornblower 2020: 314, citing also 28.19.7, Scipio tells the troops they are fighting Carthage 'without anger for *imperium* and glory'.

preserve its control of Iberia in particular. Roman–Carthaginian treaties before the first Punic war had entailed mutual and friendly or at least respectful recognition of spheres of influence, and Hannibal would have been content with a return to something like this equilibrium. It goes without saying that he expected that Carthage would continue to exploit its north African dependencies.

Almost at the end of his book 22, Livy listed the regions which went over to Hannibal in the immediate aftermath of Cannae, including – naturally enough – some of the Apulians in whose territory the battle was fought; but also the Hirpini, the Samnites except for the Pentri, all the Bruttii, some of the Lucanians, almost all the Greek coastal cities of south Italy (but Livy records proleptically the defection of those he specifies), and finally the Cisalpine Gauls or Celts.[4] He gives no detail about any of these peoples.

Livy's book 23 opens with a success which, though small, must have further raised Hannibal's hopes, and this time he does give detail, and it is illuminating. Thanks to an invitation to Hannibal from a discontented local noble called Trebius, a mountain town named Compsa, further up the River Aufidus from Cannae in the land of the Hirpini, went over to Hannibal without a struggle on hearing of the outcome of the battle. Trebius had hitherto been harassed or held in check (the verb is *premo*) by the powerful pro-Roman family the Mopsii, who now left the city. This is a classic instance of what in a Greek city would have been called *stasis* or internal division, often accompanied by violence and an approach to an external power by one of the factions. Such *stasis* during the Hannibalic war is also well attested at Italian Locri, a Greek city. Hannibal now split his army and ordered his brother Mago to accept defections in the region, or to compel the defections of those which refused.[5]

The Carthaginians were virtually unable to send supplies to Hannibal by sea from Africa.[6] They are recorded as managing to do so on only one occasion, in 215, and it is not likely that this was one of many such unrecorded successes.[7] So if Hannibal was to establish himself in Italy for the long term with a view to winning over Rome's allies, he would need to open supply lines by sea from Carthage, and that meant securing a first-rate

---

[4] Livy 22.61.11 with Briscoe and Hornblower 2020: 30.
[5] Livy 23.1.1–4. Compsa: *Barr.* map 45 B3 and Oakley 1998: 277. It was Hirpinian not Samnite, see Brunt 1971a: 94 n. 2. It was retaken by Fabius in 214, Livy 24.20.5.
[6] Livy 28.12.9, closing an admiring appraisal of Hannibal in 206, near the end of his years in Italy. This has been doubted by Erdkamp 1998, but see next n.
[7] Livy 23.41.10, Bomilcar reached Locri with soldiers, elephants, and provisions, *commeatus*. Erdkamp 1998: 179–80 thought there could have been other such shipments but admitted that if there were, they 'did not make a significant difference'.

port.⁸ His first move against an important place of this kind did not go well. He decided to 'attack Naples, so that he would have a maritime city'.⁹ There is a strategic contradiction here: the winning of allies calls for diplomacy and reassurances, but 'attack', *oppugno*, is the language of aggression and force. The same contradiction is implicit in the orders to Mago, and indeed in the whole of Hannibal's years in Italy. The citizens of Naples, Rome's oldest naval treaty ally, remained firm in their loyalty (there is no hint of a pro-Carthaginian faction), so Hannibal's attack was repelled, although with Neapolitan losses, and he had to look elsewhere.¹⁰ The importance of Hannibal's failure at Naples can hardly be exaggerated. If the Greek poet Lycophron was writing in the 190s, his unusually lucid positioning of Naples at the exact centre of his cryptic, politically aware poem may be a salute to the role its loyalty to Rome had played in the recent war.¹¹ Hannibal turned north and inland, in the direction of Capua. That is, he abandoned for the time being his efforts to win or win over a coastal city, at least on the western or 'Tyrrhenian' sea of Italy. By 215, he had won possession of Locri far to the south, in the Gulf of Tarentum, and it was to Locri that the otherwise-incompetent Carthaginian Bomilcar managed to bring supplies and reinforcements to Hannibal.¹²

Campanian Capua was a rich and proud city, some of whose citizens had Roman connections through marriage, and 300 of whose aristocratic young men were serving in the Roman army as cavalrymen. Like inland Compsa but unlike coastal Naples, it was Hellenized but not Greek by origin: the Greeks of the main colonizing period almost invariably settled on, and traded from, the coasts of the Mediterranean and Black Seas. Oscan-speaking Capua was originally Etruscan.¹³ It was supposedly founded by a Trojan companion or relative of Aeneas called Capys.¹⁴ It

---

⁸ Rankov 1996 rightly stresses the importance in the war of Roman control of good landing places (54, for Naples in particular). Again (see previous n.), Erdkamp 1998: 172–3 argued unconvincingly that Livy exaggerated Hannibal's anxiety to capture a harbour city. He conceded, however, that the Carthaginians did not seriously try to expel the Roman warships from the Mediterranean.

⁹ Livy 23.1.5; cf. Frederiksen 1984: 239 and Fronda 2010: 103. Polybius' complete account of the war ended with Cannae. From now on, we possess substantial fragments, but much of Livy's narrative derives from Polybius.

¹⁰ Naples may be the (real or imagined) setting of the stratagem at Polyaenus 6.38.10: Hannibal, unable to capture a 'coastal city of the Romans', sent merchant ships with Roman flags. 'The citizens' saw the flags, came out to greet the ships, and were slaughtered. We are not told that the city was taken (the whole population can hardly have gone to the shoreline). But the story may a worthless example of 'Punic fraud'.

¹¹ Lycophron, *Alexandra* 732–7 with Hornblower 2022: 87. More usually, Lycophron uses periphrases for names of places and individuals, but here he says 'the Neapolitai'.

¹² Livy 23.30.8 and 41.10.   ¹³ Livy 4.37.1 with Ogilvie 1965: 591–2.

¹⁴ Virgil, *Aeneid* 10.145 with Harrison 1991: 100 and Frederiksen 1984: 117–18, both discussing alternative identities for Capys. In the fifth century BCE, Hecataeus (*FGrHist* and *BNJ* 1 F 62) knew of

would be good to be sure that this foundation myth was authentically Capuan.[15] It would suggest that Capua claimed closeness to Rome – there were strong kinship ties – but also something like parity of esteem.[16]

The defection of so important a place would, after Trasimene and Cannae, be a further blow to Roman prestige in Italy; and it would – and did – deprive the Romans 'at a blow of all the resources of Campania, most importantly her corn'.[17] But the Capuans were not united in hostility to Rome, nor was their defection immediate.[18] They initially approached the Roman consul Varro, the loser at Cannae, for whom Livy invents a speech which made no attempt to conceal the magnitude of the defeat and instead played the pan-Italian card, warning the Capuans what horrors to expect from the barbarian invaders. Whatever Varro really said, it cannot have been encouraging, and in 215 the Capuans struck a treaty with Hannibal, a fateful decision for their city's future. The terms guaranteed Capuan self-government; but Hannibal supposedly went further in a speech to the Capuan senate: he promised extravagantly that Capua would 'soon be the capital of all Italy', *breui caput Italiae omni*, a clever promise which, if historical, cost him nothing in the short term.[19] But it flattered the decision-making Capuans' self-regard and encouraged their hegemonical aspirations.[20] In the years of Hannibalic control (216–211), Capua for the first time proudly issued its own coinage.[21] As for the 300 Campanian cavalrymen who had remained loyal to Rome, they pleaded that they were in effect stateless. So they were, in a most unusual gesture, awarded Roman citizenship and enrolled in the municipality of loyal Cumae.[22] In 213, a further 112 Campanian cavalrymen deserted to the praetor Gnaeus Fulvius Centumalus at Suessula, south-east of Capua.[23]

---

Capua, but it is not certain that he, rather than Stephanus of Byzantium who cited him, added that its founder Capys was a Trojan; see Jacoby's n.

[15] Frederiksen 1984: 118 claimed that 'the figure of Capys has been detected upon coins of the fourth century BC', but in the accompanying note (130 n. 10), his editor Nicholas Purcell says he has 'been unable to trace the coins to which MWF refers here'. Nor can I find anything relevant in *HN Italy*.

[16] See Fronda 2015 and Mermati 2015.

[17] Frederiksen 1984: 239, cf. Pol. 7.1.1. For Campania generally in the Hannibalic war, see Frederiksen 1984: 238–63 (ch. 11) and 285–318 (ch. 13, revised version of Frederiksen 1959) for the economy and society of Republican Capua.

[18] Livy narrates the defection of Capua at great length: 23.3–10.

[19] 'Capital': Livy 23.10.2. It has been plausibly argued that in the longer term the secession of Capua actually worked against Hannibal, because other Campanian states were alarmed at Capuan ambitions; see Fronda 2007: 104 and 2010: 144, 146–7. (He was not the first to take this line: Fronda 2010: 101 n. 5 for others.)

[20] See Fronda 2007 for these as a strong motivating factor in the Capuan revolt.

[21] See *HN Italy*: 64–6 nos. 479–510.  [22] Livy 23.31.10–11; Harris 1971: 194 and n. 1.

[23] Livy 24.47.12–13. He went on to be consul in 211: *DPRR* FULV0904.

## Hannibal's Treaty with Philip V of Macedon

It was alleged that the winter of 216–215 at Capua weakened Hannibal's army as a fighting force because of the unaccustomed luxury.[24] This is probably not much more than Roman wishful thinking. In any case, the rumours did not touch Hannibal himself.[25]

Roman garrison forces ensured that Hannibal's continuing efforts to secure a Campanian port (Cumae, Puteoli) came to nothing, as did his repeated attempts on inland Nola, where he was defeated in a minor engagement by Marcus Claudius Marcellus as propraetor, an outstanding but reckless soldier and the future captor of Syracuse.[26] This was one of Hannibal's very few defeats in the field.[27] Towards the end of 215, he left Campania for the time being and encamped for the winter next to Apulian Arpi, Greek Argyrippa, supposedly founded by the Homeric Greek hero Diomedes, near modern Foggia.[28]

### 5.2 Hannibal's Treaty with Philip V of Macedon, 215

In 215, Hannibal made one of his worst decisions: to sign a treaty of alliance with the young Macedonian king Philip V. The treaty document was intercepted and read by the Romans: their naval prefect Publius Valerius Flaccus captured the ships which carried the envoys of Philip and Hannibal.[29] The treaty, as given by Polybius, is more reliable than Livy's, as we shall see. It is more obviously the Carthaginian version.[30]

> This is a sworn treaty between Hannibal the general, Mago, Myrkanos, Barmokaros, and all other Carthaginian senators present with him, and all Carthaginians serving in his army, on the one side; and Xenophanes, son of Cleomachus of Athens, sent to us by King Philip son of Demetrius as his ambassador, on behalf of himself, the Macedonians, and their allies, on the other side.
>
> In the presence of Zeus, Hera, and Apollo; in the presence of the Genius [*daimon*] of the Carthaginians, and of Hercules, and Iolaus.[31] In the presence of Ares, Triton, and Poseidon; of the gods who accompany the army, and of the sun, moon, and earth; of rivers, harbours, and waters; of all the

---

[24] Livy 23.18.10–16, which concludes by saying that the process continued into the summer of 215.
[25] For his love affair, see pp. 151–2: it was not however at Capua.
[26] Frederiksen 1984: 242. Nola: Livy 23.46 (Livy makes Marcellus exaggerate this success later, 27.2.1). Marcellus is *DPRR* CLAUD0810; he was consul in 222, 214, 210, and 208. In addition, he was elected suffect (replacement) consul in 215 but abdicated.
[27] See p. 421.   [28] Livy 23.46.8. Diomedes: Lycophron, *Alexandra* 592. Cf. p. 363 (on the Dasii).
[29] Livy 23.33–4; *MRR* 1: 257, *DPRR* VALE0805. Flaccus had been consul in 227.
[30] For the text of the alliance, see Pol. 7.9 and Livy 23.33.9–12; *SVT* no. 528. Brizzi 2011a: 161–80.
[31] The *daimon* of the Carthaginians is perhaps Tanit (Greek Artemis), see *ICO*: 145, discussing 'Spain' no. 10B, a Punic dedication from Ibiza, about 180 BCE; see p. 357.

gods who possess Carthage; of all the gods who possess Macedonia and the rest of Greece; of all the gods of war who are witnesses to this oath.

Hannibal the general, and all other Carthaginian senators present with him, and all Carthaginians serving in his army, subject to our mutual consent, proposes to make this sworn treaty of friendship and honourable good-will. Let us be friends, close allies, and brothers, on the following conditions:

(1) King Philip and the Macedonians and the rest of the Greeks who are their allies shall protect the 'supreme Carthaginians' [i.e. the Carthaginian citizens?], Hannibal the general and those with him, and those dependants of the Carthaginians who live under the same laws; also the people of Utica, and the cities and peoples subject to Carthage, and our soldiers and allies in Italy, Gaul, and Liguria, with whom we are in alliance, and with whomsoever we may hereafter enter into alliance.

(2) The Carthaginians and those serving in this army, and the people of Utica, and all the cities and peoples, subject to Carthage, and all peoples and cities in Italy, Gaul, and Liguria, who are our allies, and all others in Italy who may hereafter become allies of the Carthaginians, shall protect and guard King Philip and the Macedonians, and such other Greeks as are his allies.

(3) We will not make plots against, nor lie in ambush for, each other; but in all sincerity and good-will, without deception or plotting, will be enemies of those who make war against the Carthaginians, except for those kings, cities, and peoples, with which we have sworn agreements and friendships.[32]

(4) We too will be enemies to those who make war against King Philip, except for those kings, cities, and peoples, with which we have sworn agreements and friendships.

(5) You will be on our side ['for us'] in the war in which we are now engaged against the Romans, until such time as the gods give us and you the victory.[33] And you will give us what help we need, and as we mutually agree to.

(6) When the gods have given us victory in our war against the Romans and their allies, if the Romans ask us to make a treaty of friendship, we will include you in the treaty, and on the following terms; first, the Romans must not wage war against you; second, they are not have control over Corcyra, Apollonia, Epidamnus, Pharus, Dimale, Parthini, or Atintania; and third, they must restore to Demetrius of Pharus all those of his friends who are now part of the commonwealth of Rome.[34]

---

[32] The manuscripts of Pol. have a word meaning 'ports' not 'peoples', but this must be a mistake.
[33] Editors expand to '*allies* for us' after 'you will be ... '; but 'for us' may be enough.
[34] 'Commonwealth', κοινόν (lit. 'common thing', often 'federation'), is an unexpected word here but must mean something like 'control' or 'dominion'.

(7) If the Romans make war on you or us, we will help each other in the war, according to the needs of either of us.

(8) Similarly, if any others do so, except for those kings, cities, and peoples, with which we have sworn agreements and friendships.

(9) If we decide to subtract from or add to this sworn treaty, we will subtract or add only as may be agreed by both of us.

The alliance brought Hannibal no obvious material benefit (except for some possibly believable Macedonian mercenaries in Hannibal's army at Zama).[35] On the contrary, the no doubt exaggerated rumours of its contents can only have increased the wariness of the Italian communities whose support he so vitally needed. Why did Hannibal do it? Perhaps he hoped to force the Romans to the negotiating table. Perhaps he simply hoped to distract them a little, and in particular to ease what was in effect a Roman blockade of the sea.[36] It was even more unwise of Philip, because the Roman senators had long and implacable memories. They did not forget his collusion with the hated and feared invader: the 'first Macedonian war' (a modern and misleading expression) of 215 or 214 to 205 between Rome and Philip was a desultory affair, because the Romans had more urgent preoccupations.[37] But once they were rid of the threat of Hannibal, they embarked on war with Philip, the 'second Macedonian war', in earnest; and their proconsul Flamininus defeated him at Cynoscephalae in 197.

The terms are differently given by Polybius and by Livy, who makes Philip promise specifically to send the largest possible fleet to help Hannibal in Italy.[38] But this is not consistent with Polybius' clause §6: 'after the gods have given us victory over the Romans', we will make peace with them on condition that they will no longer control Corcyra or the Illyrian mainland. The promises of mutual aid are much more vaguely and therefore plausibly expressed than in Livy. Polybius' version makes it clear that a 'war to annihilation', a *Vernichtungskrieg*, was not envisaged at Carthage; the stronger commitments found in Livy's text were later

---

[35] Livy 30.33.5, for a 'Macedonian legion'. This is not in Polybius and has been doubted totally, but see p. 219.
[36] Groag 1929: 88 (who however noted that Philip was no match for Rome navally); Lazenby 1978: 148.
[37] The uncertainty about the start date (Philip's pact with Hannibal, or Rome's first naval action?) is because there was no formal Roman declaration of war, unlike that against Hannibal, or Philip in 200. The hostilities against Philip were a kind of eastern theatre of the war with Carthage. They did have a definite terminus, however: the Peace of Phoenice, negotiated between Philip V and Publius Sempronius Tuditanus in 205 (*DPRR* SEMP0882). For the other signatories, see *HCP* 2: 552 on Pol. 18.1.14 'the treaty in Epirus'. But the Aetolians had without Roman permission made a separate peace with Philip a year earlier; this independence cost them dearly later on.
[38] Livy 23.33.10. For all the ancient sources, with discussion in German, see *SVT* no. 528.

fabrications, designed to justify wars of annihilation against both Carthage and Macedon.[39]

Philip had heard the news of Trasimene while presiding at the Nemean games at Argos in southern Greece, summer 217.[40] But it was the much greater Roman defeat at Cannae the following year which stirred him to offer Hannibal an actual treaty of alliance.[41] The Polybian treaty, which begins with an impressive invocation of the gods who preside over the oath, clearly translates a Punic document. From near eastern and Semitic diplomatic precedents, it has been argued that on the Carthaginian side, 'the contracting party is Hannibal himself together with the troops under his command', and that the pact was not concluded in the name of the Carthaginians.[42] This is obviously relevant to the subject of our next chapter, the degree of freedom of action and of independent policy-making possessed by Hannibal and Scipio. The status of Hannibal's Carthaginian co-jurors is crucial. The document begins 'this is a sworn treaty made between Hannibal the general, Mago, Myrkanos, Barmokaros, and all other Carthaginian senators, *gerousiastai*, present with him'.[43] We have seen, when discussing Hannibal's council of war (his *synedroi*), that these senators present with Hannibal are likely to have been formal representatives of the Punic government, attached more or less permanently to his mobile staff.[44] (It is not obvious why Mago and the other two are named, nor is anything else known about any of the three.) That is, they were not sent out specially from Carthage to conclude the treaty with Philip.[45] It has been said that 'the treaty may still have been ratified subsequently at Carthage'.[46] But we do not know this for sure, and ratification is a notoriously slippery legal concept: the home government was not going to repudiate such a solemn treaty in which their own senators were co-jurors. So this implies that Hannibal made an important decision on his own responsibility (we cannot quite say 'initiative' because that came from Philip), although he in turn presumably consulted his own *synedroi*.

Hannibal can hardly have hoped ambitiously that this alliance would open up a second front – or rather a third, in addition to Italy and Iberia.

---

[39] See *SVT* no. 528, comm. at p. 250.   [40] Pol. 5.101.3–7.
[41] Pol. 5.101 (Trasimene); Livy 23.33.4 (Cannae).   [42] Bickerman 1952: 18.
[43] Geus 1994: 188, 'Mago (7)'; 199, 'Myrkanos'; 14, 'Barmokaros'. Geus (unlike *HCP* 2: 44) rightly distinguishes the first from Mago (8), who with Bostar (5) and Gisgo (6) was sent by Hannibal to Philip but intercepted at sea by a Roman fleet: Livy 23.34.
[44] See p. 109.
[45] As seems to be implied by Bickerman 1952: 1, when he calls them 'Punic emissaries'.
[46] *HCP* 2: 43.

But any diversion of naval forces away from Italy would be welcome to him. From the perspective of the Romans, the threat from Philip was not great at this time.[47] But his alliance with Hannibal had the effect of drawing them still further into the affairs of Greece and the Mediterranean, a process which in the lifetimes of Scipio and Hannibal culminated in the Roman defeat of Antiochus III at Magnesia in Asia Minor (190).[48] There were other consequences, closer in time. Notable among these was the Roman alliance in 212 with the Aetolians of mainland Greece, the power which at this time enjoyed a majority on the ancient voting body, the so-called amphiktiony, or 'dwellers round about'. This ancient body controlled the affairs of the oracular sanctuary at Delphi, with which the Romans had very long-standing connections, or so they liked to believe.[49] The amphiktiony was not the same as the oracle, but since the Aetolians controlled the physical site, they controlled access to the oracle. As recently as the crisis of morale after Cannae, the Romans had sent to the oracle for guidance.[50] The terms of the Aetolian alliance are given by Livy; the epigraphic Greek text was discovered in 1949 at Thyrrheum in Acarnania (north-west Greece).[51] This was the first Roman treaty with a mainland Greek state and included an obligation on the Aetolians to wage immediate war on Philip by land, and on the Romans to help them with ships. The Roman intention was to stop Philip sending assistance to Hannibal; instead, the Romans would, it has been well said, fight Philip to the last Aetolian.[52] The Aetolians were unpopular among other Greeks, and as the Roman involvement in Greece continued and grew, the Romans began to regard their old friends and allies the Aetolians as expendable.

## 5.3 Syracuse

In the campaigning years 214 and 213, Roman armies nibbled away at Hannibal's military and diplomatic gains of the immediate post-Cannae

---

[47] In 209, a Carthaginian fleet was sent to Corcyra to help Philip, but this came to nothing much: Livy 27.15.7 and 30.16, with Thiel 1946: 121–4; Lazenby 1978: 163–4 and 166.
[48] 'Still further': Holleaux 1921 argued that the Romans had no serious interest in the Greek east until the end of the third century, but this view is no longer tenable in light of epigraphic evidence discovered over the century since 1921 (above all *SEG* 30.1073, from Chios; see p. 71). It entailed some arbitrary alteration and drastic downdating of events recorded in literary texts, notably Pol. 30.5.6 (the Roman friendship with Rhodes): *HCP* 3: 425.
[49] Hoffmann 1934: 129–31.    [50] Livy 22.57.5 and, for the oracle's reply, 23.11.1–6.
[51] Livy 26.24.7–15 (cf. Pol. 18.38.5–9) and *SVT* no. 536; both translated in Austin no. 77; inscription only, with translation: Sherk 1984: no. 2. Modern discussions are listed at Burton 2011: 90 n. 37, and see his own pp. 90–4.
[52] Errington 2008: 189.

period: the consul of 214, Fabius Maximus the Delayer, recovered Casilinum and other Campanian places, and in the same year the proconsul Tiberius Sempronius Gracchus (consul 215) defeated Hannibal's officer Hanno (22) at Beneventum.[53] Fabius the Delayer recaptured Hirpinian Compsa. In 213, the year of young Publius Scipio's aedileship, Fabius' like-named son, consul with Gracchus as colleague, who was now consul for the second time in three years, recaptured Arpi.

But of far greater importance than any of this was the defection of Syracuse, the greatest city of Sicily, to the Carthaginian side.[54] The complete Carthaginian takeover was not until late 214, but the process began fortuitously in 215, when the aged King Hiero II died. He had been a loyal ally of the Romans since 263 but was succeeded by a young and impulsive grandson, Hieronymus, who reversed the previous long-standing alignment. He approached Hannibal, who sent him two part-Syracusan brothers who had served with him 'for some time' (Polybius): Hippocrates and Epicydes, who were born in Carthage of a Carthaginian mother but were descended from a grandfather who had been exiled from Syracuse because he was thought to have assassinated one of the sons of the tyrant Agathocles.[55] Hiero's death at just that time was Hannibal's first piece of luck, although in view of Hiero's advanced age it cannot have been entirely unexpected.[56] His second piece of luck was the presence in his Italian entourage of two interesting and useful Carthage-born Syracusans, of mixed descent and obviously bilingual: how many such can there have been on his staff? Their personal names are common everywhere in the Greek world and are therefore uninformative.[57] That they turned out to be extremely able and enterprising was no doubt a third piece of luck. But it is

---

[53] This Gracchus: *DPRR* SEMP0866. He was not father (*DPRR*) but uncle (Münzer, *R.-E.* Sempronius no. 51 and family tree at cols. 1369–70) of the more famous Gracchus (SEMP1182) who married Scipio's daughter Cornelia II, and whose father was an otherwise unknown Publius, not recognized by *DPRR*. So SEMP0866 was great-uncle of the famous Gracchi. Hanno: Geus 1994: 122. It is possible that Hanno partially retrieved this defeat soon after: Livy 24.14–16 and 20.

[54] For the first phase of the tumultuous events at Syracuse, see Pol. 7.2–9, Livy 24.4–7 and 21–39. For the second and final phase of Syracusan narrative (Roman siege and recapture by Marcellus), see Livy 25.23–31; cf. Pol. 8.3–7 and 37. Pol. 9.10 is a moral lecture on the plundering of cities, prompted by the treatment of Syracuse after it fell. For the whole story down to the Roman recapture, see Lazenby 1978: 102–8, 115–19, and MacDonald 2015: 152–9.

[55] Pol. 7.2.3; Livy 24.6.2. The grandfather had gone to Carthage as an exile from Syracuse. This (see W/M) is the meaning of *oriundi ab Syracusis exsule auo*. Yardley 2006 wrongly translates 'they traced their origins back to Syracuse where their grandfather had been in exile' (i.e. from somewhere else), but Polybius makes it clear that he was exiled *from Syracuse*.

[56] There had been an earlier false rumour of his death: Pol. 7.3.6.

[57] But there was another Epicydes on the Carthaginian side at Syracuse, with the curious '*cognomen*' Sindon: Livy 25.28.5. Greek σινδών is a linen garment.

also a tribute to Hannibal's ability to make good appointments of individuals who, as the 'men on the spot', could take initiatives as boldly as Hannibal himself, while continuing to further his interests. Or did they so continue? This has been denied; the point is important for Hannibal's biographer and must be examined.

Hippocrates and Epicydes worked on young Hieronymus at the same time as a Syracusan embassy from Hieronymus was negotiating at Carthage. The Carthaginian authorities were persuaded to agree to Hieronymus' extravagant demands, which included acceptance of his rule over all Sicily, and they sent him ships and troops. But it was Hippocrates and Epicydes, the men on the spot, who caused the young king to abandon his grandfather's treaty with Rome and to reject the more cautious advice of his other counsellors. These included a man called Aristomachus of Corinth, the mother city of Syracuse.[58]

These men were certainly acting as Hannibal's agents and in his interests for as long as this was possible.[59] Livy specifically says that Hannibal approved of their staying at the court of the 'tyrant', that is, Hieronymus.[60] This detail is admittedly not in what survives of Polybius and may be Livy's own comment. But nothing the brothers did in Sicily, at very short notice (that is, there was no possibility of consulting Hannibal), suggests personal ambition, rather than a desire to win Syracuse for Hannibal and Carthage in a politically complicated and volatile situation. They neither of them achieved any personal goals in Sicily. Hippocrates – to anticipate events a little – died of the plague during the Roman siege; Epicydes narrowly escaped from Agrigentum to Africa and presumably Carthage, after which he is not heard of again.[61] But that was in 210, after Syracuse had fallen to Marcellus' army. It is not evidence that Epicydes had not acted on Hannibal's behalf hitherto. He was simply saving his skin.

So these were good appointments. But there is a counter-example. After Syracuse had fallen to the Romans, Hannibal sent out another general, Muttines or Muttones, an energetic Libyphoenician whom Hannibal had personally trained in the arts of war, says Livy. But this was a less successful appointment because he quarrelled with his colleagues and went over to

---

[58] Pol. 7.5.3. Corinth: Th. 6.3.2.
[59] It has been claimed that from this early point the brothers 'no longer act as Hannibal's agents but are pursuing personal goals in Sicily': Walbank and Habicht 3: 453 n. 10 (n. on Pol. 7.4.4). There is no justification for this.
[60] 24.6.3, *nec inuito Hannibale apud tyrannum manserunt.*
[61] Livy 25.26.14 (Hippocrates); 26.40.11 (Epicydes; the reference to his army at 27.8.15 under 209 is retrospective).

the Romans, after making secret approaches to Marcellus' successor Valerius Laevinus. A very rare example on the Carthaginian side of a defector of high rank and ability, he was rewarded with Roman citizenship, and an inscription shows he was honoured in 190/89 at Delphi under the name Maarkos Valerios Mottones.[62]

To return to 214: Hieronymus was assassinated at Leontini north of Syracuse, and Hippocrates and Epicydes won power. The internal convulsions which followed need not be followed in detail here. The recapture of Syracuse after a bitter siege by Marcellus in late 212 is dramatic and narrated by Livy at length, as befitted its importance. Enough of Polybius' account survives to show that Livy drew on Polybius, whose account was also leisurely and detailed.[63] Both of them narrate fully and with obvious fascination the role of the mathematician Archimedes on the Syracusan side. (Livy would record, as a tradition, that when the city fell, Archimedes was absorbed in drawing figures in the dust and was killed by an ignorant soldier, to the distress of Marcellus who took trouble, *cura*, to have him properly buried.)[64] Some of the action took place away from Syracuse, in Leontini and in faraway Agrigentum on the south coast. Syracuse itself might have held out for longer if the Carthaginian admiral Bomilcar, commanding a fleet no smaller and perhaps larger than that of Marcellus, had not unaccountably lost his nerve and sailed away. This was, it has been said 'perhaps the supreme moment of the war'.[65] It was certainly important. But we might want to reserve that description ('supreme') for the outcome of the battle of the Metaurus in 207.

## 5.4 Tarentum

Hannibal at this same time, probably spring 212, scored a spectacular success by seizing the lower part of the great port city of Tarentum, Greek Taras, modern Taranto, Sparta's only successful and fully historical colony in the Mediterranean: *Lacedaemonium Tarentum*, as Horace called it.[66] This ancient connection was long remembered: high-profile military

---

[62] Pol. 9.22.4, 'the Libyan', with *HCP* 2: 150; Livy 25.40.5 (pupil of Hannibal); 26.40.5–7 (defection); 27.5.7 and 38.41.12 (citizenship and later career). Delphi: *Syll.*$^3$ 585 lines 86–8, also listing his four sons by their *praenomina* and calling them all 'Romans' (nos. 32–6).
[63] See n. 54 for references.
[64] Livy 25.31.9–10. Cf. p. 95 for the motif of *cura* about the bodies of enemies.
[65] Livy 25.27.12 with Lazenby 1978: 115.
[66] *Odes* 3.5.56, the closing words of his tribute to Regulus (first Punic war). Taras and Sparta: Malkin 1994: 115–42.

adventurers, including some Spartan royalty, responded to invitations and pleas from Tarentum for help against their Messapian neighbours, and even against Rome (Pyrrhus). In the Hellenistic period, the mythical Spartan king Menelaus, Agamemnon's brother, was poetically represented as a precursor of these historical individuals, by making him – un-Homerically – travel west in search of his wife Helen.[67] Tarentum, in its magnificent position on the gulf named after it, possessed the only natural harbour in the gulf, the beautiful *mare Piccolo*; this gave it perennial strategic importance, enhanced by Hannibal's failure to secure a naval foothold on the west coast of Italy. Tarentum was enormously populous and wealthy; its prosperity derived from its famous wool, its purple dye, and its agricultural produce, especially olives, wine, and luxury foods.[68] Finally, it was a delightful spot with a mild climate and a reputation for luxurious living, so that for Horace it was not only 'Spartan Tarentum' but 'soft Tarentum', *molle Tarentum*: very unlike the stern mother city.[69]

Hannibal had been approached in 214 by five unnamed noble young men from there, but this came to nothing. Now another discontented group under Nico and Philomenus carried out an ingenious deception – a pretended hunting expedition – to induce the guard to open the gate so that Carthaginian troops could enter. The Roman commander Livius managed to reach the citadel, where he and a small force remained heroically, provisioned by sea, until the main part of Tarentum was recaptured by Fabius in 209.[70] Tarentum now issued coinage on the Punic standard.[71]

## 5.5 Capua

Hannibal for a short moment in mid-212 held not only Tarentum but also both Capua and Syracuse, which were the two greatest cities of Italy (after Rome) and Sicily respectively. Hannibal made huge efforts to prevent Capua from reverting to Roman control; the inhabitants were desperately short of food because of the strong Roman military presence in Campania, and Hannibal could not directly force the Romans to lift the siege. Instead

---

[67] Strabo 6.3.4. For the Spartan king Archidamus III, see Diod. 16.62–3 (against Messapians); Plut. *Pyrrhus* 13. Menelaus: see Malkin 1994: 57–64, and Hornblower 2015: 328–9 on Lycophron, *Alexandra* 853.
[68] Strabo 6.3.1; Wuilleumier 1939: 213–28; Lomas 1993: 121; *IACP* no. 71.
[69] *Satires* 2.4.34; cf. Hornblower 2011: 321; Erskine 2013: 33–4.
[70] Livy 24.13.1–5 (214). Pol. 8.24–34; 9.9.11; 10.1; cf. 13.4.6; Livy 25.7–11 and (Roman recapture) 27.15–16.
[71] *HN Italy*: 106 nos. 1078–83.

he tried diversionary tactics. In 212, he moved suddenly east to Apulia and, at the strategically well-positioned town of Herdonea, he inflicted a heavy defeat on the praetor Gnaeus Fulvius Flaccus, whose brother Quintus was one of the consuls for the year.[72] In the next year, 211, Hannibal tried an even bolder throw, the march on Rome, the 'very heart of the war', a move which he had declined after Cannae five years earlier.[73] There was no question of an attempt to capture or besiege the city: the aim was rather to draw enough Roman forces away from Campania to enable the Capuans to provision themselves until better times.[74] But by chance, both consuls were at the time in Rome recruiting what were probably two urban legions, so the city was far from defenceless.[75] It is very possible that one of the young men in the city watching Hannibal's movements was the younger Publius Scipio, the 'destined leader of the war'. If so, it is safe to assume he was not an idle bystander. Hannibal with 2,000 cavalry actually got as far as the Colline Gate and a temple of Hercules, his own supposed protector; from there, he rode up to the closest possible vantage point, from where he surveyed the walls and the lie of the city. A picturesque tradition even had him hurl a spear over the city wall.[76] There was a cavalry skirmish, and a full-scale engagement was allegedly averted only by a cloudburst.[77] Perhaps an epiphany? At any rate, this caused Hannibal to remark that he been thwarted of the capture of Rome twice, once by lack of will, *mens* (he meant after Cannae), once by bad luck, *fortuna*. Patriotic Roman exaggeration and perhaps some outright invention have been at work here. But this moment – 'Hannibal at the gates' – gave the Romans a fright which was long remembered: that phrase *Hannibal ad portas*

---

[72] Livy 25.20–1; *Barr.* map 45 C2; *DPRR* FULV0924 and 0781. This battle has often been doubted, e.g. by Erdkamp 2006: 551, as a doublet of Hannibal's defeat of a different Fulvius (Centumalus) at Herdonea in 210 (*DPRR* FULV0904). See p. 153. But despite the coincidences, its historicity is defensible, because Cn. Fulvius Flaccus was accused in 211 of *perduellio*, treason, for losing his army: Livy 26.2–3. See *MRR* 1: 271 n. 2 and Lazenby 1978: 114 against De Sanctis 1968: 445–6 n. 28.

[73] Pol. 9.5–9; Livy 26.7–11 with Beltramini 2020: 135–72. But in Latin the metaphor was 'head' not 'heart', *caput ipsum belli* (Livy 26.7.3). Hannibal's route is differently given by Pol. (who says simply 'through Samnium', 9.5.8) and Livy, who gives a direct route along the Latin Way, 26.9.2; but Livy is also aware of what looks like Pol.' indirect route, though he attributes it to Coelius Antipater.

[74] See *HCP* 2: 121–4 and map at 122; Lazenby 1978: 121–2.

[75] Pol. 9.6.5–6 with *HCP* 2: 126 for the difficulties. As for a siege, see Erdkamp 1998: 177: Hannibal could not have supplied his army in Latium for long enough to carry out a successful siege, even if he had had the equipment to do so.

[76] Livy 26.10.3; Pliny *NH* 34.32; Silius 12.563–6. The Pliny passage interestingly claims that there were three statues of Hannibal in Rome, the very city into which he hurled … etc. It has been suggested that Silius here imitates Virgil's description of Turnus hurling his spear and prowling round outside the Trojan camp, *Aen.* 9.52 and 57–8: Hardie 1994: 81 and 83; Agri 2020: 322–3.

[77] Livy 26.11.2–7. The story was cited by St Augustine, *City of God* 69, cf. Brizzi 2011a: 59–60 and 69, noting (60) the then-topical relevance of Alaric's sack of Rome, 410 CE.

became proverbial for a desperate emergency.[78] A curious tradition held that a minor god called Rediculus, 'of Retreat', appeared to Hannibal, who was so terrified by a vision, presumably of this obscure god, that he retreated.[79] Rediculus was rewarded for his help to Rome by a shrine on the Appian Way. The story is certainly of a 'divine warning' type which became attached to Hannibal; but the derivation of the divine name is probably fanciful: Rediculus is more likely to mean 'god of happy return'.[80]

But despite Hannibal's audacious effort at distraction, Capua fell later in the year 211 to the proconsul Quintus Fulvius Flaccus and was treated with exemplary harshness and cruelty. Flaccus' own outrageous behaviour features as no. 1 in Toynbee's chronologically organized list of misdemeanours by Roman public officers in 211–123 BCE, alongside Pleminius and other better-known scoundrels. Flaccus, in defiance of the wishes of the senate and his consular colleague, executed fifty-three Capuan senators after the city had unconditionally surrendered.[81] How far the initial angry Roman decisions about Capua's status – all self-government and citizen rights to be abolished, and the city's territory to be the property of the Roman people in perpetuity – were actually carried out over the next years and decades is not certain. For example, a savage order for wholesale deportation of the rebels seems never to have been carried out.[82] The city recovered its prosperity to a surprising extent in the second and first centuries BCE.[83]

At some point before or possibly just after the fall of Capua, Hannibal is said to have had a love affair. Appian put this in Lucania: '*savage man though he was, he indulged himself in unaccustomed luxury, and took a lover*'. Pliny the Elder placed it at Salapia in Apulia and says the town was famous for Hannibal's love affair with a courtesan or sex worker, *meretricio*

---

[78] Cicero, *Philippics* 1.11 and *de finibus* (*About the ends of good and evil*) 4.22. Livy used it at 23.16.2; cf. Scipio at 26.41.12, *prope in portis uictorem Hannibalem*, 'victorious Hannibal almost inside the gates'. See Halkin 1934: 24 n. 4 and (on Juvenal 7.158–64) 27 and n. 3.

[79] Festus and Paul 354–5 Lindsay (locating it outside the Porta Capena; Pliny *NH* 10.122 merely mentions the *campus*, field, of Rediculus at the second milestone). An alternative explanation might be that the supernatural warner was Hannibal's supposed model Hercules/Herakles, whose temple features in the story. But why should a different god be given a separate new shrine by the Romans? In Silius, Jupiter tells Juno to stop Hannibal: 12.691–700.

[80] Wissowa 1912: 55, but see (against the Hannibal explanation) Latte 1960: 53–4 n. 2. The Greek for 'return', *nostos*, was not personified and did not receive cult.

[81] Toynbee 1965: 2. 612–13. Flaccus' anticipation or wilful misinterpretation of the senate's instructions was variously reported: Livy 26.14–16.

[82] For the problems, Frederiksen 1984: 244–50. For the terms, see Livy 26.16.5–13 and more fully 26.34, cf. Cicero, *On the agrarian law* (*Against Rullus*) 2.88 and very briefly Pol. 7.1.1–2.

[83] Frederiksen 1984: 309–10; Torelli 1999: 8.

*amore*.⁸⁴ This was a predictable slur against the woman if she existed, or against women generally if she did not.⁸⁵ The story is not in Livy's Polybius-derived narrative, and the differently given locations are not reassuring.⁸⁶ Livy had claimed implausibly that the whole Carthaginian invading army sank into gross and debilitating indiscipline and luxury at Capua, including use of sex workers, here called by the contemptuous neuter plural word *scorta*.⁸⁷ But he says nothing of the sort about Hannibal personally, neither at Capua nor Salapia, nor anywhere else. We know very little about Hannibal's sex life apart from his Iberian wife. Certainly no allegation of sexual abuse was ever levelled at him, as far as we know.

## 5.6 Conclusion

Hannibal's situation in Italy looked bad at the start of 211. In particular, the appalling fate of Capua was a warning to any other Italian cities still contemplating going over to him in the future, or even of voluntarily continuing their present adherence to his cause. Any such adherence would have to be maintained by Carthaginian garrisons and force. The loss of Syracuse in east Sicily meant that he had to abandon hopes of reinforcements from Carthage via the west of the island; and Malta had been in Roman hands since its capture by the consul Longus in 218.⁸⁸ On the other hand, the news from Iberia in 211 was more encouraging for him: the near-simultaneous deaths in battle of the elder Publius Scipio and his brother Gnaeus meant that the way looked clearer for his brother Hasdrubal to follow him to Italy with an army. If Hannibal had known that a son and nephew of the two dead commanders was perhaps watching him from the walls of Rome, he would have given him no consideration. But that young Scipio was the 'destined leader of the war', the *fatalis dux belli*.

---

⁸⁴ App. *Hann.* 43/183 (the Greek originals of the italicized words are ἄγριος ἀνήρ ... then ἐρωμένην, feminine singular passive participle); Pliny *NH* 3.103, cf. *Barr.* map 45 C2 (Apulian Salapia). Livy says Hannibal wintered at Sal(a)pia in 214/13: 24.20.15. But the nearby places are there said to be distant Metapontium and Heraclea, which could indeed be said to be in Lucania: *Barr.* map 45 E4. So some scholars posit another Salapia in that region: cf. Seibert 1993a: 260–1 n. 29. But from Pliny's context, it is clear he meant the Apulian town. MacDonald 2015: 163 cites Appian's variant but accepts the Apulian location. She remarks 'it was the most exciting thing to have happened in Salapia for centuries'.

⁸⁵ I assume only one *meretrix* (cf. Appian), although the adjectival phrase is compatible with more than one.

⁸⁶ But it is not a roving anecdote because Hannibal is always the subject.

⁸⁷ 23.18.10–15, under 216. *Scorta*: §12.

⁸⁸ Livy 21.51.1–2; cf. p. 88 for Longus' capture. Lycophron may show awareness of the importance of Malta at this time: *Alex.* 1028 with Hornblower 2022: 97–8. See further p. 289 n. 86 (bilingual text).

## Conclusion

The war in Italy was still not going all the Romans' way. In 210, Hannibal scored a notable hit by his destruction at Apulian Herdonea of two legions under the proconsul Gnaeus Fulvius Centumalus, who was among those killed. This is probably the second of Hannibal's victories at Herdonea.[89] The veteran fighter Marcellus was consul for the third time that year.[90] He fought Hannibal indecisively at Numistro in Lucania. Frontinus nevertheless praised Hannibal's superior choice of position for his camp and treated him wrongly as the victor.[91] It was in the context of this military narrative that Livy mentioned Hannibal's move of the population of Herdonea to Thurii and Metapontum. This may have been in Polybius' mind when he spoke of Hannibal's treaty-breaking impiety in Italy, which (he says) took the form of moves of populations.[92]

After the recapture of Tarentum in 209 by the elder Fabius Maximus, more Italian communities abandoned Hannibal: the Hirpini and some Lucanians. Marcellus was elected to his fourth consulship, for the year 208, with Titus Quinctius Crispinus, praetor in 209, as his colleague.[93] They represented a yet more aggressive strategy and tried, as Fabius had not, to bring Hannibal to open battle. Crispinus began a siege of Locri but left abruptly to join Marcellus near Venusia, with a view to a showdown. This decision was a disaster. They were ambushed by Hannibal, Marcellus was killed, and Crispinus was badly wounded and died before the end of the year.[94] The two consuls elected for 207, Marcus Livius Salinator and Gaius Claudius Nero, hated each other; but they went on to cooperate by winning one of the decisive battles of the war near the River Metaurus. The dramatic story of Nero's lightning march up Italy after eluding Hannibal and the consuls' joint defeat of Hasdrubal Barca, on his way to join his brother, will be resumed in Chapter 8.

This chapter ends by provisionally comparing and explaining the different fortunes and achievements of our two parallel lives in the periods

---

[89] For this second battle of Herdonea, see Livy 27.1, *MRR* 1: 280 and Lazenby 1978: 170–1. For the first, see p. 150 n. 72. Centumalus is *DPRR* FULV0904. Polyaenus (6.38.7) reports a stratagem of Hannibal against a Fulvius, ambushed at Herdonea; if this is worth anything, the battle must be the second, since Fulvius is killed. The stratagem is political, a pretend-deserter who called in Flaccus, claiming that the 'best men', ἄριστοι, perhaps in Latin *principes*, were fed up with Carthaginian harshness.

[90] For his career and other consulships, see p. 141 n. 26.

[91] Livy 27.2.4: Hannibal's camp was on a hill, Marcellus' on level ground. Frontinus (2.2.6) regarded this as 'superior' in both senses: Hannibal's camp was 'protected by hollows and precipitous paths', so he won a victory over a 'very famous general'; see p. 338.

[92] See p. 410 on Livy 27.1.14 and Pol. 9.26.7.   [93] Crispinus: *DPRR* QUIN0916.

[94] Pol. 10.32, Livy 27.26–7. Hannibal's personal role in the ambush is clearer in Livy (esp. at 27.26.7) than in what remains of Pol. here.

covered so far. Naturally, such a comparison becomes fully possible only after 210 when Scipio entered on his command. Both men were operating overseas, in lands controlled by an imperial power. But the Carthaginian hold on Iberia was far more precarious than the Roman hold on Italy, despite important defections after the shock of Cannae. Once the main defectors (Capua, Syracuse) had been recovered and harshly punished, there was less appetite for defection. During his short period as chief commander in Iberia, Hannibal was able to build on the successes of his father and uncle, but that ceased to be true once he crossed the Pyrenees and Alps. Scipio, by contrast, continued the Iberian strategy and diplomacy of his father and uncle. He was also able to reform the Roman army and to emulate Hannibal's own tactics at Cannae. By contrast, Hannibal in Italy lacked Rome's greater capacity for replacement of manpower (the allied contribution was important), so he was not much keener on an open battle than were his Roman opponents, as long as they were pursuing a Fabian policy. So his undoubted tactical genius found limited outlet.

The old question, 'was Hannibal's failure in Italy more a political than a military failure?', can be left until we compare Hannibal and Scipio as commanders at Chapter 16.11. In particular, it will be necessary to ask how true it was, as Livy claimed and some Marxist historians have argued, that support in Italy for Carthage or Rome was divided on class lines.

CHAPTER 6

# *Overseas Commands*
## *Freedoms and Perils*

## 6.1 Introduction

The situations of Hannibal in Italy and Scipio in Iberia as overseas commanders are similar, and this is one of the most important parallels between them. Both men were operating far from home, in a world of slow and precarious communications.[1] They therefore enjoyed – or suffered from – a partial absence of control by their governments. The ambiguity expressed by those two verbs arises because a commander in the field who took an important initiative stood to gain unshared glory; but equally he would be held accountable for any decision judged to be mistaken and so would be vulnerable to attacks from political enemies. This was not a new problem. Thucydides had remarked on the 'jealousy, *phthonos*, of the leading men' at Sparta towards Brasidas, at a time when he was far away, campaigning successfully in northern Greece.[2] As for early Republican Rome, it has been interestingly argued that the origins of the *prouincia* system are to be found in the tradition of independent action by leaders of individual *gentes*, families, who were nevertheless expected to remain within their own spheres of control.[3]

## 6.2 How Much Communication with the Authorities at Home?

To say *partial* absence of control by governments is necessary caution. The degree of control exercised from home is a function of the possibility, frequency, and speed of communication, topics on which we are

---

[1] The Stanford Orbis website (https://orbis.stanford.edu/) provides sophisticated calculations of the time and cost of travel between different places in the Roman world; I owe my knowledge of it to Denis Feeney. For example, travel from (coastal) New Carthage in Iberia to Rome would take fourteen days, but from anywhere in the Iberian interior it would take between fourteen and twenty-eight days depending on distance from the sea. These figures are approximate, depending on the sea route taken, and on whether the journey was from or back to Rome. See Arnaud 2005: 149–71 and map at 154–5 for the complexities of ancient sea routes in the western Mediterranean; also Cabezas-Guzmán and Ventós 2022.
[2] 4.108.7.    [3] Drogula 2021: 37.

imperfectly and sporadically informed.[4] Ancient historians tended to report letters to or from generals in the field only when they were remarkable for some reason, like the memorably 'laconic' message sent home to Sparta after the sea battle at Cyzicus in 410 BCE by Hippocrates, the *epistoleus* (here 'second-in-command'), and intercepted by the Athenians: Xenophon quotes the eleven words of Greek, in four staccato sentences: 'Ships lost. Mindarus killed. Men starving. Don't know what to do.' In another and much longer Greek example, Thucydides reports and claims to quote in full the letter sent to Athens from Sicily by the mortally sick Nicias in 414, asking to be recalled. Only at this point, a year after he had arrived in Sicily, does Thucydides tell us that Nicias had often sent messages before this.[5] Our sources for the second Punic war appear to behave in much the same way. We have seen that after the deaths of the Scipio brothers, the Roman position in Iberia was saved by the energetic leadership of Lucius Marcius Septimius, probably a military tribune.[6] Near the beginning both of a new book and of the second Pentad of the war narrative, Livy says that Marcius' letter caused offence in the Roman senate by his usurpation of the title of propraetor. But it was decided that discussion of this matter of principle should be postponed until after the departure of the equestrians who had brought Marcius' letter; these were now sent back with a promise of the money and grain which Marcius had asked for.[7] The narrative technique is doubly notable: modern translations say, more or less unavoidably, that '*the* letter of Marcius was raised in the senate', but there has been no hint so far – there is nothing in book 25 – that he wrote a letter at all; and the equestrians who brought it are mentioned only when they are due to return with the senate's reply. The matter of the usurped title 'propraetor' made the letter unusually interesting, and this may be why Livy includes the letter at all. Should we not assume that such letters were sent routinely? Marcius is said to have received from Gnaeus Scipio a thorough training in all military matters over many years.[8] It is likely that this included the drafting and sending of concise dispatches home, an essential part of the commander's job (the future Duke of Wellington was noted for his clear succinct dispatches and written

---

[4] For reports home to the Roman senate by commanders, see Schulz 1997: 54–5. They were lodged in the treasury, the *aerarium*.
[5] Xen. *Hell.* 1.1.23 (Spartan letter); contents of letters postponed until their arrival: Th. 7.8.1 and 11.1, cf. Hdt. 1.123.4 and 125.2 with Dewald and Munson 2022: 353–4.
[6] See p. 116.  [7] Livy 26.2. See p. 353 for the senate's role in provisioning.
[8] Livy 25.37.3; very soon afterwards, there is a close verbal chime with the description of Hannibal's Libyphoenician pupil Muttines, 25.40.5 (p. 147).

orders).⁹ Publius and Gnaeus Scipio had sent at least one dispatch to Rome; like Marcius' letter, this asked for supplies, but it was also special because it dramatically raised morale at Rome and therefore qualified for inclusion in the histories.¹⁰ We have no way of knowing how many dispatches or deputations of a more routine sort were sent to and fro. Probably a lot.

The same is true of the Carthaginian side. Consider the episodes mentioned at the end of Chapter 4. In 203, emissaries from Carthage brought instructions to Hannibal's brother Mago in north Italy twice, and on the second recorded occasion they took an identical message ('return to Africa!') to his brother Hannibal in south Italy. Hannibal had been at his base near Croton for several years. But Mago, in the period since 206, had moved from Iberia to overwinter on Minorca, and from there to the Genoa region of Italy. How did the first set of emissaries know where to track him down? He must surely, in dispatches or by messengers which or whom we do not hear about, have been keeping the home authorities informed about his movements. If the information about traffic between Carthage and the generals abroad is particularly plentiful in those years, that may represent the reality: the situation was urgent as never before. Or the answer may be historiographical rather than purely historical: it may be that the historians, when selecting their material, chose to record that traffic with greater fullness than usual, so as to heighten the drama of the final phase of the long, drawn-out war.

Another episode treated already in a narrative chapter (Section 4.2) concerns the important question, should Hasdrubal try to join his brother in Italy? In Livy's book 23, the Carthaginian senate soon after Cannae ordered Hasdrubal to do this nearly a decade before he was actually able to try; that is, in 208–207. On the earlier occasion, the senate's order and Hasdrubal's reluctance to implement it was fully reported. But when the matter becomes a reality again (209), what is evidently the senate's much earlier instruction is mentioned by Hasdrubal (6) and Mago (6) at a council of war in Iberia – but only as one factor in the decisions there taken, without mention of further orders from the senate. Perhaps the commanders felt that the senate's original instructions still stood: certainly in 210, the Carthaginians are said to be assembling troops to help Hasdrubal cross to Italy. Or perhaps Livy has misleadingly omitted an explicit new instruction from Carthage (but then the mention of the earlier

---

⁹ Cf. Keegan 1987: 133.   ¹⁰ Livy 23.48.4, cf. p. 115.

order would be otiose). More probably, the commanders simply felt that urgent actions were needed, and they took them.

## 6.3 Peripheral Imperialism: Decision-Making by the Man on the Spot

The useful notion of 'peripheral imperialism' in the sense of the title of this section is borrowed from the history of modern colonial empires, to describe decision-making done without reference to home authorities.[11] It is exceptionally hard to be sure whether Hannibal's attack on Saguntum was undertaken on his own initiative, as seems likeliest, or with the authorization of Carthage.[12] The evidence for such specific authorization is not good, and his independent actions contributed heavily to the outbreak of war.

Let us now return to another key moment in the opening phase of the Hannibalic war, one for which some explicit – but not straightforward – literary evidence survives. The decision in spring 218 of Scipio's father Publius to send his army on to Iberia under his brother Gnaeus was crucial for the outcome of the entire war.[13] But we also saw that two modern authorities, writing simultaneously, have adopted somewhat divergent interpretations of this decision. For one of them, the senate had 'mandated' it, and this was 'a most important example of how explicit senatorial directives could impose limitations on magisterial freedom of action'.[14] He relies, first, on Livy's statement that Publius sent Gnaeus to Iberia so as not to leave his allotted *prouincia* 'denuded of Roman support', *nuda auxiliis Romanis*; and, second, on Publius' speech before the battle at the Ticinus, where he tells the troops that his brother Gnaeus is in Iberia 'under my auspices and because the Roman senate and people wished it'.[15] These passages, with their confident assertions about motive, are however probably mere expansions of a less explicit passage of Polybius. This makes Publius say, also in a speech before Ticinus, that he would not have come to Italy, *abandoning the Iberian expedition on which he had been sent*, if he had not thought that this was both necessary for his fatherland and certain to end in victory.[16] But although Polybius was less prone to large-scale

---

[11] Richardson 1986: 177, citing and quoting Fieldhouse 1981: 23.   [12] See p. 82.   [13] See p. 86.
[14] Eckstein 1987: 189.
[15] 21.32.3 and 40.3; *auspicium* is an essentially religious technical term: see p. 70 n. 185. The emphasis on auspices may be coloured by Augustan attitudes.
[16] Pol. 3.64.10, given by Livy in indirect speech. Cf. Richardson 1986: 33 n. 6, 'almost certainly Livy's own expansion'. Publius had been 'sent' to Iberia at 3.40.2, with the plain verb πέμπω. At 64.10, the

invention of speeches than was Livy, an exception should be made for prebattle harangues – exactly the category to which the Polybian speech just cited belongs.[17] It is not in dispute that Iberia, *Hispania*, was Publius' allotted *prouincia*, but it goes too far to speak of 'explicit senatorial directives'.[18] A new and highly dangerous situation had arisen as a result of Hannibal's dramatic and unexpected arrival in north Italy, and Publius had to respond, and fast.

The other modern view is preferable: Publius' decision 'coincided with the senate's own opinion' of the importance of Iberia, but 'that decision was made and implemented by P. Scipio himself'.[19] The literary passages are in effect of a counterfactual, rhetorical sort: 'what if Publius had in this new situation decided differently, leaving Iberia undefended and abandoning his mission?' The speaker Publius invites the answer, 'that would have been a terrible mistake'. But the reader, possessed of hindsight, is subtly invited to wonder if in that event, with much larger Roman forces, the battles of Ticinus, Trebia, and Trasimene might have gone the other way.

In the years that followed, the Scipio brothers made further decisions on what appears to be their own initiative; and after their violent deaths, the same is true of the younger Publius Scipio.[20] It has been objected that these three commands were all 'very exceptional'.[21] This is true if taken to mean 'without precedent'; but the pattern of Roman commanders, operating in Iberia with a high degree of freedom of action, would continue through the rest of the Republican period, though with fluctuating interest on the part

---

Greek word for 'had been sent' is ἀπεστάλη, passive of ἀποστέλλω. But the passive can mean just 'depart', with no implication of agency, see LSJ ἀποστέλλω (I); Powell 1939: 337, στέλλω (3) 'set forth'; *CGL* ἀποστέλλω (5), 'passive with middle sense'. So στέλλεται and ἐστάλη at Hdt. 5.43.1 and 45.1 do not imply that the Spartan Dorieus was 'sent by' (the oracle at Delphi), see Eidinow 2023: 102–3. The *Polybios-Lexikon* 1.1 ἀποστέλλω: cols. 204–5 admits only the meaning 'sent'. But perhaps Pol. makes Publius defensively choose a verb which, with its possible neutral nuance, plays down his contravention of the senate's orders.

[17] Walbank 1985: 249 and 253–4; Briscoe and Hornblower 2020: 51 and n. 129. No distinction should be drawn between direct and indirect speech. See p. 31 for speeches.
[18] Cf. Richardson 1986: 34: 'there is every reason to suspect that had the senate been consulted, their advice would have coincided with Scipio's opinion. Not only had Spain been named as a *provincia*', but the senate continued to send supplies there.
[19] Richardson 1986: 35.
[20] For example, the decision to attack New Carthage speedily; and the diplomatic sequel, to be discussed shortly.
[21] Rich 1988: 315–16 (also applying this description to the outbreak of the first Punic war). He speaks of 'the Scipios' commands in Spain'. Since he is criticizing Eckstein's distribution of attention in his ch. VII, he means all three men. The younger Scipio is more obviously exceptional than his father and uncle, although Gnaeus' position was differently anomalous. For the possibilities – *imperium* delegated by Publius? propraetor or proconsul? – see Eckstein 1987: 190 and n. 13.

of the senate.²² As for the elder Scipios, two clear examples of initiatives taken on the spot are the treaties granted to an alleged 120 Iberian communities in 217, and their abortive but prescient dealings with the African (Numidian) ruler Syphax in 213.²³

The younger Scipio behaved very similarly: his settlement of New Carthage, after the rapid assault which resulted in its capture, was nuanced and reflects 'on the spot' decision-making.²⁴ As usual after a Roman victory in Iberia, it was followed by a series of diplomatic dealings with local leaders who approached him because they sought to detach themselves from their Carthaginian alignments. One approach was in the other direction; Scipio copied his father and uncle by seeking to win over Syphax, and he narrowly avoided capture.²⁵ If this had gone wrong, Scipio's enemies at Rome would have seized on it. If he had been caught and offered for ransom, would the senate have paid?

If we look to the end of the time span of this book for possible examples of independent diplomatic action by Roman commanders and officials, there are occasions when events overtook the instructions given to envoys by the senate, so that they had to improvise. There is a simple example in 195 BCE: a triumvirate of Roman envoys at Carthage, when Hannibal had escaped overnight, addressed the Carthaginian senate and added some new points on their own initiative. But everything they said was in the spirit of their mandate.²⁶

The inscribed letters, *epistulae*, sent to Greek communities in Asia Minor by the Scipio brothers Publius and Lucius in the early 180s, after the battle of Magnesia, are expressed in precise and detailed diplomatic language and so provide evidence of a valuable sort not available for Iberia at this date.²⁷ Those Greek places had long had the 'epigraphic habit', which reached Iberia only later.²⁸ The letters certainly expressed the general wishes of the senate. But they were very probably composed at short notice – that is, without specific referral to the senate at Rome.

But by whom were such letters actually composed? These two letters are among the very earliest to have survived. Literary sources do not mention such official Roman letters until the war with Philip V, at the beginning of

---

[22] Such initiatives are a recurrent theme of Richardson 1986: 34–5, 37, 69–70, 74, 89, 96–7, 100, 119–20, 124–5, 142–4, 147, 163–5. But see 153–5 for a change after the middle of the second century, cf. 166–8, 175–8.
[23] Eckstein 1987: 198–9 on Livy 22.20.10–12 and 204–5 on Livy 24.48.1–3. [24] Livy 26.47.
[25] Eckstein 1987: 209–32. See p. 127. [26] Livy 33.49 with p. 301.
[27] The detail of letters preserved in literary sources cannot reliably be taken to express exactly what the Scipios said. For the two inscriptions, see Sherk 1969: nos. 35 and 36. Cf. Sherk 1969: 186 n. 1.
[28] The 'habit': Macmullen 1982.

the second century; after that, Titus Quinctius Flamininus (consul 198 and then proconsul) is recorded as sending many letters.²⁹ One of them survives on stone.³⁰ (The extent of Flamininus' independent decision-making is a much discussed topic in modern scholarship and can be postponed for the moment.) This sort of letter-writing was a new development, so that it has been said by the greatest modern expert that 'it would not be too rash to maintain that the Romans learned the art of letter-writing from the Greeks'. But the same expert concedes that no simple answers are available to the question of whether Roman generals composed in Greek or in Latin and then got others to translate them.³¹ The surviving letters differ in the degree to which they betray linguistically their origins in Roman minds, so that each must be examined individually, but the general form and language are usually Greek, the spirit and contents Roman.³²

In the immediate sequel to the defeat of Antiochus III at the battle of Magnesia in 190, the brothers Publius and Lucius Scipio travelled in Asia Minor and dealt with various cities; some of the results survive on stone: Lucius had been consul in the year of the battle with Publius as his legate. The better preserved of the two letters sent by the brothers is addressed to the council and people of the Carian city Heraclea under Mount Latmos and says that the city's envoys (whose names follow) have met the Romans and handed over their decrees.³³ The brothers, Lucius as consul in 190 and his brother Publius, reassure them of their own favourable attitude to all Greeks and undertake 'since you have come into our [pledge of good faith]' to take care of them. Then they grant them freedom and control of their affairs, and they accept the offered gifts and pledges. Further reassurances follow. This exchange reflects the situation directly after the defeat of the Seleucid Antiochus III at Magnesia in 190. There is 'everywhere good Koine usage and vocabulary'. But the Greek word for good faith, *pistin* (an unavoidable restoration of a gap on the stone), indicates a 'truly Roman frame of mind'; the Aetolians in 191 fell into the trap of equating this Greek word *pistis* with Latin *fides*.³⁴

The immediate historical trigger for the other letter is less obvious. It is written to the people of Colophon in Ionia and confirms the inviolability

---

[29] Sherk 1969: 186 n. 1.
[30] Sherk 1969 no. 34, to Chyretiae in Thessaly; translation at Sherk 1984: no. 4.
[31] Sherk 1969: 199.     [32] These are the conclusions of Sherk 1969: 209.
[33] Sherk 1969 no. 35 (1984 no. 14 for translation).
[34] See Sherk 1969: 200 for these two judgements about his no. 35; *koine* (two syllables) means 'common (Greek)', referring to the widespread Hellenistic form of the educated, non-dialect language. *Fides*: Livy 36.28.

(Greek *asulia*) of the nearby temple of Apollo and Claros. The date of the letter itself is certainly the same as the other, 190, Lucius' consulship. It has recently been convincingly argued, against attempts to push back to 195 the Colophonian diplomatic efforts to secure recognition of this *asulia*, that 'the Scipios sent their letter at the very beginning of the Colophonians' initiative' and that this initiative began very soon after Magnesia, in 190.[35] So again the Scipios were reacting on the spot to a brand-new situation. As for the language, the stone is very fragmentary, but most of it can safely be restored so as to correspond exactly to the opening lines of the inscribed Heraclea letter, with its 'good Koine' features.[36] Only the final few surviving words ('the temple', 'inviolability') are a departure.

The likely conclusion is that the Scipio brothers had some sort of travelling bilingual secretariat, perhaps consisting of no more than one individual, skilled at turning Roman decisions into the right sort of idiomatic chancellery Greek. But the thoughts were those of the brothers. It is unlikely, to be sure, that they made any fundamental decisions which they knew to be at variance with senatorial policy. But the newer and more unexpected the situation, the more they are likely to have acted on their own initiative. The people of Colophon had suffered very recently at the hands of Antiochus through a year-long siege.[37] So the Scipio brothers' acknowledgement of the sanctuary's inviolability was hardly a controversial act – unlike Publius Scipio's behaviour over the looting of the sanctuary at Italian Locri, to which we will turn shortly.

No letters by Hannibal to Iberian or Italian communities survive, nor are any mentioned by the literary sources. Like Scipio, he settled the internal affairs of communities such as Campanian Capua as soon as its citizens surrendered.[38] One important diplomatic document in Hannibal's name does survive, the treaty he swore with Philip V of Macedon in 215 BCE. Despite the presence of Punic co-jurors and advisers, the alliance was made and sworn by Hannibal himself, whether or not it was later ratified at Carthage.

Those co-jurors attested in 215 are a reminder that both Hannibal and Scipio were accompanied on campaign by advisers, who compensated to a certain degree for the physical remoteness of the generals from their home government. Hannibal's military advisers, his *synedroi*, are thought to have been representatives of the Carthaginian government; and Roman

---

[35] Jones 2019: 144. See p. 23.
[36] This is why Sherk 1969: 200 passes over it in his discussion of the language of Roman *epistulae*.
[37] Livy 37.26.
[38] Capua: *SVT* no. 524. For other treaties with Italian communities in the years after Cannae, mentioning only Hannibal as the Carthaginian party, see *SVT* nos. 525–7 and 531.

commanders had their *consilia*, councils of war. But Hannibal may have become increasingly isolated as the war went on.[39] In particular he was cut off from day-to-day communication with his brothers Hasdrubal and Mago; and the outspoken Maharbal (not a kinsman of Hannibal) disappears from the record soon after Cannae.[40] Scipio by contrast had Laelius and later his brother Lucius to turn to for advice. It was nevertheless on Scipio, as on Hannibal, and not on family members or panels of advisers, that responsibility – and potential blame – would lie for decisions which had to be taken urgently.[41]

## 6.4  A Case Study: Italian Locri, 215–204

Let us look at an episode and a place in which, for once, both Hannibal and Scipio played a part at different times. One of the best illustrations of how a Roman general's independent and unwise actions abroad might be used by his enemies to undermine him at home was the scandal of the Pleminius affair at Italian Locri.[42] The main surviving source is Livy, but for the events at Locri at least, he followed Polybius, whose account does not survive.[43] Here, by contrast with the treatment of Colophon, a famous sanctuary's inviolability was ignored – and by Romans answerable to none other than the younger Publius Scipio.

The local political background in a nutshell is that in 215 BCE, after but not straight after Cannae, the Locrians, who had hitherto been Roman allies, went over to the Carthaginian side.[44] A Roman attempt to besiege Locri in 208 failed, but Scipio regained Locri in 205.[45]

---

[39] As argued in Appendix 3.1.
[40] He is last heard of at Casilinum in 216, Livy 23.18.4. See Geus 1994: 195, 'Maharbal (3)'. Cf. p. 108.
[41] For the activities of Hannibal's agents Hippocrates and Epicydes at Syracuse, see p. 147, where it was maintained that they did not cease to act in Hannibal's interests as long as this was possible. But even before that, they do seem to have taken initiatives themselves.
[42] Livy's main narrative is at 29.6–9, but he returns to it at 29.16–22 under 204, speech of complaint against Pleminius by the Locrians in the senate. See also Diod. 27.4 and App. *Hann.* 55/230–1. On the Pleminius affair, see Ciaceri 1932: 191–7 and esp. Toynbee 1965: 2. 613–21, the second and longest section of his appendix on 'misdemeanours 211–123 BC'; also Smith 1993: 27–9. For Millot 2019, see n. 59.
[43] See De Sanctis 1968: 627–8. But some at least of the detail of the speech of the Locrians at Rome is probably Livy's own invention. Smith 1993: 27 considered the possibility that Polybius deliberately ignored the Pleminius affair as a minor episode, built up by Scipio's enemies to discredit him. It is likelier that the text of his report does not survive.
[44] Livy 24.1. Two brief earlier mentions of Locri's defection (under 216) anticipate that more detailed narrative: 22.61.12 and 23.30.8. At 23.41.10, under 215, the Carthaginian Bomilcar succeeds in landing reinforcements at Locri. This too must be slightly anticipatory. See Ciaceri 1932: 141 n. 3; cf. De Sanctis 1968: 242 n. 94.
[45] Livy 27.26–8; 29.7–8.

After winning control of Locri, Scipio as consul very correctly told the citizens that he was not competent to impose a settlement: they should send a deputation to the senate at Rome. He left Quintus Pleminius in charge of the city while he himself sailed to Messina in Sicily. Pleminius was a legate in the sense of staff officer of Scipio, and he was Scipio's personal appointment; it is important that despite the title *pro praetore* which Livy gives him earlier, he had never been elected to a praetorship at Rome.[46] So far, Scipio had done nothing out of the ordinary: the appointment of staff officers was a commander's prerogative.[47] Nor was he out of order when, without consulting or informing the home authorities, he left Pleminius in charge during his own absence. The trouble arose from the way Pleminius behaved at Locri and the sequel, and this shows Scipio to have been, on this occasion at least, a poor judge of men and of important matters of principle.

The wealthy Greek-speaking Locrians were an unusual and sophisticated community, who attracted the interest of Aristotle and then of Polybius in his book 12 about how to do history.[48] Women played a greater role in the religious, cultural, and economic life of this Locri, the 'Sparta of the West', than in almost any other Greek city anywhere.[49] Women were integrated into Locrian society in all its public aspects: the third-century BCE female Locrian epigrammatist Nossis wrote of Locrian battles against their Bruttian neighbours.[50] The female-centred cult of Persephone (Latin Proserpina) at Locri was important; she seems to have been associated or even identified with Aphrodite, on the evidence of the 'Locrian *pinakes*', beautifully painted terracotta boards.[51]

The wretch Pleminius and his men violated this great goddess' famous temple and removed some of its treasures with impunity.[52] It might have seemed a more trivial offence when one of them stole a silver cup from a Locrian citizen, so that some of the Roman military tribunes took it away

---

[46] Livy 29.8.3 (Scipio's instructions); 29.8.5 (legate; for this sense see *OLD legatus* (2)); 29.6.9 (propraetor), see *MRR* 1: 304. For Pleminius, see *DPRR* PLEM1026.

[47] Mommsen 1887–8: II.1. 97.

[48] 12.5–12a; he opens this long section by saying he himself visited Locri more than once and did the Locrians favours. These Italian Locrians were called 'Epizephyrian', to distinguish them from their founding settlers, the Locrians of mainland Greece.

[49] See Redfield 2003; for 'Sparta of the West', see his p. 251. The position of women at Sparta was also peculiar, and there were mythical links between the two places: the Spartans lent their heroes the Dioscuri, Castor and Pollux, to the Locrians to help them defeat Croton in the Archaic battle of the Sagra River: Diod. 8.32, Redfield 2003: 252.

[50] *Anth. Pal.* 6.132; *HE* 2795–8.    [51] Sourvinou-Inwood 1974; Redfield 2003: 366–7.

[52] Diodorus (27.4) goes further than Livy by incriminating Pleminius personally. For Diodorus' mainly but not entirely Polybian version, see De Sanctis 1968: 345.

## A Case Study: Italian Locri, 215–204                                165

from him. But this led to a fight between two groups of Roman soldiers, and Pleminius, when appealed to by his men, savagely punished the tribunes (stripping and whipping), whose supporters reacted with even greater violence and cut off Pleminius' ears and nose. Scipio as commander-in-chief sailed across from Sicilian Messina to Italian Locri and summarily judged the incident there. He exonerated Pleminius completely and continued him in office at Locri, while sending the tribunes to Rome.[53] But Pleminius seems to have been one of those people who do not take 'yes' for an answer: beside himself with anger at this (from his point of view favourable) outcome, he now mutilated the tribunes and killed them and treated some Locrian citizens with what Livy calls 'similar cruelty'.[54]

In 204, the Locrians appealed to the senate at Rome, sending an embassy whose members performed a ritual of supplication and wore deliberately filthy clothes in a display of forensic *squalor*.[55] They were shrewdly careful not to denounce the powerful Scipio himself too obviously in the long speech which Livy gives them, a *tour de force* of indignant rhetoric, which compared the impiety towards Persephone with that of Pyrrhus many decades earlier.[56] But Scipio's equally powerful enemies at Rome, notably Quintus Fabius Maximus, had no such inhibitions and tried to have him recalled. The senate voted double restoration of the impiously stolen sacred treasures, and Livy wishes us to conclude that they now felt that their religious slate was clean for the impending invasion of Africa.[57] On a proposal of a senior consular Quintus Caecilius Metellus, a supporter of Scipio, the senate instructed Marcus Pomponius Matho, praetor for Sicily and Scipio's cousin (see Family Tree 2), to proceed to his province with a heavyweight panel of advisers (*consilium*) and investigate the charges against Scipio – a highly unusual proceeding against a consul in his year of

---

[53] Livy 29.9.8. He had the right to judge it in virtue of his consular *imperium*: Mommsen 1887–8: 1.122–3 and 2.1.114. W/M ask why he did not punish the tribunes himself rather than sending them to Rome. A better question would be, why did he not send Pleminius to Rome as well as the tribunes? Pleminius was eventually sent to Rome, but not by Scipio.

[54] Livy 29.9.11, without giving details.

[55] Livy 29.16.6. For the supplication, made in Greek style, *ut Graecis mos est*, by proffering olive branches, see Naiden 2006: 227–8 (but the Locrians did not make a 'mistake' as Naiden says: they did what was natural to them as Greeks and were sympathetically heard). On the political use of symbolic *squalor*, see Lintott 1968: 16–17 for the Roman Republic, but also citing the Athenian trial of the generals after the sea battle at Arginousae in 406, to which an organized crowd posing as kin of the battle-dead turned up in mourning, wearing black with shaved heads: Xen. *Hell.* 1.7.8; on this episode, see also Lintott 1982: 157.

[56] See Lévêque 1957: 625 and n. 4. With this section of Livy, compare perhaps Hdt. 6.134–5, which may hint at an epiphany by vengeful Demeter.

[57] Levene 1993: 72–3. This is certainly one reason for Livy's full coverage of the affair. We shall see that the matter raised questions of imperial principle.

office.⁵⁸ Matho first went to Locri, where he addressed the Locrians and invited them to lodge complaints against Scipio if they wished. The Locrians replied that although he had shown too little grief at the injustices suffered by their city, they would rather have him as a friend than an enemy. So there was no further inquiry into Scipio's actions. But Pleminius was sent to Rome after all, where he probably died as a prisoner in 204. An alternative but unlikely version put about by the historian Clodius Licinus, an obscure younger contemporary of Livy, had Pleminius live on in prison in Rome until Scipio's second consulship in 194, when he tried to escape by arranging for parts of the city to be burnt down. This is generally but not universally rejected as a fiction inspired by the story of Catiline in the 60s.⁵⁹

So Scipio escaped legal reprisals, but his reputation was harmed, and rightly so. His critics added accusations of sloppy discipline and adoption of unsuitable Greek dress; he was easily able to defend himself against these specious charges. His main error of judgement, for which he did not apologize, was his arrogant exoneration of his appointee Pleminius, from whom he ought to have dissociated himself.⁶⁰ At least, it would have been wiser for him to have forwarded Pleminius to Rome for trial along with the tribunes. His decision was a judicial act taken on his own authority, although he may have consulted his *consilium*, and he was within his rights to exercise his *imperium* in this way. But it was a bad mistake.

It may be objected that Scipio's ill-advised blanket support of a subordinate's outrages does not amount to an important act of policy and is therefore not an example of 'peripheral imperialism'. On the contrary, the Pleminius affair touched on a problem of Roman imperialism which was to grow more and more acute over the next two centuries: how to treat provincials and allies. In the period of and even before the tribunate of Gaius Gracchus in the 120s, Roman *repetundae* ('recovery') legislation sought to protect the governed against the rapacity of their Roman

---

⁵⁸ Mommsen 1887–8: 2.1.116, also 117 and n. 1 for other constitutional aspects of the treatment of Pleminius; also Scullard 1970: 277 n. 132A. The *consilium* consisted (Livy 29.20.11) of ten legates, a praetor, two tribunes of the plebs, and a plebeian aedile (on the role of aediles where there were accusations of violence, see Lintott 1968: 94). For Metellus, consul in 206, see *DPRR* CAEC0891.

⁵⁹ Livy 29.21.4–13. The 194 version: 29.22.10 and 34.44.6–8. See Oakley 1992 and *FRHist* 3: 561, comm. on Clodius Licinus 64 F1: the parts of Livy 29.22.10 relating to Licinus are interpolated. See Köster 2014 on the literary treatment of Pleminius as stock villain and his suitably nasty death (agreeing with Oakley 1992 at 322–3). Millot 2019 thinks the arson attempt in 194 possibly historical and rejects the Catiline analogy, even suggesting (103–4) that it was Scipio himself, as consul, who did away with Pleminius as an embarrassment. That might, however, be thought to support the Catiline theory: it was as consul in 63 that Cicero had Catiline executed.

⁶⁰ Toynbee 1965: 2. 619–21 considers but rightly rejects the possibility that Scipio was behind the temple robberies because he was short of money and supplies.

governors, something the Classical Athenians had never contemplated in the days of their own empire.⁶¹ Cicero's speeches against Gaius Verres for his depredations in Sicily (70 BCE) address the problem in detail, and Marcus Iunius Brutus in 43 and 42 ruthlessly extorted funds from the cities of Asia Minor. In 48, Romans from Italica in Iberia tried to kill Quintus Cassius Longinus, the man left in control of the region by Caesar, in anger against his misgovernment.⁶² The last two episodes occurred early in Livy's own lifetime (born in 59). So his very full narrative of Scipio's and the senate's treatment of Locri and Pleminius had recently topical resonances when Livy was writing. To be sure, Locri was an Italian not a strictly provincial city and was a Roman ally which had, albeit under 'conditions of quasi *force majeure*', defected to the Carthaginian side, so could expect severity.⁶³ But the senate did not take this line when settling the matter, although religious anxieties before their African invasion may have played a part: they firmly declared that the injustices suffered by the Locrians were not desired by the senate and people of Rome, and that the Locrians were good men, and friends and allies.⁶⁴

No such extreme and credible story attaches to Hannibal: there is no recorded Carthaginian equivalent of Pleminius; the picture is rather of general Carthaginian cruelty and rapacity, and this may have been exaggerated by patriotic Roman sources. The briefly reported claim that, shortly before Hannibal left Italy for ever, the hitherto-inviolate sanctuary of Juno Lacinia at Croton saw the slaughter of a large number of Italian soldiers who had taken refuge there after refusing to go to Africa with their chief is incredible, not least because it would have gone down so badly with the other Italian troops who were a valuable component of his army at Zama.⁶⁵ This is part of a wider and largely unjustified Roman tendency to attribute impiety to Hannibal.

Hannibal seems to have been a rather better judge of subordinates than Scipio; at least, we do not hear that any of them let him down quite as spectacularly as Pleminius. Not that Carthaginian control of Locri, under the command of a man called Hamilcar, had been blameless or popular: on the contrary, Livy writes of the arrogance and cruelty which the Locrians

---

⁶¹ See Brunt 1990a: 319–21 (and n. 103: 'even if personal or political feuds explain why some or most charges were brought, it would remain true that injustice to subjects was a suitable pretext for assailing personal adversaries'. This is relevant to the forensic attack on Scipio).
⁶² Caesar, *Civil war* 2.20.6 with Wilson 1965: 35. For Italica, see p. 132 n. 110.
⁶³ *Force majeure*: Toynbee 1965: 2. 613.   ⁶⁴ Livy 29.19.6–7: *uiros bonos sociosque et amicos*.
⁶⁵ Livy 30.20.6. See Huss 1986: 225 and Hoyos' n. on the passage (2006: 705–6). Hannibal's own agency is in any case not categorically asserted.

had endured under a Carthaginian called Hamilcar, but he adds a specific comparison: for criminality and greed, Pleminius and his Romans far outdid Hamilcar and his Carthaginians.[66]

This Hamilcar is intriguing, and it is important to fix his identity. He is presumably the 'Hamilcar the Carthaginian, *Poenus*' mentioned as a cavalry commander when Locri went over to Carthage in 215.[67] But the addition of *Poenus* seems gratuitous in that context, and the text has been doubted.[68] It does nevertheless looks as if the two Hamilcars at Locri, separated by a decade, are one and the same man: Livy does say that the Locrians in 215 admitted 'Hamilcar and the Carthaginians' to the city, which implies he was to possess political as well as military authority. So he can probably be assumed to have been both placed and for many years retained in charge of the city by Hannibal on his own authority – in 215 at least, an instant decision was needed – and therefore to have been personally responsible for ten years of alleged 'arrogance and rapacity'. This evidently tight control was exercised despite Hannibal's promise of freedom and autonomy to the Locrians at the outset. That obvious prosopographic conclusion about Hamilcar is not, however, quite straightforward. In 208, there was an earlier and nearly successful Roman attempt to recapture Locri, when the Carthaginian commander is casually named by Livy as Mago, not Hamilcar. This Mago is said to be unsure whether he could defend the city, which shows him to have been in control of the city at that moment.[69] He is not Hannibal's younger brother; instead, he is thought to be 'Mago the Samnite', who is found operating in Bruttium in 212 and perhaps in other years also.[70] If that plausible guess is right, it is not

---

[66] 29.8.6–7 and 29.6.17.
[67] Livy 24.1.4 and 9. Geus 1994: 60 n. 249, discussing 'Hamilcar (12)' identifies the Hamilcars at Locri in Livy books 24 and 29 but acknowledges the difficulty over the intervention by Mago; see my text. Huss 1985: 346 and 404 appears not to identify the two Hamilcars at Locri, giving them separate entries in his index, but does not discuss the problem. Ciaceri 1932 identified the two Hamilcars: 1933: 142, 191, 326 (index).
[68] But another minor Hamilcar is equally unnecessarily called *Poenus* at 31.10.2. He is explicitly said to have been a survivor of the army taken across to north Italy by Hasdrubal Barca so is not identical with the man at Locri.
[69] Livy 27.28.14. Livy introduces the name Mago without explanation, as if his readers must know who he is, which might favour the identification with the 'Samnite'; but the abruptness might merely reflect compression of Polybius.
[70] Geus 1994: 189, 'Mago (10) der Samnite': 'Samnite' is a curious nickname, not an indication of actual origin (pp. 45 and 74). Active in Bruttium in 212: Livy 25.15.8, cf. the more general Pol. 9.25.1, Hannibal's friend 'Mago who commanded, χειρίζοντι, in Bruttium'. For the identification of the 'Samnite' with the Mago at Locri, see also De Sanctis 1968: 462 n. 55, HCP 2: 134, n. on Pol., just cited; Huss 1985: 387 n. 102; Feraco 2017: 351, n. on Livy 27.28.14–17.

## A Case Study: Italian Locri, 215–204

inconsistent with a continuing role for Hamilcar as the permanent governor of Locri. If, as is very plausible, Hannibal's trusted friend Mago the 'Samnite' had a roving commission in Bruttium, the large area of south Italy which included Locri, he would naturally be found defending Locri in a military crisis.[71]

Since Locri suffered from depredations at the hands of agents of both Hannibal and Scipio in the same period, it is a tempting case study for a parallel investigation of the two men and their handling of subject communities in wartime. But this is hard to execute because the evidence on the Carthaginian side is so much scantier. Modern writers have concentrated almost entirely on Pleminius and Scipio. That is understandable, because the episode as very fully narrated by Livy, using Polybius extensively, is so rich in political and religious detail. Perhaps the allegations of Carthaginian cruelty are little more than pro-Roman patriotic invention, and a better analysis of the course of events in this Greek city might be in terms of *stasis*, factional conflict.[72] Livy's introduction to the Pleminius affair is revealing: he mentions Locrian exiles at Rhegium who had been driven out by the 'opposite faction', *aduersa factio*, which had handed Locri over to Hannibal in the first place.[73] The Greek – that is, the Polybian – version of this sentence might with a few adjustments (not Hannibal but some Persian satrap, perhaps) have come straight out of a chapter of Thucydides.

The evidence on the Carthaginian side is, however, not entirely negligible, and – for example – the small prosopographic puzzle about the identity of Hamilcar (one man or two?) demands an answer. If, as we have argued to be the better view, there was only one Hamilcar at Locri throughout, the Carthaginian villain of the year 205 was as much Hannibal's appointee as Pleminius was Scipio's. And whereas Pleminius may have been left in charge by Scipio *in absentia* as a mere temporary expedient, Hamilcar was, on the view here taken, a long-standing appointment. Were ten years of Hannibal's agent Hamilcar better or worse than a few more dramatically frightful days of Scipio's Pleminius? Hard to say. Livy, as we have seen, endorsed the view that Pleminius outdid Hamilcar in

---

[71] Geus 1994: 61 n. 349 solves the Mago problem by giving his Hamilcar (10) and Mago (10) simultaneous commands of the Locrian garrison. This, too, is a perfectly plausible formulation.
[72] Cf. p. 138 for *stasis* at Compsa.
[73] Livy 29.6.5. These exiles are called *principes*, members of the upper class. This passage has a bearing on the question, whether Livy was right (24.2.8) to say that generally the Italian upper classes in the second Punic war favoured Rome, the plebs inclined to Carthage. See p. 362.

criminality and greed.[74] If the Locrians were treated so badly under Hamilcar's regime, did they go, could they have gone, to Hannibal or even to the senate at Carthage and complain? Was there any mechanism or precedent for such appeals, and what was the legal position?[75] Carthaginian law is an elusive topic.[76] None of the Greek literary sources for attempted seizures of power by ambitious Carthaginian individuals are legally informative. The most relevant text is a sentence in Justin.[77] It says that the Hundred (judges) examined the actions, *res gestae*, of returning generals.[78] It has recently been speculated that the *sufetes* 'ensured Carthaginian imperial control', but hard evidence is lacking.[79] But there was evidently a developed legal system at Carthage, and Hannibal, no less than Scipio, had his enemies at home, who would have been glad to listen to forensic accusations against one of Hannibal's officers, if such could be made. Was Hannibal himself ever attacked in this way? We cannot answer any of these questions confidently. When he finally returned to Carthage from Italy, the homeland was in mortal danger and needed his services too urgently for leisurely judicial reviews. But whereas we know for sure that Scipio acquitted his delinquent subordinate Pleminius in a formal legal tribunal, we do not know whether Hannibal ever had to hear similar accusations against Hamilcar. But if he did, then he must have judged in Hamilcar's favour, or the man would not have still been governing Locri in 205. Neither Hannibal nor Scipio consulted the home authorities before making their initial appointments: Scipio was not obliged to, under Roman law, and Hannibal's decision must have been made on the spot when Locri was captured. We do not know if he later informed the authorities at Carthage of this appointment in a letter, still less whether he needed or sought their ratification for it. Probably not. We can however say that the

---

[74] 29.8.7: probably from Polybius.
[75] Appian, *Iberian history* 5/17, says that in about 229 Hanno (18) was recalled to Carthage to hear charges made against him but gives no details. At 4/16, Appian had said that Hanno still owed an audit of his previous command.
[76] Cf. p. 65.
[77] Modern writers sometimes apologize for using Justin, e.g. Warmington 1966: 146, 'a late and admittedly unsatisfactory source'. No need. His *Philippic History* (see p. 30) is an epitome of the Augustan polymath Pompeius Trogus, who in turn used good sources such as Posidonius. For Trogus, see Yarrow 2006a: 145–42, 346–7; Yardley and Heckel 1997: 20, 'a world history that deals only marginally with Rome'. He covered Carthage in books 18–22.
[78] 19.2.5–6, on which see Newman 1887–1902: 2.406. For the improbable story in Cassius Dio that Hannibal was tried at Carthage after Zama, see p. 66.
[79] Pilkington 2019: 125. He makes interesting use of Punic epigraphy but concedes that most of these inscriptions are merely brief records of individual office-holders (127). For a judicial role exercised by the *sufetes* in 193 BCE, see Livy 34.61.15 with Huss 1985: 465.

## A Case Study: Italian Locri, 215–204

sufferings of the Locrians, if they have been correctly reported, were due to appointments made by Hannibal and Scipio acting on their own initiative.

***

One of Scipio's final acts after Ilipa and before leaving Iberia was alleged to have been to found a city, Italica, near modern Seville in the deep south. But this alleged foundation is probably a Hadrianic myth.[80] If so, we do not need to decide how far the action was Scipio's alone or was ratified by the senate.[81]

---

[80] See Chapter 4.6.
[81] But in case new evidence turns up to prove that Scipio's role was after all historical, I give two modern views. Richardson 1986: 57 thought Italica was founded by Scipio alone, 'outside the control' of the senate. Subsequent ratification: see Pina Polo 2021: 156, not specifically discussing Italica, in which he is not much interested (see p. 293 n. 112), but Graccuris and 'other new towns'. He accepts that Roman commanders decided for themselves the location and population of the new towns.

CHAPTER 7

# *Politics and Factions at Carthage and Rome*

## 7.1 Introduction: Carthage

There is perhaps no area where the disparity between our evidence for Carthage and Rome is greater than their internal politics and faction-fighting. For Carthaginian political institutions, the main source is Aristotle's *Politics*, written more than two centuries before the outbreak of the second Punic war. For actual Carthaginian political behaviour in our period, it is hard to go much beyond the crude binary opposition Barcid/anti-Barcid or Hannonid, a word derived from the personal name of Hanno (18): Livy himself talks more than once of the 'Barcine faction', but 'Hannonid' is a modern and question-begging locution. To these two groups, a third faction has been conjecturally added, a 'pro-Numidian party', which supposedly saw the advantages of alignment with king Masinissa against the coercions of the Romans. But if this faction was ever a reality, it can have had very little importance before the start of the second century BCE.[1]

Hannibal's main opponent is named as this Hanno, who makes his first appearance very early in the first Decade of Livy for his role in the debate at Carthage over Saguntum.[2] Hannibal must have had his supporters at Carthage throughout his years in Italy, but our sources show little interest in this. The fullest descriptions of Carthage's internal history and politics

---

[1] 'Barcine faction': e.g. Livy 21.2.4; see p. 48. For Carthaginian political factions in the second Punic war, and the supposedly pro-Numidian faction, see Günther 1999, plausibly rejecting the existence of the 'parties' (in a modern sense) who feature in the title of her article. For the years 237–218, see Hoyos 1994: largely negative in its dismissal of modern reconstructions. He is surely right (262–4) to deny that the Barcids before the second war with Rome had an anti-oligarchic reforming programme (contrast Hannibal after the war), and to insist (249–52) that the generalship was always elective, not the result of a sudden lurch to democracy.

[2] For a later opponent in the senate, see 30.37.7 (after Zama), Gisgo (7), about whom nothing else is known.

172

are to be found in the three sections of Livy's post-Zama narratives, of which the longest and most rewarding describes Hannibal's apparently single-handed reforms and fight against oligarchic financial corruption; the opening sentence of the relevant section of Livy begins by talking of 'the men of the faction opposed to Hannibal', not of 'Hannibal's faction'.[3] It cannot be said, however, that any of this material throws light on how exactly Carthaginian politicians operated, and what if any 'groupings' may have existed there, apart from support of or hostility to Hannibal and his family.

## 7.2 Rome

Carthage was an oligarchy, but the people had an occasional role. Was Republican Rome any sort of democracy? Until the late twentieth century, the answer would have been an obvious and puzzled 'no'. There were three electoral and judicial assemblies (*comitia*), to be sure, but they were 'timocratic' (property-weighted) rather than democratic.[4] And did not Polybius himself say that Scipio Africanus 'sought fame in an aristocratic state' (meaning an oligarchic one)?[5] But there is well-informed contemporary evidence for the opposite view: none other than Polybius' own book 6. Here he propounded a theory of checks and balances at Rome between the monarchical, oligarchic, and democratic elements and saw no problem about identifying a democratic element as the third of the trio of consuls, senate, and people.[6] In particular, he claimed that the tribunes of the plebs 'are always obliged to act as the people decree and to pay every attention to their wishes'.[7] This is a startling generalization and hardly reflects the way real-life tribunes behaved in the age of Scipio Africanus, with the possible exception of Gaius Flaminius in 231, one of the 'forerunners of the Gracchi'.[8] Perhaps the Gracchi and other tribunes and reformers of the second century BCE were influenced precisely by their reading of the mistaken and misinformed Polybius? The contradiction in that position

---

[3] 33.45.6; see Chapter 12.
[4] They were the tribal, centuriate, and curiate *comitia*. See *OCD*[4] *comitia* (A. Momigliano and T. J. Cornell).
[5] Pol. 23.14.1. See p. 266 for the obituary context, a threefold obituary in which the Greek Philopoemen is the democrat.
[6] See esp. 6.14 for the role of the people. Polybius did not, as sometimes claimed, speak in terms of a 'mixed constitution' of the sort familiar from Greek theory but of checks and balances (Derow 2015: 99, originally 1982), except that in his analysis there is no check on the senate. I cannot here discuss the disputed composition date of book 6.
[7] 6.16.4–5. [8] See p. 403 citing Taylor 1962.

has been wittily pinpointed by John North.[9] But it is inconceivable that Polybius, friend of Scipio Aemilianus and shrewd observer at first hand of the political life of Rome, was completely wrong to call Rome a democracy of some kind. At any rate, some recent scholarship has swung round to treating it as just that.[10] That represents a reaction against, and entails partial abandonment of, an older picture which assumed tight oligarchic control of decision-making, with only an occasional and exceptional assertion of a different popular will by votes of otherwise-supine assemblies. That older view has been called the 'frozen waste' theory (North again).[11]

The debate ranges widely in time: it embraces the Late as well as the Middle Republic – everything from the Punic wars to the age of Cicero – but our concern is with the age of Hannibal and Scipio, roughly the half-century from about 230–180 BCE. Within that half-century, the sixteen years of the second Punic war are not easily characterized as a very democratic-looking period of Roman politics. Fabius the Delayer and other big names in Livy's third Decade seem usually to get their political way without the need to appease obstructive tribunes of the plebs, or to take much notice of 'popular' politicians and the urban masses. (Minucius caused trouble for Fabius, but it was short-lived. The people voted the Iberian command to young Scipio but hardly in defiance of senatorial wishes.) There is, it has recently and plausibly been argued, a special reason for this: demography. Heavy military casualties among the senatorial class in 218–216, especially in its junior ranks, produced a top-heavy senate for many years to come. This helps to explain the electoral dominance of prominent senior senators and consulars after the senate was filled up again (by the formal process of 'adlection') in 216: the new arrivals would have been of lower status.[12] That being so, it may after all be reasonable to look for techniques of control, and to ask whether individuals operated alone or as members of larger entities, and if so whether these entities were temporary or lasting.

As already noted, the divisions and intrigues of Roman political life, by comparison and contrast with Carthaginian, are fairly well documented. But much of the evidence and therefore scholarly discussion relates to the

---

[9] North 2004 (originally 1990): 145: 'the most intriguing possibility of all, enabling us to have our intellectual cake and eat it too, is to combine an ignorant Polybius who invented a non-existent democratic element in the Rome he found, with a highly influential Polybius whose theories once published actually determined events'.
[10] Millar 1984, 1986, 1998; also Yacobson 2010. Against: Mouritsen 2001, 2017; Hölkeskamp 2010, 2017.
[11] North 2004: 144.    [12] Barber 2019.

Ciceronian period, the middle decades of the first century BCE, and by that time the senate's prestige and authority were much weakened by comparison with its standing in the second Punic war, at least after Cannae in 216.[13]

Republican Roman personal names are rich and complicated by comparison with Carthaginian and make possible close prosopographic analysis and conjecture, that is, the study of family ties and regional origins. In the decades up to the 1970s, some influential historians tried to explain Roman political decisions as a function of lasting relationships between powerful families and of the ascendancy or decline of 'groups'; other historians forcefully denied the existence of such groups.[14] But in the past thirty or forty years, this sort of study has gone out of fashion among historians of ancient Rome in favour of such debates as 'was Rome as democracy or not?'. It is hard to say why: it is not as if prosopography has somehow been discredited as damaging, like, say, lobotomy. Part of the explanation is that traditional prosopography is perceived as suffering from the 'fundamental limitation' that it concentrates on 'the highest echelons of society'. That is the formulation of Jürg Rüpke in the introduction to his prosopographic work on the priests of Rome, a criticism made with Ronald Syme (1903–89) explicitly in mind.[15] But 'there is more than one way of doing prosopography': Syme was interested in names as indicators of social origin and of social and geographical mobility as well as in family connections.[16] There is in any case one original and important exception to recent neglect of prosopography, John Henderson's highly

---

[13] One pair of categories in particular will not be used or examined here: *optimates* and *populares*, popular politicians (not necessarily of 'low' birth) and their aristocratic opponents. The categories are not easily applicable to Scipio's lifetime as opposed to Cicero's (the word *optimates* in a political sense is not found before the first century BCE). The key text is Cicero's speech *For Sestius* 96 with Harris 2016: 94, who stresses that popular discontent was genuine, but corrects Cicero's claim that the two categories of politician had 'always' existed, rather than from the mid-second century. See Brunt 1971b: 93–5. Despite receiving the 'adulation of the common people' after Zama (Dorey 1961: 194), Scipio was no *popularis* politician. Flaminius and Varro are treated by Livy as popular politicians, with some justice in Flaminius' case at least; but the hostile way they are described is coloured by later political divisions and animosities. It could be said that, of our two parallel lives, Hannibal was the *popularis*, taking on the selfish *optimates* of Carthage.

[14] See esp. Scullard 1973 (reprint, with new foreword, at pp. xvii–xxxiii of 1st ed. of 1951; see also preface to 2nd ed.). On the *gentes*, he was influenced by the classic work of Münzer 1920 [Eng. tr. 1999]. In his 1973 foreword, Scullard cited, summarized, and sought to answer sceptical objections, to which add now Brunt 1988: 443–502, 'Factions' (building on his own earlier work in reviews and articles); Briscoe and Hornblower 2020: 74–81. For a massively documented summary of the debate about the nature of Roman Republican politics, see Hölkeskamp 2001 (exasperated review discussion of Münzer 1999).

[15] Rüpke 2008: 5, col. 2.

[16] For these points, see *OCD*[4] 'prosopography', whence the quotation in the text. Hölkeskamp 2001 scores some hits against prosopography, but on a rather narrow definition of the word and concept. It is not all frail and boring speculations about the workings of oligarchies.

original monograph, whose subject is the family pride explored in Juvenal's eighth satire (late first century CE).[17]

Of all the groups which have been conjecturally identified as active in the years 220–160 BCE, that which concerns us most is the Aemilian-Scipionic (see Family Tree 2). Here is the argument. The connection between the Aemilii and the Cornelii Scipiones is personified by Publius Scipio Aemilianus, born an Aemilius but adoptive grandson of the Scipio who defeated his 'parallel life' Hannibal at Zama. That earlier Scipio was himself married to the daughter of Aemilius Paullus, consul in 216. The group's most conspicuous period of electoral success was in 222–216 BCE, when these two families and their possible political allies (Livii, Servilii, Minucii) dominated the consulships, as attested by the official inscribed lists of magistrates and triumphs, the *fasti*.[18] The catastrophic defeat at Cannae in 216, when Aemilius Paullus was killed, temporarily ended this dominance, which was replaced by that of Quintus Fabius Maximus the Delayer, *cunctator*. When in 211 Gnaeus and Publius Scipio were killed in Iberia, not only was young Scipio appointed to a proconsular command beginning in 210, but his near-contemporary Publius Licinius Crassus Dives, already *pontifex maximus* since 212, was elected to the censorship for 210.[19] He went on to be Scipio's colleague in the consulship of 205. All this, it is argued, indicates the success of a group. But there is no specific evidence to indicate that, as has been conjectured, Crassus had a hand in Scipio's appointment in 210.[20]

Such was the argument of H. H. Scullard (1903–83), and the Aemilian-Scipionic was one of the more convincing-looking family groups. His general method has provoked strong disagreement. The most powerful and persuasive dissenter was P. A. Brunt (1917–2005), whose approach was however indirect.[21] That is, he did not have much to say about Scullard's chosen period, the decades of and immediately after the Hannibalic war (220–160 BCE).[22] Instead his procedure was to show in detail that in the first century BCE, especially the years for which we have Cicero's detailed writings (from the 70s down to his death in 43), there is no good evidence for stable factions, and no good reason to suppose that marriage ties or shared membership of a *gens* automatically resulted in stable political alliances: brothers are sometimes found in opposing political camps. We have, he argued, no right to assume that earlier and much less

---

[17] Henderson 1997.  [18] Scullard 1973: 39–44, cf. 36 and 55.
[19] He was born in about 240, some five years before Scipio. For Crassus, see p. 118 n. 25.
[20] See p. 118.  [21] See also Meier 1966.
[22] See however Brunt 1988: 455 and n. 13 for the Hannibalic war and 447–8 on the early second century.

well-documented periods were any different.[23] For Brunt, such groups as can be identified 'tended to form around prominent individuals' such as Scipio Aemilianus, but they were neither cohesive nor durable.[24] I think Brunt had the better of the argument, and I will not seek to explain Scipio's career in terms of groups.

For the Hannibalic war, we have for the most part little more than Livy's accounts of elections (usually only the results) and the inscribed lists of magistrates, the *fasti*. Otherwise, he and the other literary sources were naturally interested in how a man as young as Scipio was appointed to so vital a command in the first place. And they have much to say about his domestic critics at the time of the Pleminius affair and the attempts in the same period to prevent him carrying the war to Africa; and above all about his enemies in the 'trials of the Scipios' in the 180s.

Young Publius Scipio was appointed by popular vote to the command in Iberia, and this appointment was not some sort of democratic assertion of impatience with the senate's leadership; but equally it cannot be explained entirely in terms of family groups of Scullard's sort. It is a mere conjecture that the senate ensured that there should be no candidate other than Scipio.

When Scipio was away campaigning in Iberia, his run of military and diplomatic successes would have made it very difficult to unseat him. On his return in late 206, he was not awarded the official triumph to which he was, as a *priuatus* – with *imperium* but without a magistracy – strictly not entitled. He hoped for it but knew the conventions and did not press his claims.[25] We are not told which senators were for it and which against.

The Pleminius affair in its Roman phase came to a head in 204.[26] Scipio's harshest critic in the senate was, not surprisingly, Fabius Maximus, the advocate of defeating Hannibal in Italy. He proposed Scipio's recall and wanted the tribunes to propose to the people the revocation of his *imperium*. But his stated reason was not Scipio's failure to deal adequately with Pleminius, but his unauthorized departure from his province of Sicily to hear the charges against Pleminius at Messina on the Italian mainland. Fabius also proposed that full restitution be made to

---

[23] Brunt 1988: 444 (cf. 449, 456, 502): 'I shall argue that factions of the kind postulated [by Scullard] were at best small and evanescent in the time of Cicero and that there is no sound reason for believing that they were more extensive in earlier times, for which there is much less evidence.' Brunt's other target was Syme 1939.

[24] Brunt 1988; 446. For scepticism about the political importance of adoption and intermarriage, see Brunt 1988: 452–4.

[25] Livy 28.38.4. See p. 135.   [26] See previous chapter.

the Locrians. Feelings ran high, says Livy, both for Scipio and against, but he gives no names.[27] Quintus Metellus made a successful counter-proposal as far as Scipio was concerned: Pomponius Matho, the new praetor for Sicily, should go there at once and conduct an inquiry, together with ten senators, two tribunes of the plebs, and one aedile. Since Scipio's mother was a Pomponia and Pomponius was Scipio's cousin, the choice of a kinsman to head the inquiry was obviously designed to favour Scipio. No elaborate theory of groups is needed to explain Metellus' line: Brunt (who did not discuss this particular episode) would presumably have regarded this as a short-term effort to save a prominent and much-needed individual from the consequences of his own actions. In any case, Pomponius' invitation to the Locrians to denounce Scipio might have backfired, unless he had advance knowledge of their probable attitude.[28]

In 203, the year after the effective end of the Pleminius affair, the consuls were two Servilii, but this was less startling a family monopoly than it might seem because one of them, Gnaeus Caepio, was a patrician, the other, Gaius Geminus, was now plebeian, and they were not closely related.[29] Geminus' brother Marcus was consul for 202, together with Tiberius Claudius Nero. These years saw attempts by several individuals, some of them Servilii, to wrest the African command from Scipio and win it for themselves or at least share it in some way. Caepio, consul in 203, tried to cross to Sicily and then Africa in pursuit of Hannibal but was prevented by a dictator specially 'appointed for that very purpose', *ad id ipsum creatus*, Publius Sulpicius Galba Maximus.[30] Similarly, Marcus Servilius Geminus and his consular colleague Claudius Nero both wanted the province of Africa, that is, to unseat or sideline Scipio. Claudius was sent to Sicily, but his fleet was destroyed by a storm.[31] This activity has been interpreted as a desertion by the Servilii of their former friends the Scipionic group, and an abandonment of their traditional loyalty to it.[32]

---

[27] Livy 29.19.6 and 10 (Fabius' proposal and the divided senatorial opinion). Scipio's departure for Messina: 29.7.2. A referee suggests that Livy's treatment of this last aspect might have been influenced by the career of Julius Caesar.

[28] Livy 29.20. Scullard's conclusion about the commission of inquiry, 'if it went to criticize, it stayed to bless' (1973: 77), simplifies the course of events unduly.

[29] Hoyos 2006: 700; family tree at Münzer 1920: 140 [1999: 132]; *DPRR* SERV0919 (Caepio) and 0931 (Geminus). 'Now' plebeian, because the Servilii Gemini had 'transferred to plebeian status' only recently: this *transitio ad plebem* was probably effected shortly before 218 by Gaius, father of the consul of 203 (Münzer 1920: 137–9 [129–32]; Scullard 1973: 35, 276).

[30] Livy 30.24.1–4; Münzer 1920: 143 [1999: 135]. 'Specially . . . ' is an exaggeration. See Wilson 2021: 172 and 378 no. 83: Galba was also appointed not only to use his superior *imperium* against the consul, but also to hold elections and perhaps (cf. Livy §4) to hear cases in Italy.

[31] Livy 30.27.1–7 and 39.1–4.   [32] Scullard 1973: 78 and 82.

But the postulated friendship and traditional loyalty are only an inference from electoral successes by the Servilii in the preceding years of supposed Aemilian-Scipionic ascendancy. The behaviour of the Servilii in 203 and 202 looks like nothing more than opportunism and ambition by individuals, and it surely needs no explanation in terms of enduring groups.

The same is surely true of Gnaeus Cornelius Lentulus, who as consul in 201 tried after Zama to continue the war against Carthage and help himself to some of the glory.[33] It was he who as a military tribune in 216 had comforted the dying consul Aemilius Paullus after Cannae.[34] That earlier momentary episode is not enough to show that he was aligned with the Aemilian-Scipionic group.

Let us return to Scipio himself. Politically, the years after Zama were a quiet period in his life; at least, he was not openly attacked. He was the highest-ranked senator (*princeps senatus*) from 199, and *censor* in the same year, the most prestigious office of state.[35] This was the period which saw the greatest prominence of Titus Quinctius Flamininus, the victor over Philip V of Macedon (197). This man's glittering career is exceptionally hard to explain satisfactorily in terms of family groups and factions, and he therefore provides an argument against the validity of such a model of politics.[36]

The only recorded instance of a family acting politically in concert is from this very decade, and it happens to concern the Cornelian *gens*: it is an election held in 193 BCE. Livy records that Publius Cornelius Scipio Nasica failed to be elected for the consulship of 192, although not only was he supported by the *gens* Cornelia, but a Cornelius (Lucius Cornelius Merula) also presided over the elections as consul.[37] This is a kind of presentation by negation, in the language of narratology: the implication here is 'he was not elected, *as you might have expected, in view of . . .* ' and so on. On this passage, Brunt commented that the family 'cannot have been in such accord the next year when he was actually elected, with his own cousin L. Scipio as a competitor'.[38] (Lucius Scipio went on to be elected consul for 190.) As for the presidency of a Cornelius, Brunt also noted, in a different context, that this too did not result in Nasica's election in 193.[39] He was also

---

[33] Livy 30.40.7–15.  [34] Livy 22.49.6–12. See p. 104.
[35] For Scipio's tenure of these positions, see Chapter 11.4.
[36] This point has often been made. See e.g. Hölkeskamp 2001: 99.
[37] 35.10.9. See p. 259. Merula is *DPRR* CORN1091.
[38] 35.24.5 with Brunt 1988: 451, and see now Pittenger 2008: 189 n. 4.
[39] Brunt 1988: 455 and n. 13, part of a convincing argument to the effect that presiding over elections conferred minimal powers.

right that, in its context (the 180s), the references to 'the Scipios' in Livy's expression 'the faction which was adverse to the Scipios', *factio quae adversus Scipiones erat*, do not mean the whole family, only the brothers Publius and Lucius Scipio, then under attack.[40]

## 7.3 The Political Aspect to the 'Trials of the Scipios'

The words just quoted (*factio . . . erat*) are taken from Livy's factually and chronologically confused, but gripping and very well written, narrative of the attacks against the Scipios in 187 (Lucius) and 184 (Publius, but he was also a target in 187).[41] These events will be treated in full later.[42] But since at first sight this seems like a battle of factions – Marcus Porcius Cato and his supporters against the Scipios and theirs – it must be considered here too. (The notorious complications and difficulties in the sources will be ignored for the moment.) On the *factio* passage itself, Briscoe in 2008 commented that 'those who think that the ancient sources show no awareness of political groupings should take note of this passage'.[43] But even in these two dramatic years, groupings were small and temporary. An example: the tribune Tiberius Sempronius Gracchus helped to prevent the imprisonment of Lucius Scipio. He also went on to be son-in-law of Publius. If we knew only these two bare facts, it would be reasonable to conclude that this was evidence of a family working together for political advantage. But in fact the sources insist, perhaps to an exaggerated degree, that Gracchus was a personal enemy of Publius, so that his action was all the more praiseworthy. The exaggeration is part of a cherished ancient right-wing contrast between Gracchus the admirable father on the one hand, and his two wicked sons on the other, the turbulent reforming tribunes of 133 and 123–122.[44]

In order to undermine the Scipios, Cato made use of a series of tribunes: in 187, two cousins called the Petillii, then another called Minucius Augurinus; and in 184 Marcus Naevius. They are obscure individuals, on whom no theory of groups can be built.[45]

The attacks on the Scipios do, nevertheless, illuminate the nature of Roman politics in the first two decades of the second century BCE, years which are full of bitter disputes about the award of triumphs and prorogation and the retention of booty. The best part of Gruen's study of the 'fall'

---

[40] Livy 38.55.3 with Brunt 1988: 447. For the word *factio*, cf. Augustus, *Res gestae* 1.1 (tendentious).
[41] 'Trials' is inexact: the opening attack was in the senate, so not strictly judicial.
[42] In Chapter 18.  [43] Briscoe 2008: 193.  [44] See esp. Cicero, *On the consular provinces* 18.
[45] For these three, see p. 389.

## The Political Aspect to the 'Trials of the Scipios'

of the Scipios is its introduction, which brings all this out very well.[46] What happened to the brothers Scipio is just one, albeit the most famous, example of the concern of the ruling class in this period to prevent ambitious individuals from upsetting the competitive equilibrium on which the state depended. Nobody must have *regnum in senatu*, 'kingship in the senate', a celebrated phrase supposedly aimed at Publius Scipio by the Petillii.[47] This concern was by no means entirely new. The new factor after 200 was the vastly increased wealth and the Mediterranean reach of Rome.

---

[46] Gruen 1995: 60–6. He does not actually believe they fell at all, so he puts inverted commas round 'fall' in his title.

[47] Livy 38.54.6. The phrase was adopted as the title of Schlag 1968.

CHAPTER 8

# *The Tipping Point*
## The Battle at the Metaurus or Sena, 207, Hannibal Aged 40

## 8.1 Introduction

We now retrace our steps chronologically to 207, having already brought Scipio home from Iberia in the next year 206, and discussed some of the successes and problems of his consulship of 205 and its aftermath, the Pleminius affair. In the north Italian events of this chapter, Hannibal and Scipio will hardly feature at all: Hannibal was stranded in south Italy, and Scipio was still in Iberia. But the battle we call the Metaurus – including its antecedents and consequences – deserves a chapter to itself because it radically affected the careers of both men: after 207, it was impossible for Hannibal to win the war. In a nutshell, Hannibal's brother Hasdrubal tried to force his way from Iberia to join Hannibal but was defeated and killed at the Metaurus River in north-eastern Italy near modern Urbino by brilliant cooperation between two personal enemies: the consuls of the year, Gaius Claudius Nero and Marcus Livius Salinator.[1] This removed Hannibal's main hope of reinforcements. He had been outwitted by Nero, who was able to set out undetected on a forced march the length of Italy to join his colleague.

Historians, ancient and modern, are fond of identifying tipping points and are liable for rhetorical purposes to exaggerate their decisiveness. And yet neither Polybius nor Livy in so many words pinpoint 207 as the beginning of the end. It was left to the Roman poets to do this. But Livy makes the point in more subtle ways. In the later part of his Book 27, he

---

[1] Livy (29.37.4) says 'Salinator' derived from what was believed (*credebant*) to be his role in the new salt-tax (*sal*, 'salt'), a controversial feature of his censorship of 204. But this cannot be right if his cognomen was inherited, perhaps from his father the decemvir in 236 attested by the *fasti*. (See p. 196) If it was so inherited, it is legitimate to call the consul of 207 'Salinator' from the start. But if consul and decemvir are identical, as some believe, the cognomen might still have been inherited; or else the *fasti* used the cognomen anachronistically, as is possible. In what follows, the consul is called Salinator for convenience because, as we shall see, there is another Livius in the frame, not to mention the historian Livy.

narrates the battle, and the Roman forced march up Italy which preceded it, and he says explicitly that the Roman victory 'was regarded', *uidebatur*, as having compensated for the humiliation of Cannae in 216. It was indeed the 'turning point of the tremendous war'.[2]

## 8.2 The Political and Religious Prelude at Rome

We may begin, not with Hasdrubal as he set out from Iberia to cross the Alps like his brother more than a decade earlier, but at Rome, with the consular elections for 207.[3] The background was that the consuls of 208, Marcellus and Titus Quinctius Crispinus, were both dead; the first was killed fighting, the other died of his battle wounds: 'they had left the state as if orphaned', *uelut orbam rem publicam reliquerant*.[4] More prosaically put, there were now, as Livy goes on to say, two leaderless consular armies in the field. Before his death, Crispinus appointed Titus Manlius Torquatus dictator to hold the elections. Of the possible candidates, Nero stood out and 'was considered excellent by the senators'.[5] The problem was to find a colleague whose moderation and prudence would counterbalance Nero's quick and excitable temperament. 'There was Marcus Livius', says Livy, dramatically starting the next sentence with the personal name in asyndeton, *M. Liuius erat*, where the verb means 'There was (a man who fitted that description, namely')[6] – but would he be willing to serve? Salinator was a gloomy individual with a grudge. He had never forgotten that when he was consul in 219, he and his colleague Aemilius Paullus had been tried for embezzlement; Salinator was convicted, but Paullus narrowly escaped. Salinator retired to the country and took no part in public life for many years. He now deliberately neglected his personal appearance, growing his hair and beard long, and wearing smelly old clothes. This is *squalor*, an old forensic technique for arousing indignation and pity.[7] He particularly resented

---

[2] Livy 27.49.5, in effect Livy's own authorial comment, not from a speech. Turning point: Münzer 1926: col. 896: 'der entscheidende Wendepunkt des gewaltigen Krieges'.

[3] Livy 27.33.6–35.14.     [4] 27.33.7. For Marcellus and Crispinus, see p. 153.

[5] Livy 27.34.1–2: *patres ... uirum quidem egregium ducebant*. He had coped well enough in Iberia as propraetor in the difficult interval between the deaths of the older Scipios and the arrival of the younger. But there is little to report in the years between. He was no Scipio, and 'outstanding', *egregius* (anyway focalized through the senators), looks like an exaggeration, influenced by the future events of 207 itself. The emphasis on speed and impulsiveness may also be retrojected from his daring decision in 207 to march north.

[6] 27.34.3, cf. 24.37.3 *L. Pinarius erat* or 24.48.2, *Syphax erat rex Numidarum*, with W/M on all three passages. This is not quite the same as the introduction of Marcius Septimius, a new character (p. 116). For asyndeton (absence of coordinator) see p. 216.

[7] For *squalor*, which has a Classical Athenian precedent, see p. 165, citing Lintott.

Claudius Nero, who had, he believed, given false testimony against him at his trial.[8] He was nevertheless persuaded – after the censors had made him change his clothes, have a haircut, and get rid of the beard – to let his name go forward and was elected, but only after voicing his grievances. Nevertheless, no Roman observer could have felt the prospects for a successful year's collaboration looked encouraging. The observer would have been dead wrong, although the two men were to fall out again during their tenure of the censorship in 204.[9]

Despite all this, Salinator may have had a cultivated and pleasanter side, if it is right that the poet Livius Andronicus of (probably) Tarentum in south Italy had been the enslaved property of Salinator's like-named father, and tutor to his children, who included Salinator himself, the future victor at the Metaurus. Livius Andronicus was freed and therefore acquired Roman citizenship, hence the *nomen* Livius – but none of these were related to the much later historian Livy/Livius.[10] Livius the poet wrote a hymn to Juno, which was sung by a girl chorus early in this crisis year 207, part of a successful attempt to appease a goddess, who had up to now favoured the Carthaginians.[11] In view of the undoubted family connection, whatever exactly it was, between Livius Andronicus and Salinator, the consul could have had a hand in the commission.[12] How much of a hand? It is true that Livy mentions only the *pontifices* (priests) and the *decemuiri*, the 'ten men', as responsible for the hymn and its performance. But there is an intriguing and attractive possibility that Salinator the consul was himself one of the *decemuiri*.[13] These were a committee of ten priests (in later times fifteen) whose main

---

[8] Livy 29.37.10 (204 BCE). See Briscoe and Hornblower 2020: 258, on Livy 22.35.3 and 273 on 22.40.3.
[9] The censorship: Livy 29.37. See further *MRR* 1: 306. It has been suggested that the entire tradition of their animosity in 207 is a retrojection from the censorship of 204 (e.g. Lazenby 1978: 181), but Livius' allegation about Nero's testimony at the old trial is not likely to be an invention: the facts would have been too well known for that. For another possible retrojection from a much later episode, see p. 108 (Arausio in 105).
[10] Palmer 1974: 108 suggested that 'Tarentum' was really an otherwise-unknown location in Rome. See Jerome's translation and expansion of Eusebius' chronicle (Fotheringham 1923: 219): *Titus Liuius tragoediarum scriptor clarus habetur, qui ob ingenii meritum a Liuio Salinatore, cuius liberos erudiebat, libertate donatus est.* Cf. Münzer 1920: 229 n. 1 [1999: 428 n. 14]. This Salinator is probably but not certainly the father of the consul of 207, not the consul himself: Appendix 8.1.
[11] Livy 27.37.7–15.
[12] Palmer 1974: 97 and 1997: 108; Feeney 2016: 226 and 325 n. 122; Farrell 2021: 140–1.
[13] Palmer 1974: 95 and 1997: 108, with which Feeney 2016 (as in previous n.) agrees.

responsibility was for matters concerning the Sibylline Books, including Secular Games, which were traditionally sanctioned by the Books.[14] Livy does not mention these Books in the context of the 207 crisis, but it is possible that the Books were consulted, and that this explains why the *decemuiri* played a part in the arrangements for the hymn.[15] They certainly seem to have taken over at some point from the *pontifices*. The theory – Salinator as both consul and *decemuir* – depends, however, on a disputed identification: for the tricky problem, see Appendix 8.1.

The hymn to Juno was only one, although the most fully reported, of the Roman state's responses to prodigy reports, which came flooding in after news of the first prodigy had arrived, a shower of stones at Veii.[16] As before Trasimene just five books earlier, and perhaps by deliberate symmetry, Livy recounts a long series of such reports and the steps taken to appease the gods.[17] But his ancient readers or hearers will have known in advance, as we certainly do, that this time the appeasement was to be successful.[18] Livy recounts all this after the consuls had taken up office and before they had conducted a levy of troops. But prodigies and their reports must be distinguished from each other: some of those listed by Livy in chapter 37 could have occurred earlier. But the birth of a grossly outsized intersex baby at Frusino seems to have been almost immediately contemporary (such a birth was disturbing because it represented a confusion of

---

[14] On the *decemuiri*, see Rüpke 2008: 8. Münzer 1920: 229 n. 1 [1999: 428 n. 14] was right that in Livy's account it was primarily, 'in erster Linie', the *decemuiri* (and *pontifices*) who were responsible for the hymn; but that need not rule out some role for Salinator, especially if he was a *decemuir* himself.

[15] W/M suggested that the Sibylline Books did in fact ordain the measures, as they did in 200, but conceded that Livy does not make this clear. Apollo's temple (27.37.11) is a clue: in Greek myth, the Sibyl was inspired by Apollo. The fullest case for associating the hymn with the Books was made by Diels 1890: 89–96, esp. 93, cf. 39. One of his reasons (95–6) was the Frusino hermaphrodite (intersex infant) whom in 207 Etruscan diviners ordered should be drowned at sea (cf. text): another outbreak in 200 BCE of such a shocking 'Zwitter' (the German word) led to an exact and explicit repeat of the measures taken in 207 'in the consulship of Gaius Claudius and Marcus Livius', including the singing of a hymn by Publius Licinius Tegula, modelled on that of Livius Andronicus; this time Livy mentions the Books as well as *decemuiri* (but not Etruscan diviners). See Livy 31.12.5–10 with Feeney 2016: 229–30 on Tegula, 'Mr Roof-tile', who is not in *DPRR*.

[16] On prodigies, see Briscoe and Hornblower 2020: 64–5, citing Rosenberger 1998 and 2007, and add Requena Jiménez 2018.

[17] Book 22, narrating the Roman disasters at Trasimene and Cannae, occupies the same (i.e. second) position in its Pentad, as does the Metaurus campaign in book 27, whose result was the opposite. For Pentads, see p. 5. Livy arguably works out the structural relationship in detail: Briscoe and Hornblower 2020: 17–19. The clearest statement of the parallel is at 27.49.5, the Metaurus seen as vindicating Cannae (p. 183).

[18] 'Or hearers' because of the possibility that Livy might have recited this gripping, patriotic passage to an audience of friends. For such recitations by historians, see Momigliano 1980: 361–76.

categories). Diviners, *haruspices*, from Etruria ordained that it should be drowned in the sea. Perhaps the Sibylline Books were consulted as well.

### 8.3 The Campaign and Battle

Livy, after recounting this highly unusual consular election and the subsequent religious measures, devotes the rest of Book 27 to a narrative of the Metaurus campaign, and it is one of his finest surviving pieces of writing.[19] Even without literary embellishment, the story would be a gripping one.

Both consuls received Italian *prouinciae*, separated by the length of the peninsula: in the north, Salinator was allotted Gaul against Hasdrubal; Nero in the south got Bruttium and Lucania against Hannibal; each had two consular armies. Together with the other commands of the year, this brought the total of legions in Italy to fifteen out of a grand total of twenty-three.[20]

The plan that Hasdrubal should leave Iberia and join Hannibal in Italy was an old one: we first hear of it soon after Cannae, as an order from the senate which Hasdrubal resisted in a letter. Then in 210, news reached Rome that Masinissa was in Carthage with a force of cavalry, and that the Carthaginians were amassing troops in Africa, all this (says Livy) with a view to facilitating Hasdrubal's crossing to Italy. Then in 209, the local Carthaginian commanders, who had not forgotten the senate's much earlier order, made a series of decisions including a march by Hasdrubal to Italy. Hasdrubal wrong-footed everyone, including his brother, by the ease and speed with which he made his crossing of the Alps. This short-term success was in the longer run disastrous for the Carthaginian cause. In the first place, Hannibal was rather late leaving his winter quarters (Ovid dates the battle at the Metaurus to 23 June, Julian calendar/end of April, Republican calendar).[21] In the second place, Hasdrubal made the mistake of laying siege to Placentia, presumably thinking he had plenty of time.[22] Hannibal knew better, because he was aware that sieges were

---

[19] 27.38–51. Particular references to Livy will not usually be given. For a commentary in Italian on book 27, see Feraco 2017.

[20] Lazenby 1978: 181; Taylor 2020a: 28 (table 1.3).

[21] Plan for Hasdrubal to join Hannibal: see p. 115, citing Livy 23.27–8 (216 or 215); 27.5.11–12 (210); 27.20.6 (209). Ovid: *Fast.* 6.770. This date has been doubted as too early (Hoffmann 1962: 142, n. to 97), but Hasdrubal crossed the Alps very fast. Cf. De Sanctis 1968: 561–2. On the Ovid line see further n. 62. The many problems of the Roman calendar (on which see esp. Rüpke 2011) cannot be gone into here.

[22] Lazenby 1978: 182 defends the decision, citing Livy's explanation that he wished to scare the local people, i.e. the Celts; he needed their help.

time-consuming, so did not hurry to leave his winter quarters. So Livy, but the explanation of Hannibal's thinking is not entirely logical.

Nero, now in south Italy, chased Hannibal around from town to town and even worsted him in an encounter at Grumentum whose scale, however, Livy may have exaggerated.[23] Hannibal was able to reach and install himself at Canusium, very close to the scene of his greatest victory at Cannae. But in the end, it was Nero the pursuer who gave Hannibal the slip.

'After withdrawing from the siege of Placentia' (Livy), Hasdrubal had sent six men on horseback carrying a letter to his brother.[24] The letter said that he would meet him in Umbria, an imprecise location, given the size of that region; he can only have meant the area east of the Apennines known as the *ager Gallicus*.[25] But before disclosing its contents, Livy artfully describes how the men got lost and were captured and interrogated – at Tarentum, from where they were taken to Nero's headquarters and interrogated again, and the letter finally opened and read.[26] That is, he tantalizingly delays revelation of the contents until the moment when the letter was read, although not by its intended recipient. This was an old technique of ancient history-writing: it maintained suspense and enabled the writer to move briskly to the actions taken in light of the letters.[27]

Nero forwarded the letter to the senators in Rome. He announced to them that he would confront Hasdrubal in Umbria and advised that a legion should be recalled from Capua, that troops should be levied in Rome, and that the urban army should be sent to Narnia at the southern end of Umbria. (This may tell against modern suspicions that Hasdrubal wrote the letter as a deliberate blind and expected it would indeed fall into Roman hands.) Locally, Nero gave out that he would attack some garrisoned place in Lucania; that is, he would remain in the south. This implies a hope that the false plan would reach Hannibal's ears through the agency of spies or deserters. In reality, he sent riders ahead to arrange for provisions to be supplied by the local populations on his intended route north. Only when

---

[23] For Grumentum, see *Barr.* map 45 C4. Exaggeration: Lazenby 1978: 185.
[24] Livy 27.43.1, where I read (with W/M, the OCT, de Selincourt, and Seibert 1993a: 386 n. 43) *postquam a Placentiae obsidione abscessit*. Walsh prints the less plausible variant *postquam ad Placentiae obsidionem accessit*, followed in the World's Classics translation: 'after commencing the siege of Placentia' (Yardley 2006: 436, cf. 619 for his use of Walsh's Teubner text).
[25] Harris 1971: 136 n. 6.
[26] Livy 27.43. It was read with the help of interpreters (§5, *litterae . . . lectae per interpretem sunt*), so the letter was in Punic, and (as Denis Feeney points out to me) 'the consul's staff obviously includes people who can read/speak Punic'.
[27] For contents of letters postponed until their arrival see p, 156; cf. Th. 7. and 11–15.

he was on the road did he reveal his true intention to his troops. Hannibal had for once been badly outwitted and out-generalled.

At Rome, there was justified terror, as great (says Livy) as when four years earlier a Carthaginian army stood at the city's walls and gates; now there was apprehension of 'two Punic wars, two mighty armies, almost two Hannibals in Italy'.[28] But there follows an extraordinary chapter narrating Nero's forced march northwards on the east side of Italy to join his colleague in the neighbourhood of Sena Gallica in Umbria, modern Senigallia. The marching soldiers were rapturously received by the Italian communities along their route and hailed as 'champions, *uindices*, of the city and empire of Rome, *urbis Romanae imperiique*'; the local men and women uttered prayers and praises as they pressed food on the troops as they passed, but these refused to take more than they needed, as they hurried on by day and night.[29] The next chapter reveals that the army's numbers were swelled by volunteers en route. The description may have been exaggerated in the patriotic telling, but it has clear implications for Rome's popularity and Carthaginian unpopularity in (at least central) Italy after a decade of incessant war.[30]

Nero sent ahead to tell his colleague Salinator that he had arrived, and to ask whether he should come secretly or openly, by day or night, and whether they should combine camps. Salinator replied that Nero should come secretly by night, and he must also have advised his colleague that that they should combine camps.[31] At a council of war, which the praetor Lucius Porcius Licinus also attended, many advocated delay so that Nero's army could rest, but Nero said this would throw away the advantage of his speedy march and rightly preferred immediate battle: the 'deception', *error*, they had carried out on both Hasdrubal and Hannibal would not last long.[32] Livy does not bother to say that this view prevailed, as it evidently did; he merely says that preparations were made for immediate battle.

---

[28] Livy 27.44.1 and ('two Hannibals') 5, on which see Stocks 2014: 174 n. 19, who aptly compares Sil. *Ital.* 15.516, Hasdrubal as a 'twin Hannibal', *geminum Hannibalem*. The reality was different: Hasdrubal was far inferior as a tactician.

[29] Livy 27.45. These gifts and offers were not entirely spontaneous and unprepared: Nero had sent riders ahead to arrange provisions, Livy 27.43.10, cf. p. 355.

[30] 27.45. See esp. Badian 1958: 144; cf. Briscoe and Hornblower 2020: 8 n. 23. There were similar scenes, on a smaller scale, on Nero's return march southwards: 27.50.2.

[31] Seibert 1993: 386–7 supposes Salinator was displeased at the arrival of his enemy Nero and even imagines his 'frosty greeting', 'frostige Begrüssung'. There is no authority for this, and he would surely have welcomed reinforcements. Seibert is right that Livy concentrates on Nero's march rather than Salinator's; but that is because the march made for a dramatic story; an explanation in terms of political bias in favour of the emperor Tiberius' ancestor is not necessary.

[32] Livy had used the word *error* in this sense at the start of the matching book 22 (1.3) about Hannibal's use of wigs as disguise; this neatly inverts the 'Punic fraud' motif.

The topography of the battle itself, and of Hasdrubal's movements in the short period leading up to it, are uncertain, puzzling, and disputed: no mass of boot-nails and weapons have yet been found, of the sort which have made possible the identification of Iberian Baecula.[33] As we shall see, the battle which we call the Metaurus is invariably associated with Sena in the ancient literary authorities until one of Horace's finest poems immortalized the Metaurus river. Salinator's camp was probably near coastal Sena, about ten miles south of the mouth of the river.[34] Hasdrubal was also, again only probably, close to Sena by the time the consuls met. He had reached the Adriatic down the route of the later road known as the *via Aemilia*, which joined Placentia to Ariminum, modern Rimini; from there the *via Flaminia*, built in 220 as censor by the same Flaminius who in 217 was killed as consul at Trasimene, runs across the Apennines and through Umbria to Rome. Hasdrubal's motive for continuing south after Fano is not obvious, but that is not a reason for denying that he did so. Perhaps he wanted to leave the via Flaminia open by forcing the praetor Lucius Porcius Licinus to pursue him, so that he could rejoin the road at a later junction upriver.[35] Or perhaps he guessed that Hannibal might take the coast road to join him.

There followed the famous moment, so well narrated by Livy, when Hasdrubal realized for sure that he was facing not one but two consuls and their armies. He had already formed his suspicions and had tried to confirm them through scouts. Then the Roman buglers sounded once from the praetor's camp – but twice from that of the consul Salinator. This told Hasdrubal beyond a doubt that there was not one consul there but two. Livy describes him speculating in anguish how Nero could have given Hannibal the slip: had his brother been defeated? Or had his own letter never reached him? Livy cannot have had any actual evidence for these thoughts, but they are plausible enough. Hasdrubal now moved north again towards the River Metaurus, presumably to avoid or at least postpone battle. Whether he actually reached the left (north) bank and the via Flaminia, or stayed on the

---

[33] For the general terrain, see *Barr.* map. 42, also 40 for the line of the via Aemilia. Map 19 ('the Metaurus campaign') of Lazenby 1978 depicts most of Italy and is too small-scale to be useful for the battle area; a more helpful map is at Caven 1980: 212 (but he wrongly says the ancient name of the mod. river Cesano, on either bank of which Caven places the two enemy camps, was Sena like the town, and his map so labels it. The true ancient name was Suasanus). Even more detailed is De Sanctis 1968 map VI, but that (next n.) assumes that the two camps were at Fanum Fortunae (mod. Fano) not Sena. Discussions: *HCP* 2: 267–70; Lazenby 1978: 182–4, 187–9; Caven 1980: 211–16; Seibert 1993a: 385–93; Hoyos 2003: 146–51; MacDonald 2015: 190–1.

[34] De Sanctis 1968: 549 and map VI places both enemy camps at Fano (cf. Walbank *HCP* 2: 268–9) and regards ancient mentions of Sena (the last important town before Ariminum) as vague and general. Lazenby 1978: 183 calls this solution 'very forced'.

[35] So Caven 1980: 212. Licinus is *DPRR* PORC0948.

right bank, is disputed and strictly insoluble; on the answer depends the further question, on which bank was the ensuing battle fought? The right bank is preferable. It fits better Livy's picture of Hasdrubal and his troops struggling with difficult terrain, and he perhaps avoided the coast road and the obvious river-crossing there, for fear of running into Licinus' patrols.[36] As before, he may have been hoping to cross the Metaurus further upriver eventually and so reach the left bank and the via Flaminia. We should not underestimate the degree of his ignorance and panic.

Although the exact location of the battle on the right bank has not been fixed, for the course of the battle we have an incomplete narrative by Polybius as well as Livy's full version. But they disagree on one important detail, the position of Hasdrubal's elephants. Hasdrubal placed his Gauls (Celts) on the left and his best troops, the Iberians, under his own command on the right, with the elephants in front of them.[37] Salinator commanded the Roman left, opposite the Iberian troops, and Nero the right. The Romans won the battle by an astutely improvised manoeuvre by Nero: unable to make headway against the enemy left, he marched some of his men round to the left of the Roman left and attacked Hasdrubal in the flank. The elephants caused trouble for both sides equally. When Hasdrubal realized the day was lost, he charged, says Livy, directly into an enemy cohort and 'as was worthy of his father Hamilcar and his brother Hannibal, he died fighting', *ut patre Hamilcare et Hannibale frater dignum erat pugnans cecidit*; so in effect committing 'suicide by Roman'. Polybius does not report the detail about the charge on horseback but agrees that he died 'in hand-to-hand combat'.[38]

Much booty was taken, but Livy's casualty total for the Carthaginians (56,000) is incredible; perhaps 10,000 out of a force of between 20,000 and 30,000 is more plausible.[39] Nero sped southwards and threw Hasdrubal's 'carefully preserved' head in front of Hannibal's camp. Livy closes his book 27 with this appalling act of impiety and with Hannibal's despairing reaction. Such post-mortem battlefield decapitation should obviously be distinguished from beheading as a method of execution, as was done on the orders of Fulvius Flaccus to some Capuan senators after their surrender, or

---

[36] Caven 1980: 214, who assumes there was a bridge at or near the river-mouth.
[37] Pol. 11.1–3; Livy 27.47–9. Livy (48.5) says the elephants were in the centre, but this is forgivable, because Polybius appears to contradict himself, first saying they were in front of the centre, but then in front of the Carthaginian right, which is more probable.
[38] Livy 27.49.4; Pol. 11.2.1. For the Greek phrase, ἐν χειρῶν νόμῳ, see *Polybios-Lexikon* 3.2 χείρ: col. 1027. See Chapter 16.2, discussing what was expected of a commander both in normal situations and in defeat.
[39] Lazenby 1978: 190; Taylor 2020a: 63 and footnote e ('preposterously high'). Walbank (*HCP* 2: 273) offers higher figures for Hasdrubal's army, c. 30,000–35,000.

on Scipio's to the mutineers of 206.[40] Nero's decapitation of Hasdrubal is more like the symbolic posthumous revenge and humiliation inflicted in Herodotus by the Scythian queen Tomyris on Cyrus the Great: she looked for his body on the battlefield, cut off the head, put it in a wineskin full of blood, and gloated over it. Such treatment of a defeated and dead enemy leader is well attested in Greek literature and history and is indicative of 'heightened emotions and a strong desire for revenge' by emphasizing and symbolizing total loss of status and power. In Roman history, the head of Crassus was insultingly treated by the Parthians after his death in the battle of Carrhae (53 BCE).[41] Livy, like Herodotus, uses the outrage on the severed head as almost the closure of a long dramatic book. Roman poetry explored and exploited the symbolism of decapitation: Virgil on Priam, Lucan on Pompey were both alluded to by Silius, for whom both actual and metaphorical decapitation were important themes.[42] In Silius, elaborating Livy, Hasdrubal's head is presented to Hannibal by Nero on the end of a spear.[43]

When the news of the Metaurus reached Rome, the rejoicing was limitless and is fully narrated by Livy.[44] Even the brief and fragmentary Metaurus narrative of the usually drier Polybius ends by describing how every sanctuary was decorated, and every temple filled with offerings and sacrificial victims; such, he says, was the mood of optimism and confidence that it seemed as if Hannibal 'was no longer in Italy', a hyperbolic figure of speech which Livy surprisingly does not pick up. The mood is in obvious contrast with the grim

---

[40] Livy 26.15.8; 28.29.11. Cf. the revolting story of a beheading carried out at dinner on the orders of Lucius Quinctius Flamininus (*DPRR* QUIN0977), brother of the famous Titus, to gratify a lover's curiosity. Livy 39.42.7–43.3 gives variant versions; the detail of the beheading is in that of Valerius Antias (*FRHist* 25 frag. 55, implying that Flamininus did it in person). See Briscoe 2008: 358–62; *FRHist* 3: 359–61 (Rich).

[41] See McHardy forthcoming on battlefield decapitation in the Greek imagination (whence the quotation). Tomyris: Hdt. 1.214; cf. Xen. *Anab.* 1.10.1 (head and right hand of the younger Cyrus cut off after the failure of his revolt against his brother Artaxerxes II); cf. Pol. 8.21.3, fate of the Seleucid usurper Achaeus. Rome: for Crassus (*DPRR* LICI1981), see Plut. *Crassus* 30 and 33 with Briscoe and Hornblower 2020: 172 (noting the contrast with Livy 22.7.5, the 'barbarian' Hannibal's search for the body of Flaminius after Trasimene, so as to give it decent burial; see p. 94–5, also citing Hannibal's respectful treatment of the head of Gracchus the proconsul in 212). Denis Feeney reminds me of Plut. *Gaius Gracchus* 17.4, the heads of Gracchus and a colleague cut off for a reward after being killed in an affray. At the end of Shakespeare's *Macbeth*, Macduff re-enters with the head of the 'usurper' Macbeth, whom he has just killed in a duel: 5.9.20–1.

[42] See Marks 2008: 72–4, citing Virg. *Aen.* 2.554–8 and Lucan, *Pharsalia* 8.708–11.

[43] *Pun.* 15.805–23, forming the closure of the book, cf. Livy's closure. Marks 2008: 78–9 sees this as foreshadowing the metaphorical decapitation, i.e. defeat and nullification, of Hannibal himself. For Augoustakis 2003, the decapitation of Hasdrubal is a kind of gender reversal and emasculation, cf. Marks 2008: 67.

[44] 27.50–1, amplifying Pol.

resilience described at the end of book 22, after the disaster at Cannae, five books (a Pentad) earlier. As we have seen, Livy makes the contrast explicit.

There was an interesting sequel. Under the year 191, Livy records that a temple of *Iuuentas*, Greek Hebe, goddess of youth, was dedicated by Gaius Licinius Lucullus, and that it had been vowed by the consul Livius Salinator 'on the day on which he destroyed Hasdrubal and his army', *quo die Hasdrubalem exercitumque eius cecidit*. Livy adds that it had, unusually, been contracted for by Salinator as censor in 204.[45] (He does not call it the 'battle of the Metaurus'.)[46] Livy had not, however, mentioned the vow anywhere in his book 27 narrative, and the opening action of book 28 moves quickly to Iberia. Nor had he mentioned it in book 29 where he narrated the censorship of Salinator and Nero. There is another indirect allusion to the Metaurus battle at the point where Livy mentions what was done with the booty from it.[47] So the vow first features in Livy under the year 191. How are his earlier silences to be explained?[48] The vow was an important detail, one would have thought. Elsewhere, Livy in different places records both a vow and its later fulfilment; thus he mentions both the *uer sacrum*, 'sacred spring', vowed after Trasimene in 217 and its fulfilment two decades later.[49] Perhaps Salinator's vow was not mentioned by his source for book 27; but even without the ease and speed of a laptop

---

[45] Livy 36.36.5–6 (possibly the date was really 197 not 191, but the difference is not relevant to the present discussion). *Iuuentas*: see Wissowa 1912: 136. The youth so honoured are the victorious soldiers of the battle; see Latte 1960: 256. The censorial contract: see Orlin 1997: 142 and n. 103 (it is unclear whether he paid for it from his share of booty); also 199. Lucullus: *DPRR* LICI1114; Rüpke 2008: 89, 770 no. 2247.

[46] See Appendix 8.2. Contrast the retrospective naming of the defeat of Antiochus III by the brothers Scipio at the battle of Magnesia (190 BCE), in the speech delivered in 187 by P. Scipio Nasica at the 'trial of the Scipios': Livy 38.58.9, *quo die ad Magnesiam signis collatis L. Scipio Antiochum deuicisset*. (But a Greek inscription, *Syll.*³ 606, has a periphrastic alternative designation of Magnesia: p. 334–5 n. 164.) Trasimene and Cannae are often named retrospectively in Livy, in both narrative and speeches; see e.g. 27.12.11, Hannibal exhorts his men to remember Trasimene and Cannae.

[47] 28.45.12: gifts of gold and silver were sent to Delphi in 205 'from the booty of Hasdrubal', *ex praeda Hasdrubalis*. Haywood (1933: 59) took this to be 'Spanish booty', presumably thinking of Scipio's victory over Hasdrubal Gisgo at Ilipa, narrated at 28.12–16 (so explicitly Scullard 1973 [1951] 131 n. 1); the reference can hardly have been to his victory over Hasdrubal Barca at Baecula in 208 (27.18–19), after which Hasdrubal gave Scipio the slip. L. does not mention booty after either of those Iberian battles, whereas the Metaurus resulted in great quantities of it, *magna praeda*, 27.49.6 (cf. Pol. 11.3.2, more than 300 talents). So this may be another allusion to the great battle won in 207 by Nero and Salinator. It is true that 28.45.12 begins by describing games held by Scipio, and that Ilipa is the more recent victory over a Hasdrubal. But the booty point makes the Metaurus likelier.

[48] Briscoe's 1981: 276 (on 36.36.5) does not draw attention to the silence but does discuss the date of the dedication. Heckel in the Oxford World's Classics edition of book 36 (Heckel 2000: 570) does notice the silence in Book 27.

[49] 22.9–10 with 33.34.1–2 and 34.44.3. The *uer sacrum* was an old rite, originally a vow to sacrifice everything born the following spring. Some humans were supposed to leave their native land, but this requirement had (probably) lapsed by now. See Briscoe and Hornblower 2020: 180.

computer he could surely have gone back and added it later.⁵⁰ So perhaps the omission was conscious and deliberate: he did not want to slow down the rapid battle narrative in book 27. But vows of Salinator's sort need further examination. The topic – a tricky but important one – is relevant to other Roman battles, both mentioned and not mentioned in the present book, so is treated in Appendix 8.2. There is a further complication in that Cicero in the *Brutus* says that Salinator vowed games for his victory. Probably the vow was for both temple and games.⁵¹

A triumph was certainly awarded to Livius Salinator after the battle, and perhaps to Nero also. But Nero's is controversial, like Salinator's vow, so it too is postponed to an appendix (Appendix 8.3).

## 8.4 Reception: The Poets

Ennius certainly mentioned Salinator's triumph specifically: *Liuius inde redit magno mactatus triumpho*, 'Livius returned from there honoured with a great triumph'.⁵² It has also been made very probable that for Ennius, the Metaurus victory of 207 was the moment at which Juno, for whom Andronicus had composed his song before the battle, was finally reconciled to Rome: 'at the time of the second Punic war, as Ennius says, Juno was appeased and began to favour the Romans'.⁵³ This was not the only reconciliation of 207, but that between the two consuls was only temporary.

The Metaurus battle seems not to have been called that generally, or perhaps at all, until Horace immortalized the name in a long Pindaric *Ode*.⁵⁴ It

---

⁵⁰ Briscoe 2008: 395 (38.52.1–6n.) invoked 'constraints of ancient book production' to argue against a theory that Livy might have gone back and revised something. But this cannot be taken to an extreme. He surely did not dictate nearly 150 books to a scribe (or team of scribes: he must have been wealthy to have the leisure to work for many years on his vast history) and then deposit them in pigeonholes in his study and make no further alterations or additions.

⁵¹ On *Brutus* 73, see further Appendix 8.4, discussing Cicero's name for the battle (Sena not Metaurus).

⁵² Ennius, *Annals* line 299, book IX frag. ii Sk. (Goldberg and Manuwald 2018a: 256–7, book IX frag. 2.); Skutsch 1985: 475, 477 for this clear allusion to the Metaurus.

⁵³ *Bello Punico secundo, ut ait Ennius, placata Iuno coepit fauere Romanis*: Goldberg and Manuwald 2018a: 240–1, Book VIII t[estimonium] 2; cf. Livy 27.37 (Livius Andronicus). For 207 as the moment, see Badian 1972: 160 n. 2; Feeney 2016: 225–9 and n. 326; Feeney 2021: 1.60; 2.270, 348–9, 354–5 and n. 46. Skutsch 1985: 466 found 207 for the reconciliation 'tempting' but (and with no reference to Badian's discussion in a book edited by Skutsch himself!) placed it eight years earlier, 'before the minor [Roman] success at Hamae' near Campanian Cumae: Livy 23.35–6, under 215 BCE. For this success, which was indeed minor, Lazenby 1978: 96. So the Juno fragment really belongs in book IX, together with the 'great triumph' fragment; see previous n. In accordance with his conclusion, Skutsch assigned the Juno fragment to Book VIII (as frag. xvi), and Goldberg and Manuwald follow him without discussion.

⁵⁴ Horace, *Odes* 4.4. Drusus is *DPRR* CLAU4194. The preceding poem but one (*Odes* 4.2) announces itself explicitly as Pindaric in line 1, *Pindarum quisquis*, where Horace pretends to be unable to rival Pindar (then does so). But 4.4 is no less Pindaric, without advertising itself as such.

celebrates a victory in 15 BCE by Nero Claudius Drusus, and his brother the future emperor Tiberius, over the Vindelici in present-day Germany: *quid debeas O Roma Neronibus / testis Metaurum flumen et Hasdrubal / deuictus*, 'the Metaurus river is witness to the debt you, O Rome, owe to the Nerones, and so too is the defeated Hasdrubal'. All modern commentators on the *Ode*, most recently Richard Thomas, note that the river is here personified as witness, *testis*, and that there are poetic precedents for this.[55] The Metaurus thus resembles Zama in its early anonymity: the name 'Zama' was first attached to Scipio's decisive defeat of Hannibal in 202 by Cornelius Nepos in the 30s BCE. Neither Polybius nor Livy call the battle by that name, although both mention Zama as a place name.[56]

Horace and Livy were close contemporaries, and it is impossible to say for certain which of them could have read or been influenced by the other. Thomas says that Livy 'presumably' wrote the end of book 27 before Horace wrote book 4 of his *Odes*, where 'presumably' leaves open the reverse possibility; we might anyway wish to allow for the possibility of partial recitation by one or other author before actual publication.[57] Livy's closural statement in book 27, that Hannibal is said to have lamented that he now recognized the future fate of Carthage, the *fortuna Carthaginis*, is neatly matched by Horace's penultimate stanza.[58] Horace has Hannibal bewailing, with deliberate verbal repetition, the death of both Hasdrubal and the hopes and fortunes of our – that is, the Carthaginian– name: *occidit occidit / spes omnis et fortuna nostri / nominis Hasdrubale interempto*.[59] Modern punctuation usually ends Hannibal's speech here, at *interempto*; but the poem continues for another four-line stanza, *nil Claudiae non perficiunt manus*, 'there is nothing that Claudian hands cannot achieve'.[60] It is not certain or agreed that Horace has now taken

---

[55] Lines 37–9. See Thomas 2011: 141, citing Catullus 64.357, the Homeric river Scamander as witness, *testis*. For Horace's imitation here of Ennius on the Great Plains as witness (African victory of Scipio in 203), see p. 211.
[56] Nepos, *Hannibal* 6.3; cf. HCP 2: 446, Yardley 2006: 710. Zama as place name: Pol. 15.5.3, Livy, 30.29.2. Livy's retrospective references to this, the final battle of the second Punic war, are periphrastic: 30.40.2, 38.46.10. Strabo is silent about Zama *as a battle*, p. 205.
[57] Thomas 2011: 149.
[58] Livy 27.51.12. Thomas (previous n.) also notes that the role of *fortuna* is traditional; his comment suggests scepticism about a direct connection between the two authors.
[59] Lines 70–3. Commentators do not help with the meaning of 'our name', but it is more likely to refer to Carthage as a whole than to a smaller entity such as the Barcid family. So D. West 1997 (Oxford World's Classics translation): 118 renders it 'the fortune of our people'.
[60] Or *perficient*, future not present tense; see Feeney 2021: 2.270.

over from Hannibal as speaker, and perhaps there is deliberate ambiguity.[61]

Otherwise, the Augustan poets have little to say about the victory at the Metaurus. There is nothing relevant in Virgil. Ovid seems to have recognized the importance of the battle of 207 BCE in his poem about the Roman calendar, but if that is what he is talking about, he does not name the Metaurus, only Hasdrubal, and that problematically.[62]

## 8.5 Conclusion

'Battle of the Metaurus' was not the standard designation for the battle of 207 BCE until Horace decided to personify a river which flowed near the battle site and in this way unintentionally turned the minor river Metaurus into a Roman 'place of memory'. It would be wrong to claim that the battle at which Hasdrubal was killed was a piece of 'invented tradition', allotted spurious importance at Rome so as to enhance the achievement in Germany of one of Augustus' stepsons.[63] On the contrary, Horace and Livy, and probably Ennius before them, were surely correct to regard the battle as a decisive contribution to the eventual Roman victory over Carthage five years later. Roman maritime supremacy in the war was virtually absolute throughout the war and meant that Hannibal could not be reinforced by sea, whereas Roman capacity for replacement of manpower was far greater, because the Romans could draw on their Italian allies, whereas Hannibal had no equivalent manpower resource.[64] Hannibal's only hope was from Iberia, and the defeat and death of his brother Hasdrubal in north Italy put an end to that hope.

If the victory entered the full limelight of Roman memory after 15 BCE, but not before, that was because it was only then that descendants of the consuls Salinator and Nero possessed sufficient military prestige to make

---

[61] See Feeney 2021: 2.269–71, part of a fine exploration (*hic finis fandi*, 234–77) of the sometimes deliberate ambiguities arising from the absence of ancient punctuation.

[62] *Fasti* 6.770, *cecidit telis Hasdrubal ipse suis*, 'Hasdrubal fell by his own weapons'. The implication of suicide contradicts both Polybius and Livy, unless his desperate final solo charge on horseback (Livy 27.49.4) can be regarded as a kind of suicide. For this reason, (unconvincing) attempts have been made to find another Hasdrubal. See De Sanctis 1968: 560–1. Ann and Peter Wiseman in their Oxford World's Classics edition (Wiseman and Wiseman 2013, note on the passage) take the reference to be to 'the battle of the Metaurus', but they add 'it is not clear why Ovid suggests a death by suicide'.

[63] For 'places of memory', see Nora 1999–2006, and for 'invented tradition' see p. 131.

[64] For the limits to the Carthaginians' ability to increase available manpower, see Taylor 2020a: 73 ('the center was ultimately hollow'), but contrast his p. 64 for their willingness to continue recruiting and fighting once the war reached Africa in 204–202. Rome's Italian allies: Brunt 1971a: 420–2, cf. Lazenby 1978: 234–5. Occasional recruitment difficulties are recorded, both at Rome and with the allies and colonies, but were surmounted. For examples, see Livy 25.5.5 and 27.38.2 (Rome, 212 and 207); p. 364 (Latin colonies in 207).

their victorious ancestors seem worth celebrating. At the time, the end of the third century, it was different. The old quarrel between the two men resurfaced during their joint censorship in 204, and perhaps this extreme rancour, rather than their earlier and untypical moment of cooperation and glory, is what stuck in Roman memories during the immediately following years and even decades. Thus, it is remarkable that in Livy's account of their acrimonious censorship there is no word about the outstanding shared military success only three years earlier and the resulting joy, and that he comments specifically on the unpopularity, *inuidia*, in which these censors were held.[65] The absence of an agreed single name for the battle will not have helped: Livy's periphrasis in Book 36, 'the day on which Hasdrubal and his army were killed' is not exactly catchy. But the facts of the battle's importance were already there from at least the time of Polybius, written in the middle of the second century, and – even earlier, by several decades – in Ennius also.

## Appendix 8.1 Livius Salinator: Both *Decemuir* and Consul?

A *decemuir* called Marcus Livius Salinator, son of Marcus and grandson of Marcus, is attested in the Capitoline records (the *fasti*) as having a presiding role (as a *magister*) at the Secular Games in 236 BCE.[66] If he was the consul of 219 and 207, he must have had a very long tenure of the life appointment of the decemvirate, at least thirty-three years.[67] But that is not inconceivable: after all, the *decemuir*'s colleague Marcus Aemilius Lepidus Numida died as late as 211.[68] But Münzer thought that the *decemuir* was not the same as but the father of the consul of 207, and this has been generally accepted.[69] In any case, there is no doubt that Gaius, son of the consul Marcus, was a *pontifex* in

---

[65] 29.37.17.
[66] A much better-attested celebration of the Secular Games (supposedly a once-in-a-century event) had taken place in 249. This throws doubt on the historicity of those of 238, but the names of the *magistri* are nevertheless thought to be genuine, to give the fraud verisimilitude. So Münzer 1926: col. 891, Livius no. 32; cf. Palmer 1974: 102–4; Rüpke 2008: 516 no. 515.
[67] The consul of 219 and 207 is *DPRR* LIVI0827.
[68] Livy 26.23.7; *MRR* I: 223 (implicitly denying identification with the consul of 207: there is no addition 'Cos. 219, 207'). The consul Salinator's death date is unknown, but must be later than his censorship of 204, which unlike some rancorous censorships was completed. As for the perceived problem of implausible longevity, see Palmer 1974: 95 (cf. 1997: 97) for the – not quite decisive – argument from Numida, for whom see *DPRR* AEMI0785 and Rüpke 2008: 77 and 516 no. 515 ('probably the same as the *decemvir* who died in 211').
[69] Münzer 1920: 229 [1999: 209]; 1926: col. 891. Livius the *decemuir* of 237 is dissociated, without argument, from the consul of 207 by Rüpke 2008: 77 and 773, followed at *DPRR* LIVI0876. Gruen 1990: 91 n. 50 takes the same view, without citing Münzer. He has an additional argument from the 'M. Livius' who was one of the five *legati* to Carthage in 218 (Livy 21.18.1), but it is not clear to me

207, having been one since 211, so the consul did at least have a close family link with one of the two colleges of priests who were energetically active in that year of alarm at the threat from Hasdrubal.[70] Unless and until new evidence emerges, it is impossible to decide finally the question whether the *decemuir* of 236 and the consul of 219 and 207 were identical, because both were called 'Marcus, son of Marcus, grandson of Marcus'. (The family used only these two *praenomina*, Gaius and Marcus, so were even more parsimonious than the Cornelii Scipiones, who used three *praenomina*.) To use the hymn itself as supporting evidence for the identification would be tempting but might reasonably be thought a circular argument. The probabilities are against the identification.

## Appendix 8.2  The Metaurus Vow and Other Vows before or during Battles

We should perhaps not be too surprised at the non-mention of Salinator's vow at the Metaurus in Livy's book 27.[71] Deferment seems to be his usual practice: this is presumably because his sources, whether archival or other, recorded the hard fact of a dedication of a temple or games but were less likely to record a vow at the time it was made – that is, usually, before a battle.[72]

This appendix will be about Roman practice, not Carthaginian. If Hannibal made pre-battle vows (as he may well have done), we do not hear of them. In his first Decade, Livy mentions Roman vows made in the heat of the battle and recorded in the battle narrative itself, such as Romulus' vow to Jupiter Stator; the dictator Camillus in 345 BCE vowed a temple to Juno Moneta 'in the middle of a battle' against the Aurunci, *inter ipsam dimicationem*, and it was dedicated the following year.[73] With this, compare, from the fifth Decade, Gaius Cicereius' vow during a battle in 173 and his dedication

---

whether he thinks the *legatus* was Salinator the *decemuir* or an otherwise unknown M. Livius. The *legatus* is usually and rightly taken to be the consul of 219. See p. 84.

[70] Gaius as *pontifex*: Livy 26.23.7 (211); Rüpke 2008: 82 and 773 no. 2274; *DPRR* LIVI0952. Münzer 1926: cols. 895–6 acknowledged – while not actually identifying consul and *decemuir*, but noting the priesthoods held by two other family members – that the honour paid to Livius Andronicus showed the consul's influence on all aspects of public life.

[71] In this appendix, ancient references are to Livy unless otherwise stated.

[72] For the political aspect of dedications of temples under the Republic, see Orlin 1997, esp. 35–75 on vows (45–66 for vows made on campaign) and 162–89 on dedications (and vows); but he does not address the problem of Livy's deferment of the mention of Metaurus vow or others, not does he discuss absence of evidence for battlefield vows made before some victories, such as Zama (see p. 201). His main concern is to stress the importance of the senate's role in the whole process. At 199–202, his appendix 1 lists state temples with deity, date, circumstances, vower, source, and dedicator.

[73] 1.12.4–7; 7.28.4 and 6. In this chronologically wide-ranging appendix, *DPRR* references will not always be given.

five years later of a temple to the same goddess. (This shows that Livy's recording practice did not change materially between the first and fifth Decades.) Appius Claudius Caecus is alleged to have vowed a temple to Bellona in 296, again during the battle, *dicitur . . . in medio pugnae discrimine*. The indirect Livian tradition relates that the consul Publius Sempronius Sophus vowed a temple to the earth god Tellus during a battle in 268 at Ausculum against the Picenes, in which there was an earthquake.[74]

The nearest to a vow made *after* a battle in Livy's surviving narrative seems to be in the closing phase of the battle of Sentinum (295): Quintus Fabius Maximus Rullianus vowed a temple to Jupiter Victor at a moment when victory was clearly assured. (The vow was certainly fulfilled but the dedication was presumably recorded in Livy's lost second Decade.)[75]

Some pre-battle vows in the first Decade are reported retrospectively only, like Salinator's. For example, a temple of Mars was dedicated in 387 BCE by Gaius Quinctius Cincinnatus as a result of a vow vaguely said to have been made 'in the Gallic war'. There is other evidence from the first Decade. At least one vow of a temple was probably recorded in the lost second Decade: Claudius Marcellus at Clastidium, in the Gallic war, vowed a temple to Honour and Virtue. This allegedly improper double temple became controversial early in his consulship of 208.[76]

In the third Decade, the consul Sempronius Tuditanus vowed a temple to Fortuna Primigenia before a successful battle fought against Hannibal near Croton in 204 BCE.[77] Livy says the vow was fulfilled by Quintus Marcius Ralla ten years later, 194 BCE, though there are difficulties about this.[78] More straightforwardly, a temple to Concord was dedicated in 217 in fulfilment of a vow made by the praetor Lucius Manlius Vulso during a mutiny in 218. The vow was not reported at the time it was made; but then nor was the mutiny.[79]

---

[74] Cicereius (*DPRR* CICE1340): 42.7.2 and 45.15.10; Claudius Caecus (*DPRR* CLAU0591): 10.19.17; Sophus (*DPRR* SEMP0701): Florus 1.14; Wissowa 1912: 195; *MRR* 1: 200.

[75] 10.29.14 with Oakley 2005b: 327; *DPRR* FABI0559.

[76] Cincinnatus (*DPRR* QUIN0466; not the famous one): 6.5.8. See the valuable collection and discussion at Oakley 1998: 267–8 (7.28.4n.), but he confines himself to the first Decade. Marcellus' controversial vow: Livy 27.25.7–10, cf. 29.11.13. The vow is not mentioned in the *periocha* to book 20, but that does not prove it was not in the full text.

[77] 29.36.8–9. with Levene 1993: 74. For Tuditanus, see *DPRR* SEMP0882; cf. pp. 104, 143 n. 57.

[78] 34.53.5–6, where however Livy wrongly calls the maker of the vow Sempronius Sophus and – again wrongly if he means Tuditanus – says the man who consecrated it was censor at the time. For the problem, Briscoe 1981: 132–3 and 2012: 431, n. on 43.13.4–5: perhaps there was a muddle between two Roman temples of Fortuna Primigenia; also Orlin 1997: 142–3. Ralla is *DPRR* MARC1115.

[79] 22.33.7–8 with Briscoe and Hornblower 2020: 250–1; *DPRR* MANL0836. The context of the mutiny must have been 21.25.8–9; see W/M. Cf. 28.38.14: on a motion of the new consul Scipio Africanus, money was granted for the games he had vowed during the Iberian mutiny narrated earlier in the

## Appendix 8.2

Since pre-battle vows are often mentioned only when they are fulfilled (that is, as a result of victories), it is not surprising that we do not hear of them as having been made before Roman defeats, although they must often have been: thus, neither of the consuls before Cannae in 216 are recorded as making any vows of temples or of anything else. In 217, Gaius Flaminius was accused of not having made the customary vows on his first day in office as consul and on departing for his campaign, but such vows are distinct from battlefield vows.[80] In a very brief speech of exhortation, Flaminius tells his troops at Trasimene later in 217 that more is achieved by force and courage than by *uotis aut imploratione*, usually and naturally translated something like 'prayers or supplications'.[81] But Levene has taken the first word to refer specifically to the common phenomenon of vows, *uota*, by Roman commanders before battle to dedicate a temple to a particular god if successful and sees Flaminius' failure to make such a vow as further evidence of his fatal irreligiosity.[82] To be sure, *uotum* is ambiguous between 'vow' and 'prayer'.[83] Levene's suggestion is ingenious, and perhaps Livy is indeed addressing the attentive reader above the heads, so to speak, of the troops. But this is a rhetorical context, and the conjunction of *uotis* with *imploratione* imposes – on the surface at least – the simple sense 'prayers' for *uotis*. So too does the envisaged audience: ordinary troops were not financially in a position to vow and dedicate temples. Levene is right, however, that Flaminius is not reported as having made a pre-battle vow of a temple. But then, the same is true of the consuls before Cannae, and those two men are not regarded by Livy as especially irreligious. If they or indeed Flaminius had made a vow of a temple, and had been victorious, Livy would not necessarily have reported this at the time, rather than at the time of the dedication years later. So a vow before a defeat would not necessarily have been mentioned either. But in any case, it has been rightly said that a battlefield vow by the commander 'always brings a favourable outcome to the battle', so it is logical that Livy does not record vows before defeats.[84]

---

book (28.24–9, cf. p. 223), where however the vow was not mentioned. The games were held the next year, 28.45.12.

[80] Livy 21.63.7–9 with Orlin 1997: 39–40 and n. 15; 49.

[81] 22.5.2. So Briscoe and Hornblower 2020: 165. The old Loeb edition by Foster had 'vows', but the new Loeb edition, with tr. by Yardley (2019), has 'prayers'. This does not seem to be conscious rejection of Levene; Yardley's tr. mostly reproduces that of his own Oxford World's Classics edition (Yardley 2006). The tr. of De Sélincourt 1965: 99 is loose: he has Flaminius 'crying out that no prayers would save them now'.

[82] Levene 1993: 42.

[83] See *OLD* 1 and 2, although it is there acknowledged that there is no sharp difference between the two senses.

[84] Oakley 1998: 268.

There are several examples in Livy's fourth Decade of temples dedicated in fulfilment of earlier pre-battle vows which Livy did not record at the time of the vow, so that the mention of the fulfilment of Salinator's hitherto-unmentioned Metaurus vow in book 36 is not the only example. In 192, Marcius Ralla, whom we have already met, dedicated two temples of Jupiter which had been vowed by Lucius Furius Purpurio, one of them when he was praetor 'in the Gallic war', the other as consul (200 and 196 BCE).[85] In 191, Publius Scipio Nasica as consul held games to Jupiter, which he had vowed during his propraetorship in Iberia (194) in the middle of a battle, *inter ipsum discrimen pugnae*.[86] After that, there is a striking clustering in book 40, all under the years 181–179 BCE.[87] The two most important battles in this cluster are as follows: first, the fulfilment in 181 by Acilius Glabrio's son of his father's vow of a temple of Piety, *Pietas*, a vow made ten years earlier on the day of Thermopylae in 191 BCE (naming the battle). Second, the censor Marcus Aemilius Lepidus' fulfilment in 179 of the vow made by Lucius Aemilius Regillus before the naval battle against Antiochus off Myonnesus in 190 BCE.[88] This last item resembles Livy on Salinator's Metaurus vow to the extent that the battle, although famous and important, is not named at the time of the dedication, although Livy had (by contrast with the Metaurus) named Myonnesus both in the battle narrative and again when the news of the victory reached Rome.[89]

In the poorly preserved first Pentad of the fifth Decade, books 41–45, Livy records both that the praetor Gaius Cicereius vowed a temple to Juno Moneta during a battle against the Corsicans in 173 BCE, and that he dedicated it five years later.[90]

From this review of the evidence, it is clear that Livy could, if he had wished, have reported Salinator's vow at time it was made, whether before

---

[85] 35.41.8; Orlin 1997: 184–5; *DPRR* FURI0967.   [86] 35.1.8 (battle and vow), 36.36.1 (the games).

[87] At 39.22.8, Livy reports the celebration in 185 of games which Lucius Scipio said had been made 'during the war with Antiochus', *bello Antiochi*, but this is not quite a battle vow. Under 181, see 40.34.4, Lucius Porcius Licinus' dedication of a temple of Venus Erycina, vowed by his father as consul during the Ligurian war (*DPRR* PORC1154, father, and 1271, son). Under 179, see 40.44.8–9, the consul Quintus Fulvius Flaccus fulfilled his vow (of games and a temple) made in a Celtiberian war; also 40.52.1, the censor Aemilius Lepidus fulfilled his vow of temples, made in the war against the Ligurians eight years earlier.

[88] Thermopylae: 40.34.6; Orlin 1997: 180–1. *DPRR* ACIL1063 (father) and 1270 (son). Briscoe 2008: 492–3 is mainly interested in whether the father was still alive at the time of the dedication but does not discuss the deferred mention of the vow. Myonnesus: 40.52.4; *DPRR* AEMI1175. Briscoe 2008: 550 does here comment on the non-mention of the vow in the narrative of the battle; that is, at 37.29.7–30.10.

[89] 37.29.10 and 37.47.3.

[90] 42.7.1 and 45.15.10. See p. 198 for the implication of this passage (no change in Livy's recording habits between first and fifth Decade).

or during the battle. But equally, there are plenty of vows reported only at the later time of the dedication of the temple. His practice did not change over time: it is true that none of the many battle vows in the fourth Decade were reported under the year in which they were made, but Cicereius in the fifth Decade is enough to refute any attempt to detect a change of pattern.

Three of Livy's silences are noteworthy. The three great battles which assured Roman dominance in the Mediterranean around 200 BCE were Zama against Hannibal (202), Cynoscephalae against Philip V of Macedon (197), and Magnesia against Antiochus III (190). Remarkably, no battle vow or subsequent dedication is recorded by the victors in any of these three battles: that is, by Publius Scipio Africanus, Titus Quinctius Flamininus, or Scipio's brother Lucius, aided by his brother Publius as *legatus* (in the sense of military adviser).[91] Should it be assumed that vows or dedications were indeed made before or during these battles, as at Metaurus/Sena and Myonnesus, but that Livy or his source failed to record them? Or should it rather be assumed that they were not made? In which case it would seem that a battle vow would indeed guarantee a favourable outcome, but that a favourable outcome did not require a battle vow. It would, however, have been rash of a Roman commander to omit a vow in such critical encounters, even if it were not actually obligatory to make one. On the other hand, a temple or games dedicated by any of those three big names could hardly have escaped the record. On balance, we should conclude that vows were not made.

## Appendix 8.3  Salinator's Triumph – or Nero's Also?

The triumph for the Metaurus victory is controversial and was perhaps so at the time. Livy is explicit that the senate granted triumphs to the consuls Livius Salinator and Claudius Nero. But he explains that the two men agreed among themselves to celebrate a *consociatus triumphus*, a 'shared triumph', although Salinator was in a chariot and Nero was on a single horse and unaccompanied by soldiers.[92] Most modern scholars, notably Mommsen, treat Nero's honour as the lesser honour of an *ouatio* (I avoid the English word 'ovation' because it has different and purely positive connotations, as in 'she was given a standing ovation'). Ennius named only Salinator ('Livius ... honoured with a great

---

[91] Aemilius Paullus, who defeated Philip V's son Perseus at the decisive battle of Pydna in 168, can very probably be added to this list, but the damaged state of the text of books 44 and 45 means that complete certainty is not possible.
[92] Livy 28.9.11. For *consociatus*, see §11. Scullard 1973: 73 and n. 3 accepted this.

triumph'), but Skutsch suggested that a lost following line of Ennius might have referred to such an *ouatio* by Nero.[93] That is a guess piled on a guess. Valerius Maximus says explicitly that Nero 'triumphed without a chariot', *sine curru triumphauit*.[94] To be sure, that absence is one diagnostic feature of an *ouatio*; but Livy does not use the word *ouatio* about Nero in 207, although he certainly had the vocabulary for it. For example, he says of Appius Claudius Centho, praetor in 175, *ouans cum in urbem iniret*, 'when he celebrated an *ouatio* on entering the city' (174 BCE). A 'triumph on the Alban Mount' might also really be an *ouatio*, like that celebrated by Quintus Minucius (Rufus) in 197.[95] But there is no mention of the Alban Mount in Livy's account of the 'shared triumph' of 207.

Let us suppose that Mommsen was right. One suggestion is that an *ouatio* granted to Nero was tendentiously represented as a shared triumph by Livy's source. Hoyos thinks that the enthusiasm for Nero displayed by the populace and 'comparative downplaying of his fellow consul (despite him being a Livius) may not be entirely unconnected with the eminence of the Claudii Nerones in Augustan Rome'.[96] Conversely, it is possible that Ennius elided Nero altogether, again tendentiously. But the best guess may be that the two consuls improvised and shared some elements of both triumph and *ouatio*.[97]

## Appendix 8.4 The Name of the Battle: Cicero in the *Brutus*, and Other Writers

Battles, even some of the most important ones of any period in history, do not always have universally agreed names; and in our sources, some ancient battles are referred to only by vague periphrasis, such as Polybius' regular retrospective designation of Trasimene as 'the battle in Etruria'. (He used the place name Trasimene only once in his surviving text, but to designate the lake not the battle.)[98] Hew Strachan has pointed out that some modern battles have had different names in different countries (Waterloo and Jutland were called respectively 'La Belle Alliance' and 'Skagerrak' in Germany), and that some are the result of deliberate cultural choices

---

[93] Skutsch 1985: 477.   [94] Val. Max. 4.1.9, clearly derived from Livy.
[95] Centho: 41.28.6; Minucius: 33.23.8. *DPRR* CLAU1290 and MINU1062.   [96] Hoyos 2006: 683.
[97] Pittenger 2008: 71. Cf. Richardson 1975: 55 ('a deliberately modified form of triumph, rather than an *ouatio*'), and Chaplin 2000: 145: the consuls' plan an essentially conservative adaptation of the triumph to an unprecedented situation.
[98] 3.84.15 and 108.9; 5.101.3; 15.11.8, with the addition 'against Flaminius'. 'Trasimene' (the lake): 3.82.9.

## Appendix 8.4

('Tannenberg').[99] As Strachan also says, geographical imprecision often explains some imprecision in naming; that would help to explain some of the difficulty about the Metaurus. We do not know what name the Carthaginians gave to Hannibal's battles when using their own language. Livy makes Hannibal refer to Trasimene and Cannae by those names when talking to Scipio before Zama; but this report is in Latin and is at best a fictional embroidery of a real speech.[100] They may well have had their own name for Zama, which was in their own part of the world. It is not easy to explain the battle name Metaurus as a matter of Roman cultural choice, given that (as we shall see) another name for the battle was current in the time of Cicero. Horace may, as we saw, have wanted a river name so as to provide himself with an arresting personification: Metaurus as river god and witness.

There is, in the surviving books of Livy – always a necessary qualification – only one other retrospective allusion to the battle of 207. When narrating the joint triumph of Salinator and Claudius Nero, Livy calls it 'the battle in Gaul', but that is partly because in the context it was important that Gaul was Salinator's province, and this is one reason why he was awarded the triumph. Nor is the *battle* ever called the Metaurus in Book 27 itself. Livy names the *river* just once, as a topographical feature.[101]

But another name for the battle was current in late Republican times. Livy records retrospectively that Salinator at the battle of 207 had made a vow of a *temple* to Iuuentas, goddess of youth. Cicero in the *Brutus*, composed early in 46 BCE, also mentions Salinator's vow.[102] But he says he vowed *games* to Iuuentas, and that the vow was made at (that is, presumably before) the 'battle of Sena', *proelium Senense*, where the adjective denotes the town of Sena Gallica (modern Senigallia) near the battle site.[103] Cicero's source for this particular detail of nomenclature is

---

[99] See Strachan 2019: ix–x. He explains that the German victory over Russia at Tannenberg in 1914 was so called in revenge for the defeat of the Teutonic Knights in 1410, and that the obvious geographical name would have been Allenstein. Denis Feeney reminds me that some American civil war battles were named differently by the two sides (Antietam/Sharpsburg, and so on).

[100] 30.30.12.    [101] 'Battle in Gaul': 28.9.12. Metaurus river: 27.47.9.

[102] §73 with Douglas 1966: 62. The Ciceronian context is a complicated discussion of the chronology of the career of the poet Livius Andronicus; see Oakley 1998: 61–3 and 63 n. 1. The problem is that Cicero's polemic (directed against the poet Lucius Accius) may provide reasons for dating Salinator's dedication to 197 BCE. At MRR 1: 335, the year 191 is accepted without question. Lucullus in the 190s dedicated a temple to Iuuentas, which had been vowed by Salinator in 207 on the day of his victory over Hasdrubal, and that is all we need for the present purpose.

[103] Probably (cf. p. 193) Salinator vowed both a temple and games (Latte 1960: 256 n. 2, Scullard 1981: 208). The temple took years to build, and was inaugurated only now, hence Livy's notice. Accius and therefore Cicero were more interested in the games aspect.

unknown. I cannot find who else in pre-Ciceronian antiquity so designated the battle, but somebody must have done. A very few modern authorities do use this name, rather than 'battle of the Metaurus', the designation which Horace popularized for all later time.[104] Livy mentions Sena as the site of the camps of the two sides. Appian in the second century CE also has this detail and mentions a 'river difficult to ford', ποταμὸν οὐκ εὔπορον, but does not name it.[105] Since he goes on to equate the battle with Cannae for importance, it seems he was here following Livy in a general way, although it is just possible that Livy was translating a now-lost sentence of Polybius.[106] Probably Appian was more familiar with Roman historians (Livy) than he was with Roman poets (Horace).

It is theoretically possible that Livy or one of his speakers had some reason to refer to the battle in one of the years after 167 BCE, which were narrated in the many lost later books. That perhaps becomes less likely as the second century wears on. By far the likeliest candidate, however, is one of Livy's very last books, precisely his narrative of the campaigns of Drusus and Tiberius, because the very brief *Periochae* (summaries) show that Drusus' campaigns 'across the Rhine' were covered in the lost books 141 and 142. That is, Livy or one of Livy's speakers might, like Horace, have noticed the role of Nero Drusus' ancestor at the battle fought back in 207 BCE. The battle was narrated but not named in the non-Livian summary (*Periocha*) of book 27 itself, nor does the river feature there.

In what is left of Polybius' account of the battle, the river is not mentioned at all, nor is the battle either named or alluded to periphrastically anywhere else in the surviving books. If he did refer to it in a lost context, he might perhaps have called it 'the battle in Umbria', by analogy with his designation of Trasimene as 'the battle in Etruria'.

No fragment of Coelius Antipater, or of any of the other relevant fragmentary Roman historians, alludes to the battle, let alone naming it. Survival of such fragments is largely a matter of chance, but it may be that

---

[104] Mommsen called it the battle 'bei Sena' when discussing Salinator's triumph: 1887–8: 1.128 and n. 1 and 3, 129 n. 3, and cf. 95 n. 2. The two standard histories of Roman religion both call it the battle at Sena (Wissowa and Latte, cited at p. 192, but that is because they are in effect paraphrasing Cicero.
[105] Livy 27.46.4 (Sena). App. *Hann.* 52/222–3.
[106] Cannae comparison: App. *Hann.* 53/224, cf. Livy 27.49.5. – Eutropius (late fourth century CE), whose account of this period certainly derives from Livy, has *apud Metaurum flumen et Senam*, 'at the Metaurus river and Sena' (3.18.2). Other Livy-derived historians (Florus 1.22.50, Valerius Maximus 7.4.4) use the Metaurus alone to fix the battle, but by their time Horace's ode had had its effect. Aurelius Victor, *On illustrious men* does not name the battle in his chapter (50) about Salinator but does so under Claudius Nero (48.2), where he calls it the battle 'at the Metaurus river and Sena'; but see Pichlmayr 1961: 216 (addenda by Gruendel to Teubner edition of 1911, citing Baehrens' suggested deletion of *Metaurum flumen*).

these writers passed over the battle briefly and without memorable comment.

Ennius certainly mentioned the triumph after the battle: see p. 193. We do not know for sure whether he named the battle or not. But if he had done, and had called it the Metaurus, we might have expected that this would have survived in the tradition. So he probably did not name it.

Livy's contemporary the Greek geographical writer Strabo mentions the Metaurus only in passing, and merely as a river in Umbria; contrast his full handling of Trasimene – both lake and battle – a very few lines earlier, and Cannae in the next book, again mentioning the Roman defeat.[107] On the other hand, the battle of Zama in north Africa, which ended the Hannibalic war, is also entirely absent from Strabo, under whatever name he might have used for it. He names 'Zama' elsewhere, to be sure, but only in book 17 as the site of Juba's palace, destroyed by the Romans at a much later date. In that book, Strabo is more interested in Scipio Aemilianus and the final defeat and sack of Carthage in 146. Naraggara, the battle name favoured by De Sanctis, is also absent from Strabo. Conversely, one book earlier, Strabo shows that he knew both of the designations of another battle with two names, Alexander's final victory over Darius III at Gaugamela – or Arbela.[108]

Ovid knew the battle but did not name it. Silius Italicus' battle narrative named both the town of Sena and the Metaurus river in different lines.[109] This is non-committal as to the actual name of the battle.

The epitome of Stephanus of Byzantium's *Ethnica* has no entry for 'Metaurus', which is a pity, because it might have cited some literary sources, as it often does. It is not absurd to look for such an entry: after all, there is one for the Ticinus, site of Hannibal's earliest Italian victory.[110]

---

[107] Strabo 5.2.10 (Metaurus; he names Sena in the previous sentence, but likewise as a place not a battle site); 5.2.9 (Trasimene), 6.3.11 (Cannae).

[108] Strabo 17.3.12 (Zama), De Sanctis 1968: 572–7; cf. Mommsen 1906: 36–48: there were two places called Naraggara and two called Zama. In the present book, the battle will be called Zama. The other name is a mouthful and not necessarily more correct. Gaugamela and Arbela: Strabo 16.1.3 and 4

[109] Ovid: see p. 195. Silius: *Pun.* 15.551 and 556.

[110] τ 126 Billerbeck: Ticinus is said to be a *polis* near Ravenna and a homonymous river. The settlement was not enough of a *polis* to qualify for inclusion in the Copenhagen Inventory (Hansen and Nielsen 2004), although Stephanus does give an ethnic: Τικίνιος.

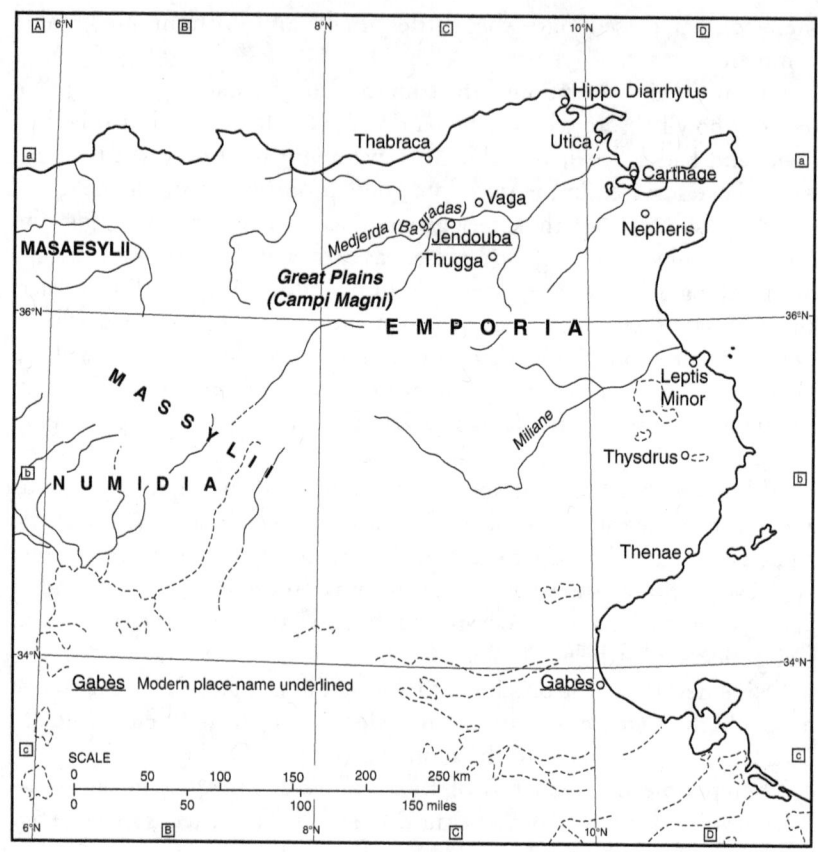

Map 3  North Africa

CHAPTER 9

# Hannibal and Scipio Meet and Fight at Last
## Zama, 202, Aged 45 and 33

## 9.1 Scipio in Africa: Battle of the Great Plains

At the end of Chapter 4, we left Scipio as consul for 205. He was given Sicily as his province, and after a political struggle Africa was added.[1] 'Scipio's games' were then staged, to great acclaim from a huge attendance.[2] Two diplomatic legates were sent to Delphi with gifts 'from the booty of Hasdrubal', *ex praeda Hasdrubalis*. This is probably a reference to the victory over Hasdrubal Barca at the Metaurus in 207, rather than to Scipio's own more recent victory over Hasdrubal son of Gisgo at Ilipa, 206.[3]

Otherwise, the expected showdown with Carthage dominated Scipio's consulship, although there were other enemies at large, notably Hannibal's other brother Mago and Philip V of Macedon. Scipio's preparations and progress were slow and cautious and have even been called 'pedestrian', in contrast with Hannibal's rapid and audacious invasion of Italy at the beginning of the war.[4] But another contrast is in order, with the impetuousness – however much exaggerated by Livy for literary effect – of two earlier Roman war commanders and consuls, Flaminius and Varro, and perhaps also Nero in 207. Scipio's run of Iberian successes had been unbroken, it is true. But his experienced, skilful, and formidable older opponent Hannibal remained essentially undefeated in the field.[5] So our knowledge of the outcome of Zama should not get in the way of a fair assessment of the steps Scipio now took.

---

[1] Livy 28.40–5; *MRR* I: 301. In this chapter, ancient references without name of author are to Livy.
[2] 28.45.12. The succinct words *ludi Scipionis* refer to games vowed by Scipio during the Iberian mutiny of 206 (where however no vow was mentioned), and for which money was voted at the start of his consulship, 28.38.14. See p. 223 for the vow.
[3] See p. 192 n. 47.   [4] So Lazenby 1978: 226–7 ('pedestrian').   [5] For minor defeats, see p. 421.

For the moment, however, Hannibal was still at large in Italy. So Scipio needed to alarm the Carthaginian authorities into recalling him, thereby satisfying those of his critics at home who thought that defeating Hannibal in Italy should be the top priority. The options are explored in speeches which Livy put into the mouths of Scipio and Fabius, now very near the end of his long life (he died in 203).[6] Fabius is made to concede that Scipio's plan in crossing to Africa was to draw Hannibal after him, *ut Hannibalem eo trahas*, but he stresses the risks and impugns Scipio's motives as self-aggrandizing. Scipio rejects the personal accusations with justified scorn and replies that he 'will indeed draw Hannibal after him, rather than being detained in Italy by him', *sed illum ego potius traham, quam ille me retineat*.[7] If Fabius had had his way, Hannibal would no doubt have been defeated in Italy sooner or later by Scipio or by another, after a massive build-up of Roman forces; but Carthage would have continued as a wealthy imperial power in north Africa and as a perceived or actual military threat.

Scipio was not allowed to levy troops, but he was granted leave to recruit volunteers.[8] He took 7,000 of these to Sicily (with 30 ships) sometime after his consulship began; but the total of his troops in Sicily was much greater, about four legions including the allied contribution. The Romans were still short of money, but not short of manpower by this stage of the war. Forces were however needed against other enemies, so they were in no position to throw everything at Carthage. For example, the province of Scipio's consular colleague Crassus was the lands of the Bruttii, where there were four legions to keep watch on Hannibal; as *pontifex maximus*, Crassus could not leave Italy. This suited Scipio, who therefore had to be given Sicily. The proximity in the north of Hannibal's remaining brother Mago fuelled existing disaffection in Etruria, against which Cornelius Cethegus, consul for 204, took some action. Sempronius Tuditanus, who would be consul in 204, is said to have had 10,000 infantry and 1,000 cavalry and 35 warships in Greece for possible use against Philip. The praetor Spurius Lucretius and the proconsul Livius Salinator moved directly against Mago; he was not defeated until 203. Scipio had new ships built at Panormus on the north coast of Sicily (modern Palermo) and sent Laelius as prefect of the fleet with some reconditioned old ships to raid Africa.[9]

---

[6] The speeches of 205: 28.40–4 with Beltramini 2023: 195–200. Fabius' death: 30.26.7–10, also Plut. *Fab.* 27.2, who says that Fabius did not see the end of the war or hear of Hannibal's defeat but died 'about the time when Hannibal left Italy'. See also *MRR* 1: 314–5 and n. 10; Ryan 1998: 179. See further p. 251 (Scipio replaces him as *princeps senatus*, senior senator, but only after an interval).

[7] 28.42.16 and (Scipio's reply) 44.9.    [8] 28.45.13; and 29.1.1 with Smith 1993: 9.

[9] For the detail of the Roman dispositions, see 28.45.13–46.13. Four legions for Sicily: the total is uncertain because Livy is unsatisfactory; the best calculations remain those of Brunt 1971a: 655–6 and Lazenby 1978: 202–3, cf. 195. Money short: 28.46.4. Other enemies: Lazenby 1978: 195. For Crassus,

Scipio's main Sicilian base was Syracuse, where he sampled Greek cultural life and was criticized for allegedly lolling around enjoying himself in this way. He had no difficulty proving, not by words but by actions – an impressive military and naval exhibition of drill and manoeuvres – that he was not neglecting his military duties.[10]

In 204, he crossed over to Africa, performing elaborate religious ceremonies.[11] He and his brother Lucius commanded the squadron of twenty warships which protected the transport ships on the right.[12] The twenty on the left were commanded by Laelius and the thirty-year-old Marcus Porcius Cato, casually mentioned as quaestor by Livy. As a result of the mature Cato's well-documented enmity towards Publius Scipio and his brother Lucius in the 180s, a cluster of anecdotes grew up about this early military service under Publius, retrojecting the later antipathy, and even antedating the quaestorship by bringing him back to Rome so as to have him share in Fabius' attacks in 205.[13] But Livy's sole mention of Cato in the entire third Decade is in the brief military report just cited, and he never mentions him in connection with the Pleminius affair which did Scipio so much reputational damage.

The dangerously low total of only forty escorting warships for so large an unarmed fleet has caused surprise among modern critics (a further twenty were available in Sicily), and Scipio's judgement has been questioned.[14] He certainly took a risk; but from the Roman point of view, the Carthaginians showed themselves, as so often in this war, conveniently unenterprising naval enemies.

---

see p. 118 n. 25; for his Bruttian command 28.38.12, and for the four legions in Bruttium 28.46.2–3 and 29.13.3 with De Sanctis 1968: 614–5 and nn. 9 and 10. Etruria and Cethegus (*DPRR* CORN0815): 29.36.10–12 with Harris 1971: 136–7, cf. 135 n. 2. For Tuditanus, see p. 104, and for the forces he was given for Greece 29.12.2. For Lucretius (*DPRR* LUCR1020) and Salinator, 28.46.7–13. Salinator was ordered to take an army of enslaved volunteers (*uolones*) to Ariminum: §13. For *uolones*, see Briscoe and Hornblower 2020: 312.

[10] 29.22.1–6 for Scipio's wordless reply to his critics. See further p. 122 for Scipio's drill exercises, citing Roselaar 2015.

[11] 29.27.1–13. For a historical commentary on book 29, see Smith 1993, and for book 30 Butler and Scullard 1953. For the elaborate naval rituals as he set sail, see pp. 223–4.

[12] The types of warships available to the Romans in this period were what Casson (1971: 97–135 at 100) calls 'polyremes', i.e. ships larger than triremes (quadriremes and especially quinqueremes). See Lazenby 1978: 16 and 273; also *CHGRW* (P. de Sousa) 357–66, esp. 357, 364, calling quinqueremes 'fives', i.e. with oars at two levels pulled by three and two men each, or at three levels, two men at the higher levels and one at the lowest. Livy's usual expressions for warships are *rostrati*, 'with a prow', or just 'long ships', but passages like 21.49.2 show he knows the word *quinqueremis*, Latin for Pol.'s πεντήρης. Pol. himself is not always consistent. At 3.41.2, he mentions ships and quinqueremes separately, but they are all presumably quinqueremes.

[13] 29.25.10; *DPRR* PORC0907. The quaestorship was certainly in 204 not 205. For a full demolition of the anecdotal tradition, Astin 1978: 12–15; cf. Smith 1993: 57.

[14] Thiel 1946: 157 (cf. 20) was particularly outraged.

The Roman landfall on Africa was preceded by an auspicious omen: when told that the nearest land was called the Beautiful Promontory, Scipio greeted it with pleasure: 'the omen pleases!', *placet omen*. As presented by Livy, this is in surely deliberate contrast with Hannibal's unhappy landfall.[15]

Established in Africa, Scipio (with the help of the Numidian king Masinissa, who had joined him with perhaps 2,000 cavalry) easily defeated the Carthaginian commander Hanno (28) by means of an ambush near a place called Salaeca, in the vicinity of the 'Tower of Agathocles'.[16] It was on this occasion that Scipio is said to have made his contemptuous joke at Hanno's expense: 'Cavalry under roofs in summer! May there be more of them, so long as they have a commander of that sort!' This is reminiscent of a remark about the consul Aemilius Paullus, also in Livy, and attributed to Hannibal at Cannae.[17]

Scipio carried out a much more elaborate ruse in winter 204–203.[18] This entailed pretending to be interested in peace terms conveyed by Syphax (Roman withdrawal from Africa in exchange for Carthaginian withdrawal from Italy) while really using the pause to gather information though his diplomatic agents about Carthaginian dispositions. In particular, he learned that the enemy's huts were of light construction – wood or reeds – and could be easily set on fire. At this time, there was evidently a formal truce, *indutiae*, between Syphax and Scipio, although both Polybius and Livy mention it only when it was about to be broken. Livy claims, as Polybius significantly does not, that the Carthaginians 'added some unfair conditions' (*iniquis ... adiectis*) and that this gave Scipio the excuse for breaking the truce.[19] This detail is probably a pro-Roman addition by one of Livy's non-Polybian sources, designed to exculpate Scipio from any suspicion of truce-breaking. Under the further pretence of an attack on Utica, he attacked and burned down the two enemy camps at night (those of Syphax and Hasdrubal (8) son of Gisgo), causing enormous loss of life as men were trapped in the flames or cut down while trying to flee unarmed and naked. Polybius, startlingly and apparently without sarcasm, praises this deed as 'in my opinion the finest of

---

[15] 29.27.12–13. See *Barr.* map 32 F1, where the spot is marked as *Pulchri/Apollinis Pr.*, north of Utica. Unhappy Hannibal: p. 214.

[16] 29.34. For the Tower of Agathocles, see App. *Libyan History* 14/56. Masinissa's cavalry force: Livy 29.29.4, and for Masinissa himself, see p. 123.

[17] 29.34.7, cf. 22.49.3. See p. 21.

[18] He wintered at a place which was called after him *castra Cornelia*, just east of Utica.

[19] See Pol. 14.2.13–14; and Livy 30.4.8 for the alleged Carthaginian additions. On the religious aspect of this incident, see p. 229.

Scipio's many fine deeds'. Livy narrates it without closural comment of this or any kind but must have been aware that it made moral nonsense of persistent high-minded Roman accusations against Hannibal of 'Punic treachery'.[20] It came close to an act of perjury.

The casualties on the Carthaginian side were so high that some at Carthage urged the immediate recall of Hannibal from Italy. But it took an even greater disaster to bring this about.[21] Hasdrubal and Syphax had escaped from the conflagration and carnage, and in spring 203 they assembled an army of perhaps 30,000 at the so-called Great Plains.[22] Syphax's adherence to the Carthaginian side is ascribed by both Polybius and Livy to the influence of his beautiful wife Sophoniba, daughter of Hasdrubal (8) son of Gisgo.[23] Battle was finally joined after some days of probing skirmishes. Scipio executed a refinement on the Ilipa formula, by which he had held back his centre. This time he placed his first-line infantry (the *hastati*) in the front to pin the enemy centre and attacked the enemy flanks with the second and third lines (the *principes* and *triarii*).[24] The Carthaginian wings collapsed, but Polybius remarks on the courageous stand of the Celtiberian troops in the Carthaginian centre: they enabled Syphax to return to his own territory and Hasdrubal to Carthage, where the news caused the senate to recall Hannibal at last. For Ennius, 'the Great Plains are a witness'. But to what? The line's remnants are a mere four words of solemn spondees, but Horace paid imitative tribute to it in his 'Metaurus Ode', which appeals to the River

---

[20] Livy 30.3–6; Pol. 14.1–5; for the closural judgment see 14.5.15, πολλῶν καὶ καλῶν διειργασμένων Σκιπίωνι κάλλιστον εἶναί μοι δοκεῖ τοῦτο τοὖργον. Walbank (*HCP* 2: 430) comments mildly that it is 'hard to reconcile with P[ol].'s remarks on ἀπάτη [deceit] in xiii.3', where Pol. remarked (§8) that Romans of his own day declare war openly and 'seldom use trickery', ταῖς ἐνέδραις σπανίως χρῶνται. That rendering of the noun is better than 'ambushes', as in the Loeb tr. and the *Polybios-Lexikon*. Punic treachery or deception, *Punica fraus*, as a recurrent theme in Livy: p. 80.

[21] The Carthaginian authorities were perhaps tolerant of mercenary casualties.

[22] Pol. 14.6.10 (recall urged). For the battle of the Great Plains, μεγάλα πέδια, see Pol. 14.7.9–8.14; Livy 30.8. For the relation between these accounts, Erdkamp 2006: 534: Livy mainly followed Pol. but exaggerated the purely Roman contribution to victory.

[23] See Geus 1994: 200–1. The tragic story of Sophoni(s)ba is elaborated by Livy. But she was not his invention. At Pol. 14.1.4 under 203, Scipio is said to reckon (wrongly) that Syphax must by now have tired of 'the young girl', ἡ παιδίσκη; the brief and casual reference shows she had featured already. At 14.7.6, when before the battle of the Great Plains she successfully urges Syphax not to abandon the Carthaginians, she is again ἡ παιδίσκη, but this time Pol. adds 'who was daughter of Hasdrubal the general and wife of Syphax, *as I have mentioned earlier*', that is, in a lost portion of narrative. Keegan 2021: 128–32 discusses Sophoniba as an example of gendered historiography.

[24] See Lazenby 1978: 210. For these three terms, see above all Pol. 6.21.7–10, part of an invaluable explanation of the organization of the Roman army. See Lazenby's glossary at 268, 272, 274 and Keppie 1998: 33–6; Rosenstein 2023: 64; and see p. 103 for the manipular army. The *triarii* consisted of older men.

Metaurus as personified 'witness', *testis*; so it must have hailed the victory's importance.[25]

Scipio seized Tunis and laid siege to Utica, adapting his warships to carry siege engines, as Marcellus had done at Syracuse. This was a mistake, because it allowed the Carthaginians to seize sixty transport ships and tow them away to Carthage, causing jubilation there.[26]

In further fighting by land against Scipio's lieutenant Laelius and Masinissa, Syphax was taken prisoner. The wretched Sophoniba now turned in desperation to Masinissa instead, who married her in haste when she appealed to him not to let her fall into Roman hands. But Scipio was having none of this and recommended self-restraint on his own model – in effect, 'get rid of her'.[27] The young woman was a casualty of high male politics, effectively forced to take poison when she was no longer regarded as convenient. There is an obvious foreshadowing of Cleopatra in some of this.[28] As for Masinissa, Scipio addressed him as 'king' and gave him, among other magnificent and symbolic gifts, a 'curule chair' and an ivory staff, *eburneus scipio*.[29] The implication is that Roman magistrates and foreign kings were equal, and this in turn has implications for Scipio's own attitudes. But also for those of the senate, which confirmed his donations in full.[30]

## 9.2 Hannibal Leaves Italy

Unfortunately for us, Polybius' narrative of Hannibal's last two years in Italy is lost, including the moment of his departure; but it was in summer 205 that he erected the altar with a bilingual inscription recording his achievements and his forces at the start of his invasion. Livy uses this as the brief closure to his book 28 and implies that it presaged the historical closure to Hannibal's

---

[25] Pol. 14.8.9 and 14. Ennius: Skutsch 1985: 130 (operis incerti fragmenta 8, *testes sunt Campi Magni*) and 754–5; Goldberg and Manuwald 2018b: 288–9, 'Scipio' frag. 2. Horace, *Odes* 4.4.38, cf. p. 194.
[26] Livy 30.9.10–10.21.
[27] 30.12–15; the Latin for 'control yourself' is the terse *uince animum*, 30.14.11. But the 'continence of Scipio', celebrated by Renaissance painters, refers to an early episode in Iberia concerning the fiancée of Allucius: Livy 26.50, cf. p. 57.
[28] And of Dido, see Conway 1922: 12. But he whitewashes Livy's Scipio (Masinissa was 'persuaded by Scipio's grave but gentle appeal to put away the beautiful Carthaginian woman who had captivated him').
[29] 30.15.11. For the *sella curulis*, see p. 113 n. 1. Did Scipio really have such a bulky object handy in north Africa? Perhaps an army carpenter hastily built an approximation of one. The staff: for a possibly relevant coin, see Scullard 1970: 268–9 n. 97. For the word *scipio* as a staff, see p. 49.
[30] Rawson 1991 [1975]: 181–3; quotation from 183; cf. 1989: 433–4. See p. 125. Senate's confirmation: Livy 30.17.7–14.

years in Italy.³¹ But he really lets himself go in the chapter which describes Hannibal's outburst of emotion when the orders came to sail home, comparing him to a man about to go into exile – although Livy acknowledges that he had already prepared a fleet in anticipation of recall and made other practical arrangements.³² Hannibal gnashes his teeth and groans, blaming the gods and men, and especially himself for not attacking Rome straight after Cannae (this detail is not at all plausible). Roman readers would have thoroughly enjoyed all this. We do not know if there was any teeth-gnashing in Polybius. But the story that many Italian troops who had refused to follow him to Africa were 'foully murdered', *foede interfectis*, at the temple of Juno Lacinia should be disbelieved. In any case, Livy does not quite say that Hannibal authorized it but uses the passive past participle.³³ An elaborate story told by Coelius Antipater, transmitted by Cicero, has Hannibal warned in an epiphanic dream by Juno that if he removed a gold column in her temple, he would lose the sight of his remaining eye. So he had a heifer made from the gold he had already taken from its centre when establishing that it really was solid gold and put this object on top of the column. The episode, whether true or not, is thought to have been narrated by Coelius under 205, the year when Hannibal inscribed his record of achievements.³⁴ But it might rather have been part of a complex of sensational 'good riddance' stories told about him on the eve of his quitting Italy, as he did in 203. He received an ill omen just before his landfall in Africa; this might belong to the same group.³⁵

Leaving aside whatever emotions or regrets Hannibal 'must have' felt, we can certainly ask what would have been in his best interests, once he had heard through his spies and from general talk that Scipio intended to cross to Africa. Starved as he was of supplies and reinforcements, he would by this time surely have been better off in Africa, which was elephant country, as Italy was not; and where his presence might be expected to win over local rulers with cavalry forces – not to mention the advantages of proximity to Carthage and its stores and granaries.³⁶ A recent military reverse in

---

³¹ 28.46.16. For the inscription, see p. 12, cf. 16. Hannibal scarcely features in book 29. At 29.36.4–9 (204), the consul Tuditanus was initially defeated by Hannibal in a minor engagement in Bruttium but retrieved the defeat when joined by the proconsul Crassus.
³² 30.20.
³³ 30.20.6. See p. 167. Diodorus (27.9) certainly makes Hannibal directly responsible and says 20,000 men were slaughtered, along with 3,000 horses and innumerable baggage animals. Similarly App. *Hann.* 59/247–9.
³⁴ *FRHist* 15 F32 (from Cicero, *On divination* 1.48), with comm. at 3: 255.   ³⁵ The omen: p. 214.
³⁶ Carthaginian elephant wealth should not however be exaggerated. For the characteristics of the ('Forest') elephants mostly used by the Carthaginians, see p. 26 n. 87.

Bruttium, though small-scale, did not hold out fair prospects of further military successes if he remained in south Italy.[37]

Whereas the arrival of Scipio's flagship had been preceded by a favourable omen, Hannibal – so the story went – was told that his prow was pointing towards a ruined tomb, so he uttered a prayer to avert the ill omen and told the helmsman to sail on. The mix of symmetry and asymmetry between Scipio's and Hannibal's omens is unmistakable; but the parallelism is, as often, a literary device.[38] Hannibal eventually landed his forces at Lepti Minus or Minor (modern Lamta) but soon moved to Hadrumetum (modern Sousse), also coastal, about 100 km south of Carthage, and from there headed overland westwards to Zama.[39]

## 9.3 Futile Diplomacy: Hannibal and Scipio Meet and Talk at Last

The two years before Zama saw much negotiation, not only between Romans and Carthaginians, but between both main parties on the one hand and the African pocket dynasts Syphax and Masinissa on the other. The diplomacy was marked by bad faith and accusations of bad faith. We have seen that despite the recurrent theme of 'Punic treachery', Scipio was guilty of at least one serious and calculated deception, that which led to the burning of the enemy camps not long after his arrival.[40] Which side had most to gain from bringing on a decisive battle? Surely the Roman, so that there must be a suspicion that Scipio did not much care if negotiations broke down, as eventually they did. But the Carthaginian senators were not united in wanting to avoid a final conflict; some of them pinned unrealistic hopes on Hannibal's return or were angered by arrogant Roman language.[41]

After the Carthaginians had been defeated at the Great Plains in 203 and their ally Syphax had been captured in a separate engagement, they sent a deputation of thirty senators to Scipio to sue for peace, blaming Hannibal for the war. Scipio offered these terms: the Carthaginians must remove their armies from Italy and Gaul, withdraw from Iberia and all the islands between Italy and Africa, hand over their navy except for twenty warships,

---

[37] Bruttium: n. 31.
[38] Livy 30.25.12. The Latin for the averting action is *abominatus*. Tränkle 1977: 24 rightly called this a clear parallelism with Scipio, 'ein deutlicher Parallelismus'.
[39] For these places, see *Barr.* map 33 G1 and for Zama map 32 D4; but for the actual battle site (not certainly identified), see n. 57.
[40] See e.g. Livy 30.22.6 for *Punica fraus*. Cf. 30.42.20, 'perfidy of the Carthaginians', *perfidia Carthaginiensium*.
[41] Pol. 15.2.2–4.

supply his army with food, and pay an indemnity (amount uncertain).[42] The Carthaginian senators accepted and were forwarded to Rome after a truce had been agreed. At Rome, the peace terms were undoubtedly ratified.[43] It was at this point that Hannibal finally left Italy, as did Mago in the north of the peninsula.

The Carthaginians now committed two acts of great folly. The first was purely opportunistic: the Roman propraetor Gnaeus Octavius had sailed from Sicily with a fleet of warships and transport ships, but contrary winds blew the now-unescorted transports to the island of Aegimurus in full view of Carthage. The Carthaginian senate ordered Hasdrubal son of Gisgo to gather up the transports together with their abundant supplies. Scipio sent three legates to Carthage in a quinquereme to protest against this violation of the truce. But on its return journey, the quinquereme was attacked by its escort of three Carthaginian triremes (warships) and forced to beach; most of the crew were killed, but the ambassadors were miraculously saved.[44] That, naturally, was the end of the truce.

The final diplomatic effort was a famous one, a personal meeting between Hannibal and Scipio, suggested by Hannibal. There is no good reason to doubt that it occurred. Scipio agreed to it, although he cannot have wanted to postpone the inevitable battle. For one thing, he will certainly have heard that one of the consuls of the new year 202, Tiberius Claudius Nero, had been given Africa as his province with *imperium* equal to Scipio's. In the event, this man took a long time to get a fleet ready, and when he did finally launch it, storms forced him back and his *imperium* lapsed.[45] But that could not have been foreseen in spring 202, and Scipio did not want to share the glory of finishing the war.

Hannibal and Scipio each took an interpreter, partly as a matter of prestige and perhaps also because neither would have been happy to trust the other's interpreter.[46] Both leaders had some linguistic facility and could speak and understand Greek, but they would not have wanted to be misunderstood or misrepresented, so probably each spoke in his own language.

---

[42] Livy 30.16.10–12.
[43] Pol. 15.1.3–4 (retrospective) is preferable to Livy's account, in which the Roman senate refused peace and the Carthaginian envoys were summarily dismissed: 30.23.8.
[44] Pol. 15.1–2 (a fragment, beginning after some of the events reported in Livy 30.24–5; see *HCP* 2: 440–1). Octavius: *DPRR* OCTA0880. Aegimurus: *Barr.* map 32 G2.
[45] Livy 30.27.1–5; 38.7; 39.1–3. This Nero (*DPRR* CLAU1032) was son of the consul of 207, the co-victor at the Metaurus.
[46] Polybius implies only one between them (15.6.3), but Livy more plausibly says *cum singulis interpretibus*, i.e. one each. For interpreters, see pp. 98–9.

So our two parallel lives met at last and spoke; but what was actually said? The detail is beyond retrieval. Both Polybius and Livy rose in their different ways to the rhetorical challenge.[47] Hannibal speaks first in both accounts, presumably because he has asked for the interview and has a final offer to make. Polybius' two speeches are of about the same length as each other, and Livy gives Scipio about the same space as had Polybius. But he makes Hannibal speak for twice as long as Scipio, about ninety lines to Polybius' forty-five: he evidently judged that Hannibal was the suppliant and must be made to elaborate his case eloquently (and perhaps unhistorically, if Plutarch was right to imply that Hannibal was a poor public speaker).[48] Certain strands are already there in Polybius, but Livy characteristically makes more of them. So Polybius' Hannibal comments on Scipio's youth; Livy has this too but takes it further by making the forty-five-year-old Hannibal describe himself as an elderly man, a *senex*: this pose of seniority helps to explain the 'patronizing' tinge which has been detected.[49] Livy expands on earlier history (in particular the responsibility for the first Punic war) to a greater extent than did Polybius. At the level of detail, his Hannibal is made to use a device characteristic of Livian speeches: asyndeton, that is, the absence of such coordinating words as 'and' (*et*, *-que*).[50] For example, Livy's Hannibal tells Scipio 'what I was at Trasimene, at Cannae, that you are today'. By contrast, Polybius' Hannibal avoids the direct comparison with his adversary: 'I am that Hannibal, who after Cannae...'.[51]

But Polybius' presentation of Scipio is in its more subdued way no less artistic than Livy's. Livy opens Scipio's speech with a vocative, which leaves us in no doubt that this is direct speech. Polybius' Scipio opens in indirect speech for the generalities about fortune but slides imperceptibly and Pindarically into direct speech for the reply to Hannibal's specific proposals.[52]

---

[47] Pol. 15.6.6–8, 14; Livy 30.30–1. See Conway 1922: 9–10 and Edlund 1967 for comparative analyses.
[48] *Moralia* 812e, cf. Mossman 2018: 78. Most of the speeches Polybius gives him are pre-battle encouragements.
[49] Pol. 15.7.1; Livy 30.30.10; Hoyos 2006: 710.
[50] The most famous Latin example is used for the dust-jacket of Adams 2021: Caesar's VENI VIDI VICI, 'I came, I saw, I conquered', written on a placard carried at his Pontic triumph in 46 BCE: Suetonius, *Diuus Iulius* 37.3 with Adams 2021: 11 (the words expressive of the rapidity of the campaign); cf. also Butler and Cary 1927: 92.
[51] Livy 30.30.12 with Adams 2021: 666, and 667 (cf. 693) for asyndeton 'bimembre' (with two elements) as seemingly 'disproportionately frequent in [Livy's] speeches, direct and indirect'. The Hannibal example is of the 'prepositional type', here combined with 'at' (*ad*). Contrast Pol. 15.7.3.
[52] Pindar: see Feeney 2021: 2.268. Translators feel it necessary to insert 'he continued' at 15.8.4, but there is no such flag in the Greek. For a similar glide, made explicit by translators, see 3.64.4–5

Hannibal's offer was that Sicily, Sardinia, and Iberia should be Roman possessions, and that the Carthaginians should never go to war against the Romans about them; likewise the other islands between Italy and Africa. Scipio rejected this more or less out of hand in Polybius, but in Livy he left the door open a chink, by suggesting that Hannibal might add an offer of compensation for the captured transport ships and the violation of the Roman envoys; the suggestion was not taken up.

The speakers share, to varying degrees in Polybius and Livy, an awareness of the fickleness of luck or fortune; but both authors make Hannibal draw on the concept much more than Scipio, perhaps a hint that Hannibal is afraid he will lose unless events take an unexpected turn.[53] This encourages us to resume our earlier speculation as to what might have been the consequences of a victory against the odds by Hannibal (and Scipio's death in battle?).[54] After all, Hannibal outnumbered Scipio in infantry and elephants, though not in cavalry. It is not likely that Hannibal would have risked another invasion of Italy, this time from the south: formidable Roman forces were gathered there. So Roman control of Italy would have been safe. But the Roman allies in Italy might at last have forced an exhausted Roman senate to accept a settlement not unfavourable to Carthage. Carthaginian maritime power and African empire would have survived, but Roman power in Iberia would have been impossible to eliminate, even allowing for the usual volatility of the Iberian leaders. The Roman reckoning with Philip V of Macedon would have had to be postponed, perhaps indefinitely, and Antiochus III would have remained untouched for the time being. But Scipio was not the only gifted Roman general remaining: perhaps after a few years Titus Quinctius Flamininus could have taken up the challenge of avenging the hypothetically dead Scipio on African soil. But after that, there will be too many possible forks in the historical road for this 'no-Scipio' direction to be worth pursuing further.

---

(Scipio's father to his troops), but that soon reverts to indirect speech. Contrast the younger Scipio's speech to the Carthaginian envoys after Zama (15.17.3–7), all of which is indirect speech. Shuckburgh turns it all into direct speech; the revised Loeb edition switches to direct speech at §4.

[53] Pol.'s Hannibal refers to τύχη, fortune or luck, three times: 15.6.6 and 8, then 7.1; his Scipio once, 8.3. Livy's Hannibal refers to *fortuna* nine times: 30.30.5, 10, 11, 12, 16, 18, 20, 21, 22, his Scipio once, 31.6. For τύχη in Pol. (but not here), see Walbank 2007. Roman *fortuna* was 'not the blind chance which Tyche so often represented; they [the Romans] contended that she liked to help the valiant': Weinstock 1971: 113 and n. 2.

[54] See pp. 95–6 for the earlier counterfactual exploration (what if Scipio had fought and died at Trasimene?).

## 9.4 The Battle of Zama

A decisive full-scale battle between our two parallel lives was now inevitable.[55] Appian's source even invented Homeric episodes of single combat between Hannibal and Scipio, and between Hannibal and Masinissa.[56]

The battle has been called 'Zama' since Nepos, but of the two main places of that name in the area, neither was the battle site.[57] At most, Zama Regia was the site of Hannibal's camp, but only until he moved to another.[58] The true battle site is strictly unknown, but was most probably in the plain at Draa el Metnan, south of El Kef (ancient Sicca).[59] Sometimes coin hoards help to locate such sites, because soldiers in antiquity often hid their savings and valuables before battles, in the hope of retrieving them later, but were killed.[60] The north African terrain is however not suited to this sort of excavation.

Numbers are hard to ascertain because we do not have Polybius' figures, unless Appian used them, which is far from certain. It seems that Hannibal's army numbered perhaps 36,000 infantry, 4,000 cavalry, and 80 elephants.[61] Scipio had 29,000 infantry and 6,000 cavalry; no elephants.[62] So Hannibal's forces were larger at about 50,000 in total, except in the cavalry arm, and his elephants turned out to be a hindrance to his own side. His first line consisted of 12,000 Celtic and other

---

[55] On the battle see now Taylor 2019b, confident, and full of interest but speculative; also Roselaar 2015: 28–9, quoting Front. *Strat.* 2.3.16. Of older accounts, Scullard 1970: 143–54 and Lazenby 1978: 218–26 are still valuable.

[56] *Libyan history* 45/189 and 46/195–8.

[57] See p. 15 (Nepos). Zama Regia (see *Barr.* map 32 D4) is probably the Zama Maior of the geographer Claudius Ptolemy (4.3.8), modern Sakiet Sidi Youssef. Zama Minor was probably modern Jama. See Lazenby 1978: 218 and map 20. For Naraggara, the site of Scipio's camp according to Livy (30.29.9) and Pol. (15.5.14 as emended from Μάργαρον), see *Barr.* map 32 B4. But there are difficulties about this identification; see again Lazenby 1978: 218.

[58] Pol. 15.5.3 and 6.1.b.

[59] Connolly 1981: 203 (site 'unknown'). See most recently Taylor 2019b: 314–15 and satellite image at fig. 1, without autopsy, and approving the choices of Walbank (*HCP* 2: 447), Lazenby 1978: 218, and Scullard 1974b. Taylor provides no general map of the agreed location within modern Tunisia, for which see rather Scullard 1974b fig. 13 or Lazenby 1978 fig. 20.

[60] See the remarkable chart 10 at Crawford 1978: 162–3, showing the close correlation between numbers of coin hoards discovered and 'periods of war and disturbance'. For the recent identification of the site of Baecula from finds of weapons and coins, see p. 123.

[61] Taylor 2019b: 317 with note c, and 2020a: 61, both relying on App. *Libyan history* 40/168–70 (50,000 total) and 41/177 (4,000 cavalry, but Taylor 2019b: 319 thinks this too low, so that Hannibal had only a 'modest but not insurmountable' disadvantage in cavalry. I am not convinced, given the frailty of the literary evidence). The total may not be far wrong, but it relies on an ancient author who later in the same context wants us to believe that the principals fought duels (Taylor acknowledges this difficulty). Perhaps Appian switched sources? On the elephants, see Charles and Rhodan 2007.

[62] Lazenby 1978: 220–1; Seibert 1993a: 467 n. 30; Taylor 2019b: 316.

mercenaries, his second of local Libyan and Carthaginian levies, and his third and best of the men he had brought from Italy. His Numidian cavalry were on the left and his Carthaginian on the right.[63] He kept his most experienced men, the veterans from the Italian period, in reserve, but that in the event was a mistake.[64]

The uncertainty about the battle site, in contrast to Trasimene, Cannae, or Baecula, means it is not possible to reconstruct the battle movements with assurance. We rely on Polybius and modern conjecture. The latest theory, in a nutshell, holds that Hannibal's strategy was to extend his third infantry line, so luring Scipio into a trap. But this failed because Scipio extended his own line and was able to hold out until his cavalry could envelop Hannibal's forces.[65]

Now for the detail. Hannibal placed his huge and no doubt terrifying total of eighty elephants in front and deployed his human forces in three lines, of which the third consisted of the Carthaginian veterans who had been with him in Italy.[66] Scipio commanded the Roman and allied centre; Masinissa and his Numidian cavalry were on the right, Laelius and the Italian cavalry on the left. With a view to neutralizing the enemy's elephants, Scipio altered his usual formation of maniples by positioning the *principes* immediately behind the *hastati*, so creating corridors through which the elephants could pass ineffectively.[67] In fact, the sound of the trumpets and bugles terrified the creatures, who turned round and charged the Numidians on their own side or escaped chaotically to the right.[68] Masinissa and Laelius each attacked the Numidian cavalry opposite them.

The infantry forces now closed in combat, 'with neither spears nor swords' (Polybius), an initially puzzling expression but clarified by Livy's 'pushing with shoulders and shields'.[69] Scipio now merged his *triarii* and *principes* so as

---

[63] For all this, see Pol. 15.11.1–4. Livy (30.33.5, cf. 30.26.3 and 31.1.10) mentions a Macedonian legion, not in Polybius. This is regarded as Roman patriotic invention (e.g. by Lazenby 1978: 222; Erdkamp 2006: 537–8; Taylor 2019b: 312) and may be an exaggeration. But it is possible that Philip did send mercenaries to help Carthage at this period: Harris 1979: 216 n. 2.

[64] Pol. 15.12.7 with Lazenby 1978: 224–5.

[65] Taylor 2019b: 315 fig. 2 for his computer-generated reconstruction of battle lines.

[66] Pol. 15.11.1–3. With the third line as a 'bulwark against cavalry encirclement', Taylor 2019b: 317–18 compares, with due reservations, Alexander's deployment at Gaugamela: Arr. *Anab.* 3.12.1. But Taylor sees Hannibal's arrangement as more than defensive, in fact as a trap.

[67] Taylor 2019b: 321.

[68] Pol. 15.9.7–8 and 15.12.2–4. Vegetius 3.24.13 seems to refer to Scipio's tactic against the elephants at Zama. See Milner 1996: 114 n. 3 (and xviii n. 2).

[69] Pol. 15.13.1, where the text has been altered to 'not with spears but with swords', (surprisingly accepted in the Loeb edition revised by Walbank and Habicht) but was defended by Walbank earlier (*HCP* 2: 459), and see now Taylor 2014: 308 and 2019b: 322. Livy 30.34.3, *ala deinde et*

to outflank Hannibal's third line.[70] The second Carthaginian line tried to fall back onto the third, which refused to admit them. The fighting between the two most experienced contingents on each side was long, bloody, and desperate.[71] But the outcome was decided by the return of Laelius and Masinissa 'providentially at the right moment'.[72] The battle was over, as was Hannibal's military career as a Carthaginian general; with a few other cavalrymen, he rode at top speed to Hadrumetum. The Carthaginian losses were reported to be a staggering 20,000 dead and another 20,000 captured. Roman losses were supposedly 1,500.[73]

## 9.5 After Zama

The terms for a second truce now offered or rather dictated were naturally harsher, but the Carthaginians were still allowed to retain control of the cities of Libya they possessed before the war, 'up to the Phoenician trenches', and to be autonomous and ungarrisoned. But they must pay an enormous indemnity (10,000 talents, payable over fifty years) and the number of ships allowed was reduced from twenty to ten. They could make no war without Roman permission and must restore to Masinissa everything he or his ancestors had controlled – a notably wide and vague clause, bound to lead to friction. Meanwhile, they must feed the Roman army for three months until a decision arrived from Rome about a (final) treaty.[74]

Hannibal must have lost no time moving to Carthage from Hadrumetum, because a memorable story has him manhandling a senator, Gisgo (7), who tried to speak against acceptance of these terms, pulling him off the platform. He apologized, reminding them that he had left Carthage at the age of nine and was out of touch with the expected civilities. On his advice, the terms were accepted.[75]

---

*umbonibus pulsantes*. For *ala* as 'shoulder', see Butler and Scullard 1953: 125, cf. Taylor 2019b: 323 n. 57. *OLD ala* (2) is deficient.

[70] Taylor 2019b: 325–6, cf. 327.
[71] Pol. 15.13.7 says that when the *hastati*, the Roman first line, got into trouble, the officers, ἡγεμόνες, of the second line, the *principes*, ἐπέστησαν τὰς αὐτῶν τάξεις. The verb is difficult but probably means that the *principes* stood firm, not that they helped the *hastati*. See Scullard 1970: 152–3 and Taylor 2019b: 313.
[72] Pol. 15.14.7, with HCP 2: 463, but the religious tinge of δαιμονίως ('divinely') should not be eliminated too completely, cf. *Polybios-Lexikon* 1.2: col. 409.
[73] Pol. 15.14–15. Casualties: Pol. 15.14.9; Livy 30.35.3; Taylor 2020a: 63.
[74] Pol. 15.18; Livy 30.37.2–6. For the limitation about the Phoenician trenches, see App. *Libyan history* 54/235. Their location is unknown: HCP 2: 466–7; Huss 1985: 421–2 n. 151.
[75] Livy 30.37.7–10; Pol. 15.19. See further p. 268. Polybius' surviving text here ceases, for the time being, to cover Roman relations with Carthage, except for a chapter describing Scipio's triumph for Zama and the death in prison of Syphax, who was led in the triumph (16.23). From now on, we

An embassy went to Rome, where one of the consuls for the new year 201, Gnaeus Cornelius Lentulus, tried to continue the war and was even given command of the fleet, not that anything came of this.[76] But although there were evidently some in the senate who wanted harsher terms than Scipio's, his command was extended, and he was given power to make peace as seemed good to himself and the ten commissioners (*legati*) who would accompany him. There was weeping at Carthage when the first instalment of the indemnity had to be found, but Hannibal is said to have smiled and was rebuked for this. He retorted that the time for tears was when they had lost their weapons, when their ships had been burned, and when they were forbidden foreign wars, rather than now, when tribute had to be paid out of their own private pockets. Meanwhile Scipio added Cirta, Syphax's former capital, to Masinissa's paternal kingdom.[77] He then set sail for Lilybaeum in western Sicily and from there proceeded to Rome.

---

mostly rely on Livy's version of Polybius. The long-lived Masinissa reappears at Pol. 31.21 (late 160s) for one episode in the long series of his predictable territorial disputes with Carthage. After that, Polybius book 36 begins the narrative of the third Punic war (events of 150–46 BCE).

[76] We have met this man before, at and after Cannae, p. 104.   [77] For all this, see 30.40–4.

CHAPTER 10

# The Religion of Hannibal and Scipio

## 10.1 Introduction: Rituals, Divination, Sacrifice, Oaths

What survives of Livy is our main literary source for Republican Roman religion; what survives of Polybius tells us far less.[1] Much of what we think we know about Hannibal's religion also goes back to Livy.[2] Roman tradition made out that Scipio was exceptionally pious (like his mother Pomponia) and had a specially close relationship with Jupiter: it was said that when he went to the Capitol to sit and commune with the god, the dogs never barked or attacked him. From Livy's choice of verb for sitting, it has been suggested that he prayed sitting down rather than standing up with arms raised, the usual posture: a sign of familiarity with the god?[3] But Hannibal was usually represented as the opposite, an impious perjurer.[4] Neither extreme tradition is convincing.[5] As for Hannibal, there are many counter-examples from Livy's own text – and from other authors, such as Pliny the Elder's report that Hannibal spared the temple of Artemis (Punic

---

[1] On Polybius book 6, see n. 50.
[2] See Levene 1993; Briscoe and Hornblower 2020: 58–74, esp. 59 n. 148.
[3] For Pomponia, see p. 42. Aulus Gellius 6.1.6; Aurelius Victor, *On illustrious men* 49.2. Cf. Livy 26.19.5, but without the dogs; Pol. 10.5.5 (he communed with the gods not only at night, i.e. in dreams, but also in the day) with *HCP* 2: 200–1. Rüpke 2007a: 13 calls Scipio an 'obvious example of individual religiosity at Rome' and argues for the unusual praying posture, though this is a lot to extract from the verb *consideret* (or *sedisset*: Aurelius Victor). Rüpke 2007a: 245 compares Scipio's relation with Jupiter as personal protective deity to Sulla's with Fortuna or Pompey's and Caesar's with Venus. These are not very precise analogies and do not take account of Scipio's own reported stress on the favour of Neptune/Poseidon.
[4] Livy 21.4.9, an arresting series of asyndeta (no coordinating 'ands', p. 216): 'no truthfulness, no integrity, no fear of the gods, no respect for oaths, no religious scruples': *nihil ueri, nihil sancti, nullus deum metus, nullum ius iurandum, nulla religio*. Polybius (9.26.7) imputed impiety to Hannibal because he broke treaties with (unspecified) Italian states by moving their populations: pp. 225 and 242.
[5] For Hannibal's religion, see esp. Huss 1986; cf. also Geus 1994: 83. Among conventional, Greek-sounding, religious expressions put into Hannibal's mouth, cf. e.g. Plut. *Marc.* 30.4 'nothing can happen against the will of the god'.

Tanit) at Saguntum from piety, *religione inductus*. On the other hand, Statius says Hannibal 'polluted the houses and temples of Saguntum'. If the second half of this reflects an independent tradition – this is very doubtful – it is not incompatible with sparing a single temple, like Alexander, who was said to have spared the house of Pindar at the destruction of Thebes in 335.[6] The same passage of Statius says that savage and perjured Hannibal owned a statuette of Hercules 'at the table' by the great sculptor Lysippus, and that it was owned by Alexander before him and Sulla after him.[7] If true, this would be unexpected evidence for Hannibal's connoisseurship in the arts, but the poem as a whole does not inspire confidence.[8] Otherwise the statue might have found a niche in Chapter 13, as illustrating Hannibal's relationship with the Greek world.

Both Hannibal and Scipio certainly attracted 'legends' of a religious sort. The Scipionic legend is famous and has been much studied, but in a way there was a Hannibalic legend too. Both sets of legends grew cumulatively over time and are therefore hard to disentangle and evaluate.[9]

It is surprising that Scipio is not attested as having made a battlefield vow of a temple or games before Zama, to be fulfilled if he won.[10] This might have been recorded only at the time of its fulfilment, like his games held in 205, which he had vowed during the Iberian mutiny. Polybius did not record this sort of thing anyway, but Livy's narratives of the Zama campaigns, and of the 190s, are detailed and unbroken. It is nevertheless possible that our information is incomplete.

Does this apparent omission mean Scipio was irreligious? Clearly not, in view of his earlier vow and its fulfilment. Nor did he neglect expected rituals of other sorts: here is one satisfyingly well-documented example. In 204, as he set out from Sicily for Africa, he ordered silence through a herald, prayed

---

[6] *NH* 16.216 with p. 82, contrast Statius, *Silvae* 4.6.83–4. Arr. *Anab*. 1.9.10.

[7] *Silvae* 4.6.75–8, cf. 105–9, calling Hannibal a 'barbarian' and other rude words (cf. p. 409); Robertson 1975: 473 and 704 n. 71.

[8] Unexpected but not inconceivable. The Austrian field marshal Prinz Eugen (Prince Eugene) wrote to his agent telling him to buy a certain painting. He gave his address, superbly, as 'besieging Belgrade'. I owe my knowledge of this to the late Jasper Griffin.

[9] See above all Walbank 1985: 120–37 for Scipio, Huss 1986 for Hannibal. Kubler 2018, a full-length study of cultural memories of the second Punic war (but with no index of any sort), does not deal with either legend as such, but concentrates on just three episodes: (1) Hannibal's crossing of the Alps, (2) Saguntum and the start of the war, and (3) Trasimene. On her treatment of (1), which does bear on the Hannibal legend because of the Heracles theme, see n. 234.

[10] For battlefield vows, see Appendix 8.2. Livy 31.49.4 reports under 200 the celebration of games vowed by Scipio 'as consul in Africa' i.e. in 205. This is problematic because he was no longer consul when he set foot in Africa in 204. Whatever the solution, this was not a battlefield vow.

elaborately for a safe return – and for much plunder – to the gods and goddesses of sea and land, sacrificed an animal 'in the traditional way', *uti mos est*, and threw its entrails into the sea. Then he gave the signal for departure, by sounding a trumpet.[11] Appian further specifies that his sacrifices were to Zeus and Poseidon, Roman Jupiter and Neptune, and this detail is sound.[12] Livy's otherwise fuller description is reminiscent, in many of its details, of an equally famous departure by sea, that of the Athenians to – rather than from – Sicily, in 415 BCE, except that those Greeks made libations (liquid sacrifices) of wine; and that particular expedition ended in disaster. This need not indicate much if any direct literary imitation of Thucydides: these were standard rituals, performed by Pindar's Jason on the stern of the *Argo*.[13] And not only by Greeks but also by Romans, in history and myth. Livy's very Roman expression *uti mos est* should be taken seriously, although we must reckon with some Greek influence: the watery god Neptune took on some attributes of the Greek Poseidon and so, like him, became associated with sea journeys.[14] Appian, describing the prelude to Octavian's unsuccessful sea battle against Sextus Pompeius in 36 BCE, says that Octavian 'offered sacrifices and poured libations into the sea from his flagship to the gentle winds, Neptune of Safety and to the waveless sea'.[15] Virgil's Anchises, after Palinurus has sounded a 'clear signal' (obviously a trumpet call), stands on the prow, fills a bowl with wine, and calls on 'the gods of the sea and the land and the weather' to grant an easy passage: it has been noted that this invocation closely resembles Scipio's in 204 BCE. Two books later, Anchises' son Aeneas is, like Scipio, about to set sail from western Sicily: he stands, garlanded with olive, on the ship's prow, pours wine into the sea, and throws sacrificial entrails after it.[16]

---

[11] Livy 29.27.1–5, probably not from Polybius, whose text on Scipio and Hannibal is missing between 11.33, Scipio's triumphant return from Iberia in 206, and 14.1, when he is already in Africa. But although Polybius is surely one of the 'Greek and Latin authors' of Livy 29.27.13, the religious departure narrative at §§1–5 is not at all in his manner. For this reason, Tränkle 1977: 22–4 was right to deny its Polybian origin. On the Livy passage, cf. Smith 1993: 9. On the striking asyndeton at 29.27.2 (the repeated *gero*), see Adams 2021: 127. Erskine 2010: 43 notes the stress on plunder.

[12] App. *Libyan history* 13/50; Wissowa 1912: 227–8 n. 3, citing the dedications *ILS* 3934 (to 'Jupiter the storm-god', *Iovis Tempestati*) and 3934a (to 'Neptune', *Neptuno*). Scipio had claimed Neptune's help at New Carthage: p. 120.

[13] Th. 6.32.1 with *CT*: 3.393–4, listing other such Greek passages attesting libations at the start of an enterprise, including Pindar, *Pythian* 4.193–201. Cf. Burkert 1979: 41: 'libation, ceremoniously pouring out liquids, plays an overwhelming role throughout Near Eastern and Mediterranean religion'.

[14] See *OCD*⁴ 'Neptunus' (J. Sch[eid]).

[15] App. *Civil War* 5.98/406; for this episode, see Hadas 1930: 125.

[16] Anchises: Virgil, *Aen.* 3.519, 527–9; Williams 1962: 166 rightly compares Scipio at Livy 29.27.1 for 'the form of the prayer'. It is a kind of 'merism', for which concept see n. 22; Aeneas: *Aen.* 5.774–6.

## Introduction

Suetonius in his *Life* of Caesar recorded an oracle, allegedly exploited by Scipio and perhaps invented in or after the Hannibalic war, according to which the Scipios were destined to be 'fortunate and invincible in Africa'. Caesar was sufficiently bothered by this to ensure that he had a man called Scipio Salvito on his staff; that *cognomen* is derived from the root for 'safe'.[17]

In the early phases of the war, Hannibal is certainly described as performing solemn ritual acts which are not dissimilar to those familiar from Greek religion.[18] A vividly reported example is his violent and personally executed sacrifice of a lamb to reinforce his oath to reward his troops: he invited the gods to kill him just as he killed the lamb by smashing its head with a stone.[19] This attitude continued until his last years in Italy; his treatment of the sanctuary of Juno Lacinia was more than respectful: his record of achievements was inscribed there, and stories that he ordered a massacre inside the sacred precinct should be disbelieved.[20] But no libations are mentioned at his departure for Carthage in 203.[21] Instead, as he watched Italy recede from the ship, he is alleged to have accused gods and men and especially himself. But this whole passage about Hannibal's extreme parting emotions is part of a hostile narrative cluster, and the reference to gods and men is a 'merism', here a way of indicating the totality of intelligent beings.[22] On the other hand, when in 218 he had

---

[17] Suet. *Caesar (diuus Iulius)* 59. *DPRR* CORN3783 prefers the spelling Salvitto, as at Pliny *NH* 7.54 (cf. Butler and Cary 1927: 124). See Weinstock 1971: 97–8, also discussing a mysterious but possibly related coin of Scipio bearing a personification of Africa, and noting that the oracle was transferred to Aemilianus in turn (147 BCE).

[18] For Bonnet 2006 (how Greek was Carthaginian religion?), see p. 290. The Punic epigraphic evidence is not very informative. For Hannibal's behaviour and attitudes, we rely entirely on non-Carthaginian writers, so that there are problems of imported cultural assumptions. For Hamilcar (1) sacrificing at Himera, see p. 228.

[19] Livy 21.45.8 with Huss 1986: 224. In Roman religion, at least, it was not usual for a magistrate to strike the killing blow in person, but the violence was not all that exceptional; see Aldrete 2014, mostly about large bovines, and not recommended for the queasy reader. See esp. Aldrete 2014: 29: magistrates did not do the actual 'dirty work'. For Hannibal's advice after Zama to his fellow-citizens at Carthage to sacrifice and pray for Roman ratification of the treaty, see Pol. 15.19.7 with Huss 1986: 225.

[20] See p. 167, 213. There are other such tendentious stories: Huss 1986: 227 nn. 32 and esp. 33, the story of the plundering of the temple in the grove of Feronia near Capena. It is ambiguous: the men restored some of the booty from piety, *religione inducti*: Livy 26.11.8–10. The Latin phrase is interestingly identical to Pliny's about Saguntum, n. 6.

[21] Years after the end of the war, in 195 during his flight by sea from Carthage to eastern exile, Hannibal ordered a sacrifice at the harbour of Cercina island (Livy 33.48.4). This and the ensuing banquet look like a pre-departure ritual but are also a ploy to enable him to sail away undetected while the other diners were drunk: p. 300.

[22] Livy 30.20.7; West 2007: 100; Adams 2021: 55 (merisms). For the unhappy departure, see p. 213–4.

set out from Gades in southern Iberia, he fulfilled his vows to Hercules (Punic Melqart) and bound himself by new ones if his affairs should prosper.[23] We do not hear of him making pre-battle vows before Cannae or Zama, his two great set-piece battles, but the same is true of his Roman opponents. Hannibal's most famous vow – never to be a friend of the Roman people – did not concern a single battle but was a pledge for a lifetime. It was allegedly made at the age of nine, and the initiative was naturally not his but his father Hamilcar's, though the boy claimed much later in life to remember it.

It is a literary and perhaps historically grounded parallel between Hannibal and Scipio that one of the earliest stories attached to the young Scipio, as also to the young Hannibal, is about a famous vow.[24] After Cannae, Scipio as a military tribune rallied survivors of the battle, held a sword over their heads, swore an oath by Jupiter Optimus Maximus not to desert the *res publica* of the Roman people, and made them swear the same oath.[25]

Solemn oaths and lists of gods introduce Hannibal's treaty with Philip V in 215.[26] The text as given by Polybius begins:

> In the presence of Zeus, Hera, and Apollo: in the presence of the genius of Carthage, of Heracles, and Iolaus: in the presence of Ares, Triton, and Poseidon; in the presence of the gods who battle for us, and of the Sun, Moon, and Earth; in the presence of Rivers, Lakes, and Waters: in the presence of all the gods who possess Carthage: in the presence of all the gods who possess Macedonia and the rest of Greece: in the presence of all the gods of the army who preside over this oath.[27]

The list is less valuable as an indication of Hannibal's own religious outlook than might have been hoped, despite the inclusion of 'Heracles', with whom he is supposed to have had a special relationship. The individual deities are, it is thought, not personal to Hannibal but are the official gods of Carthage. Nor are the identifications straightforwardly one to one: Punic deities might be identified with or assimilated to more than one Greek god.[28] Conversely, there is – for example – more than one Punic

---

[23] Livy 21.21.9.
[24] It is not quite the earliest story of all, which had him save his father at the battle at the Ticinus river: p. 59 on Polybius 10.3 and Livy 21.46.7–8. Not to mention the legend of his supernatural conception, to be discussed later, pp. 235–6.
[25] Livy 22.53. See p. 106.   [26] For the historical context and the full text, see Chapter 5.2.
[27] Pol. 7.9.2–3, Loeb tr. On the detail, see *HCP* 2: 46–52 and Huss 1986: 228–30.
[28] Barré 1983: 13.

## Introduction

candidate for identification with Poseidon, Roman Neptune.[29] But the identification of Melqart with Greek Herakles, Roman Hercules, is considered certain.[30]

Pre-battle sacrifice for divinatory purposes was a feature of Classical Greek religion, less so of Hellenistic.[31] We do not hear that either Hannibal or Scipio, both of whom were well acquainted with Greek practices and history, were regularly accompanied on campaign by favourite seers (Greek *manteis*) whose names we know, like the individuals attached to the Classical Athenian generals Tolmides and Nicias, or later Alexander. At the end of the second century BCE, the Roman general Marius took round with him a female Syrian seer called Martha and kept her in grand style: she was carried about in a litter, wearing a purple robe with garlanded spear, and she instructed him what sacrifices to make. Marius' wife had sent her along to her husband after Martha had usefully predicted the winners at a gladiatorial contest. A few decades later, Sertorius' pet white doe in Iberia, whose name has not come down to us if she had one, possessed divinatory powers, or so he claimed.[32] But no such gifted creature, and no such literally and figuratively colourful Martha figure, was to be found in the retinue of Hannibal or Scipio. Perhaps this silence is merely part of a general and unexplained decline in literary mentions of divinatory sacrifice before battles. But it has been suggested that named diviners were a feature of the early and late, but not the middle, Roman Republic; and that the return of such individuals attached to great men was 'part of the reorientation towards the dynasts'.[33]

As for Hannibal, Cassius Dio says that Hannibal was 'versed in much Punic and Greek learning, and understood divination by [inspection of] entrails'.[34] So it seems he was his own diviner, like his distant predecessor Hamilcar (1), who (allegedly) stayed in camp during the whole of the battle

---

[29] Barré 1983: 80–1.
[30] Barré 1983: 64. For the ambiguous evidence of coinage, see Yarrow 2013: 356–7, cited at p. 289.
[31] Parker 2000: 301–4 (2023: 247–51).
[32] Flower 2008: 46 and n. 66 (Tolmides and Theaenetus); 116 (Nicias and Stilbides); 91 (Alexander and Aristander). Marius and Martha: Plut. *Mar.* 17.2–5, cf. 42.8 on his respect for prophecy, μαντική; see also Front. *Strat.* 1.11.12, and Valgiglio 1956: 85–7. The doe: Plut. *Sert.* 11.2–8 with Konrad 1994: 123–4, citing other evidence, and tracing the story to Sallust. The sacred Roman chickens, who were supposed to eat greedily when the auspices were taken (if they did not, it was a bad omen), had a keeper, but he was hardly an intimate of the commander. For the ritual, the *tripudium*. see Briscoe and Hornblower 2020: 69–70 and 279, n. on Livy 22.42.8: before Cannae.
[33] North 1990: 69 and n. 49, citing Herennius Siculus, friend of Gaius Gracchus, and Caesar's Spurinna.
[34] Cassius Dio 13 frag. 54.3 with Huss 1986: 226, who also cites a story that when Prusias proposed to ignore Hannibal's advice to attack Eumenes II of Pergamum, because the entrails were unfavourable (for this war, see p. 376 and n. 38), Hannibal asked 'are you going to prefer a piece of animal flesh to a seasoned commander?': Val. Max. 3.7 ext. 6 and Cic. *On divination* 2.52 (with Stocks 2014: 22 and

of Himera (480), sacrificing for omens, and then received at Carthage what looks like Greek posthumous hero cult of a kind foreign to Carthaginian religion.[35] Whatever the truth of that story, divination was certainly part of Carthaginian religion at an earlier time than Hannibal. The Greek translation of the treatise narrating Hanno (3)'s sixth-century BCE naval expedition along the west coast of Africa mentions seers, *manteis*, who told Hanno and his crew to leave a certain island when they heard alarming sounds of flutes and cymbals (§12). Hannibal himself sacrificed at Avernus in Campania. This was the probable site of an ancient oracle of the dead, and it is possible that Hannibal made a consultation as well as a sacrifice.[36]

A more sinister type of sacrifice was notoriously attributed in antiquity to the Carthaginians: human sacrifice, especially of children, to Baal Hammon, whom the Romans identified with Jupiter and Greeks with Kronos. In modern times, allegations about this practice have been treated with scepticism as a mere racist slur.[37] But the current interpretation of the literary and archaeological evidence has returned to acceptance of the ancient view.[38] If Hannibal was believed to have engaged in human sacrifice at any stage of his career, the mostly pro-Roman literary sources would without doubt have pounced on it, but none of them does. By contrast, there was well-attested human sacrifice at Rome in both 228, the consulship of Hannibal's future enemy Fabius Maximus the Delayer, and

---

30–1); see also Plut. *On exile* 66 = *Mor.* 606c, with Huss 1986: 226 and n. 30. But in Plutarch, Hannibal says it to Antiochus, so it is unsafe to use it about Prusias specifically: p. 35. (Hannibal is the agent both times, so it is not quite a 'roving anecdote', a story told about more than one agent.) A linguistically difficult line of Ennius (374 Sk.) is thought to be a remark by Hannibal to Antiochus (it is from book XIII) and seems to imply that seers do not speak the truth about their own lives. See Skutsch 1985: 540. All this is no more evidence of general irreligiosity than Hector's 'One omen is best, to fight for one's country' (*Iliad* 12.243). 'The general should be master not servant of his seer': Plato *Laches* 199A. For the dubious story that Hannibal consulted the oracle of Ammon in Libya and received a teasing response about the location of his grave, see p. 382.

[35] Hdt. 7.167.2, all of which is accepted by Picard 1994: 366. The whole story, which has Hamilcar throwing himself on a flaming pyre and then receiving cult at Carthage and other Phoenician places, is hard to believe. It looks too Greek. As for the cult, it is an old suggestion (Stein 1889: 161; Macan 1908: 238; Huss 1985: 95 n. 21) that on this point Herodotus confused Hamilcar, as a theophoric name 'servant of Melqart' with Melqart. That is ingenious but a long shot. Since Hamilcar was half-Greek, it is tempting to think the cult might really have been Greek, for an enemy treated as hero, a familiar Greek category. But Herodotus is explicit that the cult was Carthaginian. See further p. 428.

[36] For Hanno's voyage, see p. 61. Avernus: Livy 24.12.4 and 13.6, treating the sacrifice as a pretext, but conceding that Hannibal did indeed perform the sacrifice 'for which he had come'. Consultation (?): see Hornblower 2018: 110–11.

[37] As Bonnet 2006: 372 puts it, this implies a Manichean contrast between good Greeks (or Romans) and cruel Carthaginians. But 'good' Romans sacrificed human beings.

[38] Diod. 20.14.4–5; Tertullian, *Apologeticus* 9.3; Huss 1985: 535–40 (balanced); Rives 1994 (on Tertullian); Fantar 2007: 75–7 (dismissive). Quinn 2018: 91–106, esp. 91–105 (accepting). As at Rome, the practice was intermittent and a response to crises, rather than regular.

then again after Hannibal had defeated the Romans at Cannae in 216, a year when again Fabius was prominent, succeeding the deceased consul Aemilius Paullus as a *pontifex*.[39]

Burial of the dead was one of the most serious rituals known to ancient religions. Carthaginian religion was no exception. This form of piety does not quite entail but is often accompanied by a belief in an afterlife, and there is archaeological evidence for afterlife beliefs at Carthage.[40] At a grave site in the western part of Carthaginian territory (Kef-el-Blida), a painting depicts two ladders like Jacob's ladder in the Hebrew Bible. On one of them, a man is climbing up to heaven, while the other ladder has been left behind by a dead man. Also depicted is what seems to be a 'divine conductor of souls', like the Greek Hermes; such figures are also found on lead fragments in Carthaginian graves.[41] And in a tomb near Kerkouane (Cap Bon), a fresco depicts the journey of the soul.[42]

As for Hannibal in particular, a curious speech ascribed to him by Polyaenus affirms belief in the reincarnation of valiant individuals.[43] Hannibal gave or tried to give proper burial rites to the corpses of defeated enemy commanders at Trasimene and other battles, and we noted the contrast with the consul Nero's ugly treatment of Hasdrubal's head after the battle of the Metaurus.[44] But no such flagrant and impious disrespect is ever attributed to Scipio.

But on one important occasion, soon after his arrival in Africa, Scipio does seem to have been guilty of taking opportunistic but planned military action during a truce, close to but not quite actual perjury in the religious sense of a breach of an oath made to the gods, of the kind which guaranteed a formal and permanent peace treaty. The burning of the camps of Hasdrubal and Syphax, which was made possible by spying under the pretence of Roman diplomatic visits, clearly took place during a truce, *indutiae*.[45] Such

---

[39] *MRR* I: 252; Rüpke 2008: 81 and 676 no. 1595. See p. 72.

[40] 'Belief' is a disputed term among experts in cognitive religion. Its use here does not imply access to the minds of Hannibal or any other Carthaginian. It is merely a handy word for what may reasonably be inferred from recorded behaviour and utterances.

[41] B ʿl Smm, θεὸς ψυχοπομπός; see Huss 1986: 231–2. For this depiction of the journey of the soul, see also Fantar 2007: 85.

[42] *Barr.* map 32 H3; again, Fantar 2007: 85.

[43] Polyaenus 6.38.2 (=*Excerpts of Polyaenus* 14.20): 'Hannibal convinced his men that those who died courageously in war returned to life after a short period. Moreover, he once found a man resembling a brave soldier who had died bravely, γενναίως, and urged him to say that he was the one who had died earlier' (tr. Krentz and Wheeler 1994: 603–5 and 893, adapted).

[44] See pp. 94 and 411 for the contrast between Hannibal and Nero.

[45] See p. 210 for this episode. For *indutiae*, see Täubler 1913: 29–44 (with 42 n. 2 for Pol. 14.2.13). Oakley 2005a: 538–9 (Livy 9.41.6n.).

temporary cessations of hostilities were not solemnized religiously as far as we can see; but Polybius says that Scipio sent the embassy 'so as not to appear to *paraspondein*', here 'to break faith'.[46] The verb is a powerful one, even if not used technically: it derives from σπονδαί, the 'libations' poured to the gods to seal a treaty. Livy's source evidently felt uncomfortable with this double-dealing by Scipio, so it claimed, with no Polybian authority, that the Carthaginians had made extra unreasonable demands which justified his treating the truce as at an end.

Scipio's triumph over Hannibal in 201 was a ritual procession of thanksgiving with no obvious parallel in Carthaginian life.[47] The gods so thanked by victorious generals were Jupiter Optimus Maximus and Liber-Triumpus (Dionysus Thriambos).

## 10.2 Priesthoods

Roman priesthoods were usually held for life.[48] Most were compatible with political and military careers, although tenure of some of them imposed restrictions. Scipio was a Salian priest in 190 – a 'dancing' priest of Mars – as Polybius tells us under that year, which was actually long after the year in which he is thought to have been elected. In that year, Scipio was (as we shall see shortly) temporarily paralysed by the restrictions, which lasted for the thirty days of the sacrifices.[49] The twelve Salians performed a singing and dancing ritual in the city of Rome in March and October, the start and end of the traditional campaigning season. (Their name derives from *salire*, to leap or dance.) For their duties, Polybius refers back to his earlier discussion in what must have been part of the mainly lost opening of book 6 and explains or repeats that they performed some of the principal sacrifices and could not move their residence during the thirty days of the sacrifices.[50] This meant that in 190 Scipio had to wait before joining his brother Lucius the consul for the battle of Magnesia against Antiochus III; it has been suggested that the delay was convenient for Scipio because it gave Antiochus time

---

[46] Pol. 14.2.13. *Polybios-Lexikon* 2.1 παρασπονδέω (I): col. 116. Pol. also uses it about Hannibal and Italian states at 9.6.7; cf. pp. 153, 242, 410.

[47] See further p. 245.

[48] See generally Rüpke 2008: 7–14; the Salian priesthood was an exception, see p. 14 n. 25.

[49] Pol. 21.13.10–14; more briefly Livy 37.33.7. Date of election, perhaps as early as 215 or 216: p. 14, citing Rüpke 2008. Their functions: Scullard 1981: 30, 85–6, and 195; cf. Beard 1990: 21 (table).

[50] His book 6 therefore said more about Roman religion than appears from the surviving text. The Teubner ed. of book 6 (BW, not followed by the Loeb ed.) actually prints part of the book 23 passage about the Salii twice, the first time as 6.1.9.

for second thoughts.⁵¹ But even if so, that does not mean that his obedience to the obligation to delay was a cynical fiction.

So much for the hard evidence, but it has recently been held that in Livy's presentation, Scipio had, as early as 211, begun to act as if invested with worryingly usurped priestly authority. It is claimed that by this stage 'Scipio is in danger of becoming an oracle in his own right', and that his 'pretensions to divine inspiration represented a serious threat to the established structure of the republican response to divine issues'.⁵² The interesting argument rests on the second of two 'either/or' prongs (*siue ... siue*) of Livy's speculative analysis of Scipio's claim to be guided by dreams or other divine advice. This, says Livy, was either, *siue*, from genuine *superstitio* (the first prong); or else, *siue* again, it was intended to ensure that his orders and plans would be carried out with no delay, 'just as if they had been sent as oracular pronouncements', *uelut sorte oraculi missa*. If the surprisingly cynical second prong, the second *siue*, gives Livy's own preferred view (this is likely but not certain from his habits elsewhere), that tells us something of Livy's own opinions, to be sure.⁵³ It is another matter whether Scipio's behaviour was regarded by contemporaries as any sort of danger or threat. Nor, if Livy's language is to be pressed this closely, should *uelut* be forgotten: real Roman priests did not bother with 'as if' oracles. The closing words about oracles are no more than an exaggerated and rhetorical way of making a striking point about Scipio's personal authority or charisma. In a minor way, stories circulated about his ability to tell the future: Gellius says that when faced with an apparently impregnable town in Iberia, Scipio told an ordinary soldier that the citadel would fall the day after tomorrow, and this duly occurred. Divinely conferred gift of prophecy? Or a shrewd and experienced military assessment?⁵⁴

Carthaginian priesthoods were different from Roman. They were not combined with other sorts of career, and some were held by women (the Vestals were the only securely attested female priesthood at Rome).⁵⁵ A remarkable example is the inscribed epitaph of the chief priest Batbaal, which gives her lengthy genealogy.⁵⁶ It needs an effort to imagine a female

---

[51] Scullard 1970: 205. For the ancient evidence, see n. 49.
[52] Davies 2004: 124–33; quotations from 131 and 132; accepted by Beltramini and Rocco 2020: 243: 'appropriation of the authority institutionally assigned to priests'.
[53] Livy 26.19.4. Habits elsewhere: Oakley 1998: 441 (8.7.8n.).
[54] Gellius 6.1.7–11, placed straight after the passage about Scipio communing with Jupiter at Rome, so offered as somehow miraculous.
[55] See Rüpke 2008: 8 on the possibility that there were female Salii; none are known.
[56] Huss 1985: 543–5 for Carthage. For Batbaal (including text and translation of *CIS* 1.5988), see Pilkington 2019: 127.

*pontifex maximus* at Republican Rome, as unlikely a pontiff as the mythical Pope Joan.[57] Carthaginians believed in keeping functions and career paths separate; we have seen that in Hannibal's time at least, military and political careers were similarly not intertwined, as by contrast they inextricably were in Rome.[58] Hannibal was therefore not formally a priest with a special title and functions like Scipio's; rather, he recalls Alexander's quasi-priestly role in that he performed sacrifice himself, though perhaps not usually the actual killing.[59] But Alexander had his own professional seers on campaign, whereas Hannibal is supposed, as we have seen, to have himself understood divination by animal entrails and dream interpretation. (That would not exclude the additional presence of professionals.)

## 10.3 The Hannibalic Legend

In the second century CE, the Greek prose satirist Lucian made Hannibal reject any idea that he was the son of Ammon like Alexander, or that he was a god, or that he narrated in detail dreams experienced by his mother; on the contrary, he achieved what he did as a mortal man.[60] For what this is worth as history (not a lot), it does make Hannibal reject for himself miraculous parentage like those of Alexander and Scipio. But Hannibal, not less than Scipio, attracted stories which implied that gods took special interest in him, for good or ill. Here is a small example, not from the Polybian or Livian tradition: the story that in 211 Hannibal, 'at the very gates' of Rome, *Hannibal ad portas*, was deterred and obliged to withdraw by a vision which resulted in the Roman construction of a shrine by the Appian Way to the 'Returner' god Rediculus.[61] Whatever the truth of the name's derivation, and the name is thought more likely to mean 'god of happy return', the epiphany story (which does not make quite clear that it was Rediculus whom Hannibal saw) shows the attractive force of Hannibal. Dreams will be the subject of a later section. Many of them, though not all, are stories of supernatural warnings rather than encouragement. But the undoubted historical background to Juno Lacinia's alleged and dubious warning to him in an epiphanic dream, not to steal gold from her sanctuary near Croton, is that he had singled out that sanctuary for

---

[57] For the traditions about Pope Joan, see Kelly 1986: 329–30.   [58] See p. 64 for *sufetes*.
[59] See p. 225 for Hannibal and the lamb.
[60] *Dialogues of the Dead* 12.2 (=382); Huss 1986: 232–3. For this dialogue, see Prologue. For Ammon as father of Alexander, see now the dedication SEG 59.1764 with Parker 2022: 155 (it will be *CPI* no. 519): 'King Alexander to his father Ammon'.
[61] Festus 354–5 Lindsay. See p. 151.

attention in the first place.⁶² It is, after all, where he inscribed his record of achievements in 205.

Since Juno was believed to have favoured Carthage, at any rate until her reconciliation with Rome at the time of the battle of the Metaurus in 207, it was an obvious further step to make her protect and encourage Hannibal explicitly and from the outset. But this explanatory step was not taken until Silius, who introduces the Juno motif very early. In his account, it is Juno who sends Anna (a nymph) to urge Hannibal on to fight at Cannae.⁶³ Then, after the battle, Juno dissuades Hannibal from marching on Rome: she sends down another of her agents, Somnus the sleep god, to put him out of action; but she does so in the interests of Hannibal rather than of Rome, because she wants to restrain his incautious ardour.⁶⁴ And when Hannibal is at the gates, *ad portas*, in 211 BCE, Silius ignores Rediculus (whose name would anyway not scan in Silius' hexameters because the first vowel is short, from *redeo*) and makes Jupiter tell Juno to stop him herself.⁶⁵

The role of Jupiter (Punic Baal Hammon) in provoking the war is less easy to explain that that of the perennially angry Juno. After all, Jupiter was 'the supreme god of the Roman state'.⁶⁶ Livy's source – ultimately Hannibal's historian Silenus of Caleacte, followed by Coelius, as we learn from Cicero – knew of a story that after Hannibal had taken Saguntum, Jupiter (not Juno) caused the war with Rome by sending a night-time epiphany to Hannibal of a young man of godlike appearance or beauty who said he had been ordered by Jupiter to guide him to Italy.⁶⁷ In the original Silenus/Coelius version, Hannibal is summoned to a council of the gods by Jupiter and ordered to wage war on Italy. He is given a guide, and from that point on, the dream is much the same as in Livy. His guide ordered Hannibal to follow him and fix his gaze on him; Orpheus-like, Hannibal could not resist disobeying by looking round.⁶⁸ He saw that he in his turn was followed by a massive snake, which destroyed the vegetation to the accompaniment of a huge thunderstorm; his young guide explained that this signified the destruction of Italy; he

---

⁶² Cicero, *On divination* 1.48, from Coelius. See p. 213.
⁶³ Juno's reconciliation in 207: see p. 193 for Ennius. Sil. 1.55; 8.25–43. On Silius' Juno and her relation to Virgil's, see Feeney 1991: 303.
⁶⁴ Sil. 10.337–50; Feeney 1991: 304: 'to lay Hannibal to sleep and dissuade him from overreaching himself with a march against Rome'.
⁶⁵ Sil. 12.691–700; Feeney 1991: 304.   ⁶⁶ Feeney 1991: 305.
⁶⁷ See p. 85 n. 39, citing Livy 21.22: Cicero, *On divination* 1.49. See *FGrHist* 175 Silenus F2 and *FRHist* 15 Coelius F8. On the dream, see further p. 241 n. 145.
⁶⁸ Walbank 1985: 129; cf. Hoyos 2006: 633.

was not to worry about it but to proceed with his invasion. Jupiter's paradoxical use of Hannibal here was explained by Silius Italicus as due to a desire to 'test the Romans by adversity' and increase their fame: this has been dismissed as a poetic makeshift.[69] Or was Jupiter thought of as luring Hannibal on to eventual defeat? Or was the story circulated by Hannibal himself during the war so as to convince Italian communities that his damage to Italy was not wilful, but done in fulfilment of divine purpose (so that all would be well eventually)?

Hannibal was thought by Romans to have enjoyed a special relationship with Melqart, Greek Herakles, Latin Hercules, and perhaps Hannibal did indeed believe this himself. 'I would like to find out whether this Hannibal really is, as he himself says, a rival of the travels of Hercules.' Livy or his source put these striking words into the mouth of Scipio's father at the beginning the war, referring to Hannibal's crossing of the Alps and Hercules' passage across the Alps from Iberia to Italy after he had captured the cattle of Geryon.[70] Later Roman authors adopted the Alpine comparison; the association of Herakles/Hercules with the Alps seems not to be an old Greek tradition.[71] Polybius' shorter version of this speech does not contain this detail, which may be no more than Livy's authorial embroidery of his own narrative about Hannibal's vows at Gades.[72] Silius Italicus picks up and elaborates this brief Livian theme of Hercules as role model for Hannibal: 'you will acknowledge, Alcides [a poetic name for Hercules] that I am not unlike your young self', meaning 'I am very like you when you were a mortal'.[73] Silius' Hannibal goes on to pray to Hercules that he will be at his right hand when he destroys the descendants of Troy (the Romans), just as Hercules was remembered for the first sack of Troy, an episode earlier than the main Trojan War.[74] There is a parallel with Scipio here, because like Hercules he is represented as choosing virtue instead

---

[69] Sil. 3.163–4, *gentem exercere periclis / Dardaniam*, with Feeney 1991: 304–5.
[70] See Huss 1986: 334–5. The elder Scipio's remark: Livy 21.41.7.
[71] Nep. *Hann.* 3.4 (source uncertain, with a fanciful explanation from the 'Graian' i.e. Greek Alps); Sil. 3.415–41 and 11.217–18 (the sky-scraping stones of the Alps had been trodden only by a god); Pliny *NH* 3.123. In the fourth century CE, Ammianus Marcellinus (15.10.9) put Hercules' Alpine actions on his way *towards* Iberia: all these are Latin authors, and quite late. Cf. Proctor 1971: 196–7. Earlier, Greek, accounts of Herakles' return to Greece from Iberian Tartessus took him overland but were not interested in the Alps. This crucial difference is not seen by Kubler 2018: 133–77, esp. 133–4. The first Greek source to link Hercules and the Alps is Diod. 4.19.3–4 (Augustan; probably from a mythographic handbook, not from Posidonius: Schwartz 1959: 54–5). De Witt 1941: 59–60 makes unsupported assumptions about the Hercules 'tradition'. See further Konrad 1994: 108.
[72] Pol. 3.64.   [73] 'Not unlike' is a litotes, meaning 'very like'.
[74] Sil. 1.509–14; Stocks 2014: 218–21. See Kubler 2018: 153–7, esp. 156–7 on Hercules (but nowhere citing Stocks 2014).

of pleasure.⁷⁵ Cicero, and very probably Ennius before him, made the comparison between Scipio and Hercules explicitly.⁷⁶

It would be good to know with whom Hannibal communed at the oracle of the dead in Campania, if he did. Melqart has been suggested, and this would work if we were to press the identification of Melqart with Greek Herakles, who had a double aspect as both a heroized dead mortal and a god.⁷⁷ Another obvious guess is a consultation of his father Hamilcar (9); that would be like Aeneas' conversation with his father Anchises in Virgil, *Aeneid* 6. And we have seen that the poet Silius made Scipio converse with his mother Pomponia in the underworld.⁷⁸ But this Hamilcar was not a god, he was just – dead.⁷⁹

## 10.4  The Scipionic Legend (i): Supernatural Birth

The two principal elements in the Scipionic legend are his supernatural birth (his mother Pomponia impregnated by a snake) and the divine help which was supposed to have enabled his capture of New Carthage in Iberia (209).⁸⁰ Livy treated the story of Scipio's divine birth, and his relationship with gods, early in the second half of his third Decade, having already introduced him as an adult agent in books 21 and 22, the first two books of the first half of the Decade. The immediate narrative context in book 26 is Scipio's election in 210 as commander in Iberia after his father and uncle had been killed there the previous year. The decision to postpone the topic like this was a good one, but it was not Livy's: he was following Polybius, whose character sketch of Scipio is however placed somewhat later still, after his actual arrival in Iberia.⁸¹ The two treatments have recently been subjected to close analysis.⁸² The upshot is that although there are clear

---

⁷⁵ Sil. 15.18–132 (esp. 78–9, explicit allusion to Hercules ('Amphitryoniades'), another of his poetic names, and a very handy filler of half a hexameter line); Stocks 2014: 221 with nn. 7 and 8.
⁷⁶ On the theory that Ennius 232 Sk. (Goldberg and Manuwald 2018a: 230–1), *nunc Iuppiter hac stat*, 'Jupiter now stands on our side', refers to Hannibal and the crossing of the Alps with divine help, see Kubler 2018: 135. See p. 408. Cicero: *On the republic* frag. 3 with Walbank 1985: 121; cf. n. 96.
⁷⁷ Huss 1986: 235–6. Double aspect: Hdt. 2.44.5.  ⁷⁸ 13.642–3. See p. 42.
⁷⁹ For another Hamilcar (1), who did receive cult according to Herodotus, not an easy story to believe, see p. 236, cf. 428.
⁸⁰ Modern works: Haywood 1933: 9–29; Toynbee 1965: 2.500–8; Scullard 1970: 18–23; 52–9 (New Carthage); 233–7; Walbank 1985: 120–37.
⁸¹ Livy 26.19; Pol. 10.2 and 4–5.
⁸² Beltramini and Rocco 2020, esp. 234–7 arguing that the less flattering nuances in Livy are the contribution of Livy himself rather than of Valerius Antias, who showed Scipio in a poor light on a later occasion (*FRHist* 25 F29: dishonourable sexual behaviour in Iberia), disagreeing with the rest of the tradition about the episode.

general similarities, Livy's portrait is a little more ambiguous than that of Polybius: he plays down Scipio's virtues and thinks he exploited the sometimes silly religious beliefs of others.[83] Polybius by contrast rejects the Scipionic legend and the role of luck, chance, fortune, Greek *tychē*, in Scipio's success. In his opinion, Scipio relied instead on his own outstanding qualities of cleverness and his willingness to work hard – but was happy to let his troops think he was divinely inspired.[84]

The idea that Scipio was the son of a union between a mortal woman and a god would not have struck an ancient Greek as an absurdity; but Scipio is the first clearly historical Roman to have attracted such a miraculous story.[85] The next is Octavian, the future emperor Augustus, fathered on Atia by Apollo in the shape of a snake.[86] Some prominent historical Greek individuals were held to have divine parents; Apollo (again) was supposedly the father of Seleucus, the first king of the dynasty.[87] Also in the early Hellenistic period, the Macedonian prince Demetrius the Besieger was extravagantly hailed by a poet as son of the sea god Poseidon and Aphrodite – if that is the right name for the mother and is not a scribal error for his usual consort Amphitrite.[88] We have seen that Hamilcar (1) is said to have received cult at Carthage after Himera (480); the story has clear Greek elements. Hannibal (9) did not receive cult alive or dead.

All this might seem to indicate a purely Greek source for the legend of Pomponia and the snake. But that would be too crude a solution, for two reasons: first, because Roman religious life was by now thoroughly permeated with Greek ideas and practices, and, second, because some of the

---

[83] See esp. 26.19.7: strong criticism of those who compared Scipio's allegedly divine birth with the story that Alexander the Great's mother Olympias was impregnated by a snake. See Walbank 1985: 121, also noting another parallel: with Hercules, 'who had to cope with snakes in his cradle'. Not quite the same as snaky parentage, however.

[84] Pol. 10.5.8–9, cf. the character sketch at 10.2, esp. §§9–13, which include a comparison with the Spartan Lycurgus. For Pol. and fortune, see p. 217 n. 53.

[85] I leave to one side the mythical figures of Romulus and Remus, or the implications of the flaming head of the child Servius Tullius (Livy 1.39.1).

[86] Suet. *Aug.* 94.4; Ogden 2013: 338–40; Parker 2022: 156 (Scipio and Octavian). Nothing so extravagant is told of Sulla.

[87] Justin 15.4.3; Parker 2022: 155–6, with references.

[88] *CA*: 174, 14–15. Aphrodite is an unexpected partner: in Homer, *Odyssey* 8, Poseidon is sternly unamused by her adultery with Ares. At Hesiod, *Theogony* 243, Amphitrite is scanned long, short, short, long. But in the Hellenistic poem, the goddess must be scanned long, short, long, long. This obstacle is not insuperable. The meaning of the name Amphitrite is uncertain, but it may be related to the sea god Triton (West 1966: 238), whose first syllable is long. For metrical freedom with a divine name, cf. *Il.* 5.31, Ἄρες Ἄρες, the same vocative of Ares scanned long, short, then short, long!

key contemporary or near-contemporary authors writing in Latin were 'mix-Greeks' from south Italy, a region which Greeks had begun to colonize as long ago as the eighth century.⁸⁹ When Horace said that Scipio owed his fame not to honorific inscriptions but to the 'Calabrian Muses', *Calabrae Pierides*, he was referring to Scipio's contemporary Ennius.⁹⁰ Ennius was believed to have been a personal friend of Scipio.⁹¹ He celebrated him both in epigrams, as we shall see shortly, and in a separate work, the *Scipio*, of which not much is left.⁹² Ennius, who became a Roman citizen only at the age of fifty-five in 184 BCE, famously claimed to be a man of 'three hearts', *tria corda*.⁹³ He was supposed in antiquity to have meant by this Greek, Latin, and Oscan, so his treatment of Scipio is not likely to have been entirely Roman in conception.⁹⁴

The poetic fragment of Ennius which most clearly salutes Scipio as a Greek-style hero is a two-line epigram, duly composed in the Greek epigrammatic tradition. It owes its survival to Lactantius (about 300 CE) quoting Cicero who in turn is quoting Ennius: Scipio himself is made to say that 'if it is right for anyone to climb to the regions of the celestial ones, to me alone the greatest gate of heaven is open', *si fas endo plagas caelestum ascendere cuiquam est, / mi soli caeli maxima porta patet*. Cicero in *On the Republic* adds the comment 'Yes, Africanus' (by this name on its own Cicero usually means Aemilianus,⁹⁵ but the Ennius lines are

---

⁸⁹ For 'mix-Greeks', μιξέλληνες, see Pol. 1.67.7 (cf. p. 27 n. 88). There was also a word 'mix-barbarians', μιξοβάρβαροι: Xen. *Hell.* 2.1.15 (the people of Carian Cedreae).

⁹⁰ Horace, *Odes* 4.8.19–20 = Goldberg and Manuwald 2018a: 38–9 T[estimonium] 47. Many editors think that either two or six lines of this poem are spurious – including some of the lines referring to Carthage and Hannibal – because it does not conform to a 'law' according to which the line totals of all Horace's poems are divisible by four. But Thomas 2011: 185–6 prints all of it in his text. Weinstock 1971: 294 n. 11 thought that 'even if the verses are spurious . . . the evidence they contain is valuable'.

⁹¹ Cicero said 'our Ennius was dear to the elder Africanus, and so his marble image is thought to have been placed in the tomb of the Scipios': *For Archias* 22 and an ancient commentator = Goldberg and Manuwald 2018a: 6–7, T 9; other sources less probably said that Ennius was actually buried in the tomb of the Scipios: T 49 (Livy 38.56.4); T 53 (Ovid, *Art of love* 409–10); T56 (Val. Max. 8.14.1); T 62 (Pliny *NH* 7.114) and T 99 (Jerome, *From Abraham* 1849). But tradition also connected Ennius with Scipio's enemy Cato: Nepos, *Cato* 1.4 = Goldberg and Manuwald 2018a: 30–1, T 38; T 91 (Aurelius Victor, *On illustrious men* 47.1) and T 97 (Jerome, *From Abraham* 1777).

⁹² For the seven fragments of the *Scipio*, see Goldberg and Manuwald 2018b: 286–95. Scipio must have featured in the *Annales*, but no obviously relevant lines survive.

⁹³ Feeney 2016: 188.

⁹⁴ Late citizenship: Feeney 2016: 188. 'Three hearts': Skutsch 1985: 130, *op. incert. frag.* (fragments of uncertain works) 1 = Aulus Gellius 17.17.1; Goldberg and Manuwald 2018a: 68–9, T 83, and 2018b: 316–7, unidentified works no. 16; see Gowers 2007: 228–30 for various other possible nuances of the claim. See also Henderson 2004: 101–2 and cf. Walbank 1985: 123: 'Ennius was not a Roman'.

⁹⁵ See p. 203, citing Douglas 1966: 66.

certainly about his adoptive grandfather Africanus), 'for that gate was open to Hercules too'.[96] (We have seen that Hercules is relevant to Scipio as well as to Hannibal.) The cautious opening words 'if it is right', *si fas*, should not be overlooked: at all times, some sceptical Greeks, like Plutarch much later, would have denied that it was *fas*. But the hint at a link between conquest and deification is there and may have been inspired by Hellenistic literary models and actual religious practices.[97]

Ennius in his *Scipio* asked 'how great a statue will the Roman people make, how large a column, which could speak of your achievements?'[98] His extravagant language was perhaps influenced by the very popular Hellenistic Greek writer Euhemerus of Messene, who propounded a doctrine of deification through conquest and benefaction, and whose *Sacred Record* was translated into Latin by Ennius, with some free reinterpretation and additions.[99] It has been suggested that the real-life Scipio's answer to Ennius' rhetorical question was the splendid arch, adorned with statues, which he erected on the way up to the Capitol in 190, before leaving for Asia Minor as adviser to his consular brother Lucius in the campaign against Antiochus III. But it is only an attractive modern speculation that any of the statues actually depicted Scipio himself.[100] Nor was Scipio the only military commander in this period to have erected such a monumental arch.[101]

Most of this evidence is derived from literary sources who report the doings and attitudes of the upper classes. A different sort of story about Scipio's perceived divinity is set in the final phase of his life at Liternum, when some admiring brigand chiefs arrived and, after a brief misunderstanding, were allowed to pay him (we are told)

---

[96] Skutsch 1985: 131 (*Varia* no. 1 = Cic. *On the republic* frag. 3, from Lactantius, *Divine institutes* 1.18); *FLP* Ennius frag. 44; Goldberg and Manuwald 2018b: 234–7, epigrams 3b. See Henderson 2004: 101–2. For Cicero's *On the republic*, see p. 417 (the *Dream of Scipio* in book 6), and for other epigrams by Ennius about Scipio, see p. 13.

[97] Bosworth 1999: 5 and nn. 31 and 32. See further n. 99 on Euhemerus.

[98] Goldberg and Manuwald 2018b: 294–5, *Scipio* frag. 7; Skutsch 1985: 130, fragments of uncertain works no. 3.

[99] Euhemerus: Bosworth 1999: 11 and n. 69, followed by Rüpke 2007a: 58 and 263 n.44. For Euhemerus, see *OCD*[4]. He gave his name to 'euhemerism', the idea that divinity is achieved through deeds. For the fragments of Ennius' translation, see Vahlen 1928: 223–9; Goldberg and Manuwald 2018b: 238–59.

[100] Livy 37.3.7, the only evidence; see p. 329, cf. 414 for the immediate historical context. The link with the Ennius fragment is the ingenious suggestion of Hölkeskamp 2018: 437.

[101] See Harris 1979: 261–2.

something like the reverence due to the gods. Scipio did not receive actual posthumous cult.[102] Nor did Hannibal.[103]

## 10.5 The Scipionic Legend (ii): New Carthage and Neptune

Chronologically, birth at Rome comes before anything else, but logically, the origins of the legend surely lie in the seemingly miraculous capture of New Carthage in Iberia.[104] This was the result of what Scipio presented as an epiphany of Neptune, Greek Poseidon, who had appeared to him in his sleep. He probably predicted it well in advance of the bold attack on the lagoon (Polybius), rather than just before it (Livy).[105] It was this apparent miracle, and the similarity with the deified Alexander, for whom the sea allegedly parted in Pamphylia and so did him obeisance, which is likely to have prompted thoughts of Scipio's divinity.[106] It is tempting to think that Ennius, to return to him, hinted at this epiphany in his *Scipio*, a mostly lost poem of which even the genre is not certain. 'Fierce Neptune gave the rough waves a respite', he wrote; but he continued:

> the Sun checked his horses' path as their hooves flew
> the endless rivers stood still, the trees lacked wind.[107]

The continuation shows that special pleading must be avoided, because the preternaturally calm sea is only one of a list of miraculous interruptions to the natural order. Of these, the most spectacular is that the sun stopped in his course, as it did when in Greek myth Atreus, father of Agamemnon and Menelaus, made his brother Thyestes involuntarily eat his own sons. Nor does the source Macrobius (early fifth century CE) reveal any clue as to the historical context of this *Scipio* fragment.

More secure and tangible evidence about Scipio and Neptune comes from Appian's narrative of Scipio's departure for Africa in 204, when from his flagship he poured libations to Zeus and Poseidon, that is, to Jupiter and Neptune. Long before, Herodotus had described how the Spartan king

---

[102] For the admiring deputation of brigands, see p. 394, citing Val. Max. 2.10.2. No posthumous cult: p. 418. For the late story (Pliny, *NH* 16.234) that a snake, *draco*, guarded the spirit, *manes*, of Scipio at Liternum, see p. 393.
[103] See p. 428.
[104] So, rightly, Walbank 1985: 135, summing up a long discussion: 'it seems likely, then, that the beginnings of the legend are to be seen in the events at New Carthage'.
[105] Pol. 10.11.7 and Livy 26.45.9, with Walbank 1985: 134–5. [106] See p. 121.
[107] Goldberg and Manuwald 2018b: 292–3, *Scipio* frag. 5, from Macrobius, *Saturnalia* 6.2.26.

Cleomenes, about to set off by ship, had sacrificed a bull 'to the sea', presumably meaning Poseidon.[108]

It seems from this evidence that Scipio continued to capitalize for many years on his special relationship with both Jupiter and Neptune. Whatever the truth about his pious visits to the Roman Capitol from an early age, it is unlikely that the supernatural elaboration (the silent guard dogs and so on) would have been added without the spectacular capture of New Carthage with the help of an epiphany of Neptune.

## 10.6 Dreams and Epiphanies

Not everyone claims or is alleged to have been fathered by a snake or to have been paid homage by the miraculous parting of the waters of the sea. But everyone experiences dreams.[109] They become remarkable, and therefore most relevant to this chapter, only when they take the form of divinely sent epiphanies, appearances of a divine entity to one or more of the senses of the human recipient. (In the modern world, dreams are usually of the 'episode' or narrative type, rather than the epiphany or messenger type, which seem to have been so common in antiquity.)[110] Everyone is interested in their own dreams and what they might signify; in the ancient world, the interpretation of dreams was largely a matter for specialists. An entire detailed treatise on the subject has come down to us, under the name of Artemidorus (about 200 CE).[111] From Memphis in Ptolemaic Egypt, an inscribed advertisement in verse reads 'I interpret dreams with the god's mandate. To Good Fortune. The one who interprets these is Cretan.'[112] Temple medicine entailed going to sleep ('incubation') in the sanctuary of a suitable divine healer such as Asclepius or Amphiaraus, and then consulting one of the temple staff in the morning.

Naturally, the literary sources tend to concentrate on the dreams which were supposedly experienced by commanders of the stature and

---

[108] Hdt. 6.76.2 with Hornblower and Pelling 2017: 192.
[109] Ancient dreams have attracted much recent scholarly attention of a high order, notably Harris 2009 and Thonemann 2020. One much-discussed question is how seriously dreams were taken by our literary authorities, but for the present propose that matters less than the attitudes and beliefs of the agents themselves, inasfar as these can be recovered. For dreams in Livy's third Decade, see Briscoe and Hornblower 2020: 66–72. For the literary 'Dream of Scipio' (Aemilianus), a fantasy by Cicero, see Chapter 19.6.
[110] Harris 2009: 23–46.
[111] Hammond and Thonemann 2020 (translation with notes); Thonemann 2020 (monograph).
[112] CPI no. 196.

glamour of Hannibal and Scipio, and in which supernatural figures gave advice or warnings. But lesser individuals also reported their dreams, which might feature apparitions by real people. Lucius Marcius Septimius, whom we have met as having rallied the dispirited troops in Iberia after the deaths in battle of Gnaeus and Publius Scipio (211), told his men that the dead brothers had repeatedly appeared to him in his sleep. 'They urged me', he said, 'not to leave either themselves, or their soldiers and your comrades, unbeaten in this land for eight years, or the *res publica* unavenged.'[113]

In Greece, divine warnings might be transmitted to a sleeper by anonymous and apparently mortal agents, and therefore seemingly far inferior in status to the Olympian gods, unless we are to suppose that like Homer's Athena the god or goddess took a temporary human form. The regular type of messenger was a beautiful young man of exceptional height, who stood over the recumbent recipient of the message. Herodotus describes how just such a 'tall good-looking man stood over' Hipparchus the son of the late sixth-century BCE tyrant Pisistratus and delivered an exhortation in hexameters, just like an oracular pronouncement. The message was enigmatic, again like some literary oracles, which is why Hipparchus 'communicated it to the dream interpreters'.[114]

The dream which Hannibal is said to have experienced in Iberia near the start of the war is of this sort.[115] The young man is explicitly described as being of *diuina specie*, 'of divine ... ' what? The noun *species* can mean either 'appearance' or 'beauty'. We are not told that he consulted a dream interpreter or other seer, Greek *mantis* (we have noticed the apparent absence of such professional diviners in his entourage, and in that of Scipio). He acted as his own interpreter and evidently took the dream to be encouraging.

By contrast Juno, near the end of the war, was said to have appeared to Hannibal without a messenger, to warn him against impious treatment of her temple treasure.[116] Hannibal immediately complied. In a similar way, the Persian commander Datis, on his

---

[113] Livy 25.38.5–6. For Marcius as dreamer, see p. 117.
[114] Hdt. 5.56.1–2. See also Hdt. 7.12.1 (Xerxes) and cf. *FGrHist* 532 (the 'Lindian Chronicle' from late Hellenistic Rhodes) D, 13–14.
[115] Livy 21.22.6. For the other evidence, see n. 67, and for the complex source tradition, see Devillers and Krings 2006, for whom (339) the dream was designed to assert Hannibal's authority and his divine charisma. Huss 1986: 238 suggests that this supernatural visitor was actually Herakles/Melqart. But we have seen that such young messengers in ancient reports of dream epiphanies are often left anonymous.
[116] See p. 213.

return voyage to Asia after the battle of Marathon (490 BCE) experienced a dream whose details are not recorded. But we can make a guess at its contents and warning message, because next day he ordered a search of his fleet and found a statue (presumably small) of Apollo in a Phoenician ship. He took steps to return it to Delium in mainland Boeotia, by depositing it in Apollo's sanctuary on the Aegean island Delos.[117]

Dreams can be invented or embellished: even if we had been able to interrogate our two parallel lives about their dreams the next morning, we would not know how truthful they were being. Polybius was sure that Scipio did not gain power, *dunasteia*, for his fatherland by dreams and omens.[118] We have no way of telling if he really dreamed about Neptune at New Carthage (the problem of the lagoon must surely have been preying on his mind), only that he made good rhetorical use of the idea that he did experience such a dream. Similarly, Hannibal's epiphany of an emissary from Jupiter or Baal Hammon would have been wonderfully encouraging to his troops. The predicted devastation of Italy might to a sceptical critic seem too accurate to be believable, but devastation of enemy territory meant booty and plunder for the troops, which would be an important part of the encouragement.

## 10.7 Conclusion

The parallel between Hannibal and Scipio in the religious sphere is close, once we have discounted literary bias. Despite Scipio's reputation for piety and Hannibal's for impiety and perjury, there is in reality little to choose between them. If anything, Hannibal comes off a shade better. He more than once treated the corpses of defeated Roman commanders punctiliously, while Scipio took dishonest advantage of a truce. Hannibal is said by Polybius to have shown impiety by breaking treaties with Italian cities by moving their populations but gives no examples.[119] Neither of them are attested as making vows to gods before battles, a Roman not a Carthaginian habit as far as we can see; but Scipio did fulfil a vow made during a mutiny. They both

---

[117] Hdt. 6.118.
[118] 10.2.9, from the introductory character sketch. The word for 'omen' is κληδών, found only here in the surviving text of Pol. It originally means a divinely sent message (warning, encouragement) taking the form of a chance utterance, as at Hdt. 9.91.1.
[119] 9.26.7, perhaps with Herdonea in mind: see p. 153.

## Conclusion

seem to have claimed special relationships with the gods whom Romans called Hercules (perhaps Scipio imitated Hannibal in this) and Jupiter, and they both used dream epiphanies to encourage their troops. Scipio attracted a Greek-style legend of supernatural birth, but Hannibal did not, and Lucian made him point this out.

CHAPTER 11

# Scipio Triumphant, 202–193
## Aged 33–42

## 11.1 Introduction

Livy's obituary of Scipio includes the sentence that he was a remarkable man, but in the arts of war more than of peace.[1] That is a fair verdict.[2] It is applicable to Hannibal also, as we shall see in the next chapter, although Hannibal did at least attempt to push through some radical political and economic reforms, as Scipio did not. Other countries in other periods have subsequently elected their successful top general to the top political position. It has not often worked out well. The Duke of Wellington was prime minister for two dutiful but unpopular years in 1828–30. A good story went that after presiding over his first cabinet meeting he said: 'I gave them their orders, but they wanted to stay behind and discuss them.' (This cannot be quite true because he had served for many years in the long-lived cabinet of Lord Liverpool, the 'arch mediocrity'.) Ulysses S. Grant's presidency was marred by financial corruption; not on his own part, however, and his support for Civil Rights has recently improved his reputation. Marshal Josef Pilsudski of newly independent Poland had no formal military training; he nevertheless defeated the invading Soviet Russian forces in the 'miracle on the Vistula' in 1920; but his years as political leader were increasingly unhappy as he moved away temperamentally from parliamentary democracy. Eisenhower's relaxed approach suited the times, but he was capable of energetic action when needed. Napoleon was an undeniably reforming legislator, but his capture of political power had hardly been

---

[1] 38.53.9, *uir memorabilis, bellicis tamen* ⟨*magis*⟩ *quam pacis artibus*. The sense is clear. But *magis*, 'more than', is a necessary editorial insertion. There is an echo here of Hannibal's apology for his violence towards a speaker at Carthage after Zama, when he explained that he after his long absence he had experience only of the arts of war, *militares artes*: p. 59.
[2] More or less endorsed by Dorey 1961, who concluded (198) that Scipio lacked the qualities needed by a political leader at that period.

democratic. De Gaulle was a published student of military strategy and tactics, and a two-star general (he never promoted himself). But the rapid fall of France in 1940 meant that he never had the opportunity to display his talents as a commander in the Second World War, and he had been a prisoner of war for more than half of the first.

But in ancient Rome, political honours were regarded as the natural reward for military success.[3] The consulship was the main reward but was itself a military office (unlike that of *sufete* at Carthage), so it provided the opportunity for further commands in the field. Scipio's victories in Iberia preceded his consulship of 205, but he was proconsul at Zama in 202; Titus Quinctius Flamininus began his operations against Philip V of Macedon when consul in 198 but defeated him at Cynoscephalae when proconsul the next year, 197.[4] Even in such a double system, equal brilliance in the military and political spheres was rare. Julius Caesar was a legislator of genius, like Napoleon, and undefeated in battle, unlike Napoleon; but look what happened to Caesar! Augustus was not a great soldier, although in the *Res gestae*, his inscribed record of achievements, he had to pretend that he was; but he was wise enough to find and employ a better one than himself in the person of Marcus Vipsanius Agrippa.[5]

## 11.2 Scipio's Triumph, 201

Scipio's triumph in 201 must have seemed very special to onlookers, given the small number of triumphs permitted in the entire second Punic war.[6] The triumph was a peculiarly Roman religious ritual.[7] It had, as we have seen, no known Carthaginian counterpart: we can only guess what reception Hannibal might have received after a hypothetical victory at Zama – perhaps the citizens of Carthage would have gone out to meet him and decorated him with ribbons, like a victorious Greek athlete from a Classical Greek city-state.[8] And there would surely have been a procession of some sort: such processions, Greek *pompai*, were regular and immensely popular features of public life in Classical and Hellenistic cities, including some sort

---

[3] See above all Harris 1979. Bellomo 2019 argues persuasively that Scipio and Flamininus were exceptions to the usual norm of single-year consular commands for important wars.
[4] For proconsuls, see p. 14 n. 27.   [5] *DPRR* VIPS2808.
[6] Richardson 1975: 52–3 (only about six celebrations of all sorts, depending on how we treat Salinator and Nero in 207, cf. p. 202. Contrast the thirty-six in the years 200–170). See Itgenshorst 2005: 267; Pittenger 2008: 149.
[7] See p. 230.
[8] See above all Th. 4.121.1, the Spartan general Brasidas was welcomed 'like an athlete' by the people of Scione in northern Greece.

of fifth-century imperial Athenian display of allied tribute.[9] Nearer Carthage in time and place, a famously lavish procession was held at Ptolemaic Alexandria in the earlier third century, of which a detailed if perhaps exaggerated description fortunately survives.[10] Such processions may indeed have influenced the later development of the Roman triumph, but not its earliest manifestations, which possibly had an Etruscan origin.[11] The Romans formalized their victory processions to a high degree, not by hard rules but by a set of conventions whose antiquity is obscure. As we have seen briefly, a Roman triumph was a procession to offer thanks for victory to Jupiter Optimus Maximus and Liber-Triumpus, Dionysus Thriambos.[12] (The word *triumphus* may derive from this Greek cult epithet *thriambos*, which originally had no military connotations.)[13]

The procession had to set off at the 'triumphal gate', and its destination was the temple of Jupiter on the Capitol; a full triumph could therefore be held nowhere but in the city of Rome.[14] There was nothing spontaneous about the decision to award or refuse a triumph, unlike the mass welcomes to homecoming heroes of the Classical and Hellenistic Greek world, some of whom really were heroized. The general needed special dispensation from the people to retain his *imperium* in the city, and this vote in turn depended on a request from the senate. A triumph could be celebrated only by a general who had defeated a foreign enemy; he must have fought under his own 'auspices', which meant he must be a magistrate or pro-magistrate in the full sense (it was this requirement which debarred Scipio from triumphing in 206, despite his anomalous possession of a proconsular *imperium* as a private citizen). He should have withdrawn his army to show that the province was pacified.[15] Finally, but only after 180 BCE, he must have killed 5,000 of the enemy in the same battle; this requirement is rather dubious.[16] On this last criterion, Scipio would have qualified four times over. Defeated enemies were customarily paraded (and might then

---

[9] Isocrates 8.82 with Meiggs 1972: 433–4, appendix 19, 'Tribute display at the Dionysia', and Raaflaub 2009: 107, suggesting that the Athenians were imitating Achaemenid Persia.
[10] *FGrHist* 627 Callixinus F2, with Rice 1983; Beard 2007: 168–9 is suspicious of some of the more extravagant details.
[11] For the hellenization of victory commemoration at Rome, see Bastien 2007: 151–92. Cf. already Tarn 1951: 194 for royal processions as Hellenistic equivalents of Roman triumphs.
[12] See p. 230.   [13] Varro, *On the Latin language* 6.68, perhaps fanciful.
[14] If refused a proper triumph, a general might celebrate one on the Alban Mount, about 20 km from Rome; and inside Rome the lesser honour of an *ouatio* was available. See p. 202.
[15] For *deportatio exercitus*, see Richardson 1975: 61 on Livy 26.21.3–4 (Marcellus).
[16] Val. Max. 2.8.1; Mommsen 1887–8: 1.133 and n. 7. Pittenger 2008: 113 rightly observes that this was a necessary not a sufficient condition. For the importance of the year 180, see Richardson 1975: 62 on Livy 40.38.9.

be executed afterwards, like Jugurtha a century later). Hannibal escaped this humiliating fate, as did Syphax, by a narrower margin; Cleopatra escaped it by suicide. Above all, a triumph was an opportunity for the lavish display of other types of booty, chiefly bullion. Triumphs were as much about money as about religion.

On his return from Africa, Scipio was at last allowed to celebrate a triumph, the honour he had been denied for his victories in Iberia.[17] Silius Italicus closed the final book (17) of his Hannibalic war epic with this triumph.[18] The procession was surely magnificent (Carthaginian war reparations will have ensured that), but it no use pretending that we know what it actually looked like. Appian has a full and colourful description, including paintings of cities captured and so on, but it is confusing: it oscillates between an account of Scipio's particular triumph in 201 and of Roman triumphs generally: it starts 'this is the form of the triumph, which they continue to use up to the present day'; then it continues in the present tense, although with some material specifically about the Carthaginians and Scipio. It therefore cannot be safely used to reconstruct Scipio's triumph and its décor in detail.[19]

Better evidence, although of an indirect and analogous sort, may be found in the description of Flamininus' triumph over Philip V of Macedon a few years later (194: Livy 34.52). Vast quantities of bullion and precious metals were carried; the prisoners and hostages on display included Philip's son Demetrius. Regrettably, there is nothing about paintings of cities and the like.

---

[17] See p. 135: there is no contradiction between Polybius and Livy on this point, as has been wrongly claimed. But there is a lesser contradiction: Polybius (16.23.6) thought Syphax was exhibited in the triumph and then died in prison. Livy explicitly disagreed, saying (30.45.4–5) that he had already died at Tibur; here, he famously calls Polybius *haudquaquam spernendus auctor*, 'by no means a contemptible authority', which is not patronizing but litotes (deliberate understatement) and strong praise. (45.39.7 may assert the contrary but is from a made-up speech in the mouth of Lucius Aemilius Paullus in 167. He is made to say 'many of us remember what crowds turned out when Syphax was captured'. The context is triumphal parades, to be sure, but the allusion might – disingenuously? – be to Syphax's earlier arrival in Rome.) HCP 2: 529 and Beard 2007: 120 and 359 n. 28 merely note the contradiction. Livy is likelier to be right for once; he must have had good archival reasons for rejecting Pol. so confidently.

[18] Beard 2007: 42–3 suggests his model was Ennius, who is sometimes conjectured to have ended his *Annales* with a later triumph, that of Marcus Fulvius Nobilior in 187; against this, see Goldberg and Manuwald 2018a: 310–11. But Scipio's triumph was an obvious place for Silius to conclude, and there is no evidence that Ennius did the same.

[19] Appian, *Libyan history* 66/293–300. Östenberg 2009: 189–261 argues plausibly that paintings and other representations of defeated cities and so on were for later display in temples, not (so as to avoid offending the gods) for carrying in the triumphal procession itself. Beard 2007: 150, 224, and 262 refers everything in Appian to Scipio's 201 triumph.

## 11.3 Scipio and Flamininus

After Zama, the Roman senate turned to unfinished business with the Macedonian king Philip V, who had so unwisely concluded a treaty with Hannibal in 215 at the moment of maximum Roman weakness. It brought him no advantages, but the senate did not forget. The first Macedonian war had been a holding operation, to prevent Philip from causing trouble in Italy while Hannibal was still there.[20] The domestic steps by which in 200 the Romans went to war in earnest, in the second Macedonian war, were tortuous and complicated (there was initial popular reluctance). But there is no reason to think that Scipio opposed the war for personal reasons, as has been suggested.[21] He is virtually invisible in these years, so there is no need for his modern biographer to trace in detail either the domestic Roman politics which led to the declaration of war or the negotiations with Philip which ended with his defeat at Cynoscephalae in 197. The victorious commander, who also led the negotiations with the king before and after the battle, was the young proconsul Flamininus.[22]

Why does Scipio feature so little in the story of the second Macedonian war, and what was his attitude to Flamininus? It is difficult to explain Flamininus' sudden and well-attested leap to prominence in terms of groups or factions.[23] It is possible that he married a Fabia, but the literary evidence for this is ambiguous; and in any case the *cognomen* of the relevant family of the Fabian gens was Buteo, so there was no very close connection with the family of Scipio's political and personal enemy, the recently deceased Quintus Fabius Maximus Verrucosus, the 'Delayer'.[24]

As for Scipio and the new war, he and Philip were on friendly terms a decade later when Scipio wrote him a letter, but that does not solve the alleged puzzle, as if – most improbably – in 200 he was generally known to

---

[20] Or further afield. But on the 'Macedonian legion' on the Carthaginian side at Zama, see p. 219.
[21] See p. 257, accepting the arguments of Feig Vishnia 1998.
[22] On Flamininus see (as well as Scullard 1970 and 1973): Badian 1970, Briscoe 1972 and the shorter version at 1973: 22–35; Ferrary 1988: 144; Pfeilschifter 2005: 242–324; Dmitriev 2011: 146–224 (criticized at Hornblower 2018: 76 n. 174); *DPRR* QUIN0999.
[23] See p. 179 for this example as a warning against acceptance of the 'family groups' theory.
[24] Pol. 18.10.8 says Flamininus in 198 sent a Quintus Fabius, his wife's ἀδελφιδοῦς, on a mission to Greece. That Greek noun can, like English 'nephew', mean either 'brother's son' or (as Livy explicitly took it, 32.36.10) 'sister's son'. Münzer 1920: 117 [1999: 112] thought it possible that Livy was wrong, in which case Flamininus married a Fabia. See Badian 1970: 32–3 and n. 25; Briscoe 1973: 241–2. This Fabius was probably a Buteo, praetor in 196 (*MRR* 1: 331 and 337 with 339 n. 2). *DPRR* FABI1097 merely says the praetor of 196 was 'related to' Flamininus, lists him hesitantly as 'Q. Fabius (Buteo)?', and has no separate entry for a Fabia in the relevant time frame. Brunt 1988: 448 remarked of the Pol. passage that although it refers to intrigues of friends of Flamininus, it shows no awareness that they formed a group or acted together on all occasions.

favour a king who had allied himself with Hannibal; and was therefore regarded with suspicion and somehow disqualified from the Macedonian command.[25] By the end of the 190s, Hannibal was a powerless exile, and the new Roman enemy was Antiochus III of Syria. Good personal relations with Philip, who was now helping the Romans against Antiochus and their other enemies in the east Mediterranean, made sense in those altered circumstances.

The puzzle is however surely non-existent. The first commander against Philip in this war which began in 200 was the experienced Publius Sulpicius Galba, one of the consuls of the year. He had already served in Greece – that is, against Philip – in his first consulship of 211.[26] At the start of 199, Scipio was elected censor, an office which lacked *imperium* and so precluded a military command. He was in any case not conventionally eligible for another consulship until ten years had elapsed since 205; that would not have ruled out a proconsular command, but this might have been resented by ambitious younger men hopeful for the Macedonian command. As for Scipio's personal relations with Flamininus, there is no hard evidence. But Flamininus in 201 was one of a commission of ten men appointed to distribute land in Samnium and Apulia to Scipio's veterans from the Africa campaign, and in 200 he was one of three commissioners appointed to supplement the colony at Venusia.[27] Perhaps Scipio approved of him for this reason, and also – for all we know – for his personal qualities. Both men possessed much charisma, although similarity of that sort does not always result in harmony. As chief senator, *princeps senatus*, from 199, Scipio had the right so speak first in senatorial debates, but he seems to have made very few decisive interventions.[28]

'Philhellenism' has been seen as the key to the difference or the similarity between Scipio and Flamininus, who after his defeat of Philip theatrically proclaimed the 'freedom of the Greeks' at the Isthmian festival near Corinth in 196 BCE.[29] This resulted in the award to Flamininus of something like cultic honours of a thoroughly Greek sort.[30] Philhellenism is an ambiguous term: it can mean admiration for Greek culture, or a policy favourable to

---

[25] For Scipio's letter, see p. 20.
[26] *MRR* 1: 272; *DPRR* SULP0936. Badian 1970: 34–5, cf. 37 and 48, speculated that he was influential in Flamininus' eastern appointment.
[27] *MRR* 1: 322 and 325–6.
[28] It goes too far to say, with Scullard 1970: 180, that with this appointment Scipio 'became the official leader of the senatorial oligarchy'. Few interventions: section 5.
[29] Pol. 18.46; for this festival, see p. 71.
[30] Weinstock 1971; Erskine 1994. For the fourth-century and Hellenistic Greek background, see Habicht 2017 [1970]. See further p. 420.

Greek interests. It was perfectly possible to be philhellenic in the first sense but not the second. Just how far Flamininus was politically philhellenic is much debated.[31] But in any case, the reply of the Scipio brothers, Publius and Lucius, to Antiochus' envoy Heraclides in 190 expresses much the same policy as had been laid down before Philip by Flamininus at the campaign's opening conference by the River Aoos in Epirus (198): Philip must evacuate those cities where he had garrisons.[32] These three Romans were essentially carrying out the wishes of the senate: Polybius emphasizes the role of the military council (*synedrion*) which decided what answer should be given to Heraclides, and its members were obviously expressing the senatorial line. As for the famous proclamation of the freedom of the Greeks at the Isthmia, this too surely expressed the will of the senate, notwithstanding that the style and the resulting acclaim belonged to Flamininus.[33] In his diplomacy before and after Cynoscephalae, very fully documented by Livy using Polybius, Flamininus as the 'man on the spot' will certainly have made detailed decisions on his own initiative.[34] The sources have very little to say about Scipio's attitudes and activity in the 190s down to his second consulship of 194, and modern speculation about his possible policy differences from or agreements with Flamininus are just that: speculation.[35] Scipio's speech at the beginning of his second consulship in 194 does not explicitly express a view as to the freedom of the Greeks as against the need for a Roman military presence in Greece; he urges that Macedonia should be allotted to one consul in view of the threat posed by Antiochus in combination with the Aetolians and Hannibal.[36] In any case, his line on this topic should not be retrojected to 198.

---

[31] Badian 1970: 54–5 denied that he was much of a cultural philhellene either.

[32] Livy 32.10.3 for the Aoos conference; for the Scipios, see Pol. 21.14–15, esp. 14.8: Antiochus must set free the cities of Aeolis and Ionia and retire from all his possessions on this side of the Taurus. For the similarity, see Ferrary 1988: 60 and n. 54.

[33] Badian 1958: 73–4: Flamininus contributed only the 'pomp and grandiloquence'. Twelve years later, Badian had shifted position somewhat: it was 'largely at his [Flamininus'] prompting, we may be sure', that the senate 'framed its decree after Cynoscephalae' (1970: 55). He usually expressed derision for formulations of the 'we may be sure' variety. On this point, his earlier thoughts were better.

[34] Chapter 6.

[35] See the works cited at n. 22. On one crucial point, Briscoe 1973: 34 (introduction to commentary on Livy 31–33) says of the terms imposed after Cynoscephalae that Flamininus believed that a free Greece was the best defence against Antiochus, but 'Scipio, as we shall see, probably took the opposite view' (also at 1972: 45). The promise is not fulfilled in 1973 but must refer to the earlier, longer version, 1972: 47, where Scipio is said to have seen a military presence as the greater security (no evidence cited). Briscoe's treatment is essentially a refinement of Scullard's theory of groups but sees Flamininus' election as consul for 198 as an unusual moment in Republican history: he transcended the support of 'traditional allegiances', because he had a bold strategy and clear policy, the freedom of Greece (1972: 42 = 1973: 32). This is better than the hopeless attempt to identify Flamininus' support among individuals and families.

[36] Livy 34.43; see p. 253.

## 11.4 Censor and *Princeps Senatus*, 199

The two appointments in this section were intimately connected. The office of censor, to which Scipio was elected in 199, was – like the triumph – another peculiarly Roman institution, and a very prestigious one.[37] Two censors were elected, one patrician, one plebeian, at intervals of five years in this period.[38] They held office for a year and a half, unless one of them died (as happened in 214 and 209), in which case the other laid down office immediately, or unless they quarrelled and abdicated (as happened in 92 and 65). Scipio was the patrician censor, and his plebeian colleague was Publius Aelius Paetus, consul in 201.[39] The main task of censors was the compilation of a list of Roman citizens (the census). This empowered them to remove individuals from the list for disgraceful public or private conduct, part of a general censorial supervision of morals. They also revised membership of the senate, both by control of its intake and by expulsion of existing senators. They were responsible for leasing public property and for making and selling contracts of various revenue-generating sorts. The purificatory ceremony of 'carrying out a lustration' (*lustrum condere*) marked the successful completion of the censors' term of office.

In addition, the censors appointed to an honorific position, that of *princeps senatus*, chief senator, who had the right to speak first in debates.[40] This mattered greatly because most members simply said which previous speaker they agreed with; there was a fixed order of speaking, determined chiefly by rank and age. Scipio became *princeps senatus* in 199, in succession to the deceased Fabius Maximus.[41] It follows that, in his capacity as censor, he and his plebeian colleague Paetus had originally appointed Scipio himself.[42] There was, however, nothing outrageous or unconstitutional about this, or else his enemies like Cato would have seized on it. (Indeed, in 183, after Scipio's death, Cato himself as censor and his

---

[37] Cf. p. 230.   [38] For patricians and plebeians, see p. 53.   [39] *DPRR* AELI1006.
[40] See Ryan 1998: 171–24 (and 179, cf. 231 and 232–8, for Scipio in particular).
[41] Livy 34.44.4, reporting Scipio's reappointment by the censors of 194. Fabius had died at an advanced age in 203 (p. 208), just too late for one pair of censors to replace him, so until the next pair in 199 there was no *princeps senatus*.
[42] For collegiality between censors in the appointment of a *princeps senatus*, see Ryan 1998: 234–8. It had been held that Scipio appointed himself: Mommsen 1887–8: 3. 970 and n. 2. Scullard 1970: 180 and 1973: 97, also Briscoe 1973: 33 n. 2, attributed Scipio's appointment as *princeps* to his colleague Aelius Paetus, but there is no evidence for this; as we saw, Livy reports the appointment not under 199 itself but retrospectively. In the rare cases of dispute between censors about the *princeps senatus*, the right to choose was settled by lot (Livy 27.11.9–11); one of the censors of 209, Cethegus (on whom see p. 114), wanted the senior ex-censor, but the other, Publius Sempronius Tuditanus, claimed that the lot, which had favoured him, showed the will of the gods, and he chose Fabius Maximus). Since these censors worked in general harmony, Paetus must have been happy.

colleague Lucius Valerius Flaccus appointed Flaccus to the position.)[43] But it was a bold step for a different reason. In this period, the distinction of *princeps* conventionally went to the patrician who had been censor at the earliest date.[44] In 199, there was at least one such ex-censor available, another but much less distinguished member of the Cornelian gens, Marcus Cethegus, who had been censor in 209.[45] But nobody seems to have objected to Cethegus being passed over.

If Scipio availed himself of his right to speak first, his oratory seems on Livy's evidence to have made little impression over the next years. He remained *princeps senatus* until his death in 183, having been renewed yet again in 189 and in 184.

The events of Scipio's censorship were unremarkable.[46] The most unusual feature was that he and Paetus worked together 'in conspicuous harmony', *magna inter se concordia* (perhaps a kind of presentation by negation, a glance at the bitter wrangles between Salinator and Nero in 204).[47] Since the job entailed both financial and political responsibilities, there was a parallel with Hannibal after Zama. But Hannibal was a root-and-branch reformer, whereas the Roman censors of 199 did nothing out of the ordinary: their censorship was not famous for its severity, unlike Cato's in 184, nor did they even try to impose unpopular new taxes, such as the salt tax which was attributed to Salinator and Nero. They removed nobody from the senate. They contracted sales taxes in Campanian Capua and Puteoli and transport dues at Castra, where they also enrolled 300 colonists, the number stipulated by the senate.[48] Also at Capua, they sold some

---

[43] See *MRR* 1: 375; *DPRR* VALE0930 for Flaccus; Ryan 1998: 180 and esp. 235–6 (against Plut. *Elder Cato* 17.1, which says that Cato alone appointed Flaccus); *FRHist* 3: 357 (J. W. Rich). Cf. p. 414.

[44] Ryan 1998: 225–32 argued on the basis of Livy 27.11.10 that there was no actual rule that the *princeps senatus* must be a patrician, but he acknowledged that in the second century there was an effective 'patrician monopoly on the post' (229). Censor at earliest date: see the same passage of Livy for the disputed appointment in 209, with Ryan 1998: 226.

[45] See *MRR* 1: 285 for Cethegus, on whom see p. 114. It is not certain that Gaius Claudius Nero (cens. 204, cos. 207, and hero of the Metaurus) was still alive. Scullard (1970: 180 and 1973: 97 n. 1) added Publius Licinius Crassus (cens. 210 and Scipio's colleague as cos. 205), but he was not patrician. On Ryan's view, that would not have been fatal, as we have seen; but anyway, Crassus had had to abdicate as censor because of the death of his colleague. Briscoe thinks Scipio may have been the only qualified candidate, but in view of Cethegus this seems to be wrong.

[46] Livy 32.7.1–3 summarizes. See Kienast 1954: 57. On the textual detail, see Briscoe 1973: 177–8 (there are small difficulties).

[47] *MRR* 1: 306.

[48] It is not certain (Briscoe 1973: 178) whether these were new taxes, or whether the Romans were taking over old ones previously levied by the local communities. Either way, there was no reason for disgruntlement – at least, at Rome. Castra ('camps') may be one of Hannibal's old bases in Bruttium or Campania.

## 11.5 Scipio's Interventions, or Lack of Them, in the 190s

We have seen that as *princeps senatus*, from 199 until his death sixteen years later, Scipio had the right to speak first. Did he do so in the 190s? Did he speak in the senate at all? Livy reports surprisingly few interventions. We do not have the actual minutes of speeches made in the senate, and a large allowance must be made for Livy's powers of invention and elaboration. With that important proviso, let us look at the evidence.

(i) In 195, he is reported as having 'for some considerable time opposed', *diu repugnante*, the persecution of Hannibal, 'as if it was not enough to have defeated him in war'.[50] The phrasing is careful, but presumably means not that he now spoke at length, or spoke several times in a single long debate, but that he had urged prudent generosity more than once before and now did so on this deciding occasion also. He lost the argument: a delegation was sent to investigate accusations against Hannibal, as a result of which, as we shall see in Chapter 14, he fled Carthage forever. Scipio was right, however, in that the now-exiled Hannibal in the east Mediterranean caused more trouble, or at any rate more apprehension, than he would have done if left alone.

(ii) In 195, the elections for 194 saw Scipio elected consul for the second time. This consulship was conferred in what the Romans called *suo anno*, 'in his year' – that is, after the conventional lapse of ten years since his first.[51] No special explanation is needed, given his enormous personal prestige.[52] He urged in the senate that one consul was enough for the security of Italy; the other should be sent to Macedonia, in view of the threat from Antiochus.[53] What, he asked, did they think Antiochus would do when both the Aetolians, now clearly enemies of Rome, and Hannibal,

---

[49] So Brunt's table at 1971a: 13 gives the census figures for 204 and 194 but not 199. For Capua's ferociously harsh treatment after its recovery by Rome in 211, see p. 151.
[50] Livy 33.47.5.
[51] The convention was not formalized until the *lex Villia* of 180. During the war with Hannibal, it had lapsed (e.g. Marcellus was elected consul four times between 215 and 208), but it seems to have been reasserted after the war.
[52] Badian 1968b: 125 and 137 n. 66, approving Scullard 1973 [1951]: 116, claimed that Hannibal's arrival at Antiochus' court in 195 'had scared the Roman electorate into giving Scipio Africanus a second consulship'. In fact, Scullard merely said this was 'one reason for Scipio's striking victory' – that is, only one reason. Errington 1989: 277 says Hannibal's reception by Antiochus 'helped' Scipio to the consulship of 194.
[53] Livy 34.43.

a commander famous for the disasters he had inflicted on the Romans, incited him to war? It is interesting that Scipio is here made to speak of Hannibal as a victorious leader, as if Zama had never happened. It is also interesting that both speeches, the first directly, the second indirectly, invoke the name of Hannibal. If Scipio really spoke in this way, his mind was still running on his old adversary. As for Antiochus, Scipio was speaking in a new situation created by the enmity of the Aetolians, who had been Rome's earliest allies in mainland Greece.

One anecdote about Scipio's second consulship is narrated in the sources out of any sort of chronological order but is in fact datable. He is said to have 'on one occasion', ποτέ, asked in the senate for urgently necessary funds, but the quaestor refused to open the *aerarium* (treasury) 'because of some law'. Scipio replied grandly that he would open it himself because it was owing to him that it was shut at all – that is, because his victories in Iberia and Africa had so vastly enriched the Roman treasury.[54] The reply may also be a (not very good) sort of joke, if Scipio's – highly implausible – implication is that before he came along there was so little money in the *aerarium* that it was not worth bothering to lock it.[55] In Polybius, this is the second of three anecdotes told to illustrate Scipio's character; the other much longer two relate to domestic attacks on him in 184 and 187 respectively.[56] Polybius does not spell out the implication of the *aerarium* anecdote, but it displayed a dangerous arrogance – as well as an unexpected sense of humour perhaps – and it is not surprising that it surfaces again as an aside in Livy's readable but not very reliable account of the forensic attacks on both the Scipio brothers.[57] The anecdote must belong in his consulship because a private citizen could not have demanded the keys from a quaestor.[58]

Also in his consulship, Scipio made a successful proposal that senators should be given special segregated seats in the games but is said to have later regretted having done so. The change, naturally unpopular with non-senators, was however carried out not by a senatorial decision but on the instructions of the new censors, Sextus Aelius Paetus and Cornelius Cathegus, and Scipio's exact role was differently reported.[59] In any case, it is not clear if the proposal was made in the senate itself.

---

[54] Plutarch *Mor.* 196f, Scipio apophthegms ('terse sayings') no. 9, spells this out. See further p. 387.
[55] So Briscoe 2008: 197.   [56] Pol. 23.14.56.
[57] Livy 38.55.13; see p. 386. Livy queasily followed his source Valerius Antias in dating all these attacks to 187, but this story about 194 is offered by way of retrospective comparison with Scipio's similarly arrogant actions at that later time.
[58] See *HCP* 3: 244–5 (but dating the consulship to 195 by a slip); Briscoe 2008: 196.
[59] Livy 34.44. This Paetus (brother of Scipio's own colleague as censor) is *DPRR* AELI1006. For the problem of Scipio's role, see J. W. Rich, *FRHist* 3: 348–9, discussing no. 25 Valerius Antias F 41.

These two (ignoring the games proposal and the brush with the quaestor) are the only senatorial debates between 199 and 194 in which Scipio is specifically recorded as speaking, and in the second he was consul and so possessed additional authority. In 195, there was another debate, this time not in the senate, concerning the proposal to repeal the Oppian law, which had been passed in 215 and restricted female manifestations of luxury: a so-called sumptuary law.[60] Cato, himself now consul, spoke (unsuccessfully) against the repeal, so giving a foretaste of his own austere censorship of 184. The episode is sometimes seen as in effect a personal conflict between Cato and Scipio, and so a foreshadowing of another theme of the internal politics of the 180s.[61] There is no evidence whatever for this: Livy, in a very lengthy treatment, never mentions Scipio at all in this connection. It is true that Polybius will describe the magnificent lifestyle of Scipio's wife Aemilia, but he does so in a narrative dated more than three decades later, as part of her funeral notice (she died in 163): he explains that her magnificence was displayed on religious occasions, where it could be thought to honour the gods not to aggrandize herself.[62] This does not even begin to justify the idea that Cato in 195 had Scipio, or indeed Flamininus, specifically in his sights. Scipio is simply absent from the Oppian narrative.

The mid-190s (197–194) saw a very active colonization programme in Italy, and this has been seen as a reflection of Scipio's personal efforts to protect southern Italy from invasion by Antiochus.[63] But the military and defensive explanation for the colonies has now been generally and rightly abandoned because of their small size. The rationale for the senate's policy was different. It may have been led by Scipio as *princeps senatus*, but if so we are not told this.[64]

Efforts to see traces of Scipio in everything that happened in Roman domestic and foreign policy during the 190s and especially in the years 199–194 are largely futile because they have so little foundation in the evidence.

---

Cicero, in the lost speech *For Cornelius*, defending a former tribune (Asconius 55 Stangl), stressed Scipio's later regret, but in the speech *On the responses of the haruspices* (24), before the senate, he stressed his authorship of the proposal. The apparent discrepancy is to be explained (Rich) by the different 'rhetorical requirements' of the two occasions, the one 'popular' (*popularis*), the other senatorial.

[60] Livy 34.2–8.
[61] Scullard 1970: 188–9. By contrast, Astin 1978: 27–9 rightly ignores Scipio altogether.
[62] Pol. 31.26.3–5, cited by Scullard (previous n.).
[63] Scullard 1970: 193 and 1973 (originally 1951) 117; Salmon 1969: 97–8.
[64] The better view: Schlag 1968: 48 n. 98 and Harris 1979: 221 n. 5 (the senate wanted to 'secure and take advantage of land confiscated from the Italian supporters of Hannibal'); cf. Hornblower 2018: 102 with nn. 94 and 95.

He seems to have been largely silent in public, as far as that – no doubt incomplete – evidence goes. And without Plutarch's lost *Life*, we can say nothing about his private life. The comparison with the years 211–202 is telling. Some crude statistics will make the point.

How often does Livy make Scipio speak anywhere, first during the war with Hannibal and then in the sequel?[65] The answer is that there is a very marked difference between the years 199–194 and the half of Livy's third Decade (books 21–30), which narrates Scipio's military career up to and including Zama in 202. His recorded speeches in the whole third Decade actually begin in 216 with his famous oath rallying survivors after Cannae.[66] After that, in books 26–30, Livy reports no fewer than forty-five speeches by Scipio, of varying lengths, some in direct speech, many in indirect. I give the list in a footnote (with, for brevity, book and chapter numbers only, not paragraphs).[67] The list excludes simple orders to men in battle or sieges, unless Scipio is made to say something interesting. There is only one speech in the senate, the long reply to Fabius, delivered as consul in 205. One chapter contains brief reports of letters sent by Scipio, to Syphax and Pomponius; these are not included in the list, though they were doubtless dictated. Another chapter, describing Scipio's proof that he had not been idle in Syracuse, explains that he replied to his critics with 'actions (a military display) not words'.[68] There are obvious objections to the procedure I am adopting. Livy often invents speeches, and he certainly expands and embellishes those he found in his sources, notably Polybius where we can check against him; but Polybius' war narrative is badly incomplete after Cannae, and in any case the list ignores length of speeches. This argument can be reversed: Livy was attracted to Scipio's personality, so he would be more likely to add than to subtract speeches by him.

A more serious-looking objection is that in a purely military narrative it is unsurprising that Scipio the commander (as a 'private citizen with military authority', *priuatus cum imperio*, then consul and then proconsul) was the centre of attention. But that is the point: Scipio was vocal, decisive, and eloquent in the world with which he was familiar but seems to have been less confident and articulate out of it, even in his years as *princeps*

---

[65] Polybius is very gappy after Cannae in 216 (the closure of his book 3) and again after his very full book 18, which ends in 196.
[66] 22.53.
[67] Book 26: 19, 20, 41, 43 (two), 48 (two), 49 (two), 50 (two). Book 27: 17, 18, 19 (two). Book 28: 4, 18, 19 (two), 27–9 (long speech after Iberian mutiny), 32, 34, 38, 40, 43–4 (in senate), 45. Book 29: 1, 8, 24, 25, 27 (three, prayers to gods, remark to helmsman). Book 30: 3 (disputed whether speech or letter), 5, 13, 14, 15, 16, 25, 29, 31 (reply to Hannibal), 32, 37, 44.
[68] Reply to Fabius: 28.3–4. The other chapters: 29.44 and 22.1, *res non uerba*.

*senatus* when the senate must often have looked to him for an opening opinion. To be sure, he may well have expressed opinions there in 199–194 more often than on the mere two occasions we hear of, one of them as consul for the second time; but if so, they do not seem to have been thought memorable enough to have been recorded.

We must now return to the years 201–190 as narrated by Livy in the relevant part (books 31–37) of his fourth Decade, because another obvious objection might take the form of a question: how many senatorial meetings do we know of in that period, and at how many might Scipio have been expected to speak, especially after he became *princeps senatus* in 199? Again I give a list of the total in a footnote.[69] Only the following are of special interest (several concern awards of individual triumphs).

At one meeting, it is said that the 'consulars', *consulares* (former consuls) took a certain view.[70] The word would include Scipio, but the year was 200, so he was not yet *princeps senatus*; that position was still vacant. But this passage shows that sometimes the views of individuals, or classes of them, might be mentioned. We shall see that there are further examples.

A weighty Roman decision in 200, to go to war with Philip of Macedon, was not made easily or unanimously: at first, the centuriate assembly voted against, but the war vote was carried eventually. It has been suggested that Scipio initially opposed the proposal, out of war-weariness and concern for his personal dignity. But we have seen that there is no convincing support for this in the sources: the senators themselves were not unanimous.[71]

At the important meeting of the senate at the start of 197, the senate determined that Flamininus' command should be continued.[72] There is no mention of Scipio as having expressed a view.

In 193, an individual senator, no less than Flamininus himself, plays a leading role in some complicated senatorial sessions. The detail is not here relevant, but various foreign embassies were heard in the senate itself, while some matters concerning Antiochus were referred to the commission of ten who had met the king three years earlier.[73] If Scipio expressed a view, we do not hear of it.

---

[69] Book 31 (201): 3, 4, 5 (200), 6, 9, 11–12, 48–9. Book 32 (199) 1, 8 (198), 27, 28, (with which cf. Pol. 18.11–12) (197). Book 33: 22–3, 25 (196), 37, 43 (195). Book 34: 10, 43 (194), 57–9 (193), 62. Book 35: 2, 6–8, 23 (192), 41. Book 36: 1–2, 4, 35 (with which cf. Pol. 21.3.1–4), 39–40 (191). Book 37: 1 (190). The year 189 begins at 37.48.
[70] 31.48.3. The topic was Lucius Furius' request for a triumph.
[71] See Feig Vishnia 1998: 38–9 (cf. 43–4 for the divided senate), against Briscoe 1973: 46. Cf. p. 248.
[72] 32.28.  [73] 34.57 and 59. The commission: Pol. 18.42.5 and 44.1; *MRR* 1: 337–8, under 196.

In the same year 193, the opinion of the (or some) 'senior senators', *seniores*, is singled out for mention in a debate about the situation in Iberia. That general category certainly included Scipio, an Iberian expert if anyone was, but if he was one of this particular group he is not named. Also in 193, the conduct of Scipio's brother, Lucius, the consul of the year, was discussed by the senate, and criticisms were expressed. Again there is no mention of any intervention by Publius, as might surely have been expected. At last, in 190, Scipio does speak out, to declare that if the senate allots the eastern command against Antiochus to Lucius, he will accompany his brother as legate, as indeed he went on to do.[74]

The conclusion is that on the available evidence, Scipio was notably sparing in his senatorial interventions; if so, this no doubt enhanced their effectiveness. In view of (i) and (ii) on p. 253, Scipio's own interventions, it will not do to reply that the speeches and opinions of individuals are never recorded. And there are plenty of other examples. To cite only two famous episodes from the Hannibalic war, Titus Manlius Torquatus spoke at successful length in the senatorial debate about the ransoming or not of the Roman hostages after Cannae, and we have already noticed the verbal duel between Fabius and Scipio in book 28. From Livy's fourth Decade, Scipio Nasica as consul in 191 spoke in the senate to justify his own eventually successful request for a triumph.[75]

Scipio's influence in these years varies according to context. The final sentence of Livy's book 34 describes the sending of a three-man commission to arbitrate between Masinissa and the Carthaginians in 193. Scipio was one of the three. They decided in favour of neither party, although we are told that Scipio's knowledge of the matter, and his authority, *auctoritate*, with both sides, meant that he could have settled the dispute with a mere 'nod of his head', *nutu*. That is a powerful and evocative word: Virgil's Jupiter 'made all Olympus tremble by his nod', *totum nutu tremefecit Olympum*.[76] But Livy may rather have had in mind a remark in one of Cicero's dialogues: the authority or influence, *auctoritas*, of Africanus resided generally not only on his expressed opinion, *sententia*, but on his nod, *nutu*.[77] Cicero puts this flattering observation into the mouth of

---

[74] 35.2.6 (Iberian debate); 35.6–8 (Lucius' conduct); 37.1 (eastern command).
[75] 22.60 (Torquatus); 36.40 (Nasica).
[76] 34.62.18, cf. *Aeneid* 9.106. This detail is not from Pol.: Homer's Zeus 'nods', verb not noun, e.g. *Iliad* 1.528.
[77] Cicero, *On old age*, sometimes called the *Cato maior*, 61 (also embracing Aemilius Paullus and Fabius the Delayer). The older Africanus is certainly meant, although '*Africanus* when used by C[icero] without qualification almost always means Aemilianus': Douglas 1966: 66, who gives precisely this *On old age* passage as one of the two exceptions, the other being *On the orator* 1.210 (but that has *Africanorum* in the plural, i.e. Aemilianus as well). See further p. 421.

Scipio's enemy Cato the Censor![78] The word *auctoritas* is strong.[79] On the other hand, later in the same year and back in Rome, Scipio was not only unable to secure the election of his cousin Scipio Nasica to the patrician consulship of 192; he could not even achieve that of the plebeian candidate Gaius Laelius, whom he also supported. This, says Livy, showed how little Scipio counted for.[80] He means, domestically.

It would be possible to write a history of the 190s in terms of 'what Flamininus did and was done to him', to adapt Aristotle's epigrammatic but quirky definition of history, in which Alcibiades was the chosen example.[81] Not only do we have the very full narrative of Livy and some Greek inscriptions, but a surviving *Life* of Flamininus by Plutarch, whose *Life* of Scipio is lost. It is much harder to write a history around the doings and sufferings of Scipio in those years, and it is better not to over-interpret such evidence as there is. With the start in earnest of the Roman war against Antiochus, and then the domestic attacks on the Scipio brothers in the 180s, the situation clarifies.

## 11.6 The Visit to the East: Did Scipio and Hannibal Meet and Talk?

One episode must be dealt with separately, because it is the supposed historical context of a famous personal and informal meeting between Scipio and Hannibal. If it could be shown to be historical, it would be their first such meeting since the formal face-to-face exchange before Zama, when they represented their respective states; and it would be their only other meeting at any time.

In 193, a high-powered deputation, consisting of two (originally three) experienced *consulares* whose names are known to us, arrived in Asia

---

[78] That is not absurd. The genuine Cato quotation which opens book 3 of Cicero's *On duties* also implies a respectful attitude to Scipio on Cato's part. For this item see p. 421.
[79] Augustus in the *Res gestae* (34.3) claimed it and contrasted it with *potestas*, 'power' (cf. already Cicero, *Against Piso* 8). For the perceived *auctoritas* of Hannibal, see p. 322; but the parallel is imperfect because there (Livy 36.41.2) the sense is different, his temporary influence with a particular individual (Antiochus). Soon afterwards, Livy makes Antiochus comment on the *auctoritas* of Scipio also (i.e. not only of Hannibal), in relation to Antiochus (37.37.9, cf. p. 333). But there the word has the more general sense, almost 'prestige'.
[80] See Livy 35.10.9 (Nasica) and 10 (Laelius): *adeo ne in plebeio quidem consule, cum pro Laelio niteretur, Africanus ualuit*. For this failure, see p. 179.
[81] *Poetics* 1451a 36–7. This is part of an unsatisfactory argument that poetry concerns itself with universal truths, and with what might happen, history with particulars, what did happen – as if there are no universalizing statements in history-writing!

Minor, having been sent in 194.[82] Publius Scipio was not one of the three; but an anecdotal tradition made out that he was 'part of the embassy' (*in ea fuisse legatione*) and that he met and talked to Hannibal one to one at Ephesus.[83] It will be seen shortly that he did very probably make a journey to the east in 193. But he certainly was not a member of the original trio of Roman ambassadors.[84] So for the whole story to be true, he must have joined the other ambassadors, or rather the two others, or maybe even just the one other. In that sense he could loosely be said to have been part of the reduced embassy.[85] Paetus mysteriously drops out of Livy's text between 194 and 193; and Galba had initially been left behind at Pergamum because of illness.[86] That leaves just Villius, who in the circumstances would surely have welcomed Scipio's company, contribution, and authority. But that is speculation. The further history of the embassy (Galba later rejoined his colleague Villius) can be postponed.[87]

An easier solution (it might be felt) would be to retain Scipio's conversation with Hannibal but discard the alleged connection with the embassy altogether, especially since Scipio for all his prestige does not explicitly feature in anything the embassy says or does. That is not impossible; but it would violate the 'take it or leave it' principle of not picking and choosing between elements in a story.

Livy apparently accepted the story's historicity; or at least he reported it neutrally.[88] He cited as his authority for it Claudius Quadrigarius, who in turn cited a history written in Greek by Acilius, thought to be the Gaius Acilius who is attested in 155 BCE as an interpreter from Greek into Latin.[89]

The anecdote, which is a good one, has Scipio asking Hannibal which commanders in history he rated highest. Hannibal answered (giving his reasons) by putting Alexander in first place and Pyrrhus in second. Scipio

---

[82] Livy 34.59.8 (194, all three) and 35.14.6 (193, but omitting Paetus); *MRR* I: 348. The three were Publius Sulpicius Galba Maximus (cos. 211 and 200), Publius Villius Tappulus (199; *DPRR* VILL1034), and Publius Aelius Paetus (201).

[83] Livy 35.14. 5–12; App. *Syrian history* 10.38–42; Plut. *Flam.* 21.3; see *MRR* I: 348–9. On Livy's alleged reasons for Hannibal's rankings, see the opening of Chapter 16.

[84] Scipio was consul in 194 when they set out, and therefore in Rome. He was at Carthage earlier in 193, as we saw when discussing his *nutu*. If he had sailed from Carthage to Ephesus, he would have followed the same itinerary as Hannibal two years earlier. But it is likelier that he returned to Rome and set out again some time later.

[85] See pp. 314–15.

[86] On Paetus' disappearance and Galba's illness (Livy 35.14.1 and 16.1), see p. 314.

[87] See Chapter 15.4 for the details of this phase of diplomacy with Antiochus.

[88] Livy 35.14.5. But Holleaux 1957c: 207 n. 2 thought Livy's formula *Claudius ... tradit*, 'Claudius relates', to be wary ('très peu affirmatif').

[89] *FRHist* 7 Acilius F4 and 24 Quadrigarius F 66. For comm., see *FRHist* 3: 188, E. Bispham and J. Northwood on the Acilius fragment, and 1: 224–5 for what is known about Acilius himself.

then asked for his third choice and Hannibal nominated himself. Scipio laughed and said, 'well, what would you have said if you had beaten me?'. Hannibal replied, 'Oh, in that case I would have put myself above Alexander, and above Pyrrhus, *and above all other commanders*'. A neat piece of flattery, as Livy admits: he says Scipio was baffled, *perplexus*, by the Punic cleverness, *Punico astu*, but he was also moved by the *assentatio*, flattery.[90] Appian adds that Hannibal then offered Scipio hospitality, and Scipio said he would have come gladly, but he knew that Antiochus was an object of suspicion to the Romans. Appian comments on the contrast between, on the one hand, the magnanimity of Hannibal and Scipio and, on the other hand, the small-mindedness of Flamininus, who 'killed Hannibal by the poison of Prusias' although he was no threat because Carthage had been destroyed.[91] Plutarch similarly uses the story in the context of Hannibal's more or less enforced suicide to point a contrast between Flamininus and Scipio.[92] He also reports it, more briefly, in his *Life* of Pyrrhus.[93] In the *Pyrrhus* version, he ruins the story and the joke by making Hannibal's order of excellence Pyrrhus first, Scipio second, himself third. But the cross-reference to the *Scipio* does not imply that this order was given there too, the mistake is more likely to be a mere piece of faulty memory by Plutarch.[94]

Modern academic historians enjoy spoiling a good story and have been busy demolishing this one. The epigraphist Holleaux argued influentially that since it was apparently not recorded by Scipio's admirer Polybius, who

---

[90] Gruen 2011: 126 is right that *Punicus astus*, 'Carthaginian cleverness' (Gruen) or 'Punic ingenuity' (Yardley 2000: 212), is positive. Gruen adds that Livy avoids words like *calliditas*, which would imply deviousness. This goes a shade too far: *Punicus astus* may not imply outright deception, unlike the much commoner *Punica fides* or *fraus*, but there is still a whiff of 'cunning', 'craft', 'guile' (*OLD*), as in Tacitus' description of Tiberius' 'crafty handling of foreign affairs', *consiliis et astu res externas moliri*, *Ann.* 6.32.1. On Scipio's perplexity, see Jaeger 1997: 175–6.

[91] App. *Syrian history* 11.42–44: not quite accurate: Hannibal took poison himself when Prusias was about to hand him over, and Carthage was not destroyed until 146. But it is true that Flamininus was indirectly the agent of Hannibal's death. See pp. 381–2.

[92] *Flam.* 21.3–5. For the different nuances between Livy and Plut. *Flam.* on the Hannibal–Scipio exchange, see Pelling 1997: 277: Plutarch is more concerned than Livy to emphasize Scipio's deference and respect, inasmuch as he was engaged in a reflexive exchange, designed to contrast Scipio's attitude with Flamininus' vengeful treatment of Hannibal. Schrott 2014, a 2-vol. edition of and commentary on Plutarch's *Philopoemen* and *Flamininus* (more than 800 pp.) seems unaware of his predecessor Pelling 1997, the most important contribution to the subject matter of his own book. Did none of his dissertation supervisors and examiners point out the omission? His discussion of the Ephesus meeting is at 744–6: no mention of Holleaux.

[93] 8.5, a passage which shows that Plutarch used it yet again in his lost *Scipio*; see p. 32 n. 125 for this self-reference, fragment 2 Sandbach.

[94] For other possible explanations see Pelling 1997: 276 n. 62.

was a friend of Scipio's adoptive grandson Aemilianus, it must be false.[95] The argument is weak, even on its own terms: the witty Hannibal undoubtedly comes off best from Livy's version of the exchange, and this – if we are to give weight to Polybius' supposed personal bias – might be why Polybius suppressed it, if he did, but we shall see that he may not have done. It is certainly true that Polybius did not include the anecdote in his narrative of this year; otherwise, Livy, who follows Polybius closely hereabouts, would not have bothered to cite Acilius or Quadrigarius for it. (He would not have cited Polybius by name either but would have embedded it in his narrative with no comment as to source.) It is however also true that Polybius sometimes mentions an episode out of chronological order so as to make a particular point. For example, he does not narrate the stern senatorial decision not to ransom the prisoners after Cannae in his narrative at the end of his book 3, but at the end of book 6, so as to illustrate Roman national qualities. But where might he have inserted the Ephesus meeting? There is an answer, and a good one. An attractive case has been made that it could have featured anecdotally in Polybius' book 23, at the point where he covered the synchronized deaths of Hannibal, Scipio, and Philopoemen, a discussion which survives only partially in the surviving text.[96] It is, in any case, presumptuous to insist that an event not mentioned by Polybius did not occur. He had his own unfathomable and perhaps austere criteria for inclusion and exclusion. For example, he does not mention the equally famous anecdote, also after Cannae, which has Maharbal rebuking Hannibal for not marching on Rome straightaway, and yet this story has not been generally rejected. The argument that the Ephesus meeting could not have happened, because it is not in what we have of Polybius, fails.

There is a separate question: did Scipio make, could Scipio have made, an eastern journey of the kind presupposed by the meeting? (There is no doubt that Hannibal was in the area.) Holleaux, despite his disbelief about the conversation, nevertheless thought that Scipio did visit the east in 193, and that this was how the story arose. Cassius Dio, summarized by the Byzantine writer Zonaras in the twelfth century, says that Scipio went straight to Asia after his arbitration of 193 between Carthage and Masinissa.[97] There, by conducting secret conversations with Hannibal,

---

[95] Holleaux 1957c: 189 [1913: 81], accepted on the Polybian point by Briscoe 1981: 166. Cf. also Lévêque 1957: 654. Campanile 2023: 62–3 follows Holleaux.

[96] See Pelling 1997: 278–82 (and cf. 276 n. 60). He argues that although Plutarch knew and used Livy on the Ephesus episode, he also knew Pol.'s version: Appian's Polybius-derived version is similar to Plutarch's.

[97] Zonaras 9.18.12–13. See the Loeb ed. of Dio vol. 2 p. 308, fragments of book 19.

## The Visit to the East in 193

he succeeded in reducing the latter's influence with Antiochus; but Zonaras gives no details of what was said between them. It is not easy to see why this should have been invented by Dio's source.

Some tricky Greek epigraphic evidence has also been adduced, again by Holleaux. At about this time, Publius and Lucius Scipio made several undated dedications at the Aegean island sanctuary of Delos, in which Publius is called by the usual Greek for 'consul', and Lucius is called by the equivalents of both 'praetor' and 'consul' in different dedications, if the Greek terminology is consistently precise. Another and more informative inscription records a Delian decision to crown Publius Scipio with a laurel crown at a festival of Apollo, 'being *proxenos* (proxeny was a lifetime honorific title) and benefactor of the Delians and of the sanctuary (of Apollo)' – in other words he was already *proxenos* at the time of the crowning.[98] The actual proxeny decree does not survive or at any rate has not been found (there must have been one), but it may have pre-dated the crowning by only a very short interval. Since Publius was consul in 195 and did not leave Italy, he cannot have visited Delos just then; therefore 'consul' in the dedication must refer to a later but perhaps not much later year. Much the likeliest date is 193, when on the better view the proxeny is thought to have been conferred on Publius, and when Lucius was praetor.[99] Against this, it has been objected that the proxeny might have been conferred some years later and in the absence of the recipient, but there is no reason so suppose this.[100] A very interesting inscribed decree shows that the Delians at around this time (probably 192) sent ambassadors to Rome to renew their 'closeness and friendship' with the Romans.[101]

---

[98] *Inscriptions de Délos* 442B: Publius is στρατηγός ὕπατος (consul) at line 102, Lucius is στρατηγός (praetor) at 89–91 and στρατηγός ὕπατος (consul) at 100. The *proxeny* for Publius alone: Durrbach 1921 no. 64, dating it 193 (see next n.). Tr. at Sherk 1984 no. 9, dating it 193 (no discussion, but citing Durrbach 1921). *Syll.*³ 617 (H. von Gaertringen, 1917) dated it 189, but this was before Durrbach 1921. It has several slips in the notes.

[99] Holleaux 1957c: 201 [1913: 92] accepted 189, Durrbach's suggested date in his original publication of the inscription in 1904. But Durrbach later (1921, see previous n.) changed his mind in favour of 193. He seems to have been converted by Holleaux's reconstruction in 1913 of the year 193, despite Holleaux's own retention of 189! The editor of Holleaux's collected papers, Louis Robert, added a square-bracketed reference to Durrbach 1921 (Holleaux 1957c: 201 n.4) but did not draw attention to his revised date. Schlag 1968: 133 and n. 169, and Briscoe 1981: 166 treated 189 as certain. Cf. Gruen 1984: 168 n. 68 (189 'most likely').

[100] Briscoe (previous n.), but as we saw he accepted the 189 dating. Scullard 1973: 121–2 n. 5, and at greater length 1970: 285–6 n. 163, inclined to accept the historicity of the Asian visit, calling Holleaux's reconstruction 'brilliant', but was agnostic about the anecdote.

[101] Durrbach 1921–2 no. 65 (tr. Sherk 1984 no. 10), with commentary for the delicate Delian situation (Rome did not make it a free port until 166). Closeness (the Greek word is οἰκειότης) and friendship: Hornblower 2015: 250–1 (for Lycophron on Anius, mythical king of Delos, who was a friend of Aeneas' father Anchises. For Anius see further p. 352).

Greek international sanctuaries were traditionally open to all visitors and all dedicants.[102] But this particular embassy was a strikingly partisan gesture.[103] The Delians, who controlled the sanctuary, must have been particularly nervous about their standing at Rome in the later 190s, given that at some time between 201 and 192 Antiochus' agent Menippus, a violent and dangerous character, had erected a statue on Delos of Antiochus, and that the Delians themselves had paid for statues to the king and his queen Laodice.[104] It would have made good sense at this delicate moment for the Delians to cultivate the great Publius Scipio by inviting him to Delos, to crown and honour him in person: even at this late period, proxeny was not an entirely empty diplomatic category.

Further epigraphic evidence may indicate that in 189, on the return voyage to Rome from Asia, both of the Scipio brothers, and also two other Romans, paid a brief visit to a city in northern Crete, where they were perhaps honoured in the same spirit as was Publius alone at Delos.[105]

Inasfar as Scipio's Delian benefactions towards the Delians were political (that is, not merely the gift of crowns), they may have been more hoped for than actual. The Delians made a real effort with the *stele* (pillar) bearing the inscription: it depicts both the crown, and a baton or staff to evoke the *cognomen* Scipio. The gesture would have been wasted if he never saw the object. As for Lucius, he could easily have entrusted Publius with offerings which he could not make in person in the year of his praetorship.[106] His

---

[102] Bagnall 1976: 151. The neutrality (or not) of Hellenistic Delos in particular was at one time the subject of vigorous debate. For a useful summary, see Laidlaw 1933: 279–282, cf. Constantakopoulou 2017: 45 nn. 72 and 73. The chief opponent of the idea of Delian neutrality was Tarn (esp. 1913: 429–32).

[103] The decree was duly cited by Tarn 1913: 432 in support of his denial of neutrality.

[104] Menippus statue: Durrbach 1921–22 no. 59. For Menippus, see Livy 34.57.6 and 59.3 (193), 35. 51.4, where in 192 Menippus attacked Roman troops in another sanctuary of Apollo, at Delium on the Greek mainland, killing some and capturing others; this incident, for which see p. 314, helped to precipitate the war between Antiochus and Rome.

[105] Schlag 1968: 137 acutely suggested this analogy between the Delian honours and the award (*IC* II. III.5A) by Cretan Aptera of proxeny and benefactor status to Publius and Lucius Scipio, Gnaeus Cornelius Hispallus (*cognomen* restored), and Lucius Aemilius Regillus, praetor 190 (for whom see p. 23). Aptera (east of Cydonia, modern Chania) is a finely fortified Hellenistic city on the north-west coast of Crete (*Barr.* map 60 B2), and the four men could have dropped by on their way home from Asia in 189; cf. Livy 37.60.7 for the sea route between Crete and Ephesus. Hispallus (praetor 179, cos. 176) was probably Lucius' junior officer in 190 (*MRR* 3, the Supplement: 72, cf. *DPRR* CORN1090 'title not preserved') so would surely not have been honoured in absence. Or did he make the voyage alone, bringing encouraging messages from the greater and senior three, and so was tactfully included in the Aptera list? He was certainly honoured as benefactor by Polyrrhenia, a western neighbour of Cydonia (*Barr.* map 60 A2), at this same time (*IC* II.XXIII.13); hence the Aptera restoration. It may be relevant that after Magnesia, Hannibal is said to have fled to Gortyn, in south central Crete (*Barr.* map 60 C 2): Nep. *Hann.* 9. Cf. p. 370.

[106] So Holleaux 1957c: 205.

offerings as consul can by contrast be dated to 189, on his way back from his victory at Magnesia.

The Asiatic visit has, then, not been disproved and might well be historical, Polybius notwithstanding. If so, and if Scipio and Hannibal did meet, it would not be too surprising if those two middle-aged soldiers had re-fought Zama over a drink of wine and discussed generalship.[107] Whether Hannibal really laid such an ingenious dialectical trap for Scipio might be doubted, but he had had nine years to think what he might say if they ever met, and how he might set up a question-and-answer session which would reverse the outcome of Zama – at the conversational level. But equally, the meeting, if there was one, might have been improved either orally or in writing by an ingenious third party, perhaps by a Greek who would naturally have known his Homer.[108] After all, this is the only occasion on which we hear that Scipio laughed; and Achilles smiles only once in all the *Iliad*.[109]

Another discussion of generalship is said by Cicero to have taken place at Ephesus when Hannibal was Antiochus' guest, and on that occasion Hannibal showed none of the same good humour as he did in the exchange with Scipio. He had just sat through a long boring lecture on warfare by a Greek philosopher called Phormio and testily complained at having to listen to an old man with no military experience.[110] Both stories are anecdotes, but both are believable.

---

[107] Questions and answers of this sort should not automatically be dismissed as unhistorical, or as merely idle exercises of the rhetorical schools and fantasies of satirists (thus Lucian 388, at the end of *Dialogue of the dead* no. 12 – see p. 4 – makes Scipio in the underworld claim that he himself is inferior to Alexander but superior to Hannibal: §7). For an expression of this sort of easy modern dismissiveness, see Wheeler 2001: 171. For example, when the historical Scipio was asked for his own opinion, he is credibly said to have rated Dionysius and Agathocles highest: p. 56, citing Pol. 15.35.6.
[108] The earliest source for the anecdote was the bilingual writer Acilius.  [109] 23.555.
[110] Cicero, *On the orator* 2.75–6. See p. 282 and cf. Campanile 2023: 70–1.

CHAPTER 12

# *Hannibal as Political Reformer at Carthage, 196 Aged 51*

## 12.1 Introduction: The Contrast with Scipio

Hannibal returned home to Carthage in 202 as the loser of Zama, but he remained Carthaginian general, Greek *stratēgos*, until 199.[1] The seven years of his life after Zama, spent in a city which he had left at the age of nine, were a predictably rougher experience than victorious Scipio's in the same period; and Scipio had been away for much less long. Both men had lived most of their adult lives as soldiers and had sometimes behaved in ways which violated the accepted norms of political behaviour.[2] Hannibal physically assaulted an opponent in the senate almost straightaway and had to apologize, which he did gracefully; but Scipio's occasional arrogance and anger were not openly in evidence until the 180s. As censor in 199, he nominated himself as *princeps senatus*, but this does not seem to have upset anybody. Of the two, it is Hannibal who used an elected position to carry through political and economic reforms unwelcome to the ruling oligarchy, whereas Scipio was largely quiet and accepting of the status quo. Polybius said in his obituary notice of Scipio that he 'sought fame in an aristocratic state'.[3] This is exactly right: he was as anxious for a triumph and other conventional honours as any successful Roman of his class. But there is no good evidence that he ever contemplated

---

[1] Nep. *Hann.* 7.1–3.   [2] Livy perhaps noted the similarity: see p. 390 and n. 34.
[3] 23.14.1. The immediate contrast is with the Greek (Achaean) leader Philopoemen, who 'pursued fame in a democratic state' (Pol. 23.12.8) and was believed (*HCP* 3: 235–9) to have died in the same year 183 as Scipio and Hannibal. It has been suggested (*HCP* 3: 242) that Pol. may in some lost nearby fragment have said that Hannibal, the third of the deceased trio, 'pursued fame in a *monarchic* state' (monarchy, oligarchy, and democracy are the three constitutional forms recognized, simply and exhaustively, in early Greek political thought, starting with Pindar, *Pythian* 2.86–8 and Hdt. 3.80–2; see Hornblower 2004: 79–80; cf. Pol. 6.3.5 with *HCP* 2: 638–9). That would be neat (Nicholson 2023: 316–17 is tempted but pulls back). If Pol. said this, he violated the facts for the sake of neatness, because Carthage was not a monarchy. Aristotle thought it had oligarchic, aristocratic, and democratic features (*Politics* 1273a–b, 1293b, 1316b), but not monarchical. For Carthaginian 'kings', βασιλεῖς, actually (for Aristotle) *sufetes*, i.e. the top magistrates, see p. 64. At Hdt. 3.81, Megabyxus had conflated oligarchy and aristocracy, 'rule of the best', but Aristotle distinguished them.

placing himself above the constitution, despite Iberian chiefs who greeted him as king. But in the Rome of the early second century, there was room and need for a far-sighted and energetic reformer. The Romans were the victors in the long war, to be sure, but this did not mean that there were no structural problems in exhausted Italy, many of them due precisely to the Hannibalic war, or else aggravated by it. Hannibal's legacy, in the title of Toynbee's book of 1965, will be the subject of a later discussion.[4] Scipio was no reformer, no Sulla, and no Caesar. Hannibal by contrast was an energetic left-wing innovator until forced far away from Carthage by a combination of Roman pressure and enmity at home. In some ways, he resembles Scipio's grandsons the Gracchi, especially Gaius for his populist curbing of judicial abuses, rather than Scipio himself.

## 12.2 Hannibal as Reformer

A doubtful tradition in Cassius Dio, but not in Livy, recorded that after Zama, 'Scipio was raised to great prominence, but Hannibal was tried by his countrymen (literally "among his own people"), accused of refusing to capture Rome when he could have done, and of stealing booty or plunder from Italy. He was not convicted, but not long afterwards he was appointed to the greatest office among the Carthaginians.'[5] Livy's silence is not absolutely decisive against the factual truth of the supposed trial which prompted this ancient contrast between our two parallel lives. (Dio might have noted a similarity rather than a contrast, because Scipio, too, was at a later date accused of financial impropriety: see Chapter 18.) Livy's main concern, in his narrative of Hannibal's flight in 195 (the second slice of text to be discussed shortly), was to explain the recent hostility towards him among the Carthaginian ruling class. The immediate domestic aftermath of Zama was not urgently relevant to this and might conceivably have been in Polybius. But the story is unsafe as evidence for more than an ancient tendency to compare and contrast Hannibal and Scipio. The charges as given look rather Roman. Indeed, they could have been fabricated as a suspiciously neat mirror image of two criticisms made against Scipio, for a sin of omission and another of commission: Scipio did not stop Hasdrubal from slipping out of Iberia, and he was suspected of having pocketed booty.[6] The fabricator says the Romans appointed Scipio to high office but then put him on trial, the Carthaginians tried Hannibal but then appointed him to high office.

---

[4] See Chapter 19.
[5] Dio book 17 frag. 86, from Zonaras 9.14: accepted by Seibert 1993a: 496 and (more cautiously) by MacDonald 2015: 219–21. It is rejected by Hoyos 2003: 182 on the grounds that 'not even Nepos' knows of it. 'Among his own people' is παρὰ τοῖς οἰκείοις.
[6] See p. 125 for Fabius' sneer about Hasdrubal. Booty allegation: p. 389.

Otherwise, the evidence for Hannibal's activity at Carthage until his flight in 195 consists essentially of just three extended slices of Livy's narrative, of which only the first two are about Hannibal in person at Carthage. They are: (1) the immediate sequel to Zama; (2) his reforms of the 190s, retrospectively described, enclosed by a narrative of his flight in 195; and (3) the activities of his agent Ariston in 193, after Hannibal had fled.[7] Of these three, the longest and most valuable is the second.

In the first slice, consisting of two separate chapters, we see Hannibal the realist, urging the acceptance of Roman terms dictated after Zama.[8] When they were discussed in the popular assembly, Gisgo spoke against them, and Hannibal pulled him off the platform.[9] This caused consternation, so he apologized, reminding them how long he had been away from Carthage: 'I left when I was nine and have come back after thirty-six years.'[10] He went on to discuss the peace terms. Soon afterwards, seven chapters later in Livy, Hannibal was seen smiling at the tears being shed at the financial impositions. When rebuked for this by Hasdrubal Haedus, 'the billy-goat', on the grounds that Hannibal himself was the cause of the tears, Hannibal replied that the time for weeping was when their weapons were taken from them, their ships burned, and they were forbidden foreign wars.[11] 'You are in mourning because an indemnity is being collected from private individuals. Don't make the mistake of thinking the Romans will leave you in peace, *otium*. No great state can remain quiet for long' (he means Rome) 'and it will look for enemies at home if they have none abroad.'[12] The same idea, attributed to Hannibal by his enemies, will be expressed in more obviously metaphorical and poetic language (a state will grow flabby through inaction) in the second main section, three books later.[13] More generally, the financial aspect of Hannibal's speech near the end of Livy's book 30 prepares the reader for the second main section, Hannibal's reforms near the end of book 33.

The opening and to us very valuable part of that second slice, which is mainly concerned with the account of the reforms, is the explanatory prelude to the dramatic narrative of Hannibal's secret flight from Carthage. The source of it all is very probably Polybius.[14] The actual flight is best dated to

---

[7] (1) 30.37.7–13 and 44.4–11; (2) 33.45.5–49.8; (3) 34.60–1. References in this chapter will be to Livy unless otherwise specified.

[8] The narrative reports the impossible story (30.37.13, introduced by *sunt, qui ... tradant*, 'there are some who claim') that Hannibal fled to Antiochus now rather than in 195.

[9] Geus 1994: 35, 'Gisgo (7)'.

[10] 30.37.7–10. This passage is important as establishing Hannibal's year of birth: p. 59.

[11] For his critic, see Geus 1994: 150, 'Hasdrubal (12) der Bock'.

[12] 30.44.4–11, esp. §8, *nulla magna ciuitas*, where Livy is perhaps echoing Thucydides' Alcibiades in the debate before the Sicilian expedition, 6.18.6 (415).

[13] 33.45.7.     [14] The reforms: 33.45.6–47.2. For the flight (33.47.3–49. 7), see Chapter 14.

195 with Livy.[15] But that does not necessarily mean that Hannibal's reforming activity is all to be dated to that year.[16] It may have been described 'analeptically', that is, retrospectively or as a set of flashbacks. Livy says that Hannibal had irritated many of the powerful 'by his recent activity', *recenti facto*, an imprecise phrase which would surely be compatible with a date or dates earlier than 195.[17] He was elected 'praetor' – that is, *sufete* – by the people.[18] In that capacity, he summoned a 'quaestor' (evidently a financial official of some sort), who refused the summons – seemingly foolish behaviour towards an experienced soldier.[19] But the 'quaestor' had good reasons for his confidence: he was in the process of being promoted to the arrogant and corrupt order of judges and behaved as if he already possessed his future powers. This disobedience was the catalyst for, rather than the cause of, Hannibal's wider attack on the ruling oligarchy, to the details of which we will return. His opponents incited the Romans against Hannibal, *Romanos in Hannibalem . . . instigabant*; the imperfect tense implies a process, not an event.[20] At Rome, Scipio 'resisted these for a long time', *diu repugnante*.[21] Here, *diu* similarly implies a drawn-out process rather than an event.[22] It does not mean merely that there was just one debate in the Roman senate in which Scipio held out for a long while against intervention. That is, the entire narrative of the Carthaginian reforms and their consequences at both Carthage and Rome probably covers several years, culminating in the flight. But the process came to a head in 195 when the Romans sent a three-man delegation to accuse Hannibal of plotting war in combination with Antiochus.[23]

Scipio, as we saw in the previous chapter, also had a brush with a financial official, a quaestor, in the years after Zama.[24] The parallel – two great soldiers showing impatience with petty officialdom at home, after their long years of campaigning – is real, but it is artificially exaggerated for us by Livy's choice of Latin *quaestor* to describe a Carthaginian magistrate.

---

[15] Nepos, *Hann.* 7.6 put Hannibal's flight in 196, the year after his period as *sufete*, which in turn he dated in the consulate of Marcus Claudius Marcellus, i.e. 197.

[16] For the date of the 'episode' (45.6–49.7 in its entirety), see Briscoe 1973: 335, but he does not discuss that of the reforms separately from the flight, i.e. he puts both in 195. Huss 1985: 426–7 and n. 8 has Hannibal elected *sufete* for 196 and the Roman embassy arriving in 195. Similarly Seibert 1993a: 499 and n. 17. For Nepos, see n. 15.

[17] 33.45.8.

[18] Why did Livy not render Carthaginian *sufete* by *consul*? At Carthage, as at Rome, there were two eponymous *sufetes* annually. And who was Hannibal's colleague as *sufete*? We are not told. Perhaps he was a cipher, like Marcus Calpurnius Bibulus, Julius Caesar's consular colleague in 59 (*DPRR* CALP2272): some contemporary wag called it the consulship of Julius and Caesar.

[19] 33.46.3–4. The original Punic word is uncertain, either *rab*, 'head (of finance)' or '[one of the] *mhsbm*', 'accountable ones'. See Hoyos 2003: 191 and esp. 231, appendix 14. Pol.'s Greek word would have been ταμίας. For another 'quaestor', this one in Hannibal's army in Italy, see n. 28.

[20] It presumably represents an imperfect tense in Polybius' Greek verb also. [21] 33.47.3–4.

[22] See p. 253. [23] 33.47.6–7. [24] For Scipio and his recalcitrant quaestor, see p. 254.

Hannibal's main political reform was to end the lifetime tenure of the judges, who (says Livy, with some exaggeration) dominated Carthage at this time and exercised kingly rule, *regnum*, without accountability. To offend one of their number meant to have them all against you. His first step was to arrest the disobedient 'quaestor' and denounce not only him but the whole order of judges before a meeting of the people (Livy uses the Latin *contio* for this).[25] Seeing that this went down well, he promulgated a law by which judges could henceforth hold office for one year only and could not serve for two years in succession.[26] No oligarchy will ever reform itself, and it is clear that to achieve this radical result, Hannibal used his influence and popularity with the assembly, although – like the Gracchi – he had some supporters among the leading men.[27] His curtailing of the powers of the judges seems to have been permanent, or Livy would have said so.

Hannibal's reforms of Carthage's finances were still more remarkable: here was a man who had spent his life so far in military camps, feeding his troops off the Iberian or Italian land and relying on local contributions (voluntary or forced) and on very occasional supplies sent from Africa. None of this, it might be thought, called for much of a macroeconomical skill set. But to deny him all relevant experience in accounting would be to underestimate the number of day-to-day financial calculations and decisions required from a general in command of a large army on the move.[28] In any case, we are told, this career soldier of over fifty sat down to make a detailed study of Carthaginian revenues: he totted up the taxes from transport by land and sea, and the resulting disbursements; he then calculated the amounts consumed by the ordinary and legitimate expenditures of the state, and how much had been embezzled.[29] Impressive.

Were Carthaginian state finances really in a bad way when Hannibal took a hand, and was he successful? On the one hand, in 199 the silver of the first instalment of the Carthaginian indemnity was found to be impure, and the Carthaginians had to make up the difference by borrowing at Rome.[30] This might be due to the loss of Iberia and its silver, but perhaps only to local dishonesty and peculation of the kind Hannibal put a stop to. The borrowing was no more than a short-term expedient, and anyway it shows that Carthaginian credit was good. But the whole incident must have made a poor impression at Rome.

---

[25] A *contio* at Rome was an informal public meeting.    [26] 33.46.1–7.
[27] Livy 33.46.7 says he offended 'the great part of the *principes*', i.e. not all of them.
[28] For this aspect of logistics, see p. 355 (citing Hannibal's army 'quaestor' in charge of the grain, Livy 25.13.10).
[29] 33.47.1–2.    [30] 32.2.1–2.

On the other hand, the Carthaginians had in the previous year 200 sent 200,000 bushels of wheat to Rome and a further 200,000 to the Roman army in Macedonia. These bushels were a purely *ex gratia* gesture.[31] Such extravagant liberality was not altogether wise: Carthaginian commercial and agricultural prosperity always made some Romans nervous.[32] Half a century later, Cato, the persistent advocate of the destruction of Carthage, is said to have shaken out the folds of his toga in the senate and let drop a Libyan fig. The other senators admired its size and beauty, and he reminded them that the country where it grew was only three days sailing time from Rome.[33] Cato got his way. Carthage was indeed destroyed, by Scipio Aemilianus in 146.

As for the indemnity, under the terms of 201, a total of 10,000 talents was due over fifty years in annual payments of 200 talents.[34] In 191, the Carthaginians asked to pay in one go the whole of the then outstanding portion, but the Roman senate refused.[35] One motive for the offer was probably to secure the return of their hostages, but equally the Roman senators were reluctant to lose this insurance.[36] They may also have been annoyed at this further demonstration of Carthage's financial solvency. One other main clause of the peace terms, the destruction of the war fleet, caused tears to be shed at the time, but it relieved Carthage of a heavy running expense.

Archaeology helps, but only a little, and in a very general way. Carthage's two harbours continued in active use in the first half of the second century, but it is naturally impossible to pin anything firmly to Hannibal's single tumultuous year as *sufete*. From the evidence of amphorae, it has been inferred that the loss of the overseas empire after 201 reduced the volume of Carthage's international trade, but that this was balanced by an increase in locally produced amphorae, perhaps indicating more intense exploitation of local resources.[37]

Hannibal is now about to flee to the Greek east, from which he did not return for the remaining twelve years of his life. Before we ask how he managed his escape, let us pause to ask what Greek culture meant to our two parallel lives.

---

[31] 31.19.2. Cf. Briscoe 1973: 108: 'a voluntary contribution'.
[32] One late ancient writer claims in passing that Hannibal, to keep his idle 'legions' out of trouble, put them to work planting olive trees over much of 'Africa', i.e. Libya: Sextus Aurelius Victor, *On the Caesars* 37.2–3. Presumably after Zama? MacDonald 2015: 283 n. 10 comments on this that 'Hannibal's home region of the Sahel was later known for large-scale olive production', but she adds 'this is hardly proof'.
[33] Plutarch, *Cato the Elder* 27.1–3, a famous anecdote.    [34] A talent was roughly 25 kg.
[35] 36.4.7–9.    [36] Briscoe 1981: 225.
[37] Pilkington 2019: 120 (but his focus in that book is mainly 550–202 BCE).

Map 4 Greece and the east Mediterranean

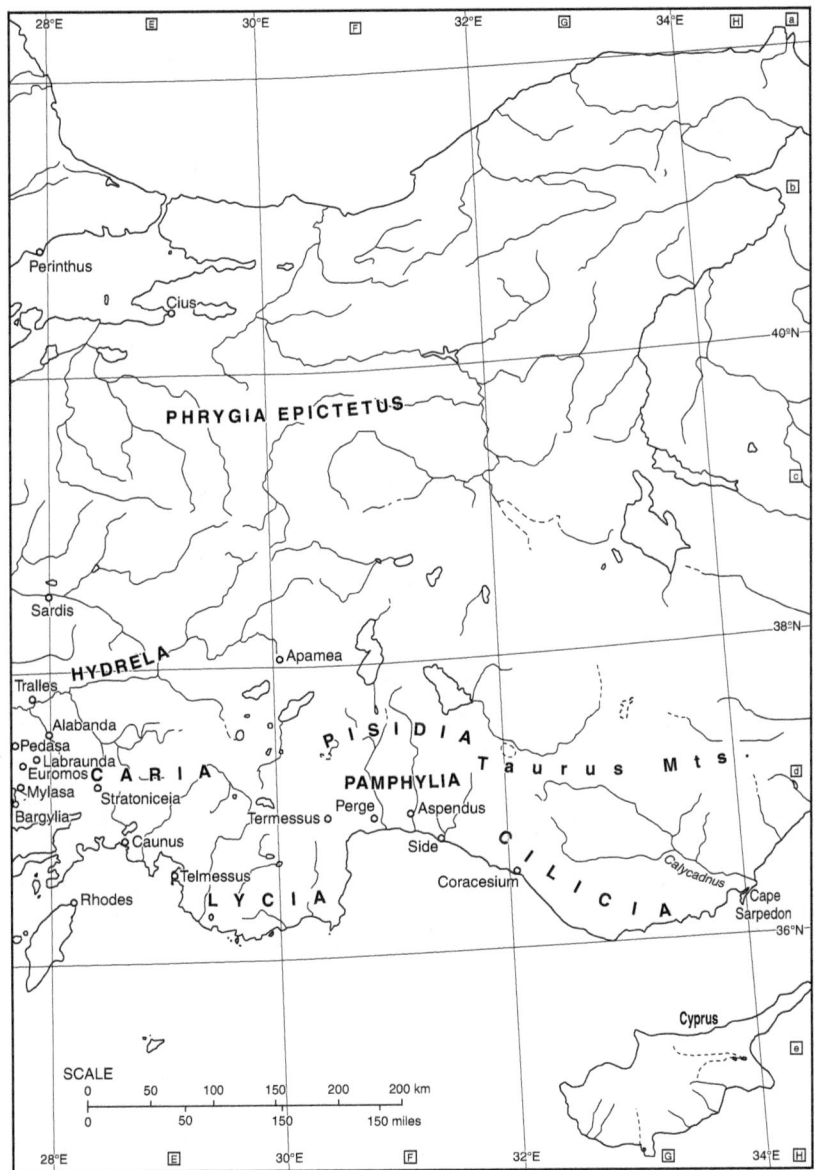

Map 4 (cont.)

CHAPTER 13

# *Hannibal, Scipio, and the Greek World*

## 13.1 Introduction

One of the most curious parallels between the lives of Scipio and Hannibal, which neither man could possibly have predicted at any time during the long recent war between their countries, was that each would end his active career acting as adviser to one of the opposing commanders in a new war, to be fought in the Greek east more than a decade after Zama. The new war was between the Romans and the Seleucid king Antiochus III, and the commanders of the two armies were Scipio's brother Lucius and Antiochus himself, at whose court Hannibal was then living. An observer of the recent war between Rome and Carthage might conceivably have guessed that Hannibal, whether victorious or not, might one day be useful to his ally of 215, Philip V of Macedon. But in the event, neither Hannibal nor Scipio played any known part in the battle of Cynoscephalae where Philip was defeated (197).

This chapter will be mainly concerned with Greek culture. But was there a political aspect, too? Hannibal has been seen as championing Greek freedom against Roman oppression: after all (it is said), some of the Italian allies who defected from Rome after Cannae were Greek cities by origin.[1] This emphasis is a refreshing corrective to the usual preoccupation with the claims of contemporary Romans such as Flamininus to be the restorers and upholders of Greek freedom, or of the Scipio brothers Publius and Lucius to be 'favourably disposed to all Greeks' and to 'grant them their freedom'.[2] But Hannibal's situation is more complex than this neat parallel might suggest. Some

---

[1] See Stepper 2001: 77, citing Livy 22.61.12.
[2] See Sherk 1984: no. 14; Austin no. 202, the Scipios' letter to Heraclea in Asia Minor.

outstandingly important Greek cities of the peninsula, notably Naples, did not join the invader. And the south Italian communities of Greek origin inherited the fractiousness of their founding communities in ways that make generalization vulnerable.[3]

## 13.2 Scipio at Syracuse; Scipio and Greek Culture

Now that we have brought our two parallel lives to the Greek-speaking east, it is a good moment to examine their exposure and attitudes to Greek language and culture. This time, we will begin with Scipio and a well-attested episode from 204. Scipio as proconsul incurred criticism at Rome for adopting a Greek lifestyle at his temporary military base, Syracuse.[4] The detail is interesting, as much for the suspicious Roman attitudes it betrays as for the supposed facts. He dressed, we are told, like a Greek not a Roman, still less like a Roman commander; he strolled round the gymnasium in Greek tunic, *pallium*, and Greek boots, *crepidi*, and occupied himself reading books (or perhaps listening to them being read to him by an enslaved person) and taking exercise.[5] His staff did much the same, and it was claimed that there was general laxness and indiscipline.[6]

Hellenistic Syracuse is not often mentioned as a cultural and literary capital in the same breath as Athens, Egyptian Alexandria, and Pergamum, but it deserves to be. In the early third century, the Sicilian historian Timaeus from Tauromenium, north of Syracuse, but for much of his life in unhappy exile at Athens, nostalgically and perhaps pointedly described Syracuse as the greatest and most beautiful city in the world.[7] In the long reign of Hiero II, which had begun in 275 and ended as recently as 216, the enormous main theatre of Syracuse (there were two) was rebuilt in stone.[8]

---

[3] This will be explored in a later chapter when discussing the battle in Italy for 'hearts and minds': Chapter 16.11.
[4] Livy 29.19.11–13 and 21.13. See also Plut. *Cato the Elder* 3.7 and other evidence cited at Prag 2007: 97 n. 171. See further n. 18.
[5] The *pallium*: Schulz 1997: 114 and n. 85 says it was against the rules for a provincial governor, *Statthalter*, to do this in wartime (but Scipio was not exactly a *Statthalter* at the time). *Crepidi*, from Greek κρηπῖδες, were regarded as non-Roman, cf. Suet. *Cal.* 52 with Wardle 1994: 337. Reading: such intellectual activity might be relevant to the problem, whether Africanus or Aemilianus was the subject of Plutarch's lost *Life* of a Scipio, paired with the intellectual Greek general Epaminondas; see Appendix 1.2. That is, the cultured and philosophically inclined Aemilianus is not automatically preferable on those grounds. Africanus read books too!
[6] He answered these accusations wordlessly, by a faultless naval and military display: Livy 29.22.1–2, cf. p. 209.
[7] *FGrHist* 566 F 40. 'Pointedly' because of the implied contrast with Athens.
[8] See Wilson 2013: 87–8 and his figs. 4.7 and 4.8.

This was a replacement for the wooden structure where long ago the visiting Athenian tragic poet Aeschylus had staged his *Women of Aitna*. The pastoral poet Theocritus hoped for Hiero's patronage – a slippery term – and addressed to him one of his finest poems, *Idyll* 16, although he had better luck with Ptolemy II Philadelphus, as shown by *Idyll* 17.[9] He nevertheless makes his two fictional emigrées Gorgo and Praxinoe in *Idyll* 15 insist proudly in Egyptian Alexandria that they are 'Syracusans, Corinthians by descent'.[10] This is surely a species of 'autofiction'. The mathematician and engineer Archimedes, a fatal casualty of the Roman sack of 212, was Hiero's friend and adviser. It has been said that 'the troubled state of Sicily in the early part of Hiero's reign left him . . . with little time for the elegant occupations of some Hellenistic princes'.[11] Maybe so. But in the more peaceful years after 241, and with Archimedes' technical help, the king commissioned a giant ship called the *Syracosia*, of which a long description survives in Athenaeus (about 200 CE), but for which the ultimate source is an otherwise unknown author called Moschion.[12] The decorated monstrosity was a work of art in itself. Like a modern luxury cruise liner, it contained both a gymnasium and a library; but it was too large for any local harbour, so because there was a corn shortage in Egypt at the time, Hiero sent it full of grain as a gift to Ptolemy III Euergetes, after renaming it the *Alexandris*.[13] Perhaps he kept back the books, which – unlike the grain – were hardly needed at the ship's destination, where the vast papyrus collection was one of the wonders of the ancient world. If so, it is attractive to imagine Scipio pulling roll after roll of Greek literary works from the pigeonholes of this formerly floating library; but it may not have survived complete and unscathed from the plunder of 212. If he was able to read the complete accounts of early Rome by Timaeus and Timaeus' outstanding contemporary Hieronymus of Cardia, he was enviably better placed than we are.[14]

---

[9] On *Idyll* 16 and the complexities of patronage, see Hunter 1996: 77–109. For *Idyll* 17, see Hunter 2003, and, on Theocritus' career, Hunter 1999: 1–2 and n. 5, resisting the 'rigid schematism' of a discrete early Sicilian period followed by a later eastern career, i.e. at Alexandria. Wilson 2013: 83 says Theocritus composed his *Idylls* (all of them?) 'at the court of Hiero's Syracuse', but this goes much too far in a western direction.

[10] 15.91.   [11] Gow 1950: 2.305.

[12] Ath. 206–9 = *FGrHist* Moschion 575 F1. See Jacoby for the likely date of the ship's construction. He suggests that Moschion hoped for a reward for his *ekphrasis* (description of a work of art), such as was given to the epigrammatist whom he quotes.

[13] Ath. 209b; Berve 1959: 69–70 and 72–4.

[14] For Hieronymus' excursus on early Rome, a great loss to scholarship and history, see *FGrHist* 154 F 13 and 11 with J. Hornblower 1981: 248–50.

The story of the *Syracosia* does not end there, because it was the subject of a long (eighteen-line) and extravagant praise epigram by one Archimelos, who was probably an Athenian, because he was rewarded by Hiero with a further gift of grain which was sent not to Egypt but to Athens' main harbour, the Piraeus.[15] Not much is known about this poet, but an old and very plausible emendation ascribes to him, and not to Archimedes as in the manuscript tradition, the authorship of a four-line epigram in the Greek *Anthology*, warning an anonymous, obviously talentless, but perhaps fictitious poet not to 'tread the difficult path of Euripides'.[16] Finally, there are detailed and perhaps intentional similarities between the *Syracosia* and the emperor Caligula's two 'floating palaces' on Lake Nemi.[17]

As for the gymnasium where Scipio is supposed to have strolled so nonchalantly, this Greek institution was regularly and at all periods the subject of Roman disparagement.[18] This was partly because of its perceived association with pederasty. (In the fourth century, Alexander's father Philip II of Macedon talent-spotted the future royal archivist Eumenes of Cardia while watching boys and youths exercising in that Greek city's gymnasium.)[19] But Sicilian gymnasia were not merely recreational: they were, as Scipio knew perfectly well, 'training grounds for citizen soldiery'.[20] This paramilitary role was hardly peculiar to Sicily.[21] But as many as twenty-one Sicilian gymnasia have been identified archaeologically on the ground, or from inscriptions, including one in Syracuse, which is thought to have been near the great altar of Hiero II.[22] The altar was itself another spectacular artistic and architectural achievement of

---

[15] *Suppl. Hell.* no. 202, again from Athenaeus (209c).
[16] *Anth. Pal.* 7.50; see Susemihl 1891–2: 2.539–40 and n. 101$^d$ and *Suppl. Hell.* no. 203? (*sic*).
[17] Suet. *Cal.* 37.2 with Wardle 1994: 282.
[18] 'Greeklings are fond of gymnasia', said the emperor Trajan, patronizingly: Pliny the Younger, *Letters* 10.40.2 with Sherwin-White 1966: 621, citing other evidence. Add Plutarch, *Greek questions* 40 (*Moralia* 274d) with Rose 1924: 188, citing Cicero, *Tusculan disputations* 4.70, who quotes a line from an uncertain tragedy of Ennius (Goldberg and Manuwald 2018b: 170–1, frag. 158): 'the beginning of disgrace is to bare bodies among citizens'. On the other hand, Marcellus founded a gymnasium at Sicilian Catana, north of Syracuse: Plut. *Marc.* 30.4–5; Rawson 1989: 433. This evidence is worth more than the conventional sneers at effeminacy put into Marcellus' mouth by Silius much later: *Pun.* 14.136–8, cited by Prag 2007: 97 n. 171.
[19] Plut. *Eum.* 1.1–2; this Eumenes was almost certainly the historian Hieronymus' uncle.
[20] Wilson 2013: 112, citing Prag 2007: 89. See also Ma 2000: 247 and 254 for the gymnasium as a paramilitary institution. Prag 2007 generally (but esp. 96–7) demonstrates the importance to Rome of Sicilian manpower.
[21] Launey 1949–50: 813–74 (unfortunately not covering Sicily).
[22] Prag 2007: 89 and nn. 113 and (Syracuse) 114 at end. Generally, Hiero II 'devoted himself to the building of temples and gymnasia' (Ath. 206e), if 'building' is the meaning of κατασκευάς in ἐσπουδάκει μὲν καὶ περὶ ἱερῶν καὶ γυμνασίων κατασκευάς. It might less attractively mean

the regime.²³ Livy was right to juxtapose book-reading and the gymnasium: libraries were often attached to gymnasia, as a fragmentary Hellenistic inscription from Sicilian Tauromenium illustrates.²⁴ That catalogue includes copies of works by Alexander's historian Callisthenes and the Sicilian historian Philistus, and of Fabius Pictor's Greek history of Rome. So the gymnasia libraries of Hellenistic Greek cities contained more than keep-fit manuals.

Finally, Scipio's Greek clothing and footwear. We may have met Scipio wearing a *pallium* before, depending on what view we take of the comic allegation that his father dragged young Scipio home half-dressed from his girlfriend or mistress, *amica*, or – on the alternative reading – boyfriend, *amicus*; probably an enslaved or non-citizen person, whatever the gender.²⁵ But as we have seen, the anecdote probably does not refer to Scipio at all.

That Scipio had a reading and conversational command of Greek cannot be doubted in view of this Syracusan evidence, and it can also be taken as certain at this period of Roman history that he acquired some elementary Greek in his far-off years of education, if not later. He and his brother sent letters in Greek to cities in Asia Minor and visited Delos and Crete.²⁶

One important way in which Scipio demonstrated respect for Greek culture was by furthering the careers of individuals from the Greek south of Italy. A well-attested example is Sextus Digitius, Mr Nimble-Fingers, of Paestum in south Italy. This individual from an allied city disputed with a Roman claimant the reward for being the first to scale the fortifications of New Carthage in 209. Feelings ran high among the soldiery between the partisans of both candidates, so Scipio's man Laelius awarded crowns to both of them and (very probably) also Roman citizenship to Digitius for that feat of heroism. So Scipio lavishly rewarded Laelius in his turn. Digitius the wall-climber was upwardly mobile in more than the literal sense. He went on to become a praetor in 194 and was allotted Hispania Citerior as his *prouincia*. An attractive case has been made that he owed his success to the protection of Scipio. Paestum was Greek Posidonia, the 'city of Poseidon', who was Scipio's divine helper at New Carthage.²⁷

---

'equipment', 'furniture', 'installations' for the interiors of those structures. For Marcellus at Catana, see n. 18.
²³ Wilson 2013: 89 with 90 fig 4.9 and colour plate II (after p. 266).
²⁴ *SEG* 26.1123, second century BCE. Cf. Prag 2007: 93–4.  ²⁵ See p. 56.
²⁶ On the authorship and composition of the letters, p. 160–1. Delos and Crete: p. 264.
²⁷ Livy 26.48.5–14 (New Carthage episode). Career: *DPRR* DIGI1138 (but his campaigning on land in Iberia was not a success, Livy 35.1.1–3). For Scipio's role in his advancement, see Torelli 1999: 79–80, following the lead of Münzer 1920: 92–5 [1999: 88–91], who had argued, in a model of applied

## 13.3 Hannibal at Capua; Hannibal and Greekness

Now for the more elusive Hannibal.[28] In his biography, Capua in some respects plays the part of Syracuse in Scipio's, because his army's winter of unaccustomed luxury there in 216–215, after Cannae, is supposed to have debilitated them as a fighting force.[29] But there are important differences: first, Capua was an Etruscan city in origin, and Oscan in language and culture, not a morally suspect Greek *polis*; and second, there is no implication in Livy that Hannibal himself succumbed to the alleged temptations.[30]

Hannibal's knowledge of Latin has been doubted – wrongly.[31] But there can be no doubt that he had a good working knowledge of Greek, although his family was not (as has been claimed) from the Greek colony of Barce in Cyrenaica.[32] The question, 'how much Greek did Hannibal know?' is hard to answer, because literary sources mention interpreters only rarely, and yet they must have been everywhere in the ancient world.[33] And Hannibal's entourage must have included people who could handle sophisticated chancellery Greek of the sort needed for the treaty with Philip.

It is Nepos who provides the main hard evidence for Hannibal's personal acquaintance with Greek language and (perhaps, and up to a point) culture. Here is what he says of Hannibal:

> His military deeds have been recorded by many, two of whom were with him in camp and also lived with him as long as fortune allowed, Silenus, and Sosylus of Sparta. Hannibal employed this Sosylus, whose place of origin was probably Caleacte in Sicily, as his teacher of Greek [literature?], *litterarum Graecarum usus est doctore*.[34]

---

prosopographic method, that Digitius was an example of Scipio bringing on 'new elements from the Hellenized south of Italy'. For the personal name Digitius at Paestum, see also Schulze 1904: 96 n. 4. Poseidon: Münzer 1920: 94, noting that Paestum sent Rome naval help at this time, and suggesting that Digitius was a ship commander. For Paestum/Posidonia (*Barr.* map 44 G5, *IACP* no. 66), a Latin colony since 273, see Fronda 2010: 207–8.

[28] On Hannibal and the Hellenistic world, see Geus 1994: 82–5.   [29] Livy 23.18.10–16. See p. 141.

[30] App. *Hann.* 43/183 and Pliny (*NH* 3.103) say that at about this time Hannibal succumbed to unaccustomed luxury and had a love affair with a local women, but this was in either Lucania or Apulia, not Capua: pp. 151–2. For Capua see pp. 139–40.

[31] Rochette 1997: 158. We should distinguish between his knowledge at the start and end of the war. On the story at Livy 22.13.6, comic Carthaginian muddle between two Italian place names, see p. 99.

[32] A recent suggestion rejected in Appendix 2.1.

[33] See Briscoe and Hornblower 2020: 197. For the parley before Zama, at which interpreters are specifically mentioned, see p. 215.

[34] Nepos, *Hann.* 13.3. For this passage in part or full, see *FGrHist* and *BNJ* 175 Silenos T2 (first sentence only) and 176 Sosylos T2 and F1 (I adopt their spelling of the personal names); the *BNJ* entries on the two authors are by Mary Williams and Duane Roller respectively. Cf. Momigliano 1975: 4. Polybius

The translation of *Graecae litterae* is crucial. Does it mean Greek language or Greek literature?[35] There is no easy answer. The second sense necessarily presupposes the first, but not the other way round, except that even elementary language teaching soon makes use of simple continuous texts. The basic sense of the plural form could be used metaphorically in Nepos' time, as in Caesar's comment that when Sulla 'laid down the dictatorship, he did not know his ABC', *nescisse litteras, qui dictaturam deposuerit*.[36] An alleged ban on Greek at early fourth-century Carthage goes *ne quis ... litteris Graecis aut sermoni studeret*, 'that nobody should study Greek language and speech', where the context (prevention of treasonable contacts) makes it likely that the target is learning to write and speak Greek, rather than studying Greek literature.[37]

Can we go further? It seems clear that the plural *litterae* was ambiguous as between the two senses, just as the now antiquated English phrase 'man of letters' implied much more than mere literacy. For the ambiguity, see Appendix 13.1, quoting the privately communicated opinion of an expert Latinist, the late J. N. Adams.

So in view of the ambiguity, we should perhaps think in terms of a spectrum of meanings and ask where on the spectrum we should expect to find Hannibal's command of Greek *litterae*. Did he soak himself in Greek literature? A busy soldier and commander like Hannibal would hardly have been interested in struggling with the dislocated word order (*hyperbaton*) of Pindar's odes or the dense abstractions of Thucydides' speeches, even if he had the time for this.[38] At most, he might have wanted to read or hear – for enjoyment as much as for professional enlightenment – the easy and militarily valuable Greek of Xenophon's *Anabasis*, or Aeneas the Tactician's collection of stratagems.[39] Perhaps Sosylus, as a Spartan, might have given him as homework one of the martial poems of his

---

compared Sosylus' history to the chatter of the barber's shop (3.20.5 = 176 T2 and F1), but that, even if it is a correct assessment (and Polybius was notoriously disparaging about other historians), is not relevant to his role as a teacher of Greek.

[35] Roller in *BNJ* has 'Greek literature' in his translation (which I have adopted except for the addition of square brackets round and a question mark after 'literature'); but in his commentary he calls Sosylus Hannibal's 'tutor of Greek' (implying language only?). Quinn 2018: 83 goes much too far: she says Sosylus taught him 'Greek language, philosophy, and history'.

[36] Suetonius, *Caesar* (*diuus Iulius*) 77.   [37] For this ban, see p. 287 and n. 71.

[38] Lucian's Hannibal claims that he achieved what he did despite being an uncultured barbarian, uneducated in the poetry of Homer or the writings of Aristotle: *Dialogue of the dead* 12 (384). The second half of this may be true, but the passage is valueless as factual evidence for it; so rightly Seibert 1993a: 32 n. 31. Brizzi 2011a: 73 calls Hannibal a 'man of Greek culture', 'Uomo di cultura greca'.

[39] See p. 99 for the 'oxen trick', which recalls something very similar in Aeneas.

fellow-countryman Tyrtaeus, whose Greek is not too hard. But prescribing for a busy soldier some suitable set books for language teaching, if Sosylus did so, is not the same as providing practical instruction. Vegetius says that Hannibal 'sought a Spartan military teacher when he was about to invade Italy', *nec minus Hannibal petiturus Italiam Lacedaemonium doctorem quaesiuit armorum.*[40] This is usually taken to be an implied reference to Sosylus.[41] If so, Vegetius has much exaggerated the historian Sosylus' known range of competence. And Hannibal had a low opinion of academic theoreticians who presumed to possess military expertise.

But if 'as long as fortune allowed' means that tutorials with Sosylus were not available to Hannibal after 202 – or perhaps after 195, when he left in a hurry for Asia Minor – he was probably thrown back on his own resources when he arrived in the Greek east. In reports of his many dealings with and advice to the kings Antiochus and Prusias in his last years, we do not hear of interpreters. That, as we have seen, is not proof of their absence in the ancient world generally, but Hannibal must surely have been able to carry on a fairly advanced Greek conversation unaided by that time. In this period, Hannibal wrote a letter in Greek to the Rhodians, perhaps warning them against Roman ambitions and deviousness.[42] He is not likely to have had access to any sort of secretariat at this time, even allowing for a general culture of enslavement; and Sosylus was far away. So its composition was probably his own work. By contrast, the bilingual (Greek–Punic) inscribed account of his *res gestae* was composed when he was commander in Greek-speaking south Italy, where help in translation and drafting was surely available to him from staff members (including Sosylus) or from friendly locals, if he needed it.[43]

Apart from Hannibal's advice in Greek to Antiochus, two stories have come down to us of conversations conducted by Hannibal during his Seleucid period, in the first of which Greek can be assumed to have been the shared language, although it was the first language of neither speaker. That was the exchange with Scipio at Ephesus in 193, already discussed.[44] In that same context, we briefly mentioned another story from that period, also explicitly set in Antiochus'

---

[40] Book 3 preface §7.
[41] Milner 1996: 63 n. 1. His rather loose translation is 'so also did Hannibal obtain the services of a Spartan tactician when he was going to invade Italy'. A *doctor* was a 'teacher, instructor, trainer' (*OLD*) and is Nepos' word for Sosylus as teacher of *litterae*.
[42] See p. 19 on Nepos, *Hann.* 13.2.   [43] For this inscribed record, see p. 12.   [44] See p. 260.

Ephesus, and this one, if reliable, would be evidence that Hannibal had at least one brush with Greek philosophy, although not a very happy one. This second story is entirely about Greek-speakers. Cicero is discussing the need for expert knowledge of a topic before you presume to speak about it.[45] He says that an elderly Peripatetic (that is, Aristotelian) philosopher called Phormio was due to give a lecture on generalship and military matters generally. The hosts of the exile Hannibal were aware of his achievements and distinction, so they invited him along, and he agreed to go. The lecture went on for several hours, but the local audience was delighted with it and asked Hannibal his opinion. 'It is said' (so Cicero), 'that his reply was not delivered in the best Greek, but it was frank, *non optime Graece, sed tamen libere respondisse fertur*: he had heard many old men who talked rubbish, *deliros senes*, but nobody who talked more rubbish than Phormio.'

The name Phormio(n) was fairly common everywhere, including at Athens and in Asia Minor.[46] But by far the likeliest candidate for the Phormio to whom this anecdote was attached – not necessarily correctly – is not a fictional but a fully historical figure.[47] He is even listed in the ancient *Life* of Aristotle attributed to Hesychius as one of Aristotle's last successors as 'scholarch' (head of the Peripatetic school of philosophy at Athens). The last five names in this list are thought to be unreliable, but there is no doubt that Phormio was a known Peripatetic philosopher.[48] If he really was scholarch, he was probably not an Athenian citizen but a metic (registered foreigner) like Aristotle himself and later scholarchs.[49] But in any case we do not know his place of origin or anything else about him. Philosophers moved freely around the Hellenistic world. So if the Hannibal story is true, Phormio is more likely to have been a visitor to Antiochus' court (and so a peripatetic philosopher in the non-technical as

---

[45] *On the orator* 2.75–6.   [46] As shown by the eight fascicles of *LGPN*.

[47] For a fictional Athenian Phormio in a third-century BCE comedy, see *LGPN* 2 (Athens and Attica): 465, Φορμίων no. 9.

[48] Rose 1886: 10 lines 19–22 at 22; cf. Susemihl 1891–2: 1.150 n. 779 (and pp. 152–3 for the Hannibal story). See esp. K. O. ('Charles') Brink 1941, for whom the Hannibal story is of interest as illustrating the 'polyhistorie' ('erudition', LSJ; better perhaps 'wide-ranging inquiry') of the Peripatos. On the Hesychius list, see Brink 1940: cols. 908–9, doubting whether the bearers of the last five names, including Phormio, were really scholarchs. Philodemus (first century BCE) wrote a treatise about the heads of the Academy but does not seem to have mentioned Phormio.

[49] It is not quite certain that he was a non-Athenian: most of the heads of the Hellenistic Athenian philosophical schools were not native Athenians, but they were often offered citizenship, and a few of them accepted it. See Habicht 1997: 108. The philosopher Phormio is not listed in either *PA* or *LGPN* vol. 2 (Athens and Attica) so is presumably there regarded as not Athenian.

well as the technical sense) than a resident sage in retirement from Athens. Either way, Phormio and his lecture would be interesting evidence for cultural life at the Seleucid court.[50] Cicero sympathizes warmly with poor Hannibal, who after all his victories on the battlefield had to sit and listen to a lecture on his own life's craft by an elderly Greek windbag who had had no military experience whatever. The aside about the level of Hannibal's Greek – imperfect but effective – is neatly plausible. Nobody has tried to disprove this story (contrast the one about the chat with Scipio) as being inconsistent with the attested movements of either Hannibal or Phormio. We should probably accept that the incident really did occur.

It is true that the story of Hannibal and Phormio has some similarity with other anecdotes of the same approximate type, in which a military man (Hannibal again, a man called Eudamidas, probably a Hellenistic Spartan king) comments adversely on the opinion of a philosopher, perhaps a Stoic, who said that only the wise man can be a good general. Our knowledge of these anecdotes is owed to Plutarch and to Stobaeus (fifth century CE).[51] They do not undermine the Phormio story.

## 13.4 Greekness at Rome and Carthage in the Time of Hannibal and Scipio

Concentration on Hannibal and Scipio as individuals will get us only so far. The broader environment will help more. Roman cultural contacts with the Greek world are a vast topic, even when the inquiry is confined to the period up to 183 BCE; they have been the subject of many excellent modern studies, and a full treatment is beyond the scope of the present work.[52] I here touch briefly on only two areas: religion and literature.

It is exceptionally difficult to identify how much that happened in Roman history during the third century BCE was new, because books 11–20 of Livy are lost, and they covered the vital years between 293 and

---

[50] But he does not feature at Bikerman 1938: 39 (on intellectuals at Seleucid courts, including the Epicurean philosopher Philonides) or in Visscher 2020.
[51] For detailed discussion, see Appendix I.3 on 'roving anecdotes'.
[52] The most valuable modern works are Hoffmann 1934; Toynbee 1965: 2, chs. 13 and 14; Galinsky 1969; Ferrary 1988; Rawson 1989; Gruen 1990 and 1992; Feeney 2016, and many chapters of Feeney 2021.

about 220 ('about' because the early part of book 21 contains some retrospective material). We have only summaries of those books. Religion is a good example.[53] The third century as a whole, and the Hannibalic war in particular, have been seen, with good reason, as a period of innovation. Wissowa even said that the year 217 was the most important in the history of Roman religion.[54] That year saw a mass of religious responses to the Trasimene disaster, and an increase in Greek elements is detectable as the war went on.[55] But the novelty should not be exaggerated.[56] Livy book 10 ends with the advice of the Sibylline books to bring the cult of Aesculapius (Greek Asklepios) from Epidaurus in the Greek Peloponnese; this duly happened in 292.[57] Borrowings from Greece do not account for all changes. Lists of portents and prodigies are few in Livy's books 1–10, but frequent in book 21 and later books. But there are various explanations for the change (perhaps a mere change in recording practice), and in any case the late writer Julius Obsequens, who collected Livy's prodigy lists, took 249 as his start point: that is, a date in the first not the second Punic war. There are other examples of religious behaviours in the Hannibalic war period which might look more traditional if we had the full text of Livy's second Decade. In any case, there was some ambiguity in religious attitudes: a Greek and a Gaul were sacrificed in 228 and 216 at the time when the Romans were reaching out militarily and diplomatically across the Adriatic towards the Greek world in the east.[58]

The creation of a literature in Latin was an astonishing feat and was largely the achievement of one man, Livius Andronicus, who was not born a Roman but was probably a half-Greek from Sparta's colony Tarentum in the south of Italy.[59] He was active in Scipio's lifetime (he produced plays at the Roman games in 240 and died in 200). His rendering of Homer's *Odyssey* into Latin was ingeniously respectful of the original, but also firmly Roman: he did not use the hexameter metre of the original, and the first line invoked, not the Greek muse,

---

[53] See, citing modern work, Briscoe and Hornblower 2020: 61–2.   [54] Wissowa 1912: 60.
[55] On the introduction in 205 of the cult of the Great Mother (*Magna Mater*) from Asia Minor, see Livy 29.10–11, *MRR* 1: 204, and modern works cited at Briscoe and Hornblower 2020: 68 with n. 203 and 72. An honorific role in this episode was played by 'Publius Scipio, son of the man who fell in Iberia' (Livy 29.14.8); this is Nasica son of Gnaeus, not his first cousin Scipio Africanus, son of Publius, as wrongly identified by Warde Fowler 1911: 330. See Smith 1993: 45.
[56] For earlier, some much earlier, Roman contacts with Delphi, see p. 145.
[57] 10.47; *MRR* 1: 182.   [58] For the sacrifice, see p. 71.
[59] Toynbee 1965: 2. 416–34; Feeney 2016; Farrell 2021. For Livius Andronicus, p. 184 (discussing Livius Salinator). On the hellenism of the comic playwright Plautus (after 200): Adams 2003: 351–2; Feeney 2016: 61–2, 88.

but the Roman goddesses of inspiration, the *Camenae*. Towards the end of the third century, Fabius Pictor wrote his history in Greek, and although his work was not yet in the public domain, he was a natural choice for the embassy sent to Delphi in 216.[60] Young Scipio was still in Rome in that year and so was a witness to the atmosphere of fear which was generated by Hannibal, and which promoted the request to Delphi. For the 'three hearts' of Ennius, see p. 237.

Let us turn to Carthage.[61] Hannibal's late-life exposure to the elderly Greek philosopher Phormio was not a success, and he may never have been able to read Aristotle's *Politics* for himself. But it is important that Carthage's constitution is there treated by way of a direct comparison with Sparta and Crete, almost as if it were a Greek *polis* or region. At least one gifted Carthaginian could cope with Aristotle, although it would be unwise to build too many generalizations on him.[62] This man was a truly remarkable individual, a distinguished home-grown philosopher, whose lifetime (about 187–110 BCE) overlapped with that of Hannibal. His original name was Hasdrubal, like Hannibal's brother, but this was changed, presumably by himself not a teacher, to the Greek Kleitomachos, Latin Clitomachus. (Cicero mentions him several times.)[63] This was a radical onomastic change because the new name was not theophoric like Hasdrubal, which derives from Baal. His father was Diognetos, a theophoric Greek name from Zeus, so he may have been of mixed Carthaginian–Greek parentage.[64] Clitomachus left Carthage for Athens in his mid-twenties and became a pupil of Carneades (214–129 BCE), the most important exponent of the philosophy of the 'New' or 'Sceptical' Academy (the Academy took its name from the gymnasium dedicated to

---

[60] Livy 22.57.5 and 23.11.1–6 with Briscoe and Hornblower 2020: 68–9 and 310.
[61] See p. 290 for Greek features of Carthage's religious life, discussing Bonnet 2006.
[62] Geus 1994: 12 lists another second-century BCE philosopher (an 'Academic', i.e. Platonic pupil of Lakydes) called Ariston, a Carthaginian with a Greek name; compare Hannibal's Tyrian agent Ariston, p. 310; or the Carthaginian Philippus (not a philosopher) at Livy 39.42.8 with Walsh 1994: 159: 'the Greek name need occasion no surprise; Carthage was by this date a Hellenistic city'. (True enough. But Briscoe 2008: 360 thinks it may have been a nickname.)
[63] Diogenes Laertius, *Lives of the philosophers* 4.67. He has often been discussed. See Momigliano 1975: 5; Huss 1985: 53 and 505; Geus 1994: 150–3 'Hasdrubal (13)'; Habicht 1997: 274 and n. 30; *OCD*[4] 'Clitomachus'; Gruen 2011: 137; Feeney 2016: 204. Cf. Corsten 2019: 147 for the change of name. At least one other philosopher underwent a less culturally drastic name change at Athens: Theophrastus, 'divine speaker', started as Tyrtamos but was renamed by his teacher Aristotle: Diog. Laert. 5.38. This man's original name is unique and of uncertain derivation. It may have 'sounded barbarian' (Parker 2019b: 4 and n. 5), but its bearer was certainly a Greek, from Eresus on Lesbos. Parker notes that Plato too was said to have started out with a different name, but the truth of this has been doubted.
[64] Steph. Byz. Καρχηδών, κ 104 Billerbeck, the only evidence; Geus 1994: 150.

a local hero called Hekademos, who received cult in the district of Athens where Plato had his school).[65] Carneades was also originally from north Africa (but from the Greek city of Cyrene, a 'granddaughter' foundation of Sparta via Sparta's Aegean colony Thera/Santorini), and it would not be too difficult to write a Mary Renault-style story exploiting the well-attested personal connection between the two men.[66] Clitomachus was author of a huge number of purely philosophical treatises setting out the doctrines of Carneades, who himself wrote nothing, like Socrates and Jesus of Nazareth. But Clitomachus/Hasdrubal did not forget his homeland, because he also took time to compose a book 'to console his Carthaginian fellow-citizens, now in captivity', *consolandi causa ad captiuos, ciues suos*, after their city was sacked in 146.[67] Eventually, he rose to be scholarch of the Academy.

Later writers did not forget Clitomachus' origins either. Cicero called him 'clever, as might be expected for a Carthaginian, and very studious and diligent', *et homo acutus, ut Poenus, et ualde studiosus et diligens*. The comment is not necessarily patronizing.[68] This is an extraordinary career, and although much of it was spent in Athens, he must surely have had some training in Greek philosophy in Greek at what had very recently been Hannibal's Carthage, before emigrating to Athens (we shall shortly meet four Greek philosophers at Carthage from what may be an earlier date).[69] It is true that our main source Diogenes Laertius says that already at Carthage Clitomachus did philosophy 'in his own language' (the word for 'language' is φωνή, lit. 'voice' or 'speech'), but Diogenes may here just be drawing false inferences.[70] It would be a mistake to explain it by

---

[65] See *OCD*⁴ 'Carneades' and 'Academy'.

[66] Clitomachus was with Carneades until his old age, *usque ad senectutem* (presumably Carneades' old age, although in that case one might have expected 'until his death', *usque ad mortem*): Cicero, *Academics* 2.98. Mary Renault (1905–83): compare the philosophers in her historical novel about fourth-century Sicily, *The mask of Apollo*.

[67] Cicero, *Tusculan disputations* 3.54, proving that Clitomachus' book was available to be read a century later.

[68] *Academica* 2.98. Reid 1885 (commentary on the *Acad.*): 295, starts by saying the Latin means 'clever, as might be expected from a Carthaginian'. He continues, however: 'But Nep. *Epam* [*inondas*] 5.2 *exercitatum in dicendo, ut Thebanum scilicet*, '[skilled at speaking] considering that he was a Theban', the Thebans being slow of speech. The *ut* in these clauses conveys two quite different meanings, according to the context.' In the second passage, *scilicet* may hint at the more patronizing nuance. If Cicero also meant to be patronizing, cf. Thucydides on Brasidas: 'good at speaking – for a Spartan': 4.84.2. But, as Denis Feeney points out to me, Cicero may be saying that he had 'not only the native quickness you would expect from a Carthaginian, but also habits of industry'. Reinhardt 2023: 61 translates 'a man who was sharp, as one would expect from a Carthaginian'.

[69] Training at Carthage: so, very plausibly, Feeney 2016: 204.    [70] So Feeney, as in previous n.

appealing to the startling notice of a senatorial decree at Carthage imposing a ban on reading and speaking Greek in future, said to have been passed in the early fourth century, and designed to prevent anyone from speaking or writing to an enemy without an interpreter.[71] The story seems most improbable.[72] But if there is any truth in it, it is likely to have been a mere short-lived panic measure passed in the wars with Dionysius I, prompted – says Justin – by some alleged treasonable communication in Greek with Dionysius. The amount of Carthaginian intermarriage with Greeks would have made any such ban very hard to enforce.[73] In any case, we learn from the late (second century CE) philosopher Iamblichus that four Carthaginians of the Pythagorean school of philosophy were active at Carthage in perhaps the fourth century BCE. Their very Greek-looking names were Anthes (or Anthen), Hodius, Leocritus, and Miltiades, but Iamblichus gives their ethnics unequivocally.[74]

Carthage in Hannibal's boyhood was a booming and blooming commercial centre with no doubt a high standard of living.[75] This continued to be true well after the defeat at Zama and into the lifetime of Hasdrubal-Clitomachus, although arguably on a somewhat less international scale. Greek traders and businessmen, always proficient linguists themselves, then as now, must have helped to make the city an attractively multilingual society.[76] Punic-speaking traders reached Athens from the east, as can be seen today from archaeological material in the Piraeus and Athens and other museums, but it is surprising – perhaps a mere accident of survival? – that none of the eighteen

---

[71] Justin 20.5.13: *facto senatus consulto, ne quis postea Karthaginiensis aut litteris Graecis aut sermoni studeret, ne aut loqui cum hoste aut scribere sine interprete posset.* See p. 280.
[72] Huss 1985: 143 n. 15 thought the whole treason story improbable. Quinn 2018: 83 says the ban cannot have lasted long, citing Hannibal's employment of Sosylus.
[73] I owe this point also to Denis Feeney. For intermarriage with Greeks (like the parents of Hasdrubal/ Clitomachus) see pp. 62 and 146 on Hdt. 7.166, and on the two Syracusan-born Carthaginians of mixed descent on Hannibal's staff.
[74] Iamblichus, *Life of Pythagoras* (or *On the Pythagorean life*) 27.128 and 36.267; Geus 1994: 11, 172, 173, 198–9. For the sixth-century BCE philosopher Pythagoras, see *OCD*⁴ 'Pythagoras (1)' (C. H. K[ahn]). Masson 2000: 223–4 suggests, in rejection of Iamblichus, that the four, 'tous porteurs de bons noms grecs', came from Greek Chalcedon in Bithynia, not Carthage, Καλχηδών not Καρχηδών. Cf. *LGPN* VA (2010): 33, Ἄνθην; 343,r Ὅδιος; 267, Λεώκριτος; 318, Μιλτιάδης. This works better for Hodios than for the others, cf. Homer *Iliad* 2.856, *FGrHist* 156 Arrian frags. 97–8 for the name in Bithynia; but it is also found at Miletus and Samothrace.
[75] For this aspect of the series of treaties between Rome and Carthage before the Punic wars, see p. 62, citing Palmer 1997.
[76] For inscriptional evidence for Greek–Punic code-switching in north Africa, some as early as the second century BCE, see Adams 2003: 240–2.

surviving inscribed monuments are actually for Carthaginians.[77] Other epigraphic evidence, in the form of decrees, indicates the presence of Carthaginian diplomats and traders at Classical Athens.[78] There is even, as an inscription shows, contact with inland Thebes.[79] In Carthage itself, Punic artists and craftsmen and architects were influenced by Greek models (this, rather than 'the presence of Greek hands', is thought to be the explanation of strikingly Greek subjects and handling).[80] From the first half of the third century, we hear of a sculptor called Boethus son of Apollodorus, who despite those two Greek names was certainly a Carthaginian, but perhaps of partially Greek descent.[81] Ptolemaic Egypt to the east was the nearest Hellenistic kingdom to Carthage geographically and was an obvious source of artistic and other models, as coins may illustrate.[82] Carthage's even nearer neighbour Cyrene was for the most of the Hellenistic period under direct Ptolemaic control, and sometimes not; but either way it was a flourishing Greek *polis* – the home city of Callimachus and of the multi-talented Eratosthenes as well as of Carneades – as was Cyrene's own daughter-city to the west, Euesperides, the modern Benghazi. It is even possible that touring Greek dramatic troupes visited Carthage.[83] There were limits, however: no Hellenistic Carthaginian victor at the panhellenic games can be pointed to, whereas a metrical Greek inscription celebrates a prince from Phoenician Sidon called Diotimus (like Diognetus, a good theophoric Greek name derived from Zeus), who won the chariot race at the Nemean games in mainland Greece, about 200 BCE.[84] The poet's patron was able to assert his Greekness by alluding to the mythical foundation of Greek Thebes by Cadmus the Phoenician, son of Sidonian Agenor. No Carthaginian athlete or charioteer seems to have wanted to find

---

[77] See Bäbler 1998: 115–55 for archaeologically attested Phoenicians at Athens, with catalogue at 240–50, nos. 51–68. She has no separate section on Carthaginians.
[78] For diplomacy between Carthage and Athens in the late fifth century, see O/R no. 189 (cf. p. 63). An inscription from the fourth century (*SEG* 35.70, about 333) is a proxeny decree for two Tyrians and has been conjectured to relate to a Carthaginian trade delegation: a recently identified fragment adds 'from Carthage' at line 2; and see line 6 for import of corn to Athens.
[79] R/O no. 43, mid-fourth century.
[80] Boardman 1994: 62–4 and figs. 3.15–20, esp. 18, Greek-looking Hellenistic votive relief to Persephone, dedicated at Carthage in Punic by a Punic official, Milkyaton.
[81] Paus. 5.17.4 and epigraphic evidence: Geus 1994: 15–16 and nn. 57–60.
[82] See the two very similar coins (Carthaginian, *c.* 300, Ptolemaic, *c.* 320) at Quinn 2018: 122 fig. 6.2, both depicting Herakles (Punic Melqart) on the obverse.
[83] Feeney 2016: 205 and 319 nn. 26 and 27.
[84] Austin no 140. For Diognetus, father of Clitomachus, see p. 285.

a way to turn the mythical Tyrian founder of Carthage, Dido/Elissa, into any sort of a Greek.[85]

But, given the centuries-old Carthaginian presence on Sicily, especially in the west, the most important and perennial locus of Carthaginian–Greek contacts was naturally Sicily (and Malta).[86] Intermarriage specifically mentioned in literary sources tends to be associated with Syracuse in the east of Sicily, but Carthaginians with Greek personal names could have had a parent from virtually anywhere on the island. Ubiquitous and literally tangible evidence for cultural interaction was the fine Siculo-Punic coinage, minted in the west to pay soldiers. The inspiration of some of the coins is the bronze issues of Agathocles, Greek tyrant of Syracuse, and the script is bilingual. But this does not mean that 'Greek is a rejection of Punic'. The facial types are 'commonplace within idealized Hellenistic portraiture'.[87] Siculo-Punic silver tetradrachms from about 300 BCE depicting a male head covered with a lion-scalp have been much discussed. Melqart or Heracles? Perhaps simultaneously both.[88] (This has implications for our next aspect, Carthaginian religion.) Beautiful though some of these coins are, the most spectacular example of Greek–Carthaginian cultural interaction is a fifth-century marble statue found in 1979 at Motya, modern Mozia, a tiny island just off the far west coast of Sicily: the 'Motya charioteer'. The resemblance to Greek exemplars is palpable, notably to a famous statue of a charioteer at Delphi.[89] But to categorize it as booty from a Greek city of Sicily risks making patronizing assumptions about the quality and abilities of local Punic workshops; and statues of that size and weight are awkward to move and need

---

[85] For Dido/Elissa, see Geus 1994: 204–7. A Greek pedigree could have been achieved indirectly, by invoking the tradition connecting Agenor with Tyre as well as Sidon, as at Hdt. 1.2.1 with 4.147.4 (Agenor king of Tyre as father of both Europa and Cadmus), Curtius Rufus 4.4.15 and 19 (with Atkinson 1980: 312, citing also Paus. 5.25.12); cf. Quinn 2018: 47 and 227 nn. 22 and 23.

[86] For Malta, see the bilingual Greek–Punic inscription *IG* 12.600 (*ICO*: 15–17, Malta no. 1, with fig. 1 and plate 1), on which see Adams 2003: 200, Yarrow 2013: 357, and Hornblower 2022: 98, n. on Lycophron, *Alexandra* 1027 (where 'Melite' is almost certainly Malta, which was not conquered by the Romans until 218, see Livy 21.51.1–2, cf. p. 88 for the capture by the consul Longus). This text and *IG* 12.953, an honorary decree from Malta for a Syracusan, are both late third century BCE. The Punic-speaking population will not have been evicted after the Roman takeover.

[87] Yarrow 2013: 354–64, discussing Siculo-Punic issues and the coinage of the Mercenary revolt of 241–238 BCE; quotations from 361 and 363. On the Siculo-Punic mints and coinage, *ACGC*: 227–8 and 233–5 is still useful.

[88] So Yarrow 2013: 357. (cf. 356, questioning whether the distinction is even meaningful).

[89] Motya: *Barr.* map 47 A3. Punic inscriptions from Motya: *ICO*: 60–1 and 63–5, Sicily nos. 10, 13, 14, dedications to Baal Hammon). For the Delphi charioteer, see Smith 2007: 127 figs. 30 and 31.

large cranes.⁹⁰ One adventurous theory associates the statue with the Carthaginian cult allegedly paid to Hamilcar (1) after Himera (480).

Let us now return to Carthaginian religion, already touched on when discussing Hannibal and religion, and ask specifically about the degree of its Greekness.⁹¹ In a cautious study, Bonnet does not deny a degree of Carthaginian 'permeability' to some features of Greek religion. An example: the Sicilian Diodorus, probably using the Sicilian Timaeus, reports that in the early fourth century the Carthaginians adopted the pre-eminently Sicilian cults of Persephone and Demeter, including setting up special priesthoods for them. Bonnet regards this as something other than an act of 'hellenization'.⁹² Instead, she regards it as a religious *captatio beneuolentiae* (an attempt to win over the goodwill of a potentially hostile deity), comparable to the Roman adoption of the cults of Venus Erycina (of Sicilian) Eryx or Cybele.⁹³ That may be so, but such recruitment is one of the ways in which religions of distinct cultures interacted and lost their separateness, whatever abstract word we use for the process; and 'hellenization' is as good as any, once stripped of any offensive implication of *de haut en bas* – that is, the imposition of a higher on a lower culture, and therefore of cultural domination. 'Hellenism' is a less loaded term, but vaguer in that it does not convey the notion of a process.⁹⁴ But if Diodorus' report is reliable, it is evidence for good awareness of Greek religion by Carthaginians and a willingness to import and adopt the religious aspect of hellenism for their own purposes.⁹⁵

By contrast with her treatment of adoption of cults, Bonnet regards the story of the foundation of Carthage as a Greek-style foundation legend, although there is no Greek parallel whatever for the crucial feature, the

---

⁹⁰ For the Motya statue, usually on display at the Mozia museum, see Bell 1995; Hornblower 2004: 197 and fig. 3 at 198 (photos); and above all Smith 2007: 133–4 (whence the point about cranes) and 132 figs. 37–9 (photos). Smith notes the 'strong Greek presence' at fifth-century BCE Motya. Fentress 2013: 160 is very brief; cites Bell but not Smith.

⁹¹ Bonnet 2006.

⁹² Bonnet 2006: 373–4, on Diod. 14.77.4–5: 'Parler d'hellénisation de Carthage à propos de l'introduction de Déméter et Korè [Persephone, Latin Proserpina] semble donc abusif [improper]' (374). The cult of Demeter and daughter Kore was massively popular in Sicily, as shown by the quantity of deposits displayed in the museum at Agrigento, Ancient Greek Akragas. For Timaeus as Diodorus' source here, see Meister 1967: 95.

⁹³ For Venus of Eryx, see p. 96. A drastic extension of this idea was the 'calling out' of the enemy's gods to one's own side, but this was effective only between closely similar communities, such as between Rome and Etruscan cities. For such *euocatio deorum*, see esp. Livy 5.21 (Etruscan Veii), with Ogilvie 1965: 674.

⁹⁴ See *OCD*⁴ 'Hellenism, Hellenization', and the works there cited.

⁹⁵ On Hercules/Melqart, already discussed under coinage, see p. 227 (the oaths in the treaty of 215 with Philip V).

slicing up of an ox-hide.⁹⁶ Common sense nevertheless suggests that, given Carthage's maritime situation and the evidence for Carthaginian intermarriage with Greeks, it would be astonishing if Greek religion had left only slight traces there.

## 13.5 City Foundations in Iberia: The Barcids

This section will be broader than purely biographical in the narrow sense. It will take in the direct families and relatives by marriage of Hannibal and Scipio.

Cities have been founded in every inhabited continent and every period, and city-states are far from being a Greek invention.⁹⁷ But one useful approach to the 'Greekness' of Hannibal (and family) is to examine their respective city foundations, real or alleged, and to ask what they might owe to Greek attitudes and practices, especially in the way new cities were named. The section will end by looking at New Carthage and other Carthaginian city foundations, asking more generally how, in their apparent aims and their geographical positioning they resembled or differed from Greek city foundations. Neither Hannibal nor Scipio is known to have founded cities in Iberia, if we discount Scipio's alleged and very dubiously attested foundation of Italica as a Hadrianic fiction.⁹⁸ More believable but still vulnerable traditions held that Hannibal did help to found cities in Asia Minor in the time of his exile.⁹⁹ But there are no such traditions about Scipio. His 'exile' at Italian Liternum at the end of his life was brief and internal. In the early 180s, he and his brother ordered the affairs of Greek cities in Asia Minor, always in accordance with the senate's wishes or known policies. But it was not until Pompey in the 60s BCE that a Roman commander created or re-founded cities in that part of the world.

Carthage and Rome both claimed to have been founded from pre-existing cities of the east Mediterranean: Tyre and Troy, except that Roman mythology contrived to combine the ancient Aeneas story with the Indigenous myth of the much younger Romulus.¹⁰⁰ So neither Hannibal's home city nor Scipio's were themselves thought of as Greek

---

⁹⁶ Bonnet 2006: 370–1, following Scheid and Svenbro 1985. The ox-hide: see pp. 377–8.
⁹⁷ For a comparative study of thirty city-state cultures, see Hansen 2000, and for a further six, Hansen 2002.
⁹⁸ See Chapter 4.6 for Scipio and Italica.
⁹⁹ These traditions will be dealt with in Chapter 17.5.
¹⁰⁰ Tyre: as for the reality, Quinn 2018: 129 is sceptical (too sceptical perhaps) about the 'notion that Carthage was originally a formal or even informal Tyrian colony'. Rome and Troy: see Alföldi 1957; Cornell 1975; Wiseman 1995; Erskine 2001; and Hornblower 2018: 52, 111–19.

foundations. Indeed, it has been well said that 'when the Romans decided that they were ultimately Trojans, they were in effect saying that they were neither Greeks nor Etruscans'.[101] Nevertheless, Greek city foundations had from the eighth century been a largely Mediterranean-wide and Black Sea phenomenon: Greeks settled 'like ants or frogs round a pond', as Plato made Socrates put it.[102] Other cultures must surely have looked to the Greek example.

Since the time of Alexander the Great's father Philip II of Macedon, new cities were often 'eponymous', that is, they were named by or after a mortal man or woman.[103] Carthage's north African neighbours to its east, the Ptolemies, were not themselves very active city founders, unlike the Seleucids; but their kingdom included the greatest and most successful of all eponymous foundations, Egyptian Alexandria, the personal work of Alexander himself (rather than named after him by someone else). Greek colonial cities often paid hero cult to a founder or *oikist*.[104] This was not confined to the Archaic and Classical periods: Alexander was honoured at Egyptian Alexandria as the 'Founder'; and at early Hellenistic Ai Khanum in Bactria (northern Afghanistan), there was a *temenos* or religious precinct to a Thessalian called Cineas, evidently a founder or *oikist*.[105] Neither Carthage nor Rome went in for cult of this sort, nor is cult of any sort attested for either Hannibal or Scipio.[106]

There was a second and very simple way in which new Classical and especially Hellenistic cities were named: by reproducing the place name of the founding city or of a city in the old home region. So in the Archaic period, Locri in south Italy was settled by Locrians from central Greece. This was a form of nostalgia, sometimes suggested by similarities of new and old terrain, or by perceived familiarity of other sorts. Appian lists a large number of cities in Syria such as Edessa, Beroia, and Pella which were named after Macedonian predecessors, and Thessalians serving with Alexander convinced themselves that they had found long-lost kin in Armenia.[107] We have seen that Theocritus' fictitious ladies in Sicilian

---

[101] Momigliano 1989: 56 (= 1984: 384), cf. Dench 2005: 220 on Rome's 'not-quite-Greek Trojan roots'.
[102] *Phaedo* 109a–b. The surprising and perhaps unattractive ants are usually omitted when this picturesque passage is quoted by modern scholars, as it often is (e.g. at Brown 1971: 11). *Largely successful*: there were many failed Greek attempts at overseas settlement.
[103] For an annotated list, Fraser 2009: 324–76; see also Cohen 1995, 2006, and 2013. For Alexander's cities see Fraser 1996, and, for Egyptian Alexandria, Fraser 1972.
[104] See e.g. Hdt. 6.38.1, Miltiades.   [105] See Cohen 2013: 225–44.   [106] See pp. 428, 418–19.
[107] App. *Syrian history* 57/297–8 with Cohen 2006: 177; Thessalians in Armenia: Strabo 11.14.12 with Lane Fox 2018: 198. For Syrian Larisa as named for the Thessalian Larisa, see Diod. 33.4a with Cohen 2006: 117 and Lane Fox 2018: 211–12.

Syracuse can even say 'we are Corinthians', because Syracuse was a Corinthian foundation long before.[108]

The Barcid family in Iberia were energetic city founders: Hannibal's father Hamilcar (9) founded Leuke Akra, probably on the site of modern Alicante.[109] More important was his son-in-law Hasdrubal (5)'s foundation in 228 of 'New Carthage'.[110] In fact, the Punic name of the original, African, Carthage, *Qart-Chadasht*, itself means 'New City' in Punic. There was no question of calling the Iberian Carthage by the name of its human founder, in the Greek manner. But the decision to call it simply 'Carthage' was perhaps influenced by the Hellenistic Greek practice we have just noticed: calling a new and distant city by a familiar name, in fact the name of the actual metropolis.

It might be objected that since 'Carthage' just means 'New City' in Punic, a second Punic 'New City' somewhere else would not call the metropolis to mind. This approach is too literal. The ancient Greek name for modern Naples, Italian Napoli, was Neapolis, and this too means New City. It is absurd to suppose that every time that great city was named, the notion of newness was mentally present. So too with Carthage: in whatever language, Iberian Carthage was much more than just the New City.

Diodorus says that Hasdrubal founded 'another city', but that is all we know about it.[111] Hannibal's own period as commander in Iberia was short: he had no time for city founding. At any rate, there is none that we hear of. All the evidence for him in this role is from his last years as a royal pensioner in Asia Minor.

The founder of Iberian Italica was not Scipio Africanus, as Appian claimed. But in any case the founder, whoever he was, named it after his country, not after himself, like a Hellenistic ruler.[112] It was not until the proconsul Tiberius Sempronius Gracchus, father of the famous Gracchi brothers and son-in-law of Scipio Africanus, founded Graccuris in Iberia (178) that a Roman presumed to name a city or

---

[108] Theoc. *Idyll* 15.91; see p. 276.   [109] See p. 68 on Diod. 25.10.3.
[110] Latin *noua Carthago*, as at Livy 26.42.2. But Latin authors often called it just 'Carthage', as at Livy 22.19.19.3; conversely, for Polybius it was sometimes 'New City', Καινὴ πόλις (as at 3.95.2, and see 5.1.3), but also sometimes just 'Carthage', Καρχηδών (as at 10.9.3); at its first mention, he says specifically that some call it 'Carthage', some 'New City' (2.13.1). Cf. *HCP* 1: 167. For the foundation, see p. 69, cf. 60.
[111] Diod. 25.12.
[112] Not Scipio: Chapter 4.6. Pina Polo 2021: 155 briefly observes that Italica was one of four specified Roman foundations in the Iberian peninsula 'in the same period' (this is vaguely defined as 'pre-Caesarian', p. 154) which did not receive the name of an imperator; but otherwise says nothing about Italica. He seems to be avoiding the Scipio problem!

town after himself.¹¹³ But once Scipio is removed from the Italica story, there is no telling whether the foundation of Italica antedated or postdated that of Graccuris.

Iberian Graccuris was founded in 178 by Tiberius Sempronius Gracchus.¹¹⁴ Some Italian assize or market towns, Latin *fora*, founded in the second century, also bore the names of their founders, but none is definitely earlier than Graccuris.¹¹⁵ The place name Graccuris is curious and without obvious parallel. The town is attested by only two literary sources, and some coins from the time of the emperor Tiberius (14–37 CE), which spell it Graccurris.

First, the summary (*periocha*) of Livy book 41. This says that Gracchus 'established the town Graccuris in Iberia as a memorial to his own works', *monimentumque operum suorum Graccurim, oppidum in Hispania, constituit.*¹¹⁶ (We have most of Livy book 41, but the text of Livy's fifth Decade is unsatisfactory and missing at the crucial place.) Second, the eighth-century CE epitome of the grammarian Pompeius Festus (second century CE) says that Graccuris was an Iberian place, and that it had previously been called Ilurcis.¹¹⁷ If Gracchus was imitating a Hellenistic king (although surely such self-aggrandizement would have been politically dangerous in the 170s), one might have expected the name to be Graccheia, on the analogy of Alexandr(e)ia, for example, or Seleukeia/Seleucia or indeed Caesare(i)a later on, to give them their Greek spellings.

The actual suffix is thought to be related to a Basque word *uri/urri* meaning 'city'.¹¹⁸ The entry in 'Festus' is compatible with a subsequent

---

¹¹³ The main evidence is Livy *Periocha* 41.2.

¹¹⁴ *MRR* 1: 395–6; *Barr.* map 25 D3. See Pina Polo 2021: 146–7, 155–6 (arguing that the senate approved the foundation, but only after the event; cf. p. 171) and 160); also Harris 1989: 128–9 and Levene 2023: 2.635. I am indebted to David Levene for help with Graccuris, especially for an advance sight of his commentary on *Periochae* 41.2. Richardson 1986 regularly spells it Gracchurris (*sic*) without explaining why.

¹¹⁵ Pina Polo 2021: 156 n. 64. One of these was Forum Sempronii, mod. Fossombrone, founded by (Sempronius) Gracchus at about the same time as Iberian Graccuris. For fora as market towns or assize towns (i.e. civic centres where provincial governors held their courts), see *OCD*⁴ forum and conventus (2).

¹¹⁶ The place name at Livy *Periocha* 41 is a correction (based on Paul's epitome of Festus, see next n.); the manuscripts have *Gracchorum* or *Graccorum*. Levene (see n. 114) prefers *Graccuris*, partly because of the evidence of the later coins. *Monimentum* and *monumentum* are variant spellings.

¹¹⁷ That entry is generally cited as 'Fest. 86 L[indsay]', but it is not an actual fragment of Festus but part of Paul the Deacon's later epitome, itself an epitome of Augustus' friend Verrius Flaccus. So something may have dropped out en route from Verrius. Festus' interests were primarily etymological, and the entry gives purely historical facts, unless we count the statement that it was previously called Ilurcis.

¹¹⁸ Knapp 1977: 109, cited by Levene (see n. 114). See also Pina Polo 2021: 147 ('perhaps an indigenous suffix that could have meant "city"').

renaming in Gracchus' honour by the locals; but the *periocha* is explicit that the naming was by Gracchus himself, and that presumably reflects a missing sentence of Livy. So it should be respected. If Graccuris was really a partly Iberian name, given by Gracchus himself, it might throw an interesting light on his attitude towards the local inhabitants, who may have formed part of the intended population.[119]

Roman colonies on the sites of pre-existing Greek cities in south Italy were given encouraging new names, sometimes martial, so that south Italian Thurii became Copia, 'Abundance' and Hipponium became Vibo Valentia, two words conveying the ideas of military strength and valour.[120] Roman colonies on the sites of pre-existing Greek cities in south Italy were given encouraging new names, sometimes martial, so that south Italian Thurii became Copia, 'Abundance' and Hipponium became Vibo Valentia, two words conveying the ideas of military strength and valour. This sort of onomastic optimism was an old Greek habit of mind, too. Many Mediterranean cities were optimistically called 'Olbia' – 'happy', 'prosperous' – not only the best-known Milesian foundation in the Black Sea region: Stephanus of Byzantium lists no fewer than nine Olbias.[121]

Some Roman foundations or re-foundations were 'theophoric', that is, named for a god. Gracchus himself (the father) was one of the three commissioners (*triumuiri*) who founded the Italian colony Saturnia in 183.[122] When his son Gaius wanted to send a colony to the site of Carthage, its name was to be Junonia, after Juno, who was supposed to have transferred her support from Carthage to Rome. By contrast with all these choices, the name Italica would imply that many of the settlers were Italians.[123] The name, like that of (Iberian) Carthage, recalled the home region, by a form of onomastic nostalgia somewhat like the naming of Italian Locri after Greek Locri.

## 13.6 Conclusion

For both Hannibal and Scipio, Greek language and culture were to some extent foreign, but in the two decades either side of 200 BCE, they were also familiar and unavoidable parts of life for both Carthaginians and Romans. For Rome, this hardly needs illustration. As for Carthage, the career of the philosopher Hasdrubal/Clitomachus may have been unusual, but that it

---

[119] But Levene tells me he would not wish to relate the partly Iberian name to the Iberian element in the city's population.
[120] For these two places and their renaming, see Hornblower 2018: 60, 64, 75.    [121] o 41 Bill.
[122] Livy 39.55.9; *MRR* 1: 380.    [123] See p. 130.

was possible at all says something important about his early home milieu, which was clearly not a stranger to philosophy. Lucian's frivolous portrait of Hannibal as a self-confessed untutored barbarian is part of an implied false contrast with Scipio, but in any case Strabo in the time of Augustus could casually speak of the 'barbarization' of much of Greek south Italy, meaning its Romanization.[124] Neither Hannibal nor Scipio wrote much in Greek, but then nor did they write much in their own respective languages either. Scipio at Syracuse in 204 displayed a positive enthusiasm for a Greek lifestyle, but it was Hannibal who spent his last years at Greek-speaking courts and may have helped their rulers to found eponymous cities of a Hellenistic type. Neither man aimed at kingship or sought to name cities after himself.

## Appendix 13.1    Hannibal and 'Learning Greek *Litterae*'

For the two aspects of the word see *OLD littera* 1, 2, and 3 (the basic senses), 8 and 9 (literature). But I wanted more specific and thorough guidance about Nepos' likely meaning, so on 1 October 2020, I consulted Jim Adams by email, and he replied as follows. He began by referring me to the 'important part ... of the very good long article on *littera* in the *TLL* which draws attention to ambiguities'.[125] He continued:

> *littera* can of course mean 'letter, grapheme' but it often in the plural refers to writings. If you 'learn Greek letters' it may be understood that you are learning the language at the same time. It would not seem very convincing to attempt to pin down the type of phrase I think Nepos has to mean specifically 'to learn the Greek alphabet'. There is bound to be at least an ambiguity. The *TLL* quotes Jerome's Vulgate John 19.20 *erat scriptum Hebraice* ['it was written in Hebrew'] alongside Luke 23.38 *erat superscriptio inscripta super illum ... litteris Graecis, Latinis et Hebreicis* ['there was a superscription above him ... in Greek, Latin, and Hebrew *litterae*'], where the second passage has to allude to languages as well as alphabets.[126] If you took the latter passage dead literally the inscription or whatever might have been written in just one language, but transliterated from the alphabet of that language into two other alphabets as well.

---

[124] 6.1.2, making exceptions for Rhegium, Tarentum and Naples. See Bowersock 1965: 81 n. 8.

[125] *TLL littera* IV, 1527.79–81: *respicitur l i n g u a* (*sing. collect*.; *usus praeparatur locutionibus pluralibus uelut* '[litter]is Punicis scribere, insculpere' (*v. sub i*) *uel* '[litter]as Graecas discere' (*v. sub ii*), *ubi etiam linguae notio subaudiri potest*' ['where the notion of language may also be implied'].

[126] Both of these biblical texts refer to the multilingual (Greek, Latin, Hebrew) notice (*superscriptio* or *titulus*) fixed above Jesus' head on the cross. It read 'The King of the Jews', words which Pontius Pilate famously refused to qualify under pressure (he was asked to change it to 'he *said* he was ... '), saying 'what I have written, I have written'. Cf. Barrett 1955: 457 on the whole John passage (19.19–22).

So Adams judged that we cannot pin Nepos' Latin down, and we must accept this. Another approach might have been via Sosylus, a Greek himself, who is surely Nepos' source here and would presumably have used the Greek word *grammata* (γράμματα), which Nepos translated as *litterae*. The Greek word can mean 'a man's writings'.[127] But when it does so, it is usually in the singular, *gramma*. To teach someone Greek *grammata* would most naturally be taken to mean teaching them the Greek language.[128] But this point can hardly be pressed.

---

[127] LSJ⁹ γράμμα III.3; cf. *CGL* (§10).
[128] Herodotus (4.78.1) says that the half-Greek Scythian Scyles was taught Greek γλῶσσα (lit. 'tongue') and γράμματα, how to speak and write Greek, by his Greek mother.

CHAPTER 14

# Hannibal Flees to Antiochus III; His Intrigues; 195–193
## Aged 52–54

### 14.1 Introduction

Hannibal was forced by domestic enemy intrigues and Roman pressure to flee from Carthage in secret, probably in 195.[1] Livy's source for his departure is probably Polybius, whose own sources cannot be certainly identified.[2] The narrative of the flight has been thought to look suspiciously like that of Themistocles to Persia by sea, as described by Thucydides, and that is presumably taken to indicate Livy's use of an inferior and sensationalist Latin writer. But the similarities are slight and general.[3] For political exiles in the ancient world, a royal or satrapal court was a natural refuge, and a clandestine escape was the natural solution.[4] It is true that there are occasional Thucydidean touches, but they are not from the Themistocles narrative.[5] In any case, Polybius was perfectly capable of dramatic or tragic narrative, as indeed was Thucydides himself.[6] (This is not to deny that Livy sometimes 'improved' what he found in Polybius.) For once, let us follow Livy's story in full.[7] It is a good one, conspicuously favourable to Hannibal, and rightly admiring of his coolness and ingenuity under pressure.

---

[1] We now resume Hannibal's story from Chapter 12. To recapitulate, in Livy, his flight (33.47.3–49.7) is narrated immediately after the account of his reforms (33.45.6–47.2). Together, these two interlocking passages form the second main slice of narrative about Hannibal between Zama and 195. See p. 268.
[2] Source: Briscoe 1973: 335–6. (Tränkle 1977 does not discuss the passage.) For the date, see n. 20.
[3] Th. 1.135–8; cf. Briscoe (n. 2).
[4] Refuges: from the fifth century, cf. O/R 121 (Ionian Erythrae) 27, 'those who have fled to the Medes', i.e. the Persian satrap; Th. 1.115.4 (discontented Samians).
[5] Unless we count Th. 1.136.1, Themistocles realized in advance what was afoot, cf. Livy 33.47.9, Hannibal saw through this. On the shared mentions of Ephesus, see p. 302 and n. 22.
[6] Cf. Livy 40.3–5, the horrific and certainly Polybian story of Theoxena and her children, with Walbank 1985: 215–16.
[7] Detailed references will not always be given.

## 14.2 The Flight from Carthaginian Territory: How Did He Manage It?

Hannibal's flight was precipitated by the arrival of three Roman envoys, whose official mission was to lay before the Carthaginian senate the accusation that Hannibal was plotting war (that is, against Rome) in combination with Antiochus.[8] They were two senior consular figures, Gnaeus Servilius Caepio, consul in 203, and Marcus Claudius Marcellus, consul in 196, and with them a younger man, Quintus Terentius Culleo, who went on to be praetor in 187.[9] But Hannibal's domestic enemies persuaded these Roman visitors to pretend that they had come to settle the Carthaginians' quarrel with Masinissa (Livy does not spell out the aim of this ploy, but it was evidently to detain an unsuspecting Hannibal in the city so that his enemies could destroy him). Hannibal alone saw through this; he realized that the Romans would not grant peace to Carthage unless an implacable war, *inexpiabile bellum*, was waged against him alone (that is, by the Romans).

He decided to yield to circumstances and fate or fortune, *fortuna* (this probably represents Greek τύχη, a favourite Polybian word and concept).[10] He had long made preparations for flight, and now he passed the day in the forum to avert suspicion. As soon as darkness fell, he went to the city gate in civilian clothes, with two companions who did not know what he was planning to do. Horses were waiting ready where he had ordered, and in the night he crossed the large area called Byzacium and reached his private castle, *turris*, on the sea between Acylla or Acholla and Thapsus (this is the first time we have heard of this evidence for Hannibal's personal wealth).[11] A fully equipped and manned ship was waiting. And so he left Africa, lamenting his country's fate more often than his own. He crossed to the island of Cercina the same day.[12]

---

[8] In what follows, brackets enclose explanatory or other comments on the Livian narrative.
[9] *MRR* I: 341; *DPRR* CLAU0997 (son of the conqueror of Syracuse, CLAU0810) and SERV0919 for the consulars. For Culleo, see *DPRR* TERE1135. He regarded Scipio as the author of his liberty, *libertatis auctor*, because of his release when he was a prisoner of war, and marched in his triumph wearing a cap of freedom (Livy 30.43.11 and 45.5). For younger men accompanying senior ambassadors (so as to do routine work like keeping a record?), cf. p. 264 n. 105, Hispallus on Crete. Sculllard 1973: 284 suggested that Culleo was appointed to the embassy as a supporter of Scipio (this is doubtful) and because he had local knowledge of Carthage from the time of his detention (but they were hardly going to get lost in the city). No doubt the embassy was also accompanied by enslaved people for menial tasks, but they are ignored by the ancient sources as usual.
[10] Walbank 2007; cf. p. 217 n. 53.
[11] For these places, see *Barr.* map 33. On that map, Byzacium stretches across 1–2 F–G; Acholla (so marked) is at H2, south of Thapsus at H1.
[12] *Barr.* map 33 H3. Cercina features in the story of another escape from (the site of) Carthage, that of Gaius Marius: Plut. *Mar.* 40.10.

In Cercina harbour, he found several Phoenician ships laden with merchandise. A crowd gathered to greet him as he stepped ashore, so when they questioned him he gave out that he had been sent on a mission to Tyre, the mother-city of Carthage. 'Mother' and 'daughter' cities were not always this friendly in the ancient world – witness the perennially bad relations between Greek Corinth and Corcyra – but there is plenty of evidence for this particular closeness. At the end of Alexander's prolonged siege of Tyre in 332 BCE, we hear of Carthaginian sacred envoys who happened to have come to the metropolis to pay honour to Hercules, 'according to an ancient custom'.[13]

But Hannibal was afraid that one of these ships might set out by night for Thapsus or Hadrumetum with the news that he had been sighted at Cercina. So he arranged a sacrifice and invited the ships' captains to a banquet on the seashore, including a huge improvised sunshade, really a kind of marquee, made from ships' sails and sailyards, because it was midsummer and very hot. Partying went on until far into the night, accompanied by heavy drinking. (The real purpose of the sunshade was to immobilize the ships.) Hannibal slipped away under cover of darkness, and when the others woke up, everybody had a hangover, *crapula*, and the crews had to waste several hours putting the ships back together again: a clever and amusing stratagem, as good as anything in Polyaenus or Frontinus.[14]

Back in Carthage, a crowd turned up to visit Hannibal's townhouse as usual (this sounds very like the Roman civic ritual of the morning greeting, *salutatio*.[15] But great men everywhere in the ancient world no doubt had their clients and hangers-on and the detail is believable). No Hannibal! People demanded to be told where he was: had he escaped, as indeed he had, or had he been murdered by Roman treachery? Opinions and sympathies were divided. Eventually news came that he had been sighted on Cercina.

The three Roman envoys announced in the (Carthaginian) senate that their own senate had discovered, first, that the earlier war against Philip of Macedon had been largely fomented by Hannibal (this was surely improvised nonsense); second, that he had sent letters and messengers to King Antiochus and the Aetolians; and third, that he had been plotting the defection of Carthage – that is, from the terms of its treaty with the Romans. They added that he had certainly gone to Antiochus (only a guess, but a correct one) and would not rest until he had incited the whole world to war. He must not go unpunished, if the Carthaginians

---

[13] Quinn 2018: 113–16, citing other evidence. Tyre: Arrian, *Anabasis* 2.24.5.
[14] Livy 33.48. See p. 225 n. 21 for the sacrifice.   [15] See *OLD* (2).

wanted to satisfy the Roman people that none of his actions had been carried out by their wishes, or with their official approval. The Carthaginians replied that they would do whatever the Romans decided was fair. (The Romans cannot have known that Hannibal would have vanished overnight, nor did they have time to consult the senate, so part of their speech must have been re-purposed and delivered on their own initiative – if they really spoke in this vein at all.)[16]

With this, Livy's strictly Carthaginian narrative breaks off for the moment. But Nepos adds some plausible extras in the same spirit as Livy's closure. Carthaginian ships pursued Hannibal to no avail, his property was confiscated, his townhouse was demolished, and he was formally condemned to exile.[17] The razing of the house of a condemned man was a solemn religious penalty in both Greek and Roman law.[18] Our knowledge of Carthaginian penal law is too slight to allow us to say that this detail betrays itself as fiction.

Livy follows the movements of Hannibal, who set sail for the other end of the Mediterranean. He put in first at Carthage's mother-city Tyre, which was now in the Seleucid sphere of influence.[19] From there, he moved north to a suburb of the Seleucid western capital Syrian Antioch called Daphne, where he met Antiochus' oldest son, another Antiochus, celebrating a festival.[20] This Antiochus was here deputizing for his father as crown prince, but he never became king because in 193 he predeceased his father, who was therefore succeeded in 187 by his second son Seleucus IV.[21]

---

[16] For this example of overseas improvisation, see p. 160.

[17] *Hannibal* 7.7. Town house: Nepos says *domus* but presumably does not mean his castle on the coast; razing a house was a public act of execration, which would be pointless at a remote coastal spot.

[18] Connor 1985. For Rome of the late Republic, see Cicero's speech *On his house*.

[19] Since the fifth Syrian war, 202–195 BCE. The 'Syrian wars', of which there were at least six, were between the Ptolemies and Seleucids. The term is misleading because they were not only for control of Syria (Austin: 286–7).

[20] Livy 33.49.6. For this, the most important of the many Antiochs, see Cohen 2006: 86–93 (calling it 'Antioch near Daphne'); Fraser 2009: 328–9; *Barr.* map 67 C4. Western capital: the eastern was Babylon. For Daphne, see *HCP* 3: 449 on Pol. 30.25.1 (Antiochus IV's competitively lavish celebration there in 166). The festival confirms that Hannibal's midsummer flight should be dated to 195 (cf. already Holleaux 1957b [1908]: 181), because an inscription published in 1964 (eventually *SEG* 36.1280) shows the festival was celebrated in 197; it was probably not annual but held every other year, so the next was 195. Briscoe 1973: 335 and 341; Cohen 2006: 82, 89 n. 17.

[21] For this Antiochus, see Livy 33.19.9 (where he is one of the 'two sons') and 35.15.2 (his death). On the difficulties of the former passage, see Briscoe 1973: 285, discussing Holleaux 1942b: 183–4. He is the 'Antiochus the son' mentioned alongside his father 'the great king Antiochus' and his mother, Queen Laodice, in *SEG* 36.1280 (previous n.). Cohen 2006: 82, discussing Hannibal's brief meeting with this prince at Daphne, mistakenly calls him 'the future Antiochus IV', who succeeded to the throne in 175 and was the youngest of the three sons of Antiochus III, two of whom were, confusingly, called Antiochus.

Antiochus the king was away, but Hannibal caught up with him at Ionian Ephesus. Themistocles had also fetched up here long ago, but Ephesus with its harbour Coressus was a very common (dis)embarkation point.[22] Antiochus had hitherto been wobbling about war with Rome, but Hannibal's arrival gave the push needed to shift him in that direction. It was at Ephesus that Hannibal is reported to have met Scipio, where they had their famous conversation about generalship. This tradition can and should be accepted.[23]

---

[22] Th. 1.137.2 for Themistocles and e.g. Hdt. 5.54.1 and 100: Ephesus and Coressus.   [23] See p. 262.

CHAPTER 15

# Hannibal and Scipio as Military Advisers in the Late 190s: The Road to Magnesia, 190
### Aged 57 and 45

## 15.1 Introduction: The Seleucids

The evidence for Hannibal's flight in 195 was full, detailed, and lively.[1] This is a welcome change, given how little we know about internal affairs at Carthage. He did not lose all contact with Carthage even two years after his dramatic escape.[2] But now that we have brought him to Ephesus and then Antioch, the western capital of the Seleucid king Antiochus III, we may stand back and look at the Seleucids as a dynasty, before returning to Hannibal and then the war between Rome and Antiochus.[3]

The three great Hellenistic dynasties which dominated the eastern Greek world in the years up to 200 BCE were the Ptolemies of Egypt, the Antigonids, and the Seleucids (the last two cannot be located geographically as easily the Ptolemies).[4] It is worth asking what Hannibal's options were in the mid-190s. When he was contemplating exile, and he had had plenty of time to do this before the actual and probably inevitable moment came (he was nothing if not a realist), the first two dynasties were ruled out as providers of refuge. Egypt in the 190s was unstable under its boy king, Ptolemy V, and its foreign policy was all over the place.[5] But at no point would the king's advisers – who were anyway divided among themselves – have been so foolish as to risk offering hospitality to Roman enemy number one. Hannibal's former ally, the Antigonid Philip V of Macedon was defeated by the Romans in 197 and became their ally. Attalid Pergamum was another ally. That left only the court of Antiochus.

---

[1] Chapter 14.   [2] For the Ariston affair, see p. 310.
[3] For the war and its antecedents, see Grainger 2002: very favourable to Antiochus as a supposedly rational agent.
[4] The west Greeks had their own powerful and well-attested dynasts, whose capital was usually Syracuse (the Deinomenids in the fifth century; Agathocles; Hiero II). But there were intervals of non-monarchic government. By the end of the third century, Sicily was a Roman province.
[5] Gruen 1984: 679–85.

The evidence for the three dynasties differs in quality and bulk. The survival of vast numbers of documentary papyri in the special climate of Egypt, and the quantity of inscriptional evidence, some of it bilingual or trilingual in Greek, demotic, and hieroglyphic Egyptian, make it possible to study Ptolemaic interaction with indigenous Egyptian culture.[6] It is difficult to say how far the men working in the library and 'museum' at Ptolemaic Egyptian Alexandria, and the poets Callimachus, Theocritus, and Apollonius Rhodius, can be regarded as agents and servants of anti-Seleucid Ptolemaic policies.[7] The Seleucids had no Greek literary or cultural centre to compare with Alexandria, although there was a 'public library' at Syrian Antioch, of which the poet Euphorion of Chalcis was the head, appointed by Antiochus III.[8] Much earlier, a Babylonian priest (and so Seleucid subject) called Berossus, who has been much discussed in recent years, wrote a *Babyloniaca*, in which an anti-Egyptian slant has been ingeniously detected.[9] But the closeness of his relationship to Antiochus I has sometimes been overstated: it relies on one late and difficult piece of biographical evidence or *testimonium*.[10] The reign of Antiochus III, with which we are primarily concerned, produced three main figures, all intriguing, but all fragmentary:[11] Euphorion, the poet Simonides of Magnesia, and Hegesianax son of Diogenes of Alexandria

---

[6] The inscriptions from Egypt itself, Greek, bilingual, and trilingual, are being collected in the three volumes of *CPI* (see Abbreviations) Part 1. It is hoped to collect the Greek inscriptions from the Ptolemaic possessions outside Egypt (for which see Bagnall 1976) in a future Part 2.

[7] Fraser 1996: 34–6 solved (in my opinion) an old puzzle, the multiple 'false' Alexandrias in literary lists. He argued that Ptolemaic Alexandrian scholars sought to counter the greatest achievement of the Seleucids, the founding of new cities, by renaming many actually Seleucid cities as Alexandrias (Alexander the Great was 'the Founder' of their own city). More tentatively and conjecturally – cf. Visscher 2020: 4 and n. 11 – Fraser argued (36–9) that Seleucid writers replied with a 'Seleucus Romance', reasserting Seleucus I's role. The implied analogy here is with the 'Alexander Romance', a pseudo-historical narrative. Visscher 2020: 120–53 suggests that anti-Seleucid polemic is reflected in Callimachus, esp. frag. 110 Pf., the 'lock of Berenice'; cf. Visscher 2020 160–2 on the *Hymn to Delos*. But these, and the other literary texts she examines, are not obviously anti-Seleucid and can easily be read 'straight', so her theory solves no puzzle.

[8] See Lightfoot: 203 (Euphorion T 1; cf. Visscher 2020: 170). Visscher 2020 examines the evidence for literature in the Seleucid empire. Much of it is fragmentary, and some of it actually Ptolemaic, see previous n.

[9] Dillery 2015: 270–1. Heller 2014, reviewing Haubold and others, 2013, cautions against exaggerating Berossus' importance.

[10] See *FGrHist* and *BNJ* 680 T2, from the Christian writer Tatian: Berossus 'composed the history of the Chaldaeans for Antiochos (I)', tr. G. De Breucker, *BNJ*. Kuhrt 1987: 55 misquotes Tarn (1951: 41) as saying Berossus wrote 'at royal command'. Tarn's actual words were 'at the request of Antiochos'. Even this went too far. At most, the Greek might imply he dedicated his work to him (Kuhrt 1987: 54, Kosmin 2014: 271). The verb is κατατάσσω ('arrange'? 'narrate'?) with the dative.

[11] Visscher 2020: 154–99. She claims (156) that Antiochus III's reign 'represented a high point in the Seleucids' patronage of poets, writers, and intellectuals'.

Troas, who is the most important for our purposes. Euphorion recorded a prophecy that Seleucus, the founder of the dynasty, would rule Asia.[12] Simonides celebrated Antiochus I's victory over the Gauls, but that was a long time earlier. Hegesianax was to a much greater extent a player on the contemporary stage. He was used on several crucial missions by Antiochus III, including an embassy to Rome in 193. In that same year, as an inscription shows, he was honoured with proxeny at Delphi, which at that time was still controlled by Antiochus' new friends the Aetolians.[13] In his history, he sought to subvert at least one cherished Roman tradition by denying that Aeneas went to Italy from Troy.[14] The Trojan theme seems to have become an even more prominent element in Roman thinking during the 190s.[15] Antiochus had a riposte ready for this: before he momentously crossed to Greece in 192, he made a point of sacrificing to Athena at Ilium (Troy).[16]

The second dynasty, the Antigonids, liked to pretend that they were descended from the ancient Argead dynasty of Macedon which boasted mythical Argive origins.[17] That was certainly a family connection worth their stressing, however tenuous the reality. The Argead Macedonian king Amyntas and his son Alexander I are prominent in books 5 and 8 of Herodotus, and their successors are well known from Thucydides and then the historians and orators of the fourth century, above all Demosthenes. But the reality was that the Antigonids were as much upstarts as the Ptolemies and Seleucids.

The evidence for the Antigonids is largely Greek. The epigraphy of Macedonia is rich, and its published quantity has increased greatly in recent years.[18] The Hellenistic family did not always control the Macedonian heartland: its recovery in 277 was effected by Antigonus Gonatas, who died in 239. Philip V, whom Flamininus defeated at Cynoscephalae in 197, had succeeded to the throne in 221 after the reigns

---

[12] Frag. 119 Lightfoot; Visscher 2020: 180.
[13] *Syll.*³ 585 lines 43–4. Was he a – perhaps self-imposed – exile from Alexandria Troas? Along with Smyrna and Lampsacus, it resisted Antiochus in 192, Livy 35.42.2. He would not be the first or last exiled Greek historian, starting with Herodotus and Thucydides.
[14] *FGrHist* and *BNJ* 45.   [15] See Hornblower 2018: 190 and nn. 17 and 18.
[16] Livy 35.43.3, calling the goddess Minerva.
[17] Hdt. 5.22.2 and Th. 5.80.2 (Argos). Pol. 5.10.10 (Philip V's claim) with *HCP* 1: 548. Antigonus 'the One-Eyed', first of the new dynasty, may have been related to Philip II in some now unrecoverable way. For Antigonus see Briant 1973, and on Hieronymus of Cardia's first-hand literary portrait of this obviously unforgettable man, see J. Hornblower 1981: 211–23.
[18] A special tribute must be paid here to the work of Miltiades Hatzopoulos. See (a selection) Hatzopoulos 1994, 1996, 2016, and 2021.

of his father Demetrius II and of Demetrius' cousin and Philip's guardian, Antigonus Doson.[19]

Like the Antigonids, the Ptolemies and Seleucids emerged only in the period after the death of Alexander in 323, and both were founded by former commanders in his army, who became known dynastically as Ptolemy I Soter and Seleucus I Nicator.[20] Of the two monarchies, the Seleucid was the younger by a decade, and Seleucus was actually helped back to power at Babylon – allotted to him soon after Alexander's death – by the first Ptolemy. Diodorus, drawing on the history of Alexander's Successors written by the near-contemporary Hieronymus of Cardia, romantically describes how in 312 he achieved this with no more than the 800 infantry and 200 cavalry given him by Ptolemy.[21]

The Seleucids have left very little papyrus evidence, but plenty of coins and Greek inscriptions, especially but not only from Asia Minor.[22] In addition, Babylonian cuneiform texts are a kind of counterpart to the non-Greek evidence from Egypt. The Seleucids have been intensely studied and reinterpreted in recent years. One influential approach has been a deliberate and provocatively expressed shift of scholarly emphasis away from Asia Minor and the Aegean (the main preoccupation of the surviving ancient literary sources), presenting them as an essentially Mesopotamian power and playing down their origins in the Greco-Macedonian world.[23] This has reversed a modern as well as an ancient bias; but has been overdone. It had already (in 1958) been shown that 'native individuals' constituted only about 2.5 per cent of the Seleucid ruling class.[24] For that sort of reason, it has been well said that the Seleucids 'did not forget that they were Macedonian kings'.[25] This is relevant to the non-Greek outsider

---

[19] For Gonatas, see Tarn 1913, still the best biography of a Hellenistic ruler. For Doson, Le Bohec 1993; for Philip V, Walbank 1940 and (correcting some aspects of Pol.'s treatment of him) Nicholson 2023 (316–24 for a comparison with Hannibal).

[20] For Ptolemy I, see Seibert 1969 and Anson 2023; for the whole dynasty, Hölbl 2001 and (for military matters) Fischer-Bovet 2014. For Seleucus I, Mehl 1986, Grainger 1990 and Kosmin 2014 (a very favourable and not entirely convincing re-evaluation of Seleucus as a geopolitical thinker of genius).

[21] Diod. 19.90.1.   [22] For Antiochus III and the cities of Asia Minor, see Ma 1999.

[23] See esp. Kuhrt and Sherwin-White 1987, then Sherwin-White and Kuhrt 1993.

[24] Habicht 2006b: 30 [originally 1958]. Habicht treated Seleucid history in detail twice more: Habicht 2006d (mainly the period after 188) and 2006c (relations with Athens).

[25] See Walbank 1988: 112, ending an important review of Kuhrt and Sherwin-White 1987. He noted the absence of Syrians and Babylonians from the Seleucid army at the battles of Raphia (217) and Magnesia (190), and in Antiochus IV's grand quasi-military procession held at Daphne (166), for which see p. 301 n. 20.

Hannibal's very limited role at the court of Antiochus III.[26] By contrast, in 219 BCE (the start of the fourth Syrian war), a learned Greek doctor from Seleucia in Pieria called Apollophanes had easily persuaded the same Antiochus to adopt his own initially successful military plan of operations in Syria.[27] As a result, Apollophanes' home city Seleucia was won back from Ptolemy IV. Another named Greek is known to have switched to Antiochus' wealthier court from Philip's.[28]

## 15.2 Antiochus in the Mid-190s

By 196, Antiochus III had been on the throne for many years, in fact since 222, but the reign had not been an unqualified military or political success. The fourth Syrian war against Ptolemy III, which had begun so well for him, ended in defeat at Raphia (217). The fifth Syrian war (202–195) went better for him. Before that, his 'march up country' (*anabasis*) began in 212. It was an attempt to reassert Seleucid control in the eastern satrapies, but he was obliged to leave the local rulers of Parthia and Bactria in place. He was nevertheless unofficially accorded the title 'the Great' for these limited and essentially diplomatic achievements.[29] He did not return to the west of the empire until 205. In the years after 203, Antiochus made territorial gains in Caria and Ionia and recovered control of Syria and Palestine in the Middle East (this was the outcome of the fifth Syrian war). He also began to assert by force what he regarded as ancestral claims to European Thrace. Friction with Rome had already begun by the time Hannibal arrived at Antioch.

At the Isthmian games in 196, Flamininus had proclaimed the 'freedom of the Greeks', including those in Asia.[30] The extra words had clear implications for Antiochus. He sent envoys, Hegesianax the historian and Lysias, who were heard by the ten Roman *legati*.[31] These insisted that the menacing but vaguely expressed Asiatic provision meant what it said.[32] That is, Antiochus was to keep his hands off the cities which were autonomous; this meant above all Smyrna and Lampsacus, both of which

---

[26] See Habicht 2006b: 30: Hannibal 'in every respect an exceptional phenomenon' and 'even he always remained an outsider' in the inner circle surrounding Antiochus III.
[27] Pol. 5.56 and 58 with Habicht 2006b: 32. [28] See p. 318 for Alexander the Acarnanian.
[29] Errington 1989: 249–50. Errington 2008: 178 is somewhat less severe.
[30] Pol. 18.44.2; see p. 71, cf. 249.
[31] After defeating an enemy, the Romans sent out 'ten legates' or diplomatic commissioners, *decem legati*, to settle the conquered territory. See Yarrow 2012 for the history of the institution.
[32] Pol. 18.47.1–4 (naming Hegesianax and Lysias; on both, see HCP 2: 615–16).

had complained to the Roman senate about Antiochus' hostile attentions.[33] He was to make war on none of them and to withdraw from those previously subject to Ptolemy and Philip. He was ordered not to cross to Europe with an army (he had already done so). Finally, the envoys were informed that a Roman deputation would visit Antiochus himself. This duly happened in 196 at Lysimachia in European Thrace, a city which had been destroyed by Thracians in perhaps 198 after a brief occupation by Philip V, and which Antiochus was now in process of rebuilding. For what follows we have the accounts of both Polybius and Livy. They agree that one ostensible purpose of the mission was to mediate or arbitrate between Antiochus and Ptolemy.[34]

The Roman envoys at Lysimachia, in the person of their spokesman Lucius Cornelius Lentulus, repeated the demands just listed and added that no thinking person could interpret Antiochus' presence in Europe as anything but preparatory to an attack on the Romans. Antiochus had had time to prepare his reply, and it was a masterpiece; perhaps he was helped to arrive at and formulate it by Hegesianax, who will have known how to exploit history and political analogy for forensic purposes.[35] The king refuted the Romans point by point. He politely asked the Romans not to bother themselves about the affairs of Asia, any more than he concerned himself with the affairs of Italy. He had crossed to Europe to recover the Chersonese and the cities of Thrace because he had an ancestral claim to those places, which were 'spear-won' by Seleucus I as a result of his defeat of Lysimachus at Corupedium (281 BCE). 'Spear-won territory', *doriktetos chora*, was an accepted and important Hellenistic concept, and a familiar slogan in Hieronymus' narrative of the Successors of Alexander, which was closely and extensively followed in the non-Sicilian parts of books 18–20 of Diodorus.[36] In particular, Antiochus' occupation and resettlement of Lysimachia was, the king said, not directed against the Romans but done with a view to providing a residence for his son Seleucus, his eventual

---

[33] Smyrna was an important Aeolian coastal city in central Asia Minor. Lampsacus was further north, on the Asiatic side of the Hellespont. For both places, see Livy 33.38.1–3 and for Lampsacus see also *Syll.*³ 591 (Austin no. 197, Sherk 1984 no. 5, Lampsacene honours to an ambassador to Massilia and Rome). The inscription, on whose importance see Battistoni 2009: 83–9, shows that Lampsacus pleaded an indirect and complicated kinship tie with Rome via Troy, from which Rome claimed to have been founded after the Trojan war. Lampsacus was a member of the league of cities of the Troy region and was founded by Phocaeans from western Asia Minor, as was Massilia in southern Gaul. Massilia had a long-standing treaty with Rome.

[34] Pol. 18.50–52; Livy 33.38.10–14; App. *Syr.* 1.3 with Brodersen 1991: 80. For Lysimachia, see also Cohen 1995: 82–7; Fraser 2009: 358. Arbitration: Ager 1996: 216.

[35] Lentulus (cos. 199) is *DPRR* CORN1023. Cf. Livy 34.58 for Hegesianax's arguments at Rome in 193.

[36] J. Hornblower 1981: 53.

successor as Seleucus IV. As for Ptolemy (he calmly continued), he would settle with him amicably and indeed had decided to join him in a marriage alliance, by betrothing his daughter Cleopatra to Ptolemy V. The marriage duly took place in 193.

The king's dispute with Smyrna and Lampsacus was dealt with separately, after representatives of those cities were brought forward and heard: Parmenio and Pythodorus from Lampsacus and Coeranus from Smyrna. Antiochus now, and for the first time, displayed a real or possibly simulated flash of temper. He interrupted a long speech by Parmenio (had this man been going on too elaborately about Lampsacus' kinship tie with Rome?) and announced grandly that it was his pleasure to submit to arbitration by the Rhodians, not the Romans. A clever point: the Rhodians were not only friends of the Romans at this time but were well known for providing reliable 'foreign judges' to settle international disputes. The Romans, on the other hand, regarded arbitration cynically, as a way of extending their influence.[37] The Roman delegates were unable to respond adequately. But Antiochus and his advisers, knowing what had happened to Philip on the battlefield and afterwards, cannot have thought that this was the end of the matter. There was now a comical interlude, prompted by a rumour that young Ptolemy V of Egypt had died.[38] Both parties pretended not to have heard the rumour, but both acted on it: Lentulus asked for breathing space to consult with Ptolemy (despite believing him to be dead). Antiochus allegedly saw a chance to take over Egypt, so he sailed south to Ephesus then Lycia, where he discovered that the rumour was false. His onward journey from here was a series of disasters: first a mutiny, then a storm which caused the loss of many of his ships and men. He wintered at Antioch. He sent an embassy to Flamininus in Greece to ask for a formal alliance with Rome. When this arrived in spring 195, Flamininus said that in the absence of the ten *legati* he had no opinion to express and advised that they go to Rome with their request.[39] They do not seem to have done so, and as far as we know – and these years are unusually well documented – there was no further diplomatic contact between Rome and Antiochus until the arrival at his court in 193 of three envoys sent in 194.[40]

---

[37] Cf. the Rhodian judges, δικαστὰς Ῥοδίους, at Pol. 28.7.9, with *HCP* 3: 335–6 (and *SEG* 51.431) for the retention of the Rhodians in Pol.'s text, an important detail. Ager 1996: 217, discussing the present episode, perhaps overemphasizes Rhodian neutrality. For the Roman attitude to arbitration, see Bispham 2014: 239–40.
[38] Livy 33.41. The word is *rumor* (41.1) not *fama*, for which see p. 310, but the idea is the same.
[39] Livy 33.41.5 (196) and 34.25.2 (195). See Briscoe 1973: 326 and 198: 89.
[40] For this embassy, see p. 314.

Such was the position when Hannibal, now an exile from Carthage, turned up at Ephesus, where he was welcomed by the crown prince Antiochus.[41] His father Antiochus the king, his navy depleted, was at Antioch, where Hannibal went to meet him.

## 15.3 The Ariston Affair

Hannibal was, however, not quite finished with Carthage, or Carthage with Hannibal. But this time he acted vicariously, through a spy called Ariston, a Tyrian whom he had met by chance in Ephesus. (The personal name Ariston is Greek, and a common one everywhere, derived from a superlative which meant 'best'. So it either indicates Greek intermarriage in his family or is a hellenized version of a similar-sounding Phoenician name.)[42] The mission failed, but the story is illuminating, not least about the power of *fama*, rumour, at Carthage, as at Rome.[43] The Greek equivalent is *fēmē*.[44] It is a favourite word of Polybius, but it is not certain that this word and notion featured so prominently in the Polybian original of the Ariston story.[45] Livy may have touched up a simpler narrative rhetorically, as he often did.

At the end of book 34, Livy picks up Hannibal's story where he left off at the end of book 33. He flags this explicitly by saying that he had fled to Antiochus 'as was said earlier'. This authorial reminder may also have been in his main source here, Polybius.[46] The main narrative has now reached 193, but some of its introductory material looks as if it is spread over the whole two years since Hannibal's arrival.

The narrative actually begins at Rome in 193: three envoys had been sent to Antiochus; but they had only just set off when some different, unnamed, *legati* brought word from Carthage that Antiochus was 'beyond doubt', *haud dubie*, preparing for war, with Hannibal as his agent, *minister*, and this caused anxiety at the prospect of a simultaneous war against Carthage. Livy does not here use the word *fama*, 'rumour', but that is what he means. He then explains the rational grounds for this Roman anxiety. Hannibal, he says, was held in great honour by the king, who had long, *diu*, been

---

[41] See p. 301.
[42] See p. 285 n. 62 for such bi-cultural names. The Latin form is *Aristo*, but (exceptionally) I retain the Greek because of the onomastic aspect.
[43] For the importance of *fama*, see Hardie 2012.
[44] Hardie 2012: 50–7. In the text I have printed the Greek noun with 'f', rather than the conventional 'ph', to bring out the derivation of the Latin noun from the Greek (cf. *OLD*).
[45] *Polybios-Lexikon* 3.2 φήμη: cols. 890–1; sub-heading on rumour, 'Gerücht', at 890.
[46] 34.60–2. The 'flag': 60.2. Such internal cross-references are common in Pol.

contemplating war with Rome and thought Hannibal the ideal man to contribute to discussions of this.[47] Hannibal always gave him exactly the same advice: Italy should be the theatre of choice. It would provide an invader with provisions and fighting men, whereas no king or nation would be a match for Roman armies abroad, supplied with Italian manpower and resources. He asked for himself 100 decked warships, 10,000 infantry, and 1,000 cavalry, with which he would sail first for Africa, where he was confident that he could persuade the Carthaginians to rebel. If they were hesitant, he would raise a war against the Romans in some region of Italy. Antiochus ought to cross over to Europe with all his remaining forces and base his army in Greece, not moving it across to Italy but holding it in readiness to do so, which would be enough to create the appearance of a move, and to ignite rumour, *fama*. This time, Livy does use that actual word. The plan sounds highly optimistic, and the vague multiples of ten are not reassuring. But the report might nevertheless be historical: Hannibal perhaps guessed that big talk of this kind would work best on a man like Antiochus. It is bad method to pick and choose details from a story like this. We must take it or leave it, and there is no good reason not to take it.[48]

A three-line fragment of Ennius, quoted by Aulus Gellius, is part of a speech or more likely soliloquy by Antiochus. It seems at first sight to contradict the usual picture of Hannibal as warmonger:

> Hannibal, that brave soul, urges me
> not to wage war, whom my heart took to be
> the greatest persuader and vigorous mainstay of war.[49]

Without more by way of context or exact date, it is impossible to assess these lines with any confidence, but they are usually explained as a purely limited disagreement: perhaps Hannibal was arguing not against war absolutely, but against Antiochus' intention to restrict the war to Greece.[50] It has also (taken absolutely) been interpreted as a poetic

---

[47] 34.60.2–6. Again, Livy will hereafter be followed closely, with references and explanatory comments in footnotes.

[48] Badian 1968b: 132 is extraordinarily confident: he says that Ariston, whose existence and mission he evidently accepts, 'was clumsy enough to be caught', and 'there is no reason whatever to think he was the only [envoy] Hannibal sent'. (This last assertion could easily be reversed.) Antiochus had 'done nothing to stop these intrigues', but 'on the other hand he had never committed himself to public support for Hannibal'.

[49] 371–3 Sk. (Book XIII frag. 3). The tr. at Goldberg and Manuwald 2018a: 299 uses 'heart' for both *pectus* at line 371 and *cor* at 372, but we need different English words for different Latin ones. For *pectus* as 'soul', see *OLD* (4).

[50] Briscoe 1981: 141; Skutsch 1985: 537.

expression by Antiochus of surprise and shock that Hannibal could so confound expectations.[51]

Hannibal needed to prepare the ground at Carthage, but he decided not to send a letter in case it was intercepted, as had happened with the treaty with Philip V more than two decades earlier. Instead, he needed a reliable oral messenger. He now sent Ariston to Carthage with instructions: he had tried him out on trivial undertakings first and had both given him generous rewards and promised him more, all with the king's approval. He told Ariston the names of people he needed to contact and gave him secret codes so that they would know that the instructions really did come from him. But when he arrived at Carthage, Hannibal's enemies were as quick as his friends to realize why Ariston had come. To begin with, there was just gossip 'at social gatherings and dinner-parties' (more *fama*, in effect; this particular double expression is a Livian favourite). But then in the Carthaginian senate some members complained openly that Hannibal's exile was useless if even in his absence he could make trouble and provoke civil disturbance by his intrigues. They then gave a pretty accurate account of 'Ariston the Tyrian visitor' and his mission, and they (correctly and importantly) associated Antiochus with Hannibal in their complaints. There was a general outcry: Ariston should be summoned and interrogated; if he refused to talk, he should be sent to Rome, escorted by ambassadors. 'We have been punished enough for the reckless actions of one man. Private citizens can misbehave at their own peril, but the state must be not only free of guilt but free of the rumour, *fama*, of guilt.' (Here Livy does again use the actual word *fama*, which has played an implied role more than once already.)

Ariston was interrogated, and he pleaded his strongest argument: he had brought no letter to anybody. But he was not able to explain satisfactorily why he had come at all, and he faltered when it was pointed out that he had been in contact only with members of the 'Barcine faction'.[52] There was then a dispute between those who wanted him arrested and detained as a spy, and those who urged that there was no need for such drastic steps and that to arrest visitors without reason would set a bad precedent: after all, Carthaginians might find themselves treated the same way at Tyre and other trading centres. The matter was adjourned for the day.

---

[51] Stocks 2014: 59–60 suggests that Ennius' Antiochus is commenting on 'the Roman Hannibal's status as a product of people's (mis)conceptions'.

[52] For this expression, see p. 48.

## The Ariston Affair

Ariston now resorted to Carthaginian ingenuity against Carthaginians. That evening, he hung up a written tablet in the busiest part of the city where the magistrates sat every day, then at night 'he climbed on board his ship and escaped', *nauem conscendit et profugit*.[53] Next day, when the *sufetes* took their seats, they read the tablet, which said that Ariston had brought no message for any private individual, but a public one for the senators.[54] Since his incrimination had been made so openly and generally, there was less enthusiasm for pursuing the small number of suspects. But envoys were sent to Rome to put the affair before the consuls and to complain about the wrongs inflicted by Masinissa, the Numidian ruler who had contributed to Scipio's victory at Zama and had been rewarded extravagantly and at the expense of Carthage.

Masinissa had heard all about this: yet more *fama*. He was aware that the Carthaginians were in bad odour at Rome and at odds with each other, and that the people suspected their leaders because of the information supplied by Ariston. So he saw his chance and began to provoke and damage them in various ways (listed by Livy but not here detailed). Hearing that the Carthaginians were sending a deputation to Rome, he did the same himself. The news about 'the Tyrian visitor' filled the Roman senate with alarm at the prospect of simultaneous war with both Antiochus and Carthage. (This is 'ring-composition': that is, the narrative returns to where it started. In literary and thematic terms, we are back at the point where Livy began the narrative of Hannibal's attempted manipulation of Antiochus and the Ariston affair, all of which was supplied in order to explain the grounds for the senate's fear of a double war. But in terms of the actual sequence of events, the latest news or rumour served to heighten that earlier anxiety.)[55] The Romans' suspicions were increased by the Carthaginian failure to keep a proper guard on either the man or his ship after they had decided he should be arrested and sent to Rome. (This, if true, is rumour not fact: we have not actually been told about any such firm decision, only that there were conflicting opinions, one of which was to arrest him, and that the matter was then adjourned.)

We may leave Livy's narrative there; the final section of his book 34 continues with a detailed account of the complicated Carthaginian dispute with Masinissa, ending with the sending of an embassy including Scipio, which did not, however, reach a conclusion. Ariston disappears from both

---

[53] 34.61.14.
[54] As often in an ancient historian, the contents of the writing are (p. 156) disclosed when received and read, not when written.
[55] 34.62.6, cf. 34.60.1.

Carthage and history with the four crisp words quoted earlier, ending *profugit*.

The Ariston story illustrates the pervasive, important, and damaging effect of rumour, *fama*. When he sent Ariston, Hannibal cannot have foreseen the exact course of events at Carthage. But if he did indeed want to provoke a war, as he probably did, those events acted in his favour by the suspicions generated or amplified by *fama*, first at Rome, then at Carthage, then at Rome again. Writing in 1959, during the Cold War of modern times between the USSR and USA, Ernst Badian, himself a kind of 'cold warrior' (that is, a consistent supporter of American policy towards Russia), gave his article about Rome and Antiochus the subtitle 'a study in cold war'.[56] That was striking but not really appropriate, because the ancient tensions soon morphed into a hot war. It was precipitated by Antiochus' occupation of the strategically important Greek harbour city of Thessalian Demetrias (previously Pagasai, and modern Volos), and by a massacre of Roman soldiers at Delium, a sanctuary of Apollo in Greece, perpetrated by Antiochus' officer. The war was settled on the battlefield of Magnesia.[57] A better subtitle, as far as the Ariston affair goes, might be 'a study in *fama*'.

## 15.4 Hannibal's Childhood Oath Again

We have seen that three Roman consular envoys, Sulpicius Galba, Publius Villius Tappulus, and Aelius Paetus, were sent to Antiochus in 194, but only two of them arrived in Asia Minor in 193. In between, Paetus drops out of the narrative altogether.[58] En route, the other two visited Eumenes II of Pergamum, who was frantically pushing the Romans to war against Antiochus. Galba was left behind ill at Pergamum. This was the embassy – or what remained of it – which Scipio seems to have joined (perhaps at a stage when it was only a one-man embassy), and which is said to have been the context of his celebrated conversation with Hannibal about

---

[56] Badian 1968b was first published in 1959. For his politics, see Harris 2017b: 8, 13.
[57] For Menippus and the Delium massacre, see Livy 35.51, cf. p. 264. Badian 1968b: 139 n. 100 calls this an 'impious massacre' but thinks the Romans had taken 'deliberate advantage of the *asylia* [inviolability] of the place'. That is too cynical.
[58] See p. 260 for the embassy, citing the two relevant Livy passages. To repeat, they are 34.59.8 (194) and 35.13.6 (193), with an explicit back-reference (to book 34), but without Paetus. He has not simply dropped out of the text of the second passage through scribal error, because Villius alone is said in the next chapter to talk frequently with Hannibal at Ephesus (35.14.2, no mention of Paetus). It may be that Pol. somewhere provided an explanation of Paetus' disappearance but that Livy omitted it.

generalship.⁵⁹ Its progress therefore needs to be followed in a little detail. At Ephesus, Villius made a point of talking frequently to Hannibal, so compromising him in Antiochus' eyes. From there, Villius travelled to Phrygian Apamea (east of Ephesus) to meet Antiochus. But it was there that King Antiochus heard of the death of his son, the younger Antiochus, so Villius tactfully made himself scarce and returned to Pergamum. By that time, Galba had recovered, and both the Roman ambassadors made their way together from Pergamum to Ephesus.⁶⁰ There is no way of telling exactly when in this complicated and lengthy sequence Scipio arrived at Ephesus.

This Roman diplomatic visit is the context of another famous story about Hannibal: his childhood oath 'never to show goodwill towards the Romans'. Polybius gave the full story at the start of the Hannibalic war (as did Livy), and he evidently gave it again under 193, where however we have only Livy's second version of the clearly Polybian original.⁶¹ This is fuller and less absolutely worded than Livy's uncontextualized first version. In the two surviving fuller versions, the Greek and the Latin, Villius plays a devious role. He cultivates Hannibal assiduously, with a view to making Antiochus suspicious of him.⁶² He succeeds in this until Hannibal tells Antiochus the oath story to reassure him, and his trust is duly restored. There are two separate problems here: (1) did Hannibal's father really make him swear the oath? and (2) did the reassurance story really happen? The oath itself might be unhistorical, but Hannibal in a tight spot like this could perfectly well have told an unhistorical story (after all, who was in a position to contradict him?). That Antiochus 'never had much use for Hannibal's advice' (as has been asserted) would not disprove (2), even if it were clearly correct as an assessment of Antiochus' attitude.⁶³

A brief story given only by Nepos has Hannibal in 193 sailing as far as Carthage's neighbour Cyrene with five ships in an attempt to solicit help from Carthage.⁶⁴ He never got there. The authorities at Carthage got wind

---

⁵⁹ On Livy 35.13 and 14, see p. 262, defending the historicity of the conversation.
⁶⁰ See Livy 35.15.1–16.1 with Holleaux 1957c: 169 n. 1, stressing *ambo*, 'both' at 16.1. A little earlier (15.1), Antiochus hears of the arrival of the Roman ambassadors, *legatorum*, plural. That is vaguely put, but these are presumably Villius and Galba (not Paetus), as they certainly are at 15.9. For the crown prince Antiochus, see p. 301, and for this Apamea (there were several), *Barr.* map 65 D1 and Fraser 2009: 338 no. 3.
⁶¹ Pol. 3.11.1–12.1; Livy 21.1.4, 35.19.3. See p. 51 for the oath in its chronological place.
⁶² Livy 35.14.14.
⁶³ 'Never had much use': Badian 1968b: 139 n. 92. Antiochus' attitude is a good deal more complicated than this.
⁶⁴ *Hann.* 8.1–2.

of his proximity, and they exiled Hannibal's brother Mago, says Nepos. This is a bad mistake by Nepos, because this Mago was by now long dead. The story has been defended but is suspect. The supposed relation to the Ariston episode, which is altogether unmentioned by Nepos, is not clear.[65]

### 15.5 The Roman Decision for War

The trouble began with the Aetolians, a long-established confederacy in central Greece with a poor reputation as uncivilized and piratical.[66] The immediate problem was this: the Roman senate decided it could not tolerate Antiochus' occupation, with Aetolian encouragement, of two strategically vital Greek places, the Thessalian city Demetrias (recently seized by the Aetolians) and Euboean Chalcis. But the 'truest cause', in Thucydidean terms, was the collision between, on the one hand, Antiochus' claim to the spear-won territory (*doriktetos chora*) of Seleucus I (including European Thrace) and his belief that Asia Minor was his by right, and on the other hand the growing assumption at Rome that the outside world should obey Roman orders.[67] We should once again add the precipitating effect of rumour, *fama*. Livy makes this point explicitly under 192, talking in anticipation of 'an expectation [at Rome] of the war with Antiochus which had not yet begun': there were 'wild and untraceable rumours, some truth combined with much falsehood'.[68]

The Aetolians were the Romans' first allies in Greece (from 212), and, for the Romans, Aetolian control of the amphiktiony which in turn controlled the oracular sanctuary of Delphi was part of the reason for the alliance.[69] But the Aetolians were unpopular with other Greeks, and this meant that, as Roman interest in Greek affairs increased, the Aetolian connection became an embarrassment. The cause or pretext for Rome's progressive coolness towards the Aetolians was the separate peace treaty they had made with Philip V in 206, in breach of their obligations under their alliance

---

[65] Defended: Seibert 1993a: 513–14 and nn. 42 and 43, who sought to connect it with a hypothetical visit by Hannibal at this time to the oracle of Zeus Ammon (at the Siwah oasis), which said that Hannibal would die 'on Libyan soil' (Pausanias 8.11.11).

[66] Scholten 2000: 22. They were already a league in the mid-fifth century (R/O no. 128, treaty with Sparta). Thucydides reports the opinion that many of their communities ate raw meat, the sign of a barbarian (3.94.4). Piracy: Austin nos. 43 and 106. Aetolia is the only part of mainland Greece not included in Pausanias' guide to Greece (second century CE).

[67] Th. 1.23. Cf. Derow 2015: 134, summarizing what he convincingly takes to be Polybius' view: the Romans sought 'to be obeyed by everyone with whom they dealt'.

[68] *expectatio nondum coepti cum Antiocho belli . . . rumores temere sine ullis auctoribus orti multa falsa ueris miscebant*: Livy 35.23.1–2; cf. Harris 1979: 222.

[69] See p. 145.

with Rome of 212.⁷⁰ This angered the Romans at the time because the peace was made without their authorization.⁷¹ But only a year later, the Romans themselves and their allies ended the first Macedonian war by a treaty, the Peace of Phoenice. In 200, the Romans were reported by a Macedonian speaker as having delivered a rude rebuff to a recent Aetolian embassy at Rome: 'why do you come to us, Aetolians, you who made a peace with Philip without Roman authority?'⁷² The Aetolians were still fighting on the Roman side at Cynoscephalae in 197; but when after the battle they protested at Flamininus' refusal to grant them cities in Thessaly despite the terms of the 212 alliance, he told them that the alliance had ended when the Aetolians abandoned the Romans and made peace with Philip.⁷³ The Aetolians took this snub badly, and Polybius calls this episode a 'beginning of great evils', a phrase which already had a very long history.⁷⁴ It was, he continues, the 'spark' which ignited the wars with the Aetolian league and Antiochus.⁷⁵ In his threefold taxonomy of causes in book 3 – an extension of Thucydides' twofold system of underlying cause and pretext – he had said that Antiochus' landing at Demetrias was the beginning, *archē*, of the war between Rome and Antiochus. There the 'cause' of the war was the anger of the Aetolians, and the pretext was the liberation of Greece which they and Antiochus proclaimed.⁷⁶ But here in book 18, the description of the anger of the Aetolians as a 'spark' looks more like an *archē*, a beginning, than a 'cause'.

In 193, the disgruntled Aetolians started to stir things up in a serious way.⁷⁷ At a meeting of their league at Naupactus, their elected leader Thoas complained that after Cynoscephalae the Romans had shown the least honour to the Aetolians, although they were mainly responsible for the

---

⁷⁰ The alliance treaty stipulated that if either party to the alliance made peace with Philip, that peace should be valid only if Philip were to cease hostilities against the other party: Livy 26.24.12.
⁷¹ *Irati quod sine auctoritate sua*: Livy 29.12.1 and 4.
⁷² *Quid ad nos uenitis, Aetoli, sine quorum auctoritate pacem cum Philippo fecistis?* (lit. 'to us, Aetolians, without whose authority you made . . .'): Livy 31.29.4. The rebuff was delivered in 201. (Not 202. For the correct date see Derow 2015: 137.)
⁷³ 18.38.8 (and §7 for the provision that captured towns were to go to the Aetolians, mobile booty to the Romans; for this, see also Sherk 1984: no. 2).
⁷⁴ Pol. 18.39.1. On the phrase 'beginning of evils' (ἀρχὴ κακῶν or variants), see Hornblower 2013: 125 on Hdt. 5.28 and esp. 5.97.3, Athenian ships sent to help the Ionian revolt an ἀρχὴ κακῶν for Greeks and barbarians. The sequence began with the 'evil-beginning' ships sent to abduct Helen, Homer, *Iliad* 5.63. Cf. also Th. 2.12.3. Pol. was also reprising himself: at 11.5.9, a Greek speaker (identity uncertain) used it in 207 to warn the Aetolians to make peace with Philip. Walbank (*HCP* 2: 277) thought it might have become (merely?) proverbial, but the shared Aetolian reference is pointed.
⁷⁵ 18.39.2. 'Spark' is σπινθήρ, a word found here only in all the surviving text of Polybius. It was not yet a dead metaphor.
⁷⁶ Pol. 3.7.1–3, anticipating his own much later narrative. ⁷⁷ Livy 35.12.

victory (this last claim was a considerable exaggeration). On Thoas' motion, envoys were sent to the courts of three kings: Nicander to Philip V, Damocritus to the Spartan king Nabis, and Dicaearchus to Antiochus. The complex events at Sparta need not detain us (Nabis ended up being killed – by the Aetolians). To Philip, Nicander talked up the combined strength of the Aetolians and of Antiochus, whose entourage now included the great commander Hannibal, an enemy of Rome from his birth and prodigiously good at killing Romans.[78] As for Nicander, his later history is recounted by Polybius in a long prolepsis. Forgiven by Philip, he ended his days at Rome, where he may have been one of Polybius' informants.[79]

At Antiochus' court, Dicaearchus listed Aetolian resources, and lied freely about Philip and Nabis, making out that they were already on board diplomatically. Antiochus' own man Minnio also prodded the king to war, although ignorant of foreign affairs and basing his optimism on the king's successes in Syria and Asia.[80] Soon after, Alexander the Acarnanian had his say at a meeting of Antiochus' council of advisers, and he too made out that Philip was eager to turn on the Romans. (This is the man whom we have met already, as a friend of Philip V who had left him for the richer court of Antiochus.)[81] Hannibal did not attend this meeting, temporarily in royal disfavour because of his suspiciously friendly chats with Villius; but this is the moment when he was able to win back the king's trust by telling the story of his childhood oath. Hannibal featured among the recommendations of Alexander the Acarnanian: he should be sent to Africa to cause a diversion. This implies no very high opinion of Hannibal.

Actions as well as words had their effect on Antiochus. The Aetolian takeover of Demetrias – the 'beginning' of the war according to Polybius, as we have seen – is reported at some length by Livy as a mixture of guile, folly, and force.[82] Their success was partly made possible by the false rumour, one of several such (*inter cetera uana*), that the Romans planned to give Demetrias back to Philip. In late 192, the Romans, says Livy, were already preparing for 'the new war', but this had not yet been declared.[83]

---

[78] 35.12.14. No mention of Zama, and different rhetorical use will be made of Hannibal's fame by Nicander's compatriot Thoas when addressing Antiochus himself, p. 319.
[79] Pol. 20.11 with Walbank and Habicht vol. 5: 265 n. 31.
[80] Livy 35.15.8. The fifth Syrian war against Egypt had gone well for Antiochus: p. 307.
[81] Livy 35.18.1–2 with Habicht 2006b: 35. Cf. p. 307.
[82] Livy 35.31–4 (cf. p. 316 for Polybius on the 'beginning'). Livy must be reflecting Polybius – as usual hereabouts – when he concludes that madness, *furor*, a very strong word, had seized the Aetolians and their magistrates: 35.33.11.
[83] Livy 35.31.5 and 42.1.

Antiochus was still in Asia Minor when Thoas the Aetolian brought news that he was now in control of Demetrias; and in the same way that this man had lied in Greece about the size of the king's forces, so he now told similar lies about how the Greeks would flock to the beaches to welcome the royal fleet. Thoas also presumed to lecture the mature and experienced king on his job, by offering him at length the benefit of his opinion of Hannibal, including a not very tactful hint of a risk that Hannibal's fame on the battlefield might eclipse the king's own.[84] This whole section of Livy is Polybian, although Livy was always liable to embellish speeches in particular, so we cannot press every detail. This speech is nevertheless worth giving in full. (The Latin is in indirect speech, but I turn it into direct, with a small amount of paraphrase.)[85]

> It would be a mistake for you to detach any part of Your Majesty's fleet, but if you do send some ships, Hannibal is the last person you should appoint to command them. He is an exile and a Carthaginian, whose misfortune and character alike could no doubt suggest to him a thousand new schemes every day. His very military reputation, by which he might ingratiate himself to you as if by a dowry, is too great for a king's subordinate commander.[86] It is the king who should be the focus of every eye, the king who should be seen to be the sole leader and commander.[87] If Hannibal lost a fleet or an army, the effect would the same as if another general were responsible. But what if he were successful? In that case the glory would be his, not Your Majesty's. On the other hand, if fortune grants victory over the Romans in the whole war, what hope would there be that Hannibal would be willing to live under a king, subject to one man, when he had scarcely endured subjection to his native land?[88] That is not how he has behaved from his youth up: his hopes and thoughts have embraced dominion over the whole world, so it is not likely that in old age he would tolerate a master. Your Majesty has no need of Hannibal as military commander; at most you could use him as a companion and adviser. The benefit from his intellect

---

[84] 'Mature': Errington 2008: 218 even calls him ageing at this time. This is too strong, even allowing for lower life expectancy in antiquity and a vigorous career of campaigning. He was about fifty.

[85] Livy 35.42. On this speech, see Walsh 1961: 243–4, listing the 'wealth of rhetorical figures' and rightly insisting that indirect speech in Livy can be as effective rhetorically as direct: this particular speech, he argues, characterizes Thoas as fearful and jealous, while also serving to 'portray the increasing influence of Hannibal over Antiochus'.

[86] The unexpected dowry comparison, *uelut dote*, hints at dynastic marriages such as that concluded at about this time between Seleucids and Ptolemies.

[87] An adaptation of a famous Homeric precept which became proverbial: *Iliad* 2.204, 'a plurality of rulers is not a good thing: let there be one ruler, one king'.

[88] 'Live under': *uicturum* is future active participle of both *uinco*, 'conquer' and *uiuo*, 'live'. But although *uincendi* (from *uinco*) has just occurred, and 'to conquer under a king' is not impossible here, 'to live' is generally and rightly taken to be the meaning. There would have been no ambiguity in Pol.'s Greek, assuming this sentence is a direct translation.

would be limited – neither dangerous nor useless. But if greater results were demanded of him, that would be a burden on both giver and receiver.

The following chapter of Livy begins with a very Polybian generalizing comment on the envy to which inferior people are prone, because they hate every kind of excellence in others.[89] Nicander in his address to Philip had also acknowledged Hannibal's military prowess but used it more crudely to list it among Antiochus' assets. Whether or not Thoas spoke exactly as in Livy's report, the speech is said to have had the effect of deciding Antiochus to abandon his plan of 'sending Hannibal' (that is, as commander in chief), 'which had been his only good thought at the start of the war'. So Polybius seems to have discounted Thoas' opinion.

Although Polybius had said that Antiochus' landing at Demetrias was the 'spark' which ignited the war, it was the ugly episode at Delium, the slaughter by Antiochus' officer Menippus of Roman troops inside the sanctuary of Apollo, which led proximately to the Roman decision for war.[90]

### 15.6 The War until Magnesia

At Demetrias, Antiochus held a conference attended by Aetolian leaders and other Greeks – and by Hannibal, who had 'for some time now', *iam diu*, not been party to such policy deliberations. Livy gives Hannibal a long speech. It is clearly taken from Polybius because Appian has a briefer version, but making the same essential points.[91] Hannibal urges that Philip should be brought into a military alliance by all possible means. He even cites his enemy Thoas' view that Philip was like a chained wild beast, eager to attack the Romans. But if Philip could not be induced to join the king, then at least he should be prevented from joining the Romans: Antiochus' son Seleucus, now at Lysimachia, should devastate Macedonia so as to force Philip to defend his own territory. Hannibal reminded the king of his earlier advice (to take the war across to Italy). He should split his fleet and station part of it at Corcyra, modern Corfu, to forestall a Roman crossing, and send the rest to Italy.[92] Hannibal ends by admitting that he does not have experience of every sort of warfare but claims he does know a thing or two about how to make war against the

---

[89] 35.43.1. [90] Livy 35.51 (see pp. 264, 314); 36.1.1–2, 6.3. Cf. *HCP* 3: 65.
[91] Livy 36.6.7 (Hannibal excluded); 36.7.1–21 (his speech). App. *Syr.* 14/54–9 with Brodersen 1991: 115–17.
[92] But for a Seleucid fleet to enter the Adriatic was easier said than done.

Romans. The admission perhaps betrays the historian's knowledge of Hannibal's naval defeat at the hands of the Rhodians the following year. Nowhere in the speech does he mention his own earlier alliance with Philip (215), which had gained him little and had served only to anger the Roman senate, but it was surely in his mind. One important detail was the suggestion about Corcyra.[93] If this advice was genuinely given, it showed shrewd foresight, although to station a naval force in the Roman-controlled Adriatic would not be easy.

Antiochus, says Livy, acted on none of this advice, except that he sent Polyxenidas the Rhodian to bring a fleet and land forces from Asia. This man was an exile, who would play a prominent role in the naval war which followed.[94] Since the Rhodians, the greatest sailors of the Hellenistic world, were active Roman allies, this side of the war was fought between Rhodian captains on both sides.[95] Antiochus moved to Chalcis, where he had an affair with a young local woman and married her; the further story that he indulged in prolonged debauchery is generally discounted.[96] But after a winter of inactivity and no progress, he chose to blame the Aetolians and especially Thoas for their empty promises, *uana promissa*, and decided that Hannibal had been right after all: he calls him admirably wise and almost a prophet, *uates*.[97] Antiochus' attitude to Hannibal as adviser is curiously volatile, and this will need an explanation, which we will try to provide.

What of Philip V, on whom both Nicander and then Hannibal placed such hopes? It is true that Livy claims that Philip was wobbling between Rome and Antiochus even at this late stage but turned decisively against Antiochus when the latter supposedly incited a man called Philip of Megalopolis to bury the bones of the Macedonian dead at Cynoscephalae, a provocative act because it implied neglect by Philip.[98] Whether or not this was the whole story, when war breaks out we will find Philip helping the Romans during the campaign in Greece, which

---

[93] See p. 324 on Cephallenia, the large island south of Corcyra, setting of *Captain Corelli's mandolin*.
[94] Livy 36.8.2. Already mentioned at 35.50.7, but with no introduction or ethnic. Polybius gave his ethnic at 10.29.6 (a fragment of the Parthian narrative, 209) but not the fact of the exile. Later (37.10.1), Livy will specify that he was a Rhodian exile, *exul Rhodius*. The narrative delay of that detail is explicable: Polyxenidas' exile was relevant at that point because of his enmity with the Rhodian commander Pausistratus.
[95] For the naval war, see Van Gelder 1900: 134–9; Thiel 1946: 255–361.
[96] Bar-Kochva 1976: 95–6 with 244–5 n. 5, listing modern views, cf. also his p. 262 n. 18.
[97] Livy 36.15.1–2.
[98] Livy 36.8.3–6. For a bitter epigram by Alcaeus of Messene on the non-burial, see *HE* 28–33 (Alcaeus no. IV, *Anth. Pal.* 7.247), and commentary. For Philip's witty reply, see *Anth. Pal.* 16.26B (Loeb ed.) or the commentaries on 7.247 in *HE* and Beckby.

culminated in the battle of Thermopylae. He was rewarded by the release of his son Demetrius, a hostage at Rome since the defeat of 197.[99]

The Roman consul for 191, Manius Acilius Glabrio, took the land army across the Adriatic unopposed (proving that Hannibal was right to urge that this be prevented). The fleet was commanded by Gaius Livius Salinator (son of the victor of the Metaurus), who took it into the Aegean. Antiochus decided, disastrously, to make a stand at Thermopylae with his own limited forces and his Aetolian allies, whose numbers were also much smaller than he had hoped and expected. Glabrio routed Antiochus' troops, ably supported by the famous Cato as military tribune. Cato destroyed the Aetolians stationed at one of the mountain peaks called Callidromus. Antiochus escaped across the Aegean to Ephesus, and the self-serving Cato as legate brought the news to Rome just ahead of Lucius Scipio as legate, whom the consul had sent off earlier with the same mission, a mysterious duplication of roles.[100]

Hannibal is nowhere mentioned in the Thermopylae narrative.[101] When he is next heard of, he is at Ephesus, presumably left behind by Antiochus when he crossed the Aegean to Demetrias in Greece. That was a pity, from the Seleucid point of view. It is hard to believe that Hannibal would have advised the foolish attempt to hold Thermopylae against heavily superior forces: the defence of Thermopylae by the Spartans and some allies in 480 against the might of Xerxes' army had, after all, been glorious but a total defeat. At Ephesus, everybody else assured the king– himself quite unworried, *securus admodum*, about the war with Rome – that the Romans would not cross to Asia. But Hannibal alone disagreed, and 'his influence, *auctoritas*, with the king was then at its height', *Hannibal unus, cuius eo tempore uel maxima apud regem auctoritate erat.*[102] (This kind of focussing device, 'everyone else ... But x alone ... ', is Homeric and Herodotean.)[103] His reasons are given by Livy in indirect speech, but let us pretend to hear his voice in direct speech. Evidently, his spoken Greek was by now both

---

[99] See e.g. Livy 36.13.1 for Philip's help; Pol. 21.3.3 (Demetrius). Livy had said at 36.4.1 that Philip promised lavish material help to the Romans, at a time when his own narrative implies that he was still was open to persuasion by the other side. This has been dismissed as apocryphal (Walbank 1940: 200 n. 3), but Briscoe 1981: 224 suggests plausibly that the offer may have been historical but was made after the events at 36.8.

[100] Livy 36.15–21. For Glabrio, see *DPRR* ACIL1063 and for Salinator junior, LIVI0952.

[101] For the fighting, see Bar-Kochva 1976: 158–62.

[102] Livy 36.41.2. Here *auctoritas* refers to influence with a particular individual. For the word used by Livy (37.37.9) about Scipio, but with a different and more general sense ('authority', almost 'prestige'), see p. 259.

[103] 'x alone': see Hornblower 2013: 249 on Hdt. 5.92.1 (Soklees' speech) cf. p. 105.

fluent and pungent, if this report is at all accurate (we do not have the Polybian original, which Livy may well have elaborated).[104]

> I do not doubt that they will come; I'm only surprised that they aren't in Asia already. The crossing from Greece to Asia is shorter than that from Italy to Greece, and Your Majesty is a much stronger reason than are the Aetolians. Rome is as powerful by sea as on land: a fleet of theirs has for some time been stationed at Cape Malea, and I gather that fresh ships and a fresh commander have recently arrived from Italy, and they mean business.[105] You should forget any thought of peace; that is an idle hope. Very soon you will have to fight the Romans for Asia itself by land and sea, and either stop them acquiring world supremacy or lose your own kingdom.

Again, Antiochus thought that Hannibal alone foresaw and foretold the truth, but this time he acted on his advice.[106] The king himself set out for the Chersonese to strengthen the area with garrisons in case the Romans came by land, ordered Polyxenidas to prepare and launch a fleet, and sent spies round the islands. Salinator had reached Delos but was stuck there for a while by unfavourable winds. Polyxenidas urged immediate battle. Everyone agreed – presumably including Hannibal – so Polyxenidas got his way but was defeated by the Romans, in combination with their ally, King Eumenes II of Pergamum, in a sea battle off Corycus on the Ionian mainland east of Chios.[107] Then a Rhodian contingent, commanded by Pausistratus, joined these in pursuit of Pausistratus' personal enemy Polyxenidas to Ephesus.[108]

At Rome, Lucius Scipio was elected consul for 190, and his brother Publius announced that if Lucius was given Greece as his *prouincia*, he would accompany him 'as legate'.[109] Greece was duly assigned to Lucius and Italy to his consular colleague Laelius.[110] But it was further agreed that Lucius should take his army across to Asia 'if that seemed to be in the state's interests', *si e re publica uideretur*. The parallel between Hannibal and Scipio Africanus is neatly drawn by Livy, purporting to give the sentiments of the senators. They were, he says, keen to see which would be the more effective: the defeated Hannibal's help to Antiochus, or the victor Scipio

---

[104] Livy 36.41.2–5.
[105] The Latin for 'much stronger reason' is *multo maiorem causam*. Yardley 2000: 288 translates 'much more important target'. Cape Malea is the southernmost tip of the Peloponnese.
[106] Compare Livy 36.15.2.
[107] *Barr.* map 56 D5, 'KORYKOS MONS' (to be distinguished from the better-known Cilician Corycus).
[108] Livy 36.41–3.   [109] Livy 37.1.9. See further Section 15.8.   [110] See further p. 324.

Africanus' help to his brother Lucius the consul, and to the Roman legions.[111]

After the defeat at Corycus, Antiochus at Ephesus devoted himself to refitting his fleet; he sent Hannibal to Syria to bring back Phoenician ships and told Polyxenidas to repair his existing ships and build others, and to do so all the more energetically in view of his earlier reverse.[112] There follows in Livy an elaborate tale of deception, by which Polyxenidas pretended to wish to return to his native Rhodes and promised Pausistratus, the Rhodian commander, that he would hand over the Seleucid fleet, or most of it, as the reward for his reinstatement. The upshot was that Pausistratus and many fine officers were killed and many Rhodian ships sunk; but the angry Rhodians immediately replaced the dead Pausistratus with a supposedly more cautious commander called Eudamus and sent out a replacement fleet.[113] It is tempting to see the mind of Hannibal, another exile, behind the subterfuge, but there is no evidence for this; if there were, the literary sources would not have missed the chance to label this as 'Punic deceit'.

A new Roman naval commander, the praetor Lucius Aemilius Regillus, was on his way, but Salinator remained active for the moment: he won an admittedly costly naval victory over the Lycians off Patara before sailing to Greece to meet the Scipio brothers in Thessaly, and then returning to Italy.[114] When Regillus reached Piraeus, the harbour town of Athens, he met four ships which Salinator had recently sent to Corcyra's southern island neighbour Cephallenia so as to secure the Adriatic crossing against 'piracy', *latrocinium*. But since he himself had already left eighteen ships there for the same purpose, he took the four across to Asia with him.[115] This Roman attention to the vital Adriatic highway recalls Hannibal's neglected advice that Antiochus should send part of his fleet to Corcyra to forestall or delay a Roman invasion.

The Roman and Rhodian fleets were assembled at Samos when news, *fama*, arrived of an enemy fleet on its way from Syria. This was commanded by Hannibal and Apollonius, a Seleucid courtier. A large Rhodian fleet, put together from several locations, set off to forestall him. Ship numbers were thirty-eight Rhodian and forty-seven Seleucid, so Hannibal had a far from trivial numerical advantage.[116]

---

[111] 37.1.9–10. Cf. Balsdon 1972: 226.   [112] Livy 37.8.   [113] Livy 37.10–12.
[114] Livy 37.14–16. For Regillus, see p. 264 n. 105 (Cretan honours).
[115] Livy 37.13.11–14.2; Thiel 1946: 326–7. In 191, the praetor Atilius Serranus had sent his legate Aulus Postumius with 'a few ships' to Cephallenia (Livy 36.12.9), but they seem to have been withdrawn soon after: Thiel 1946: 259 and n. 307.
[116] The *fama*: Livy 37.22.2. Numbers: Thiel 1946: 340–1. Nepos *Hann.* 8.4 says the advantage was the other way round.

## The War until Magnesia 325

The ensuing naval engagement was the last – or perhaps only the penultimate – battle which Hannibal fought; but no name is attached to it in the ancient sources.[117] It took place off the coast of Pamphylia between Side (which the Seleucid fleet had reached) and to the west of Side the Eurymedon River, where the Athenian Cimon had won a famous victory over the Persians in the fifth century.[118] Hannibal commanded the left wing which stood out to sea, Apollonius the right, but Hannibal was probably commander in chief, despite the usual ancient implications of the right wing as more prestigious.[119] The Rhodian admiral Eudamus engaged prematurely with only five ships and was punished for this mistake by being hard pressed by Hannibal. But Rhodian seamanship, always first-class, began to prevail over Seleucid superior numbers.[120] The Rhodian sailors' morale was greatly raised when one of their ships sank a much larger enemy seven-bank vessel. The Seleucid right wing, that on the landward side under Apollonius, was defeated by the Rhodian left, and this local victory released ships from that part of the Rhodian fleet to help Eudamus when he gave the appropriate signal, so that Hannibal and his part of the fleet had no option but to flee.[121] The Rhodians did not pursue (they were tired and weakened by seasonal sickness), although there were soon recriminations about this; but nor did the defeated Hannibal dare to move west beyond Lycia.

The importance of this Rhodian victory was immense, and it has even been claimed that it was greater than the more famous subsequent Roman victory at Myonnesus.[122] It meant that the two Seleucid fleets, that of Polyxenidas at Ephesus and Hannibal's reinforcements, could not combine, and this failure opened the way for the Roman army of the Scipios to cross over unopposed to Asia at the Hellespont for the decisive land campaign of Magnesia. It is a corollary of this importance that Hannibal's mission to Phoenicia did not at all mean that he was being sidelined. His personal prestige apart, his purely linguistic qualifications

---

[117] Livy 37.23–4. The Polybian original is not a conventional battle description and probably derives from Rhodian oral or written sources. The Rhodians are not spared, which makes it more believable. Thiel 1946: 276, 338 n. 571 calls it the 'battle of Side'. His detailed account, an annotated version of Livy by a Dutch naval historian of strong opinions, is at 338–45. Hannibal's last battle of all was supposedly a naval victory in 184, commanding Prusias' fleet against Eumenes II of Pergamum: p. 375–6.
[118] *Barr.* map 65 F4.
[119] Thiel 1946: 341 n. 578, pointing out e.g. that Polyxenidas commanded the left at Myonnesus. Usual implications and further exceptions: *CHGRW*: 404–5 (P. Sabin).
[120] For their manoeuvres, see *CHGRW*: 435 (P. de Sousa), also calling it the battle of Side (cf. n. 117).
[121] The signal given was for dispersed ships to come together. [122] Thiel 1946: 345.

were also relevant: he will surely have been able to converse fluently with his Phoenician hosts and listen intelligently as they discussed naval technicalities with him. He was not a sailor by experience, but he was a quick learner.

Hannibal, presumably stuck on the south coast of Asia Minor (his movements are not recorded), did not take part on the losing side in Regillus' naval victory in September 190 at Myonnesus, a little island north of Samos.[123] Again, the Rhodians were the real heroes. This was the end of the naval war. Antiochus promptly and perhaps unnecessarily abandoned Lysimachia, and the Roman land army was free to enter Asia Minor.[124] The Scipios were even able to use Lysimachia as their own base because Antiochus left valuable stores there.

It is hard to believe that Hannibal offered Antiochus no specific military advice about the Magnesia campaign, but if so we do not hear details from Polybius or Livy. An alleged sarcastic and menacing remark about the magnificent appearance of Antiochus' army may however belong here. It is reported by Gellius. The king, so the story goes, asked Hannibal if he thought his forces would be 'enough' for the Romans, and he replied, 'enough and more than enough, *however greedy they are*'. The joke seems clear enough, but Gellius felt it necessary to explain that he meant 'enough for [Roman] booty'.[125]

After the battle of Magnesia was won, the joy at Rome at the news of the Scipios' victory was because 'at the start of the war', *ineuntibus id bellum*, Antiochus had seemed formidable partly on account of his own strength and partly because he possessed Hannibal as 'director of his campaign', *rector militiae*.[126] But this should not be over-interpreted. It is explicitly retrospective (*ineuntibus*), and the focalization is important: it is a report of or conjecture about Roman impressions and past fears. It has been suggested that one of Antiochus' main dispositions for the battle – to place his elephants in reserve behind his main lines – shows that he wanted to avoid Hannibal's mistake at Zama.[127] If so, and it is no more than a conjecture, this might be evidence of conversations with Hannibal himself at some earlier date. But Hannibal does not actually feature again in Livy's narrative until the Roman demand at Apamea in 189 that he be surrendered, along with Thoas the Aetolian and other named individuals.[128] The

---

[123] Livy 37.2–30; Thiel 1946: 346–57 (352–57 for the battle).
[124] Livy 37.31.1 (abandonment of Lysimachia).   [125] Aulus Gellius 5.5.   [126] Livy 37.51.9.
[127] Bar-Kochva 1976: 172, cf. 169. See p. 335.
[128] Livy 38.38.18, anticipated by Scipio Africanus in his speech to the Seleucid envoy Zeuxis immediately after the battle, 37.45.16–17.

## 15.7 Hannibal as Adviser: Conclusions

Antiochus' attitude to and treatment of Hannibal is ambiguous and calls for an explanation. On the one hand his advice is frequently reported by Livy (using Polybius) and in detail: he is given no fewer than three speeches. The first is in the context of the Ariston affair in 193. Here, Hannibal is said to have been held in great honour by the king, and his advice, given in indirect speech, is emphatically said to have been 'always one and the same'. In other words, this is 'iterative presentation': that is, there had been other such speeches which the historian has not bothered to record. Then, second, there is the long direct speech in which Hannibal urges the enlistment of Philip and the sending of part of a fleet to Corcyra. The third speech (indirect) warns the king that the Romans are indeed about to cross to Asia. At this point, Antiochus does finally act on his advice. A further indicator of Hannibal's perceived importance is the large space allotted in Livy to Thoas' verbal attack on him.[129]

Each time Hannibal offers advice we are told that the king valued him highly and on two occasions that he regarded him as some sort of prophet, even once using the word *uates*. But the usual context is Antiochus' subsequent regret and annoyance, after the event, that he had failed to act as Hannibal had advised. This failure is partly due to the jealousy on the part of the likes of Thoas. But the easily active effect of that jealousy on the king in turn needs an explanation. Suspicion temporarily generated by Hannibal's conversations with Villius was no doubt one factor and was no doubt spitefully fanned by Hannibal's enemies at court; but we are told that these suspicions were soon removed by his telling the story of the childhood oath. A more profound cause was this: hostility to a Carthaginian among courtiers and Greek visitors *spoke to the king's own inherited prejudices*. The Seleucids had never been much disposed to employ non-Greeks. Hannibal was very much the exception, and, as has been well said, he remained an 'outsider'.[130]

Finally, how good was Hannibal's advice? It needs to be broken up according to stages. The initial reported suggestion, an outright invasion of Italy, was not realistic, even with the proviso that Antiochus himself should

---

[129] 34.60.2–3 (first); 36.7 (second); 36.41 (third); 35.42 (Thoas).
[130] See Habicht, as quoted at p. 307 n. 26.

stay in Greece. Hannibal was here envisaging a replay of his own spectacular initial run of successes at the start of his war with Rome; but this was not 218, and the Romans were not to be taken by surprise again; their mobilization since then had been immense; and the Italian communities had for the most part not been won over to the Carthaginian side. Perhaps Hannibal simply wanted war and thought this was the best way to fire up the king's ambitions. Hannibal was, however, more sensible in urging that a naval squadron should seek to deny the Adriatic passage to the Romans, and that, if that tall order failed, they should be confronted at the Hellespont. He shared with Scipio the view that Philip's attitude was crucial (he could have added that of Prusias I of Bithynia). Finally, Hannibal was undoubtedly correct in his prediction that the Romans would cross to Asia, and very soon.

### 15.8 Scipio as Adviser

Publius' offer that if Lucius was assigned Greece, he would serve as his *legatus* (in the military not diplomatic sense) was accepted enthusiastically.[131] However exactly this unusual appointment came about, Publius' formal status as military legate is clear.[132] It is natural to suppose that the intention was that he should be both 'legate and adviser' to his brother the consul in this year.[133] The modern expansion 'and adviser' is a reasonable one. Polybius' description of Publius Scipio's official status in 190 does not survive, if he provided one at all.[134] But his Greek word for a Latin military *legatus* was *presbeutes*, which retains the Latin ambiguity between *legatus* as an envoy or ambassador, and as a senator attached to the staff of a consul in an advisory capacity.[135] Such

---

[131] Livy 37.1.9–10.
[132] Cicero (*Philippics* 11.17) says the senate nearly transferred the Asiatic command to Laelius but when Publius offered to serve on Lucius' staff, no change was made. This may be right; see Scullard 1973 [1951]: 128 and 1970: 202 and 286–7 n. 165; Briscoe 1981: 291. But the basic fact – officially he was a mere *legatus* – would be unaffected. See Scullard 1973: 284–5 (app. xvi, 'Scipio Africanus on L. Scipio's staff') against the theory that Publius was granted proconsular power. (Elsewhere, Cicero says that it was the senate which asked Publius to go as legate: *pro Murena* 32. That is unlikely: Briscoe and cf. Kienast 1954: 145 n. 53.) Schulz 1997: 58 is right that the situation was exceptional.
[133] So explicitly Gruen 1984: 638.
[134] We do have Appian, who says Publius was appointed (not πρεσβευτής but) σύμβουλος, 'adviser', to his brother because of Lucius' lack of military experience and ability (*Syrian history* 21/100), but this is Appian's usual word for military *legati* (*HCP* 1: 718) and is not disparaging. In Classical Sparta, such 'advisers' were a mark of disgrace, appointed when a king or other commander was thought to have done badly: Th. 2.85.1, Cnemus; 5.63.4, Agis. But there was no such implication at Rome.
[135] Pol. 6.35.4, παρ' ἕκαστον τῶν πρεσβευτῶν καὶ συμβούλων, 'for each of the *legati* and members of the *consilium*', with Walbank *HCP* 1: 717, whose tr. I adopt, as also his definition of such *legati*. See

military *legati* 'would be important members of the general's *consilium*'.¹³⁶ But our superior knowledge that Scipio was in the event absent from the battle makes it easy to forget an obvious likelihood: the expectation and hope at Rome was probably that if it came to blows with Antiochus, the great Publius Scipio would fight and exercise military command of some sort, not merely advise. The counterfactual question is therefore worth putting: if Scipio had arrived from Elaea in time for the battle and in robust health, what role would his brother Lucius the consul have given him?¹³⁷ It seems that there was no legal obstacle to using *legati* in this admittedly anomalous way.¹³⁸

Let us pause in Rome before following Publius Scipio Africanus to Asia Minor on his last if vicarious campaign. Before setting out, he erected a spectacular monumental arch (*fornix*) on the way leading up to the Capitol. The idea was not unprecedented, but this structure was memorably magnificent.¹³⁹ It was adorned with marble basins and seven gilded statues, possibly representing famous ancestors as well as himself, although that is conjecture. The whole assemblage is an example of what has been called 'intersignification', a term coined as a physical counterpart to 'intertextuality', to convey the interplay between genres and the interrelation and contrast with pre-existing monuments.¹⁴⁰ (The idea of such a family monument was well established in Greek sanctuaries: a notable fourth-century BCE precursor was the *sungenikon* of Daochos of Thessaly at Delphi.)¹⁴¹ On Scipio's arch, there were, in addition, two equestrian statues, perhaps of the Dioscuri Castor and Pollux, or perhaps of Scipio's father and uncle – or were the horsemen polysemically meant to evoke mythical and historical pairs at one and the same time? Scipio's arch may

---

also Pol. 35.4.5 and *Polybios-Lexikon* 2.2 πρεσβευτής: cols. 696–7, 'Unterfeldherr, Gehilfe eines Feldherr' (subordinate commander, assistant to a commander). Walbank notes (with Mommsen 1887–8: 696) that the first attested examples of 'senatorial *legati* attached to the consul in an advisory capacity' are from the wars with Philip (Livy 32.28.12) and, precisely, Antiochus (36.1.8, Lucius Flamininus). For possible earlier precedents, see Kienast 1954: 146 n. 54. See also Schulz 1997: 166–7.

¹³⁶ *HCP* I: 718.

¹³⁷ As for Hannibal, even if he were present in western Asia Minor, and available for a military command at Magnesia, would Antiochus have wanted this? Thoas the Aetolian's warning about Hannibal stealing the king's glory was not a bad one.

¹³⁸ Mommsen 1887–8: 1. 230 and 2 (1). 696–700. See also Keppie 1998: 40 for the delegation by the magistrate of 'part of his forces and duties' to a senatorial legate.

¹³⁹ Livy 37.3.7 with Briscoe 1981: 294–5 and Harris 1979: 261–2, additional note VI, 'the fame of victorious commanders as it was reflected in the monuments'.

¹⁴⁰ See Hölkeskamp 2018: 422–4 for 'intersignification', and 437–8 for Scipio's *fornix*.

¹⁴¹ *Syll.*³ 274 with Hornblower 1982: 248 and n. 209 (the Mausoleum at Halicarnassus may be another fourth-century example).

have been intended competitively, as a response to a statue of Fabius the Delayer erected in 209 next to Heracles the ancestor of the Fabian *gens*.[142]

We must return to Scipio's mission in 190. If we accept that Publius Scipio was indeed envisaged at the outset as *at least* an adviser to his brother Lucius, as is plausible enough, the contrast between the quantum of coverage in our sources of Hannibal and of Publius as advisers to their own sides is striking. Publius was sent, at his own suggestion, as legate of his brother Lucius the consul. But the only speech of Publius to Lucius recorded by Livy, reflecting Polybius, is a mere seven lines of direct speech at the start of the campaign (addressing him as *L. Scipio!*).[143] It emphasizes the crucial importance of Philip V and urges Lucius to test his intentions.[144] Lucius duly did so, by sending Publius' future son-in-law the young Tiberius Sempronius Gracchus, who went on to be the father of the Gracchi. Scipio and Hannibal evidently but independently agreed about the crucial importance of Philip (or had this topic come up in their conversations at Ephesus?).

In fact, the longest advice offered by Scipio in the whole year 190 is not offered to his brother at all, but to Antiochus! This vigorous direct speech to the king's envoy includes the slangy asyndeton 'go tell him', *abi nuntia*, often used in comedy to slaves and subordinates.[145] The same peremptory expression is used in Livy's book 22 on separate occasions by two consuls, Gaius Flaminius and Lucius Aemilius Paullus, so Livy's partiality to this lively Latin idiom would be a clue that not all his detail derives from Polybius, even we did not for once have Polybius' original, which is much shorter and in indirect speech.[146] Livy, it has been said, 'never tires of bringing Africanus into dramatic prominence', and this kind of rhetorical

---

[142] Hölkeskamp 2018: 437–8. See also Bosworth 1999: 11, cited at p. 238, for a suggested link with the writings on human deification of Euhemerus of Messene and his translator Ennius.

[143] The use of both *praenomen* and shared *cognomen* to a brother is a quaintly formal address, and it is not clear what if anything Livy meant to convey by it. Dickey 2007: 261 and n. 11 cites it as a prose example of a brother using his brother's name rather than e.g. *frater*. She also cites Livy 40.12.9, the Macedonian prince Demetrius addresses his brother as *Perseu* (vocative), but the single Greek name is not quite comparable. Livy's source Polybius would have made Scipio use *praenomen* only.

[144] Livy 37.7.8–10. Polybius, in the context of Scipio's capture of New Carthage, mentions that he wrote a letter to Philip (Pol. 10.9.3, making him 'fragmentary historian' no. 232 in both *FGrHist* and *BNJ*); cf. p. 20. It has been suggested that Scipio sent it at this time, 190, to persuade Philip to allow the Romans to pass through Macedonia, but see *HCP* 2: 204. It cannot be dated precisely.

[145] 37.36.8. See Adams 2021: 281 (such pairings probably reflect 'ordinary (assertive) speech'); cf. Briscoe and Hornblower 2020: 55, 159–60, with indebtedness to the late Jim Adams.

[146] Livy 22.3.13 and 49.10, cf. Pol. 21.15.5–11. Both Shuckburgh and the revised Loeb translations of Pol. (Habicht and Walbank) switch to direct speech for part of 37.36.

elaboration of speeches is one way of doing so.[147] (But the habit is far from being confined to speeches made by Scipio rather than by anyone else.)

The historical background is that the Romans crossed to Asia, but Scipio, as long-standing Salian priest, had to be left behind for religious reasons, which made it impossible for him to move locations during the entire month of March, sacred to Mars.[148] At some unknown point, Scipio's son, another Lucius like his uncle, had been captured, it is not known by whom exactly.[149]

Antiochus, very uneasy now that the Roman army had crossed over from Europe, sent his envoy Heraclides of Byzantium with public promises of large concessions, territorial and financial.[150] To Scipio privately Heraclides made the same proposals, but added a personal one: an offer from the king to release young Lucius without ransom – and he unwisely went further and offered a bribe of money, as much as Scipio asked for, if he would help him get the peace terms. Scipio courteously accepted the release of his son but naturally refused the bribe.[151] He told Antiochus, in effect, that his main proposals were all very well but should have been made before not after the Romans were on his doorstep. He should pay not half but the whole amount of Roman expenditure. In reciprocity for the gift of his son, he gave the king a counter-gift, a piece of simple but good advice: at all costs, avoid fighting against the Romans. But Seleucid prestige was at stake, and Antiochus went ahead nevertheless – disastrously, despite his numerical superiority. Scipio had sized up the military odds and knew that numbers were only one element in the calculation: he will have heard a report of the recent battle at Thermopylae, and perhaps also of the battle in 201 at the Panion in Syria, where Antiochus had won against a Ptolemaic army thanks to his elephants, but where his phalanx had underperformed badly.[152]

This same year (190) is the context of other specific recorded pieces of advice given by Scipio, but again not directed at his brother Lucius. Instead, these were sent in collaboration with him. For example, the brothers wrote

---

[147] Walsh 1961: 235, but rightly adding 'it is his custom to reproduce substantially the content while rearranging the form', and so on. That is, it is Livy's general custom.
[148] See p. 230, citing Pol. 21.13.10–14 and Livy 37.33.7. For the alleged date of Scipio's election as Salian priest in some year before 211, see p. 14 n. 25, citing Rüpke 2008.
[149] The prisoner (*DPRR* CORN1331) was not Publius, the older of the two sons. See Briscoe 1981: 339.
[150] Pol. 21.13–15; Livy 37.34–5. He undertook to abandon his claims to Lampsacus, Smyrna and Alexandria Troas, and some other Asia Minor places, and to pay half the Romans' expenses.
[151] The son's release featured later in the accusations at Rome against Scipio, Livy 38.51.2; see p. 392.
[152] Pol. 16.18–19.

a number of letters jointly, including a famous letter to Prusias I of Bithynia, who was hesitant as to which side to back, to reassure him that the Romans had no objection of principle to kings; on the contrary, they had left some in place and even strengthened them.[153] This letter was successful and made a difference to the balance of strengths at Magnesia.

If Publius wanted to be present in some capacity at the battle, as would have been natural for the great soldier, he was persistently out of luck, because he fell ill at Elaea, south of Pergamum.[154] On hearing of this, Antiochus immediately sent his son back *gratis* with an escort, and Scipio now gave the strangest piece of advice of all those considered in the present chapter. Livy again gives it in direct speech. He told the escort 'please tell the king that I thank him; but the only way I can show my gratitude is to advise him not to join battle until he has heard that I have returned to camp', *ne ante in aciem descendat quam in castra me redisse audierit.*[155] This repeats his earlier warning, but the 'until' clause is indeed cryptic.[156] What can he have meant? (Always assuming this additional piece of advice is historical, and Appian also has it, so it was presumably in Polybius.)[157] There remain various possibilities, after treachery has been ruled out.[158] Perhaps Scipio hoped to be able to broker a last-minute deal. Or perhaps – since the immediate context is an expression of gratitude for his son – he wanted to give a life for a life and ensure Antiochus' personal safety in the event of his defeat.[159] That might mean that he wanted to keep the Seleucid empire in existence under its present ruler, but (like Philip's Antigonid kingdom) in geographically reduced and submissive form.[160] That sort of client arrangement, consisting of

---

[153] Pol. 21.11.3–12, cf. Livy 37.25. See p. 23.    [154] Livy 37.37.6; *Barr.* map 56 E4.

[155] 37.37.8. Not in Polybius, but (n. 169) there is a gap in the surviving narrative.

[156] Cryptic is Scullard's word: 1973 [1951]: 130 and 1970: 205. Balsdon 1972: 228 called it 'extraordinary', Briscoe 1981: 344 'obscure'. But McDonald (1938: 159) said it 'should not be considered enigmatic' (because Scipio hoped for a peaceful last-minute settlement). This is part of his general exalted view of Scipio's 'Hellenistic' foreign policy.

[157] App. *Syr.* 30/151, with Brodersen 1991: 172 and n. 4, agreeing with McDonald (previous n.). Polybius remains Appian's chief source in his Magnesia narrative, but he took over from someone else his over-emphasis on the role of Gnaeus Domitius Ahenobarbus (n. 169), for whom see *DPRR* DOMI1110.

[158] For the possibilities, see Scullard 1973[1951]: 130–1 and (repeated word for word twenty years later) 1970: 205.

[159] Fear of this eventuality is far from absurd. Two of Alexander's successors, Antigonus 'the One-Eyed' in 301 at Ipsus and Lysimachus in 281 at Corupedium, had fallen in battle, both fighting against Antiochus' ancestor Seleucus I. So this was Seleucid family history. Indeed, Magnesia was fought on the very site of Corupedium! (Bar-Kochva 1976: 163).

[160] See again McDonald 1938: 159.

mutual but unequal obligation, rather than direct control, would be normal for this period. Or did he want the glory of yet another grand military victory for himself? This last theory would imply that he would have been happy to rob his brother of the prize, which is conceivable only if relations between the two were not quite as good as is usually assumed (e.g. was Publius going behind Lucius' back when he entered into this private correspondence with the king and gave him advice?).[161] But in any case, only Lucius as commanding magistrate could qualify for any post-war award of a triumph. Rather, Publius may have feared possible Roman military mistakes (his brother's included), but it is hard to see why that consideration should have been expected to appeal to Antiochus. The preferable solution is the first: Scipio still hoped that a showdown on the battlefield might be avoided by diplomacy, and with a not uncharacteristic touch of arrogance believed that he himself was the best person to arrange such a political settlement, given his good personal relations with Antiochus. This solution helps to explain Antiochus' otherwise puzzling delays and hesitations before committing his numerically superior forces.

The advice to avoid battle if possible was good, but Antiochus followed it only very partially. Livy says that he had confidence in the size of his army of 60,000 infantry and 12,000 cavalry, as against a Roman and Attalid Pergamene force of less than 30,000.[162] 'But', says Livy immediately afterwards, 'he was much moved by Scipio's authority, *auctoritas*: in view of the uncertainties of war he had placed all his hopes on him as support for his complete success.'[163] So he retreated across the River Phrygius to the region of Magnesia (mod. Manisa) 'by the Sipylus', a mountain; this designation was to distinguish it from the better-known Magnesia on the river Maeander further south.[164] He fortified his position in case he

---

[161] So Baldson 1972: 227, part of an exasperated attempt to salvage the reputation of the always scrupulously correct Lucius at the expense of the 'irresponsible' Publius.
[162] Taylor 2014: 315 therefore calls Magnesia 'one of the great lopsided victories of ancient history'.
[163] Or, 'for every possible outcome': Livy 37.37.9. The Latin (with which cf. 7.23.4) is *in quo ad incertos belli euentus omni fortunae posuerat subsidia* (adopting *omni* for *omnis*, with Briscoe 1981: 345, a suggestion not noticed in Walsh's 1989 OCT). It is not easy to render this except either clumsily or by paraphrase. 'Support', *subsidia*, does not mean that he expected Scipio to fight against his own side, or to fight less vigorously like a corrupt boxer, but that he thought that his advice was valuable.
[164] The Phrygius River provides another good illustration of the way ancient battles, even decisive ones, did not instantly and everywhere acquire canonical names. (Cf. Appendix 8.4.). We saw (p. 192 n. 46) that a speaker in 187 calls the battle *ad Magnesiam* (Livy 38.58.9). But we also there saw

wanted to delay matters, *si extrahere tempus uellet*.[165] He was perhaps still hoping that Publius Scipio would turn up and work some diplomatic miracle.

As it turned out, Publius missed the actual battle of Magnesia and did not join his brother the consul until Lucius had arrived, victorious, at Sardis.[166] It is inconceivable that there had been no conversations between Publius and Lucius about possible strategy and tactics while the brothers were on their way from Italy, and before Publius was detained first by religion then illness. But nothing whatever is reported, with the sole exception of Publius' early and emphatic advice to sound out Philip. So when in modern treatments he is, for example, described as 'to a great extent the director of diplomatic and military operations' in 190, that makes assumptions which may well be valid up to a point but certainly cannot have related to the precise situation at Magnesia, if only for the obvious reason that the king's final dispositions of his huge and ethnically varied army could not have been known or guessed at in advance.[167]

### 15.9 Conclusion: Two Advisers Compared

To sum up: actual evidence for Publius Scipio as adviser to his brother is lacking, with the sole exception of what to do about Philip. Paradoxically, there is far more evidence, including several speeches, which make Scipio give advice to Rome's enemy Antiochus, so to that extent the parallel with Hannibal is even closer than might have been expected. But Hannibal wanted the king to make war, Scipio strongly advised him against it. In an obvious sense, Scipio was right, in that Antiochus went down to a smashing defeat; but we have seen that some of Hannibal's detailed suggestions would have been worth following and might have averted the catastrophe, or reduced its scale, by military and diplomatic successes which could have weakened the Roman negotiating position in advance.[168]

---

that a short near-contemporary decree recording Achaean honours to Attalus of Pergamum calls it 'the battle in Lydia by the River Phrygius' (*Syll*.³ 606): quite a mouthful.

[165] Livy 37.37.9–11.   [166] Livy 37.45.3.

[167] 'To a great extent': *MRR* 1: 358, entry for Publius under 'Legates, Lieutenants'. But see Scullard 1970: 206.

[168] Errington 1989: 285 commented (without reference to Hannibal) that 'if Antiochus had played his cards sensibly, the Roman march into Asia could have been made into a nightmare'.

## 15.10 Magnesia

So the decisive battle of Magnesia was fought in the absence of both Hannibal and Scipio, but both were absent presences.[169] Lucius moved his army in Antiochus' direction, and there was skirmishing for two days; but Antiochus still declined battle.[170] Eventually, the two commanders committed their whole forces. The Romans, whose army included troops led by Eumenes II of Pergamum and his brother Attalus (future King Attalus II), were greatly outnumbered in both infantry and cavalry. As at Trasimene in 217, there was a mist or fog, which Livy says was to the greater disadvantage of the Seleucid side, particularly their archers, whose bowstrings were softened by the damp (but it is not clear why their opponents' bowstrings were less affected).[171] Antiochus' terrifying scythe-chariots and his camels were easily routed by Eumenes' Cretan and Thracian slingers and archers; the camels and the chariot-pulling horses bolted and were scattered in all directions.[172] This spectacular upset was followed by the destruction of the Seleucid 'cataphracts' (heavy cavalry) by their opponents' cavalry. On the right wing, commanded by Antiochus himself, the Roman legionaries had got the worst of it, but the Seleucids over-pursued, and the Romans were rallied by Marcus Aemilius Lepidus, a military tribune.[173] He and Attalus drove the Seleucids back. Antiochus was forced to accept defeat and fled to Sardis.

Peace terms were imposed immediately by Publius Scipio and then ratified at Apamea the following year by ten Roman *legati* (of the diplomatic sort). They were predictably harsher than those held out before the battle: Antiochus must pay the entire cost of the war in an indemnity of 15,000 talents, quit Europe, and abandon his possessions this side of the Taurus mountain range. For our purposes, the most important clause was

---

[169] Pol.'s battle narrative is lost. It would have been in a gap of bk, 21 between 15.13 (Antiochus rejects Publius Scipio's first advice not to fight) and 16.1, which begins 'After the Romans had defeated Antiochus they occupied Sardis and its citadel'. But it is the basis for Livy 37.37–44. The best modern treatments: Bar-Kochva 1976: 163–72 and Taylor 2014: 315–16; see also De Sanctis 1969 [1923]: 188–97. Balsdon 1972: 229–30 rightly rejects Appian (*Syrian history* 30/152–36/189), who gave undue prominence to Gnaeus Domitius Ahenobarbus (so that Scullard 1973 [1951]: 131 and 1970: 206 even called Ahenobarbus 'the effective commander'; cf. Will 1979–82: 2.213). Brodersen 1991: 174 agrees with Balsdon about Ahenobarbus but has a minor qualification about Appian at 176 n. 4.

[170] 37.38–39.1.   [171] 37.41.2–4, cf. 22.4.6 and 6.9.

[172] As noted earlier (p. 326), Antiochus avoided the mistake of Zama and kept his elephants in reserve, but Bar-Kochba (1976: 172) says he was 'amazingly short-sighted not to have applied the same conclusion to his chariots!'. In any case, even the elephants eventually caused trouble for his own side: App. *Syr.* 35/183. See *CHGRW*: 421–2 (P. Sabin) and cf. 218.

[173] *DPRR* AEMI1180.

the demand for the surrender of Hannibal, who did not wait to be handed over but went on his travels again. Scipio's troubles at Rome were also about to begin, and the fate of the payment to Lucius of the first instalment of the indemnity (500 talents) was raised by two hostile tribunes in the senate in 187, put up to it by Cato. But here we will leave the narrative of our parallel lives for the time being.

CHAPTER 16

# *Hannibal and Scipio*
## *The Military Comparison*

## 16.1 Introduction

The comparison between our two parallel lives as commanders, tacticians, and strategists, and discussion of their relative places in military history, is a perennially attractive topic.[1] The argument could hardly have begun at a much earlier date than it did. Less than a decade after Zama (that is, in 193), Hannibal and Scipio are themselves said to have talked about this during a meeting at Ephesus, and there is no compelling reason to disbelieve the story in outline.[2] Magnesia in 190 was the last great battle of their joint lifetimes, if not quite the last battle ever fought by Hannibal if he really won a naval victory as Prusias' commander.[3] So this is a suitable moment to stand back and try to form our own comparative estimate. The discussion will need to range far more widely than just battle tactics: if Livy's version of the Ephesus conversation is to be trusted in all its detail – which is admittedly not easy to believe – this need was recognized by Hannibal himself.[4] Even if the reasons are really those of Livy or his source, they neatly illustrate conventional ancient attitudes. Hannibal's grounds for putting Alexander in first place were that with a small army he defeated much larger ones, and that he went with it to the ends of the earth. He rated Pyrrhus second because he was the first to show how to lay out a camp (interesting but hardly true, surely), to choose a location (for battle, presumably), and to deploy his troops skilfully; he also knew how to endear himself to the people, so that the peoples of Italy preferred him to the Roman people.[5] Much of this, but especially the final and political point,

---

[1] See Quesada Sanz 2015: 81–2 on modern assessments.   [2] See Chapter 11.6.
[3] See p. 375 for this battle.   [4] 35.14.5–12.
[5] Camp layout ('castrametation'): Rosenstein 2023: 65 n. 2, cites Livy (as in previous n.) and Front. *Strat.* 4.1.14 for Roman admiration for Pyrrhus' castrametation, but also Plut. *Pyrrhus* 16.7 for the converse, Pyrrhus' admiration for Roman.

will be relevant to the present chapter, except that the evidence hardly allows us to say whether Hannibal or Scipio was better at laying out a camp.[6]

The available literary sources are full and detailed, even without the lost biography of Scipio by Plutarch and without a surviving biography of Hannibal until that of Nepos.[7] This chapter will deal with the most important aspects in turn. Full understanding of one such aspect is largely denied to us, in the absence of personal diaries and letters home: the ordinary soldiers' experience of and attitudes to their commanders – the 'face of battle' approach.[8] It has been suggested that one main reason for Scipio's success – often explained in terms of his reforms to the Roman army as it was in 211 and his superior tactics – may simply have been his ability to give his men more confidence.[9] The same could no doubt be said of Hannibal also, and perhaps with even greater plausibility: Scipio had to deal with one large-scale mutiny (in Iberia, 206), but Hannibal never did, as far as we know. Polybius singles this point out for praise in his obituary assessment of Hannibal: he says that despite the extraordinarily difficult circumstances of his seventeen years of campaigning, no one ever dreamed of conspiring against him, nor was he ever deserted by those who had joined him. The second of those claims is not quite true in view of the defection of the high-ranking Libyphoenician Muttines to the Romans,

---

[6] Front. *Strat.* 2.2.6 judged Hannibal to have made a good choice of camp position at Numistro in Italy before his indecisive battle against Marcellus (Livy 27.2). Bellón, Rueda, Lechuga, and Moreno 2016: 78 and n. 30 think Frontinus means to explain how Hannibal, on higher ground, was able to escape afterwards. But Frontinus does not quite say this. See p. 153: the value of the item is reduced by Frontinus' belief that Hannibal won the battle. He didn't.

[7] See Appendix 1.1 for the main ancient sources and 1.2 for the Plutarch problem. Among modern military treatments of Hannibal's war against Rome, the second Punic war, see esp. Lazenby 1978 and the contributors to Hoyos 2011 (edited collection on the three Punic wars) part 3. De Sanctis 1968 [1913] remains fundamental.

[8] John Keegan's 'Face of battle' (Keegan 1976) was pioneering; he did not however address Classical antiquity in 1976. Keegan 1987, on six great commanders and their different styles of leadership, has a chapter on Alexander, but not on Scipio or Hannibal. His book has been influential on modern historians of ancient Greek warfare; note the subtitle of Hansen 1991, and the book's dedication: 'To John Keegan for *The Face of Battle*'. Sabin 2000 is, despite its title ('The face of Roman battle'), confined to heavy infantry clashes. Sabin 1996: 61 observes that the evidence for the Punic wars is less immediate and so less amenable to 'face of battle' treatment than that for Classical Greece, but Daly 2002 applied it to Cannae. For a bad-tempered critique of 'face of battle' approaches inspired by Keegan, see Wheeler 2001, the second half of which gathers contradictory statistics on the efficiency of missiles. It is not made clear how this weakens or is relevant to the 'face of battle' model.

[9] Harris 2008, discussing the view of Sabin in *CHGRW* (430–3) that generalship was what counted most in the Roman wars against Carthage and the major Hellenistic states. 'This conclusion could be questioned, but if it is right it is probably not because Scipio Africanus was a better tactician than his opponents or looked after the supplies better, but because he gave his men more confidence.'

a personal blow to Hannibal, who had trained him.[10] On the other hand, the Iberian mutiny quashed by Scipio was prompted precisely by the correct news that he was seriously ill, and this was aggravated in turn by *fama*, rumour, including false or possibly fake news of his death.[11] That should be taken as an indication that his personality was a crucial factor in maintaining loyalty and discipline. The mutiny is not evidence that he was generally unpopular with the rank and file.

## 16.2 First Rule: Stay Alive!

Before we address the military success of Hannibal and Scipio and ask how much they learned from others – including from each other – we should acknowledge a kind of negative achievement, without which their stories could have been cut short at any moment. In a word, each of them ensured that he *survived*. Self-preservation was particularly discussed with reference to the death in 208 of Marcellus, who recklessly exposed himself and was killed in a mere skirmish. This prompted disapproving comment from Polybius, followed by Plutarch, both of whom drew a comparison with Hannibal, who was never wounded.[12] (Again, not quite true.[13] He was one-eyed because of the rigours of the Alps crossing; he did not lose the other eye fighting, like Philip II of Macedon at the siege of Methone in 354.) The agreed conclusion of those two ancient historians is that it is irresponsible of a commander to expose himself in battle. After his defeat at Zama in 202, Hannibal fled at high speed on horseback to Hadrumetum, having (as Polybius says) 'done everything that could have been done by a good and experienced commander'.[14]

---

[10] Pol. 23.13. Conspiracies: Hannibal's intriguing wigs of different colours (p. 27) imply that he was afraid of assassination, but by whom? Perhaps Roman agents. His own men and officers would not have been fooled. Muttines: Livy 26.40.7; see p. 182.

[11] Livy 28.24.1 and 15, For the pervasive effect of *fama*, see generally p. 310, citing Hardie 2012.

[12] Pol. 10.32–3, Plut. *Marc.* 33.2 (= *comparison between Marcellus and Pelopidas* 3.2). From Livy's fuller version (27.27), we learn that in the same encounter Marcellus' consular colleague Crispinus received serious wounds. He died from them soon afterwards, leaving the state 'orphaned' i.e. with no consul (27.33.6–7). Their joint presence doubled the risk (the opposite mistake to the catastrophic division and so dilution of forces by Scipio's father and uncle in Iberia. But at least neither of those were consuls at the time). Next year, 207, the consuls took the same risk at the Metaurus but were better prepared. Hannibal never wounded: Pol. (10.33.2, he never met with disaster, ἐσφάλη, despite many great battles, so careful was he of his own safety) is less specific than Plut., who says μηδὲ τρωθέντα τὸν Ἀννίβαν, 'Hannibal was never wounded'. 'Disaster' is a relative term. Hannibal suffered some minor land defeats: p. 421.

[13] See n. 17.

[14] Pol. 15.15.3. Horace, *Odes* 4.8.15 apparently wrote of the 'rapid flight', *celeres fugae*, of Hannibal (after Zama). The words have been ingeniously emended to *celebres fugae*, 'famous routs', but see Thomas 2011: 191; on the textual problems of the whole central part of that difficult poem. see p. 237 n. 90.

Five years earlier, his brother Hasdrubal, after defeat at the Metaurus, fell in hand-to-hand combat, perhaps after charging straight at a Roman cohort. Polybius comments that as long as he had reasonable hopes of achieving something worthy of his past, he was supremely careful of his own safety (but all hope was now gone).[15] The difference between the brothers, both of whom Polybius praises for their different behaviour in defeat, is presumably that Hannibal thought correctly that he could still be of service to his country, but Hasdrubal, also correctly, did not. But Polybius actually praises Hannibal for the simpler reason that he had done his soldierly best. Again, Polybius praises Hamilcar (9), father of both Hannibal and Hasdrubal, for dying in a manner 'worthy of his great achievements, fighting against the most warlike and powerful enemies, acquitting himself boldly and bravely at the moment of danger'. But although Polybius' language about Hamilcar is vague, and he does not praise him for freely exposing his person, he is praised for dying fighting, with no suggestion that he should have been more careful.[16] As for Hannibal himself, we have seen that he is praised for the opposite: avoiding reckless exposure. But Livy, in his character sketch of Hannibal, positioned before the war had even started, says he was the first to enter the battle and the last to leave it. This whole passage is however an imitation of Sallust, and the details will not bear much weight; of more value is Livy's narrative record of two wounds, one of them sustained through incaution.[17] But lurking here is one half of the accepted ideal of generalship; the other half is 'stay alive!'. There is an underlying tension here, which will need further discussion.[18]

Scipio was similarly careful of his own safety and never had to decide what to do with himself after a total defeat on the battlefield: he died in his bed – most unusually for an ancient commander with a long career behind him.[19] Frontinus reports a story that when 'Scipio Africanus' was scolded by some people for being insufficiently pugnacious, he replied that his mother had given birth to a general not a warrior. But this Scipio is more

---

[15] Pol.11.2.1 and 9; Livy 27.49.4. See p. 190.
[16] Pol. 2.1.8. See 68–9 and nn. for the correct translation of Pol.; and for Diodorus and Appian, who each give different versions again.
[17] Livy 21.4.8. He probably sustained a minor battle wound near Placentia, early in the war (218): see p. 91 for Livy 21.57.8, a wound not mentioned by Polybius. He had been more seriously wounded at Saguntum in 219 (Livy 21.7.10), on approaching the walls 'with insufficient caution', *incautius*. His youngest brother Mago (6) died of battle wounds, although not immediately (p. 136).
[18] See Wheeler 1991, who shows that the Homeric warrior ethic, personified by Achilles, never gave way entirely to a purely directive role, but that personal intervention by commanders was not usually a feature of the initial phase of battle. For the same tension in modern times (the heroic but controversial death in action of Colonel 'H' Jones, battalion commander at Goose Green in the UK's Falklands campaign of 1982), see Freedman 2022: 142.
[19] Wheeler 1991: 147.

## First Rule: Stay Alive! 341

likely to be Aemilianus than the man we usually call Africanus.[20] Polybius, looking back at Scipio's earlier life in the context of his appointment to Iberia, says that by saving his father's life at the River Ticinus in 218, he acquired a reputation for bravery: a late source even claims he received precisely twenty-seven wounds.[21] But Polybius adds, on a probable emendation of the text, that after this he *seldom* threw himself into danger 'when his country reposed her hopes of success on him – conduct characteristic not of a commander who relies on luck, but on one gifted with intelligence'. The interpretation of the passage is difficult but not trivial and is addressed in a footnote which can be ignored by readers not concerned about or impatient with textual details.[22] Soon after that passage, Polybius says that at the capture of New Carthage in Iberia (209), Scipio 'threw himself into the danger, but as far as possible he did so safely': three strong men covered him with their shields.[23] The phraseology ('threw himself') is virtually identical with that used a little earlier.[24] So this is almost an example of 'correction in stride', by which an author immediately cancels or qualifies an earlier statement.[25] As for the three stout shield-bearers, such protection of a commander may have been normal Roman practice, and so

---

[20] Front. *Strat.* 4.7.4: *Scipio Africanus fertur dixisse, cum eum parum quidam pugnacem dicerent: 'imperatorem me mater peperit, non bellatorem.'* Wheeler 1991: 121 and 154 n. 4 referred it without discussion to Africanus. But Astin 1967: 263, for whom it is no. 44 in his appendix of sayings of Aemilianus, *dicta Scipionis*, admitted it is strictly uncertain, *incertum*, as between the two, but plausibly preferred Aemilianus because of the similarity with his nos. 42a, 42b, 43a, and 43b, and assigned it to the Numantine campaign of 134 BCE. The sentiment feels unsuited to Africanus, but that is a subjective impression.

[21] Servius on Virg. *Aen.* 10.800; Scullard 1930: 37 n. 1.

[22] Pol. 10.3.7, λοιπὸν ἤδη σπανίως αὐτὸν ἐδίδου κατὰ τοὺς ὕστερον καιροὺς εἰς τοὺς κατ' ἰδίαν κινδύνους. This adopts Dindorf's emendation σπανίως, 'seldom' (accepted by Habicht and Walbank, Loeb ed.) for the manuscript reading πάντως, printed by BW and accepted by Shuckburgh, who translated it 'freely', which would produce the opposite sense. Cf. *HCP* 2: 199: πάντως is inconsistent with 10.13.1, New Carthage: see text. The *Polybios-Lexikon* registers the emendation under σπάνιος (3.1 col. 56) but not under δίδωμι or πάντως.

The Greek for 'threw himself into danger' (cf. *Polybios-Lexikon* 1.2 δίδωμι: col. 535) is αὐτὸν ἐδίδου, lit. 'he gave himself' (LSJ δίδωμι II.4 has 'give oneself up'). The Loeb ed. has 'exposed his person', which is the right sense, but the Greek is vaguer than this. Shuckburgh had 'exposed himself to every sort of danger', which is better.

The rationale for emending to 'seldom' (not to some word for 'never') is to reduce the conflict with 13.1, i.e. 'although after 218 he seldom threw himself into danger (3.7); he nevertheless so threw himself now, 210 (13.1) – but only after taking proper precautions'.

[23] Pol. 10.13.1; Livy 26.44.7. See p. 120. The Greek for 'safely' is ἀσφαλῶς, an adverb which conveys a hint of caution.

[24] The Greek of 10.13.1 is ἐδίδου μὲν αὐτὸν εἰς τὸν κίνδυνον, this time translated in the Loeb ed. 'took part in the battle'. That is too free and obscures the chime with 10.3.7.

[25] Hornblower 2013: 281, citing Lattimore 1958. If the MS reading πάντως were retained (n. 22), it would be an even clearer example of this device, in effect: 'he always threw himself into danger after 218 (10.3.7) ... He threw himself into the danger in 209 – but this time he did so *safely*'. Shuckburgh managed to produce plausible translations on that reading.

not evidence for Scipio's special care of his own person.²⁶ At Trasimene in 217, the consul Gaius Flaminius had been similarly protected, although his rash impulsiveness and that of other popular leaders is a constant theme of Livy's narrative in book 22.²⁷ He certainly died in the fighting by the lake.²⁸ Even Alexander was protected by the shields of his comrades at the taking of the town of the Malli tribe in 326, but that was only after he had recklessly jumped down from the wall into the citadel on his own and had been so seriously wounded that he lost consciousness.²⁹ To return to Scipio, in the fierce fighting to retake Iberian Ilourgeia in 206, he is said to have approached the walls and exposed himself to 'no small danger', *haud mediocri periculo*, which caused anxiety among the troops, who hurried to plant siege ladders.³⁰

The attitudes of the literary sources, especially the Greek ones, are in fact ambiguous, and they probably vary according to personal prejudice about the individual concerned. No writer in any period of antiquity chides Alexander for his many wounds; on the contrary, they are represented as a badge of honour, as frontal wounds often were.³¹ Arrian, a Greek writing under the Roman Empire of the second century CE, and a man with experience of high office and of military leadership, makes Alexander, in what is no doubt a speech of Arrian's own invention, invite his mutinous troops at Opis to strip and display their wounds. 'In my case', he is made to say, 'there is no part of the body, or none in front, that has been left unwounded', and he goes on at some rhetorical length.³² What if he had

---

²⁶ Scullard 1970: 228 says indignantly that these three men 'did not shelter a coward'.
²⁷ See Briscoe and Hornblower 2020: 46, listing passages.
²⁸ Livy 22.6.4 with Briscoe and Hornblower 2020: 168 (Flaminius). Livy makes Flaminius fight fearlessly and energetically at Trasimene, but this contradicts his source Polybius, who makes him display 'the utmost dismay and dejection'. See Briscoe and Hornblower 2020: 165 on Livy 22.5.1 and the different Pol. 3.84.6.
²⁹ Arrian, *Anab.* 6.9–12.   ³⁰ Livy 28.19.17; cf. p. 128.
³¹ Wounds in the back were considered shameful. See McHardy forthcoming.
³² *Anab.* 7.10.1–2. Keegan 1987: 58 quotes this speech. The only weakness of the Alexander chapter of Keegan's *Mask of command* (Keegan 1987: 13–91, summarized and endorsed by Lawrence Freedman 2022: 461) is that, despite his warning about rhetoric at 55, he is too inclined to treat speeches in Arrian as straightforwardly usable, authentic utterances at the level of detail. But at least he sees that the ancient world has something for the student of military command. Michael Howard explains in the preface to *War in European history* (no subtitle) that he will start in about 1000 CE as being 'the millennium for which we have reliable records' (Howard 1976: ix). So much for Thucydides, Xenophon, Hieronymus of Cardia, Polybius, and Caesar, to go no later. Contrast Strachan 2013: 152: 'the evolution of military thought is a story that starts at the bottom, with the practical and tactical guidance of the ancients, from Xenophon to Vegetius, and works its way up', and cf. 257 (perceptive remarks on Edward Luttwak, the Byzantine emperor Maurice, and Thucydides). Freedman's history of strategy has a chapter 3 'the Greeks' (Freedman 2013: 21–41, including at 29–38 a treatment of Thucydides from an International Relations point of view. The Romans are

been killed rather than just badly wounded at the town of the Malli? It nearly happened, but Arrian expresses no adverse criticism of the sort so emphatically expressed by Polybius and Plutarch about Marcellus.

Similarly, the almost-simultaneous deaths in battle of Scipio's father and uncle Gnaeus and Publius in Iberia attracted little hostile comment from the ancient literary sources, although it was clearly a mistake on their parts to separate from each other and so divide and reduce their forces. Livy is the main source, but he drew on Polybius, who in his surviving text does explicitly represent Scipio as anxious to avoid his father's fate.[33]

For a Greek general on the losing side of a 'hoplite' (heavy-armed infantry) battle to be killed in the ensuing rout was not uncommon.[34] It was more unusual that at Amphipolis in 422, the commanders on both sides fell. But the Athenian Cleon is nevertheless treated as a coward (Thucydides snidely focalizes some of this through the soldiers), whereas the Spartan Brasidas dies a hero's death – literally: he is given hero cult in the Greek religious sense (but at Amphipolis not Sparta).[35]

It has been plausibly argued that there was a gradual shift in the expected role of ancient commanders from 'heroic leader' to that of 'battle manager'. That would help to explain the ambiguity of attitude already noted; and it has even been suggested, rather less plausibly, that such a change is detectable in a single man's habits, those of Alexander as described by Arrian. The Homeric recklessness he displayed at the Granicus River, his first battle against a Persian army, is supposed to give way to a more graduated approach in the later battles (cool direction at first, then a plunge in at the decisive point). This puts more weight on Arrian than he can bear. The 'integrated ideal' is expressed by Plutarch about Pyrrhus, who is said to have exposed his person in battle but nevertheless managed to direct the fighting as if supervising it from a distance.[36]

The conclusion must be that our main sources usually treat both Hannibal and Scipio with admiration and even some affection and would not dream of taxing them with cowardice for staying alive, as both

---

represented by p. 43 on Vegetius, in chapter 4). His *Command* (Freedman 2022) has the subtitle *The politics of military operations from Korea to Ukraine* but has insights applicable to the ancient world and touches on Alexander as we have seen. The epigraph (p. 31, cf. 34–5) to chapter 2 'The fury of the legions' is a sentence, including those five words, 'falsely attributed to Marcus Flavinius, second century CE' – a Roman centurion invented in the France of *c*. 1960!

[33] Livy 26.32–6; Pol. 10.7.1–2; see further next section. [34] Lazenby 1991: 98 gives a long list.
[35] Amphipolis: Th. 5.10–11. Cleon as coward: 5.7.2
[36] *Pyrrh.* 16.11 (Teubner ed., 16.7–8 Loeb ed.). For this passage, see Wheeler 1991: 121; *CHGW*: 407–8. For something like this compromise attitude, cf. Cicero (no military man), *On duties* 1.81.

men did. They both obeyed rule no. 1 for a commander, which was: lead your men in person, be visible, but do not get yourself killed.

### 16.3 Family Inheritance

Commanders of the calibre of Hannibal and Scipio are not likely to have paid much or any attention to theoretical military writings and doctrine, as opposed (perhaps) to collections of stratagems and narratives like the *Anabasis* of Xenophon or histories of Alexander's campaigns like that of Ptolemy I. Anecdotal evidence, in particular a plausible and circumstantial story told by Cicero, attributes to Hannibal outright contempt for Greek philosophers who presumed to lecture on the art of war without first-hand experience of battle.[37] He and Scipio (or some members of their entourages) might however have been familiar with Greek collections of stratagems, written as much to entertain as to instruct. The only surviving example from before their time is that of Aeneas Tacticus (fourth century BCE), but there may have been others.

More relevant, surely, was the example of close kin. The families of both Hannibal and Scipio unintentionally provided their sons with one important exemplary lesson in the importance of rule no. 1 (and provided us with a parallel between the two lives who are the subjects of this book): their older relatives died prematurely and in avoidable situations which were their undoing. If we accept that Hannibal's father Hamilcar (9) met a premature death fighting in 229, Hannibal avoided his father's fate not only at the time but ever after. He may even have witnessed it, if Diodorus' different account can be trusted. Hannibal's brother-in-law Hasdrubal was assassinated in 221. Hannibal was not going to be caught out that way, so he adopted his system of different-coloured wigs as a precaution against assassination. That is not likely to have been his only defence.

Scipio was at his most vulnerable in Iberia: by the time he returned to Italy and to his election for the consulship of 205, Roman mobilization had been massive, and there was not much likelihood of an easy defeat. But at New Carthage in 209, his situation was very different, and Polybius says explicitly that he had learned at Rome how things stood in Iberia and knew about the Celtiberian treachery and the separation of the Roman armies; so he had 'reached the conclusion that his father's defeat was due to these

---

[37] Cicero, *On the orator* 2.75–6. See p. 282.

causes'.³⁸ He therefore decided on a rapid attack on New Carthage. Polybius could have expanded 'his father's defeat' to include that of his uncle Gnaeus.

As for the 'treachery', Scipio and Hannibal were both well aware from their parents' careers and eventual fates that the local Iberian leaders and the Celtiberians would incline opportunistically towards whichever side looked to be in the ascendant at the moment. From the Iberians' point of view, why not? They had no wish to be the subjects of any foreign invader but did not have the strength to throw him out.³⁹ Diplomacy was therefore the key for Hannibal and Scipio in Iberia, and this was also true of their later dealings with north African princes, above all Syphax and Masinissa, whose cavalry forces were coveted.⁴⁰ Both of these latter rulers wavered for a long time between Rome and Carthage. Syphax ended on the 'wrong' – that is, Carthaginian – side.

Inevitably, given the nature of the literary sources, we know much more about Roman diplomacy with the local Iberian leaders than about Carthaginian diplomacy. The story is told largely from the Roman point of view, as a matter of Roman commanders, mainly the three Scipios, prising local loyalties away from Carthage. But this implies, correctly, that at earlier dates such leaders had attached themselves to the Carthaginians, not necessarily with reluctance. Hamilcar (9), says Polybius, spent nine years making many of the Iberians subject to Carthage by warfare, *and many by persuasion*.⁴¹ The final words of this brief sentence are a partial corrective to the pro-Roman tradition which held that the Carthaginians had made themselves hated in Iberia by their 'arrogance'. And Hannibal and perhaps also his brother-in-law Hasdrubal married daughters of Iberian chiefs or kings.⁴² No Republican Roman commander in Iberia ever did this, not even Quintus Sertorius, in his years

---

³⁸ Pol. 10.7.1–2, which may derive from Scipio's friend Laelius and so be more than mere inferred motivation by Polybius. It was explicated and expanded by Scullard 1930: 61: he did not want to engage all three enemies at once with a numerically inferior army, but 'if he made a dash at one of the three and upon his refusing battle found himself shut in somewhere by the other forces coming up to help, he feared that he might meet the same fate as his father and uncle'.
³⁹ So too in the Peloponnesian war the kings of Macedon switched sides often, to keep their independence; partisan modern historians criticize this as mere inconstancy.
⁴⁰ Connolly 1981: 149 was right that Scipio's persuasion of Masinissa was 'absolutely decisive'.
⁴¹ Pol. 2.1.7, condensed by Livy at 21.2.1 (more usually he amplifies Pol.). Livy says he 'spent nine years increasing the Carthaginian empire in Iberia', without specifying diplomacy: *nouem annis in Hispania augendo Punico imperio gessit*.
⁴² Hasdrubal: Diod. 25.12, with Richardson 1986: 19; but this is wrong unless his marriage to Hamilcar (9)'s daughter had ended in her death, see p. 50 n. 61. For Hannibal, see p. 43. Hamilcar gave his daughter to a Numidian prince called Naravas (Pol. 1.78.8–9). See Family Tree 1.

of defiant independence from Roman control. But in the end, the Carthaginians did indeed fail to gain enough of the local support without which they could not win the war. The reasons for Roman political and diplomatic success in Iberia, Italy, and north Africa (but above all Italy itself) during the Hannibalic war will be the subject of Section 16.9. For the present purpose, we need notice only that in Iberia, Gnaeus and Publius Scipio had anticipated and provided a model for the diplomatic techniques later followed by young Scipio. For example, the older Publius returned some hostages to their families in 217 and won great goodwill by this.[43]

## 16.4 The Creation of a New Sort of Army: Hannibal?

Carthage and Rome were exceptional among Hellenistic states in having founded empires while possessing republican governments.[44] All empires (indeed all governments, ultimately) rely on force, so the armies commanded by Hannibal and Scipio, and what those two men did to and then with their armies, need comparison.

Modern analysts, when assessing Scipio's phenomenal military success, rightly insist on his army reforms: his adaptation of the Roman army during his Iberian years was at least as important as his conduct of sieges (above all at New Carthage) and battles, culminating at Zama. But Hannibal's organizational achievement may have been no smaller, although it is much harder to retrieve details. One difficulty he faced was language. A degree of linguistic diversity was a feature of both Carthaginian and Roman armies, but Polybius was surely right to think that, of the two, Carthaginian forces were far more ethnically and linguistically mixed.[45] That was the situation in about 240 BCE, long before Hannibal took command, but forty years later it had not changed very much. Before Zama, Hannibal addressed different speeches of exhortation to his motley units, who 'had neither language, nor customs, nor laws, nor weapons, nor dress, nor physical appearance in common'.[46] If this was really true,

---

[43] See p. 115 on the Bostar–Abelux affair.
[44] *CHGRW*: 372 (J. P. Roth). Another partial exception is the maritime republic of Rhodes, if we regard its extensive territorial holdings on mainland Asia Minor (its *peraia*) as a form of empire, and why not so regard it?
[45] See p. 27 n. 88, citing esp. 1.67. At §4 of that chapter, he actually claims, not very plausibly, that this was deliberate policy, to prevent the troops from easily combining in mutiny. For the regional variety of Latin in the Republic, see Adams 2007: 118–87.
[46] Livy 30.33.8, from Polybius. For varieties of weaponry in Hannibal's army at Cannae, see Livy 22.46.

## A New Sort of Army: Hannibal? 347

Hannibal presumably made some use of interpreters. To instil corporate loyalty in such circumstances cannot have been easy.[47]

But in this area, too, we should remember the family inheritance and perhaps not credit Hannibal himself with too much. 'In Spain the Barcids had created what was virtually a professional army', wrote Scullard, adding that 'long years of practice had given it a freedom and elasticity of movement which the Romans lacked'.[48] He cites no actual evidence for this – reasonably enough, since he was there writing as a biographer of Scipio.[49] The assertion is plausible, but hard to substantiate. Carthage certainly made heavy use of mercenary soldiers. This emerges most clearly from Polybius' opening book 1, which narrates the long and bloody war fought by Carthage against its discontented mercenaries.[50] To that extent, many individual soldiers in Carthage's armies and fleets were professionals, but that is not what is usually meant by 'a professional army'. The 'mercenary war' did not stop the Carthaginians from relying heavily on mercenaries alongside citizen soldiers and cavalry, right up to Zama.[51] There was nevertheless, after the first war against Rome, a shift from such reliance to a policy or strategy of conscription in Iberia and Numidia.[52]

As for 'freedom and elasticity of movement', this seems – in the absence of specific Iberian evidence from before 218[53] – to be no more (and no less) than an inference or retrojection from Hannibal's early defeats of Roman armies at the Ticinus, Trebia, and Cannae. (Trasimene, as an ambush, is less relevant.) At each of those battles, he pinned the enemy centre and attacked on the flanks and in the rear.[54] Roman armies lacked the mobility

---

[47] This is not a purely ancient problem. Cf. Strachan 2013: 219 (quoted approvingly by Freedman 2022: 8): officers have to be 'sensitive to others' culture'.
[48] Scullard 1930: 262, repeated 1970: 225, except that the 1930 version more sweepingly ran 'entirely lacked'.
[49] In his posthumously published *CAH* chapter on 'the Carthaginians in Spain' (Scullard 1989), he did not return to this aspect.
[50] See e.g. Pol. 1.60, 65.3.
[51] See Taylor 2020a: 66 (noting that citizens enjoyed 'special political status within Carthaginian armies'). De Souza (*CHGRW*: 367) suggested that by 241 Carthaginian citizens abroad were exempt from military service but inferred from Diod. 24.11.2 that they served in the fleet at the battle of the Aegates islands in that year.
[52] Tayor 2020a: 185–6 for the way in which 'Carthage swapped strategies over time'.
[53] Battles in this theatre and period are mentioned, to be sure. But for example that in which Hamilcar lost his life is reported by Polybius (2.1.5–8) so briefly as to be useless for the military historian, except for what it says about Hamilcar's own death; see Section 2. In any case, Diodorus and Appian gave different versions, as we have seen. Generally, Diodorus book 25 and Appian, *Iberian history* are, like Polybius on whom they depend, unhelpfully vague or silent on the military activity and reforms (if any) of the Barcids in Iberia, as are the opening chapters of Livy book 21: also Polybian.
[54] Lazenby 1978: 73, generalizing from the tactics at the Ticinus.

and experience to respond adequately until the younger Scipio made his changes. In other words, Carthaginian success is on this theory analysable only as a function of Roman failure and is assumed, perhaps rightly, to be the result of Carthaginian training and campaigning on Iberian soil in years for which detailed battle descriptions do not survive. If Polybius anywhere examined the structure of the Carthaginian army in the way he examined the Roman one in books 6 and 18, we would be much better off (but in that case a few fragments of such an obviously valuable lost treatment would surely have come down to us). Scullard may have been right. But the possibility remains that what Hannibal did in 218–216 was new, his own tactical and organizational contribution, and a brilliant one too.

Writing long afterwards, Vegetius (about 400 CE) judged that in the second Punic war the Romans, hitherto victorious everywhere, were no match for Hannibal in the second Punic war because they were enervated as a result of their 'inactivity', *otium*, and their unfamiliarity with warfare during the long peace since the first Punic war.[55] This understates recent and not-so-recent Roman fighting against Gauls and other enemies. There is, however, some truth in the suggestion that the Romans had become militarily complacent through long success and therefore underestimated their new and innovative opponent. But what of Hannibal? This essentially negative verdict, according to which his (initial) military superiority was merely a function of Roman inadequacy, does far less than justice to his positive achievements, which must have been partly organizational.

The lack of good detailed literary evidence for the Carthaginian military successes in Iberia after the end of the mercenaries war (241–238) is presumably to be explained by simple lack of interest on the part of the sources, above all the primary and prime source Polybius, and indeed on the part of the Romans themselves, who had other preoccupations in these years between the first and second Punic wars (Illyria; north Italy and the Celts). Polybius' book 2 contains almost nothing about Iberia after chapter 1, which concluded with the death of Hamilcar, already discussed, and the transfer of command to his son-in-law Hasdrubal. Polybius briefly returns to Hasdrubal to narrate his foundation of New Carthage and says vividly that the Romans realized they had been 'asleep' hitherto and had allowed

---

[55] Veg. 1.28.8: *cum post primum Punicum bellum uiginti et quod excurrit annorum pax ita Romanos illos ubique uictores otio et armorum desuetudine eneruauerit ut secundo Punico bello Hannibali pares esse non possent.* For Vegetius generally see Appendix 1.3, and for this sense of *otium* see *OLD* 5. For the continuation of this Vegetius passage (about Scipio), see pp. 350–51.

## A New Sort of Army: Scipio

Carthage to build up a large body of troops.[56] The result, Polybius explains, was the 'Ebro treaty' of (probably) the mid-220s. The brief *periocha* of Livy's lost book 20 contains not a word about Iberia or even Carthage, for what that absence is worth (these brief summaries of surviving books have many omissions, some surprising, so the same is presumably true of the lost books also). He seems to have postponed the first mention of the Ebro treaty to the retrospective material at the start of the third Decade.[57] That Decade is in effect a monograph on the Roman war against Hannibal, and so Livy wanted it to be self-contained (but he also made sure it was integrated thematically into his larger treatment of Roman history).

### 16.5 The Creation of a New Sort of Army: Scipio

For this section we can safely drop the cautious question mark which we placed after 'Hannibal' for the title of the previous section. Scipio has even been credited with building a 'New Model Army': the phrase alludes to the military reforms of Oliver Cromwell in the English civil war of the mid-seventeenth century.[58] The Iberian battles of Baecula and Ilipa are fully narrated by Polybius and by Livy, whose source was Polybius. In both battles, but even more successfully in the second, Scipio abandoned one main feature of the three-tier formation which had contributed to the slaughter at Cannae. Traditionally, the powerful front rank, the *hastati*, delivered what was supposed to be an overwhelming punch to the enemy centre, and casualties were replaced by members of the ranks behind; in effect, a tactical reserve.[59] But starting with Baecula, Scipio's best troops were positioned on the flanks, and at Ilipa the Roman wings performed an additional and complicated manoeuvre which allowed them to outflank the enemy wings.[60] This flexibility was Scipio's achievement, but the teacher was Hannibal: after all, Scipio had been present at Cannae as military tribune and witnessed the unfolding disaster.

The Roman army at Cannae was formed of small units called maniples, 'handfuls'. The Roman manipular army, itself an innovation of the fourth or early third century BCE, was designedly more flexible than the

---

[56] 2.13.4, εὑρόντες δὲ σφᾶς ἐπικεκοιμημένους ἐν τοῖς ἔμπροσθεν χρόνοις καὶ προειμένους εἰς τὸ μεγάλην χεῖρα κατασκευάσασθαι Καρχηδονίους. He means 'in Iberia', from the context.
[57] 21.2.7.   [58] Scullard 1970: 229.   [59] Scullard 1970: 74; *CHGRW*: 406 (P. Sabin).
[60] For the details of both battles see pp. 123–8.

Greek-style hoplite (heavy-armed) phalanx which it replaced.[61] The change, which was anticipated by Xenophon's army, the 'Ten Thousand', at the start of the fourth century, was a response to the new threats posed by hill peoples such as the Samnites.[62] But in set-piece battles, the manipular army had relied on the application of overwhelming weight and force to the enemy centre (at Cannae, the maniples were unusually deep and unwieldy); and though frightening, this was not enough against a mobile and intelligent opponent who could hold his nerve.[63] The beginnings of an even newer arrangement by 'cohorts', a word first attested (in a transliterated Greek form and as an explanatory aside) in Polybius' account of Ilipa, are controversial. Largely because of this Polybius passage, its introduction was for long ascribed to Scipio Africanus. But it is nowadays agreed that the cohort, made up of three maniples, did not become the main tactical unit of the Roman army until sometime in the second century BCE. That is, well after the time of Scipio's campaigns, and perhaps in the context of the incessant Roman warfare in Iberia, which was far from ended by Scipio's victories at Baecula and Ilipa.[64]

The difference between Scipio's tactics and the defeats of 218–216 were not so much structural as due above all to the intense training which he imposed in the period after the capture of New Carthage.[65] This entailed prolonged weapon training, formation drill, and the manufacture and handling of new weapons, all supervised by Scipio personally.[66] It was, says Polybius in an explicit quotation from Xenophon, 'a workshop of war'.[67] Vegetius continues his passage about the second Punic war by

---

[61] For the Roman supersession of the phalanx by the system of maniples, and for what that change entailed, see Zhmodikov 2000; Rawlings 2007: 55–8; Roth 2009: 53; Taylor 2014; Lee 2020: 15–16; Rosenstein 2023: 64–5 (the manipular system in place by the 280s, the confrontation with Pyrrhus). Manipular legions were formed essentially of three ranks (*hastati*, *principes*, and *triarii*, cf. p. 211 citing Pol. book 6), each consisting of ten maniples of sixty. There were gaps between the maniples, at least at the start of a battle.

[62] For these suggestions, see *CHGRW*: 219 (Wheeler).

[63] Scullard 1930: 266–7 and 1970: 228; Lazenby 1978: 142 and 146–50.

[64] Pol. 11.23.1 with *HCP* 2: 312. The cohort: see Taylor 2019a: 81–2. Warfare in Iberia far from ended: Livy 28.12.12 makes the point well (it was not finally subdued until his own time).

[65] Pol. 10.20. See p. 122, citing Roselaar 2015.

[66] New weapons in every sense: it has been suggested (Scullard 1970: 65, Carter 2006: 159, appendix on 'Training for the *Gladius Hispaniensis*') that Scipio was responsible for the Roman change from a short thrusting sword to a long slashing type, the *gladius Hispaniensis* or Iberian sword (Livy 31.34.4), for which see Quesada Sanz 1997 and Taylor 2014: 306. Photographs at Bendala Galán 2015a: 383. It is thought to have been introduced between 216 (Cannae) and 209 (New Carthage). But Taylor 2019a: 78 thinks it may owe less to Scipio's 'prowess as a military innovator' and more to the 'pre-existing popularity of the sword within the ranks after nine years of campaigning'.

[67] Pol. 10.20.7, ἐργαστήριον ... πολέμου; Xen. *Agesilaus* 1.26, cf. *Hellenica* 3.4.17.

saying that after the loss of so many consuls, generals, and armies, the Romans were finally able to prevail only after they were able to learn [to engage in] actual performance, *usus*, and training, *exercitium*.⁶⁸ The last word is surely a reference to Scipio's successful efforts at New Carthage.⁶⁹ It is inconceivable that Hannibal's men were able to achieve what they did at Trasimene, Cannae, and earlier without having undergone similarly rigorous and intelligent training before he ever set out to cross the Alps. But we have no specific information, nor do we know how much had already been done by Hamilcar and his son-in-law Hasdrubal. As for the success of Scipio and the Romans, a contemporary of Vegetius and another Latin author, the pagan Symmachus, put a different explanation into the mouth of personified Rome, addressing the Roman emperor Valentinian II in 384 CE. Pleading for the restoration of a pagan altar of Victory, Rome says that it was the ancestral rituals (*sacra*) 'which drove back Hannibal from my walls'.⁷⁰

## 16.6 Logistics

When Livy made Hannibal place Alexander above all generals for 'taking his army to the ends of the earth', he can be read as uttering no more than vacuous hyperbole: after all, Alexander was forced by a mutiny to turn back at the River Hyphasis (modern Beas), before he could reach the Ganges. Livy's Hannibal was however right to marvel at Alexander's achievement in what we would nowadays be called logistics.⁷¹ He managed, with one main exception (the death march through the Gedrosian desert, modern Beluchistan), to keep his army supplied with food and other essentials when far from home or from friendly and well-stocked city bases. Apart from material essentials such as mules and fodder, crucial other needs were

---

⁶⁸ 1.28.9: *tot itaque consulibus, tot ducibus, tot exercitibus amissis, tunc demum ad uictoriam peruenerunt cum usum exercitiumque condiscere potuerunt*. See p. 348 for the preceding passage. For the tr. of *usus* here adopted, see *OLD* 6 (out of 14 senses). Sense 7, 'practical experience', would also do. Milner 1996: 28 translates *usus* 'military science', but there is no textual or other justification for this. My square brackets round 'to engage in' indicate that I supplied them to make a decent English sentence, while giving what I take to be the correct meaning. For *exercitium*, see Veg. 1.26.1, cf. p. 122 n. 57.
⁶⁹ So rightly Milner 1996: 28 n. 4, his footnote on the passage.
⁷⁰ Symmachus, *Dispatches to the emperor* (*Relationes*) 3.8–10, aptly quoted by Warrior 2006: 128–9.
⁷¹ For logistics in Roman Republican warfare, see Erdkamp 1998 (no index), Roth 1999, and *CHGRW* 386–8 (Roth again); see also Rosenstein 2023 (on payment, *stipendium*). The pioneering work was Engels 1978, on the logistics of Alexander's Macedonian army, with corrections at Badian 1979 (a positive review). Destruction of crops, and the extent of the devastation of Italy, are discussed in a later chapter (19.2).

advance intelligence, local interpreters, and a good grasp of road systems and of physical obstacles. Arrangements for medicines and for medical staff of some sort should surely be added to the definition of 'logistics'.[72] And one of Scipio Aemilianus' purges of his Iberian army was to get rid of merchants, sex workers, and even the seers and diviners, whom the demoralized troops had got into the habit of consulting, out of fear at all the military reverses.[73] None of these were exactly new phenomena by the Hellenistic period. In the time of the Trojan war, the miraculous but unfortunate mythical daughters of Anius king of Delos were said to have kept Agamemnon's Greek army fed for years; Thucydides turned his realistic eye to the problems of supply raised by Homer's *Iliad*; Asclepius' Homeric sons Podalirius and Machaon were army doctors; and Calchas the infallible army seer is met with early in the *Iliad*.[74] But prolonged distant warfare was more common in the wider eastern worlds opened up by Alexander's conquests.

In the west, Hannibal and Scipio both campaigned for long periods in foreign countries, Hannibal in Italy, Scipio in Iberia and north Africa.[75] But their situations were different from those of Hellenistic commanders in the far east. Roman armies in at least eastern and central Iberia were regularly kept supplied from Italy, right from the start of the second Punic war (but Scipio's capture of the abundance of New Carthage greatly eased the Roman logistical situation).[76] A key passage of Livy relates that in 195 Cato in Iberia sent supplies back to Italy because 'the war will feed itself', *bellum se ipsum alet*, a famous remark; the implication is that Cato's self-denying or virtue-signalling action was unusual, and that normally supplies came in to Iberia from elsewhere.[77] In the centre and west of the Iberian peninsula (as far as Lusitania, modern Portugal), Roman armies were out of range of such help; but much of the Iberian campaigning by the three Scipios in the second Punic war was in areas which could be and were

---

[72] Erdkamp 1998 is primarily concerned with food but mentions mule transport of sick and wounded (75).
[73] App. *Iberian history* 85/367. Hannibal was not troubled by excess of seers: p. 227.
[74] Lycophron, *Alexandra* 570–85; Th. 1.11.1; *Iliad* 2.731–2 and 11.833; 1.68–72.
[75] Hannibal also campaigned in Iberia early in his career, but a Carthaginian presence was well established in the peninsula by that time, so it was hardly a foreign country.
[76] For the importance of New Carthage in this respect, see Roth 1999: 171 (also 258 and 304), citing Livy 26.43.8 and 26.47.5–10.
[77] Pol. 3.106.7 (216 BCE): the senate 'sent the generals in Iberia all the supplies they needed' (but the Greek for 'supplies' is vague, πάντα τὰ κατεπείγοντα πρὸς τὴν χρείαν, lit. 'all that was urgent for their needs'); Livy 22.11.6, Carthaginians intercept transport ships carrying supplies/provisions (see *OLD commeatus* 4) to the army in Iberia. See also 22.22.1 (with Roth 1999: 282) and 23.48.4. Cato: Livy 34.9.12. See Erdkamp 1998: 92–3, 95, 115.

supported from home.⁷⁸ 'Home' means by the orders of the people and senate. Polybius' account of Roman political and military arrangements rightly emphasizes that the armies need constant supplies and 'without the senate's agreement, no food or clothing or pay can be provided, so that the plans of the commanders are nullified if the senate chooses to be deliberately obstructive'.⁷⁹

Naturally there were limits to what could be transported by ship. Scipio's army in Iberia will certainly have included large numbers of pack animals, mostly mules, although these unheroic creatures rarely feature explicitly in the literary record: the Greek word for mule, *hēmionos* (literally 'half-donkey') occurs only once in the entire surviving text of Polybius, and that in the context of Antiochus III's' negotiations in 212 with Xerxes, king of Armenia.⁸⁰ It has been well said that 'Wellington was confronted in Spain with basically the same geographical problems as the Scipios, and had the same mules and ox-carts to solve these problems with'.⁸¹

When near the end of the war Scipio crossed over to Africa for the campaign which ended with total victory at Zama, he had no such logistical problems: he ordered a mighty fleet of transport ships to assemble at Lilybaeum at the western end of Sicily, about 400 in total. If anything, his mistake was to set sail with dangerously few escorting warships. He had previously requisitioned corn from the cities of Sicily, deliberately sparing that from Italy.⁸²

Hannibal's logistical situation was much harder than Scipio's throughout, and therefore his achievement was the greater.⁸³ Polybius was right to

---

⁷⁸ For this important geographical distinction, see Erdkamp 1998: 155. For the letter of the older Scipios to the senate about supplies see p. 115.
⁷⁹ 6.15.2–5, which starts by speaking of consul, people, and senate but then places the emphasis firmly on senate. See Roth 1999: 246. I avoid the usual description of book 6 as his account of the Roman 'constitution', because Greek *politeia* has a broader meaning, almost 'way of 'life' (LSJ 2), and book 6 has much about military matters.
⁸⁰ Pol. 8.23.5, 1,000 mules with their trappings handed over by Xerxes (the Loeb ed. prints this at the end of book 8). The 'mules of Marius', *muli Mariani*, were not real mules but a facetious name for his troops, who had to carry their own equipment (Front. *Strat*. 4.1.7). See Roth 1999: 206. Marius was not the first Roman commander to reduce dependence on pack animals, but the Scipio associated with one such reform was Aemilianus not Africanus (Appian, as in n. 73). Female mules were preferred for transporting humans, castrated mules as pack animals. See Oakley 2005b: 422, n. on *clitellae*, 'pack-saddles', mentioned at Livy 10.40.8.
⁸¹ Erdkamp 1998: 25, referring to the 'Peninsular war' of 1808–13.
⁸² Livy 29.24.9. For the 400 total, see 29.26.3 and p. 209 for the deficiency in warships. Corn from Sicily: 29.1.14, cf. Erdkamp 1998: 87; Roth 1999: 161 (cf. 193) on this and all Scipio's preparations.
⁸³ Roth 1999: 333 concludes his book by praising Scipio, Sertorius, Caesar, Corbulo, and other Roman commanders for understanding the use of supply as 'a potent military weapon both on the defense and the offense'. He has often cited Hannibal's logistical arrangements, so it was ungenerous not to find a way to add him to the list.

emphasize it in his character sketch of Hannibal, where however the focus is on the difficulties of the initial march to Italy.[84] Thereafter, Hannibal was not kept supplied by sea from Carthage (only one such shipment is known to have got through), and this is why he was so anxious, after Cannae, to secure a naval base on the west coast of Italy.[85] His war had to 'feed itself', and he achieved this with an astonishing degree of success.[86] His most often mentioned animal companions were his elephants and horses. But like Scipio, he needed less glamorous creatures as well, and in their thousands. Hannibal's stratagem of the oxen with the flaming horns is not normally cited in connection with the prosaic topic of logistics, but it has been called the most famous example of a herd of cattle accompanying an army.[87]

For an army in hostile or even friendly territory, foraging was a perennial part of life, but this too is mentioned only sporadically.[88] Foragers, who were simply normal but unarmed soldiers on foraging duty, needed protection. A precious comment by Livy reveals that in 217, Hannibal in south-east Italy 'was in the habit of sending out' two-thirds of his army to forage, but that he cautiously reversed the proportions soon after, in a tense situation.[89]

The foragers on that occasion had set out from Gereonium; Hannibal had taken and burned the city but left some of its buildings intact to serve as granaries.[90] Such magazines (storage depots for foodstuffs) were crucially important to both sides during the war in Italy.[91] Hannibal showed great improvisatory skill in capturing Roman magazines and then using them himself: he did so at Clastidium near Placentia (modern Piacenza) in the north, and again at Cannae in the south, to which supplies were shipped down the River Aufidus from Canusium. Indeed, the loss of the grain stores at Cannae was one of the factors which led to the disastrous Roman decision to fight there. All these efforts to feed and provide for an

---

[84] Pol. 9.24.4–8 (where he is said to have listened without comment to the suggestion of Hannibal (10) 'the 'single-combat-man' that the troops must be taught to eat human flesh. For this man see p. 45 n. 31).

[85] Erdkamp 1998: 172–3 and 179–80 challenged both of these related propositions, but for rejection of his arguments see p. 138. The one shipment: Livy 23.41.10, Bomilcar.

[86] Livy's claim (22.40.9) that he was seriously short of supplies before Cannae is a Roman myth: see p. 101, citing Erdkamp 1992: 132 and n. 7. Roth 1999: 171 takes it at face value.

[87] Erdkamp 1998: 32 n. 21. See p. 99 for the stratagem.

[88] See Roth 1999: 117–55, ch. 3 'forage, requisition and pillage'.

[89] 22.23.10 (*mittebat*, imperfect) and 24.4, with Briscoe and Hornblower 2020: 226–7. See Roth 1999: 291.

[90] Not securely identified but placed near Larinum in the territory of the Frentani at *Barr.* map 45 A1.

[91] See Erdkamp 1998: 46–83, ch. 3, 'magazines and transport'; Roth 1999: 15–222, ch. 4, 'supply lines'.

army on the move called for an ability on Hannibal's part for making complex financial calculations. He is mentioned as having a 'quaestor' in his army entourage, some sort of financial officer, who was responsible for the army's corn; but the crucial big decisions were his to make. Literary sources say nothing about his work on the production of coins and choice of types, but, for example, Carthaginian 'elephant' coins struck in the Bruttium region in 218–211 must attest his close attention. All this would be good experience and training for the soldier who, in the seven years after Zama, pushed through some radical economic reforms at Carthage.[92]

Hannibal in Italy moved around a lot, partly to keep the Romans guessing and disrupt their logistical planning, partly so as not to exhaust the natural produce of an area, which would have lost him political support.[93] Only after the defeat of his brother at the Metaurus in 207 did he stay put in Bruttium. But by then, he knew he was finished militarily.

The political factor in supply is stressed by the largely pro-Roman sources. Here are two memorable examples. First, in 216 an Apulian woman called Busa from Canusium gave grain, clothing, money, and shelter to large numbers of Roman survivors of Cannae and was thanked by the senate for this after the war. This item is in Livy only, but we have seen that here epigraphy comes to the rescue by indicating that she was fully historical and not a patriotic figment: this munificent benefactor may have been daughter of an obviously wealthy man called Bouzos from Canusium, who is attested in a third-century Greek honorific inscription found at that important Hellenistic commercial hub, Delos. And there must have been a record in the archives of the vote of thanks. Second, in 207 the soldiers of the consul Claudius Nero on their forced march up Italy to join his consular colleague Livius Salinator were showered with bounty for themselves and their pack animals (*iumenta*, a general term), although they are said, in a possibly partisan compliment, to have accepted only as much as they needed.[94] It was not easy for Hannibal the invader to elicit this sort of practically demonstrated enthusiasm.

---

[92] The 'quaestor': Livy 25.13.10 with Erdkamp 1998: 103. For the Carthaginian coins from south-west Italy, see *HN Italy* : 161–3 nos. 2013–32 (cf. p. 29), and Yarrow 2021: 123–4 and figs. 3.15–16. The reforms: Chapter 12.

[93] Clastidium and Cannae: Pol. 3.69.1 and 107.2–7; Roth 1999: 182, 188, and cf. 285. Decision to fight: Erdkamp 1998: 48ᵃ and 52.

[94] Livy 22.52.7 (with Hornblower 2019 for Bouzos, cf. p. 104) and 27.45.10 (Nero). Nero had sent riders ahead to arrange for provisions: 27.43.10, cf. p. 188.

In this largely hostile environment, Hannibal needed fresh drafts of men from home or Iberia, as well as fresh supplies, but Roman control of the shipping lanes, and Hasdrubal's defeat in 207, closed off all options. The manpower figures tell the tale. The number of Roman legions in all theatres had climbed by 212 to twenty-five, the highest total of the war, an impressive increase from the seventeen at Cannae (eight of them fought against Hannibal).[95] In 203, before Zama, there were twenty. By contrast, Hannibal's available forces steadily and inevitably declined, so that when he finally left Italy, he may have had no more than 12,000 men. He did very well to extricate them at all in the circumstances.[96]

## 16.7 Weaponry

Weaponry is a branch of logistics, in that troops must constantly be kept resupplied, a need specially acute for Hannibal, who could not call on home resources. He did not encumber himself with a siege train, and his troops either carried their weapons themselves or used pack animals. Part of his solution to the difficult problem of replacement of weapons was to help himself to the best of what could be captured from the enemy.[97]

On the battlefield, the ethnic variety of his forces was on frightening and noisy display: Polybius' description of the Carthaginian infantry at Cannae, echoed by Livy, includes a description of the near-naked Celts with long swords and the Iberians in purple-bordered linen tunics with shorter swords; their oval shields were similar.[98] Of his skirmishers, the slingers were from the Balearic islands (there was no shortage of leather and

---

[95] See Taylor 2020a: 62 for 212 as the year which probably saw the 'shift toward Roman dominance' in manpower.

[96] See Briscoe and Hornblower 2020: 81–4 (84 n. 278 for the situation after the heavy losses at Cannae), drawing on the tables at Toynbee 1965: 2. 650–1 and Brunt 1971a: 418 and their discussions, still the fullest and best treatments, not superseded by Taylor 2020a in level of detail. Normal legionary strength was 4,500 infantry + 300 cavalry. The allied element (played down in the literary sources) was additional and substantial, supposedly in a 1:1 proportion, but the allies supplied three times as many cavalry.

[97] Pol. 3.114.1: at Cannae, his African troops were 'armed in the Roman fashion' (καθοπλισμὸς Ῥωμαϊκός) because they were equipped with a selection of weapons 'captured in (the) previous battles'. So translators, but the Greek actually has the singular, 'previous battle' (προγεγενημένης μάχης), which would refer to Trasimene only (?); translators seem to suppose the noun vaguely means 'the fighting' here, but I cannot find clear justification for this in LSJ or the *Polybios-Lexikon* 1.4: col. 1515.

[98] Pol. 3.114.2–4; Livy 22.46.5 with Briscoe and Hornblower 2020: 288. Shields: see Pol. 2.30.3 with *HCP* 1: 206 for the 'Galllic θυρεός'.

stones for them in Italy).⁹⁹ His Numidian cavalry were apparently armed with missile weapons.¹⁰⁰

Scipio's infantry carried large shields and throwing-spears, together with the new type of 'Iberian sword', in the use of which they were very probably trained at New Carthage.¹⁰¹ These swords can only have been manufactured locally. But by the time he crossed to Africa in 204, the workshops of Italy and Sicily were available to him.

## 16.8 Battle Tactics

Hannibal's victory at Cannae would perhaps have been impossible without something else: advance intelligence of the usual Roman dispositions.¹⁰² He had a good spy network. However sensible any arrangement of forces might have been in the abstract, mechanical repetition would make it vulnerable, and a good commander knew how to improvise. At Ilipa, Scipio outwitted Hasdrubal Gisgo by initially copying the enemy's 'best-troops-in-the-centre' formation for several days of evening deployment, but then changing everything at the last moment, first by his dispositions (placing his strongest force on the wings), and second by attacking early in the day before the enemy had even breakfasted.¹⁰³ Hannibal had done the second at the battle on the Trebia, but something of the sort had long ago been done by the Spartan Lysander at Aegospotami in 405 BCE, the sea battle which ended the Peloponnesian war.¹⁰⁴ It was an established part of a good commander's repertoire of stratagems.

Tactics, then, were a matter not only of how to fight but when. This is what the Greeks called *kairos*, and they even personified it: the right moment, the right opportunity. Part of the secret of a good general was knowing exactly when to commit forces which he had initially held back. It has been held that the first exponent of a tactical reserve was the Theban Epaminondas at Leuctra in 371, who may, in Plutarch's scheme of parallels, have been the twin of Scipio the victor at Zama. But Epaminondas'

---

⁹⁹ Pol. 3.33.11, cf. 72.7; Livy 22.4.3 (Trasimene), with Briscoe and Hornblower 2020: 164. Cf. Livy 21.55 (Trebia). Balearic slingers used stones, Rhodians used lead projectiles. For Balearic slingers, see also Lycophron, *Alexandra* 633–41. For Punic inscriptions from Ibiza, see *ICO*: 141–7, 'Spain' nos. 4–12, esp. 143–5 no. 10B line 4 of a Punic dedication to Tanit, about 180 BCE, perhaps the '*daimon* of the Carthaginians' in Hannibal's oath of 215, see p. 141.
¹⁰⁰ Pol. 3.71.10, with Lazenby 1978: 15.   ¹⁰¹ See p. 350 n. 66.
¹⁰² For this suggestion, see p. 103 n. 50.
¹⁰³ Pol. 11.22.4 (Scipio had made sure his own men had breakfasted) with Roth 1999: 54. Vegetius 3.20 may have Scipio's dispositions at Ilipa in mind: see Milner 1996: 106 n. 1.
¹⁰⁴ Trebia: Pol. 3.71.10, Livy 21.54.8. Xen. *Hell.* 2.1.22–8, esp. §7: on the fifth morning of waiting, the Athenians had as usual scattered to buy food, when Lysander struck.

priority is disputed, not least because there are earlier examples.[105] In any case, Scipio's innovation – the best troops on the flanks – did away with the main advantage of the old three-tier Roman system, which was the reserve function expected of the ranks arranged behind the *hastati*. (At the battle of the Great Plains, however, he placed the *hastati* in the front and attacked the wings with the *principes* and *triarii*).[106] At Zama, Hannibal kept back his veterans from his Italian days as a reserve, but this was a mistake.[107]

But it was the cavalry arm which decided Zama, and by that stage of the war Scipio's cavalry were better and much more numerous than Hannibal's.[108] The reasons for this were diplomatic and political. Hannibal's many elephants were not an asset, although always frightening to troops unused to the sight and sound of them. In general, Scipio seems wisely to have avoided making much use of them.

### 16.9 Punic Deception – or Roman?

If Scipio's 'breakfast' ploy at Ilipa had been carried out by Hannibal or another Carthaginian commander, the trick would have been treated by pro-Roman writers as yet another example of 'Punic deception', 'Punic fraud': *Punica fraus*.[109] And indeed we saw that Hannibal had done the same at the Trebia, though without attracting adverse comment. But there is *fraus* and *fraus*. The more serious sort entailed actual oath-breaking, and of this Scipio was undoubtedly guilty on one important occasion near the end of the war. The ruse of winter 204/3, by which he burnt the enemy camps with much loss of life, was a shameless breach of a formal truce with Syphax.[110] It is not easy to convict Hannibal of anything as deplorable as this: the rights or wrongs of his attack on Saguntum are too obscure for analysis. But it is true that Polybius regarded Hannibal's movement of

---

[105] Cawkwell 2011: 309–10 (originally 1972). But even with the qualification at his n. 46, Cawkwell perhaps exaggerated Epaminondas' innovativeness. For criticisms of various sorts, see Lazenby 1991: 98–9 and *CHGRW*: 219 (E. L. Wheeler).

[106] See p. 211.

[107] Lazenby 1978: 256 lists among Hannibal's military strengths his 'retention of his third line as a reserve' and even claims further down the page, with Zama in particular in mind, that this was 'the first example of a true reserve in the history of warfare'. This is not easily compatible with his own analysis at pp. 224–5, based on Pol. 15.12–14.

[108] See p. 218, rejecting the arguments of Taylor 2019b, who tries to reduce Scipio's advantage in cavalry numbers.

[109] See e.g. Livy 22.48.1 with Briscoe and Hornblower 2020: 291. See further their p. 328 on 22.61.4 for discussion of an example in Livy of 'Roman fraud', as we might call it. Cf also p. 188 above (mutiny suppressed).

[110] Livy 30.33.3–6; for the historical context, see p. 210 and for the religious aspect pp. 229–30.

Italian populations as a species of impiety, because it entailed breaking treaties.[111]

As for deceptions of a purely military sort, such as Scipio's 'breakfast' ploy, or the oxen with the flaming twigs on their horns which allowed Hannibal to elude Fabius, there would be no gain in totting up examples known or alleged to have been carried out by each of Hannibal and Scipio, and then awarding one point for each success.[112] The most successful and important deception of the whole war was that carried out by a Roman commander against Hannibal, but the commander was not Scipio: that Nero in 207 was cunningly able to elude Hannibal and join Salinator at the Metaurus was a failure of Hannibal's usually first-rate military intelligence.[113]

The guileful Odysseus was always as much of an acceptable model in ancient warfare as was Homer's Achilles, who claimed to 'hate like the gates of Hades the man who says one thing and hides another in his heart'. In the poem, the remark is directed pointedly at Odysseus himself.[114]

In book 10 of Homer's *Iliad*, the so-called *Doloneia*, Odysseus leads a night-time ambush on the Trojans, resulting in the death of Dolon.[115] Ambushes were regarded as a kind of deception or trickery, and this is reflected in ancient Greek and Latin terminology.[116] Hannibal's most famous ambush – surely made possible by excellent advance intelligence – was at Lake Trasimene, where Livy's narrative deliberately evokes night-fighting like the *Doloneia*.[117] But the surprise death in action of the great Marcellus was also the result of an ambush by Hannibal. Ancient warfare

---

[111] See p. 242.
[112] The flaming oxen: p. 99. As it happens, Scipio played a 'cattle trick' on the Iberian Andobales in 206: he drove his own cattle ahead to tempt the enemy to seize them, Pol. 11.32.2–3 with Roth 1999: 28 and n. 132 (noting that the same trick was played by some Iberians on Julius Caesar). Generally, there is the problem that tricks are attractive candidates for anecdotal treatment and so not always above suspicion. But one trick by Hannibal comes with good credentials, is not a roving anecdote (Appendix 1.3), and must win some sort of prize for ingenuity – and humour: the marquee made from sails which enabled him to escape from Cercina while the ships' sailors slept off their hangovers after a feast engineered by himself: Livy 33.48 with p. 300.
[113] Livy 27.45–6; cf. pp. 187–8.
[114] Hom. *Il.* 9.312–13. Cf. Freedman 2013: 23–5, and see n. 18 above (the Falklands).
[115] For present purposes, it is irrelevant whether or not book 10 is part of the original Homeric conception.
[116] The standard Greek poetic word for 'ambush', λόχος, was used of the Wooden ('Trojan' but really Greek) Horse filled with soldiers at Hom. *Od.* 4.277. For λόχος in Hellenistic prose, see Pol. 8.35.1 (ambush) and 7.9.8 (trickery) with *Polybios-Lexikon* 1.4 λόχος: col. 1497, cf. *CGL*: 881. The more usual prose word for ambush was ἐνέδρα, and this too can also mean 'trickery' in Polybius. See *Polybios-Lexikon* 1.2 cols. 803–4 under ἐνέδρα and ἐνεδρεύω, also *CGL*: 492. Latin *insidiae* is similarly not confined to 'ambush'; see *OLD*.
[117] For Greek dislike of fighting at night or in fog, see Ajax's prayer to Zeus (p. 94 n. 96).

was, however, full of this sort of thing. When, for example, Scipio ambushed Hanno at Salaeca, he hardly needed Hannibal's example to teach him.[118] Every young Roman aristocrat would have been told about the Caudine Forks disaster on Italian soil in earlier Roman history (321 BCE).[119]

Finally, should disguises be reckoned as a kind of military deception? If so, Hannibal's wigs made him a prime deceiver. And if Hannibal (10) the 'single-combat-man' was a physical double of the famous Hannibal, he might have resembled one of those unfortunate medieval lookalikes whose job was to impersonate a king in battle.[120]

## 16.10 Other Sorts of Fighting

The first Punic war was not fought only by sea, but it was decided there, at the Aegates Islands off Sicily. In the second Punic, or Hannibalic, war, there was not a single naval battle of any consequence from start to finish. There were some naval operations in Iberia early in the war, in which Scipio's uncle Gnaeus was successful, but they were on a small scale, although good for morale at Rome, coming as they did after the disaster at Trasimene.[121] But this does not mean that the sea was unimportant in the Hannibalic war.[122] On the contrary, Roman numerical superiority in warships meant that Roman maritime supremacy was virtually absolute, and this in turn meant that Hannibal was to a great extent cut off from Carthage. This is important and cannot plausibly be denied.[123] A very few reinforcements did get across; but the only certain example is the shipment which Bomilcar brought to Locri.[124] The same Bomilcar was, however, guilty soon afterwards of an abject refusal to confront Marcellus at Syracuse when he more than enough ships to do so.[125] The absence of first-rate Carthaginian naval commanders is extraordinary: were there really none to be found, or is the explanation rather to be sought in politics at Carthage, where some highly placed individuals undoubtedly wanted Hannibal to fail? To this negative factor must be added a positive: the firm adherence to the Romans of their coastal friends and allies. Hannibal, straight after

---

[118] Livy 27.26–7 (Marcellus); 29.34 (Hanno). See pp. 153 and 210.
[119] See Oakley 2005a: 52–3; Briscoe and Hornblower 2020: 41.   [120] For this suggestion, p. 45 n. 31.
[121] Pol. 3.96, Livy 22.19–21 with Briscoe and Hornblower 2020: 210–16, cf. 13 n. 69 (effect on morale).
[122] This was rightly and vigorously argued for in great detail by Thiel 1946. See also Rankov 1996, stressing Roman control of Italian landing places.
[123] For the figures, see Lazenby 1978: 31 (the upshot is that Carthage had between 50 and 100 fewer warships than Rome at the start of the war in 218). Against the denial of Erdkamp 1998, see p. 138.
[124] Livy 23.41.10.   [125] Livy 25.27.12.

Cannae in 216, tried to win control of Naples because he realized his imperative need for a good harbour city.[126] He failed to do so because enough of the leading Neapolitans preferred to stick with Rome even at this, the lowest point of Roman fortunes since the city was sacked by the Gauls in 386. We will return in the next section to the political dimension of the war in Italy.

At all events, it follows from this evidence that Hannibal and Scipio never confronted each other at sea. Nor indeed did either of them lead a navy against anyone else either – at least during the war between their two countries. A decade after the end of that war, the nautically inexperienced Hannibal, on behalf of the Seleucid king Antiochus III, fought and lost a sea battle off southern Asia Minor against Rome's allies the Rhodians, one of the most successful maritime powers of the ancient world. And a story fraught with bizarre improbabilities of detail made Hannibal win a sea battle for his Bithynian host Prusias against the Pergamene fleet.[127]

Scipio spent very little time afloat as far as we can see and took some risks which might have got him into trouble if his luck had not held, and if the Carthaginians had been a little more enterprising. For example, his arrangements for the naval escorting of his invasion army across to Africa for what became the Zama campaign were arguably inadequate.[128]

Sieges did not bring Hannibal and Scipio into direct conflict with each other, any more than did the war at sea. Saguntum held out against Hannibal for eight months; resistance was desperate, perhaps because the inhabitants kept on hoping that help would come from Rome. It never did.[129] This was a siege won by the long throttling squeeze, in traditional style, with nothing inspired about it.[130] By contrast, Scipio's capture of New Carthage in 209 was rapid and brilliant; he was able to present his success as achieved with the help of the sea god Neptune (Poseidon), so that in a way this was after all a victory on water. The near-miraculous fording of the lagoon contributed enormously to his image as the charismatic 'divinely assisted leader of the war', *fatalis dux*. Then, back in Italy, Scipio was able to take Locri after an earlier Roman attempt at a siege had failed. It was at Locri that the forces of Hannibal and Scipio very nearly came to blows for the only time before Zama.[131]

---

[126] Livy 23.1. See p. 139.  [127] For these engagements see pp. 325 and 375.  [128] See p. 209.
[129] Lazenby 1978: 26.
[130] In Italy, Hannibal mostly did not conduct sieges, not only through lack of equipment (he did sometimes improvise on the spot) but more likely to avoid spending long periods of time in one place. See Lazenby 1978: 87.
[131] See p. 136.

## 16.11 The Political Dimension: 'Hearts and Minds'

Naples stayed loyal to Rome in 216, and Masinissa and his cavalry tipped the balance at Zama. After wobbling, Masinissa fought for Rome and Scipio in the end, because that was in his best interests. Scipio had won him over and recognized him as king. This was in perfect accordance with senatorial policy, as was Scipio's much earlier treatment of Iberian chieftains. But all of these petty rulers would no doubt have swung the other way if they had thought Hannibal had a realistic chance of succeeding. Hannibal – cut off from Carthage by sea and never reinforced from Iberia – lacked the Roman capacity for replacement of manpower, and this was a function of Roman political ascendancy in Italy.

Hannibal's aim in invading Italy was not to destroy Roman power but to end Roman dominance in Italy by dismantling their system of alliances and friendships.[132] His battle victories were a means to that end; but was the end achievable? What made Italian communities reluctant to join him? One answer is to invoke Livy's much-discussed generalization, prompted by events at Croton in the far south of Italy, that 'all the Italian cities were infected by a single disease, so that a division opened up between *optimates* and *plebes*, the senate favoured the Romans, the plebs inclined towards the Carthaginians'.[133] The local upper classes usually had the local power to determine the direction taken by their cities. Most of what follows will be about south Italy, where Hannibal was operating after his initial military successes in 218–216, and to which therefore most of the detailed ancient literary evidence applies; much modern analysis necessarily follows suit.[134]

It is not in dispute that the Romans of the Republican period favoured the propertied classes, and not only in Italy.[135] This was clearly demonstrated by Flamininus' decisions in Greece after Cynoscephalae.[136] The Italian situation is more ambiguous at the level of detail, and modern views are divided about it on ideological lines, just as Livy thought was true of ancient Italian cities. The polar opposites were argued for many years ago now in monographs which are still the best introduction because of their

---

[132] Livy 22.58.3, with Briscoe and Hornblower 2020: 314, and cf. 5.   [133] 24.2.8.
[134] So Fronda 2010 is confined to south Italy. For Etruria and Umbria in the second Punic war, see Harris 1971: 131–44. For disaffection in Etruria, cf. p. 208.
[135] One (post-Hannibalic) institution in particular served to cement upper-class loyalties to Rome, the 'Latin right' (*ius Latii*), by which, after the mid-second century, magistrates in Italian municipalities became entitled to Roman citizenship.
[136] Briscoe 1974: 62–3; De Ste. Croix 1981: 307. On Flamininus' attitude, see Livy 34.31.17 (in the mouth of Nabis of Sparta) and his inscribed letter to Chyretiae in Greek Thessaly (Sherk 1969: no. 33, translation at Sherk 1984: no. 4); on the latter, see Hornblower 2018: 119 n. 58 and works cited.

close attention to the detail, combined with a clear grasp of its implications. The Marxist Geoffrey de Ste. Croix generally sought to uphold Livy's assessment.[137] He was replying in particular to the anti-Marxist Ernst Badian, who had argued that Livy 'occasionally contradicts his own thesis'.[138] At Italian Locri, the position was complicated.[139] Livy begins his Locri narrative by saying that the Locrians went over to Carthage after the 'multitude' had been betrayed by the upper classes, the *principes* (literally 'chief men'), whatever exactly 'betrayed' means there. But in 205, we hear that some Locrian *principes* were in exile at Rhegium after being driven out by the 'opposite faction', which had handed over Locri to Hannibal.[140] It is very difficult to construct a consistent political narrative in ideological terms from scattered and imprecise statements of this sort (and there are others).[141] For example, might the 'opposite faction' not be the plebs but another set of *principes*? In which case, there need be no contradiction with the 'betrayal' passage, which implied that it was the *principes* who took Locri over to Carthage. There is much to be said for the view that Hannibal at Locri, Croton, and elsewhere (notably Apulia) was 'playing on local rivalries to gain more allies'.[142] In Apulia, the Dasii family played a prominent but oscillating role, broadly hinted at by the poet Lycophron in his *Alexandra*.[143] On the other hand, it is has also been convincingly argued that Hannibal's very success in winning over the ruling group in one powerful state, Capua, deterred other Campanian states from revolting, precisely because they feared Capuan hegemonic aspirations.[144]

---

[137] De Ste. Croix 1981: 519–21.
[138] Badian 1958: 147–8 and 148 n. 1, accepted by Harris 1971: 142–3. (For Badian's own politics, see p. 314, citing Harris 2017b). See also, in the same spirit, Toynbee 1965: 1.266 n. 3; Lazenby 1978: 88; Fronda 2010: 173; Terrenato 2019: 131–2 (but this book lacks specific discussion of anywhere except untypical Capua). For Capua, see esp. Fronda 2007 and 2010: 103–47, and for the coins see Yarrow 2012: 120–2.
[139] As De Ste. Croix 1981: 520 acknowledges, when introducing a careful collection and examination of Livy's evidence. For events at Locri, see Chapter 6.4.
[140] Livy 23.30.8 and 29.6.5.
[141] None of the passages cited by De Ste. Croix is conclusive. At 24.1.8, Livy says Locri went over to Hannibal *haud dubio in speciem consensu*, which De Ste. Croix takes to mean the decision is 'represented as virtually unanimous'. But *species* suggests rather the (mere) *appearance* of unanimity, cf. Yardley 2006: 195 'what *looked like* clear unanimity' (italics added). See *OLD species* 6 (b).
[142] Lomas 1993: 70, who stresses that dislike and fear of the neighbouring Bruttians were at least as much a factor as attitudes to Rome or Carthage; cf. Fronda 2010: 161.
[143] Line 623. The Dasii of Arpi and Salapia: Torelli 1999: 89–118 (on the Romanization of Daunia) at 102; Hornblower 2015: 266–7, 399. (But DAZOU, i.e. of Dazou, coins, e.g. *HN Italy*: 76–7 nos. 633 and 642 from Arpi, are best not associated with Arpi's revolt to Hannibal: see Yarrow 2021: 115. But they do attest the family's earlier local importance.)
[144] Fronda 2007: 104 and 2010: 144, 146–7. For Capua's secession from Rome, see p. 140.

Elsewhere too, for example at Nola in Campania, feelings and support evidently oscillated, as was only to be expected given that the balance of military success had not yet tilted decisively against Hannibal, as it did after the Metaurus in 207.[145] Only then did the defeat and death of Hannibal's brother Hasdrubal signify the death of Hannibal's hopes, as Horace was to put it.

But it is precisely in the context of the run-up to the Metaurus campaign in 207 that Livy records the most extreme and visible Italian support for the Roman cause, and at that moment Hasdrubal's defeat was far from inevitable. Nero's forced march up the length of Italy to join his colleague Salinator was accompanied by rapturous displays of welcoming enthusiasm, with no discernible class differentiation. A little earlier, Livy had reported the remarkable and continuing adherence to Rome of eighteen of the thirty Latin colonies in Italy, despite their confessed difficulties in meeting Roman military demands.[146]

Polybius wrote of allied awe and respect for Rome, using two nouns with chiming prefixes, *kataplēxis* and *kataxiosis*.[147] The first of these words is a hint at fear of the reprisals which awaited disaffected communities once they had been recovered by the Romans – notably Capua, which was treated with exemplary harshness. But the other noun, 'respect', conveys something more positive, perhaps admiration for Roman culture and values generally, including stamina in adversity. Here too fear played a part, but it was fear of the Gauls or Celts, from whose ferocity Roman power protected the peoples of Italy.[148] There were, after all, terrifying-looking Celts in Hannibal's army. And Hannibal's treaty with Philip V of Macedon in 215, one of his biggest mistakes, must have caused nervousness in Italy generally, not only at Rome. By contrast with such alien and threatening 'barbarians', as they were perceived to be, many of the Italians worshipped the same defining gods as the Romans, so that respect for Rome was also, to some degree, self-respect.[149]

---

[145] De Ste. Croix 1981: 519–20.
[146] Livy 27.45.6–7 and 27.9–10 with p. 188. See Badian 1958: 144; Briscoe and Hornblower 2020: 8 n. 23.
[147] 3.90.14, κατάπληξις καὶ καταξίωσις (cf. p. 98). On this passage see esp. Harris 2016: 31–2; also Briscoe and Hornblower 2020: 8 and n. 23.
[148] Gabba 1989: 208, citing Pol. 2.23.11–13.
[149] For this good point, see Lazenby 1978: 234. But he confined it to the Latins – also a good point. In the Greek-speaking south, the Neapolitans, for example, shared some of the Olympic pantheon with the Macedonians. But they thought of themselves not as kin to Macedonians but as proud Athenians by descent. A Hellenistic torch race at Naples to the Siren Parthenope was inaugurated in the fifth century by the Athenian general Diotimos son of Strombichos: *FGrHist* and *BNJ* 566 Timaeus F98. Fronda 2010: 133 notes that even if Hannibal was seen by some at Naples as some sort

Straight after Cannae, these various motives – respect, fear of reprisals, gratitude for protection against the perceived menace from Gaul and other foreign forces including Macedon – suddenly lost their potency: hence the string of defecting Italian communities with which Livy book 22 closes. But Roman resilience did not waver, as symbolized by the thanks to the defeated consul Varro for 'not despairing of the *res publica*'. By these words, Livy was also metahistorically assuring his readers that the *res publica* was not finished.[150]

What did Hannibal have to offer the Italian communities for his part? Freedom and autonomy at Locri initially, but that promise was not kept.[151] It was sound policy to set free Italian prisoners without ransom after victories, as he certainly did; but if that policy was to continue to work, more victories on the scale of Trasimene and Cannae were needed, and Fabian strategy consisted precisely of denying him those. For many years to come, and in the absence of adequate material and financial help from the Carthaginian homeland or the silver mines of Iberia, Hannibal was forced to feed his army off the lands of the peoples he claimed to be liberating: an uneasy and ultimately insoluble contradiction. His moves of the populations of Italian cities were regarded as impious treaty-breaking by Polybius.[152] When we examine this aspect of Hannibal's legacy, we will return to the devastation and disruption he caused, which had been 'predicted' by the young man in Hannibal's epiphany dream at the outset. In the end, his failure in Italy was indeed a political not a military failure. It has been interestingly and counterfactually argued that Hannibal might have succeeded if he had taken different routes from those he did and had concentrated on different parts of Italy.[153] It is right that political circumstances varied widely in Italy from city to city and region to region: as the Austrian diplomat Metternich remarked in 1814, 'Italy is a geographical expression'. It

---

of 'Hellenistic liberator' (cf. 168 on Locri for the 'Hellenistic' part of this), that did not make a dent in Neapolitan loyalties to Rome. Fronda (143) stresses rather hostility to Capuan hegemonical ambitions.

[150] Livy 22.61.14 (Varro thanked). Macedon: Hannibal's unwise treaty with Philip V in 215 will surely have caused alarm in Italy generally, not only at Rome.

[151] See the next section for the promise at Locri – and the actuality, the decade of Carthaginian military control there.

[152] 9.26.7, without giving examples, but Herdonea is possible: see p. 242, cf. 359.

[153] Fronda 2010: 34–52; also 288–300. He is right that political circumstances varied widely from city to city. It cannot have been easy for Hannibal to stay mentally on top of all these local variations and fluctuations. Polybius makes this exact point in the course of his character sketch of Hannibal: 9.26.3.

cannot have been easy for Hannibal to stay mentally on top of all these local variations and fluctuations.

## 16.12 Man Management

Inevitably, we think and talk of how the individual commanders Hannibal and Scipio behaved in Italy and Iberia; but that is crude simplification. They could not be everywhere at once, and an important part of generalship is to appoint and support good subordinates as deputies. The best and perhaps only place where we can make a detailed comparison between our parallel lives is Italian Locri, which we have examined at length.[154] Here very briefly are the conclusions again.

Scipio's appointment of Pleminius in 205 turned out to have been a disastrous error, which Scipio compounded by misplaced leniency, and which haunted him into the 180s. The evidence for Hannibal's treatment of Locri is harder to assess because of the poverty of the Carthaginian name pool. But if it is right that Hamilcar (12) the cavalry commander of 215 was the same man who was in effectively uninterrupted control of Locri for the next ten years, it follows that he was responsible for the Carthaginian rapacity which Livy nevertheless compares favourably to the outrages of Pleminius. And there is not much sign of the freedom and autonomy which Hannibal had promised the Locrian authorities at the time of the Carthaginian takeover of their city.[155] It would be a mistake to take Livy's generalization about class struggle as evidence for Hannibal's support of democracies.[156] Locri and other wartime places were inevitably subject to military government, and much depended on the personality of the governor, whether a Roman or a Carthaginian. The misjudgement perpetrated by Scipio, who had a large Roman officer class to choose from – at least when he was consul in Italy – is less excusable than anything done by Hannibal, whose available pool of talent in Italy was small and grew ever smaller.

---

[154] Chapter 6.4.
[155] Livy 24.1.13. Terrenato 2019: 268 writes that 'it is impossible to know what terms Carthage or Syracuse offered to their prospective allies, except in the case of Hannibal and Capua'. This ignores Locri, which he does not mention. Contrast Lomas 1993: 68–9, who sees the importance of Livy's evidence about Locri, as does Fronda 2010: 159–71 and 274–8 (but neither he nor Terranato discuss or even cite De Ste. Croix 1981: 519–21). Fronda is correct (171) that the Locrians' revolt from Rome surely affected their ancient nearby colonies Hipponium and Medma, for which see Th. 5.5.3.
[156] So rightly Hoyos 2006: 654.

Both Scipio and Hannibal had excellent relations with their men. Only one serious mutiny is recorded in Scipio's armies (towards the end of his Iberian period), and he punished the leaders with no stricter discipline than any other commander of his period.[157] It is astonishing that Hannibal's men never mutinied in Italy: even Alexander, surely the ancient world's most charismatic commander, was forced by a mutiny to turn back. Hannibal's relations with his senior officers seem to have been excellent. They were allowed freedom to comment and criticize; this was most famously true of Maharbal, who wanted a snap march on Rome. If there is truth in Plutarch's attractive anecdote about the high-ranking officer Gisgo (6), who just before Cannae expressed nervousness about the enemy numbers confronting them, it shows that Hannibal was on good-humoured terms of equality with his immediate subordinates. It also shows that he knew how to praise them – a vital skill in a general.[158] As for the rank and file soldiery, Hannibal's shrewd instinct for their psychology is illustrated by the lively story of the object lesson or *paradeigma* by which, instead of a speech of encouragement before the battle of the Ticinus, he offered them the choice of conquest or death.[159] This wordless approach was perhaps specially appropriate in view of the linguistic variety of his army.

## 16.13 Conclusion

In terms of battle tactics alone, there is no doubt that Hannibal was the teacher and Scipio the pupil.[160] Without Cannae, there would have been no Baecula and no Ilipa. But as all teachers know, the able pupil can outclass and outstrip the teacher, and that in the end is what happened, at Zama.

If we take a broader view, Scipio's military task in Iberia, Italy, and north Africa was arguably easy by comparison to Hannibal's achievement in maintaining, unsupported from home, a long-term presence in Italy, and for those thirteen years eluding and frustrating the enemy's commanders, the energetic Marcellus as well as the Delayer Fabius. Scipio, by contrast, never lacked for supplies – or for manpower,

---

[157] This is not to underestimate the importance of the 206 mutiny. See p. 128, citing Chrissanthos 1997.
[158] See p. 109, citing Plut. *Fab.* 15.2–3. For an attested exception, the disgruntled Muttines, see p. 147.
[159] See p. 88: the story is in both Pol. and Livy.
[160] Cf. Brizzi 2007a: 211, 'the master and the pupil'.

Rome's greatest asset.[161] Because of Rome's greater capacity for military replacement, especially through the contribution of the Italian allies, time was progressively on his side and against Hannibal's. Both men, however, had their jealous enemies at home and were brought down by them, the one driven into actual exile at the courts of Hellenistic kings, the other forced by legal prosecution into a kind of internal exile at Liternum. The next two chapters will cover these sorry stories.

---

[161] Supplies: the mutineers of 206 complained that there were delays in their payment, not that they were not being paid at all: see p. 128 (genuine grievances). Manpower: Scipio in Iberia had four legions at his disposal for most of his time there (chart at De Sanctis 1968: 615, cf. Brunt 1971a: 679), not to mention troops recruited locally. He was even said to have contributed materially to the forces in Italy in the crisis year 207: Livy 27.38.11.

CHAPTER 17

# Hannibal's Years of Wandering, 190–183
## Aged 57–64

### 17.1 Introduction

After Antiochus' defeat at Magnesia, the Romans insisted that he surrender Hannibal, who however hoisted his sails again, in search of other places of refuge.[1] Like Cleopatra, he had no intention of gracing a Roman triumph, although he did not take Cleopatra's way out by suicide – at least, not yet. It is very possible that not all his movements are known to us, but he seems to have gone first to southern Crete (Gortyn), then back to Asia Minor and the court of Artaxias, king of Armenia.[2] Finally he fled to Prusias I of Bithynia, the enemy of Rome's friends the rulers of Pergamum.

Juvenal, writing three centuries after the miserable end of Hannibal's life, jumped straight from his defeat by Scipio in 202 to his Bithynian stay.[3] He ignored the earlier phase of Hannibal's wandering years as guest and adviser of Antiochus, and the visits to Crete and Armenia. The artistic

---

[1] See p. 336, from where our narrative now resumes. Lucius Scipio triumphed in 189: Pol. 21.24.17.
[2] Walbank, *HCP* 3: 756, reversed this, the usually accepted order (cf. e.g. Seibert 1993a: 522–4). Discussing the Cretan visit, he said Hannibal 'had already spent some time in Armenia'. Of the sources he cited, Strabo (11.14.6) gave no date, but Plutarch (*Lucullus* 31.4) wrote that 'it is said' that Hannibal went to Armenia 'after Antiochus had been defeated by the Romans'. This need not mean 'immediately after' (cf. nn. 4 and 59 on Livy 39.51.1), and Plutarch goes on to imply a leisurely Armenian stay. The logical order of visits is surely Crete, then Asia Minor, then another kingdom of Asia Minor. In any case, Walbank himself (n. 15) entertained the possibility that Labeo on Crete in 189 (see pp. 370–71) was pursuing Hannibal, which would imply that Gortyn was Hannibal's first stop. (By 'already spent', Walbank cannot have meant that the lengthy Armenian visit happened *while Hannibal was a guest of Antiochus*; this would contradict Plutarch, whom Walbank cites, and is against all probability.)
[3] 10.159–66. The manuscripts include an unsatisfactory line 160, *nempe et in exilium praeceps fugit atque ibi magnus ...*, 'for he fled instantly into exile, and there the great man ... ', that is, he fled immediately after his defeat. Nisbet 1995: 25 acutely suggested deleting the line as untypical padding, which moreover contains a factual error: Hannibal did not leave Carthage until seven years after Zama. The interpolator perhaps felt uncomfortable at the abrupt transition from Zama to Bithynia (so Nisbet).

reason for this choice is obvious: Juvenal was not writing biography and wanted to hurry on to Hannibal's dramatic death by more or less enforced self-poisoning after the realization that Prusias intended to betray him to the Romans. Juvenal was not the only ancient writer to ignore the later part of the wanderings. Livy related nothing of Hannibal between his period with Antiochus and his end in 183.[4] If Polybius did recount anything about Hannibal's wanderings – as is possible – Livy omitted it, despite his manifest interest in Hannibal as a person.[5] As it is, the seven years between 190 and 183 have to be reconstructed from Nepos, Justin, and stray pieces of evidence from other late writers. It is time to attempt a narrative.

## 17.2 First Stop Crete

Hannibal's first attested destination (his starting port is unknown) was distant Gortyn in southern Crete, taking plenty of cash with him.[6] At about the same time, one of the Roman praetors for 189, Quintus Fabius Labeo, wanted some military glory and a triumph, so he left Ephesus to sort out affairs on Crete and recover Roman and Italian prisoners said to be enslaved there; he sent messengers round to the cities of Crete inviting them to discuss matters of joint concern to the Cretans and Romans.[7] The cities of Hellenistic Crete were constantly at war with each other, and at this moment the western city of Cydonia, modern Chania, was fighting against an exceptional coalition of Gortyn and Cnossus. More usually, Gortyn in the south and Cnossus in the north, the two greatest cities of the island, were at war against each other, as inscriptions show.[8] Livy, drawing on Polybius but with additions from elsewhere, makes no mention of Hannibal here. But a connection with him has often been conjectured, as also between Hannibal's presence at Gortyn and the epigraphically

---

[4] For which see Livy 39.50.11–52.9, where (52.7–9) he is one of the three famous and neatly synchronized deaths of the year, along with those of Scipio and Philopoemen (cf. Pol. 23.13). Livy's reference at 39.51.1 to Prusias sheltering Hannibal 'after the flight from Antiochus', *fuga Antiochi* (for the genitive in this sense, see n. 59), might be taken to show Livy knew nothing of Crete or Bithynia, but that is probably too strict, cf. n. 2 on Plutarch's *Lucullus*.

[5] Walbank (*HCP* 3: 756) thought Pol. 'must have mentioned Hannibal's wanderings somewhere between' the Roman order for his extradition and his death; 'a likely point would be his arrival at Prusias' court'.

[6] Nepos, *Hann.* 9.1–4; Justin 32.4.3–5. If he had managed to return to western Asia Minor after the naval battle near Side, his obvious embarkation point was Ephesus, cf. Livy 37.60.4 for Labeo's itinerary. But Seibert 1993a: 522 assumes he went from Side itself. The idea that he went to Crete from Armenia is here rejected; see n. 2.

[7] Livy 37.60; *MRR* 1: 361; *DPRR* FABI1117.

[8] Cf. *SVT* 641 (= Pol. 22.15.1–6, Chaniotis 1996: no. 40) with Errington's commentary (in German); *HCP* 3: 201.

attested missions of the Scipio brothers Publius and Lucius, together with Gnaeus Cornelius Hispallus and Lucius Aemilius Regillus, to Cretan Aptera, and (with Hispallus only) to Cretan Polyrrhenia.[9] If chasing Hannibal was really part of the purpose of Labeo's visit, it is very surprising that Livy does not say so, given that he is – if rather contemptuously – well informed about the man's motives. An ingenious modern suggestion is that Livy's 'matters of joint concern to the Cretans and Romans' is a concealed allusion to Hannibal's presence.[10] But why should they have felt the need for secrecy? The inscriptions, which are short and honorific, could hardly be expected to mention Hannibal. Labeo duly got his triumph in 188, despite having ostensibly achieved very little.[11]

Hannibal, says Nepos, pretended to hide his money in amphorae, with some gold on top.[12] This was a very old type of ploy, by which people pretended to be wealthier than they were.[13] But he really (so the story went) deposited it in bronze statues or statuettes which he took with him when he left. Nepos has him then depart for the court of Prusias directly, without explaining why (nor does he mention Armenia at any point).[14] An interesting fragment of Polybius has been referred to this financial subterfuge. It is preserved in a collection of excerpts about embassies, made under the Byzantine emperor Constantine VII Porphyrogenitus in the tenth century CE, and runs as follows: 'for because he knew that the perception was that he had more money with him, he made his behaviour conform to this assumption in every way'.[15] If this old suggestion is right (it was first made

---

[9] For the Cretan honours to the Scipios, Hispallus, and Regillus, see p. 264. Chaniotis 1996: 42 regarded it as certain, 'sicher', that Labeo's visit and those of the Scipios and colleagues were connected to Hannibal's flight to Gortyn. Cf. more cautiously HCP 3:163 ('perhaps') and IC IV: 24 (M. Guarducci). Briscoe 1981: 394 was 'unconvinced', as far as Labeo was concerned. But Seibert 1993a: 523 appears to explain Hannibal's flight from Crete as caused by Labeo's visit.
[10] Van Effenterre 1948: 262.   [11] Livy 38.47.5; MRR 1: 366.
[12] An amphora was a long two-handled pot with a pointed end for easy transport or storage of liquids.
[13] Hdt. 3.123, cf. Th. 6.46.3. Seibert 1993a: 522–3 n. 6 called it a widespread cliché and suggested that it was invented to fill out the sparse information available about Hannibal's later period. Similarly MacDonald 2015: 225 (who calls the whole Gortyn visit a 'rumour'). On the trick, see also Syme 1995: 348, quoted at n. 17. See also Appendix 1.3.
[14] Justin says, surely wrongly, that he was on Crete 'for a long time', diu: Van Effenterre 1948: 261–2 n. 6.
[15] Frag. no. 233 BW, no. 234 Habicht and Walbank, Loeb ed. See Walbank HCP 3: 757, cited at n. 5. For the manuscript tradition of the excerpts, see Moore 1965: 127 and 137–65. Walbank says Casaubon referred the fragment to Hannibal's visit to Gortyn 'during his wanderings, after escaping from the Syrian court following Magnesia'. Walbank here presumably had in mind the whole sequence of 'wanderings [which Hannibal undertook] after . . . Magnesia'; he cannot consistently mean that the Gortyn visit followed Magnesia immediately. Indeed it did so, on the order of events here accepted; but that would contradict his own view (n. 1) that the first stop was Armenia.

by the Renaissance scholar Isaac Casaubon, 1559–1614), it would show that Polybius did indeed narrate Hannibal's stay in Crete.[16]

To sum up: there is no specific ancient evidence in support of the purely modern hypothesis of a connection between Hannibal's presence on Crete and the arrival of these various high-ranking Romans. As always in the study of the poorly documented ancient world, we should resist the temptation to bring all our few data into connection with each other, especially when Livy himself does not make that connection.

Did Hannibal go to Crete at all?[17] Casaubon's suggestion about the placing of the Polybius fragment was brilliant, but hardly conclusive; and Livy says nothing about Hannibal on Crete. The single piece of 'evidence' for what he actually did while he was there is an anecdote about a ruse of a familiar ancient sort. Let us however assume that there is some kernel of factual truth in the visit itself. The puzzle about the Roman visitors has distracted scholarly attention from a more basic question: why should Hannibal have picked Crete as a refuge? It does not seem quite enough to say that he hoped to be safe there from the Romans.[18] It was an unexpected choice.[19] After all, his other three destinations after leaving Carthage in 195 were all royal courts in Asia Minor, where exiled pensioners like himself were not hard to come across, although the famous deracinated Carthaginian general was no doubt an unusual spectacle. If we were writing a historical novel or film script about Hannibal, we might indulge in some free guesswork on the following lines.[20] Hannibal never intended Crete as more than a port of call on a longer and western Mediterranean voyage. His real destination was Carthage, where he knew that there was justified

---

[16] BW (footnote on frag. 233) ascribed it to the later Dutch scholar Tiberius Hemsterhuys (1685–1766).

[17] A doubt is implied by Syme 1995: 348: 'before making for Bithynia, the refugee went to Crete and stayed there for some time. *Such at least* [my italics] is the account of Cornelius Nepos and Justin'. Plutarch (*Flam.* 20.4) says Hannibal 'wandered for a long time before finally' ending up in Bithynia (πλανηθεὶς πολλά, τέλος) so may have known the Crete tradition (he certainly knew about Armenia) without going into details.

[18] With Hoffmann 1962: 125 or Seibert 1993a: 522.

[19] The Ptolemies always had a strong interest in Crete and maintained a garrison at Itanos in the east. See Bagnall 1976: 117–23. But (p. 303) it is unlikely that Hannibal would have approached a Ptolemaic representative on Crete or anywhere else.

[20] A film *Hannibal* does exist (1958, in colour, Italian-made but with English dialogue, starring Victor Mature). It is dire. Hannibal falls in love with Sylvia (Rita Gam), niece of Roman senator Fabius Maximus. This doesn't go well. Enough said. For the film of the battle of Cannae shown at the site museum see p. 101. A good full-length biopic of Hannibal would be an attractive idea. I have not seen the Mussolini-era propaganda film *Scipione Africano* (1937), directed by Carmine Gallone. Oddly enough, Scipio was played by an actor called *Annibale* Ninchi. (Camillo Pilotto was Hannibal.) See p. 26 for an unfulfilled plan to make a film about Hannibal starring Denzel Washington.

discontent at Roman conniving at Masinissa's constant provocations.[21] But he also knew how many enemies he still had there. So he cautiously dropped in first at the main city of Crete in search of the Carthaginian *proxenos*, that is, a local dignitary who looked after the interests of the many Carthaginian traders who landed on the island. But this well-informed man soon disabused Hannibal of any such hopes of return to his homeland and sent him on his way, back to the east. That is pure fantasy, but it would make sense.

## 17.3 Second Stop Armenia

The evidence for Hannibal's time in Armenia consists entirely of two literary texts about his foundation of Artaxata: Strabo (five words) and Plutarch's *Lucullus* (a little fuller).[22] The actual foundation can be postponed for the moment. Three questions remain: why did he go to Armenia at all? What else did he do there? Why did he leave?

Armenia was a Seleucid satrapy until after Antiochus' defeat in 190, when according to Strabo its two satraps at the time, Artaxias in the north and Zariadris in the south, became kings; that is, they threw off their dependence, a recurrent feature of Seleucid history (the Attalid dynasty of Pergamum had started in the same way, as did some of the kingdoms in the far east of the Hellenistic world). A little further on in his text, Strabo said much the same but this time added that the two *joined the Romans* and were called kings – in that order.[23] The only way of making sense of Hannibal's decision to try his luck in Armenia in 189 is to reverse that sequence and to suppose that there was a gap of a few years between the satraps' declaration of independence from Antiochus and the start of the Roman alignment.[24] Since Artaxias' half of the kingdom adjoined the Black Sea, Hannibal could have arrived there – discreetly and perhaps circuitously – by ship, rather than by land through Seleucid territory proper.

Armenia around 200 BCE was an attractive and cultured place, as seven intriguing Greek rock inscriptions attest. They vary in content. One of them refers to the Archaic Greek poet Hesiod and his brother Perses, and

---

[21] If we could believe in the oracle about his dying in 'Libya', which he is supposed to have known about (see p. 382), that might imply he had not abandoned thoughts of a return to his homeland.
[22] Strabo 11.14.6; Plut. *Luc.* 31.4–5. On the foundation, see p. 378.   [23] Strabo 11.14.5 and 15.
[24] Seibert 1993a: 523–4 n. 11. Cf. Hoffmann 1962: 126, who says that Artaxias was not party to the treaty between Rome and Antiochus and so was outside the Roman sphere of influence. He does not say when he thought the two ex-satraps joined Rome.

another is a collection of extracts from dramatic poetry in iambic rhythm, including three lines from the *Hippolytus* of Euripides; perhaps these two texts had an educational function. Two others are letters. Another is a list of the Macedonian months, a further sign that the Seleucids did not wish to lose sight of their origins.[25]

Plutarch, in his (for us lucky) digression about Artaxata in the context of Lucius Licinius Lucullus' eastern campaigns in 68 BCE, said that Hannibal gave King Artaxias 'many useful suggestions and instructions', of which the advice about founding a city on the excellent but neglected site of the future Artaxata was only one.[26] We would like to know more about how else Hannibal made himself useful to the king, but that is all we get. It does, however, imply a more than momentary role as adviser, and therefore a more than passing visit. The dates of his stay are not recoverable, but we should probably allow him a couple of years at the Bithynian court before his death in 183. So perhaps 189–185.

But Hannibal's luck ran out yet again. We do not know whether Roman pressure was applied to Artaxias, or whether he simply grew nervous about his helpful and interesting, but dangerously controversial guest. In any case, whether Hannibal jumped or was pushed, he evidently moved on, and for the last time.

### 17.4 Third Stop Bithynia

For Hannibal, however desperate his situation, to move west from distant Armenia to Prusias' Bithynia, well within the reach of the ever-lengthening arm of Rome, was a surprising and risky decision by both host and guest, given that Prusias had so recently been persuaded by the Scipios not to join Antiochus against Rome. Previously Prusias, who had married into the Antigonid dynasty, had been an ally of Philip V and was enrolled on his side in the treaty which in 205 ended the first Macedonian war between Rome and Philip.[27] Hannibal's gamble is explicable only in terms of the long-standing hostility between Bithynia and Pergamum, whose Attalid

---

[25] See p. 306 for this culturally retentive aspect of the Seleucids. For the inscriptions, see Sherwin-White (S. M.) and Kuhrt 1993: 190–7, esp. 194–7 with plates 23–6. For the Greek inscriptions, see now Canali de Rossi 2004 nos. 9–15.

[26] *Luc.* 31.4. *MRR* 2: 139–40; *DPRR* LICI1903. The source might be Sallust, cited at *Luc.* 33.3; see Scardigli 1997: 263–4. But there are other possibilities. Chris Pelling tells me that he thinks Sallust 'a very reasonable bet'; see Pelling forthcoming on Plutarch's use of Sallust in the *Lucullus*. I thank him for making this chapter available to me in advance.

[27] Pol. 15.22.1 (the marriage connection); Livy 29.12.14 (the 'Peace of Phoenice').

rulers were consistent in their support of the Romans.[28] Prusias had, probably soon after Eumenes II succeeded Attalus I (197), annexed valuable territory belonging to Pergamum.[29] At the peace conference held at Apamea in 189 or 188, the Romans formally awarded this territory to Eumenes.[30] But for five years, they did nothing to enforce this decision, evidently not wishing to displease either of the two kings. When they finally sent Flamininus to impose peace between the warring sides, they were partly moved to do so by annoyance at Prusias' hospitality to Hannibal, although it seems that Flamininus may have had no specific instructions to demand Hannibal's surrender (or death). We will return to that at the end of this chapter.

The second of the three wars between these two fractious neighbouring kingdoms (soon after 188, lasting until 183) was in full swing when Hannibal arrived.[31] The only two actions recorded of him in Bithynia until he took poison there are: first, his possible role in the foundation of the city of Prusa; and second, a naval victory fought on behalf of Prusias against Eumenes II of Pergamum in perhaps 184. The tradition about Prusa has its problems, but the sea battle is even more problematic.

The only accounts of this battle are in Nepos and Justin.[32] Nepos' account is really no more than a pair of stratagems, of which Justin gives only the second and more fantastic. It is not preserved anywhere in Livy or his usual source for this period Polybius, although they seem to have enjoyed describing the much more unusual but also more believable trick by which Hannibal slipped away from the island of Cercina by turning ships' sails into a marquee to delay pursuit by their drowsy owners after an all-night party which he had organized.[33] The first of the two Bithynian stratagems is a deception by which the opposing Pergamene sailors were led to believe that their flagship had retreated. This is not impossible. But the second, narrated at greater length, has Hannibal firing pots full of venomous snakes from catapults at the enemy ships. The Pergamene sailors laughed at first, until they realized what the pots contained. This tale is

---

[28] For the sequence of wars, see Habicht 2006e (1956), esp. 1–12 with updating appendix at 289; more briefly, 2006d: 176 (originally *CAH* 8: 325 and 328).
[29] Habicht 2006b: 5–6.
[30] Livy 38.39.15, preferable to Pol. 21.46.10, which must be emended. See Habicht 2006b: 2 and n. 6 and *HCP* 3: 172–3. For Apamea (the city), see p. 315.
[31] The first war was between 208 and 205, the third between 156 and 154 (Habicht 2006b: 5 and 13). For the dates of the second, see Habicht 2006b: 3 and 7–12.
[32] Nep. *Hann.* 10–11; Justin 32.4.6–8 with *CHGRW*: 441–2 and 447 (P. de Sousa).
[33] We saw (n. 5) that Walbank believed that Polybius must have mentioned Hannibal's wanderings and probably said something about them when Hannibal arrived at Prusias' court.

accepted by most modern scholars with virtual unanimity, sometimes combined with admiration for Hannibal's ingenuity.[34] Only a few historians in modern times have had trouble believing it.[35] The fullest discussion of this and other such stories, with numerous suggested ancient, medieval, and modern parallels, is by Adrienne Mayor in a book about unconventional warfare in the ancient world. She accepts the truth of all the 'scorpion bomb' (and similar) stratagems she cites and calls this one 'another creative zoological ploy' by Hannibal, comparable to his use of cattle with flaming twigs on their horns (a much more credible device).[36]

The whole battle tale, including and especially the anecdote about the potted snakes, was surely attached to a Carthaginian as an illustration of the 'Punic deception', *Punica fraus*, which was such a commonplace in ethnically stereotypical Roman thinking at all periods.[37] What better or more famous exponent of *fraus* than Hannibal could there possibly have been? It may be that Hannibal did indeed provide Rome's supposed friend Prusias with military and perhaps specifically naval help in his war against Rome's other and more reliable friend Eumenes.[38] That would go some way to explain why Roman patience with Prusias and his Pergamene war ran out just when it did. But even if so, we cannot pretend to know what precise form Hannibal's help took. In any case, Pergamum was the eventual victor in the series of wars, and one theory sees the great altar of

---

[34] McShane 1964: 160 n. 38; Seibert 1993b: 526 and n. 28, Hoyos 2003: 206 (a 'characteristic surprise touch'); de Sousa in 2007 (as in n. 32); and MacDonald 2015: 225 ('one of [Hannibal's] most impressive manoeuvres').

[35] Niese 1883–1903: 3.71 n. 4 called the whole Nepos narrative 'anecdotisch', citing (i) Front. *Strat.* 4.7.10, Hannibal demonstrates the same trick – but to Antiochus – and (ii) Galen vol. xiv Kühn p. 231, an unnamed 'Carthaginian' hurls pots full of wild animals, θηρίον, at the Romans (no mention of ships). This does not quite make it a 'roving anecdote' because Hannibal could be the principal agent in all of them (see Appendix 1.3 p. 35). Habicht 2006e: 1–12, in a full discussion of the war between Prusias and Eumenes and its causes, did not bother to discuss or even cite the snakes story, though he accepted that Prusias used Hannibal in his war against Eumenes (2006e: 11, cf. 2006d: 176 [*CAH* 8: 328]: 'Hannibal defeated Eumenes in a naval engagement'). A referee pertinently asks, 'where would anyone get SO MANY snakes?'.

See also Syme 1995: 348: Hannibal's vicissitudes stimulated 'curiosity – and invention ... Annalists and moralists enlarge plausibly upon the guile and sagacity of the Carthaginian'. Syme then lists the 'series of suitable anecdotes', including 'the trick he played on greedy Cretans' and 'the device of serpents in pots'. Cf. Briscoe 2008: 392, citing Syme on 'the legends surrounding Hannibal's sojourn in Bithynia'.

[36] Mayor 2022: 191–202, esp. 199–200 for the Hannibal story (but not citing Galen (see previous n.). See her pp. 191–6 for Herodian 3.9.3–8, a siege of Hatra by Septimius Severus in 198–9 CE: the defenders are said to have filled pots with venomous invertebrates, which Mayor identifies as scorpions.

[37] See p. 80, cf. 214.

[38] For the story that Hannibal once rebuked Prusias for not attacking Eumenes because of unfavourable entrails, see p. 227 n. 34, cf. p. 35. It was also told about Hannibal and Antiochus.

Pergamum, whose sculptures are now in Berlin, as a celebration of Pergamene victories over Prusias.³⁹

We have almost reached Hannibal's final days. But before we arrive there, let us examine, all in one place, the traditions about his city foundations in Asia Minor.

## 17.5 Hannibal and City Foundations in Asia Minor

Two cities in Asia Minor were traditionally founded by Hannibal in his years of exile. I shall deal with them in reverse chronological order, the more controversial first. Since Hannibal was not himself a king, any such foundations could only have been carried out, if genuinely Hannibalic at all, as the agent or helper of actual kings. The second such king was Hannibal's third royal host (and his eventual betrayer) in historical fact, the Bithynian king Prusias I. (The Seleucids at an earlier period were great founders of eponymous cities, but no tradition makes Hannibal found a city on behalf of his first royal host, Antiochus III.) For Hannibal's part in Prusias' eponymous city Prusa or Prusias, modern Turkish Bursa, in Bithynia, the only explicit evidence is a passage in the elder Pliny.⁴⁰ It was on the site of the former Cius. Hannibal's role has been much discussed, with no scholarly agreement, but there may be some truth in it.⁴¹

If it is fiction, the connection with Hannibal and Carthage might be due to mere similarity of names: a foundation legend known to Virgil represented Carthage as a 'Bursa', in effect the same word as 'Prusa'. The Punic word meant 'citadel', but in Greek a *bursa* was a strip of ox-hide. The

---

³⁹ Robertson 1975: 538. But for the view that the altar should be dated a few decades later (middle of the second century), see Rotroff 1996, citing ceramic evidence.

⁴⁰ *NH* 5.148; Arrian (of Nicomedia) *FGrHist* 156 F 29, B 63 Roos, line 8 (from the *Bithyniaca*), briefly gives the foundation by Prusias, but without mention of Hannibal. Bithynia was Arrian's home region, so he knew what he was talking about. On the other hand, the fragment is part of Tzetzes' long poem the *Chiliades*, and we cannot be sure that on this point it reproduced Arrian in full – or correctly. In any case (Cohen 1995: 403), there is no necessary contradiction with Pliny: Hannibal could have supervised the foundation in some way.

⁴¹ Barr. map 52 F4, marked PRUSA. See Cohen 1995: 403–4 (dating it to 188 or 187); Syme 1995: 348–55, appendix D, 'The foundation of Prusa ad Olympum'; Fraser 2009: 361: 'founded in c. 184 by Prusias I with the alleged help of Hannibal'. Cohen thought it 'quite possible' that Hannibal supervised the foundation on behalf of Prusias. Syme 1995: 349 said of Hannibal's alleged foundation that though it is 'more plausible than Artaxata, Prusa may also be fiction – or, at the best, a variant in the story of the wanderings, not received into the vulgate'. Syme was mainly concerned with a possible earlier foundation – by Croesus? To yield this result, Strabo 12.4.3 must be emended. Corsten 1989 suggested that the first founder was a sixth-century Bithynian commander called Prouses (an attested Bithynian name), and the city was then re-founded by king Prusias. He claims some archaeological support for the sixth-century date. He is non-committal about Hannibal.

legend is narrated by Venus early in Virgil's *Aeneid*.[42] It is of a 'trickster' type familiar to comparative anthropologists; but it is not Greek, as has been thought, by an understandable but wrong assumption.[43] In the mythical tradition, Queen Dido and her companions purchased the site of the future Carthage by a bargain which gave them as much land as could be enclosed in an ox's hide. Their trick was to slice the hide up into extremely narrow strips so as to delineate a large and habitable area. If Hannibal had founded Bithynian Prusa/Bursa on his own initiative, it would have been tempting to speculate that this name hinted at another 'New Carthage', but in the east to match the one in the west, and named for the founder's homeland, not for the founder. But King Prusias gets in the way of any such theory. If it is wrong, it does not reduce the likelihood of Hannibal's participation.

The first alleged city foundation is Artaxata in Armenia, 'founded by Hannibal for Artaxias the king', according to Strabo; the tradition is reported much more elaborately by Plutarch, who calls Artaxata the 'metropolis' (which here means 'capital') of Armenia.[44] He says that after Antiochus had been defeated by the Romans, Hannibal moved to Artaxias' court and became the king's valuable teacher and adviser.[45] This tradition is stronger and more circumstantial than that about Prusa and can be accepted more confidently. If Hannibal was the guest of Artaxias (which is perfectly possible) and Prusias (which is certain), and if those kings were

---

[42] *Aeneid* 1.367. See Austin 1971: 133–4, quoting Servius' explanation and Justin's version (18.5.9); cf. Starks 1999: 268–71 (Virgil's version not hostile to Dido); Gruen 2011: 135 n. 104. See also the exchange between Masinissa and the Carthaginians at Livy 34.62.11–12.

[43] Köhler 1866 says an English oral informant told him of a similar derivation for London's Hyde = *hide* Park (!); Frazer 1888; Jackson 2013 (North American peoples). The story is taken to be of Greek origin by Scheid and Svenbro 1985, followed by Bonnet 2006: 370–1. It looks so clever that it *ought* to be Greek – but it isn't! There is no ancient Greek parallel for the ox-hide trickery motif. Scheid and Svenbro 1985: 332 adduce (sub-section called 'la cité bovine') the cow followed by Cadmus, founder of Greek Thebes. This well-known helpful animal motif is very different from slicing up the creature's hide. The famous story (adduced at their p. 337) of Gaius Popillius Laenas (*DPRR* POPI1328) drawing a circle round Antiochus IV to order him out of Egypt in 168 (*MRR* 1: 430) is even less relevant to a trick with strips of ox-hide, which are what we want.

[44] Strabo 11.14.6; Plut. *Luc.* 31.4–5; *Barr.* map 89 G1. See Brizzi 1983 and Cohen 2013: 46. Not in Fraser 2009. For doubters, see Seibert 1993a: 524. And see Syme (as in n. 41) for Artaxata as less plausible than Prusa, which he thought might be fiction. On the contrary, the probabilities are the opposite, Artaxata less problematic than Prusa. Barceló 2004: 242, Brizzi 2007a: 295–6, and Marek 2023: 98 accept both Artaxata and Prusa. Is it more than coincidence that the emperor Constantine made a nephew with the resonant name Hannibalianus ruler of Armenia? (He did not last long.) See Sextus Aurelius Victor, *On the Caesars* 41.20; Jones 1964: 85, 132, *PLRE* 1: 407, Hannibalianus (2); Marek 2023: 565. For the personal name, see further p. 414 n. 105.

[45] On this visit, and on Plutarch's source here (Sallust?), cf. n. 26 (on Artaxata).

both known to have founded cities, it would be natural and perhaps correct for ancient writers to associate Hannibal with those royal foundations.

## 17.6 Fourth and Final Stop a Bithynian Country Estate: Hannibal's Death, 183

The evidence for Hannibal's life between 190 and 183 is sparse and precarious. By contrast, his dramatic, not so say melodramatic, death at a Bithynian country estate attracted enormous attention from ancient writers. No fewer than twelve 'other sources' – that is, other than Livy – have been collected by Livy's modern commentator.[46] To these thirteen, some of whom naturally cite each other, we should add a fourteenth: Juvenal for the lines on Hannibal in *Satire* 10.[47] It is no objection to say that Juvenal relied on other written sources: so did everybody else on the list, right back to whoever first wrote down the testimony of an eyewitness, if there was one. In any case, Juvenal's is the first surviving text to give one piquant detail: the victor of Cannae, says Juvenal, was killed not by martial weapons (an assortment is listed rhetorically) but by a ring, an *ānulus* – in which poison was concealed, as the helpful scholiast or ancient commentator tells us. But in Juvenal, we get only that one noun *ānulus* at the start of the line, followed by a pause and an abrupt change of subject.[48] This super-emphatic presentation would be unintelligibly riddling unless the ring story was already embedded in the tradition. The detail of the ring was much later picked up by Aurelius Victor.[49] The poison-ring has some similarity to the hollow bracelet in which the Athenian orator Demosthenes is said by Plutarch, quoting the Hellenistic polymath Eratosthenes, to have concealed the poison with which he killed himself.[50] Indeed, the whole narrative in which Plutarch gave the variant versions of Demosthenes' death, most of them by poison imbibed in one ingenious way or another, resembles the competing traditions about Hannibal's end, several of them, including Livy, gathered by Plutarch in the same highly characteristic fashion in his *Flamininus*.[51]

---

[46] Briscoe 2008: 391 on Livy 39.51, cf. *FRHist* 3: 361 (J. W. Rich) on no. 25 Valerius Antias frag. 56.
[47] Or even a fifteenth in view of Livy 39.56.7, where Antias is cited for an impossible variant about the Scipios.
[48] The whole passage is 10.163–6 and *ānulus* starts line 166.   [49] *On illustrious men* 42.6.
[50] Plut. *Demosth.* 30.3, citing *FGrHist* 241 F31.
[51] Plut. *Flam.* 20.5–6; cf. *Demosth.* 29.4–30.5. In the *Phocion*, Plutarch devotes a whole chapter (36) to the hero's death by poison and includes some anecdotes, but there is no hint that it was anything but state-administered hemlock.

Of the prose sources for Hannibal's death, Plutarch provided what is certainly the most interesting, polished, and rewarding account. The *Flamininus* is, unusually, paired with a *contemporary* Greek *Life*, the *Philopoemen*, and Plutarch presses the parallels between the deaths of Hannibal and Philopoemen (in underground caves) particularly hard and effectively when narrating their ends.[52] And it is the context of Hannibal's death that Plutarch tells the story of Scipio's much earlier meeting with Hannibal at Ephesus, and Hannibal's witty handling of Scipio's question, 'who was the greatest commander ever?'.[53] Plutarch offered this as an illustration of the difference in character between the generous Scipio and Flamininus.

Multiplicity of sources does not, however, imply unanimity on details: on the contrary. The essential narrative is this.[54] In 183, the now elderly Flamininus arrived at Prusias' court to remonstrate. (About what? We will have to return to this.) Hannibal in his country residence knew this meant the game was up. He had long foreseen the need to make a secret escape so had already constructed seven tunnels for a getaway; but Prusias had posted soldiers to surround the building and catch him when he tried to slip out through a back entrance. Hannibal realized this and took his own life.

Were the soldiers Bithynians, as in Livy and Plutarch, or Romans as in Nepos? Bithynian, surely.[55] Did he ask a slave to strangle him? Or take poison hidden in a ring? Or drink bull's blood like Midas or Themistocles? Plutarch aired these parallels. Or did Hannibal accidentally wound himself while escaping on a horse and then die of septicaemia, as one source alleged?[56] Why did Plutarch specify seven tunnels, not two or six or eight? Seven is often a magical or fairy-tale or story-telling number. In any case the tunnels play no important part in the narrative: the end comes when Hannibal tries to leave the building by a back door, that is, at ground level. Was Flamininus the only Roman to bring about Hannibal's death, or

---

[52] See Pelling 1997: 253–4 and 2002: 351–2 for the deliberate resemblances with the parallel *Life* or rather death of Philopoemen, and for Plutarch's moral disapproval of Flamininus' pointless vindictiveness towards Hannibal (ending with a contrast with the humanity of Scipio); cf. also 2002: 375 for the placing of the material in the *Flamininus*. Plutarch's account of Hannibal's death is discussed at Schrott 2014: 729–39; but on this unsatisfactory book, see p. 261 n. 92.

[53] *Flam.* 21.3–5. See p. 261, and cf. p. 32 n. 125: Plutarch was fond of this good story, which he also narrates in the *Pyrrhus* and in the lost *Scipio*.

[54] See esp. Nep. *Hann.* 12; Plut. *Flam.* 20–1 (the detail of the seven tunnels is at 20.4).

[55] Briscoe 2008: 393.

[56] Paus. 8.11.10–11. But this is part of the story of an invented oracle about Hannibal's place of death. See p. 316 cf. 382. The model is the Persian king Cambyses' death, Hdt. 3.64.2–4, and the reminiscence may have been prompted by the story of the oracle given to Cambyses that he would die at 'Ecbatana'.

did Lucius Scipio and Scipio Nasica also have a hand in it? That is highly unlikely.[57]

The discrepancies in the sources about the exact manner and circumstances of the death show no more than that nobody knew the facts for certain (the same is true of Demosthenes). How many people witnessed it? How did the news get into circulation? If someone – an enslaved person, or perhaps a soldier – had been interrogated by Flamininus or Prusias, as is possible, we might have hoped for fewer and less discrepant variants.[58]

But nobody denies that Hannibal died when he did. A more serious problem for the political historian is the role of Flamininus and the Roman senate. Plutarch and Appian took the view that Flamininus had been sent to Bithynia for other reasons and decided on his own initiative to ask for Hannibal's extradition. Justin said he was sent to end the war with Pergamum and to demand the surrender of Hannibal. Livy equivocated: he was positive that Prusias was suspect at Rome because he had given refuge to Hannibal 'after the flight from Antiochus' and because he was making war against Eumenes.[59] But he did not say why exactly he thought Flamininus had come. Like Plutarch, he gave Hannibal a speech blaming Flamininus – but also cursing Prusias for his breach of the laws of hospitality. In both Livy and Plutarch, Hannibal bitterly contrasts the Romans' treatment of him with their behaviour towards Pyrrhus, to whom they had given advance warning of an attempt to poison him.[60] In reality, it is hardly likely that Hannibal would come up with such an edifying and well-informed example from earlier Roman history at such a moment.

Livy professed himself to be uncertain whether Prusias was acting as a result of a reprimand by Flamininus, or whether he simply wanted to oblige him on his own initiative. Polybius' account of the actual death does not survive, except for a bare and incidental mention of Flamininus'

---

[57] See Livy's afterthought at 39.56.7 citing Valerius Antias, *FRHist* 25 frag. 56. 'Almost certainly total invention', according to Briscoe 2008: 392. Rich (*FRHist* 3: 362) is less sure, because both Scipios would have made plausible envoys. But he concludes that three ex-consuls would have been 'an unusually strong team'; and that the presence of the Scipios was indeed an invention.

[58] Note the role of Hannibal's helpful *puer* at Nep. *Hann.* 12.4: that noun does not necessarily mean a 'boy'; like Greek παῖς it can mean an enslaved male of any age. If he is historical, was he perhaps the first to tell the tale? There is also the enslaved strangler, but that is part of a decidedly minority version.

[59] App. *Syrian history* 11/43; Justin 32.4.8; Livy 39.51.1, where the Latin is *post fugam Antiochi*. For *fuga* with the genitive, meaning 'flight from', see *OLD* 7b. Livy elides Crete and Bithynia.

[60] Livy 39.51.11–12, Plut. *Flam.* 20.6, cf. Plut. *Pyrrh.* 21. For the possibility that the Pyrrhus contrast was already in Polybius, see Briscoe 2008: 394, comparing the use made of the same contrast at Livy 42.47.6, which is Polybian.

mission to Prusias.⁶¹ But his lost version was probably that which was later adopted by Plutarch and Appian, from which Flamininus emerges shabbily.⁶² It is likely that Livy departed from it (or rather he wriggled on the topic) because he or his source wanted to defend Flamininus against criticism.⁶³ Several of the sources, starting with Antias, but also Nepos and other even later writers, specifically incriminated the Roman senate.⁶⁴ This is plausible enough. The senators may have known perfectly well what they were doing when they chose a man known to be as ruthless and cunning as Flamininus for the mission to Prusias and did not need to spell out what was expected of him in regard to Hannibal.⁶⁵ As for the difference between a demand for extradition on the one hand and extrajudicial murder or effectively enforced suicide on the other, it was slight: after Hannibal's escape from Antiochus in 190, nobody can have expected that he would let himself be taken alive back to Rome.

## 17.7  Hannibal's Grave

Where was Hannibal buried? A Greek verse oracle, not attested before the second century CE, had allegedly told Hannibal in an iambic line that 'a Libyan clod of earth will hide the body of Hannibal'.⁶⁶ In Plutarch, it is just 'a certain oracle', and Appian is similarly unspecific; but Pausanias has him consulting the oracle of Zeus Ammon in Libya, east of Carthage. The word for 'Libyan' is 'Libyssa', a feminine adjective in Greek; but 'Libyssa' was also a place name in Bithynia.⁶⁷ The teasing oracle about the place of death is of a familiar type, and not in the ancient world only: the Persian king Cambyses misunderstood such an oracle to mean the wrong Ecbatana, and at the end of his life Shakespeare's Henry IV remembered a prophecy that he would die in Jerusalem (on a crusade, as he had

---

⁶¹ Pol. 23.5.1 with *HCP* 3: 221. This is nevertheless one of Briscoe's list of 'other sources'.
⁶² Plutarch makes Hannibal's death a result of Flamininus' own initiative, as part of his characterization of Flamininus in terms of φιλοτιμία, ambition. So Pelling 1997: 307.
⁶³ Briscoe 2008: 392.    ⁶⁴ Antias: see n. 57. Nepos: *Hann.* 12.2.
⁶⁵ See, in particular, his nastily hands-clean role in the murder in 196 of the Boeotian leader Brachylles, a murky business altogether: Pol. 18.43.3–12, Livy 33.27–9.
⁶⁶ Plut. *Flam.* 20.6; App. *Syrian history* 11/44; Pausanias 8.11.11; Zonaras 9.21.7. Iambic: oracular responses were usually in hexameters, but these iambics are not in themselves fatal to authenticity, cf. Hdt. 1.174.5 (a Pythian oracle in iambics).
⁶⁷ The noun for 'clod', βῶλος, is usually feminine, hence Λίβυσσα. Bithynian Libyssa: Pliny, *NH* 5.148 (a few lines after the mention of Hannibal's foundation of Prusa), and Claudius Ptolemy 5.1.13; *Barr.* map 52 F3. (On Appian's slightly different explanation of the Bithynian place name, see Brodersen 1991: 107.)

assumed), which turned out to be the Jerusalem Chamber at Westminster Abbey in London.[68]

An even later tradition further developed the story of Hannibal's Bithynian tomb, and in a remarkable direction. The Byzantine writer Tzetzes says that Hannibal died by taking poison in Bithynia near a village called Libyssa. He then repeats the oracle story but ends: 'the later emperor of the Romans, Severus, who was a descendant of the Libyans, put on this man's tomb a white piece of marble to honour the commander Hannibal'.[69] Aurelius Victor even claimed to know the text of the inscription, a half-hexameter: *Hannibal hic situs est*, 'here lies Hannibal'.[70] But (Septimius) Severus, the 'African emperor' (193–211 CE), is probably a mistake by Tzetzes for Severus' son Caracalla, who according to Herodian erected statues of Sulla and Hannibal, among others.[71] The passage should therefore not be used as evidence for Severus' supposed policy of Africanizing. Rather, it illustrates Caracalla's 'lunatic devotion to the great generals and warriors of the past'.[72] It would go too far to deny the existence of the tomb altogether: Pliny says it was at Libyssa in his day. But in modern times, no such tomb has ever been found.[73]

---

[68] Hdt. 3.64.3–5, cf. Cleomenes of Sparta at 6.80, the 'wrong' Argos; Shakespeare, *2 Henry IV* 4.5.232–40.

[69] *Chiliades* 1.798–805. The whole Hannibal section is at lines 700–803.

[70] *On illustrious men* 42.6. Cf. p. 13.

[71] But a referee comments: 'I wouldn't rule out Severus so fast. His influence and interventions in this region were extensive because of his decisive win in the region allowing for his uncontested rule. If I were a local community with Hannibal's tomb I'd be fast to exploit that to win his favor.'

[72] Barnes 1967: 97 n. 75a, whose solution is here followed. 'African emperor' is part of the title of Birley 1988, a biography of Severus. Here are some flagrant examples of Tzetzes' inaccuracy in the Hannibal section: at 750–69, he dates Cannae (really 216 BCE) after the battle of the Metaurus (really 207) and transfers the earthquake which happened at Trasimene (217) to Cannae. Herodian: 4.8.5.

[73] *NH* 5.148, *ubi nunc*. Never found: Seibert 1993a: 528 and n. 46.

CHAPTER 18

# *The Downfall and Death of Scipio, 187–183*
## *Aged 48–52*

## 18.1 Introduction

That Hannibal after his return was in effect evicted from Carthage is not surprising: some sort of hostile reaction was predictable, although it is a probably a myth that defeated Carthaginian generals were judicially crucified in their home city. Gnaeus Manlius Vulso, who is made to assert this in a speech in 187, qualifies it with 'they are said', *dicuntur*. (He says, absurdly, that this happened even after a victory, if the strategy was considered faulty.) It is true that the final sentence of Livy's book 22 complacently contrasts the formal thanks awarded to Varro after his defeat at Cannae with what would have happened at Carthage to someone in his position: he would have faced every conceivable kind of punishment, *nihil recusandum supplicii foret.*[1] But this is worthless rhetoric: when Livy wrote those words, he knew perfectly well that nothing of the sort happened to Hannibal after Zama.[2] The surprise is rather that Hannibal's flight was delayed for so many years, and even then it came about as a result of sudden severe Roman pressure as well as growing domestic enmity. The downfall of Scipio, not only a very great military man but *princeps senatus*, twice consul, and an ex-censor, is much harder to comprehend. The long drawn-out episode was much discussed in antiquity and modern times.[3]

---

[1] Vulso: 38.48.13; *DPRR* MANL1103. Livy on Varro: 22.61.15. A myth: see Briscoe and Hornblower 2020: 331. The only reliably attested known instances of crucifixions of generals are (i) that of Hanno at Messana (Pol. 1.11.5), but this action may have been taken by his soldiers, not by the authorities at Carthage: *HCP* 1: 62. This seems to have been what happened (ii) to a Hannibal (Geus no. 3) in Sardinia: Pol. 1.24.6 and Livy *periocha* 17, *a militibus suis in crucem sublatus est*. Orosius (4.8.4) calls it a stoning.

[2] For Dio's unreliable story that he was put on trial but acquitted, see p. 66. His source is not clear.

[3] The fullest source is Livy 38.50.4–60.10. Pol. 23.14 is important but is not a sustained narrative, rather an anecdotal obituary fragment. See also Gellius 4.18 and 6.19, probably from Nepos' lost work *Exempla*, cf. 6.18.11; Fraccaro 1950: 273 and n. 32. Of modern treatments see esp. Fraccaro 1950:

Scipio suffered the disgrace of two forensic or quasi-forensic attacks (the 'trials of the Scipios') and died soon after the second, in humiliating retirement. This may seem a puzzling display of ingratitude and petty jealousy.[4] 'Ingratitude' is perhaps the wrong word to use in discussing high-level Roman politics in the early second century, although Scipio himself invoked the notion indignantly, as we shall see; and Livy (following Antias) says that Rome's treatment of Scipio was even more ungrateful, *ingratiorem*, than Carthage's of Hannibal.[5] The Roman system of *repetundae*, extortion trials, was developed and formalized in the course of the second century; the key piece of legislation was the *lex Calpurnia* of 149 BCE, and this was taken further by Gaius Gracchus.[6] Altruistic or paternalistic concern for the welfare of injured provincials was only part of the reason for the growing Roman use of the lawcourts in this way. The thinking evidently was that no one individual, however gifted and successful on the battlefield, must be allowed to become too wealthy from booty, or too politically powerful.[7] Gratitude was beside the point. Something of this equalizing or competitive attitude helps to explain why Scipio came so spectacularly to grief, not helped by a definite personal arrogance. He was not actually accused directly of mistreating provincials or allies, although his handling of the Locrian complaints against Pleminius may have harmed his reputation permanently; at any rate, it features (along with his supposed *luxuria* at Syracuse) among the charges against Publius.[8] That is admittedly from part of the narrative which Livy took from Valerius Antias, and which is generally discounted.[9] It is nevertheless plausible to imagine that the old Pleminius scandal was remembered against Scipio at this time, for two reasons. First, because it illustrated his personal high-handedness.

---

263–393 and 394–415 (originally 1911 and 1939); Scullard 1973: 133–52 and 290–303 (app. IV, ancient evidence listed at 290 n. 1); Kienast 1954: 57–67; Astin 1978: 62–73 (the last two as part of biographies of Cato); Walsh 1993: 4–7 and 183–95; Gruen 1995; Briscoe 2008: 170–207 (comm. on the Livy section, with introduction); J. W. Rich, *FRHist* 3: 352–8, comm. on no. 25 (Antias) frags. 49–52; *HCP* 3: 242–7. For admiring modern literary discussions of Livy's account, see n. 17.

[4] Gruen 1995: 88 reduces the humiliation almost to vanishing point ('that he retired in ignominy or semi-exile is pure romance'. This goes much too far).

[5] Livy 38.50.7. As for the actual word 'ungrateful', an alleged epitaph made Scipio tell his ungrateful fatherland, *ingrata patria*, that it does not have his bones, i.e., he is not buried at Rome but at Liternum. See p. 16 n. 34, with a suggestion about the story's origin.

[6] *Lex Calpurnia*: see *MRR* 1: 459: the establishment of a standing court for extortion cases was achieved by the tribune Lucius Calpurnius Piso, *DPRR* CALP1510.

[7] Good formulation at Gruen 1995: 62: the senators sought to 'balance distinctions within their own ranks'. See Drogula 2021 (cited at p. 155) for a comparable theory of the origins of the *prouincia* system as a compromise between individual initiatives by families and the growing need of the state to limit such action.

[8] Livy 38.51.1.  [9] Fraccaro 1950: 305.

And second, to rake it up again would have suited the mood of the times: as Gruen has well shown, by way of background to an analysis of the attacks on the Scipios, the newly wealthy and powerful Rome of the 190s and 180s saw many bitter struggles by commanders to obtain triumphs and prorogations, and to avoid trouble about booty. All this was an expression of the 'tensions between personal aspirations and the corporate interests of the ruling class'.[10]

The name of Marcus Porcius Cato, 'Cato the Censor (*Censorius*)' or 'Cato the Elder', is inextricably associated with Scipio's downfall, although his exact contribution to it is far from clear, as we shall see.[11] He is *the* censor because of the famous severity of his tenure of that office in 184, and he is the Elder (Latin *maior*) to distinguish him from his great-grandson, Caesar's enemy Cato the Younger (*minor*). Plutarch wrote *Lives* of both, paired with upright Athenians of the fifth and fourth centuries respectively, Aristides and Phocion. In his *Life* of the elder Cato, Plutarch touched on his undoubted hostility to the Scipios only briefly in chapters 15 (Publius) and 18 (Lucius); in his lost *Life* of Publius, he will surely have provided a lot more detail.[12] Cato's tough line on the Oppian law about luxury (as consul in 195) was not directed at Scipio, or rather at Aemilia, his ostentatiously grand wife (as she was unfairly represented).[13] Whatever Cato's private attitudes, it was not until after he returned from Iberia to a triumph (194) that he himself had the prestige to attack the Scipios. Earlier evidence should not be manipulated so as to imply open hostilities not attested in the sources – for example, by antedating his quaestorship. That, however, is a detail: the truth is, Cato hated Scipio, it is as simple as that.[14] But this was compatible with a degree of respect.[15]

John Rich in 2013 called the trials of the Scipios 'one of the most thorny problems in Roman history', and many similar modern formulations can

---

[10] Gruen 1995: 60–6, esp. 62 ('tensions'). This is not to accept Gruen's conclusions about the treatment of the Scipios in particular, later in the article. See p. 391 on the attempt to try Publius in 184, and on the forensic use of Pleminius affair, see further p. 392.
[11] For Cato, see p. 209 (the quaestorship of 204).
[12] He certainly wrote one, notwithstanding the problem about whether Africanus or Aemilianus was paired with Epaminondas. See Appendix 1.2.
[13] See p. 255.
[14] Astin 978: 70 asks: 'deep-seated hostility' or not? At first, he says there must be 'cautious reserve about those passages which refer in general terms to deep and long-standing enmity' but later says it is likely that Cato 'viewed with some disfavour the flamboyant, ambitious Scipio' and 'there are grounds to suspect an underlying antipathy'. This seems an excessively fine set of distinctions.
[15] See pp. 259 n. 78 and 421 for Cato's quotation of a paradoxical remark by Scipio about leisure and solitude; this opens book 3 of Cicero, *On duties*.

be found.¹⁶ The chronology of the events is difficult to get straight (there is a discrepancy of four years between the two main ancient lines of tradition), and the nature of the charges and much else is confused or unclear; the attacks were both senatorial and forensic, and the first was aimed at brother Lucius as well as Publius, which occasionally adds to the muddle in the sources. The main attacks were separate and took place in two years, 187 and then 184, which was both the year of Cato's censorship and the year before Scipio's death. In both years, the real target was Publius, but in the earlier year, the attacks were ostensibly aimed at Lucius. The prosecutions were brought by private individuals, in the absence of a system of state prosecution.

The narrative of our chief source, Livy, is an undeniably good read and can be highly recommended if one is not much bothered about what exactly happened and when.¹⁷ If Polybius wrote up the trials fully and sequentially anywhere (that is, apart from an anecdotal and retrospective passage in the course of an obituary), Livy would appear to have used him very little, which would be surprising. So Polybius probably did not provide a conventional and sequential narrative.¹⁸ Instead, Livy drew for the most part, with obvious unease, on Valerius Antias, while professing – or artfully feigning? – despair at the many discrepant versions he found, including the relevant speeches.¹⁹ Theoretically, the plural language of the relevant sentence (especially *multa alia*, 'many other versions') could embrace a now lost Polybian account. It is however very doubtful whether Polybius would have covered the same events twice, or whether he would have thought a blow-by-blow coverage of the attacks and trials relevant to his great international theme.²⁰ But it is clear, even from the mutilated and incomplete state in which we have it (fragments preserved in the Suda,

---

¹⁶ *FRHist* 3: 352.
¹⁷ Luce 1977: 92–104; Jaeger 1997: 132–76; she admits it is 'apparently incoherent' as a piece of straight history (136–7) but admires it for its brilliant capture of Africanus' traits (133). Those are, in fact, exactly what Polybius was quite explicitly trying to capture. Chaplin 2000: 91 adds that Livy was also, in the mouth of Scipio Nasica, characterizing Lucius. See also Henderson 2004: 96–9; Haimson Lushkov 2010; cf. Pausch 2011: 189 n. 364. For Rossi 2004, and Beltramini and Rocco 2020, see n. 34.
¹⁸ Pol.'s anecdote about Scipio's second consulship of 194, when the quaestor would not open the treasury for him (23.14.5–6, cf. p. 254), lies behind Livy 38.55.13. Livy's figures at 38.55.10–13 are also ultimately from Polybius: Briscoe 2008: 177. See also n. 21 on Livy 39.52.1.
¹⁹ 38.56.1. The narrative derived from Antias is at 38.50.5–55.7 and 38.58.1–60.10; it is interrupted by a complex digression, 38.55.8–57.8. At 38.55.8, Livy begins to admit to discomfort about his sources. There follows some Polybian material (previous n.). Chapters 56–7 discuss variant versions of the trial and Publius' death, followed by an account of the relations between Gracchus and the Scipios. Briscoe 2008: 177–9 suggests that Claudius Quadrigarius and Lucius Calpurnius Piso might be the sources.
²⁰ Cf. *HCP* 3: 243: Pol. 'appears not to have dealt separately in his *Histories* with the trials of the Scipios'. Walbank suggests family tradition or Laelius as the source of the anecdotes.

a Byzantine lexicon, one of them very short), that the original triptych constituting Polybius' notices of the three important deaths of 183 – Philopoemen, Hannibal, and Scipio – must have been a *tour de force*.[21] More often acknowledged, in recent treatments, are the literary strengths of Livy's much longer performance in book 38 about the trials ('performance' because it would have made a fine recitation piece). The approximate synchronism between the deaths is historical fact, not a literary choice; but Livy's decision to bunch the three synchronized obituaries is indebted to Polybius. His material about Scipio here (book 39) is feeble and fussy by comparison with that of Polybius.[22] He uses it as the peg for a frigid excursus on the disagreement of the sources about the date of Scipio's death. By contrast, Polybius preferred to illustrate Scipio's character by three vivid, succinct, and well-constructed anecdotes. Livy's assessment of Scipio in book 38 is much better: it begins with the judgement that he was more remarkable in war than in peace.[23]

## 18.2   The Attacks of 187

For the modern historian, the biggest problem about Livy on the trials is that his main source Antias put everything – including Scipio's death – in 187, and for most of the time Livy, despite qualms about his sources, seems to go along with this. But – to anticipate – by far the likelier sequence is this, in a nutshell: in 187, Publius was indirectly attacked in the senate and then Lucius himself was put on trial.[24] In 184, there was an attempt to try Publius, whose accuser was a tribune called Marcus Naevius. Scipio died in 183. He was still *princeps senatus* when he died, having been reappointed for the last time by the censors for 184, Cato and Valerius Flaccus; but when he died the following year, those censors had not quite completed their *lustrum*, and they appointed Flaccus himself to take his place.[25]

---

[21] That it is incomplete is suggested by Livy 39.52.1, citing Polybius for the date of the deaths; but this date is not in the surviving Greek text. Briscoe 2008: 395 observes that 52.1 ought to have been printed in modern texts of Polybius as a fragment of book 23. Perhaps. But Livy, who unlike us had a full text of Pol. at his elbow, may have been making his own inference from Pol.'s placing of all three deaths in Olympiad year 183/2 (Philopoemen certainly died in 183).
[22] Livy 39.52.   [23] Livy 38.53.9–11. 'Better in war': see p. 244.
[24] Briscoe 2008: 171; *FRHist* 3: 354–5 and 356 (Rich in 2013, but these two scholars were aware of each other's work on the topic), both essentially accepting the conclusions of the foundational studies by Fraccaro and Scullard (n. 3).
[25] *FRHist* 3: 357 (J. W. Rich); Scipio had similarly appointed himself *princeps senatus* in his own censorship (199); see p. 251 (where *lustrum* is also explained).

In 187, Cato made his first move, not in a court of law at first, but in the senate. He put up two tribunes called Petillius, probably cousins, to demand an account of the 500 talents which Lucius Scipio had received from Antiochus after his defeat at Magnesia, as payment of the first instalment of the total war indemnity of 15,000 talents.[26] There followed a celebrated intervention by Publius, who correctly regarded this demand as an attack on himself. He tore up the account book, taking it amiss (as Gellius puts it in a fine formulation) that he, to whom the empire and the *res publica* owed its salvation, should be asked for an account of booty.[27] It has often been pointed out that Publius' gesture, though an excellent piece of theatre, destroyed the evidence which could have absolved Lucius from blame. There was and is in fact genuine unclarity as to whether Lucius was blameworthy. If the money was indeed to be regarded as booty, *praeda*, Lucius was within his conventional rights when he used it to pay his troops, as he certainly had done; but not if it was state funds, as might be argued from the sum's mention in the formal armistice terms. In any case, the matter was dropped – in the senate, of which, after all Publius was leader, *princeps*.

But Cato was by no means finished with the Scipios. He now arranged for an otherwise unknown tribune of 187 called Gaius Minucius Augurinus to prosecute Lucius before a popular court of some sort (this second and more serious attack is altogether omitted by Polybius in his anecdotal chapter).[28] Minucius fined Lucius for misappropriating or refusing to account for the 500 talents – and ordered his arrest and his imprisonment for not providing the sureties demanded; such harshness was abnormal.[29] But young Tiberius Sempronius Gracchus, alone of all the tribunes, prevented the imprisonment by interposing his veto, *intercessio* (a precious tribunician privilege). Although Gracchus went on to marry Scipio's daughter Cornelia II, that event took place after Scipio's death, and Gracchus' veto of 187 is not evidence for personal friendship with the Scipios in that year. On the contrary, he is often represented in the sources as a personal enemy, *inimicissimus*, of Publius Scipio; but some of that is exaggeration, part of a later aristocratic tradition which sought to contrast

---

[26] Briscoe 2008: 180. For the Petillii, see *DPRR* PETI1218 (Quintus Petillius) and 1219 (Quintus Petillius Spurinus).

[27] Pol. 23.14.7–11; Gellius 4.18.7–12; Livy 38.55.10–12 with Briscoe 2008: 172 and 196.

[28] See *MRR* 3: 188–9, a change of mind from 1: 376, where the tribunates of both Minucius Augurinus and Gracchus were dated 184. *DPRR* MINU1245 retains 184 for Minucius Augurinus but accepts 187 for Gracchus (SEMP1182).

[29] *FRHist* 3: 354 (J. W. Rich).

the upright father with the 'delinquent' sons Tiberius and Gaius, the famous tribunes of 133 and 123.[30]

Livy says that Publius returned in haste from a subordinate mission to Etruria when he heard of Lucius' troubles, and that he was just in time to manhandle some tribunes of the plebs who were taking his brother off to prison. If he did, that would have been a violation of the *sacrosanctitas*, the personal inviolability, of tribunes. But the entire story of the Etruscan mission and its violent sequel is most likely a fiction.[31] It was probably invented to produce yet another dramatic intervention by the impetuous Publius. It is, however, conceivable that Publius did some small job in Etruria in the 180s, which was then falsely transposed to 187.[32] Be that as it may, the more interesting aspect is Livy's use of it. The story prompts him to remark that on this occasion Scipio acted 'with more loyalty to family than to the state', *magis pie quam ciuiliter*.[33] Whether these words are Livy's authorial contribution or reflect a formulation by, say, Claudius Quadrigarius, it was Livy's decision to include them, and this has been seen as part of a deliberate ambivalence in his portrayal of Scipio: he was, it is claimed, displaying a 'Hannibal-like insubordination'.[34] That is a neat point: are we meant to recall Hannibal's physical attack on Gisgo (7), the Carthaginian who spoke against peace after Zama? But on that occasion Hannibal is reported as having apologized graciously as being a military man, whereas it is not recorded that Scipio apologized at all. The parallel is informative about Livy's perceptions and intentions; how far it is a historical parallel and therefore usable for evaluation of the man Scipio is another question. The whole story of the return from Etruria may be worthless.

In any case, it seems certain that Lucius was not convicted, not least because he held games the next year. It is also most unlikely that after

---

[30] 38.56.9–10. Briscoe 2008: 186 actually makes Gracchus a supporter of Cato in 187 but thinks neither man actually wanted to see Lucius hauled off to prison. But against Gracchus' support of Cato, see Val. Max. 3.7.7 with Fraccaro 1950: 291 and n. 88. For the contrast between Gracchus and his sons, see e.g. Cic. *On the consular provinces* 18; Fraccaro 1950: 292.

[31] 38.56.8. See Fraccaro 1950: 326–7. It is not mentioned by Gellius; it may go back to Claudius Quadrigarius, see Briscoe 2008: 178.

[32] So Scullard 1973: 296–7.

[33] 38.56.9. This forgets that Scipio was defending his own interests and reputation as well as his brother's.

[34] Rossi 2004: 379; cf. Beltramini and Rocco 2020: 231, who suggest that Livy in 38.50–60 (as also in his account of the Pleminius affair) raises questions about Scipio's integrity. That is more obvious over Pleminius, but there is a similarity: his misplaced loyalty to a criminal subordinate has some resemblance to his excess of *pietas* to his brother. (But Scipio could not have been called *pius* towards Pleminius: subordinates owed *pietas* to their commanders, but not vice versa, cf. *OLD pius* 3d, *pietas* 4b.)

a conviction he could have been an energetic competitor for the censorship of 184, as he certainly was, although he was not elected.[35] But the reputational damage to the brothers was done, and it was great.

## 18.3 The Attack on Publius Alone in 184

In the year of Cato's censorship, Publius himself had to undergo the humiliating preliminaries of a trial, again instigated by Cato, but this time the accuser was very probably a tribune of the plebs called Marcus Naevius.[36] (The family name or *nomen* is that of the well-known poet, but this is probably mere coincidence and has led to confusion, ancient and modern.)[37] Livy knew of this tradition, but he also knew that Antias had named the accusers as the Petillii (again). This is most easily explained as a duplication from Lucius' trial of 187.

Polybius in his obituary of Scipio chose to position this trial first of his three anecdotes, although it was the last in temporal sequence: a good choice. He begins 'when someone attempted to bring him to trial before the people, making many bitter accusations'. This formulation alone should be enough to disprove attempts to argue the entire trial away as a fiction.[38] Polybius continues 'he came forward and said nothing more than it was not fitting, *prepon*, for the Roman people to listen to anyone who accused Publius Cornelius Scipio [note the grand third-person use of the full three names, the *tria nomina*], to whom the people owed the power of speech. So everyone dispersed.'[39]

That is all that Polybius had to say on the subject. The trial was never taken to a conclusion; that was never its purpose. Polybius did not specify the actual charges, but the other sources give them variously.[40] They seem to have been an approximate rerun of the 187 allegations. Gellius, whose source was Nepos, said he was accused – 'among other unworthy

---

[35] Livy 39.22.8; cf. Gruen 1995: 88.
[36] Regular juries were composed of senators, but a tribune could call a *consilium plebis*, an assembly of the people.
[37] Gellius 4.18.3; *FRHist* 3: 355–6. Marcus Naevius is reliably and independently attested as tribune in 184: Livy 39.52.4, from the 'books of magistrates'. Cf. *MRR* 1: 376; *DPRR* NAEV1246. The poet is NAEV5288.
[38] As by Gruen 1995: 86, against whom see Briscoe 2008: 176.
[39] Pol. 23.14.2–4. Tradition romantically added that Scipio pointed out that it was the anniversary of Zama and invited everyone to accompany him to the Capitol and give thanks to Jupiter. See Livy 38.51.7–14, Gellius 4.18.3–6; *HCP* 3: 244, citing other evidence but regarding the anniversary story as 'improbable'. Pittenger 2008: 125 remarks that Scipio was symbolically re-enacting his triumphal procession after Zama.
[40] Scullard 1973: 30.

charges' – of taking money so that peace would be made on terms more favourable to the king: obviously false, and amounting to a charge of treason.[41] If Antias can be believed, Antiochus' return of Scipio's son Lucius without ransom was also dredged up. This might be one of the other 'unworthy charges' vaguely mentioned by Gellius; others might have been the ancient scandal about Pleminius, and the Greek-style self-indulgence at Syracuse, both of which were taken by Livy from Antias.[42]

All the ancient accounts agreed that Scipio then retired to his villa near Liternum. In Antias' account, Lucius pleaded his brother's illness, *morbus*, as the reason for his non-attendance.[43] But even on its own terms, the factually and chronologically unsafe chapter makes clear that this was a mere excuse.[44] It was what might be called a 'diplomatic illness'.[45] The real reason was Publius' pride. Soon the whole matter was dropped.

### 18.4 A Campanian Villa: Scipio's Death, 183

The previous chapter closed with Hannibal's death and burial at a Bithynian country estate. Now for another country residence, and another death. We are lucky to possess an ancient description of Scipio's villa near the Campanian town of Liternum, although the villa, as opposed to the town, has not been found or excavated.[46] The younger Seneca in the first century CE sent his friend Gaius Lucilius a chatty letter which began excitedly 'I am writing this to you while lying down in the actual villa of Scipio Africanus', whose achievements he went straight on to praise in warm terms.[47] In this opening sentence, he also mentioned an evidently

---

[41] Gellius 4.18.  [42] For all three, see Livy 38.51.1–2.  [43] Livy 38.52.3, also 8 and 10.
[44] But a plausible one. We hear of two illnesses of Scipio which were bad enough to affect in a small way the course of history, one at an earlier date (28.24.1, under 206), a 'grave illness' which helped precipitate the serious mutiny in Iberia. And in 190, he missed the battle of Magnesia from illness. Hannibal's health seems, apart from the eye disease of 217, to have been more robust, if that can be inferred from the silence of the sources.
[45] When the then-new British prime minister Harold Macmillan visited Moscow in 1958, the failure of the Russian leader Nikita Kruschchev to see him was explained by toothache, believed at the time to have been of the 'diplomatic' sort.
[46] *Barr.* map 44 F4, on the coast between Cumae and Volturnum; mod. Lago di Patria. It became a Roman colony in 194. Scipio may have bought the estate in 205, the year of his consulship, when the state was selling land in the region: Livy 28.46.4–5; Frank 1933: 208.
[47] Letter 86. Scullard 1970: 290 n. 179. On this letter, see Griffin 1976: 182 n. 3; Henderson 2004: 54–61 (text and translation) and 93–170 (at 57 and 93, he translates *uilla* 'manor'). Griffin says Scipio took history less seriously than philosophy and relied on collections of examples, *exempla*. At 277 with n. 4, she cautions against trusting that 'I' and 'we' in Seneca's dialogues and letters are autobiographical but observes that this letter includes an important convincing detail at §14, cf. 21: (Vetulenus) Aegialus, the estate's present freedman owner, independently attested at Pliny, *NH* 14.49; see Henderson 2004: 160–3; but cf. Griffin 2004/5 (review of Henderson 2004): 285.

uninscribed altar which he thought might be Scipio's tomb, but this was just a star-struck tourist's fancy, and his remark that Scipio's spirit was aloft, having returned to heaven whence it came, is negligible evidence for apotheosis. Seneca remarked that Rome owed to Scipio his own exile no less than Hannibal's. Seneca proceeded to give a detailed description of what was obviously an impressive and delightful country estate, with a walled plantation of trees, fortified towers, and a large concealed well; but he did not stop to ask himself whether there might have been improvements and expansion since Scipio's day.[48] He was particularly struck by the small, poorly illuminated, old-fashioned bath installation and said that Scipio washed there, after – of course! – working the land himself, in the good old way (that is, he conformed to a familiar model of antique Roman simplicity).[49] There is no mention of slaves. Seneca goes on moralizing, for much of the letter, about the modest bath house and about austere ancient Roman bathing habits, drawing a contrast with his own luxurious day.

From another first-century CE source, the elder Pliny, we hear that Scipio planted an olive tree on the Liternum estate, which was still visible in Pliny's time; there was also a large myrtle tree nearby.[50] In a cave (*specus*) below them, a snake was said to keep guard over the shade or spirit, *manes*, of Scipio. This sounds like a broad hint at hero cult in the technical Greek chthonian (underworld) sense, rather than a simple allusion to the story of his mother Pomponia's miraculous impregnation.[51]

It is certain that Publius Scipio died here in 183.[52] What exactly did he die of? Plutarch's lost *Life* would have told us. His modern biographer Scullard says, without giving evidence, that he was 'old and ill' when he retired to Liternum.[53] Scipio was actually fifty-three, which is elderly rather than old by ancient standards, and the detail of the death from illness seems to be taken from Orosius.[54] But this late (fifth-century Christian) writer mixed up Liternum with Amiternum in the Sabine country as the place of death, and this does not inspire confidence in his grasp of detail. Orosius

---

[48] See §§ 3 and 4–8.
[49] Compare the old-style frugal Romans listed at Horace, *Odes* 1.12.40–44, with Nisbet and Hubbard 1970: 159–60.
[50] *NH* 16.234 with Henderson 2004: 164 and Griffin 2004/5: 285.
[51] Cf. Ogden 2013: 250. For Pomponia, see p. 42.
[52] On the date see Polybius, cited (but rejected) by Livy, 39.52.1. For 183, see *HCP* 3: 237–9; Briscoe 2008: 395; *FRHist* 3: 357 (J. W. Rich). Livy (38.56.1) was uncertain about the location of Scipio's tomb and at 55.2 gives as a *fama* (here 'mere story') that he died and was buried at Rome. It was surely at Liternum that he died and had his tomb, although there was a statue to him at Rome. See Briscoe 2008: 197–8.
[53] 1973 [1951]: 151; 1970: 223.   [54] Orosius 4.20.29, *morbo periit*.

might nevertheless be right; or he might be merely making wrong assumptions, based on a too-rapid reading of Livy. Either way, we can only speculate on the specific cause of death. It could have been a devastating stroke or a sudden massive heart attack, brought on by stress, for which Cato's rancorous persecution would have been responsible.[55] But that is mere conjecture.

There is a charming anecdote about Scipio in this final phase; it is moving, and perhaps also true; at any rate, I should like to think so. Valerius Maximus relates that some pirate or brigand chiefs – anyway, not a conventionally respectable diplomatic legation – made their way to Scipio's villa near coastal Liternum.[56] The grizzled veteran of Baecula, Ilipa, and Zama made the obvious assumption that they intended violence and prepared to defend himself and his property, stationing the enslaved members of his household on the roof. When the brigands realized this, they dismissed their fighting men and laid aside their arms. They shouted up that they were not there as enemies but as admirers of the *uirtus*, martial excellence, of so great a man; it was, says Valerius, as if (*tamquam*) they were seeking some favour from heaven. When Scipio's slaves reported this to him, he ordered the gates to be unbolted, then invited the visitors in. They paid reverence to the very doorposts, as if, (*quasi*) to a holy altar or temple, embraced Scipio, and gave him gifts, of the sort which are usually offered to the *numen*, the divine nature, of the immortal gods.[57]

---

[55] For the sources for Scipio's death, see De Sanctis 1969: 582 n. 277.
[56] 2.10.2, *conplures praedonum duces*; Scullard 1970: 290 n. 179.
[57] For this episode in the context of Scipio and religion, see pp. 238 and 428 n. 2. (It is not evidence for cult in the strong sense: note 'as if', twice.)

CHAPTER 19

# *Afterlives*

## 19.1 'Hannibal's Legacy' in Italy

Hannibal and Scipio lived on after their deaths in 183, but their legacies were very different: the parallels get fewer. The inverted commas round the title of this section are a salute to the two-volume 1965 late-life masterpiece *Hannibal's legacy* by Arnold Toynbee (1889–1975).[1] That whole work's subtitle was 'The Hannibalic war's effect on Roman life', and the individual volumes had the sub-subtitles 'Rome and her neighbours before Hannibal's entry' (vol. 1) and ' . . . after Hannibal's exit' (vol. 2).[2] Toynbee's message, to simplify greatly, was that although the Romans won the war against Hannibal militarily and politically, the war was in the longer term economically and socially catastrophic for the winners. Livy himself had remarked at the start of his war narrative that 'the eventual victors came closer to ruin than their opponents'.[3]

The reception of *Hannibal's legacy* makes in my view for an interesting episode of modern intellectual history, and an episode relevant to the present undertaking. Toynbee was a big if controversial name in his time, and he has conditioned later approaches to the period of Roman history covered in this account of parallel lives. (Some readers may disagree

---

[1] Toynbee 1965. 'Late-life masterpiece': cf. p. 1 on Bullock. The main biographical essays on Toynbee are by William McNeill and Fergus Millar. They reached differing conclusions about *Hannibal's legacy*: 'Thus his two stately tomes codified existing scholarship on Roman republican history between 266 and 133 B.C. rather than offering any important new hypotheses' (McNeill 1977: 462). 'The sheer size of the work, and the ponderous prose in which it is written, combined with the relative absence of archaeological, documentary, and epigraphic evidence, have given it, very misleadingly, an old-fashioned appearance, and it has had less impact than it should have done. But it is in fact the most important work on the period' (Millar 2004: 184).

[2] Strictly, these sub-subtitles in combination exclude the years 218–203 – almost the entire Hannibalic war itself! But he did not mean that: he has much to say about the war years. For example, he analysed the reaction of the peoples of Italy to Hannibal.

[3] 21.1.2.

with 'interesting'.[4] They are invited to skip forward to the next section.)[5] *Hannibal's legacy* is still arguably under-appreciated and has certainly been less than adequately grappled with as a whole, although it was reviewed seriously and usually admiringly – albeit sometimes with heavy reservations – by many of what were then some of the top names in the study of ancient, especially Roman, history.[6]

By contrast, Moses Finley's response (in the *New Statesman*) was phrased in characteristically scornful, even offensive, language (he says his own response is one of 'boredom' and 'repulsion'). Other and later reviewers naturally mentioned for comparison Toynbee's earlier and much-reviled twelve-volume *A study of history*,[7] but Finley takes this line to a negative extreme: 'We at once know where we are ... it is *A study of history* once again'.[8] That was unjust and one-sided. Three weeks before Finley's review appeared, the *Times Literary Supplement* of 2 December 1965 had carried an anonymous but well-informed full-page review 'TOYNBEE RETURNS TO ROME'. It concluded: 'These are very minor blemishes on a great work of synthesis, solidly based on the most scrupulous scholarship. Those historians of a narrower range who thought that Professor Toynbee's bold venture into universal history [sc. in *A Study of history*] had ruined him as a serious historian have been utterly refuted.' The *TLS* has now lifted the old anonymity rule, and the archive reveals that the reviewer was A. H. M. Jones – like Finley, a fellow of Jesus College Cambridge at that time, where he was professor of ancient history, and Finley's immediate predecessor in that role.

---

[4] Like two referees of the present book. In deference, I have shortened the discussion and relegated some of it to footnotes but not dumped it completely, as urged to do.

[5] Following the precedent of Syme 1939: vii ('the reader who is repelled' etc.).

[6] Reviews: Momigliano 1969: 633–5 (originally in the now defunct BBC magazine *The Listener*, 2 December 1965); Jones 1965; Picard 1966; Scullard 1966; Walbank 1966; Broughton 1967; Salmon 1967; Staveley 1967; Oost 1967; Vogt 1967; Gabba 1976: 154–61, Eng. tr. of Italian original, *RFIC* 106 (1968): 68–75. Brunt was another admirer. But he did not actually review *Hannibal's legacy*, although nobody in any country was better qualified to do so. In the preface to his own important large-scale work on Italian manpower (Brunt 1971a: viii), he praised *Hannibal's legacy* warmly, describing himself as 'an admirer of its range, erudition and lucidity'. He added that it had anticipated some of his conclusions and forced him to rethink others and to 'take issue with [Toynbee] on many important points'. Crawford 2009: 75 says incorrectly that *Hannibal's legacy* is 'not cited in the Preface' to Brunt 1971a. That preface is therefore inconsistent with Crawford's claim that Brunt shared Crawford's own low opinion of Toynbee's book.

[7] See e.g. Walbank 1966: 385: after calling *Hannibal's legacy* a *tour de force*, he says 'it is the method of *A Study of History*, but applied with more checks and to a more restricted field'. The earlier work is not mentioned again in a long and positive review.

[8] Finley 1965: 1003. It might be conjectured that Finley was never likely to look kindly on an author who in the earlier work had notoriously called Judaism a 'fossil' civilization. See Eban and Aridan 2006 for that debate. But this background evidently did not bother the equally Jewish Momigliano.

That same day, 2 December 1965, saw the publication of Momigliano's short but warm notice of *Hannibal's legacy* in *The Listener*. Of the 'two majestic volumes', Momigliano shrewdly remarked that 'as a whole, this latest work cannot be easily interpreted as a further development of Toynbee's recent books, such as volume twelve of the *Study of History*, the *Historian's Approach to Religion*, and the travel books on the East … Here to my surprise (and I am bound to add, to my delight) Toynbee turns westward' to Rome, including Roman religion. After a not obviously relevant digression about Theodor Mommsen, he concluded that Toynbee 'has given the English readers a history which, while it does not supersede Beloch, De Sanctis, and Fraccaro, is a worthy companion to them'.

*Hannibal's legacy* is still routinely gestured at more or less politely by historians of ancient Rome, but actual scholarly engagement with the detail of the book gets less and less frequent.[9] Only an interesting and valuable chapter-length essay by Tim Cornell in 1996 reappraised Toynbee head-on (and at the same time Brunt's critique of Toynbee), but even this is now more than a quarter of a century old, and was inevitably restricted in scope. He took the devastation of Italy as his main case study; the debate has moved on a long way even since Cornell wrote. His general conclusion was that 'there is still much to be said for Toynbee's thesis: the agrarian problems of Italy in the second century BC, and the resulting political turmoil, can still be viewed as Hannibal's legacy'.[10]

Now, more than half a century after Toynbee, a full re-examination would be very welcome and would need a monograph of its own, by a Roman historian familiar with the chief archaeological developments in Italy over the past fifty years.[11] The present half-chapter does not pretend to do that job, for which the present author is anyway not qualified. In

---

[9] Cornell and Ando both borrow Toynbee's book title for their own titles – as does the present section. Ando (2019: 57–8) briefly praises *Hannibal's legacy*, summarizes two of its main theses, and calls it neglected. Cornell 1996 (not cited by Ando) grapples with *Hannibal's legacy* in admirable detail. Rosenstein 2004: 3–62 and 141–69 says much about Brunt 1971a, but very little about Toynbee. Fronda 2010: 67 n. 56, on the 'supposedly devastating effects' of the war on south-east Italy, notes the Toynbee–Brunt argument but does not return to either of them at 67–73, his main discussion, though citing both elsewhere for details, e.g. on legionary numbers. Taylor 2020a lists *Hannibal's legacy* in its bibliography but I can find no citation in the actual book. Pittenger 2008: 159 n. 1 regards Toynbee's central thesis as 'unassailable'. Roselaar 2019: ch. 3.2 is more critical (Toynbee's thesis about the decline of Italian agriculture part exaggerated, part wrong).

[10] Cornell 1996: 113.

[11] But for a pessimistic assessment of the value of survey archaeology in southern Etruria to the understanding of the Gracchan crisis, see De Ligt 2012: 179–82. Cf. also Cornell 1996: 110: the archaeological evidence 'too partial and too enigmatic'.

particular, one aspect of Toynbee's achievement will be scarcely touched on: his lengthy and important discussion of the creation of a Latin literary language on the Greek model. This was ahead of its time, and its value as such has been generously recognised by Denis Feeney.[12]

The UCL anthropologist Mary Douglas (1921–2007) used to say that most reviews of books on anthropology could be summarized as follows: 'it's obvious, and anyway it's wrong'. A reading at a single session of some of the main reviews of *Hannibal's legacy* can leave a similar impression. But there is no doubt that the author's theme was an important one, addressed in an enduringly important work. His agenda will be reflected in two of the section titles which follow.

## 19.2  Hannibal's Dream: The Devastation of Italy

How bad was Hannibal's devastation of Italy? On this point, Brunt argued at length, against Toynbee, that it was not all that serious or lasting, and we must now return to this debate. But Toynbee was not the first to claim that Hannibal destroyed Italian agriculture; indeed, the claim was perhaps first made in the future tense. Hannibal's dream was an epiphany sent by 'Jupiter' at the start of the war and reported by Silenus, Coelius Antipater, and Livy. Hannibal's guide, a young man of divine appearance (or 'beauty'), is said to have ordered Hannibal to follow him and fix his gaze on him. Hannibal disobeyed by looking round and saw that he in his turn was followed by a massive snake which destroyed the vegetation to the accompaniment of a huge thunderstorm; his guide explained that this signified the destruction of Italy; he was not to worry about it but to proceed with his invasion.[13]

Was the young speaker in the epiphany factually correct in his prophecy? The Greek and Latin sources who report him presumably thought so. And was Toynbee correct in his analysis? Brunt began by observing that Toynbee should have made it clearer that Hannibal's devastations mainly affected allied territory not Roman (Toynbee did argue that the south of Italy was affected much worse than the north).[14] Brunt's detailed method was to challenge the mostly Livian evidence on which Toynbee relied,

---

[12] Toynbee 1965: 2. 416–34, ch. XIII, 'The creation of a literature in Latin on the pattern of the literature in Greek'; Feeney 2016: x, 13.
[13] Livy 21.22.6–9.
[14] Brunt 1971a: 269 against Toynbee 1965: 2. 10–34 on the devastation of south-eastern Italy and Sicily in the second Punic war. Brunt went too far, see Cornell 1996: 111–12. Erdkamp 1998: 270–1 agreed with Toynbee that the Hannibalic war ruined the south of Italy more than the north.

replacing it either with scattered remarks by Polybius (who, as we have seen throughout the present book, survives only very partially for the Hannibalic war) or with arguments from general probability.[15] For example, Fabius the Delayer is said by Livy to have ordered the evacuation of unfortified towns and to have told all those living in lands vulnerable to damage from Hannibal's forces to leave after burning their houses and crops.[16] But Brunt argued that Hannibal was still able to live off the land until at least autumn 216, so the edict, 'if ever issued in the terms reported, was pretty ineffective'.[17] Against Toynbee's use of Livy, he counter-cited Polybius, who says that in 217 Hannibal was told by his scouts that there was plenty of corn in Apulia. Brunt took much the same sceptical line about Fabius' further and similar edict of 215, which he found 'hard to believe' was correctly reported.[18] As for northern Italy, which was not Toynbee's primary concern in the relevant chapter, Brunt observed plausibly that Hannibal spent much too little time in the area to have inflicted very serious losses.[19] Both Toynbee and Brunt wrote too early to take account of the arguments of Hanson about Classical Greece, but equally applicable to Roman Italy: the destruction of crops is a very slow and difficult business. It was left to Cornell to bring this comparativist insight into the argument.[20]

Brunt did not seek to minimize the hardships endured (starvation, disease from undernourishment). He also noted correctly that both sides – not only Hannibal's Carthaginians – resorted to devastations, if only to provide themselves with food and their livestock with fodder; and more recent researchers agree. Brunt provided a long list of Roman pillaging activities, mostly taken from Livy, but ending with a generalizing remark by Polybius about the effects of war on the Italian cities, inflicted by both incoming and outgoing soldiers.[21]

We ought however to go further than Brunt – or rather in a different direction – and add the powerful psychological factor, and the purely visual impact of the burning of fertile parts of Italy.[22] This is vividly brought out in the speeches about impotent watching, which Livy puts in the mouths of

---

[15] See esp. Brunt 1971a: 273; cf. Cornell 1996: 104–13.    [16] 22.11.4–5, 217 BCE.
[17] Brunt 1971a: 271 and n. 4; contrast Toynbee 1965: 2. 12–13.
[18] Pol. 3.100.1; Fabius: Livy 23.32.14.    [19] Brunt 1971a: 270.
[20] Hanson 1983; Cornell 1996: 107; cf. Rosenstein 2004: 28 (but see Erdkamp 1998: 210–22 for qualifications to Hanson's thesis).
[21] Brunt 1971a: 276 and n. 1; Pol. 9.26.9. More recent researchers: Cornell 1996: 107–11; Fronda 2010: 68 and n. 58.
[22] So rightly Fronda 2010: 68 n. 58. See already Cornell 1996: 107, invoking Hanson on Classical Greece.

Marcus Minucius Rufus and Marcus Metilius, however exaggerated the rhetoric of their complaints against Fabius' policy of inactivity and its results.[23] Hannibal and his depredations came as a shock. Virtually no inhabitants of the Italian peninsula can have had any memory of the last large-scale foreign invasion of Italy, that of Pyrrhus in the 270s, which was brief.[24] The trauma of Hannibal's lengthy presence, however great or small the actual damage he wrought, will not have been easily forgotten. To that extent, Hannibal's dream may have been a true prophecy. Perceptions are a kind of reality.

Hannibal was caught in a kind of strategic fork: one prong was that he wanted and needed the political support of Italian communities, but the other prong was his unavoidable reliance on the simply stolen or at best harshly requisitioned crops of those same communities, in the absence of more than very occasional relief supplies from Iberia or Carthage. And unlike the Romans, he had no obvious compensating benefits to confer. The Polybius chapter cited earlier ends by saying that Hannibal was notorious among the Carthaginians as greedy for money and among the Romans as cruel, *ōmos*.[25] He precedes this by saying, interestingly, that we must allow for the influence of his friends and 'the force of circumstances'.[26] The 'friends' are not specified (perhaps self-serving Italian politicians rather than Carthaginian advisers?), but the 'circumstances' are surely the difficulty of living off a land while at the same time hoping for the goodwill of those who tilled it. Polybius even records seriously the belief that Hannibal's acts of cruelty in Italy were really the work of another Hannibal altogether, Hannibal (10) the 'single-combat-man', *Monomachos*.[27]

The 1960s are a long time ago now, but it cannot be said that on this topic any very clear consensus has emerged since the thorough investigations of Toynbee and Brunt. The short-term impact of Hannibal's (and Rome's own) infliction of devastation – both material and psychological – is not

---

[23] Livy 22.14 (with Toynbee 1965: 2. 31) and 22.25; for Minucius, see p. 99, and for the tribune Metilius, *DPRR* METI0859. On Livy's insistent stress on the visual effect, see Briscoe and Hornblower 2020: 199, n. on Livy 22.14.4. Cornell 1989b: 391 aptly cites an anecdote about Pyrrhus (Cassius Dio book 9, fragment 40.27), who allegedly said that the Italian districts of his friends had been ravaged to such an extent that it was impossible to tell if they had ever been inhabited.

[24] But there were Gallic threats from the north, and Carthaginian naval incursions.

[25] 9.26.7–10.  [26] ἡ τῶν πραγμάτων περίστασις.

[27] 9.24.4–8 (see §6 and p. 109 n. 179, cf. 354 n. 84, for his cannibalism suggestion). Geus 1994: 94 'Hannibal (10)' doubts his existence, as does Brizzi 2011a: 43 (a 'kind of symbol'), but see p. 45 n. 31 (he might have been a battle double or lookalike). See generally Brizzi 2011: 35–57 on 'Hannibal's double' and the possible sources for him. Cf. also *HCP* 2: 153.

denied, but it is thought unlikely that they caused large-scale depopulation.[28] Even harshly punished Capua was prosperous and populous again in the second and first centuries BCE, a surprising urban renaissance, studied by Frederiksen.[29] It is to population and manpower that we now turn.

## 19.3 Manpower and the Land

Roman and Italian manpower losses in the war were enormous. All estimates are approximate, but on the best recent calculation, about 120,000 men were lost in battle between 218 and 203 (that is a 'net figure', one which excludes something like 25,000 deaths from non-military causes).[30] But that is evidence for Hannibal's immediate wartime effect rather than for his longer-term legacy. For the period 203–163 BCE, the census figures indicate a staggering growth rate of 1.1%.[31] De Ligt thinks that this represents a rapid recovery in the number of adult male Romans and Campanians only, rather than in the female population: mortality in the Hannibalic war had been highly selective.[32] He concludes that by the time of the Gracchi brothers (130s–120s), there was a decline in the number of *assidui*, that is, those who met the minimum property qualification for legionary service, as opposed to the *proletarii*, who did not.

Manpower and the land are intimately connected: in particular, legionary absences for years at a time were bound to affect the agrarian history of Italy; service in Iberia in particular (which continued for decades after Hannibal had left Italy) was specially unpopular. The situation faced by Scipio's grandsons the Gracchi brothers in their tribunates, in 133 and 123/2 respectively, was a perceived agrarian as well as a manpower crisis. The older brother Tiberius is reliably reported – by his brother Gaius – to have been worried about the rural poor in Etruria.[33] If, as is likely, he was alluding to a decline in the number of *assidui*, modern demographically expert historians think he was right. Appian describes the spread of estates

---

[28] Cornell 1996; Fronda 2010: 68 n. 58; at 72–3, he remarks on the loyalty to Rome of Canusium, despite devastation by Hannibal, and explains this (92–3) in terms of inter-city rivalries. It could be extended so as to account for other apparent regional anomalies in the Italian reaction to devastation.
[29] Frederiksen 1984: 308–10; Torelli 1999: 8.
[30] De Ligt 2012: 140–1. 'Enormous' is his word (143).
[31] De Ligt 2012: 142. 'Staggering' is again his word. In the end, De Ligt (2012: 134, after a long discussion of the debate) accepts the theory of Beloch and Brunt that the Augustan and later censuses included women and children, but Republican ones did not. Harris 2007: 516 confidently rejected this theory; Rosenstein 2004: 12–13 noted the objections to it but was non-committal.
[32] De Ligt 2012: 142–50, a complex argument.
[33] Plut. *Ti. Gr.* 8.9 = *FRHist* no. 11, C. Sempronius Gracchus, frag. 2.

worked by enslaved people as part of the same phenomenon.[34] Inasfar as the actions of the Gracchi have been held both in antiquity and modern times to have caused the fall of the Roman republic, and Hannibal's invasion to have led to the Gracchi (this second proposition is Toynbee's thesis in a nutshell), his legacy was enormous. But how much of this did Hannibal really cause? Few topics in Roman history have been so much studied and debated as the violently curtailed reforming efforts of the Gracchi, including the background and aftermath to those reforms.[35] This is not the place to do more than try to identify Hannibal's indubitable relevance.

One category of land was at the heart of the problem: *ager publicus*, 'public land' won by conquest.[36] The Gracchi sought to redistribute much of this land, which had been possessed – possibly illegally, as we shall see – by the wealthy; their reform aimed to create smallholdings and so increase military manpower. But archaeology suggests that the extent of large landholdings, *latifundia*, may have been exaggerated by the literary sources, who echo Gracchan rhetoric; and anyway, there is some evidence that this was an old problem, one that antedated Hannibal's arrival. In particular, the same Gaius Flaminius whom Hannibal defeated at Lake Trasimene in 217 had as tribune in 232 carried against senatorial opposition a law allotting parts of the *ager publicus* to Roman citizens. Polybius or his hostile source called this the 'first step in the demoralization of the populace'.[37] There is also an attested law which restricted individual holdings of *ager publicus* to 500 *iugera*, about 125 hectares. One principal ancient source for it, Cicero's contemporary Varro, put it in the fourth century, and this is well defended by Cornell against those who would down-date it to the first half of the second, perhaps the 160s, when Cato mentioned it in a speech.[38] It is not agreed just how much weight we

---

[34] See App. *Civil war* 1.7/26–10/40. The evidence for the Gracchi (epigraphic as well as literary) is collected at Greenidge and Clay 1960: 1–23; simplified Eng. tr.: Stockton 1981: 1–24. For warnings about distortions in Appian, see Gargola 2008.

[35] Only a few modern works can be singled out. Brunt 1971b: 63–97 is readable and still valuable, though some of his demographic assumptions have been revised or challenged. For a mainly political narrative, Lintott 1994b. More recent demographically based analyses: Rosenstein 2004: 141–69 (and 2011) and De Ligt 2012: 143–82, the best modern discussion, exemplary in its control of demographic evidence, caution, and fair-minded recognition of the difficulties in the solutions it accepts.

[36] See Roselaar 2010 (esp. 146–256 on the second century and the Gracchi).

[37] Pol. 2.21.7–8; see also *MRR* I: 225 for other testimonies. For the second century 'well before' Tiberius Gracchus, see Harris 2007: 524.

[38] Varro, *Rerum rusticarum libri tres* (*On agricultural matters, three books*) 1.2.9; Greenidge and Clay 1960: 4; Cornell 1989a: 328–9 and 1996: 99 against e.g. Lintott 1994b: 55 and Gabba 1989: 203.

should allow to the evidence for such 'forerunners of the Gracchi'.[39] Most probably, the Hannibalic war exacerbated but did not create the problem of encroachment by the unsupervised rich on *ager publicus*.

Causes can be indirect as well as direct. Let us return to Iberia. Its history provides a reasonable argument that Hannibal, by forcing the Romans to fight the war initially in Iberia indirectly, caused the recruitment problems which the Gracchi tried to solve.[40] Military service in distant Iberia was progressively unpopular and agriculturally damaging during the second century.[41] It has been held that one reason was that soldiers were unable to visit their homes even during the winter months, although this was not a novelty generated by the war with Hannibal.[42] But Hannibal's straightforward and personal causal role in this surely ended with the war against him. It is at first sight a mystery why the Roman senate chose to continue with the arduous conquest of the whole of Iberia even after the settlement with the Carthaginians at the end of the third century imposed their evacuation. After that date, there was no real threat from that direction. The simple and no doubt correct answer is the lure of Iberian mineral wealth and the expectation of booty; the hunger for triumphs was also a powerful factor.[43] But during the second century, self-enrichment seems for various reasons to have been decreasingly compelling as a motive for the ordinary Roman legionary squaddie.[44]

The causes of the Gracchan crisis in Italy were multi-factorial. Hannibal's war is part of the explanation, but so are (second) the post-202 decision to subdue Iberia whatever the cost in manpower and human misery, and (third) long-standing senatorial greed for Italian land, combined with persistent refusal to accept, or even compromise with, tribunician attempts to limit occupation of *ager publicus*.

---

[39] The title of Taylor 1962, which remains an important article.
[40] Toynbee 1965: 2. 61–2 had already insisted on the unique importance of Iberian warfare in 'uprooting the Roman peasant conscript soldier'.
[41] Toynbee 1965: 2. 96; Astin 1967: 168–9; Lintott 1994a: 36–7.
[42] So Brunt 1971b: 13 (about Sicily and Greece as well as Iberia). But Rosenstein 2004: 43–52 (cf. 142) argues strongly that there was never a time when Roman soldiers regularly obtained leave to go home in the autumn and winter for agricultural work, so that the Hannibalic war did not effect a radical change in this respect.
[43] For both mystery and answer, see Harris 1979: 208–10. Iberian mines: Johnston and Kaufman 2019: 409–10, with modern scientific references, and for their exploitation by the Romans, Pol. 34.9.8–9 (a 'fragment' from Pol.'s geographical book, consisting of a quotation by Strabo, 3.2.10; see *HCP* 3: 605–6), Diod. 5.36. According to Pliny, *NH* 33.97, in Hannibal's time the mines at Baebulo (conjecturally placed south of Castulo, *Barr.* map 27 B4) yielded 300 pounds of silver a day. Loot and triumphs: Taylor 2020a: 124–5, cf. the modern works on triumphs cited at p. 14 n. 28.
[44] Astin 1967: 168.

A fourth factor was already alluded to by Appian: agricultural slavery, the working of the Italian land by enslaved people. Modern historians have until recently held that the introduction of the 'slave mode of production' between about 200 and 133 greatly worsened the situation of free workers, especially in central Italy.[45] The link between military success and conquest on the one hand, and the growth of agricultural slavery in Italy on the other, was forcibly, perhaps too forcibly, asserted by Hopkins; to the extent that the victory over Carthage in 202 began the process, Hannibal would be relevant. But the theory that Italy's enslaved population increased dramatically in the second century is no longer widely accepted.[46] Cornell invokes the 'third-century' gap (the sparseness of evidence for anything at all, between 293 and the start of the Hannibalic war, the period of Livy's lost second Decade) to argue that the origins of the slave-based economy in Italy go back to the fourth century.[47] A similar sort of reasoning against over-dependence on what survives of Livy can be found elsewhere. Torelli has asserted, in respectful but explicit correction of Toynbee, that 'a closer analysis of the archaeological evidence more and more shows' that the destruction of south Italy is better associated not with Hannibal but with the Roman conquest of sixty or seventy years earlier, or with the campaigns of Pyrrhus.[48]

A fifth, final, and very long-term factor, not so far mentioned, is debt.[49] This too cannot be discussed in detail here, but no popular politician before Catiline in the 60s BCE tried to do anything to alleviate it.[50] So the debt problem continued well into the late Republic.[51] The war with Hannibal adversely affected the better-off as well as the poor. The strain of the war led in 211 to the phasing out of the existing coinage system and the creation of a new one based on the silver *denarius*, financed by state levies on private property.[52] But as the Roman military situation improved,

---

[45] See Morel 2007: 504–5; De Ligt 2012: 154–7.
[46] See Rosenstein 2004: 10–12; Roselaar 2019 (as in n. 9).
[47] Hopkins 1978, esp. 56 for Hannibal; reservations at De Ligt 2012: 163–5. Stronger denials at Cornell 1989a: 334 and 1996: 98; see also De Haas 2023: 146.
[48] Torelli 1999: 8, but giving no references for this point.   [49] See Cornell 1989a: 329–33.
[50] Catiline (Lucius Sergius Catilina): *DPRR* SERG1998. Brunt 1971b: 63 hesitantly ascribed a law on debt relief to the tribune Gaius Flaminius in 232 on the strength of Festus 470, lines 32–3 Lindsay (very fragmentary), which mentions a *lege [Fla> minia* in a suitable context; but he withdrew this suggestion at 1988: 505, endnote 5 to ch. 1.
[51] Brunt 1971a: 644 and 1988: 61–3.
[52] See Crawford 1985, but new evidence from Morgantina in Sicily suggests that the monetary shift was less drastic and sudden than previously thought. See Walthall 2017. A silver *denarius* was roughly a day's pay for a skilled worker.

booty began to flow in, and annual Carthaginian payments of reparations eased Roman finances further after 202.

## 19.4 Hannibal's Legacy at Carthage

Hannibal went down to total battle defeat at Zama. But to call him the defeated and Scipio the victor is too simple, if we take the longer view. The Roman republic's troubles in the second century BCE can be regarded as at least partially due to the war against Hannibal: on this view – Toynbee's view – his legacy was his revenge. Argument revolves round the extent to which the destructive processes were already at work before 218, and about whether Toynbee anyway exaggerated them. But what of Hannibal's legacy at Carthage? A century after his birth, in 146, his home city was destroyed after what we call the third Punic war, a far shorter and far more one-sided conflict than either the first or the second war. Our knowledge of domestic affairs and politics at Carthage (and its local dependencies) in its final fifty-five years of existence after Zama is very poor by comparison with our information about Rome and Italy and the campaigning in Iberia. We do not even know for sure whether Hannibal's structural reforms of the 190s were lasting, or whether they ended with or soon after his hasty departure for the east. The Carthaginians' prosperity returned fairly rapidly, so that they were even able to ask to be able to pay off the indemnity sooner than stipulated. The offer was refused.[53]

So we are reduced to asking counterfactual questions. If it is true, as Rich has concluded, that the actual origins of the second war lay in the 'wrath of the Barcids', Hannibal and his father Hamilcar can be regarded as having ultimately caused the fall of Carthage.[54] So we can ask, what if Hannibal had not attacked Saguntum? And what if he had won at Zama? On either radical hypothesis, could the Romans and Carthaginians have continued to coexist peacefully, as they had in earlier centuries?[55] What if Hannibal had indeed lost at Zama, but the settlement after Zama had allowed much less latitude to Masinissa, whose provocations against Carthage eventually led to the final war? Hannibal can hardly be held responsible for those.

Such speculations are in the end futile. The Barcids may have been the most active proponents of war at and before its outbreak, but Hannibal must have had some support back home at Carthage thereafter. The home authorities could certainly have done much more for him than they did; but his military isolation – very little by way of reinforcement from either

---

[53] See p. 271. [54] Rich 1996. [55] For 'Rome and Carthage at peace', see Palmer 1997.

Iberia or north Africa – was due in large part to Roman control of the sea, and especially Italian landing places.[56] Hannibal was, after all, accompanied on campaign by senior Carthaginian advisers, who were thoroughly implicated in his single worst mistake, the alliance with Philip V of Macedon. It took Scipio's arrival in force on African soil to induce the Carthaginian decision-makers at home to recall Hannibal and Mago, and even that was not done immediately. Naturally, Hannibal's Carthaginian enemies later sought to represent Hannibal as solely responsible for 'both starting and waging the war', but that was a self-serving simplification.[57] The direct reasons for the eventual destruction of Carthage are more plausibly to be sought in the Romans' own actions and attitudes as they became more used to acting imperialistically after 200, and only indirectly and partially in the much earlier actions of Hannibal. That is perhaps as far as we can go – as regards the short term.

Carthage did however begin to revive after another century had passed. Gaius Gracchus' attempt to plant a colony on the site failed badly.[58] It was to be called Junonia, but we have seen that this was an unfortunate choice: Juno was supposed to have abandoned her hatred of Rome, but this act of outright replacement was perhaps a step too far. Carthage was however successfully colonized by Augustus, who was carrying out a plan of Caesar, and it became the capital of the province called Africa Proconsularis. Later still, it was a great Christian religious and educational centre. But Hannibal's memory had little to do with any of this. We have seen, however, that his Bithynian grave is said to have received admiring attention from an emperor likelier to have been Caracalla than the 'African emperor' Septimius Severus.[59] But with this not very convincing story, we enter into the literary afterlife of Hannibal, to which we now turn.

## 19.5  Hannibal's Literary Legacy

A hostile or merely sceptical critic, faced with the title of this section, might exclaim in protest: 'but why a separate section?[60] Most of what you have written already is derived from Hannibal's ancient literary legacy! Your footnotes are full of references to Polybius and Livy, both of whose works are literary constructs. Even your cherished notion of a parallel between

---

[56] See Rankov 1996.
[57] See Livy 33.45.8, under 195 BCE: *prioris belli per illum unum non magis gesti quam moti*.
[58] Plut. *Gaius Gracchus* 10.1–11.3; other evidence at Greenidge and Clay 1960: 43.  [59] See p. 383.
[60] Scipio's afterlife will be treated differently, because the starting point is a particular prose narrative text, which will then be exploited in both historical and literary ways.

him and Scipio is already there in the sources.' There is some truth in the objection.[61] The sources and resources available for the biographer of a modern figure are admittedly very different in kind from anything that can be used for two individuals who lived in the late third and early second centuries BCE: contemporary memoirs and diaries, archival evidence, officially or unofficially gathered statistics – which is not meant to imply naively that such dry data are free from bias. In the very rare situation where modern historians of the Roman republic do have access to seemingly 'hard' evidence, namely census figures, there is radical disagreement about what these signify and their basis of computation; in any case, they come down to us in literary sources (so that one common expedient is to emend the figures when they do not suit a demographic theory). They were also vulnerable to political manipulation. Nor do inscriptions automatically have unimpeachable status: the letters sent to Greek cities by Publius and Lucius Scipio are valuable because contemporary, but they had a pro-Roman political purpose.

As for the specific parallel between Hannibal and Scipio, to which we will return generally in the next and final chapter, the obvious reason why it features prominently and explicitly at a particular moment in the ancient sources is pure coincidence: the two men (and a third, Philopoemen) died in the same year, 183, neither of them on the battlefield. This naturally prompted ancient reflections of a comparative sort, especially for a reason which (it will be argued in the next chapter) is not coincidental: the last days of each man were spent unhappily, rejected and in actual or effective exile. The word 'ungrateful' was too tempting to be avoided.

That comparison was obvious enough. More sophisticated types of literary parallel, especially in Livy's third Decade (218–201 BCE), have been detected in modern times, thanks to very close readings of Livy; Polybius has not yet attracted as much interest of this sort. The characteristics ascribed in Livy to Scipio and Hannibal are seen almost to effect a merger into one composite hero (or villain, if a deterioration in Scipio's character is accepted, and Hannibal treated as the negative foil).[62] The culmination of the process comes at the end of the first century CE, in the creation by Silius Italicus in his *Punica* of a 'Roman Hannibal', to adopt the title of a fine modern treatment by Claire Stocks. Silius, writing when he did, had the luxury of being able to draw on a very long Greek and

---

[61] Livy 37.1.9–10 (on the rival merits of Hannibal and Scipio as advisers to Antiochus and Lucius Scipio respectively) is a good example of an explicit parallel which is focalized through the Roman senators but is probably a literary construct (cf. pp. 323–4).
[62] See Rossi 2004; Beltramini and Rocco 2020.

Roman literary tradition, in poetry and prose.[63] We have looked at one example when discussing the 'Hannibalic legend': the identification of Hannibal with Hercules rests in part on a literary novelty not found in older Greek writers, the motif that Hercules crossed the Alps (Ennius may already have hinted that Hannibal owed this achievement to unspecified divine help).[64] Silius picks this up, but he also runs with a comparison between Hannibal and Scipio, who like Hercules/Herakles at the crossroads chose the goddess Virtue.[65]

This section will address the main themes in Hannibal's ancient reception, rather than trudging through the literary evidence author by author.[66] Poets will feature more often than prose authors, but we will touch on Cicero and Seneca the younger.

The immediate impact of Hannibal in Italy was traumatic and frightful, and this goes far to explain the literary insistence on the theme of Hannibal's *cruelty*. (The Carthaginians in Iberia were generally regarded as having made themselves hated for their arrogance, but Hannibal is not singled out.) Ennius made Hannibal cry 'he who strikes an enemy will be Carthaginian with me/whoever he is, from whatever country'.[67] Livy placed his version of this before the Ticinus battle but concretized it to make Hannibal actually promise Carthaginian citizenship to his allies (the promise is historically improbable but might have been addressed to Numidian neighbours of Carthage).[68] Silius moves it along in time to Cannae, the climax of his epic, and adds that allies might become citizens of Carthage 'if they lift up a hand bloody with Roman slaughter'. It may indeed be that Silius, while echoing Ennius, added this gory motif.[69] But the fragment of Ennius is short, and since he went on to write that 'Punic harsh arrogance severed their [the Romans'] hamstrings' at Cannae, he was capable of such gory elaboration.[70] Polybius characterized Hannibal as impious, greedy, and cruel, *ōmos*, but attributed this to friends and circumstances. (Polybius used the bad influence of advisers to explain the

---

[63] Stocks 2014 has good discussions not only of Silius and the many authors before him who wrote about Hannibal (prose, poetry, Greek, Latin), but of Homer and other epic models, to whose heroes Silius' Hannibal (and Scipio) are fruitfully compared.
[64] Ennius 232 Sk.; Goldberg and Manuwald 2018a: 231, *nunc Iupiter hac stat*, see p. 235 n. 76.
[65] See Stocks 2014: 221.
[66] For which see Barceló 2004: 246–58, 'Nachleben' (also on his modern reception); Brizzi 2011a: 59–77 and 2011b.
[67] *Annals* 234–5 Sk.; Goldberg and Manuwald 2018a: 231.   [68] 21.45.6; Walsh 2003: 209.
[69] *Punica* 9.209–11. These various passages are assembled and well analysed by Stocks 2014: 60. She says 'the famed barbarity of the Roman Hannibal is now on display', i.e., is Silius' contribution.
[70] *Annals* 287 Sk.; Goldberg and Manuwald 2018a: 251.

deterioration in the character of Philip V, but we do not have enough of his Hannibal narrative in the original Greek to know whether he took the same line.) Livy's opening character sketch of Hannibal treats him as a mix of good and bad qualities, and in the second category 'inhuman cruelty' is prominent. But most of this passage is influenced by Sallust on Catiline and Jugurtha and contains material contradicted by Livy's own narrative, especially on deception and perjury.[71] Elsewhere, Livy expresses, by implication, high praise for Hannibal and admiration for his achievements and motives; a good example is Livy's reworking of the briefer and less memorable Polybian version of Hannibal's speech before the battle at the Ticinus.[72] Nevertheless, the epithet 'cruel' was attached to Hannibal almost as a matter of course, as for Cicero before Livy and Seneca the younger after him.[73] Statius called Hannibal a savage (*atrox*), perjured, haughty barbarian, in the context of the story that Hannibal was one of three famous owners of a famous statuette of Hercules by Lysippus.[74] No story of sexual abuse or violence by Hannibal survives, although it would have been an obvious way of defaming a barbarian. We can discount the alleged affair of this 'fierce man' (Appian) with an Italian woman. The story is merely said to exhibit untypical self-indulgence or luxury, *truphē*.[75]

An aspect of the cruelty theme is devastation, and its hateful psychological effect. Hannibal's dream, with which we began that section, is a literary device, handled in a literary way. The great age of the Hellenistic Greek poets was over by the end of the second century BCE, except for some of the epigrammatists.[76] But a Greek poet who may have been a contemporary of Hannibal was Lycophron, the author of the *Alexandra*. That long poem's marked preoccupation with the Greek-speaking south of Italy may reflect the trauma of Hannibal's presence in the Croton region and his visits to Campanian sites such as the oracle of the dead at Avernus.[77] Hannibal is never named in the poem, but the same is true of Virgil's *Aeneid* (but admittedly the Virgilian allusion is transparent,

---

[71] Pol. 10.26.7–10 with *HCP* 2: 231 on the reasons for Philip V's deterioration. Hannibal: Pol: see p. 400; Livy 21.4.2–10 (cruelty at §9); Levene 2010: 100–1; Briscoe and Hornblower 2020: 170. The first paragraphs (§§2–4) have the best claim to be about the real Hannibal.

[72] Livy 21.43–4 with p. 88.

[73] Cic. *On duties* 1.38, *crudelis Hannibal*; Sen. *On anger* 2.5.4; Stocks 2014: 22–3 and 32.

[74] *Silvae* 4.6.77–8 for the first three epithets, and 'barbarian Hannibal' at 106–7; cf. Stocks 2014: 190.

[75] App. *Hann.* 43/183; see p. 151.

[76] See p. 120 for a possible allusion to Scipio at New Carthage in an epigram by Antiphilus (first century CE).

[77] For an argument to this effect, see Hornblower 2018, and for the early second-century date (controversial) see briefly 2022: xx–xxiii. For Lycophron's untypically forthright interest in Naples, which Hannibal importantly failed to win over, see p. 139.

as Lycophron's allusions never are). It is just possible that Ennius was aware of the *Alexandra* in both his *Annals* and his poem *Scipio*.[78]

The accusation of *deceit* is part of a common but by no means universal literary ethnic stereotype about Carthaginians, *Punica fraus*.[79] It would not otherwise be specific to Hannibal, so Livy makes it specific by saying his *fraus* was 'more than Punic'.[80] After the accusation of cruelty, Livy continues to paint the negative side of the picture: Hannibal was irreligious and had no regard for oaths.[81] 'Punic deception' is a constant theme in Livy and other sources and is repeated by Cicero soon before Livy was writing.[82] Livy does, however, at the start of the third Decade, use the arresting expression 'Roman dishonesty', *fraus Romanorum*, about the Roman acquisition of Sardinia after the first Punic war. This is focalized through Hannibal's father Hamilcar and reflects Polybius' authorial opinion, so is Livian only at two removes.[83] But it shows that Livy was capable of reversing the stereotype. As for Hannibal, we have seen more than once that the authorial accusation against him of irreligiosity in general and perjury in particular is not sustained by the Livian narrative.

Polybius' list of Hannibal's bad qualities includes impiety, *asebeia*, consisting of violation of treaties by transferring populations elsewhere. He gives no examples but may have been thinking of the treatment of Herdonea (population moved to Metapontum and Thurii).[84] Polybius anyway excuses all these vaguely specified failings by 'force of circumstance', as we have seen.

In Livy's introductory sketch, Hannibal's qualities are presented as a mix. The positive elements begin the catalogue: they are duller than the negative and are little more than a string of clichés about the ideal commander, who shares the hardships of his troops, needs little sleep,

---

[78] With the bristling spears at Lyc. *Alex.* 252 compare Ennius, *Annals* 384 Sk. and frag. 6 of Ennius' *Scipio* (Goldberg and Manuwald 2018b: 293–4).

[79] See p. 80 for the theme in Livy. Gruen 2011: 115–40 (ch. 4, '*Punica fides*'), argued (124–5) that Polybius did not usually subscribe to or transmit the stereotype (but Pol. 3.78.3–4 calls Hannibal's wigs a Phoenician, i.e. Punic, stratagem, cf. Gruen 2011: 121 and Briscoe and Hornblower 2020: 144).

[80] Gruen 2011: 133. See Wittchow 2009: 153–77 for Livy on Hannibal's deceit and trickery.

[81] 21.4.9.

[82] On the difficult Ennius fragment 473 Sk. (Goldberg and Manuwald 2018a: 365), see Skutsch 1985: 633–4, but I confess to not fully understanding Skutsch here. It is anyway not straightforward evidence that Ennius treated Hannibal as perjurer. Cicero: see *On duties* 1.38, 'treaty-breakers', with Stocks 2014: 23. But Gruen 2011: 132–3 with n. 85 shows that Cicero was not consistent: later in *On duties* (1.108), *calliditas*, 'cleverness', is ascribed positively to both Hannibal and Fabius Maximus. In Virgil, Carthaginian Dido hurls the taunt *perfide*, 'perfidious', at Rome's founder Aeneas: *Aen.* 4.305; Gruen 2011: 135.

[83] Livy 21.1.5; cf. Pol. 3.30.4.

[84] Pol. 9.26.7 with *HCP* 2:155, citing Livy 27.1.14 (Herdonea). See p. 153.

doesn't wear special clothes, and so on (what about Hannibal's wigs?). One of the clichés – he was 'first in and last out of battle' – goes dead against the rest of the ancient tradition, which on the contrary praised Hannibal for precisely avoiding reckless exposure of this person, of the sort which cost Marcellus his life.[85]

More interesting positive qualities have to be excavated from the literary narratives. Hannibal's *humanity and piety* are implied by Livy (thus contradicting himself) rather than asserted. After three of his victories in Italy, Hannibal honoured the universal duty of piety towards the dead by seeking out – not always successfully – the bodies of the opposing commanders, Flaminius, Paullus, and Marcellus, so as to give them honourable burial. But after defeating Hannibal's brother Hasdrubal at the Metaurus in the north of Italy, the consul Nero threw his enemy's head before Hannibal's camp far away in the south. Livy does not draw the contrast explicitly, but more subtly does so by the little word *cura*, about the actions of both Hannibal and Nero, who preserved the head 'carefully' just as Hannibal searched 'carefully' for the bodies.[86] The first-century CE poet Lucan picked up this motif of the 'more-than-Roman non-Roman Hannibal' when he rebukes Caesar for leaving the dead unburied and not following Hannibal's example, the 'Carthaginian who buried his consular enemy' and thereby observed 'the customs of humanity'.[87]

The most enduring Hannibalic motif is, however, that of the *consummate commander*. This is a paradox because he was, after all, unconditionally defeated at the end of the war which we call by his name. But for Juvenal, he is without qualification the supreme general, *dux summus*.[88] He is there defeated only by mortality, like Alexander, and like the rest of us. There was no special need for Juvenal to use a non-Roman general on whom to hang these reflections on the futility of military success, except that the Alpine adventure and the elephants caught people's imaginations, in antiquity as now: even Lucretius could not resist. (Seneca expressed impatience with this attitude.)[89] It was a minor but real advantage that for

---

[85] On the duty of a commander to stay alive, see Chapter 16.2.
[86] For the decapitation motif in Greek and Latin history and literature, see p. 191.
[87] Lucan, *Civil war* 7.799–801, *non illum Poenus humator / consulis et Libyca succensae lampade Cannae / conpellunt, hominum ritus ut servet in hoste*, with Stocks 2014: 67–8 (Hannibal 'a better Roman').
[88] 10.147, the line which begins the part of the poem about his crossing of the Alps.
[89] Seneca: see n. 104. When Lucretius (5.1302–4) says – incorrectly – that it was the Carthaginians, the *Poeni*, who taught elephants to fight in battle, he has Hannibal in mind. He calls the beasts *anguimanus*, 'serpent-handed' (1303), meaning their trunks. Cf. Macaulay, *Prophecy of Capys* stanza 25 on Pyrrhus' invasion of Italy: 'The Greek shall come against thee / the conqueror of the East, / beside him stalks to battle / the huge earth-shaking beast, / the beast on whom the castle / with all its

most poets the name 'Hannibal' was dactylic (for convenience the three syllables were usually taken to be long, short, and short) and metrically handy in all its forms.[90] By contrast, poets always struggled with the name 'Scipio'.

Virgil does not name Hannibal, but a poet does not need crude denomination. Nobody has ever doubted that when Dido prays magnificently 'may you, some avenger, arise from my bones', *exoriare aliquis nostris ex ossibus ultor*, her mind's eye is looking forward to Hannibal.[91] The poet is also deliberately looking back to Aeschylus' Cassandra, who prophesied that 'my avenger will one day come', meaning Orestes the killer of Cassandra's own killer Clytemnestra.[92] Unlike Dido, Cassandra has prophetic powers, so she can use the confident future tense. But one important detail can easily be overlooked: Virgil, like Juvenal after him, must be thinking of the Hannibal of the first two victorious years of his invasion, when he defeated the Romans in four battles, each more catastrophic for them than the last. There is an alternative possibility – Virgil had not read Toynbee, but perhaps Dido is hinting vaguely and additionally that her revenge, executed by Hannibal, did not stop with Cannae in 216 or even with his death in 183: Rome continued to suffer from his invasion and depredations.

By contrast, Horace more realistically concentrates on the defeat of Hannibal, rather than on his early successes, while acknowledging the magnitude of the threat he had posed.[93] And the non-Virgilian genres he preferred mean that he is happy to name Hannibal, as in the 'Metaurus Ode' in book 4. In the preceding book of *Odes*, 'Pyrrhus, mighty Antiochus and dread Hannibal', are the three great adversaries overthrown by older and tougher generations of Romans.[94] 'With Hannibal ... the chronological order is disregarded to provide a proper rhetorical climax.'[95] The threat posed by Hannibal features again in the *Odes* as

---

guards doth stand, / the beast who hath between his eyes /*the serpent for a hand*.' Cf. Scullard 1974a: 102.

[90] But for a minority literary tradition which made the third syllable long, see Goldberg and Manuwald 2018b: 290–3, Ennius, *Scipio* frag. 4, from Aulus Gellius 4.7.1–5; *FLP*: 28, Q. Ennius frag 32. The name Hannibal, like Hasdrubal, is 'theophoric', from Baal, a long syllable. This is presumably why Courtney (commentary in *FLP*) thinks the long third syllable of Hannibal is 'probably the original quantity'.

[91] *Aeneid* 4.625, cf. p. 76. See Brizzi 2011a: 73. As if there was any doubt, Virgil gives Sychaeus' nurse the name Barce (*Aeneid* 4.632), a clear allusion to the Barcid Hannibal: cf. p. 76.

[92] *Agamemnon* 1280; Fraenkel 1950: 3. 596; Hornblower 2018: 120.

[93] For Horace's Hannibal, see Stocks 2014: 27–9.    [94] 3.6.35–6, *Hannibalemque dirum*.

[95] Nisbet and Rudd 2004: 110. On the epithet *dirum*, they remark that it was Hannibal's conventional epithet, citing Quintilian 8.2.9 and Juvenal 7.161.

part of Horace's argument that it was not Scipio's achievements or their inscribed commemoration which made him famous but the 'Calabrian Muses' – that is, Ennius. The relevant lines are however textually problematic, so much so that some scholars have actually deleted large chunks of the poem, including precisely the references to Hannibal.[96]

Those authors who attached anecdotes to Hannibal, when in truth any great general would have done for the purpose in mind, were mostly paying tribute to the Hannibal of Livy book 22, the narrative of Trasimene and Cannae, when his smashing victories brought Rome close to panic.[97] Thus Lucretius in the first century BCE took Hannibal's invasion as the paradigmatic national terror.[98] Cicero's story of Hannibal's encounter with the independently attested Phormio the philosopher at Ephesus may be historical; but some other such tales are roving anecdotes, in which Hannibal effectively denotes a very successful/famous general.[99] The story of Hannibal's comment to Prusias about divination was also told about another of Hannibal's royal hosts, Antiochus; Cicero was one of the authors who picked it up and ran with it. Cicero was noticeably prone to use Hannibal as an example, an *exemplum*.[100] It was perhaps Cicero who turned the cry 'Hannibal at the gates!' *Hannibal ad portas* into something like a proverb for a dire emergency. He paid the archetypical enemy Hannibal striking compliments in one of his defence speeches: after enumerating the positives (intelligence, courage, achievements, *consilium uirtus res gestae*), he concludes 'his own citizens threw him out, but one can see how our enemy is celebrated in our historical literature and our memories'.[101] Perhaps as a young man in his twenties, Cicero himself remembered how the Samnite leader Pontius Telesinus in 82 BCE caused a brief panic before he was defeated at the Colline gate by Sulla. The danger is said to have called Hannibal to people's minds.[102] A few years later,

---

[96] 4.8.16, *Hannibalis minae*. See p. 237 n. 90, cf. 339 n. 14 for the textual problems.

[97] In the first two lines of Marlowe's *Doctor Faustus*, Trasimene, 'where Mars did mate the Carthaginians', is made to stand for warfare, which will *not* be the play's subject.

[98] 3.832–7, a celebrated argument against fear of death: just as we who are now living did not care 'when the Carthaginians came at us from all sides to the clash of battle', *ad confligendum uenientibus undique Poenis*, so we should not worry about what will happen when we are dead. The words do not suit the first or third Punic wars.

[99] See Appendix 1.3. Sometimes Scipio may be used in the same way: see n. 123 for Cicero's story of his alleged refusal of a statue at Corinth.

[100] Divination: p. 227 n. 34. See Stocks 2014: 22–4. For Cicero's use of *exempla*, see Van der Blom 2010.

[101] *In defence of Sestius* 142 with Stocks 2014: 24 on Rome's 'love-hate' relationship with him. See also Syme 1958: 526 on Silius' paradoxically expressed admiration for Hannibal's 'wicked courage and energy' (*improba uirtus*, 1.58).

[102] Velleius Paterculus 2.27.1 (comparison with Hannibal only) and Florus 2.9.22 ('more terrible than Pyrrhus and Hannibal', *atrocius Pyrrho et Hannibale*).

Sertorius, that other 'one-eyed man against Rome', also evoked thoughts of Hannibal.[103] Only Cleopatra played this role better in Roman literature – and life.

The admiringly obsessive attitude towards Hannibal lasted a very long time. Nepos and Valerius Maximus exhibited it. Seneca the younger criticized it.[104] Vegetius and Symmachus in the late fourth century CE still regarded Hannibal as the archetypical enemy of Rome and found different ways to explain his eventual failure.[105] Nor was the obsession purely literary: no fewer than three statues of Hannibal at Rome were known to the elder Pliny in the first century CE. By contrast, the extravagantly decorated monumental arch, *fornix*, erected by Scipio in 190 BCE on the way up to the Capitol, is known only from a sentence in Livy.[106]

To trace Hannibal's reputation after antiquity lies beyond the scope of this book. One detail is irresistible, at a time when ancient onomastic studies are at their highest ever level thanks to the near completion of the *Lexicon of Greek Personal Names*: the name Hannibal. The continuing onomastic popularity in Italy of Rome's greatest enemy, hounded into exile and forced to take his own life by poison, is a little mysterious. The Italian (Bolognese) parents of the best known Annibale, the Renaissance painter Carracci (1560–1609), probably named their son not immediately after the victor of Cannae, but after two somewhat earlier rulers of Bologna called Annibale Bentivoglio I and II. But that merely pushes the question back a few generations. There was even a not very Hannibalic pope whose birth name was Annibale: he was Leo XII (pope from 1823 to 1829).

---

[103] Konrad 1994: 31–3 (cf. 109) on Plut. *Sert.* 1.8: comparison with Sertorius, for which see also App. *Civil wars* 1.112/522 (Sertorius as Hannibal reincarnated).

[104] Seneca: in the preface to book 3 (§6) of the *Natural questions*, complaining that historians wrote about how Hannibal crossed the Alps and unexpectedly brought war to Italy after the inflicting defeats in Iberia, then how he went into exile. See Stocks 2014: 32–3.

[105] See pp. 348, 351. And Ammianus compared Rome's defeat at Adrianople (378) to Cannae: 31.13.19. We saw (p. 378) that in the early fourth century, a nephew of the emperor Constantine bore the interesting name Hannibalianus; a little earlier, another Hannibalianus was one of Diocletian's praetorian prefects: *ILS* 8929; Jones 1964: 50; a third (Afranius H.) was cos. 292 CE. See *PLRE* 1: 407–8, Hannibalianus nos. 1–3. These men, clustered around 300 CE, are indirect evidence for Romans who were actually called Hannibal (see next paragraph for the name Hannibal after antiquity). In Rome of the Classical period, the ending –ianus would have indicated a biological as opposed to adoptive father Hannibal (cf. p. 46) but that is not true at this late date, as Benet Salway kindly confirms to me, explaining that names in –ianus might now celebrate both paternal and maternal descent. He further suggests that 'Marcus Afranius Hannibal' (rather than 'Hannibalianus') could be restored at the damaged *AE* 2011, 990 (Pannonian dedication, mid-second century CE), and that this man might therefore be a father or grandfather of the Afranius cited above. For the survival of the name Hannibal in purely Punic contexts (Augustan north Africa), Birley 1988: 28.

[106] See p. 329, citing Livy 37.3.7 and Hölkeskamp 2018: 437–8.

Obviously, the derivation from pagan Baal was by then forgotten.[107] And the name is still in use in Italy. But we should not dig too deep. The many parents who nowadays call their daughters Jocasta and Cassandra are not deterred by dark thoughts of the violent ends suffered by their mythical originals: they are probably just attracted by the sound of the names.[108]

## 19.6 Scipio's Legacy

Scipio Africanus had an afterlife of the most literal and sensational sort. One day in 149 BCE, in the consulship of Manius Manilius (and Lucius Marcius Censorinus), his young adoptive grandson Aemilianus, then serving as military tribune, visited King Masinissa, now an old man and near to death.[109] The very full report that has come down to us is spoken by the younger Scipio in the first person singular. The king was delighted to entertain another and junior Publius Cornelius Scipio: by the mere mention of that name, said Masinissa, he 'felt refreshed', *recreor*. Africanus was 'the best of men, never defeated', *illius optimi atque inuictissimi uiri*. By the evening, they had had quite a few drinks and got to talking about the great Scipio. When they finally parted to go to bed, young Scipio fell into a more than usually deep sleep. Not surprisingly after such a day, and such a conversation, he had a dream in which the ghost of his grandfather Africanus appeared to him and delivered a long speech. The young man was careful to explain afterwards that he recognized him from his sculpted or painted likeness, *ex imagine*, rather than from life. (When the military tribune Marcius told his troops in a dark hour that he had seen Scipio's very recently killed father and uncle in a dream, he did not need to explain how he recognized them.)[110]

The illustrious family ghost turned out to have the gift of prophecy. He predicted correctly that his young relative would destroy Carthage and win a triumph for this. (We might want to comment that whereas Hannibal supposedly experienced a prophetic and epiphanic dream in which he received from a supernatural visitor a prophecy about the devastation of Italy, Scipio went one better and himself posthumously delivered a similar

---

[107] See Kelly 1986: 304–6 for Annibale Sermattei della Genga: 'a simple devout man, morally strong but lacking the flair of leadership ... when he died he was profoundly unpopular'.
[108] The most famous modern bearer is fictional, Hannibal Lecter in Thomas Harris' *The silence of the lambs* and in the film based on it. The reason for the choice of name is said not to be known for sure, but presumably the rhyme with 'cannibal' is behind it. See p. 372 n. 20 for the wretchedly bad Italian film about the real, i.e. ancient, Hannibal, and for another Italian film, about Scipio.
[109] This consular date is factually correct, see *MRR* 1: 459.
[110] See Livy 25.38.5–6 with p. 117 for Marcius' dream.

prophecy, but about Carthage.) Aemilianus would then receive in his own right the additional *cognomen* Africanus, which at present he held by inheritance. 'But later', warns the ghost, 'you will find the state, the *res publica*, disturbed by the plans of my (other) grandson' (a reference to Tiberius Gracchus, son of Cornelia and of the older Gracchus, whom we have met for his role in the trials of the Scipios). At this point, the ghost appears to go off the narrative rails by prophesying 'but you will, as *dictator*, re-establish the *res publica*'. Now Aemilianus was never *dictator*.[111] So this looks at first sight like 'misdirection' of a sort familiar from Greek tragedy, such as Hermes' not-quite-accurate summarizing speech at the start of Euripides' *Ion*. But no, like a good oracle, the ghost cunningly saves himself from error by adding a proviso: 'if only you escape the impious hands of your kinsmen'. This alludes to the rumours that Aemilianus' sudden and unexplained death in 129 was the work of Gaius Gracchus and family. But the mystery death was a fact.

'But, Africanus,' says Africanus, confusingly addressing his grandson by his own *cognomen*, 'you should know that those who have preserved, helped, or enlarged their fatherland have a special place reserved for them in heaven.' The young man is frightened more by the thought of plots by his relatives than of death itself and asks whether the older Scipio and his own biological father Aemilius Paullus, and others thought of as totally extinguished, are really still alive. 'Yes indeed,' says the ghost, and to prove the point Paullus also magically appears, so that father and son can embrace. The son now enthusiastically wishes to join the blessed dead, but Paullus explains that he must wait until divinely freed from the prison of the body. Duty is the way to the stars. Young Scipio now has a vision of the stars, upon which the ghost of the older Scipio picks up the thread of explanation and continues speaking for the rest of the dream. At this point, we must leave his lecture, which expounds at length the secrets and sounds of the celestial bodies and selective human immortality. At last, the young man awakes and remembers every word.

Probably nobody would have been more surprised than that practically minded soldier the senior Scipio to have been informed that in the afterlife he would himself become a seer, possessed not only of conventional powers of prophecy but of the still more vatic ability to comprehend and divulge the nature of the cosmos.[112] 'What,' it may be objected, 'of Scipio the

---

[111] Weinstock 1971: 219 with n. 9 wrote of the 'planned dictatorship of the younger Scipio'.
[112] I reject the fanciful modern theory that Livy sought to present Scipio as a kind of 'oracle in his own right'. See p. 231.

nocturnal communer with Jupiter on the Capitol?' But that mystic is part of the Scipionic legend, itself largely a fiction, and indeed it may help to explain how the real Scipio could be cast in a vatic role.[113]

'Cast' is the right word. For the entire *Dream* narrative is a fantastic first-century BCE fiction. It is the supremely creative work of Cicero, who was emulating the 'Myth of Er' which closed Plato's *Republic*. The sixth and final book of Cicero's own treatise *On the republic* included the *Dream of Scipio*, the *Somnium Scipionis*. This sixth book as a whole would be known to us only from fragments, were it not that by good luck Macrobius in the fifth century CE wrote a commentary on the *Somnium*, and this enables the reconstruction of the original *Dream*.[114] The *Dream* was and always has been famous and an object of fascination. Petrarch (1304–74) in his Latin epic the *Africa*, a panegyric of Scipio, drew not only on the third Decade of Livy but on the *Dream*.[115] The *Dream* itself was set to music in one act by the Freemason Mozart, with a libretto by Metastasio after Cicero.[116]

The philosophy and cosmology of the *Dream* are not our concern. But the *Dream* does usefully touch on themes which are helpful for the understanding of Scipio's legacy and which we will use as organizing devices. The first two are: Scipio as *the undefeated general*, and Scipio as *the best of men* (this will allow us glance again at the long-lived motif of the '(sexual) Continence of Scipio'). Both these tributes are expressed by Masinissa – or rather 'Masinissa'; but that eloquent Ciceronian construct was right to confess by implication that he owed much to the older Scipio, who had in historical fact recognized him as king and ally. This ensured that Masinissa, by the crucial role of his cavalry at Zama, would have the post-war standing to be awarded in effect a free hand to make trouble for Carthage long after 202. It would be no wonder if he really did have fond memories of his benefactor and friend.

From the ghost's speech, we can extract three more themes: the third is the positive importance of the *shared cognomen*, that is, *Africanus*. The

---

[113] There is no telling how far the legend was self-promotion. See p. 242. The most we can say for sure is that Scipio claimed Neptune's/Poseidon's help at New Carthage and made libations to Jupiter and Neptune in 204.

[114] The *Dream* is included in modern texts of Cicero's *de re publica* (for the Latin, with English tr. see Keyes 1928: 260–83, Loeb edition), and in some texts of Macrobius (e.g. Willis 1970: 155–63, Teubner ed., Latin only, no tr.).

[115] See Bernardo 1962; Scullard 1970: 242–3; Pfeiffer 1976: 6–8 (esp. 6–7 for the role of Ennius in the poem); extract from the *Africa* in Perosa and Sparrow 1979: 4–6, lines 693–773, the death of Sophoni(s)ba (English footnotes but no tr.).

[116] Dent 1947: 24: his future and hated employer Archbishop Colloredo of Salzburg was enthroned to 'the formal and uninspired strains of Mozart's *Il Sogno di Scipione*'.

fourth is the idea that the older Scipio enjoys a *special place in heaven*, that is *cult* in a loose sense of the word (cue the 'Scipionic legend' once more, this time very briefly). But a fifth and negative theme also emerges: *hostility to the Gracchi*, the older Scipio's grandsons. The *Dream* craftily imputes this hostility not to selfish senatorial enemies of reform, but to the morally flawless ghost.

We need not take these themes in the above order. Then we can close by exploring one or two legacies absent from the *Dream*.

Hannibal's line (for which see Family Tree 1) ended with him, as far as we know.[117] Nor are any children of his two brothers recorded. But the Cornelii Scipiones were proudly prominent both before and (especially if Africanus' adoptive grandson is included) after the Scipio who is half of the subject of this book, and his *name or names* were a key element of his legacy.[118] The Roman system of nomenclature for adopted children meant that the identity of the child became virtually merged in that of the adopter. The man we call, for convenience, 'Octavian' and then 'Augustus' was usually simply 'Caesar' to his contemporaries, strongly evoking the assassinated but deified dictator who had adopted the young man in his will, so that he soon became *diui filius*, son of a god. In Cicero's *Dream*, Masinissa, and Scipio's ghost, were right to stress the value of the names Publius Cornelius Scipio to the young Aemilianus, born an Aemilius; and after the final fall of Carthage, the additional *cognomen* Africanus strengthened the connection further. Long after the sudden death of Aemilianus in 129, the family ensured that the great Scipio's memory was kept green: the surviving inscribed *elogium* of him is Augustan in date.[119]

One extreme form of commemoration is *cult*. We must now return to the question of Scipio's posthumous cult.[120] His ghost in the *Dream* makes a clear if implicit claim to his own celestial status when he says that those who 'preserved, helped, or enlarged their fatherland have a special place reserved for them in heaven'. Weinstock, half a century ago, pronounced the evidence for Scipio's cult to be 'good'.[121] He ought to have

---

[117] The tradition in Silius that he had a son by his Iberian wife, supposedly called Imilce, is to be rejected. The wife, but not her name, is historical. See p. 43.
[118] For Scipio Africanus' own children, see 58. Cornelia II stands out, rather than her brothers Publius and Lucius.
[119] For Caesar's use of a Scipio called Salvito or Salvitto to nullify an oracle about Scipionic invincibility in Africa, see p. 225. The emperor Gordian I as a Scipionic 'Africanus': *Hist. Aug.* 20.9.4–6.
[120] For attitudes at Rome to cult at Rome and deification, see Cole 2013, esp. 97–102 for Africanus and the *Dream*.
[121] Weinstock 1971: 294 and n. 11, also 356: 'no doubt'. At 177, he admits that Scipio surprisingly did not enjoy the title of '(new) founder', although a saviour of Rome.

## Scipio's Legacy

acknowledged that it is much less good than that for Scipio's contemporary Titus Quinctius Flamininus, who, as Greek inscriptions attest, received cultic honours in his lifetime as opposed to merely posthumously, a vital distinction in this area.[122] Admittedly, Weinstock at that point in his book had his eye on Roman evidence, which for Scipio's period does not have the explicit character of the inscriptions for Flamininus. It is not impossible that at some future date, Greek inscriptions from Asia Minor awarding cultic honours to Publius (and Lucius?) Scipio after 190 may turn up, but that has not happened yet.[123]

Weinstock, who cited Cicero's *Dream* elsewhere, does not adduce the *Dream*, which is after all a lengthy fragment of Cicero's *On the republic*, in connection with Scipio's 'apotheosis' (as he calls it in his index of names and subjects). He does, however, cite a passage from Lactantius – preserved as another but much shorter fragment of Cicero's *On the republic* – along with the two-line epigram of Ennius in which Scipio says, 'to me alone the greatest gate of heaven is open'.[124]

Cornelia (II), Scipio's daughter and mother of the Gracchi, is alleged to have written in a letter that she expected that after her death she would be 'invoked as a parent god', *ubi mortua ero, parentabis mihi et inuocabis deum parentem*.[125] For Weinstock, this showed that 'the private cult [of Scipio] certainly survived in the family', but puzzling though the Latin words are, they prove nothing about an actual cult of Scipio, rather than at most constituting some sort of claim by herself to an extraordinarily distinguished status. As Scullard says, the letter, whose authenticity is very doubtful, is 'best left out of discussion'.[126]

All this is very well if we are happy to equate 'cult' in a general sort of way with apotheosis, or merely with the sentiment – perhaps only the literary trope – that a man or woman's earthly achievements made that person

---

[122] See, for hero cult, Jones 2010. A particularly interesting but difficult case is that of the fifth-century BCE Athenian Hagnon. The chief disputed text is Thucydides 5.11.1.

[123] Weinstock 1971: 249 n. 7 cited the Delian inscription *Syll.*³ 617, which honoured Scipio for his virtue and piety. But that is far short of cult. Cicero (*On the orator* 2.262, collecting bold uses of words) tells a story that *Scipio maior* was promised a statue by the Corinthians in a place where there were statues of other *imperatores* but said he disliked squadrons, *turmales*, 'crowds'. Scullard 1970: 287 dated this to 190–189.

[124] See p. 237.

[125] The letter is included in H. Peter, *HRR* 2: 38–40, as frag. 15 of Cornelius Nepos' *On illustrious men* (the relevant words are at p. 39 lines 20–3), but not in *FRHist* no. 45, which deliberately excludes frags. of that work, as Briscoe and Drummond explain at 1: 396.

[126] Weinstock 1971: 295 and n. 1. But see Scullard 1970: 247 n. 11; also Walbank 1985 (originally 1967): 122–3 (a 'red herring').

somehow more than human.¹²⁷ If, however, we look for such hard diagnostic cultic features as a priesthood of Scipio, we will be disappointed. Contrast, for example, the Greek (Eretrian) inscription honouring Flamininus with a holiday, sacrifices, and the wearing of wreaths.¹²⁸ As late as Tiberius' reign (14–37 CE), a long, inscribed decree about the imperial cult from Gytheum, harbour town of Sparta, listed six days of a festival which, the decree ordains, should be celebrated in honour of six named individuals, of whom the first five are members of the imperial family starting with Augustus, but the sixth, by an astonishing survival, is Flamininus.¹²⁹ Even later, Plutarch said that 'in our own time' (about 100 CE) there was a priest of Flamininus at Euboean Chalcis, and sacrifices and a hymn of praise (a 'paean', which Plutarch quotes).¹³⁰ As legacies and afterlives go, this far outdoes his contemporary and rival Scipio Africanus, who was not on present evidence inserted into the richly documented Hellenistic cult of mortals in anything like this explicit and long-lasting way.

Scipio the *undefeated general* (the counterpart of Hannibal the consummate commander) is less historically problematic than Scipio the recipient of cult, and much of the present book attests to the ancient literary tradition to this effect, starting with Ennius and Polybius.¹³¹ (Ennius was supposedly buried in the tomb of the Scipios; or more probably it was only a bust of him that was placed there.) Ennius' epigram for Scipio ran 'here he lies, to whom nobody, neither citizen nor foreigner, was able to render recompense for his efforts in proportion to his deeds, *pro factis*'.¹³² 'Deeds' surely refers to military achievements above all, as does *res gestae* ('achievements', literally 'things done') in a fragment of Ennius' mostly lost work the *Scipio*.¹³³

---

¹²⁷ See p. 238 (Euhemerus). Probable examples of trope: Cicero, *On friendship* (also known as the *Laelius*) 14, and Seneca's sententious remark at the start of Letter 86 about Scipio's spirit returning to heaven. Quasi-divine status could be hinted at even for the uncharismatic Fabius Maximus the Delayer: on Livy's extravagances of language at 22.29–30, see Briscoe and Hornblower 2020: 41, 239–40, 242; cf. Weinstock 1971: 149–50, 295 n. 4, and Hardie 2015б: 261.
¹²⁸ Sherk 1984: no. 6D, Eretria on the island of Euboea.
¹²⁹ *SEG* 11.923 lines 7–12. Price 1984: 106 summarized this incorrectly, overlooking Flamininus ('six days with each day designated in honour of a different member of the imperial house').
¹³⁰ Plut. *Flam.* 16.4, ἔτι δὲ καὶ καθ'ἡμᾶς.
¹³¹ Some lines of Naevius concern a youthful indiscretion by one 'whose achievements were great and many, and who has unique pre-eminence in the world'. Aulus Gellius took this to be the great Scipio, but there are problems. See p. 56.
¹³² For Ennius on Scipio, see Henderson 2004: 101–3.
¹³³ The fragments of this are collected by Goldberg and Manuwald 2018b: 286–95. For Ennius on Scipio's *res gestae*, see 294–5, frag. 7, from the *Historia Augusta*, a late and problematic prose work.

## Scipio's Legacy

In Cicero's writings other than the *Dream*, the elder Africanus is mentioned several times in the dialogue *On old age* (or *Cato the elder*), which imagines a Platonic conversation between Scipio Aemilianus, Laelius, and Cato the Elder or Censor.[134] After some genuine introductory dialogue, Cato, in good Socratic fashion, monopolizes the rest. 'Cato' is made to comment on the authority, *auctoritas*, of Scipio the elder (and of Paullus and Fabius Maximus the Delayer).[135] Obviously, Scipio's military pre-eminence is the main reason for his exceptional standing: Scipio the politician came nowhere near, and in several ways was even something of a failure. The third book of Cicero's *On duties* opens with a quotation transmitted via the real Cato: Scipio, according to Cato, used to say that he was never less at leisure than when he was at leisure, and never less alone than when alone.[136] Cicero then develops this theme with only a passing allusion (§2) to Scipio's glorious services to the state, *rei publicae pulcherrima munera*. Elsewhere in the treatise, it is rather Scipio's father and uncle who are the archetypical brave men, the *fortes uiri*.[137] Surprisingly, the older Scipio Africanus is never once mentioned in all Cicero's voluminous correspondence; he features anecdotally from time to time in his other works.

Scipio was undefeated in Iberia, but he did let Hannibal's brother Hasdrubal give him the slip after Baecula, as Livy makes Fabius point out. Nor did Scipio himself leave Iberia behind as anything like a fully conquered and pacified territory. One joint legacy of both Hannibal and Scipio (and of their fathers) was the decades-long, exhausting, and in manpower terms expensive Roman reduction of the Iberian peninsula.

On the other hand, Scipio's most enduring military legacy was arguably the infantry reforms he effected in Iberia, which made the Roman army more flexible than in the dark days of 218 and 217. This – together with Masinissa's cavalry – explains how at Zama he was able to defeat Hannibal, himself undefeated on land until then, except in the occasional minor skirmish.[138] The fictional Masinissa of the *Dream* could hardly be expected

---

[134] See Douglas 1966: 66 for Cicero's use of the *cognomen Africanus* on its own (he usually but not quite always means Aemilianus).
[135] §61. See p. 258, discussing Scipio' status in 199 and after.
[136] 3.1–2 cf. p. 259. Pliny, *NH* preface §30 said Cato claimed to have learned soldiering from both Scipio and Hannibal; cf. Milner 1996: 99 n. 5. This is not inconsistent with personal dislike of Scipio.
[137] 3.16, where they are linked with the Decii family who sacrificed themselves for Rome in 340 and 295 BCE, and see 1.61 where Scipio's father and uncle are part of another and longer list of men notable for their greatness of spirit, *animi magnitudo*.
[138] At sea (not his métier) he was defeated by the navally expert Rhodians in a sea battle near Side in 190 (p. 325). On land, Hannibal was defeated by Marcellus at Nola in 215 (p. 141), and the consul Nero

to mention this prosaic organizational aspect, which has to be reconstructed from the prose historians. Scipio's military changes were not remembered in the same personal way[139] as those of Marius a century later, whose soldiers were called 'Marius' mules' because they had to carry their own equipment.[140]

Virgil called the Scipiadae 'twins, two thunderbolts of war' *geminos, duo fulmina belli*. This may be deliberately polysemic; not only the uncle and father of Scipio Africanus, but also Africanus and his adoptive grandson Scipio Aemilianus.[141] The celebration of Scipio as mighty conqueror naturally did not end with Cicero, Livy, and Virgil: Scipio makes an appearance, daringly scanned as a dactyl and with a laudatory epithet, in an unexpected corner of Ovid's poetry, the *Art of love*: Ennius deserved to be buried next to you, great Scipio, *Scipio magne*.[142] Seneca's letter 86 opens with a conventional military tribute; he weakly contrasts Scipio to the 'crazy', *furiosus*, Persian king Cambyses.[143] Silius Italicus placed the real Roman Scipio alongside a literary construct, the 'Roman Hannibal'. Lucian in the *Dialogues of the dead* made Hannibal say he is not son of Ammon and is implausibly made to claim to be an untutored barbarian.[144]

Where Scipio attracted special admiration was for his avoidance of the kingly title, when his victories on the battlefield meant it might have been his for the asking. That happened in the aftermath of the battle of Baecula *in Iberia*. That possibility was hardly valid *at Rome* in the years around 200 but was highly topical in the time of Caesar. Scipio, like Wellington, was remembered as a respecter of the constitutional status quo and certainly not as a surprise left-wing reformer like Hannibal.

In that respect Scipio was, so conservative senatorial commentators insisted, the *polar opposite of the Gracchi*, his turbulent grandsons the tribunes Tiberius and Gracchus; and this is another of the themes of the Ciceronian *Dream*. In *On duties*, Cicero says that agrarian strife destroyed the Gracchi, sons of that excellent man Tiberius Gracchus, grandsons of Africanus. Father and grandfather are not here mentioned helpfully for purposes of identification, but to suggest a lamentable decline from

---

scored a success against him at Grumentum in 207 before the Metaurus battle (p. 187). That was not important in itself, but the prelude to the Metaurus campaign did see Hannibal badly outwitted for once (pp. 182, 188). Finally, he suffered a reverse in Bruttium in 204 (p. 214).

[139] It has been suggested that Scipio in Iberia invented a new kind of sword, but this is not certain: pp. 122 n. 56 and 350 n. 66.
[140] See p. 353 n. 80.   [141] See pp. 49–50 on *Aeneid* 6.843 and Lucretius 3.1034.
[142] *Art of love* 3.409–10.   [143] Seneca the Elder mentioned Scipio in the *Controversies*: p. 54.
[144] Lucian: see p. 4.

admirable ancestry.¹⁴⁵ The contrast between the tribunes and their father the older Tiberius Gracchus is drawn elsewhere also.¹⁴⁶

The theme of the *moral excellence* of Scipio is conveyed in the *Dream* by 'Masinissa' with his one word *optimus*.¹⁴⁷ Scipio's treatment of the beautiful Sophoniba shortly before Zama was found admirable in antiquity and beyond for its sexual restraint, although it may well seem repellent to modern taste (she was forced to suicide when no longer useful). But it was his chivalrous behaviour after the capture of New Carthage in 210 which chiefly fired the imagination of later writers and artists; but there was an uncomfortable alternative tradition in Polybius: Scipio the 'womanizer'.¹⁴⁸ The nobler tradition may be part of the picture of Scipio as a Roman Alexander, as depicted in Veronese's huge and sumptuous painting of Alexander, Hephaistion, and the women of Darius, now in the National Gallery in London. Handel turned Scipio's 'continence' into an opera *Scipione*, based (very) loosely on the New Carthage episode; but Scipio was not lucky as an operatic subject, because the *Oxford concise dictionary of opera* calls *Scipione* 'comparatively dull'.¹⁴⁹ Paintings of a *Continence of Scipio* are extraordinarily numerous: Bellini, van Dyck (now at Christ Church, Oxford), Poussin, Giulio Romano, Tiepolo, Reynolds, to name only the most famous.

Scipio has not come down to posterity as specially cruel: here is an obvious contrast with Hannibal. On the contrary, Polybius said he was agreed to be benevolent and magnanimous.¹⁵⁰ But savage actions are recorded of him in Iberia. One of his final acts in Iberia (206) was to order the massacre at Ilourgeia after its defection.¹⁵¹ The punishment of the mutineers soon afterwards appears (and was) ruthless but was in line with Roman military practice.¹⁵² An earlier episode (209) raises an important moral question. He gave the order to kill the population of New Carthage and spare nobody – not even the animals – although this too was said by Polybius to be the Roman custom. It is also relevant that this slaughter took place after the capture of the city but before the final surrender, after which the prisoners, including some enslaved people, were treated well, so

---

¹⁴⁵ This is part of a pervasive rhetoric of decline in the Republican period, a topic which cannot be gone into here.
¹⁴⁶ 2.80 and 2.43.
¹⁴⁷ Marks 2005 (esp. 270) argues that Scipio was portrayed by Silius as a model of a good king in every respect including virtue and is therefore being held out as an example for Domitian.
¹⁴⁸ Livy 29.49–50.   ¹⁴⁹ Rosenthal and Warrack 1979: 218 col. 2. For Mozart, see n. 116.
¹⁵⁰ Pol. 10.3.1, εὐεργετικὸς καὶ μεγαλόψυχος.   ¹⁵¹ Livy 28.19.6–8; p. 128.   ¹⁵² See pp. 128, 338.

that they allegedly felt goodwill.¹⁵³ The distinction between capture and surrender is important and was usually observed in Roman warfare.¹⁵⁴ But if Carthage had won the war, and a Carthaginian historian had written it up, Scipio's reputation would not have looked so gentlemanly.¹⁵⁵

Not featured in the *Dream* are Scipio's legacies in the literal sense of *financial bequests*. We are surprisingly well informed about this topic. Although Seneca in letter 86 claimed to detect evidence of old-style frugality at Scipio's Liternum villa, he was setting up a routine moralizing contrast with deplorable modern luxury. Polybius explained that the elder Scipio had promised dowries of fifty talents (300,000 *denarii*) to each of his two daughters; his wife Aemilia, who had money of her own, paid half of this on their marriage, and Aemilianus paid the rest before it was strictly due.¹⁵⁶ Tenney Frank reckoned that Scipio may have been worth as much as a million *denarii*.¹⁵⁷ Whatever the exact truth of that calculation, he was clearly a very wealthy man. Hannibal left nothing. Nepos said that his property was confiscated and his town house ritually demolished.¹⁵⁸ His seaside castle no doubt came under the heading 'property'.

We ended the Hannibal half of this chapter with his Renaissance and later onomastic afterlife, so let us jump ahead in time and do the same for Scipio – always remembering that the ancient name did not belong to one man but to a whole large and long-lived branch of the *gens Cornelia*. There are, for example, the prolific Venetian author Francesco Scipione Maffei

---

[153] Pol. 10.15.4–6 and 10.17.6–15; see p. 121. The fate of captured cities was an old literary motif (Paul 1982) but was much more than that for Pol., who in 146 had seen Carthage go down in flames. He certainly thought hard about the topic, cf. the moralizing 9.10, prompted by the fall of Syracuse to the Romans; but his reflections are all about property not persons. Nicholson 2023: 204 n. 108, in a study of Polybius on Philip V, says that Scipio's moral 'excellence' contrasts with the examples of 'negative' Roman behaviour she has just listed; but Scipio's orders after the taking of New Carthage but before the surrender are one of her negative examples. Enslaved people: this is the meaning of χειροτέχναι, 'skilled manual labourers', at 10.17.15, cf. §9 with *Polybios-Lexikon* 3.2: col. 1037 (cf. p. 121): here, they are said to hope to be freed. See *HCP* 2: 216 on 10.16.1, and cf. the much-discussed Th. 7.27.5, with *CT* 3: 591–2.

[154] See *CHGRW*: 397 (Roth), citing Sallust, *Jugurthine war* 91.7, where this is called a 'law of war', *ius belli*: Marius at African Capsa had the adult citizens killed despite surrender at §5.

[155] 'Portrait of a Roman gentleman, from Livy' was the title of Conway 1922, article on Livy's Scipio by one of the editors of the original OCT texts of the third Decade.

[156] Pol. 31.27, a long, legally complicated, anecdotal chapter. See *HCP* 3: 505–9, esp. 506–7.

[157] Frank 1933: 209; Scullard 1970: 291. For the value of the *denarius*, see n. 52. In addition to his Liternum villa (p. 392), he owned a town house, on the site of which in 169 his son-in-law Gracchus built the *basilica Sempronia*: Livy 44.16.10; *MRR* 1: 424; Rüpke 2007a: 27 and 260 n. 51. Briscoe 2012: 517 notes that this is the 'only evidence for the location of the house of Scipio'. It was superseded by the *basilica Iulia*. Gracchus' construction does not imply any sort of cult of Scipio: a Roman basilica was a large secular building, a kind of covered hall, see *OCD*⁴. The sense 'church' is a later, Christian development.

[158] Nep. *Hann.* 7.7. See p. 301.

(1675–1755) or, even more illustrious, Cardinal Scipione Borghese of Galleria Borghese fame (1577–1633). There were other cardinals with the name. But no actual pope was born a Scipione, so Hannibal is one up there. The vogue for such old Roman names is much easier to explain than is the popularity of Annibale. Like the names of Julius Caesar (Julio Cesare) Scaliger, father of the even more distinguished Joseph Justus Scaliger, they evoked, sometimes with absurd pretensions, Rome's ancient greatness.[159] Some Italian families of the Renaissance actually deluded themselves that they were the descendants of the great ancient Roman *gentes*: the powerful Colonna family, which produced one pope, Martin V in the fifteenth century, supposedly traced itself fraudulently back to the Julio-Claudians.[160]

But although there is a sense in which a person's life can be prolonged by a name (so adopted Romans retained their original family name as an added *cognomen*), and naming a child 'after' someone can indicate parental admiration or affection, motives for name-choice may be as trivial as mere desire for euphony. The real pathway to immortality is through biography. Horace said it best:

> many brave men were alive before Agamemnon; but they are all crushed by long night, unwept and unknown, because they lack a sacred bard.[161]

From this point of view, the modern afterlives of Hannibal and Scipio have been very different. Hannibal has never lacked 'sacred bards' in the shape of prose biographers. In my References, which are naturally selective, there are no fewer than nine biographies of Hannibal published in the past hundred years.[162] There is only one of Scipio worth the mention, that of Scullard in 1970, which was an excellent fusion of two much earlier books, one on Scipio as commander in the second Punic war, the other on Roman politics from 220 to 150 BCE.[163] There was a crop of Scipio books in various

---

[159] But the elder Scaliger's pretensions took the different form of a specious claim to be a member of the aristocratic Della Scala family. See Grafton 1983: 102.

[160] Gibbon ch. 69 n. 118 Bury, n. 99 Womersley. In modern times, the most surprising appearance of the name 'Scipio Africanus' is as the by-name of 'Sam' Mussabini (1867–1927), athletics trainer of mixed (including Italian) descent, most famous as the coach of Harold Abrahams for the Olympic Games of 1924. In the 1981 film *Chariots of Fire*, he was played by Ian Holm and is commemorated by a blue plaque in the south London suburb Herne Hill.

[161] *Odes* 4.9.25–8.

[162] Groag 1929; Hoffmann 1962; Seibert 1993a and 1993b; Barceló 2004; Brizzi 2007b; Hoyos 2003 and 2008; MacDonald 2015. For modern double treatments of Hannibal and Scipio, see p. 5. None of them are on the scale of the present work, or are otherwise comparable to it, nor are they serious biographies of either man.

[163] Scullard 1970, weaving together Scullard 1930 and 1951. Haywood 1933 was not a biography but a series of thematic studies.

languages during the 1920s, including a popular treatment by the soldier and influential military theorist Sir Basil Liddell Hart.[164] The reason for the curious concentration in that decade may have something to do with understandably lively interest in warfare and battles after the first world war. But why the imbalance between Hannibal and Scipio? The brilliant romantic loser will never lack for a sacred bard: Rommel comes to mind, another supremely able general defeated in Africa and eventually forced to suicide. But another part of the explanation for recent neglect of Scipio may be that the close study of Roman politics, especially through prosopography, is out of fashion, and after 206 Scipio's career, including his downfall, has to be examined as a largely political story.[165] His adoptive grandson Scipio Aemilianus, and his enemy Cato the Censor, were both the subjects of detailed political biographies written towards the end of the period when such books were still approved of by scholarly taste, and that period includes Scullard 1970.[166] I do not mean to imply that the only available non-military approach to the lives of Hannibal and Scipio is political, but politics cannot be avoided. The second Punic war has hardly been neglected in the last five decades, and Scipio's family has been well studied as a whole, including an important Spanish collection of essays on the activities of all the Scipios in Iberia.[167] Perhaps the recent completion of the digital prosopography of the Roman Republic will lead to a revival of attention to the careers of Scipio, and his family and associates, in their purely Roman and domestic aspects.[168] And there has certainly been fine recent work on literary treatments of Scipio as well as of Hannibal, as I hope the present chapter has shown.

---

[164] Liddell Hart 1926. Near the end of his life, the Greek scholar and controversial British politician Enoch Powell (1912–98) wrote an introduction to a reprint of 1992.
[165] On prosopography, see p. 175.
[166] Astin 1967 (Aemilianus); Kienast 1954 and Astin 1978 (Cato).
[167] Etcheto 2012; Bendala Galán 2015a (Iberia).
[168] Rüpke's important *Fasti sacerdotum* (Rüpke 2008), which has 'prosopography' in its subtitle, may also lead to a new way of using prosopography, less concentrated on what he calls the 'highest echelons' (cf. p. 175 with n. 15); but Scipio himself features there only for his tenure of a Salian priesthood. See Rüpke 2008: 642 no. 1372 for Scipio's 'biography' from this point of view.

CHAPTER 20

# *Conclusion*
## *Parallel Lives*

The careers of our two parallel lives followed similar trajectories in obvious respects.[1] Precocious children of successful military leaders whose lives were cut violently short in Iberia, they both enjoyed dazzling early battlefield successes. Militarily, Hannibal was the teacher and Scipio the eventually more successful pupil, and Hannibal's logistical achievement during his long years cut off in Italy was more impressive than Scipio's in Iberia. After Scipio defeated Hannibal at Zama in 202, both men were for several years politically active in their home cities – neither of them entirely successfully, but in different ways and for different reasons. In the late 190s, by a curious turn of events, they found themselves advising one side each in the Roman war against the Seleucid king Antiochus III; Scipio even contrived to give sensible advice to both of the opposing commanders. But their fellow citizens rejected them both absolutely – Hannibal had to flee Carthage in 195, Scipio faced humiliating legal attacks in 187 and 184 – and they died in the same year 183, the one hunted down in distant eastern exile, the other in local disgrace. Why these dramatic trajectories?

Of the two, Hannibal's fate is more easily explained. He had, after all, been comprehensively defeated on the battlefield by Scipio, and although it was only a cherished Roman myth that defeated Carthaginian generals were crucified – even Livy pretended to subscribe to it, although knowing full well that nothing of the sort happened after Zama – Hannibal was never going to recover from this failure. In fact, it is surprising that he managed to win elected office and carry out radical domestic reforms before Roman pressure forced him out, a full seven years after the defeat.

The downfall of victorious Scipio is more of a puzzle. It can best be approached after continuing to explore some of the less obvious parallels

---

[1] In this chapter, ancient and modern references will not usually be repeated from earlier chapters, and there will be very few back-references to those chapters.

between the two men. The most illuminating are negative but are no less important for that.

Neither Hannibal nor Scipio received cult in the strong sense of the word; Weinstock thought that Scipio did, but on present evidence this was true, if at all, only in the weak sense that he was regarded by some as possessed of superhuman qualities and may have encouraged such beliefs.[2] His contemporary Flamininus did received actual cultic honours in the Greek east, so this was far from unthinkable for a Roman proconsul in the early second century. Scipio could legitimately have been hailed as one of the 'saviours' or '(re)founders' of Rome, titles with cultic implications in the Greek world, but he does not seem to have been.[3]

If Hannibal had won at Zama, was Carthage enough of a Hellenistic state for any of his admirers to become actual worshippers? There is some (earlier, Greek, dubious) evidence for posthumous cult paid at Carthage to the half-Greek Hamilcar (1), who had thrown himself onto a flaming pyre after his defeat at Himera (480 BCE).[4] But it is highly unlikely that Hannibal received cult of any sort. Certainly none is attested. There was a Hannibalic as well as a Scipionic 'legend', but neither cluster of stories amounted to cult except in a very loose modern sense, 'personality cult'.

Neither Hannibal nor Scipio named a new or refounded city after themselves in the manner of Hellenistic rulers. Exiled Hannibal in the east probably helped two of his royal hosts to found cities in Asia Minor (first in Armenia, then Bithynia), but this purely adjutant role meant that there was no question of a Hannibalopolis. Scipio is reliably associated with no act of city foundation, whether named for himself or not. That he founded Iberian Italica was a Hadrianic fiction. A very few decades later, his future son-in-law Tiberius Gracchus named an Iberian city Graccuris after himself and got away with it.

More generally, neither Hannibal nor Scipio seem to have aimed at, and certainly did not achieve, anything like a monarchical position anywhere in the world. Scipio was offered the title of king in Iberia but did not accept, while enigmatically expressing a wish to be regarded as 'kingly'. The days of the Roman general with a client army, able to make demands and impose

---

[2] See pp. 418–19. The homage paid at Liternum by the brigands (p. 394) is, if historical, not evidence for organized civic cult.
[3] For Scipio as unrecognized saviour, see Weinstock 1971: 165 (no oak wreath). As for Scipio as founder, the nearest text Weinstock can find (1971: 180 n. 2) is *In defence of Sestius* 143, but there he is one of a long list of great Roman names who 'stabilized', *stabiliuerunt*, the *res publica*, the state, and deserved to be treated like the immortal gods. (The plural *Scipiones* is not significant: every name in the list is in the plural.)
[4] See p. 228 on Hdt. 7.167.2.

his will as something like an autocrat, were in the future. Gaius Marius, at the end of the second century, helped to make such a position possible by abolishing the property qualification for recruitment but was not able to sustain his pre-eminence for long after defeating Jugurtha. Scipio's veterans were easily granted land, which was duly assigned by a ten-man commission appointed in 201. There is no sign of the senatorial apprehension and resistance to such a grant, of the sort which Pompey encountered in the late 60s, and which took him into partnership with Julius Caesar, whose violent and in effect sole consulship of 59 would have been unthinkable in Scipio's world. On the other hand, Scipio in 205 was not allowed by the senate to conduct a levy of troops for his African campaign but was permitted to recruit volunteers, and he had to accept this. The senate was firmly in charge.

Hannibal was in command of an army when recalled to Africa, but although he is recorded (perhaps unreliably) as loudly lamenting his departure, there was no question of disobedience. If part of Hannibal's legacy was, as Toynbee argued, to turn Rome into something like a Hellenistic kingdom, that was not because Hannibal himself behaved like an independent Hellenistic king.

But that obedience raises one of the most interesting and (for the future) significant parallels between Hannibal and Scipio, which is to be found in the area of overseas commands. Both men campaigned for long periods in distant and hostile theatres of war, Hannibal in Italy and Scipio in Iberia. They were not entirely isolated and insulated: Hannibal was accompanied by formal advisers, *synedroi* in the Greek word, and by close family members, although it is arguable that his loneliness became more pronounced during his years in Italy. Scipio also had his advisers and friends around him on campaign. But slow and poor communications with Carthage and Rome respectively meant that far-reaching decisions often had to be taken by the man on the spot, in exercise of what modern historians call 'peripheral imperialism'. On the Roman side, perhaps the most important decision of the war was made on his own initiative by Scipio's father Publius, namely, to fight the war in Iberia, at least initially. The younger Scipio inherited this commitment, and the general policies and diplomacy of both his father and his uncle Gnaeus. But decisions such as the younger Scipio's bold and successful attack on New Carthage in 210 had to be made in a hurry, and although Scipio surely sent home more messages and messengers than we hear of, reports of actions already taken are not the same as requests for advance approval. Snap decisions were a general's to make, and sheer distance increased the scope for such independent action. This had implications for future Roman history. Syme remarked of Caesar at the end of his life that 'at Rome he was hampered: abroad he might enjoy his conscious mastery of men and events, as before in Gaul'.[5]

Much the same is true of Hannibal – to a still controversial degree, his attack on Saguntum, perhaps also the decision to cross the Alps, were his initiatives – although post-war recriminations by his political enemies naturally exaggerated his sole responsibility for inciting and then waging the war. There is no parallel in Scipio's career to Hannibal's apparently large share in responsibility for the momentous decision to attack Saguntum, a decision which led to war. Scipio made decisions on his own initiative, but he entered a war which was in no way of his making. Hannibal's communications with his brother Hasdrubal, who in 207 followed him across the Alps from Iberia in the bold adventure which came to grief at the Metaurus River, look like a purely family matter.

One crucial aspect of overseas command over vast regions is the appointment of subordinates and lieutenants to govern conquered places or areas. Such local appointments were to a large degree a commander's prerogative and needed to be made quickly without stopping to consult the home authorities and waiting weeks for a reply. In one originally Greek city of southern Italy, Locri, it is possible to compare the appointments made by Hannibal and Scipio. Hannibal's deputy at Locri, a man called Hamilcar, appears to have been guilty of ten years of alleged arrogance and rapacity ('appears' because of a frustrating prosopographic uncertainty caused by the poverty of Carthaginian personal names: a Hamilcar was in charge at Locri at the beginning and end of the relevant period, and it is probable, but not quite certain, that they are the one and the same man). But when the Romans reconquered Locri, Scipio put the criminally violent Pleminius in charge, by a disastrous error of judgement, and compounded the error by the over-lenient way he dealt with the matter afterwards. This was evidence of a definite personal arrogance which was again on display during his political troubles in the 180s. Since Carthaginian imperialism in the full sense ended in 202, apart from precarious control of a small part of north Africa for a further half-century, the Hamilcar episode had no sequels.[6] But the Pleminius affair certainly did. Toynbee included a long chronologically arranged annex to one of his chapters, listing 'acts of Roman public officers, 211–123 B. C. that were misdemeanours in the Roman "Establishment's" eyes'. The Pleminius affair is no. 2 in the list

---

[5] Syme 1939: 53.  [6] Pilkington 2019 ends his study of Carthaginian imperialism in 202.

of 32.[7] The Roman senatorial class took gradual steps to restrict extortion by governors, starting with the *lex Calpurnia* of 149, but this was not the result of disinterested altruism but was a very public expression of insistence that no member of its own class should acquire too much prestige – or booty. The trials of the Scipios (Publius and his brother Lucius) in the 180s can and should be seen as just one episode, if the most celebrated, in this vindictive equalizing process, one which gained increasing momentum after 200 as the profits of empire flowed in. Disputes over the award of triumphs were another manifestation. All this was well and convincingly argued for by Gruen in the opening pages of his essay on the 'fall' of the Scipios.[8]

Neither Hannibal not Scipio suffered legal or other reprisals as a result of the bad appointments they had made at Locri on their own initiatives, except that Scipio incurred some reputational damage. As for Hannibal, there was no mechanism by which a Greek city in Italy could appeal to Carthage against outrageous treatment. Hannibal's appointment of Hamilcar was more defensible than Scipio's of Pleminius in one respect: the pool of officer talent available to Hannibal in a remote corner of Italy after many years of hostile occupation was far smaller than that enjoyed by Scipio as consul in 205.

Neither man was a great success as a politician in the post-Zama period; Hannibal did at least bravely and single-handedly carry through unpopular reforms designed to curb oligarchic corruption, but it is not known how long they lasted after his hasty exit from Carthage. Scipio was heaped with honours after returning from Iberia (two consulships in 205 and 194, the censorship, many years as senior senator, *princeps senatus*), but he seems to have had little or no interest in political or economic reform and spoke rarely in the senate, if the literary record is anything like complete. That he was much better as a soldier than as a politician was already remarked in antiquity.

Nor was either man very effective as adviser to Antiochus in the run-up to the decisive battle of Magnesia in 190. Scipio's actual role was as *legatus* to his consular brother Lucius, in what was then the fairly new advisory sense of that Latin word. Only a few words of that advice have come down to us ('make sure you sound out Philip of Macedon's intentions'), but there was unquestionably more of it than we hear of, and much of it will have been strategic and tactical: Lucius did after all win the battle, in the absence

---

[7] Toynbee 1965: 2. 608–45 (Annex to ch. xv).
[8] Gruen 1995; the inverted commas are his. They express a doubt which I do not share.

through illness of Publius. As for Antiochus, he made a habit of asking Hannibal for advice, ignoring it, and then explaining to everybody afterwards that he wished he had followed it. The explanation for this puzzling pattern of behaviour may be that – as Habicht showed in 1958 – the Seleucid dynasty was traditionally reluctant to employ foreigners rather than Greeks or Macedonians. Envious courtiers will have been well aware of this. Scipio was also in friendly communication with Antiochus and, as an expression of gratitude for the return of his son without ransom, urged him to avoid battle 'until you hear that I have returned to camp'. Whatever the meaning of this puzzling qualification (did Scipio grandly think he alone had the stature to arrange a last-minute diplomatic settlement?), it was followed only very partially. And it gave Scipio's domestic enemies ammunition against him later on.

We started this chapter by postponing the question: 'why did Scipio fall?' and can now return to it. He lived too early to be able to set himself above the constitution by means of a client army, that is, by force, even if he had wanted to do any such thing. The legal attacks to which he was exposed towards the end of his life were and are famous; but they were not qualitatively exceptional, in a wealthy period when many successful military commanders were vulnerable to such equalizing manoeuvres. The strong personal antipathy and envy felt towards Scipio himself by venomous individuals, especially but not only the implacable Cato, are a further undeniable factor.[9] And, as we have seen, no individual, however patriotic, must be allowed to win too much glory. Finally, Scipio's own arrogance and impatience with criticism did not help him: tearing up account books when charged with financial impropriety was a memorable piece of theatre, but it was not clever tactics to destroy the evidence in that way. His clearly expressed opinion was that a general's outstanding military achievements ought to confer immunity from challenge by those petty folk who owed their very liberty to the general. Anecdotal evidence suggests that Hannibal was also capable of expressing haughty pride in his soldierly calling; but his took the innocuous form of raising a laugh by an irritated outburst after a lecture by an elderly Greek philosopher who had tried to tell him his job at tedious length.

Hannibal perhaps had a more developed sense of humour than Scipio: witness the cheerful quip, recorded by Plutarch, by which he rallied his gloomy officer Gisgo before Cannae; and the comically ingenious means

---

[9] Syme 1939: 26 applied the epithet 'implacable' to Cato's like-named descendant.

by which he gave his hungover pursuers the slip at Cercina in 195.[10] Hannibal certainly had the better of his verbal exchange with Scipio at Ephesus, from which he emerges as the wittier of the two and thus the victor after all, Zama notwithstanding. But such brief episodes, always assuming they are historical and have been correctly reported, are hardly a sound basis for serious comparative generalizations.

Generally, the personalities of our two parallel lives called for Plutarch's biographical skills; even without such full treatments, it is safe to say that there was a streak of arrogance in Scipio's make-up. But he showed magnanimity towards Hannibal in the 190s at a time when others at Rome wanted his blood; Plutarch drew a favourable contrast with the vindictiveness of Flamininus. Hannibal's character is inevitably more elusive, given the sources' distribution of attention, but his treatment of the corpses of his defeated consular enemies displayed humanity and respect as well as piety.[11] His most extravagant reported display of emotion is Livy's highly rhetorical account of his lamentation on leaving Italy, but some details of this are implausible.

The supposed personal characteristics of our two lives have been mainly explored in this book as part of their traditional literary portraits. Hannibal is regularly presented, especially but not only by the poets, as the cruel barbarian, but Polybius interestingly sought to extenuate this and even recorded the absurd belief that his cruel acts were really the work of his 'double', Hannibal (10) the 'single-combat-man'. The episode of Hannibal's shockingly unfair punishment of the guide whose Latin he himself misunderstood may have been invented simply to paint him as cruel. Hannibal's reputation for impiety was unsubstantiated by good evidence. One implausible story did double duty as illustrating both his supposed cruelty and impiety: the alleged massacre in the sanctuary of Juno Lacinia. He was regularly treated as an exemplar of 'Punic fraud' or deception, but Scipio practised 'Roman fraud' on occasion. Anecdotes circulated about Scipio's supposed chivalry (or was he really a womanizer?) and were picked up in later centuries.

These considerations prompt a final comparative glance at posthumous reputations, the topic of the preceding chapter. In one respect, our two parallel lives were unequal: with the early and important exception of the admiring Ennius, the poets found Scipio a much less congenial subject

---

[10] For two sarcastic jokes by Hannibal at an enemy's expense, see Livy 22.49.3 and 29.34.7, with p. 21; for other jokes by Hannibal see pp. 109, 261, 326. For jokes by Scipio, see p. 210 and perhaps 254.
[11] On Hannibal's character, see Geus 1994: 90–3.

than Hannibal.¹² This was no mere matter of metrical convenience. It is true that the name Scipio was intractable for most poetic purposes: he could not be made a dactyl, long-short-short, without violating the natural quantity of the first vowel. He could be made dactylic only by forced association with others of his family, as half of the 'twin Scipiadae', whatever exactly that expression denoted. But strictly speaking, the name Hannibal was also intractable, as ancient pedants pointed out to no avail (the name was theophoric, formed from the god Baal, so the last syllable ought to have been long).

The reason for Hannibal's greater poetic popularity are to be looked for elsewhere. Like Cleopatra, the frightening but in the end vanquished foreign enemy exercised perennial fascination (especially when associated with Alps and elephants). Cicero made this point in effect. Hannibal was the glamorous loser, and history or at any rate popular perception is often kind to such men.

I hope that the parallel narrative and thematic treatments of two important lives from the ancient world may have contributed something extra, beyond what would have been possible by the telling of their separate stories in separate monographs. Both of their careers were shaped by their long overseas commands. In turn those careers helped to shape their own and each other's societies. Hannibal's did so by causing the end of Hellenistic Carthage in the longer term, Scipio's by achieving Carthage's defeat in the short term. Hannibal's did so by his damaging legacy in Roman Italy, Scipio's by showing what use a more ruthlessly ambitious Roman individual than himself might make of a prolonged and successful career in a far-off location such as Iberia. Scipio was the more conventional of the two men, after his highly unconventional start (granted *imperium* as a private citizen, in some respects anticipating the young Pompey).¹³

---

[12] Much later, Silius Italicus towards the end of his *Punica* versified part of the 'Scipionic legend' in extreme (Homeric and Herodotean) fashion; but the man whom Claire Stocks aptly calls the 'Roman Hannibal' is his main focus of interest, and Cannae (216 BCE) his epic's centrepiece.

[13] Fisher 2016: 111–12, concluding his brief but interesting chapter 'Legacy', exaggerates Scipio's unwelcome 'tendency towards individualism'. He cites in support Diodorus (29.21): 'because of his great achievements, Scipio wielded more influence than seemed compatible with the dignity of the state'. But this, written in the Late Republic, goes further than its source for the whole passage, which was Polybius 23.14 (see Schwartz 1959: 75). Polybius there (§1) stresses his influence both with the masses and the senate (on this passage see Lintott 1999: 23). Fisher says Scipio 'broke constitutional rules repeatedly during the war' (he concedes that this was not so after the war) and 'had recourse to popular support'. All this goes too far. It is true that the people played an important part in Scipio's original grant of imperium, but the senate's role was paramount in the renewals of that imperium (whatever resentful jealousy may have been felt by some individual senators): see Livy 27.7.17 (209), 27.22.7 (208), cf. 30.1.10 (203). Scipio was no popularis politician, as we have seen (p. 175). Polybius, near the beginning of the passage just cited, says he had influence both with the masses and the senate (see Lintott 1999: 23). For the opening sentence ('Scipio sought fame in an aristocratic state'), see p. 173, cf. 266.

He was the perfect soldier, but not a man with any desire to change the status quo, that is, the aristocratic ascendancy into which he was born. His men liked and respected him, but he had an arrogance which helped to undo him at the end; Hannibal also displayed impatience with fools, but unlike Scipio he knew how to apologize, and perhaps had a better sense of humour. He was a more isolated and under-supported figure than Scipio for most of his long years in Italy (and was more or less entirely alone in his years of wandering). In Italy, he faced and for a long time surmounted greater military and logistical challenges than his rival Scipio, and unlike him he tried to carry out a programme of radical political reform of the oligarchy into which he had been born.

# References

Journal abbreviations as in *OCD*⁴.

Adams, J. N. (2003) *Bilingualism and the Latin language*, Cambridge
Adams, J. N. (2007) *The regional diversification of Latin*, Cambridge
Adams, J. N. (2021) *Asyndeton and its interpretation in Latin literature: history, patterns, textual criticism*, Cambridge
Adler, E. (2011) *Valorizing the barbarian: enemy speeches in Roman historiography*, Austin TX
Africa, T. W. (1970) 'The one-eyed men against Rome: an exercise in euhemerism', *Historia* 19: 528–38
Ager, S. (1996) *Interstate arbitration in the Greek world, 337–90 BC*, Berkeley, CA
Agri, D. (2020) 'Opening up texts: Flavian interactions in Statius' *Thebaid* and Silius Italicus' *Punica*', *CQ* 70: 310–31
Aldrete, G. (2014) 'Hammers, axes, bulls, and blood: some practical aspects of Roman animal sacrifice', *JRS* 104: 28–50
Alföldi, A. (1957) *Die Trojanischen Urahnen der Römer*, Basel
Alter, R. (2011) *The art of biblical narrative*², New York
Ameling, W. (1993) *Karthago: Studien zu Militär, Staat und Gesellschaft*. Vestigia 45, Munich
Ameling, W. (1997) Review of Geus 1994, *Klio* 97: 243–4
Ando, C. (2019) 'Hannibal's legacy: sovereignty and territoriality in Republican Rome', in K.-J. Hölkeskamp, S. Karataş, and R. Roth (eds.), *Empire, hegemony or anarchy? Rome and Italy, 201–31 BCE*, Stuttgart: 55–81
Anson, E. M. (2023) *Ptolemy I Soter: themes and issues*, London
Applebaum, S. (1979) *Jews and Greeks in ancient Cyrene*, Leiden
Aranegui Gascó, C. (2006) 'From Arse to Saguntum', in L. Abad Casal, S. Keay, and S. F. Ramallo Asensio (eds.), *Early Roman towns in Hispania Tarraconensis*. JRA Supp. series 62, Portsmouth, RI: 63–74
Arnaud, P. (2005) *Les routes de la navigation antique: itinéraires en Méditerranée*, Paris
Astin, A. E. (1967) *Scipio Aemilianus*, Oxford
Astin, A. E. (1978) *Cato the censor*, Oxford
Atkinson, J. E. (1980) *A commentary on Q. Curtius Rufus' Historiae Magni Alexandri Books 3 and 4*, Amsterdam

Aubet, M. E. S. (2019) 'Tyre and its colonial expansion', in C. López-Ruiz and B. Doak (eds.), *The Oxford handbook of the Phoenician and Punic Mediterranean*, Oxford: 75–85

Augoustakis, A. (2003) '*Rapit infidum victor caput*: ekphrasis and gender reversal in Silius Italicus', in P. Thibodeau and P. Haskell (eds.), *Being there together: essays in honor of Michael C. J. Putnam on the occasion of his seventieth birthday*, Afton: 110–27

Augoustakis, A. and M. Fucecchi (eds.) (2022) *Silius Italicus and the tradition of the Roman historical epos*, Leiden and Boston

Austin, R. G. (ed.) (1971) *Aeneidos liber primus*, Oxford

Aymard, A. (1967a) *Études d'histoire ancienne*, Paris

Aymard, A. (1967b) 'Polybe, Scipion l'Africain et le titre de "roi"', in *Études d'histoire ancienne*, Paris: 387–95

Bäbler, B. (1998) *Fleissige Thrakerinnen und wehrhafte Skythen: Nichtgriechen im klassischen Athen und ihre archäologische Hinterlassenschaft*, Stuttgart

Badian, E. (1958) *Foreign clientelae (264–70 BC)*, Oxford

Badian, E. (1968a) *Studies in Greek and Roman history*, Oxford

Badian, E. (1968b) 'Rome and Antiochus the Great: a study in cold war', in *Studies in Greek and Roman history*, Oxford: 112–39 (originally *CP* 54 (1959): 81–99)

Badian, E. (1970) *Titus Quinctius Flamininus. Philhellenism and Realpolitik*. Semple lectures, 2nd series, Cincinnati, OH

Badian, E. (1972) 'Ennius and his friends', in O. Skutsch (ed.), *Ennius*, Vandoeuvres: 151–208

Badian, E. (1979) 'Alexander's mules' [review of Engels 1978], *New York Review of Books* 26 no. 20 (20 December): 54–6

Baglione, M. P. (1976) 'Su alcune serie parallele di bronzo coniato', in *Contributi introduttivi allo studio della monetazione etrusca: Atti Convegno Napoli 1975*, Rome, 153–80

Bagnall, R. S. (1976) *The administration of the Ptolemaic possessions outside Egypt*, Leiden

Bakker, M. de, B. van den Berg, and J. Klooster (eds.) (2022) *Emotions and narrative in ancient literature and beyond: studies in honour of Irene de Jong*, Leiden

Balsdon, J. P. V. D. (1972) 'L. Cornelius Scipio: a salvage operation', *Historia* 21: 224–34

Barber, C. M. (2019) *Uncovering a 'lost generation' in the senate: demography and the Hannibalic war*, London

Barceló, P. A. (2004) *Hannibal: Stratege und Staatsmann*, Stuttgart

Bar-Kochva, B. (1976) *The Seleucid army: organization and tactics in the great campaigns*, Cambridge

Barnes, T. D. (1967) 'The family and career of Septimius Severus', *Historia* 16: 87–107

Barré, M. L. (1983) *The god-list in the treaty between Hannibal and Philip V of Macedonia: a study in light of the ancient Near Eastern treaty tradition*, Baltimore, MD

Barrett, C. K. (1955) *The gospel according to St John: an introduction with commentary and notes on the Greek text*, London
Bastien, J.-L. (2007) *Triomphe romain et son utilisation politique à Rome aux trois siècles de la république*, Rome
Battistoni, F. (2009) 'Rome, kinship and diplomacy', in C. Eilers (ed.), *Diplomats and diplomacy in the Roman world*, Leiden: 73–97
Beard, M. (1990) 'Priesthood in the Roman Republic', in M. Beard and J. North (eds.), *Pagan priests: religion and power in the ancient world*, London: 19–48
Beard, M. (2007) *The Roman triumph*, Cambridge, MA
Beard, M. and J. North (eds.) (1990) *Pagan priests: religion and power in the ancient world*, London
Bechtel, F. (1917) *Die historischen Personennamen des Griechischen bis zur Kaiserzeit*, Halle
Beck, H. (2011) 'The reasons for the war', in D. Hoyos (ed.), *A companion to the Punic wars*, Oxford: 225–41
Bell, M. (1995) 'The Motya charioteer and Pindar's *Isthmian 2*', *MAAR* 40: 1–42
Bellomo, M. (2019) *Il comando militare a Roma nell'eta delle guerre puniche*, Stuttgart
Bellón, J. P., C. Rueda, M. A. Lechuga, and M. I. Moreno (2016) 'An archaeological analysis of a battlefield of the second Punic war', *JRA* 29: 73–104
Bellón Ruiz, J. P., M. Á. L. Lechuga Chica, J. L. López Castro, and V. Martínez Hahnmüller (2015) 'La conquista de Andalucía Oriental: de Baria a Castulo', in M. Bendala Galán (ed.), *Los Escipiones: Roma conquista Hispania*, Madrid: 180–203
Beltramini, L. (2020) *Commento al libro XXVI di Tito Livio*, Pisa
Beltramini, L. (2023) 'Le conseguenze della vittoria. Scipione e la riflessione sull' imperialismo Romano in Livio', *Histos* 17: 182–215
Beltramini, L. and M. Rocco (2020) 'Livy on Scipio Africanus: the commander's portrait', *CQ* 70: 230–46
Bendala Galán, M. (ed.) (2015a) *Los Escipiones: Roma conquista Hispania*, Madrid
Bendala Galán, M. (2015b) 'Los Escipiones y la Roma de su tiempo: panorama social y urbano', in M. Bendala Galán (ed.), *Los Escipiones: Roma conquista Hispania*, Madrid: 35–57
Bennett, C. E. and M. B. McElwain (1925) *Frontinus: Stratagems; Aqueducts of Rome*. Loeb Classical Library, Cambridge, MA
Bernard, S., L. M. Mignone, and D.-E. Padilla Peralta (eds.) (2023) *Making the Middle Republic: new approaches to Rome and Italy, c. 400–200 BCE*, Cambridge
Bernardo, A. (1962) *Petrarch: Scipio, and the 'Africa': the birth of humanism's dream*, Baltimore
Berve, H. (1959) *König Hieron II*. Bayerische Akad. Wiss. ph.-hist. Kl. Abhandlungen, neue Folge 47, Munich
Bickerman, E. (1944) 'An oath of Hannibal', *TAPA* 75: 87–102
Bickerman, E. (1952) 'Hannibal's covenant', *AJP* 73: 1–23
Bickerman, E. (1980) *The chronology of the ancient world*, revised ed., London
Bikerman, E. (identical with the above) (1938) *Institutions des Séleucides*, Paris

Birley, A. R. (1988) *Septimius Severus the African emperor*, 2nd ed., London
Bispham, E. (2014) '*Roma iudex*. Interstate arbitration and Rome's Mediterranean hegemony', in, J. Dubouloz, S. Pittia, and G. Sabatini (eds.), *L'imperium Romanum en perspective: Les savoirs d'empire dans la République romaine et leur héritage dans l'Europe médiévale et modern*, Paris: 231–42
Boardman, J. (1994) *The diffusion of Classical art in antiquity*, London
Bondanella, P. (ed. and tr.) (2005), *Niccolò Macchiavelli*, The Prince, with introduction by M. Viroli. Oxford World's Classics, Oxford
Bonnet, C. (2006) 'Identité et altérité religieuses: à propos de l'hellénisation de Carthage', *Pallas* 70: 365–79
Bonnet, C. (2019) 'The Hellenistic period and hellenization in Phoenicia', in C. López-Ruiz and B. Doak (eds.), *The Oxford handbook of the Phoenician and Punic Mediterranean*, Oxford: 99–110
Bosworth, B. (1999) 'Augustus, the *Res Gestae* and Hellenistic theories of apotheosis', *JRS* 89: 1–18
Bouiron, M. (2022) *Stéphane de Byzance. Les ethniques comme source historique: l'exemple de l'Europe occidentale*, Turnhout
Bowersock, G. W. (1965) *Augustus and the Greek world*, Oxford
Bradford, A. S. (1977) *A prosopography of Lacedaemonians from the death of Alexander the Great, 323 B.C., to the sack of Sparta by Alaric, A.D. 396*. Vestigia 27, Munich
Brennon, T. C. (2000) *The praetorship in the Roman Republic*, Cambridge
Bresson, A. (2007) 'Rhodes, Rome et les pirates Tyrrhéniens' in P. Brun (ed.), *Scripta Anatolica: hommages à P. Debord*, Bordeaux: 145–64
Briant, P. (1973) *Antigone le Borgne: Les débuts de sa carrière et les problèmes de l'assembleé Macédonienne*, Paris
Brink K. O. (1940) 'Peripatos', *R.-E. Supp.* 7: cols. 899–949
Brink, K. O. (1941) 'Phormio (8)', *R.-E.* 20: col. 540
Briscoe, J. (1972) 'Flamininus and Roman politics, 200–189 B.C.', *Latomus* 31: 22–53
Briscoe, J. (1973) *A commentary on Livy books* XXXI–XXXIII, Oxford
Briscoe, J. (1974) 'Rome and the class struggle in the Greek states 200–146 BC', in M. I. Finley (ed.), *Studies in ancient society*, London: 53–73 [originally *Past and Present* 36 (1967): 3–20]
Briscoe, J. (1980) Review of Harris 1979, *CR* 30: 86–8
Briscoe, J. (1981) *A commentary on Livy books* XXXIV–XXXVII, Oxford
Briscoe J. (1989) 'The second Punic war', $CAH^2$ viii: 44–80.
Briscoe, J. (2008) *A commentary on Livy books 38–40*, Oxford
Briscoe, J. (2012) *A commentary on Livy books 41–45*, Oxford
Briscoe, J. (2018) *Liviana: studies on Livy*, Oxford
Briscoe, J. (2019) *Valerius Maximus*, facta et dicta memorabilia, *Book 8: text, introduction, and commentary*, Berlin
Briscoe, J. and S. Hornblower (2020) *Livy book* XXII, Cambridge

Brizzi, G. (1983) 'Ancora su Annibale e l'ellenismo: la fondazione di Artaxata e l'iscrizione di Era Lacinia', *Atti del I congresso internazionale di studi fenici e punici* I, Rome: 234–51

Brizzi, G. (2007a) *Scipione e Annibale: la guerra per salvare Roma*, Rome and Bari

Brizzi, G. (2007b) *'Moi, Hannibal...' Mémoires d'un homme de guerre*, Nantes (tr. of Italian version, 2003)

Brizzi, G. (2011a) *Metus Punicus: studi e ricerche su Annibale e Roma*, Imola

Brizzi, G. (2011b) 'Carthage and Hannibal in Roman and Greek memory', in D. Hoyos (ed.), *A companion to the Punic wars*, Oxford: 483–98

Brodersen, K. (1991) *Appians Antiochike (Syriake 1,1–44.232). Text und Kommentar nebst einem Anhang: Plethons Syriake-Exzerpt*, Munich

Broughton, T. R. S. : *see* Abbreviations under *MRR*

Broughton, T. R. S. (1967) Review of Toynbee 1965, *AHR* 72: 127–9

Brown, P. (1971) *The world of late antiquity*, London

Bruère, R. T. (1952) 'Silius Italicus *Punica* 3.62–162 and 4.763–822', *CP* 47: 219–27

Brunt, P. A. (1971a) *Italian manpower 225 B.C.–A.D. 14*, Oxford [a postscript to the 1987 reprint has the page numbers 717–27, which in 1971 numbered the indexes]

Brunt, P. A. (1971b) *Social conflicts in the Roman Republic*, London

Brunt, P. A. (1976) *Arrian: History of Alexander and Indica*, vol. 1. Loeb Classical Library, Cambridge, MA

Brunt, P. A. (1988) *The fall of the Roman Republic and related essays*, Oxford

Brunt, P. A. (1990a) *Roman Imperial themes*, Oxford

Brunt, P. A. (1990b) '*Laus imperii*', in *Roman Imperial themes*: 288–323 [enlarged and revised version of Garnsey and Whittaker 1978: 159–91]

Brunt, P. A. and J. M. Moore (eds.) (1967) *Res gestae divi Augusti: The achievements of the divine Augustus*, Oxford

Bullock, A. (1952) *Hitler: a study in tyranny*, London

Bullock, A. (1993) [1991] *Hitler and Stalin: parallel lives*, London

Burkert, W. (1979) *Structure and history in Greek mythology and ritual*, Berkeley, CA

Burton, P. J. (2011) *Friendship and empire: Roman diplomacy and imperialism in the Middle Republic (353–146 BC)*, Cambridge

Burton, P. J. (2019) *Roman imperialism*, Leiden

Butler, H. E. and M. Cary (eds.) (1927) *C. Suetoni Tranquilli Divus Iulius*, Oxford

Butler, H. E. and H. H. Scullard (eds.) (1953) *Livy book xxx*, 6th ed. London

Caballos Rufino A. (ed.) (2010) *Ciudades romanas de Hispania (7) Itálica-Santiponce: Municipium y Colonia Aelia Augusta Italicensium*, Rome

Caballos Rufino, A. and P. León Alonso (eds.) (1997) *Italica MMCC: actas de las jornadas del 2200 aniversario de la fundacion de Itálica (Sevilla 8–11 noviembre 1994)*, Seville

Cabezas-Guzmán, G. and G. R. Ventós (2022) 'Rome and the north-western Mediterranean: ports-of-call and sea routes', in T. Ñaco del Hoyo, J. Principal, and M. Dobson (eds.), *Rome and the north-western Mediterranean: integration and connectivity, c. 150–70 BC*, Oxford: 237–244

Campanile, D. (2023) 'Annibale a Efeso', *SCO* 69: 59–76
Canali de Rossi, F. (2004) *Inschriften griechischer Städte aus Kleinasien* vol. 65. *Iscrizioni dello Estremo Oriente Greco: un repertorio*, Cologne
Carey, C. (2019) *Great battles: Thermopylae*, Oxford
Carter, M. (2006) 'Buttons and wooden swords: Polybius 10.20.3, Livy 26.51 and the *rudis*', *CP* 101: 153–60
Casson, L. (1971) *Ships and seamanship in the ancient world*, Princeton, NJ
Castanyer, P., M. Santos, and J. Tremoleda (2015) 'Una nueva fortificación de época republicana en Empúries: una base militar para la conquista de Hispania', in M. Bendala Galán (ed.), *Los Escipiones: Roma conquista Hispania*, Madrid: 106–27
Caven, B. (1980) *The Punic wars*, London
Cawkwell, G. (1972) 'Epaminondas and Thebes', *CQ* 22: 254–78 (= 2011: 299–33)
Cawkwell, G. (2011) *Cyrene to Chaeronea: selected essays on Ancient Greek history*, Oxford
Chaniotis, A. (1996) *Die Verträge zwischen kretischen Poleis in der hellenistischen Zeit*, Stuttgart
Chaplin, J. (2000) *Livy's exemplary history*, Oxford
Charles, M. B. (2008) 'African forest elephants and turrets in the ancient world', *Phoenix* 62: 338–62
Charles, M. B. and P. Rhodan (2007) '*Magister elephantorum*: a reappraisal of Hannibal's use of elephants', *Classical World* 100: 363–89
Chaves Tristan, F. (2010) 'Numismática italicense', in A. Caballos Rufino (ed.), *Ciudades romanas de Hispania (7) Itálica-Santiponce: Municipium y Colonia Aelia Augusta Italicensium*, Rome: 127–35
Chrissanthos, S. (1997) 'Scipio and the mutiny at Sucro', *Historia* 46: 172–84
Christ, K. von (1970) 'Hannibal und Scipio Africanus', in *Die Grossen der Weltgeschichte*, vol. 1, Zurich: 771–83
Ciaceri, E. (1932) *Storia della Magna Grecia*, vol. iii, Milan, Genoa, Rome, and Naples
Coarelli, F. (2001) '*Origo Sagunti*: l'origine mitica di Sagunto e l'alleanza con Roma'. in V. Fromentin and S. Gotteland (eds.), *Origines gentium*, Paris: 321–6
Coarelli, F. (2002) 'I ritratti di "Mario" e di "Silla" in Monaco', *Eutopia* 2.1: 47–75
Coarelli, F. (2015) 'La tumba de los Escipiones', in M. Bendala Galán (ed.), *Los Escipiones: Roma conquista Hispania*, Madrid: 58–65
Cohen, G. (1995) *The Hellenistic settlements in Europe, the islands, and Asia Minor*, Berkeley, CA
Cohen, G. (2006) *The Hellenistic settlements in Syria, the Red Sea basin and north Africa*, Berkeley, CA
Cohen, G. (2013) *The Hellenistic settlements in the East from Armenia and Mesopotamia to Bactria and India*, Berkeley, CA
Cole, S. (2013) *Cicero and the rise of deification at Rome*, Cambridge
Connolly, P. (1981) *Greece and Rome at war*, London
Connor, W. R. (1985) 'The razing of the house in Greek society', *TAPA* 115: 79–102

Constantakopoulou, C. (2017) *Aegean interactions: Delos and its networks in the third century*, Oxford
Conway, R. S. (1922) 'The portrait of a Roman gentleman, from Livy', *Bulletin of the John Rylands library* 7: 1–15 [offprint in Institute of Classical Studies library, London, 119D SCI, in a bound volume of pamphlets on Scipio, bequeathed by H. H. Scullard]
Cooley, A. E. (2009) *Res gestae divi Augusti: text, translation, and commentary*, Cambridge
Cornell, T. (1975) 'Aeneas and the twins: the development of the Roman foundation legend', *PCPhS* 21: 1–23
Cornell, T. (1989a) 'The recovery of Rome', $CAH^2$ vii. 2: 309–50
Cornell, T. (1989b) 'The conquest of Italy', $CAH^2$ vii. 2: 351–419
Cornell, T. (1996) 'Hannibal's legacy: the effects of the Hannibalic war in Italy', in T. Cornell, B. Rankov, and P. Sabin (eds.), *The second Punic war: a reappraisal*, London: 97–117
Cornell, T., B. Rankov, and P. Sabin (eds.) (1996) *The second Punic war: a reappraisal*. BICS Supp. 67, London
Cornwell, H. and G. Woolf (eds.) (2022) *Gendering Roman imperialism*, Leiden
Corsten, T. (1989) 'Zur Gründung von Prusa ad Olympum', *Tyche* 4: 33–4
Corsten, T. (2019) 'Name changes of individuals', in R. Parker (ed.), *Changing names: tradition and innovation in Greek onomastics*, London: 138–52
Crawford, M. (1978) *The Roman Republic*, London
Crawford, M. H. (1985) *Coinage and money under the Roman republic*, Berkeley, CA
Crawford, M. (2009) 'Peter Astbury Brunt 1917–2005', *Proceedings of the British Academy* 161: 63–83
Dabrowa, E. (ed.) (2001) *Roman military studies*. Electrum 5, Krakow
Daly, G. (2002) *Cannae: the experience of battle in the second Punic war*, London
Davies, J. K. (1971) *Athenian propertied families 600–300 BC*, Oxford
Davies, J. P. (2004) *Rome's religious history: Livy, Tacitus and Ammianus on their gods*, Cambridge
De Haas, T. (2023) 'Rural transformations in Middle Republican Italy: an archaeological perspective', in S. Bernard, L. M. Mignone, and D.-E. Padilla Peralta (eds.), *Making the Middle Republic: new approaches to Rome and Italy, c. 400–200 BCE*, Cambridge: 132–63
De Ligt, L. (2012) *Peasants, citizens and soldiers: studies in the demographic history of Roman Italy 225 BC–AD 100*, Cambridge
De Ligt, L. and S. J. Northwood (eds.) (2008) *People, land, and politics: demographic developments and the transformation of Italy, 300 BC–AD 14*, Leiden
De Lisle, C. (2019) 'The Punic wars (264–146 BCE)', in C. López-Ruiz and B. Doak (eds.), *The Oxford handbook of the Phoenician and Punic Mediterranean*, Oxford: 169–96
Dench, E. (2005) *Romulus' asylum: Roman identities from the age of Alexander to the age of Hadrian*, Oxford
Dent, E. J. (1947) *Mozart's operas: a critical study*, 2nd ed., Oxford

Derow, P. S. (2015) *Rome, Polybius, and the East*, Oxford
Derow, P. S. and W. G. Forrest (2015) 'An inscription from Chios', in P. S. Derow, *Rome, Polybius, and the East*, Oxford: 243–64
De Sanctis, G. (1964) *Storia dei Romani*, vol. iv.3, Florence
De Sanctis, G. (1968) [1912] *Storia dei Romani*, vol. iii.2, Florence
De Sanctis, G. (1969) [1923] *Storia dei Romani*, vol. iv.1, Florence
De Selincourt, A. (1965) *Livy: the war with Hannibal*. Penguin Classics, London
De Ste. Croix, G. E. M. (1981) *The class struggle in the ancient Greek world*, London
Devillers, O. and V. Krings (2006) 'Le songe d'Hannibal: quelques réflexions sur la tradition littéraire', *Pallas* 70: 337–46
Dewald, C. and R. V. Munson (2022) *Herodotus Histories book 1*, Cambridge
De Witt, N. J. (1941) 'Rome and the "Road of Hercules"', *TAPA* 72: 59–69
Díaz Fernández, A. (ed.) (2021a) *Provinces and provincial command in Republican Rome: genesis, development and governance*. Libera res publica 4, Zaragoza
Díaz Fernández, A. (2021b) 'When did a *provincia* become a province? On the institutional development of a Roman republican concept', in A. Díaz Fernández (ed.), *Provinces and provincial command in Republican Rome: genesis, development and governance*, Zaragoza: 41–69
Dickey, E. (2007) *Latin forms of address: From Plautus to Apuleius*, Oxford
Dickson, P. and J. Harris (2008) 'Alan Louis Charles Bullock 1914–2004', *Proceedings of the British Academy* 153: 125–46
Diels, H. (1890) *Sibyllinische Blätter*, Berlin
Dillery, J. (2015) *Clio's other sons: Berossus and Manetho*, Ann Arbor, MI
Dilke, O. A. W. (1985) *Greek and Roman maps*, London
Dmitriev, S. (2011) *The Greek slogan of freedom and early Roman politics in Greece*, Oxford and New York
Dorey, T. A. (1961) 'Scipio Africanus as a party leader', *Klio* 39: 191–8
Dridi, H. (2019) 'Early Carthage from its foundation to the battle of Himera (ca. 814–480 BCE)', in C. López-Ruiz and B. Doak (eds.), *The Oxford handbook of the Phoenician and Punic Mediterranean*, Oxford: 141–54
Drogula, F. K. (2021) 'From the beginning: the origins of the *provincia* and its unique advantages in Republican Rome', in A. Díaz Fernández (ed.), *Provinces and provincial command in Republican Rome: genesis, development and governance*, Zaragoza: 19–40
Douglas, A. E. (ed.) (1966) *M. Tulli Ciceronis Brutus*, Oxford
Dubuisson, M. (1977) 'οἱ ἀμφί τινα, οἱ περί τινα: l'évolution des sens et des emplois', diss. Liège
Duff, J. D. (1934) *Silius Italicus. Punica*. Loeb Classical Library, 2 vols., Cambridge, MA
Durrbach, F. (1921) *Choix d'inscriptions de Délos*, Paris
Eban, A. and N. Aridan (2006) 'The Toynbee heresy', *Israel Studies* 11: 91–107
Eckstein, A. M. (1982) 'Human sacrifice and fear of military disaster in Republican Rome', *AJAH* 7: 69–95
Eckstein, A. M. (1987) *Senate and general: individual decision-making and Roman foreign relations, 264–194 B. C.*, Berkeley, CA

Eckstein, A. M. (2006) *Mediterranean anarchy, interstate war, and the rise of Rome*, Berkeley, CA
Eckstein, A. M. (2008) *Rome enters the Greek East: from anarchy to hierarchy in the Hellenistic Mediterranean, 230–170 BC*, Oxford
Eckstein, A. M. (2012) 'Polybius, the Gallic crisis, and the Ebro treaty', *CP* 107: 206–29
Edlund, I. (1967) 'Before Zama: a comparison between Polybios' and Livy's descriptions of the meeting between Hannibal and Scipio', *Eranos* 65: 146–78
Edwards, C. (1993) *The politics of immorality in ancient Rome*, Cambridge
Ehrenberg, V. E. (1928) 'Maharbal (1) and (2)', *R.-E.* 14: cols. 521–2
Eidinow, E. (2023) 'Oracular failure in Ancient Greek culture', in R. D. Woodard (ed.), *Divination and prophecy in the Ancient Greek world*, Cambridge: 93–115
Elter, A. (1907) *Donarum pateras*, Bonn
Engels, D. W. (1978) *Alexander the Great and the logistics of the Macedonian army*, Berkeley, CA
Erdkamp, P. (1992) 'Polybius, Livy and the "Fabian strategy"', *Anc. Soc.* 23: 127–47
Erdkamp, P. (1998) *Hunger and the sword: warfare and food supply in Roman Republican wars (264–30 BC)*, Leiden
Erdkamp. P. (2006) 'Late annalistic battle-scenes in Livy (books 21–44)', *Mnemosyne* 59: 525–63
Erdkamp, P. (ed.) (2007) *A companion to the Roman army*, Oxford
Errington, R. M. (1989) 'Rome against Philip and Antiochus', *CAH²* viii: 244–89
Errington, R. M. (2008) *A history of the Hellenistic world 323–30 BC*, Oxford
Erskine, A. (1994) 'The Romans as common benefactors', *Historia* 43: 70–87
Erskine, A. (2001) *Troy between Greece and Rome: local tradition and imperial power*, Oxford
Erskine, A. (2010) *Roman imperialism*, Edinburgh
Erskine, A. (2013) 'The view from the east', in J. R. W. Prag and J. Quinn (eds.), *The Hellenistic West: rethinking the ancient Mediterranean*, Cambridge: 14–34
Etcheto, H. (2012) *Les Scipions: famille et pouvoir à Rome à l'époque républicaine*, Paris
Fantar, M. H. (2007) *Carthage: the Punic city*, Tunis
Farney, G. D. and G. Bradley (eds.) (2015) *The peoples of Ancient Italy*, Berlin
Farrell, J. (2021) 'Latin', in J. B. Lande and D. Feeney (eds.), *How literatures begin*, Princeton, NJ: 131–48
Feeney, D. C. (1991) *The gods in epic: poets and critics of the Classical tradition*, Oxford
Feeney, D. C. (2016) *Beyond Greek: the beginnings of Latin literature*, Cambridge, MA
Feeney, D. C. (2021) *Explorations in Latin literature*, 2 vols., Cambridge
Feig Vishnia, R. (1998) 'The refusal of the centuriate assembly to declare war on Macedon (200 BC): a reappraisal', *Scripta Classica Israelica* 17: 34–44
Fentress, E. (2013) 'Strangers in the city: elite communication in the Hellenistic central Mediterranean', in J. R. W. Prag and J. Quinn (eds.), *The Hellenistic West: rethinking the ancient Mediterranean*, Cambridge: 156–78

Feraco, F. (2017) *Tito Livio, ab urbe condita liber* XXVII, Bari

Ferrary, J.-L. (1988) *Philhellénisme et impérialisme: aspects idéologiques de la conquête romaine du monde hellénistique de la seconde guerre de Macédoine à la guerre contre Mithridate*, BEFAR 271, Paris

Ferris, T. (2020) *Short life in a strange world: birth to death in 42 panels*, London

Fieldhouse, D. K. (1981) *Colonialism 1870–1945*, London

Finley, M. I. (1965) Review of Toynbee 1965, *New Statesman* 70: 1003–4 (24 December 1965)

Fischer-Bovet, C. (2014) *Army and society in Ptolemaic Egypt*, Cambridge

Fisher, G. (2016) *Hannibal and Scipio*, Stroud

Fitzgerald, W. and E. Gowers (eds.) (2007) *Ennius perennis: the* Annals *and beyond*, Cambridge

Flower, H. (1996) *Ancestor masks and aristocratic power in Roman culture*, Oxford

Flower, M. (2008) *The seer in Ancient Greece*, Berkeley

Foster, B. O. (1929) *Livy Books* XXI–XXII, Cambridge, MA

Fotheringham, J. K. (ed.) (1923) *Eusebii Pamphili chronici canones, Latine uertit, adauxit, ad sua tempora produxit S. Eusebius Hieronymus*, Oxford

Fraccaro, P. (1950) *Opuscula vol. 1: scritti di carattere generale; studi Catoniani; i processi degli Scipioni*, Pavia

Fraenkel, E. (1950) *Aeschylus* Agamemnon, 3 vols., Oxford

Fragoulaki, M. (2013) *Kinship in Thucydides: intercommunal ties and historical narrative*, Oxford

Frank, T. (1933) *An economic survey of ancient Rome. Vol. 1, Rome and Italy of the Republic*, Baltimore

Fraser, P. M. (1972) *Ptolemaic Alexandria*, 3 vols., Oxford

Fraser, P. M. (1994) 'The world of Theophrastus', in S. Hornblower (ed.), *Greek historiography*, Oxford: 167–91

Fraser, P. M. (1996) *The cities of Alexander the Great*, Oxford

Fraser, P. M. (2000) 'Ethnics as personal names', in S. Hornblower and E. Matthews (eds.), *Greek personal names: their value as evidence*, Oxford: 149–57

Fraser, P. M. (2009) *Greek ethnic terminology*, Oxford

Frazer, J. G. (1888) 'Hide-measured lands', *CR* 2. 10: 322

Frederiksen, M. (1959) 'Republican Capua: a social and economic study', *PBSR* 14: 80–130 (revised version at 1984: 285–318)

Frederiksen, M. (1984) *Campania*, ed. N. Purcell, Rome

Freedman, L. (2013) *Strategy: a history*, Oxford

Freedman, L. (2022) *Command: the politics of military operations from Korea to Ukraine*, London

Fronda, M. (2007) 'Hegemony and rivalry: the revolt of Capua revisited', *Phoenix* 61: 83–108

Fronda, M. (2010) *Between Rome and Carthage: southern Italy during the second Punic war*, Cambridge

Fronda, M. (2011) 'Hannibal: tactics, strategy, and geostrategy', in D. Hoyos (ed.), *A companion to the Punic wars*, Oxford: 242–59

Fronda, M. (2015) 'The Italians in the second Punic war', in G. D. Farney and G. Bradley (eds.), *The peoples of Ancient Italy*, Berlin: 215–30
Gabba, E. (1976) *Republican Rome: the army and the allies*, tr. P. J. Cuff, London
Gabba, E. (1989) 'Rome and Italy in the second century B.C.', *CAH*² viii: 197–243
Galinsky, K. (1969) *Aeneas, Sicily, and Rome*, Princeton, NJ
Galsterer, H. (1997) 'Die Stadt Italica: Status und Verwaltung', in A. Caballos Rufino and P. León Alonso (eds.), *Italica MMCC: actas de las jornadas del 2200 aniversario de la fundacion de Itálica (Sevilla 8–11 noviembre 1994)*, Seville: 49–64
Gargola, D. (2008) 'The Gracchan land reform and Appian's representation of an agrarian crisis', in L. De Ligt and S. J. Northwood (eds.), *People, land, and politics: demographic developments and the transformation of Italy, 300 BC–AD 14*, Leiden: 487–518
Garnsey, P. D. A. and C. R. Whittaker (eds.) (1978) *Imperialism in the ancient world*, Cambridge
Georgiadou, A. (1997) *Plutarch's* Pelopidas: *a historical and philological commentary*, Leipzig
Geus, K. (1994) *Prosopographie der literarisch bezeugten Karthager*, Leuven
Ginelli, F. (2021) *Cornelius Nepos: the commanders of the fifth century BC*, Oxford
Goldberg, S. and G. Manuwald (2018a) *Fragmentary Republican Latin I, Ennius: testimonia, epic fragments*, Cambridge, MA
Goldberg, S. and G. Manuwald (2018b) *Fragmentary Republican Latin II, Ennius: dramatic fragments, minor works*, Cambridge, MA
Gorman, R. (2001) 'οἱ περί τινα in Strabo', *ZPE* 136: 201–13
Gorman, R. (2003) 'Polybius and the evidence for periphrastic οἱ περί', *Mnemosyne* 56: 129–44
Gow, A. S. F. (1950) *Theocritus: edited with a translation and commentary*, 2 vols., Cambridge
Gowers, E. (2007) 'The *cor* of Ennius', in W. Fitzgerald and E. Gowers (eds.), *Ennius perennis: the* Annals *and beyond*, Cambridge: 17–37
Grafton, A. (1983) *Joseph Scaliger: a study in the history of Classical scholarship*, vol. I. *Textual criticism and exegesis*, Oxford
Grainger, J. D. (1990) *Seleukos Nikator: constructing a Hellenistic kingdom*, London
Grainger, J. D. (2002) *The Roman war of Antiochos the Great*, Leiden
Greenidge, A. H. J. and A. M. Clay (1960) *Sources for Roman history 133–70 B.C.*, 2nd ed., collected and arranged; rev. E. W. Gray, Oxford
Grethlein, J. and C. Krebs (eds.) (2012) *Time and narrative in ancient historiography: the 'plupast' from Herodotus to Appian*, Cambridge
Griffin, M. (1976) *Seneca: a philosopher in politics*, Oxford
Griffin, M. (2004/5) Review of Henderson 2004, *Hermathena* 177/8: 282–5
Griffiths, A. H. (1970) 'Six passages in Callimachus and the *Anthology*', *BICS* 17: 32–43
Groag, E. (1929) *Hannibal als Politiker*, Vienna
Gruen, E. S. (1984) *The Hellenistic world and the coming of Rome*, Berkeley, CA
Gruen, E. S. (1990) *Studies in Greek culture and Roman policy*, Leiden
Gruen, E. S. (1993) *Culture and national identity in Republican Rome*, London

Gruen. E. S. (1995) 'The 'fall' of the Scipios', in I. Malkin and Z. W. Rubinsohn (eds.), *Leaders and masses in the Roman world*, Leiden: 59–90

Gruen, E. S. (2011) *Rethinking the other in antiquity*, Princeton, NJ

Günther, L.-M. (1999) 'Carthaginian parties during the Punic Wars', *Mediterranean Historical Review* 14: 18–30

Habicht, C. (1997) *Athens from Alexander to Antony*, Cambridge, MA

Habicht, C. (2006a) *The Hellenistic monarchies: selected papers*, tr. P. Stevenson, Ann Arbor, MI

Habicht, C. (2006b) [1958] 'The ruling class in the Hellenistic monarchies', in *The Hellenistic monarchies: selected papers*, tr. P. Stevenson, Ann Arbor, MI: 26–40 with appendix at 290

Habicht, C. (2006c) [1989] 'Athens and the Seleucids', in *The Hellenistic monarchies: selected papers*, tr. P. Stevenson, Ann Arbor, MI: 155–73

Habicht, C. (2006d) [1989] 'The Seleucids and their rivals', in *The Hellenistic monarchies: selected papers*, tr. P. Stevenson, Ann Arbor, MI: 174–242 [originally $CAH^2$ VIII: 324–87]

Habicht, C. (2006e) [1958] 'On the wars between Pergamon and Bithynia', in *The Hellenistic monarchies: selected papers*, tr. P. Stevenson, Ann Arbor, MI: 1–21 with updating appendix at 289

Habicht C. (2017) [1970] *Divine honours for mortal men in Greek cities: the early cases*, tr. J. N. Dillon, Ann Arbor, MI

Hadas, M. (1930) *Sextus Pompey*, New York

Haimson Lushkov, A. (2010) 'Intertextuality and source-criticism in the Scipionic trials', in W. Polleichtner (ed.), *Livy and intertextuality: papers of a conference held at the University of Texas, Oct. 3, 2009*, Trier: 93–133

Halkin, L. (1934) 'Hannibal ad portas!', *Les Etudes Classiques* 3: 437–40

Hamilton, J. R. (1969) *Plutarch* Alexander: *a commentary*, Oxford

Hammond, M. and P. Thonemann (2020) *Artemidorus: the interpretation of dreams*. Oxford World's Classics, Oxford

Hansen, M. H. (ed.) (2000) *A comparative study of thirty city-state cultures: an investigation conducted by the Copenhagen Polis Centre*, Copenhagen

Hansen, M. H. (ed.) (2002) *A comparative study of six city-state cultures*, Copenhagen

Hansen, M. H. and T. H. Nielsen (eds.) (2004) *An inventory of Archaic and Classical poleis*, Oxford

Hanson, V. D. (1983) *Warfare and agriculture in ancient Greece*, Pisa

Hanson, V. D. (ed.) (1991) *Hoplites: the Classical Greek battle experience*, London

Harder, A., R. Regtuit, P. Stork, and G. Wakker (eds.) (2002) *'Noch einmal zu ... ': Kleine Schriften von Stephan Radt zu seinem 75. Geburtstag*, Leiden

Hardie, P. (1994) *Virgil Aeneid* IX, Cambridge

Hardie, P. (2012) *Rumour and renown: representations of fama in Western literature*, Cambridge

Harris, W. V. (1971) *Rome in Etruria and Umbria*, Oxford

Harris, W. V. (1979) *War and imperialism in Republican Rome 327–70 BC*, Oxford

Harris, W. V. (ed.) (1984) *The imperialism of mid-republican Rome*, Rome

Harris, W. V. (1989) 'Roman expansion in the west', *CAH²* viii: 107–62
Harris, W. V. (2007) 'The late Republic', in W. Scheidel, I. Morris, and R. Saller (eds.), *The Cambridge economic history of the Greco-Roman world*, Cambridge: 511–39
Harris, W. V. (2008) Review of *CHGRW*, *TLS*, 12 December: 30
Harris, W. V. (2009) *Dreams and experience in Classical antiquity*, Cambridge, MA
Harris, W. V. (2016) *Roman power: a thousand years of empire*, Cambridge
Harris, W. V. (2017a) 'Rome at sea: the beginnings of Roman naval power', *Greece and Rome* 64: 14–26
Harris, W. V. (2017b) 'Ernst Badian 1925–2011', *Biographical memoirs of the British Academy* 16: 3–17
Harris, W. V. (2021) 'The Roman conquest of Italy in recent historiography', *Studi Storici* 3: 771–91
Harrison, S. J. (1991) *Vergil* Aeneid *10*, Oxford
Hartmann, A. V. and B. Heuser (eds.) (2001) *War, peace and world orders in European history*, London
Hatzopoulos, M. B. (1994) *Cultes et rites de passage en Macédoine*, Athens
Hatzopoulos, M. B. (1996) *Macedonian institutions under the kings*, 2 vols., Athens
Hatzopoulos, M. B. (2016) *Découvrir la Macédoine antique: le terrain, les stèles, l'histoire. Recueil d'études de Miltiade B. Hatzopoulos*, Paris
Hatzopoulos, M. B. (2021) *Ancient Macedonia*, Berlin
Haubold, J., G. B. Lanfranchi, R. Rollinger and J. M. Steele (eds.) (2013) *The world of Berossus*. Classsica et Orientalia 5, Wiesbaden
Haywood, R. M. (1933) *Studies on Scipio Africanus*, Baltimore, MD
Heckel, W. (2000) Introduction and notes to J. C. Yardley, *Livy: the dawn of the Roman empire. Books 31–40*. Oxford World's Classics, Oxford
Heller, A. (2014) Review of Haubold, Lanfranchi, Rollinger, and Steele 2013, *BMCR* 2014.05.50
Henderson, J. (1997) *Figuring out Roman nobility: Juvenal's eighth Satire*, Exeter
Henderson, J. (2004) *Morals and villas in Seneca's letters: places to dwell*, Cambridge
Hennig, R. (1944) *Terrae incognitae* vol. 1 (all published), Leiden
Henze, W. (1900) 'Cornelius Scipio Africanus, P.', *R.-E.* 4: cols. 1462–70, 'Cornelius' no. 336
Hill, A. M. (2020) 'Hamilcar of Barce? Discerning Barcid proto-history and Polybius' *mixellēnes*', *JHS* 140: 69–105
Hobsbawm, E. and T. Ranger (eds.) 1983. *The invention of tradition*, Cambridge
Hobson, M. (2019) 'Carthage after the Punic wars and the neo-Punic legacy', in C. López-Ruiz and B. Doak (eds.), *The Oxford handbook of the Phoenician and Punic Mediterranean*, Oxford: 183–96
Hoffmann, W. (1934) *Rom und die griechische Welt im 4. Jahrhundert*. Philologus Supp. xxvii Heft 1, Leipzig
Hoffmann, W. (1951) 'Die römische Kriegserklärung an Karthago im Jahre 218', *Rh. Mus.* 84: 69–88
Hoffmann, W. (1962) *Hannibal*, Göttingen
Hölbl, G. (2001) *A history of the Ptolemaic empire*, tr. T. Saavedra, London

Holford-Strevens, L. (2003) *Aulus Gellius: an Antonine scholar and his achievement*, Oxford

Hölkeskamp, K.-J. (2001) 'Fact(ions) or fiction? Friedrich Münzer and the aristocracy of the Roman Republic – then and now' [review-discussion of Münzer 1999], *International Journal of the Classical Tradition* 8: 92–105

Hölkeskamp, K.-J. (2010) *Reconstructing the Roman Republic: an ancient political culture and modern research*, Princeton

Hölkeskamp, K.-J. (2017) *Libera res publica: die politische Kultur des antiken Rom – Positionen und Perspektiven*, Stuttgart

Hölkeskamp, K.-J. (2018) '*Memoria* by multiplication: the Cornelii Scipiones in monumental memory', in K. Sandberg and C. Smith (eds.), *Omnium annalium monumenta: historical writing and historical evidence in Republican Rome*. Boston: 422–76

Holleaux, M. (1921) *Rome, la Grèce et les monarchies hellénistiques au 3me siècle*, Paris

Holleaux, M. (1942a) *Études d'épigraphie et d'histoire grecques*, vol. iii, *Lagides et Séleucides*, ed. L. Robert, Paris

Holleaux, M. (1942b) 'Ardys et Mithridate', in *Études d'épigraphie et d'histoire grecques*, vol. iii, *Lagides et Séleucides*, ed. L. Robert, Paris: 183–93

Holleaux, M. (1957a) *Études d'épigraphie et d'histoire grecques*, vol. v, *Rome, la Macédoine et l'orient grec*, ed. L. Robert, Paris: 184–207

Holleaux, M. (1957b) [1908] 'La rencontre d'Hannibal et d'Antiochos le grand à Éphèse', in *Études d'épigraphie et d'histoire grecques*, vol. v, *Rome, la Macédoine et l'orient grec*, ed. L. Robert, Paris: 179–83

Holleaux, M. (1957c) [1913] 'L'entretien de Scipion l'Africain et d'Hannibal', in *Études d'épigraphie et d'histoire grecques*, vol. v, *Rome, la Macédoine et l'orient grec*, ed. L. Robert, Paris : 184–207

Holzinger, C. von (1895) *Lycophron's* Alexandra, Leipzig

Hopkins, K. (1978) *Conquerors and slaves*, Cambridge

Hornblower, J. (1981) *Hieronymus of Cardia*, Oxford

Hornblower, S. (1982) *Mausolus*, Oxford

Hornblower, S. (ed.) (1994) *Greek historiography*, Oxford

Hornblower, S. (2004), *Thucydides and Pindar: historical narrative and the world of epinikian poetry*, Oxford

Hornblower, S. (2011) *Thucydidean themes*, Oxford

Hornblower, S. (2013) *Herodotus Histories Book* v, Cambridge

Hornblower, S. (2015) *Lykophron: Alexandra. Greek text, introduction, translation, and commentary*, Oxford

Hornblower, S. (2016) '"What Alcibiades did and suffered" – but not what he looked like: physical appearance in the ancient Greek historians', *Syllecta Classica* 27: 93–107

Hornblower, S. (2018) *Lykophron's Alexandra, Rome, and the Hellenistic world*, Oxford

Hornblower, S. (2019) 'Livy, Busa the female benefactor, and the evidence of Delian epigraphy', *ZPE* 210: 71–5

Hornblower, S. (2022) *Lykophron* Alexandra. Oxford World's Classics, Oxford
Hornblower, S. and C. Morgan (eds.) (2007) *Pindar's poetry, patrons, and festivals: from Archaic Greece to the Roman Empire*, Oxford
Hornblower, S. *and* C. Pelling (2017) *Herodotus Histories Book* VI, Cambridge
Howard, M. (1976) *War in European history*, Oxford
Hoyos, D. (1994) 'Barcid 'proconsuls' and Punic politics. 237–18 B.C.', *Rh. Mus.* 137: 246–74
Hoyos, D. (2002) 'The battle-site of Ilipa', *Klio* 84: 101–13
Hoyos, D. (2003) *Hannibal's dynasty: power and politics in the western Mediterranean, 247–183 BC*, London and New York
Hoyos, D. (2006) Introduction and notes to J. C. Yardley (tr.), *Livy, Hannibal's war. Books 21–30*. Oxford World's Classics, Oxford
Hoyos, D. (2008) *Hannibal: Rome's greatest enemy*, Exeter
Hoyos, D. (ed.) (2011) *A companion to the Punic wars*, Oxford
Hoyos, D. (2019) 'Classical-Hellenistic Carthage before the Punic wars', in C. López-Ruiz and B. Doak (eds.), *The Oxford handbook of the Phoenician and Punic Mediterranean*, Oxford: 155–68
Hübner, G. (1993) *Die Applikenkeramik von Pergamon: eine Bildersprache im Dienst des Herrscherkultes*, Berlin
Hunter, R. (1996) *Theocritus and the archaeology of Greek poetry*, Cambridge
Hunter, R. (1999) *Theocritus: a selection. Idylls 1, 3, 4, 6, 7, 10, 11 and 13*, Cambridge
Hunter, R. (2003) *Theocritus: Encomium of Ptolemy Philadelphus*, Cambridge
Huss, W. (1985) *Geschichte der Karthager*, Munich
Huss, W. (1986) 'Hannibal und die Religion', *Studia Phoenicia* 4: 223–38
Itgenshorst, T. (2005) *Tota illa pompa: Der Triumph in der römischen Republik*, Göttingen
Jackson, J. B. (2013) 'The story of colonialism, or rethinking the ox-hide purchase in North America and beyond', *Journal of American Folklore* 126: 31–54
Jaeger, M. (1997) *Livy's written Rome*, Ann Arbor, MI
Jaeger, M. (2006) 'Livy, Hannibal's monument, and the temple of Juno at Croton', *TAPA* 136: 389–414
Jiménez Sancho, A. (2021) 'Italica' in T. Nogales Basarrate (ed.), *Ciudades romanas de Hispania. Cities of Roman Hispania*, Rome: 189–200
Johnston, P. A. and B. Kaufman (2019) 'Metallurgy and other technologies', in C. López-Ruiz and B. Doak (eds.), *The Oxford handbook of the Phoenician and Punic Mediterranean*, Oxford: 401–22
Jones, A. H. M. (1964) *The later Roman Empire*, Oxford
Jones, A. H. M. (1965) 'Toynbee returns to Rome' [review of Toynbee 1965], *Times Literary Supplement*, 2 December (published anonymously at the time; identity now revealed by the *TLS* archive).
Jones, A. H. M. (1971) *The cities of the eastern Roman provinces*, 2nd ed., Oxford
Jones, C. P. (2010) *New heroes in antiquity: from Achilles to Antinous*, Cambridge, MA
Jones, C. P. (2019) 'The siege of Colophon and the immunity of Claros', *ZPE* 210: 137–46

Keay, S. (1997) 'Early Roman Italica and the romanization of western Baetica', in A. Caballos Rufino and P. León Alonso (eds.), *Italica MMCC: actas de las jornadas del 2200 aniversario de la fundacion de Itálica (Sevilla 8–11 noviembre 1994)*, Seville: 21–47

Keay, S. (2013) 'Were the Iberians Hellenised?' in J. R. W. Prag and J. Quinn (eds.), *The Hellenistic West: rethinking the ancient Mediterranean*, Cambridge: 300–19

Keegan, J. (1976) *The face of battle: a study of Agincourt, Waterloo, and the Somme*, London

Keegan, J. (1987) *The mask of command*, London

Keegan, P. (2021) *Livy's women: crisis, resolution, and the female in Rome's foundation history*, Abingdon

Kelly, J. (1986) *The Oxford dictionary of popes*, Oxford

Kempf, C. (ed.) (1888) *Valerius Maximus*, Leipzig

Keppie, L. (1998) *The making of the Roman army*, 2nd ed., London

Keyes, C. W. (1928) *Cicero* de republica, de legibus. Loeb Classical Library, Cambridge, MA

Kidd, I. G. (1988) *Posidonius vol. II: the commentary (ii). Fragments 150–293*, Cambridge

Kienast, D. (1954) *Cato der Zensor: seine Persönlichkeit und seine Zeit*, Heidelberg

Klotz, A. (1940) *Livius und seine Vorgänger*, Stuttgart

Knapp, R. (1977) *Aspects of the Roman experience in Iberia 206–100 BC*, Valladolid

Köhler, R. (1866) 'Sagen von Landerwerbung durch zerschnittene Häute', *Orient und Occident* 3: 185–7

Konrad, C. F. (1994) *Plutarch's* Sertorius*: a historical commentary*, Chapel Hill, NC

Konrad, C. K. (2022) *The challenge to the auspices: studies in magisterial power in the Middle Roman Republic*, Oxford

Kosmin, P. (2014) *The land of the elephant kings: space, territory, and ideology in the Seleucid empire*, Cambridge, MA

Köster, I. (2014) 'How to kill a Roman villain: the deaths of Quintus Pleminius', *CJ* 109: 309–32

Krasser, H., D. Pausch, and I. Petrovic (eds.) (2007) *Triplici invectus triumpho: Der römische Triumph in augusteischer Zeit*, Stuttgart

Krentz, P. and E. L. Wheeler (eds. and tr.) (1994) *Polyaenus* Stratagems of war, 2 vols., Chicago

Kubler, A. (2018) *La mémoire culturelle de la deuxième guerre punique.* Schweizerische Beiträge zur Altertumswissenschaft 45, Basel

Kuhrt, A. and S. Sherwin-White (eds.) (1987) *Hellenism in the east*, London

Kuhrt, A. (1987) 'Berossus' Babyloniaka and Seleucid rule in Babylonia', in A. Kuhrt and S. Sherwin-White (eds.), *Hellenism in the east*, London: 32–56

Laidlaw, W. A. (1933) *A history of Delos*, Oxford

Laird, A. (1999) *Powers of expression, expressions of power: speech presentation in Latin literature*, Oxford

Lane Fox, R. (2018) 'Macedonians and *nostoi*', in S. Hornblower and G. Biffis (eds.), *The returning hero: nostoi and traditions of Mediterranean settlement*, Oxford: 193–212

Latte, K. (1960) *Römische Religionsgeschichte*, Munich

Lattimore, R. (1958) 'The composition of the *History* of Herodotus', *CP* 53: 9–21

Launey, M. (1949–50) *Recherches sur les armées hellénistiques*, 2 vols., Paris

Lazenby, J. F. (1978) *Hannibal's war*, Warminster

Lazenby, J. F. (1991) 'The killing zone', in V. D. Hanson (ed.), *Hoplites: the Classical Greek battle experience*, London: 87–109

Lazenby, J. F. (1996a) *The first Punic war*, London

Lazenby, J. F. (1996b) 'Was Maharbal right?', in T. Cornell, B. Rankov, and P. Sabin (eds.), *The second Punic war: a reappraisal*, London: 39–48

Le Bohec, S. (1993) *Antigonos Dôsôn roi de Macédoine*, Nancy

Lee, A. D. (2020) *Warfare in the Roman world*, Cambridge

Levene, D. S. (1993) *Religion in Livy*, Leiden

Levene, D. S. (2010) *Livy on the Hannibalic war*, Oxford

Levene, D. S. (2023) *Livy: the fragments and periochae.* 2 vols., Oxford

Lévêque, P. (1957) *Pyrrhos*, Paris

Liddell Hart, B. H. (1926) *Scipio Africanus: greater than Napoleon*, London

Lintott, A. W. (1968) *Violence in Republican Rome*, Oxford

Lintott, A. W. (1982) *Violence, civil strife and revolution in the Classical city*, London

Lintott, A. W. (1987) 'Democracy in the Middle Republic', *ZSS* 104: 34–52

Lintott, A. W. (1994a) 'The Roman empire and its problems in the late second century', *CAH*² ix: 16–39

Lintott, A. W. (1994b) 'Political history, 146–95 BC', *CAH*² ix: 40–103

Lintott, A. W. (1999) *The constitution of the Roman republic*, Oxford

Lobur, J. A. (2021) *Cornelius Nepos: a study in the evidence and influence*, Ann Arbor, MI

Lomas, K. (1993) *Rome and the Western Greeks 350 BC–AD 200: conquest and acculturation in southern Italy*, London

López-Bertran, M. (2019) 'Funerary ritual', in C. López-Ruiz and B. Doak (eds.), *The Oxford handbook of the Phoenician and Punic Mediterranean*, Oxford: 293–309

López-Ruiz, C. (2019) 'Phoenician literature', in C. López-Ruiz and B. Doak (eds.), *The Oxford handbook of the Phoenician and Punic Mediterranean*, Oxford: 257–69

López-Ruiz, C. and B. Doak (eds.) (2019) *The Oxford handbook of the Phoenician and Punic Mediterranean*, Oxford

*Los Escipiones*: see Bendala Galán

Luce, T. J. (1977) *Livy: the composition of his history*, Princeton, NJ

Ma, J. (1999) *Antiochos III and the cities of western Asia Minor*, Oxford

Ma, J. (2000) 'Fighting poleis of the Hellenistic world', in H. Van Wees (ed.), *War and violence in ancient Greece*, London: 337–76

Macan, R. W. (1908) *Herodotus: the seventh, eighth, and ninth books*, vol. 1 part 1, London

MacDonald, E. (2015) *Hannibal: a Hellenistic life*, New Haven, CT and London
Machado, D. (2021) 'Deconstructing *disciplina*: disentangling ancient and modern ideologies of military discipline in the Middle Republic', *AJP* 142: 387–424
Machiavelli, N. (written 1513, published posthumously 1532, Rome and Florence) *The Prince* see Bondanella 2005
Mackie, N. (1988) '*Hispaniae*' [review of Richardson 1986], *CR* 38: 318–19
MacMullen, R. (1982) 'The epigraphic habit in the Roman Empire', *AJP* 103: 233–46
McCarty, M. (2019) 'The tophet and infant sacrifice', in C. López-Ruiz and B. Doak (eds.), *The Oxford handbook of the Phoenician and Punic Mediterranean*, Oxford: 311–25
McDonald, A. H. (1938) 'Scipio Africanus and Roman politics in the second century B.C.', *JRS* 28: 152–64
McGing, B. (ed.) (2019) *Appian* Roman History, vol. 1. Loeb Classical Library, Cambridge, MA
McHardy, F. (forthcoming) 'Battlefield decapitation and mutilation in the Ancient Greek imagination', in H.-M. Chidwick (ed.), *The body of the combatant in the Classical world*, London
McNeill, W. H. (1977) 'Arnold Joseph Toynbee, 1889–1975', *PBA* 63: 441–69
McShane, R. B. (1964) *The foreign policy of the Attalids of Pergamum*. Illinois studies in the social sciences 53, Urbana, IL
Malkin, I. (1994) *Myth and territory in the Spartan Mediterranean*, Cambridge
Marek, C. (2023) *Rom und der Orient. Reiche. Götter. Könige*, Munich
Marks, R. (2005) *From Republic to Empire: Scipio Africanus in the* Punica *of Silius Italicus*, Frankfurt
Marks, R. (2008) 'Getting ahead: decapitation as political metaphor in Silius Italicus' *Punica*', *Mnemosyne* 61: 66–88
Marshall, P. K. (ed.) (1977) *Corneli Nepotis vitae cum fragmentis*, Leipzig
Masson, O. (2000) *Onomastica graeca selecta* III, Geneva
Mayor, A. (2022) *Greek fire, poison arrows, and scorpion bombs: unconventional warfare in the ancient world*, 2nd ed., Princeton, NJ (1st ed., 2003, had different sub-title)
Mehl, A. (1986) *Seleukos Nikator und sein Reich*, Louvain
Meier, C. (1966) *Res publica amissa*, Wiesbaden
Meiggs, R. (1972) *The Athenian empire*, Oxford
Meister, K. (1967) 'Die sizilische Geschichte bei Diodor von den Anfängen bis zum Tod des Agathokles: Quellenuntersuchungen zu Buch IV–XXI', diss. Erlangen
Meister, K. (1990) 'Autobiographische Literatur und Memoiren (Hypomnemata) (*FGrH* 227–38)', in H. Verdin, G. Schepens, and E. De Kayser (eds.), *Purposes of history: Studies in Greek historiography from the fifth to the second centuries* BC. Studia hellenistica 30, Leuven: 83–9
Mermati, F. (2015) 'The Campanians', in G. D. Farney and G. Bradley (eds.), *The peoples of Ancient Italy*, Berlin: 385–418

Meyer, E. (1923) 'Hannibal und Scipio', in E. Marcks and K. A. von Müller (eds.), *Meister der Politik*, vol. 1², Stuttgart and Berlin: 99–146
Millar, F. (1977) *The emperor in the Roman world*, London
Millar, F. (1984) 'The political character of the Classical Roman Republic, 200–151 BC', *JRS* 64: 1–219
Millar, F. (1986) 'Politics, persuasion, and the people before the Social war', *JRS* 66: 1–11
Millar, F. (1998) *The crowd in the Late Republic*, Ann Arbor, MI
Millar, F. (2004) 'Arnold Joseph Toynbee', *ODNB* 55: 178–85
Millot, R. (2019), 'Complot au Carcer: un nouveau regard sur l'affaire Pleminius (204–194 av. J.-C.)', *Dialogues d'histoire ancienne*, 45: 89–110
Milner, N. P. (1996) *Vegetius: Epitome of military science. Translated with notes and introduction*, 2nd ed., Liverpool
Miltsios, N. (2013) *The shaping of narrative in Polybius*, Berlin and Boston
Mineo, B. (2009) 'Vies parallèles dans le récit Livien: Hannibal et Scipion', *Interférences* 5
Moeller, W. O. (1975) 'Once more the one-eyed man against Rome', *Historia* 24: 402–10
Momigliano, A. (1966) *Studies in historiography*, London
Momigliano, A. (1969) *Quarto contributo alla storia degli studi classici e del mondo antico*, Rome
Momigliano, A. (1971) *The development of Greek biography*, Cambridge, MA
Momigliano, A. (1975) *Alien wisdom: the limits of hellenization*, Cambridge
Momigliano, A. (1977) *Essays in ancient and modern historiography*, Oxford
Momigliano, A. (1980) *Sesto contributo alla storia degli studi classici e del mondo antico*, Rome
Momigliano, A. (1984) *Settimo contributo alla storia degli studi classici e del mondo antico*, Rome
Momigliano, A. (1989) 'The origins of Rome', *CAH* VII² 2: 52–112 [= 1984: 379–436]
Momigliano, A. (1994) *Studies on modern scholarship*, ed. G. Bowersock and T. J. Cornell, Berkeley, CA
Mommsen. T. (1887–8) *Römisches Staatsrecht*, 3rd ed., 3 vols., Leipzig
Mommsen, T. (1906) *Historische Schriften*, vol. 1, Berlin
Moore, D. W. (2020) *Polybius: experience and the lessons of history*, Leiden
Moore, R. M. (1965) *The manuscript tradition of Polybius*, Cambridge
Morel, J.-P. (2007) 'Early Rome and Italy', in W. Scheidel, I. Morris, and R. Saller (eds.), *The Cambridge economic history of the Greco-Roman world*, Cambridge: 487–510
Moretti, L. (1957) *Olympionikai*, Rome
Mossman, J. (2018) 'Additional lives: Hannibal, Scipio, and Epaminondas', in J. North and P. Mack (eds.), *The afterlife of Plutarch*, BICS Supp. 137, London: 75–83
Mouritsen, H. (2001) *Plebs and politics in the Late Roman Republic*, Cambridge
Mouritsen, H. (2017) *Politics in the Roman Republic*, Cambridge

Münzer, F. (1900a) 'Cornelius Scipio Aemilianus Africanus, P.', *R.-E.* 4: cols. 1439–62, 'Cornelius' no. 335
Münzer, F. (1900b) 'Cornelius Scipio Asiagenes, L.', *R.-E.* 4: cols. 1439–62, 'Cornelius' no. 337
Münzer, F. (1920) *Römische Adelsparteien und Adelsfamilien*, Stuttgart
Münzer, F. (1926) 'Livius Salinator, M.', *R.-E.* 25: cols. 891–99, 'Livius' no. 33
Münzer, F. (1999) *Roman aristocratic parties and families*, Baltimore [tr. by T. Ridley of Münzer 1920, with full name-index]
Naiden, F. S. (2006) *Ancient supplication*, New York and Oxford
Newman, W. L. (1887–1902) *The Politics of Aristotle*, 4 vols., Oxford
Nicholson, E. (2023) *Philip of Macedon in Polybius' Histories: politics, history, and fiction*, Oxford
Nicolet, C. (1974) *L'ordre équestre à l'époque républicaine (312–43 av. J.-C.)*, Paris
Niese, B. (1883–1903) *Geschichte der griechischen und makedonischen Staaten*, 3 vols., Gotha
Nisbet, R. G. M. (1995) *Collected papers on Latin literature*, ed. S. J. Harrison, Oxford
Nisbet, R. G. M. and M. Hubbard (1970) *A commentary on Horace, Odes, Book* I, Oxford
Nisbet, R. G. M. and N. Rudd (2004) *A commentary on Horace, Odes, Book* III, Oxford
Nogales Basarrate, T. (ed.) (2021) *Ciudades romanas de* Hispania. *Cities of Roman Hispania*, Rome
Nora, P. (1999–2006) *Rethinking France: les lieux de mémoire*, Chicago
Norden, E. (1915) *Ennius und Vergilius*, Berlin
Norden, E. (1927) *Vergilius Aeneis Buch* VI, 3rd ed., Stuttgart and Leipzig
North, J. A. (1990) 'Diviners and divination at Rome', in M. Beard and J. North (eds.), *Pagan priests: religion and power in the ancient world*, London: 51–71
North, J. A. (2004) 'Democratic politics in Republican Rome', in R. Osborne (ed.), *Studies in Ancient Greek and Roman society*, Cambridge: 140–58, reprinted from *Past and Present* 126: 3–21 (1990), with 2003 postscript at 156–8
Oakley, S. P. (1992) 'Livy and Clodius Licinus', *CQ* 42: 547–51
Oakley, S. P. (1997) *A commentary on Livy books* VI–X, vol. i, *introduction and book* VI, Oxford
Oakley, S. P. (1998) *A commentary on Livy books* VI–X, vol. ii, *books* VII *and* VIII, Oxford
Oakley, S. P. (2005a) *A commentary on Livy books* VI–X, vol. iii, *book* IX, Oxford
Oakley, S. P. (2005b) *A commentary on Livy books* VI–X, vol. iv, *book* X, Oxford
Oakley, S. P. (2019a) 'Livy on Cannae: a literary overview', in L. Van Gils, I. de Jong, and C. Kroon (eds.), *Textual strategies in ancient war narrative: Thermopylae, Cannae and beyond*, Leiden and Boston: 157–90
Oakley S. P. (2019b) 'Hannibal reaches the Alps: Livy 21,32,6 –33,1 and Polybius 3, 50, 1–51, 3', in G. Baldo and L. Beltramini (eds.), *A primordio Urbis: Un itinerario per gli studi liviani*, Turnhout: 272–52
Ogilvie, R. M. (1965) *A commentary on Livy books 1–5*, Oxford

Ogden, D. (2013) *Drakōn: dragon myth and serpent cult in the Greek and Roman worlds*, Oxford
Oost, S. I. (1967) Review of Toynbee 1965, *CP* 62: 144–6
Opper, T. (2008) *Hadrian: empire and conflict*, London
Orlin, E. (1997) *Temples, religion and politics in the Roman Republic*, Leiden
Osborne, R. (ed.) (2004) *Studies in Ancient Greek and Roman society*, Cambridge
Östenberg, I. (2009) *Staging the world: spoils, captives, and representations in the Roman triumphal procession*, Oxford
Padilla Monge, A. (2017) 'Escipión e *Italica*. algunas notas', *Polis. Rivista de ideas y formas politicas de la Antigüedad* 29: 69–100
Palmer, R. E. A. (1974) *Roman religion and Roman empire*, Philadelphia, PA
Palmer, R. E. A. (1997) *Rome and Carthage at peace*. Historia Einzelschrift 113, Stuttgart
Parker, R. (1983) *Miasma: pollution and purification in early Greek religion*, Oxford
Parker, R. (2000) 'Sacrifice and battle', in H. Van Wees (ed.), *War and violence in ancient Greece*, London: 299–314 (2023: 245–57)
Parker, R. (2017) *Greek gods abroad: Names, natures, and transformations*, Berkeley, CA
Parker, R. (ed.) (2019a) *Changing names: tradition and innovation in Greek onomastics*. PBA 222, London
Parker, R. (2019b) 'Introduction', in *Changing names: tradition and innovation in Greek onomastics*, London: 1–20
Parker, R. (2022) 'Θεῶν φίλτρα: sexual union between gods and mortals', in E. Pachoumi (ed.), *Conceptualising divine unions in the Greek and Near Eastern worlds*, Leiden and Boston: 148–67
Parker, R. (2023) *Cleomenes on the Acropolis and other studies in Greek religion and society*. Kernos Supplement 42, Liège
Paul, G. M. (1982) '*Urbs capta*. Sketch of a literary motif', *Phoenix* 36: 144–55
Pausch, D. (2011) *Livius und der Leser: Narrative Strukturen in* ab urbe condita. Zetemata 140, Munich
Pédech, P. (1964) *La méthode historique de Polybe*, Paris
Pelling, C. B. R. (1990) 'Childhood and personality in Greek biography', in Pelling (ed.), *Characterization and individuality in Greek literature*, Oxford, 212–44
Pelling, C. B. R. (1997) *Plutarco: Filopoimene e Tito Flaminino* (introduction and commentaries; Greek text translated by E. Milandri), Milan
Pelling, C. B. R. (2002) *Plutarch and history: eighteen studies*, London
Pelling. C. B. R. (2019) *Herodotus and the reason why*, Austin, TX
Pelling, C. B. R. (forthcoming) 'Sallust and the Imperial Greek historians', in C. Krebs (ed.), *Blackwell companion to Sallust*, Oxford
Pena, M. (1985) 'Apuntes y observaciones sobre las primeras fundaciones romanas en Hispania', *Estudios de la Antigüedad* 1: 50–3
Perosa, A. and J. Sparrow (eds.) (1979) *Renaissance Latin verse: an anthology*, London
Pfeiffer, R. (1976) *History of Classical scholarship 1300–1850*, Oxford

Pfeilschifter, R. (2005) *Titus Quinctius Flamininus: Untersuchungen zur römischen Griechenlandpolitik*. Hypomnemata 162, Göttingen

Picard, G. C. (1966) Review of Toynbee 1965, *Rev. Arch.* n.s. 2: 372–3

Picard, G. C. (1994) 'Carthage from the battle at Himera to Agathocles' invasion (480–308 B.C.), *CAH²* VI: 361–80

Pichlmayr, F. (1961) *Sexti Aurelii Victori liber de Caesaribus*, Leipzig, reprint of 1911 edition, with addenda by R. Gruendel

Pilkington, N. (2019) *The Carthaginian empire 550–202 BCE*, London

Pina Polo, F. (2021) 'Foundations of provincial towns as memorials of *imperatores*: the case of Hispania', in A. Díaz Fernández (ed.), *Provinces and provincial command in Republican Rome: genesis, development and governance*, Zaragoza: 145–64

Pina Polo, F. and A. Díaz Fernández (2019) *The quaestorship in the Roman Republic*, Berlin

Pittenger, M. R. P. (2008) *Contested triumphs: politics, pageantry, and performance in Livy's Republican Rome*, Berkeley, CA

Polleichtner, W. (ed.) (2010) *Livy and intertextuality: papers of a conference held at the University of Texas, Oct. 3, 2009*, Trier

Poralla, P. (1913) *Prosopographie der Lakedaimonier bis auf die Zeit Alexanders des Grossen*, Breslau

Powell, J. E. (1939) *A lexicon to Herodotus*, Cambridge

Prag, J. R. W. (2007) '*Auxilia* and *gymnasia*: a Sicilian model of Roman imperialism', *JRS* 97: 68–100

Prag, J. R. W. and J. Quinn (eds.) (2013) *The Hellenistic West: rethinking the ancient Mediterranean*, Cambridge

Price, S. R. F. (1984) *Rituals and power: the Roman imperial cult in Asia Minor*, Cambridge

Proctor, D. (1971) *Hannibal's march in history*, Oxford

Quesada Sanz, F. (1997) '*Gladius Hispaniensis*: an archaeological view from Iberia', *Journal of Roman military equipment studies* 8: 251–70

Quesada Sanz, F. (2006) 'Not so different: individual fighting techniques and small unit tactics of Roman and Iberian armies within the framework of warfare in the Hellenistic age', *Pallas* 70: 245–63

Quesada Sanz, F. (2015) 'Los Escipiones, generales de Roma', in M. Bendala Galán (ed.), *Los Escipiones: Roma conquista Hispania*, Madrid: 66–89

Quinn, J. (2018) *In search of the Phoenicians*, Princeton, NJ

Raaflaub, K. (2009), 'Learning from the enemy: Athenian and Persian instruments of empire', in J. Ma, N. Papakarzadas , and R. Parker *(eds.), Interpreting the Athenian Empire*, London: 89–124

Radt, S. (2002) 'οἱ περί τινα in Strabo', *ZPE* 139: 46

Ramallo Asensio, S. and M. M. Ros Sala (2015) 'De *Qart Hadast* a *Carthago Nova*: la conquista de Escipión como trasfondo', in M. Bendala Galán (ed.), *Los Escipiones: Roma conquista Hispania*, Madrid: 163–79

Rankov, B. (1996) 'The second Punic war at sea', in T. Cornell, B. Rankov, and P. Sabin (eds.), *The second Punic war: a reappraisal*, London: 49–57

Rawlings, L. (2007) 'Army and battle during the conquest of Italy (350–264 BC)', in P. Erdkamp (ed.), *A companion to the Roman army*, Oxford: 45–62
Rawson, E. (1989) 'Roman tradition and the Greek world', *CAH*² viii: 422–76
Rawson, E. (1991) *Roman culture and society: collected papers*, Oxford
Redfield, J. (2003) *The Locrian maidens: love and death in Greek Italy*, Chicago
Reeve, M. D. (2004) *Vegetius: Epitoma rei militaris*. OCT, Oxford
Reid, J. S. (1885) *M. Tulli Ciceronis Academica*, London
Reid, J. S. (1908) *M. Tulli Ciceronis pro L. Cornelio Balbo oratio*, Cambridge
Reinhardt, T. (2023) *Cicero's* Academici libri *and* Lucullus*: a commentary with introduction and translations*, Oxford
Requena Jiménez, M. (2018) 'Prodigies in Republican Rome: the absence of God' *Klio* 100: 480–500
Rice, E. E. (1983) *The grand procession of Ptolemy Philadelphus*, Oxford
Ribbeck, O. (1888) *Comicorum Romanorum fragmenta*, 3rd ed., Leipzig
Rich, J. W. (1985) 'The outbreak of the second Punic war' [review of Schwarte 1983], *CR* 35: 135–6
Rich, J. W. (1988) 'Senate, generals, and Roman foreign relations' [review of Eckstein 1987], *CR* 38: 315–17
Rich, J. W. (1993) 'War, greed and glory: the causes of Roman war-making in the middle Republic', in J. W. Rich and G. Shipley (eds.), *War and society in the Roman world*, London: 38–62
Rich, J. W. (1996) 'The origins of the second Punic war', in T. Cornell, B. Rankov, and P. Sabin (eds.), *The second Punic war: a reappraisal*, London: 1–37
Rich, J. W. (2001) 'Warfare and external relations in the middle Roman Republic', in A. V. Hartmann and B. Heuser (eds.), *War, peace and world orders in European history*, London: 62–71
Richardson, J. S. (1975) 'The triumph, the praetors, and the senate in the early second century B. C.', *JRS* 65: 50–63
Richardson, J. S. (1986) *Hispaniae: Spain and the development of Roman imperialism 218–82 BC*, Cambridge
Richardson, J. S. (2008) *The language of empire: Rome and the idea of empire from the third century* BC *to the second century* AD, Cambridge
Rigsby, K. J. (1996) Asylia: *territorial inviolability in the Hellenistic world*, Berkeley, CA, Los Angeles, and London
Rivers, J. B. (1994) 'Tertullian on child-sacrifice', *Mus. Helv.* 51: 54–63
Robertson, C. M. (1975) *A history of Greek art*, Cambridge
Robinson, E. S. G. (1956) 'Punic coins of Spain and their bearing on the Roman Republican series', in R. A. G. Carson and C. H. V. Sutherland (eds.), *Essays in Roman coinage presented to H. Mattingly*, Oxford: 34–53
Rochette, B. (1997) 'Sur le bilinguisme dans les armées d'Hannibal', *LEC* 65: 153–9
Rodriguez, O. and F. J. García Fernández (2015) 'Itálica: la fundación de Publio Cornelio Escipión Africano en el corazón de la Hispania púnica', in M. Bendala Galán (ed.), *Los Escipiones: Roma conquista Hispania*, Madrid: 223–43
Roller, D. W. (2021) *Three ancient geographical treatises in translation: Hanno, the King Nikomedes Periodos, and Avienus*, London

Rose, H. J. (1924) *The* Roman Questions *of Plutarch*, Oxford
Roselaar, S. (2010) *Public land in the Roman Republic: a social and economic history of* ager publicus, *396–89* BC, Oxford
Roselaar, S. (2015) 'Battle formation in the Roman Republic: parade show or practical purpose?', *Revue Internationale d'histoire militaire ancienne* 2: 23–53
Roselaar, S. (2019) *Italy's economic revolution: integration and economy in Republican Italy*, Oxford
Rosenberger, V. (1998) *Gezähmte Götter: Das Prodigienwesen in der römischen Republik*, Stuttgart
Rosenberger, V. (2007) 'Republican *nobiles*: controlling the *res publica*', in J. Rüpke (ed.), *A companion to Roman religion*, Oxford: 292–30
Rosenstein, N. (1990) *Imperatores victi: military defeat and aristocratic competition in the Middle and Late Republic*, Berkeley, CA
Rosenstein, N. (2004) *Rome at war: farms, families, and death in the Middle Republic*, Chapel Hill, NC
Rosenstein, N. (2011) 'Italy: economy and demography after Hannibal's war', in D. Hoyos (ed.), *A companion to the Punic wars*, Oxford: 411–29
Rosenstein, N. (2023) 'Paying for conquest in the Middle Republic', in S. Bernard, L. M. Mignone, and D.-E. Padilla Peralta (eds.), *Making the Middle Republic: new approaches to Rome and Italy, c. 400–200* BCE, Cambridge: 64–79
Rosenthal, H. and J. Warrack (1979) *The concise Oxford dictionary of opera*, 2nd ed., Oxford
Rossbach, O. (1886) *L. Annaei Flori epitomae libri* II, Leipzig
Rossi, A. (2004) 'Parallel lives: Hannibal and Scipio in Livy's third Decade', *TAPA* 134: 359–81
Roth, J. P. (1999) *The logistics of the Roman army at war, 264* B.C. – A. D. *235*, Leiden
Roth, J. P. (2009) *Roman warfare*, Cambridge
Rotroff, S. (1996) Review of Hübner 1993, *Gnomon* 68: 356–61
Ruiz de Arbulo, J. (2015) '*Tarraco*, "obra de los Escioiones" y algo más', in M. Bendala Galán (ed.), *Los Escipiones: Roma conquista Hispania*, Madrid: 128–47
Ruiz Valderez, E. (ed.) (2017) *Ciudades romanas de Hispania (5) Cartagena, Colonia Julia Nova Carthago*, Rome
Rüpke, J. (2007a) *Religion of the Romans*, Cambridge
Rüpke, J. (ed.) (2007b) *A companion to Roman religion*, Oxford
Rüpke, J. (2008) *Fasti sacerdotum: a prosopography of pagan, Jewish, and Christian religious officials in the city of Rome, 300* BC *to* AD *499*, tr. D. M. B. Richardson, Oxford
Rüpke, J. (2011) *The Roman calendar from Numa to Constantine: time, history, and the* fasti, Chichester
Russell, D. A. (1972) *Plutarch*, London
Ryan, F. X. (1998) *Rank and participation in the Republican senate*, Stuttgart

Sabin, P. (1996) 'The mechanics of battle in the second Punic war', in T. Cornell, B. Rankov, and P. Sabin (eds.), *The second Punic war: a reappraisal*, London: 59–79

Sabin, P. (2000) 'The face of Roman battle', *JRS* 90: 1–17

Sacks, K. S. (1975) 'Polybius' other view of Aetolia', *JHS* 95: 92–106

Sailor, S. (2002) 'Denzel as Afrocentrist Hannibal', UPI news, 17 July 2002: https://www.upi.com/Odd_News/2002/07/17/Analysis-Denzel-as-Afrocentrist-Hannibal/74691026927936/

Saller, R. P. (1994) *Patriarchy, property, and death in the Roman family*, Cambridge

Salmon, E. T. (1967) Review of Toynbee 1965, *AJP* 88: 461–5

Salmon, E. T. (1969) *Roman colonisation under the Republic*, London

Salway, B. (1994) 'What's in a name? A survey of Roman onomastic patterns from c. 700 B.C to A.D. 700', *JRS* 84: 124–45

Sandbach, F. H. (1969) *Plutarch. Moralia vol.* XV: *the fragments*. Loeb Classical Library, Cambridge, MA

Saunders, T. J. (1995) *Aristotle, Politics books* I *and* II, tr. with commentary, Oxford

Scardigli, B. (1997) Introduction and notes to S. Fuscagni and B. Scardigli (eds.), *Plutarco: Cimone e Lucullo*, Milan

Scheid, J. and J. Svenbro (1985) 'Byrsa: la ruse d'Élissa et la fondation de Carthage', *Annales ESC* 40: 328–42

Scheidel, W., I. Morris, and R. Saller (eds.) (2007) *The Cambridge economic history of the Greco-Roman world*, Cambridge

Schlag, U. (1968) *Regnum in senatu: das Wirken römischer Staatsmänner von 200 bis 191 v. Chr.*, Stuttgart

Schmitt, H. (1964) *Untersuchungen zur Geschichte Antiochos des Grossen und seiner Zeit*, Historia Einzelschrift 6, Wiesbaden

Scholten, J. B. (2000) *The politics of plunder: Aitolians and their* koinon *in the early Hellenistic era, 279–217* B.C., Berkeley, CA

Schrott, P. (2014) *Plutarchs* Philopoimen *und* Titus Quinctius Flamininus: *eine philologisch-historische Kommentierung*, Hamburg

Schulz, R. (1997) *Herrschaft und Regierung: Roms Regiment in den Provinzen in der Zeit der Republik*, Paderborn

Schulze, W. (1904) *Zur Geschichte lateinischer Eigennamen*, Berlin

Schwarte, K.-H. (1983) *Der Ausbruch des zweiten Punischen Krieges: Rechtsfrage und Überlieferung*. Historia Einzelschrift 43, Wiesbaden

Schwartz, E. (1959) *Griechische Geschichtschreiber*, Leipzig

Scullard, H. H. (1930) *Scipio Africanus in the second Punic war*, Cambridge

Scullard, H. H. (1966) Review of Toynbee 1965, *History* 51: 199–201

Scullard, H. H. (1970) *Scipio Africanus: soldier and politician*, London

Scullard, H. H. (1973 [1951]) *Roman politics 220–150* BC, Oxford

Scullard, H. H. (1974a) *The elephant in the Greek and Roman world*, London

Scullard, H. H. (1974b) 'The site of the battle of Zama', in J. Evans (ed.), *Polis and imperium: studies in honour of Edward Togo Salmon*, Toronto: 225–31

Scullard, H. H. (1981) *Festivals and ceremonies of the Roman Republic*, London

Scullard, H. H. (1989) 'The Carthaginians in Spain', $CAH^2$ VIII: 17–43

Seel, O. (1972) *M. Iuniani Iustini epitoma historiarum Philippicarum Pompei Trogi*, Stuttgart
Seibert, J. (1969) *Untersuchungen zur Geschichte Ptolemaios I*, Munich
Seibert. J. (1993a) *Hannibal*, Darmstadt
Seibert, J. (1993b) *Forschungen zu Hannibal*, Darmstadt
Serrati, J. (1999) Review of Ameling 1993, *CR* 49: 289–90
Sherk, R. K. (1969) *Roman documents from the Greek East*, Baltimore, MD
Sherk, R. K. (1984) *Rome and the Greek East to the death of Augustus*, Cambridge
Sherwin-White, A. N. (1966) *The letters of Pliny: a historical and social commentary*, Oxford
Sherwin-White, S. and A. Kuhrt (1993) *From Samarkhand to Sardis: a new approach to the Seleucid empire*, London
Skutsch, O. (1985) *The Annals of Quintus Ennius*, Oxford
Smith, C. and L. M. Yarrow (eds.) (2012a) *Polybius, cultural politics, and imperialism*, Oxford
Smith, C. and L. M. Yarrow (2012b) 'Introduction', in C. Smith and L. M. Yarrow (eds.), *Polybius, cultural politics, and imperialism*, Oxford: 1–14
Smith. P. (1993) *Scipio Africanus and Rome's invasion of Africa: a historical commentary on Titus Livius book* XXIX. McGill University monographs in Classical archaeology and history vol. 13, Amsterdam
Smith, R. R. R. (1988) *Hellenistic royal portraits*, Oxford
Smith, R. R. R. (2007) 'Pindar, athletes, and the early Greek statue habit', in S. Hornblower and C. Morgan (eds.), *Pindar's poetry, patrons, and festivals: from Archaic Greece to the Roman Empire*, Oxford: 83–139
Snowden, F. M. (1970) *Blacks in antiquity: Ethiopians in the Greco-Roman experience*, Cambridge MA
Sourvinou-Inwood, C. (1974) 'The Boston relief and the religion of Locri Epizephyrii', *JHS* 94: 126–37
Starks, J. H. (1999) '*Fides Aineia*: the transference of Punic stereotypes in the *Aeneid*', *CJ* 94: 255–83
Staveley, E. T. (1967) Review of Toynbee 1965, *JRS* 57: 244–6
Stein, H. (1889) *Herodotos erklärt*, vol. $4^5$ (book 7), Berlin
Stepper, R. (2001) 'Roman-Carthaginian relations: from co-operation to annihilation', in A. V. Hartmann and B. Heuser (eds.), *War, peace and world orders in European history*, London: 72–83
Stocks, C. (2014) *The Roman Hannibal: remembering the enemy in Silius Italicus' Punica*, Liverpool
Stockton, D. L. (1981) *From the Gracchi to Sulla: sources for Roman history, 133–80 BC*, LACTOR 13, London
Strachan, H. (2013) *The direction of war: contemporary strategy in historical perspective*, Cambridge
Strachan, H. (2019) Foreword to C. Carey, *Great battles: Thermopylae*, Oxford: xii–xi
Strunk, T. E. (2021) 'History by analogy: Cato the Younger and Caesar in Livy's account of the second Punic war', *AHB* 35: 74–91

Sumner, G. V. (1973) *The orators in Cicero's Brutus: Prosopography and chronology*, Toronto
Suolahti, J. (1955) *The junior officers of the Roman army in the Republican period: a study on social structure*, Helsinki
Susemihl, F. (1891–2) *Geschichte der griechischen Litteratur in der Alexandrinerzeit*, 2 vols., Leipzig
Syme, R. (1939) *The Roman revolution*, Oxford
Syme, R. (1958) *Tacitus*, Oxford
Syme, R. (1964) 'Hadrian and Italica', *JRS* 54: 142–9 [= Syme 1979: 617–28]
Syme, R. (1979) *Roman papers*, vol. II, ed. E. Badian, Oxford
Syme, R. (1995) *Anatolica: studies in Strabo*, ed. A. Birley, Oxford
Tan, J. (2013) 'Booty and the Roman assembly in 264 B.C.', *Historia* 62: 417–19
Tarn, W. W. (1913) *Antigonos Gonatas*, Oxford
Tarn, W. W. (1948) *Alexander the Great II (sources and studies)*, Cambridge
Tarn, W. W. (1951) *The Greeks in Bactria and India*, 2nd ed., Cambridge
Täubler, E. (1913) *Imperium Romanum: Studien zur Entwicklungsgeschichte des römischen Reiches*, vol. I (all published), Berlin
Taylor, L. R. (1960) *The voting districts of the Roman Republic*. Papers and monographs of the American Academy in Rome XX, Rome
Taylor, L. R. (1962) 'Forerunners of the Gracchi', *JRS* 52: 21–7
Taylor, M. J. (2014) 'Roman infantry tactics in the Mid-Republic: a reassessment', *Historia* 63: 301–22
Taylor, M. J. (2019a) 'Tactical reform in the Late Roman Republic: the view from Italy', *Historia* 68: 76–94
Taylor, M. J. (2019b) 'Reconstructing the battle of Zama', *CJ* 114: 310–29
Taylor, M. J. (2020a) *Soldiers and silver: mobilizing resources in the age of Roman conquest*, Austin, TX
Taylor, M. J. (2020b) 'Panoply and identity during the Roman Republic', *PBSR* 88: 31–65
Taylor, M. J. (2022) 'Conquest and continence: Roman sexual politics at the dawn of empire', in H. Cornwell and G. Woolf (eds.), *Gendering Roman imperialism*, Leiden: 128–45
Terrenato, N. (2019) *The early Roman expansion into Italy: elite negotiation and family agendas*, Cambridge
Thiel, J. H. (1946) *Studies on the history of Roman sea-power in Republican times*, Amsterdam
Thomas, R. F. (2011) *Horace Odes Book IV and Carmen saeculare*, Cambridge
Thonemann, P. (2018) 'Review of J.-L. Brumeaux, *Vercingétorix*', *TLS*, 1 June 2018
Thonemann, P. (2020) *An ancient dream manual: Artemidorus' The Interpretation of dreams*, Oxford
Tipps, G. K. (1991) 'The *rogum Scipionis* and Gnaeus Scipio's last stand', *Classical World* 85: 81–90
Torelli, M. (1999) *Tota Italia: essays in the cultural transformation of Roman Italy*, Oxford
Toynbee, A. J. (1965) *Hannibal's legacy*, 2 vols., London

Toynbee, A. J. (1969) *Some problems in Greek history*, Oxford
Toynbee, J. M. C., (1978) *Roman historical portraits*, Ithaca, NY
Tränkle, H. (1977) *Livius und Polybius*, Basel and Stuttgart
Trevor-Roper, H. (1940) *Archbishop Laud*, London
Tröster, M. (2009) Review of Eckstein 2008, *Gnomon* 81: 42–5
Tupet, A.-M. (1980) 'Le serment d'Hannibal chez Silius Italicus', *Bull. Assoc. G. Budé*: 186–93
Vahlen, J. (1928) *Ennianae poesis reliquiae*, 2nd ed., Leipzig
Valgiglio, E. (ed.) (1956) *Plutarco: Vita di Mario*, Florence
Van der Blom, H. (2010) *Cicero's role models: the political strategy of a newcomer*, Oxford
Van Effenterre, H. (1948) *La Crète et le monde grec de Plato à Polybe*, Paris
Van Gelder, H. (1900) *Geschichte der alten Rhodier*, The Hague
Van Gils, L, I. de Jong, and C. Kroon (eds.) (2019) *Textual strategies in ancient war narrative: Thermopylae, Cannae and beyond*, Leiden and Boston
Van Gils, L. and C. Kroon (2022) 'Common ground and the presentation of emotions: fright and horror in Livy's historiography', in M. de Bakker, B. van den Berg, and J. Klooster (eds.), *Emotions and narrative in ancient literature and beyond: studies in honour of Irene de Jong*, Leiden: 523–39
Van Wees, H. (ed.) (2000) *War and violence in ancient Greece*, London
Visscher, M. (2020) *Beyond Alexandria: literature and empire in the Seleucid world*, Oxford
Vogt, J. (1967) 'Toynbees Rückkehr zur römischen Geschichte', *Historia* 16: 119–28
Vollenweider, M.-L. (1974) *Die Porträtgemmen der römischen Republik*, 2 vols., Mainz
Walbank, F. W. (1940) *Philip of Macedon*, Cambridge
Walbank, F. W. (1966) Review of Toynbee 1965, *CR* 16: 384–8
Walbank, F. W. (1985) *Selected papers*, Cambridge
Walbank, F. W. (1988) Review of Kuhrt and Sherwin-White 1987, *Liverpool Classical Monthly* 13: 108–12
Walbank, F. W. (2007) 'Fortune (*tychē*) in Polybius', in J. Marincola (ed.), *A companion to Greek and Roman historiography*, Oxford, 349–55
Wallace-Hadrill, A. (2008) *Rome's cultural revolution*, Cambridge
Walsh, P. G. (1961) *Livy: his historical aims and methods*, Cambridge
Walsh, P. G. (1993) *Livy book XXXVIII (189–187 B. C.): edited with an introduction, translation & commentary*, Warminster
Walsh, P. G. (1994) *Livy book XXXIX (187–183 B. C.): edited with an introduction, translation & commentary*, Warminster
Walsh, P. (2003) [1985] *Livy book XXI: edited with an introduction, notes & vocabulary*, London
Walthall, D. A. (2017) 'Numismatic material from late third-century contexts at Morgantina (Sicily)', *American Journal of Numismatics* 29: 110–24
Warde Fowler, W. (1911) *The religious experience of the Roman people*, London
Wardle, D. (1994) *Suetonius' Life of Caligula: a commentary*, Brussels

Warmington, B. H. (1966) *Carthage*, Harmondsworth
Warrior, V. M. (2006) *Roman religion*, Cambridge
Weinstock, S. (1971) *Divus Julius*, Oxford
West, D. (1997) *Horace: the complete odes and epodes*, Oxford
West, M. L. (1966) *Hesiod: Theogony*, Oxford
West, M. L. (2007) *Indo-European poetry and myth*, Oxford
West, M. L. (2013) *The epic cycle: A commentary on the lost Troy epics*, Oxford
Wheeler, E. L. (1991) 'The general as hoplite', in V. D. Hanson (ed.), *Hoplites: the Classical Greek battle experience*, London: 121–70
Wheeler, E. L. (2001) 'Firepower: missile weapons and the "face of battle"', in E. Dabrowa (ed.), *Roman military studies*, Krakow: 169–84
Whittaker, C. R. (1978) 'Carthaginian imperialism in the fifth and fourth centuries', in P. D. A. Garnsey and C. R. Whittaker (eds.), *Imperialism in the ancient world*, Cambridge: 59–90
Will, E. (1979–82) *Histoire politique du monde hellénistique (323–30 av. J. C.)*, 2nd ed., 2 vols., Nancy
Williams, J. (2015) 'From Jerusalem to the ends of the earth: the meaning of Paul's two names at Acts 13.9', in R. Ash, J. Mossman, and F. B. Titchener (eds.), *Fame and infamy: essays for Christopher Pelling on characterization in Greek and Roman biography and historiography*, Oxford: 327–34
Williams, R. D. (ed.) (1962) *Virgil Aeneid* III, Oxford
Willis, J. (1970) *Ambrosii Theodosii Macrobii opera vol. II: Commentarii in somnium Scipionis*, Leipzig
Wilson, A. J. N. (1965) *Emigration from Italy in the Republican age of Rome*, Manchester
Wilson, M. B. (2021) *Dictator: the evolution of the Roman dictatorship*, Ann Arbor, MI
Wilson, R. J. A. (2013) 'Hellenistic Sicily c. 270–100 BC', in J. R. W. Prag and J. Quinn (eds.), *The Hellenistic West: rethinking the ancient Mediterranean*, Cambridge: 79–119
Wiseman, T. P. (1971) *New men in the Roman senate 139 B. C. – 14 A. D.*, Oxford
Wiseman. T. P. (1995) *Remus: a Roman myth*, Cambridge
Wiseman, A. and Wiseman, P. (2013) *Ovid Fasti*, Oxford World's Classics, Oxford
Wissowa, G. (1912) *Religion und Kultus der Römer*, 2nd ed., Munich
Wittchow, F. (2009) *Ars Romana: List und Improvisation in der Augusteischen Literatur*, Heidelberg
Wollner, B. (1987) *Die Kompetenzen der karthagischen Feldherrn*, Frankfurt am Main
Wuilleumier, P. (1939) *Tarente, des origines à la conquête romaine*, Paris
Xella, P. (2019) 'Religion', in, in C. López-Ruiz and B. Doak (eds.), *The Oxford handbook of the Phoenician and Punic Mediterranean*, Oxford: 273–92
Yacobson, A. (2010) 'Traditional political culture and the people's role in the Roman Republic', *Historia* 59: 282–302
Yardley, J. C. (tr.) (2000) *Livy: the dawn of the Roman empire. Books 31–40*. Oxford World's Classics, Oxford

Yardley, J. C. (2003) *Justin and Pompeius Trogus*, Toronto
Yardley, J. C. (tr.) (2006) *Livy: Hannibal's war. Books 21–30*. Oxford World's Classics, Oxford
Yardley, J. C. and W. Heckel (1997) *Justin, Epitome of the Philippic History of Pompeius Trogus*, vol. I, books 11–12: *Alexander the Great*, Oxford
Yardley, J. C., D. Hoyos, and J. Briscoe (2019) *Livy, History of Rome books 21–22*, Loeb Classical Library, Cambridge, MA
Yarrow, L. M. (2006a) *Historiography at the end of the Republic: provincial perspectives on Roman rule*, Oxford
Yarrow, L. M. (2006b) 'Lucius Mummius and the spoils of Corinth', *SCI* 25: 57–70
Yarrow, L. M. (2012) '*Decem legati*: a flexible institution, rigidly perceived', in C. Smith and L. M. Yarrow (eds.), *Polybius, cultural politics, and imperialism*, Oxford: 168–83
Yarrow, L. M. (2013) 'Heracles, coinage, and the West: three Hellenistic case-studies', in J. R. W. Prag and J. Quinn (eds.), *The Hellenistic West: rethinking the ancient Mediterranean*, Cambridge: 348–66
Yarrow, L. (2021) *The Roman Republic to 49 BCE: using coins as sources*, Cambridge
Zhmodikov, A. (2000) 'Roman Republican heavy infantrymen in battle (IV–II centuries B. C.)', *Historia* 49: 67–78
Ziegler, K. (1949) *Plutarchos von Chaironeia*, Stuttgart [separate advance printing of *R.-E.* 2 (1951): cols. 636–962]
Ziegler, K. and H. Gärtner (eds.) (1980) *Plutarchus vitae parallelae* vol. IV, indices, Leipzig

# Index

Notes: Roman names are entered under family name or *nomen*, not *cognomen*, so 'Pomponius' not 'Matho'; but there are cross-references for important individuals ('Scipio *see* Cornelius', 'Flamininus *see* Quinctius'). Better-known Latin authors are listed once only (no cross-references), under their familiar English forms, e.g. 'Cicero', 'Seneca', 'Ovid', 'Virgil'.

'cos.' = consul.

The famous Hannibal is listed as 'Hannibal (9)' (his number in Geus 1994), and Scipio as 'Cornelius Scipio Africanus, Publius'; he is sometimes also referred to in the index as just 'Africanus'.

Abelux, 115
Acarnania, 145
Acciaiuoli, Donato, 4
Achaeus (Seleucid usurper), 25, 191
Achilles, 123
   as ancient military model, 359
   smiles once only in *Iliad*, 265
Acilius Glabrio, Manius (cos. 191)
   crosses Adriatic unopposed, 322
   vows temple to Piety, 200
Acilius Glabrio, Manius (suffect cos. 154)
   fulfils father's vow of temple to Piety, 200
Acilius, Gaius, 265
   historian and interpreter, 260
Acylla or Acholla, 299
address, form of
   Scipio's to brother Lucius, 330
adlection, 174
adoption, 46
aediles, curule, 14, 113
Aegates islands, 67
Aegospotami, 357
Aelius Paetus, Publius (cos. 201, censor 199), 314
   on diplomatic mission to Asia Minor (194–193), 260
   plebeian censor with Scipio as patrician colleague, 251
Aemilia, 43, 58
   magnificent lifestyle, 255, 386
   personal wealth, 424

Aemilianus
   Plutarch life of?, 32
Aemilius Lepidus, Marcus (cos. 187)
   fulfils vow made by Regillus before Myonnesus, 200
Aemilius Lepidus Numida, Marcus
   as long-lived decemuir, 196
Aemilius Lepidus, Marcus (military tribune 190), 335
Aemilius Paullus, Lucius (cos. 216), 21, 43, 47, 70, 84
   commanded Roman right wing at Cannae, 102
   death at Cannae, 104
   father-in-law of Africanus, 176
   tried for embezzlement, 183
Aemilius Paullus, Lucius (conqueror of Macedon, 168), 47, 54, 56
Aemilius Regillus, Lucius (praetor 190), 200, 324
   honoured at Cretan Aptera, 264
Aeneas, 60, 81, 96, 139
   as founder of Rome
     combined with Romulus legend, 291
   talks to Anchises in *Aeneid* 6, 235
   voyage to Italy denied by Hegesianax, 305
Aeneas Tacticus, 344
Aeneas the Tactician, 99
   read by Hannibal?, 280
*aerarium*. *See* treasury
Aeschylus, 22
   his Cassandra echoed by Virgil's Dido, 412
   visited Syracuse, 276

# Index

Aetolians
  as a cause of Roman war against Antiochus, 316
  breach with Rome, 317
  control Delphic amphiktiony, 145, 316
  controlled Delphi when Hegesianax honoured there (193), 305
  destroyed by Cato at Callidromus, 322
  misunderstand *fides*, 161
  Scipio on
    as inciting Antiochus to war, 253
    unpopular in Greece, 145, 316
Africanus. *See* Cornelius Scipio
  as *cognomen*, 14, 32, 46, 89
Agamemnon, 149, 239
Agathocles, 62, 108, 146
  bronze coinage of, 289
  rated highly by Scipio, 56, 265
  Tower of, 210
Agenor, 288
ager Gallicus, 187
ager publicus
  public land and Gracchan reforms, 402
Agesilaus, 9
Agrigentum, 148
Ai Khanum (Bactria)
  founder Cineas had cult at, 292
Alaric
  sack of Rome, 150
Alcaeus of Messene
  on Philip V's failure to bury dead after Cynoscephalae, 321
Alcibiades
  echoed by Livy, 268
Alcides
  poetic name for Hercules, 234
Alexander Romance, 304
Alexander the Acarnanian
  prods Antiochus to war, 318
  switched from Philip V to Antiochus III, 306, 307, 314, 318
Alexander the Great, 4, 25, 49, 55, 57, 71, 75, 87, 90, 93
  as quasi-priest, 232
  at town of the Malli people
    protected by comrades after wounded, 342
  city foundations of, 134
  forced by mutiny to turn back, 351
  owned statuette by Lysippus, 223
  rated top general by Hannibal, 337
  sea does him obeisance, 121, 239
  siege of Tyre, 300
  spared house of Pindar, 223
Alexandria
  as city name, 49
  Eschate, 134

Alexandria (Egyptian)
  as greatest eponymous foundation, 292
  built on site of earlier settlements, 129
  processions at, 246
Alexandria Troas
  Antiochus offers to abandon claims to, 331
  home town of Hegesianax, 305
  resisted Antiochus III (192), 305
Alexandris. *See* Syracosia
allies, Roman
  military contribution, 101
Allobroges, 86
Alps, 11, 83
  Hannibal's crossing of, 85–8
  Hannibal's route, 87
  Hasdrubal crosses, 186
  Hercules' crossing of, 234
altars
  at Pergamum (the 'Great Altar'), 376
  at Syracuse
    great altar of Hiero II, 277
Althaea, 79
ambushes, 210
  as deception, 359
  Marcellus killed in, 153
Ammianus Marcellinus, 234, 414
Ammon, 232
  Hannibal consults oracle?, 316
Amphiaraus, 240
amphiktiony, Delphic, 145
Amphipolis, 343
  Brasidas heroized at, 343
anabasis
  march up country
    of Antiochus III, 307
    of Xenophon, 9
  title of historical works by Xenophon and Arrian, 9
Anchises
  friend of Anius of Delos, 263
  talks to Aeneas in Aeneid 6, 235
Andobales, 23, 86, 116, 128
  shifts support to Scipio, 121
anecdotes, roving, 388
anger
  divine, 92
Anius, mythical king of Delos, 263
  magical daughters keep Agamemnon's army supplied, 352
Anna (nymph)
  sent by Juno, 233
Annaeus Florus
  on Maharbal, 111
annalistic historians, 29
Anthes, 287

Anticlea, 42
Antigonid dynasty, 305
Antigonus 'the One-eyed', 87
   defeated and killed by Seleucus I at Ipsus (301), 332
   related somehow to Philip II, 305
Antigonus Doson
   guardian of Philip V, 306
Antigonus Gonatas
   as king without a kingdom, 125
   recovered Macedonian heartland (277), 305
Antioch
   Syrian
      as Seleucid western capital, 301
Antiochus (crown prince)
   Hannibal meets at Daphne, 301
   predeceased father Antiochus III (187), 302
Antiochus I
   and Berossus, 304
Antiochus III, 3, 15, 22, 35, 51
   ambiguity towards Hannibal's advice the explanation, 327–8
   becomes 'the Great', 307
   career until 196 assessed, 307
   has affair with young woman at Euboean Chalcis, 321
   makes offers to Scipio Africanus before Magnesia, 331
   on Hannibal as adviser opinion volatile, 321
   sacrifices to Athena at Ilium (Troy), 305
   statues of
      on Delos, 264
Antiochus IV
   humiliated by Laenas, 84
   military parade at Daphne, 301, 306
   ordered out of Egypt by Popillius Laenas, 378
Antiphilus (epigrammatist), 409
   on the treacherous heron at New Carthage, 120
Aoos conference, 250
Antoninus Pius (emperor), 39
Apamea
   peace of
      Eumenes II awarded territory disputed with Prusias, 375
      Hannibal's surrender demanded, 326, 335
Apamea (Phrygian), 315
Apennines, 92, 98
Aphrodite
   and Persephone at Locri, 164
Apollo, 141, 242, 263
   Sibyl inspired by, 185
Apollonia, 142
Apollonius (Seleucid courtier)
   co-commands Seleucid fleet with Hannibal, 324
Apollonius Rhodius
   and Ptolemaic policies, 304
Apollophanes of Seleucia
   Greek doctor who persuaded Antiochus III of military plan, 307
appearance, personal, 25
Appian, 30, 50, 69
   lists Syrian cities named after Macedonian predecessors, 292
   mentions man from Italica in 143 BCE, 132
   on discussion between Hannibal and Scipio at Ephesus, 261
   on dispositions at Cannae, 102
   on Hannibal's love affair, 151
   on Hannibal's request for instructions about Saguntum, 83
   on Italica, 128
   on libations by Octavian, 224
   on Metaurus (by implication), 204
   on Scipio's problematic warning to Antiochus before Magnesia, 332
   on Scipio's sacrifices on sailing for Africa, 224, 239
   on Sertorius as Hannibal reincarnated, 414
   on spread of estates in Italy, 401
   on triumphs, 247
Appian Way
   shrine of Rediculus, 151
Appuleius Saturninus, Lucius, 49
Aptera (Crete)
   honours to Scipio and brother Lucius, 264
Apulia, 68, 97, 138, 150
Arausio
   battle of, 108
arbitration
   cynical Roman attitude to, 309
Arcadia, 73
archaeology
   and Carthaginian imperialism, 63
   and child sacrifice at Carthage, 228
   and destruction of Italy, 404
   and latifundia, 402
   attesting gymnasia in Sicily, 277
   centuriation
      at Graccuris, 294
   Great Altar of Pergamum, 376
   Iberian, 29
   in Italy, 397
   of Baecula, 123
   of Cannae, 101
   of Carthage, 271
      evidence for afterlife beliefs, 229
      foundation date and, 60

of Italica, 133
of New Carthage, 123
Punic traders at Athens attested by, 287
survey
  in southern Etruria, 397
Archidamus III of Sparta
  helps Tarentum, 149
Archimedes, 95
  friend and adviser of Hiero II, 276
  helped to design the Syracosia (ship), 276
  killed at fall of Syracuse, 148, 276
  not author of epigram on Syracosia, 277
Archimelos
  epigrammatist
    praised the *Syracosia*, 277
Ares, 141
Arginousae
  forensic mourning after battle, 165
*Argo*, 224
Argyrippa
  founded by Diomedes, 141
Ariminum, 88
Aristides and Phocion
  famously upright Athenians, 386
Aristobulus, 34
Aristomachus of Corinth, 147
Ariston (agent of Hannibal), 48, 268, 327
  name of, 285
  the Ariston affair, a study in *fama*, 310–14
Ariston (Carthaginian philosopher)
  Greek name of, 285
Aristophanes
  on Cleon, 101
Aristotle, 12
  interested in Locri, 164
  on Alcibiades, 259
  on Carthage, 63, 172
    denied Carthage monarchical, 266
  Phormio as Aristotelian, 285
Armenia
  at time of Hannibal's stay, 373
  Greek rock inscriptions, 373
  kinship with Thessaly, 292
Arno, 96
Arpi, 363
  Hannibal encamps at, 141
  recaptured by Fabius son of the Delayer, 146
Arretium, 92
Arrian, 34
  on Alexander's wounds, 342
  on Prusa
    does not mention Hannibal, 377
arrogance
  alleged Carthaginian, 121, 167

Artaxata
  Hannibal as founder of, 373, 378
Artaxias king of Armenia
  Hannibal at court of, 369, 374
Artemidorus
  on dreams, 240
Artemis, 141
Asclepius, 240, 352
  and incubation, 240
Asopius, 118
assemblies
  at Rome, 173
assidui
  defined, 401
Astarte, 96
*asulia*, 162. *See* inviolability of sanctuaries
asyndeton, 224
  absence of co-ordinator, 183
  Livy makes Hannibal use before Zama, 216
  Livy makes Scipio use slangy example, 330
Athena
  at Ilium (Troy)
    Antiochus III sacrifices to, 305
  takes human form in Homer, 241
Athens
  and Carthage, 63
  and Naples, 364
  Carthaginians at, 287
  deme system, 46
  departure of Athenian expedition to Sicily, 224
  philosophical schools at, 282
  son of admiral Phormio sent out at request of Acarnanians, 118
  Spartan fear of, 80
  Timaeus prefers Syracuse to, 275
  trade with Carthage, 63
  tribute displayed at, 246
Atilius Regulus, Marcus (cos. 217), 102
Atintania, 142
Atreus, 239
Attalid dynasty of Pergamum. *See* Eumenes, Attalus
Attalus II, 335
auctoritas, 421. *See* nod
  defined, 258
  of Scipio, 258
Aufidus, 101
Augustine
  on Alaric, 150
Augustus, 13, 46
  Res gestae, 17, 245
    contrasts *auctoritas* and *potestas*, 259
    *factio* used tendentiously, 180
    uses first person singular, 15
Aurelius Victor, Sextus, 30

Aurelius Victor, Sextus (cont.)
  on Hannibal's death, 379
  on Metaurus, 204
Ausculum
  battle, 198
auspices, 70, 158, 246
  and tripudium, 227

Baal, 49, 51, 111
  Hammon, 228
    role in provoking the war, 233
Babylon
  as eastern Seleucid capital, 301
Bactria (northern Afghanistan). See Ai Khanum
Baecula, 14, 349
  course of battle, 124
  site recently identified, 123
Baetis, 116
Balearic, 11
  islands
    slingers from, 11, 356
Barca and Barcids, 45, 47–9, 172
  faction, at time of Ariston affair, 312
Barcas (mythical figure), 76
Barce, 279
  nurse in Virgil, 76
Barce, city in Cyrenaica, 49
Barke, 4, 72
Barmokaros
  swears treaty with Philip V, 141
basileus.
  Scipio hailed as king, 122
Batbaal
  female chief priest at Carthage, 231
battle managers
  and heroic leaders, 343
beards, 25, 26
Beautiful Promontory
  as good omen for Scipio, 210
beginning of evils
  history of expression, 317
beheading
  as method of execution, 190
belief
  disputed term, 229
Bellona
  war goddess, 198
Belus, 76
benefactions
  and Euhemeran doctrines of deification, 238
Beneventum, 54, 98
Beroia, 292
Berossus
  anti-Egyptian?, 304
  closeness to Antiochus I exaggerated, 304

bilingualism, 10, 16, 17, 98, 146, 212
  Malta evidence, 289
  Pyrgi tablet, 93
biography
  ancient, 9, 20
  and past presumptive, 7
  confers immortality, 425
  only one ancient of Hannibal, 30
  sometimes disparaged, 1
Bithynia, 12
  wars with Attalid Pergamum, 374
Boccaccio
  praised Busa, 105
Boeotian
  Plutarch as, 33
Bomilcar
  fails to relieve Syracuse, 148
  incompetent, 139, 360
  reaches Locri, 138
Bomilcar (1), 65
booty, 66, 79, 86, 242, 317, 326, 385
  displayed in triumphs, 247
  from Carthage
    eased Roman finances after Zama, 405
  from Metaurus, 190, 207
  from New Carthage, 121
  from Saguntum, 83
  Scipio prays for, 224
Bostar, 115
Bouzos, 68, 104
Brachylles
  Flamininus' part in his murder, 382
Brasidas, 38
  compared to Maharbal, 107
  death and heroization, 343
  good at speaking – for a Spartan, 286
  leading Spartans jealous of, 155
  welcomed 'as athlete' at Scione, 245
breakfast
  and stratagems, 90, 127, 357, 359
Bruttium, 138, 169, 214
  battles against Locri, 164
  Crassus' province, 208
buglers
  as give-away at Metaurus, 189
Bullock, Alan, 1, 6
burial
  failure of Philip V to bury dead after Cynoscephalae, 321
  Hannibal tries to give to Roman commanders, 94, 229
Busa, 68, 104
  logistical importance of, 355
Byzacium, 299

## Index

Cadmus, 378
Caecilius Metellus, Lucius (military tribune 216), 106
Caecilius Metellus, Quintus (cos. 206), 165, 178
Caecilius Metellus Scipio, Quintus, 49
Caere, 93
Caesar. *See* Julius
Caleacte (Sicily). *See* Silenus
Cales, 99
Caligula
  floating palaces at Lake Nemi modelled on the Syracosia?, 277
Callicula, 99
Callimachus, 288
  as anti-Seleucid poet?, 304
  Hymn to Delos anti-Seleucid?, 304
Callisthenes
  works of in Tauromenium library catalogue, 278
Calvus
  as *cognomen* ('Baldy'), 45
Cambyses (Persian king)
  deceived by ambiguous oracle, 380
  Seneca contrasts with Scipio(!), 422
Camillus
  vow as dictator to Juno Moneta, 197
Campania, 15, 66, 104
  attitudes to Hannibal in, 364
  cavalrymen loyal to Rome, 140
  fertility of, 98
Cannae, 2, 26
  as granary, 101
  battle, 2, 11, 18, 26, 101–5
  cinema at, 101
  citadel, 101
  numbers at, 101
cannibalism
  Hannibal (10) suggests to Hannibal (9), 354
Canusium, 26, 68, 101
  coin from, 26, 106
  Hannibal at, in 207, 187
  Romans escape to after Cannae, 104
Cape Bon peninsula, 63
captatio beneuolentiae
  defined, 290
captured cities
  treatment of, 121, 128
Capua, 25, 162
  Etruscan origin, 279
  goes over to Hannibal, 140
  harsh Roman treatment of, after surrender, 151, 364
  hegemonical aspirations, 140, 363, 365
  importance of, 139–41
  luxurious living at, 141, 152
  Hannibal not personally implicated, 279
  Oscan in language and culture, 279
  prosperous again in second and first centuries BCE, 401
  siege of, 149
Caracalla (Roman emperor)
  and Hannibal's tomb, 383
Carneades, 36
  teacher of Clitomachus, 285
Carrhae
  battle, 191
Cartala, 79
Carthage, 4, 60
  alleged ban on Greek at, 280, 287
  and Boeotian Thebes, 288
  and Greek culture, 285–90
  archaeology and financial situation after Zama, 271
  army, 27, 79, 101, 110, 143, 167, 211, 218, 219, 347
    allied and other non-Carthaginian elements, 64
    cavalry, 64
    linguistically and ethnically diverse, 26, 65, 346
    sacred band, 64
    switch to conscription, 347
  authorities at recall Hannibal, 211
  constitution, 63
  destroyed by Scipio Aemilianus, 271
  domestic affairs after Zama, 267–71
  eventual revival, 406
  factions, 172
  finances
    not in bad shape in 190s, 270
  foundation and position, 56
  gerousia (elders), 64
  imperial but republican power, 346
  indemnity, 271
  intermarriage with Greeks. *See* intermarriage
  Junonia planned on site of, 295
  law, 65
  magistrates, 65
  mercenaries, 43, 67, 219, 347
  oligarchy but with democratic features, 173
  ox-hide story of foundation, 290
  ox-hide trick, 378
  philosophy and philosophers at, 285–7
  religion, 65, 285, 290–1
    afterlife beliefs, 229
    divination part of, 228
  revenues calculated by Hannibal, 270
  senate, 64
  sends Hannibal few reinforcements or supplies, 138, 354, 360
  separation of powers, 64

Carthage (cont.)
    sufetes at, 12, 64
    touring Greek dramatic groups at?, 288
    trade, 271, 287
Carvilius, Spurius, 55
Casilinum, 98
Casinum, 98
Cassander, 131
Cassius Dio, 36
    claims Hannibal tried after Zama, 66, 267
    on Barc(h)ids, 47
    on Scipio's movements (193), 262
    says Hannibal understood divination, 227
castle
    Hannibal's
        on coast of Africa, 299
Castor and Pollux, 329
    sent by Sparta to help Locri against
        Croton, 164
Castra
    transport dues at, 252
castrametation (camp layout)
    Pyrrhus'
        admired by the Romans, 337
Castulo, 52, 116
casualties, 211
    at Cannae, 104
    at Ilipa, 127
    at Metaurus, 190
    at Trasimene, 94
    at Zama, 220
Catana (Sicily)
    Marcellus founds gymnasium at,
        277
cataphracts, Seleucid
    heavy cavalry
        destroyed at Magnesia, 335
Cato. See Porcius Cato
Caudine Forks (321)
    as ambush, 360
causes of second Punic war, 80–3
cavalry
    at Zama, 218
    Carthaginian superiority in, 103
    Hannibal's, 11, 89
    Roman weakness in, 89, 101, 103
        redressed by Numidians, 127
Cedreae (in Caria)
    mixobarbaroi at, 237
Celtiberian
    defined, 116
Celts, 85, 89
    4,000 killed at Cannae, 104
    armour of, 356
    at Zama, 218

Ducarius, 94
    importance for Hannibal, 85
censors, 14
    collegiality between, 251
    could appoint one of selves princeps
        senatus, 251
    duties of, 251
    lacked imperium, 249
    Nero and Salinator as, in 204, 196
    Scipio as, 14, 249
census
    censors compiled lists of Roman citizens, 251
    figures
        evidence of, 401
        for 199 not known, 253
        vulnerable to manipulation, 407
centuriation
    at Graccuris, 294
    defined, 293
Cephallenia, 321
Cercina, 359
    Hannibal at, 299
Chalcis (Euboea)
    occupied by Antiochus, 316
characterization
    in Livy's speeches, 31
checks and balances
    Polybius on, 173
chief senator. See princeps senatus
Chyretiae (Thessaly)
    Flamininus' letter to, 362
Cicereius, Gaius
    vow during battle, 197, 200
Cicero, 13, 15, 20, 33, 35
    compares Scipio and Hercules, 235
    compromise view of generalship, 343
    confused about Marcius Septimius, 116
    'Dream of Scipio'
        as emulation of Plato, 417
    full names and tribe, 46
    often uses Hannibal as example, 413
    on cleverness of Clitomachus, 286
    on consular commands in 190, 328
    on demolition of house as mark of
        execration, 301
    on 'Hannibal ad portas', 151
    on Livius Andronicus, 203
    on Metaurus, 203
    on optimates and populares, 175
    on Phormio, 35, 265, 344
        comments on Hannibal's Greek, 282
    on rapacity of provincial governors, 167
    on Salinator's vow at Metaurus, 193
    on Scipio and special seats in games, 255
    on Scipio as hero, 237

on Scipio's nod, 258
on Sena, 204
Cimbri, 108
Cimon
  victory at Eurymedon (466), 325
Cineas
  cult of as founder of Ai Khanum, 292
Cirta
  Masinissa given, 221
Cisalpine Gaul, 85, 92
city foundations. *See* foundations, of cities
Cius
  former site of Prusa, 377
Civilis
  one-eyed, 87
class conflict in Italy
  how successfully exploited by Hannibal?, 362–6
Claudius Caecus, Appius (cos. 296)
  vows temple to Bellona during battle, 198
Claudius Centho, Appius (praetor 175)
  ouatio, 202
Claudius Marcellus, Marcus (cos. 208), 3, 33, 95, 183
  body of, 95
  defeats Hannibal at Nora, 141
  fights Hannibal indecisively at Numistro, 153
  founds gymnasium at Sicilian Catana, 277
  killed in ambush by Hannibal, 153
  recaptures Syracuse, 146
  reckless of own life, 68, 339
Claudius Marcellus, Marcus (cos.196)
  on embassy to Carthage (195), 299
Claudius Marcellus, Marcus (cos.152), 131
Claudius Nero, Gaius (victor at Metaurus), 84, 90, 108, 126, 153
  arranges food supplies for army on way north, 188, 355
  considered 'outstanding' in 208, 183
  impious treatment of Hasdrubal's head, 95, 191
  in Iberia, 44, 95, 117
  why hated by Salinator, 184
Claudius Nero, Tiberius (cos. 202), 215
Claudius Ptolemy
  on Italica, 131
  on Libyssa, 382
Claudius Pulcher, Appius (military tribune 216), 106
Claudius Quadrigarius
  on meeting between Hannibal and Scipio at Ephesus, 260
Cleomenes I of Sparta
  deceived by ambiguous oracle, 383
  sacrificed bull to sea god Poseidon, 240

Cleon, 101
  treated as coward by Thucydides, 343
Cleopatra, 1, 212
  comparison with Hannibal, 28, 247, 369, 414, 434
Cleopatra (daughter of Antiochus III)
  betrothed to Ptolemy V, 309
Clitomachus (philosopher), 285–7
  name changed from Hasdrubal, 285
  wrote book of consolation for fall of Carthage, 286
code-switching, 99
  Greek–Punic
    in north Africa, 287
Coelius Antipater, 17, 233
  Metaurus not alluded to, 204
  on Hannibal's dream of Juno, 213
Coeranus
  envoy from Smyrna, at Lysimachia conference, 309
*cognomen*, 14, 46, 74
cohorts
  Polybius on, 350
coins
  Carthaginian
    resemble coins of Ptolemaic Egypt, 288
  from Canusium, 25, 106
  from Capua, 140
  Hannibal's role in choice of types, 355
  of Capua, 363
  of Dasii family, 363
  of Greek Italy, 29
  of Hannibal, 27
  of Scipio, 25, 225
  Siculo-Punic, 289
  Tarentum issues of Carthaginian type, 149
Col de Clapier, 87
Colichas, 23
Colline Gate, 150
colonies, Roman
  given encouraging names, 295
colonization
  in Italy (197–194), 255
Colophon, 23, 163
comitia, 173
communications
  slowness of, 155
comparison between Hannibal and Scipio
  provisional (207), 153
Compsa
  goes over to Hannibal, 138
  recaptured by Fabius the Delayer, 146

Concord
  temple to vowed by Vulso during mutiny, 198
*consulares* (former consuls), 257
consuls, 10, 14, 44
Corcyra
  Hannibal advises stationing of Seleucid fleet at, 320
  in treaty between Hannibal and Philip, 142
Corduba, 131, 133
  founded by Marcellus (cos. 152), 131
Corinth
  as mother city of Syracuse, 147, 276, 293
  fall of, 132
Cornelia II, 58
  and cult of Scipio?, 419
  daughter of Africanus, mother of the Gracchi, 43
Cornelii Scipiones, 53
Cornelius Cethegus, Marcus (cos. 204), 114
Cornelius Hispallus, Gnaeus (praetor 179, cos. 176)
  as example of younger man on embassy of seniors, 299
  honoured at Cretan Aptera, 264
  honoured at Cretan Polyrrhenia, 264
Cornelius Lentulus, Gnaeus (cos. 201), 104, 179
  tries to continue war after Zama, 221
Cornelius Lentulus, Lucius (cos. 199)
  at Lysimachia conference, 308
Cornelius Merula, Lucius (cos. 193)
  presides over consular elections for 192, 179
Cornelius Nepos. *See* Nepos
Cornelius Scipio, Lucius, son of Africanus, 44
  birth year, 58
  captured by Antiochus but returned to father, 331
Cornelius Scipio, Publius, father of Africanus, 14, 44, 84
  killed fighting in Iberia, 116, 343
  on Hannibal as would-be Hercules, 234
  takes momentous decision to fight war in Iberia, 86, 115, 158
Cornelius Scipio, Publius, son of Africanus, 44
  birth year, 58
Cornelius Scipio Aemilianus Africanus, Publius, 4, 38, 47
  as friend of Polybius, 100
  clears out camp-followers and seers from army, 352
  dreams about his adoptive grandfather, 415
Cornelius Scipio Africanus, Publius, 1
  advances career of Digitius, 278
  advisory roles to brother Lucius and Antiochus assessed, 328–34

and Ennius, 30
and Flamininus, 248–51
and Hercules, 234, 408
and recalcitrant quaestor, 254, 387
as legate of brother Lucius, 15, 323
as princeps senatus
  how often did he speak?, 251–9
as Salian priest, 14, 331
  flamboyant clothes and panoply, 25
  movements restricted in 190, 230
as talking ghost, 47, 415
at Syracuse, 57
  adopts Greek dress, frequents gymnasium, 275
  book-reading, 275
birth year, 2
brigand chiefs show him reverence, 238, 394, 428
celebrates triumph (201), 230, 245–8
censor, 251–3
charges against in 184:, 392
consul for second time (194), 253
'Continence of', 57, 423
Crete visit, 264
death at Liternum, 392–4
denied triumph in 205, 135
despicable treatment of Sophoniba, 212, 423
did not invent manipular army, 350
discusses generalship with Hannibal at Ephesus, 97, 260, 337
dishonest ruse in Africa (204), 210, 230
Ennius and, 13
family and youth, 53–9
financial assets at death, 424
first visit to Africa, 127
flowing hair of, 25, 123
forensic attacks on (180s), 386–92
games (205), 207
hated by Cato, 386
how often wounded?, 341
in the 'Dream of Scipio' by Cicero, 415–20
jokes by. *See* jokes by Scipio
letter to Philip V, 20, 248, 330
letters from, 22–4
letters to Asia Minor cities, 23, 161
makes few interventions in senate, 258
meets Hannibal at Ephesus (193)?, 259–65
meets Hannibal before Zama, 215–17
monumental arch, 238, 329, 414
name Scipio
  afterlife of, 424
  scansion of, 48
no attested vow before or during Zama, 201, 223
no cult of, 239, 292, 394, 418, 419
nod of, as indicating authority, 258
not a man to apologize, 166, 390, 435

not a *popularis* politician, 175
not opposed to second Macedonian war, 248, 257
oath after Cannae, 106, 226
opposes persecution of Hannibal, 253
problematic last-minute advice to Antiochus before Magnesia, 332
rated Dionysius I and Agathocles highest of all, 56
saves father at Ticinus, 59, 89, 113
sexual attitudes and sex life, 56–8, 122
special relationship with Jupiter, 222
strategy at Zama, 219
suppresses mutiny in Iberia (206), 128, 338, 367
vows games during, 223
tactical preferences, 349
the 'Scipionic legend', 25, 55, 121, 223, 235
villa at Liternum
described by Seneca the Younger, 392
visit to Delos, 263
war aims, 137
wife Aemilia, 43, 58
witnessed Hannibal's march on Rome (211)?, 150
Cornelius Scipio Asiagenes, Lucius, 3, 13, 179
and aedileship, 114
at battle of Thermopylae (191), 322
celebrates games vowed during war with Antiochus, 200
commands warships on crossing to Africa, 209
Crete visit, 264
debate (193) about conduct of, 258
elected consul (for 190), 323
had hand in Hannibal's death?, 381
letters to Asia Minor cities, 23, 161
Cornelius Scipio Calvus, Gnaeus, uncle of Africanus, 14, 44, 86
funeral mound, 116, 131
killed fighting in Iberia, 116, 343
Cornelius Scipio Hispallus, Gnaeus (praetor 179, cos. 176), 58
Cornelius Scipio Nasica, Publius
fails to be elected consul (in 192 for 191), 179
Cornelius Scipio Nasica, Publius (cos. 191)
fails to be elected consul for 192, 259
had hand in Hannibal's death?, 381
speech in senate, 258
vows and holds games to Jupiter, 200
Cornelius Scipio Salvito, 225, 418
Cornelius Sulla Felix, Lucius
and Fortuna, 222
'illiterate' for resigning dictatorship, 280
owned statuette by Lysippus, 223
correction in stride
narrative technique, 341

Corsica, 67, 72, 81, 200
Corupedium
Seleucus I defeated Lysimachus at (281), 308, 332
Corycus (Ionia)
sea battle off, 323
councils of war.
Carthaginian, 109
counterfactuals, 95, 96, 105, 208, 217, 329, 405
cranes
needed to move large statues, 290
crepidi
Greek boots
Scipio wears at Syracuse, 275
Crete
Aristotle compares Carthage to, 285
dream interpreter from, 240
epigraphy. *See* Aptera, Polyrrhenia, Gortyn
Hannibal at, 369
Ptolemaic interest in, 372
Publius and Lucius Scipio visit, 264
Croesus
and Prusa?, 377
Croton, 11, 12, 18, 198
Hannibal's base in last years of war in Italy, 18
Livy analyses political divides at, 362
crucifixion, 61, 99
of generals at Carthage (dubious), 66, 384, 427
cult
for mortals, 236
cultic honours
to Flamininus, 249
Cumae, 60, 61, 193
Hannibal's attempt on, 141
curule magistrates, 113
Cybele
Roman adoption of cult, 290
Cydonia, 264
Cynoscephalae, 248
Aetolian contribution to Roman victory, 317
Philip V neglects dead after defeat at, 321
Cyprus, 93
Cyrenaica, 4, 279
Cyrene
Hannibal at (193)?, 315
Cyropolis, 134
Cyrus the Great, 50, 89
posthumous humiliation of head, 191
Cyrus the Younger
decapitated, 191
Cyzicus
battle, 156

Damocritus (Aetolian envoy)
sent to Nabis of Sparta, 318

Daochos of Thessaly
  family monument at Delphi
    compared to Scipio's monumental arch, 329
Daphne
  Antiochus IV stages military parade at, 301, 306
  suburb of Antioch
    Hannibal arrives at, 301
Darius III (Persian king), 57
Dasii
  important Apulian family, 141
  oscillating role of, 363
dates, 10
Datis (Persian commander)
  acts on warning dream, 241
Daunia, 97, 98
debt
  and Gracchan programme, 404
Decades (in Livy), 5
decapitation, 95, 191
decemuiri
  Salinator cos. 208 probably not one, 184, 196
deception, Punic, 214. *See* Punic deception
Decii
  self-sacrificing Roman family, 421
decision-making, 155
  by commanders, 158–63
  on the spot, 86
dedications, 19, 22, 93, 96, 141, 192, 338, 357
  by Alexander to father Ammon, 232
  by Publius and Lucius Scipio at Delos, 263
  of temples or games, 197
deification
  through conquest
    Euhemerus and, 238
Delium
  Datis at, 242
  Menippus at, 264, 320
Delos
  and Datis, 242
  epigraphy, 22
    Bouzos, 68, 104, 355
    kinship with Romans, 264
    Scipio and brother Lucius, 263
  neutrality of, 264
  the Delians as friends and kin of Romans, 263
Delphi, 62, 71
  Aetolian control of amphiktiony, 305, 316
  booty from Metaurus sent to, 207
  charioteer statue at
    resembles Motya statue, 289
  Daochos monument at, 329
  Muttines honoured at, 148
  Roman contacts with, 71, 145, 285

demagogues
  Flaminius and Varro represented as, 92
Demaratus
  interrogation of mother, 42
demes, of Attica, 46
Demeter
  Sicilian cult of, 290
Demetrias (Thessaly)
  and Aetolians, 316, 318
  Antiochus occupies, 316, 319
  conference at
    attended by Hannibal, 320
Demetrius II, 125
  of Macedon
    father of Philip V, 141
    unbearded, 25
Demetrius of Pharus, 142
Demetrius the Besieger, 36, 125
  son of Poseidon and (?) Aphrodite, 236
Demetrius, son of Philip V, 247
  addresses brother as 'Perseu', 330
  hostage at Rome
    released after Thermopylae, 322
democracies
  Hannibal's alleged support for, 366
demography
  explains Roman undemocratic features in second Punic war, 174
demolition of house
  as mark of disgrace
    Carthage and Rome, 301
Demosthenes, 305
  variant versons of death, 379
deportatio exercitus
  withdrawal of army a condition for a triumph, 246
Dercylidas
  as 'Sisyphus', 74
destruction of crops
  as slow and difficult, 399
devastation
  of Italy
    how bad and how lasting?, 398–401
Dicaearchus (Aetolian envoy)
  sent to Antiochus III, 318
dictators, 90, 96
Dido, 60, 76
  and Hannibal, 212
  not given Greek ancestry, 289
  ox-hide trick to obtain site of Carthage, 378
Digitius, Sextus, 121
  rewarded by Scipio for role at New Carthage, 278
Dimale, 142

Diodorus, 30, 68
  on cult of Persephone and Demeter, 290
  used Hieronymus in books 18–20, 308
Diogenes Laertius
  on Clitimachus, 286
Diognetos
  father of Clitomachus
    name theophoric, 285
Diognetus, 288
Diomedes
  founds Argyrippa (Arpi), 141
Dionysius I, 37, 62, 112, 287
  Carthaginian wars against, 65
  rated highly by Scipio, 56, 265
Dionysius of Halicarnassus, 1
Dionysus
  Thriambos, 230, 246
Dioscuri, 164, 329
Diotimos son of Strombichos
  Athenian general
    at Naples, 28, 364
diplomacy
  in Iberia, 115, 122
divination, 109, 186, 213
  by auspices, 70
  Hannibal versed in, 227, 232
  military, 35
  part of Carthaginian religion, 228
  pre-battle sacrifices as, 227
diviners
  Scipio Aemilianus expels from Iberian army, 352
Domitian (Roman emperor)
  foil to Scipio (in Silius), 423
Domitius Ahenobarbus, Gnaeus (cos. 192)
  role at Magnesia exaggerated by Appian, 332, 335
Dorieus (Spartan), 159
doriktetos chora, 316
  spear-won territory
    as important Hellenistic concept, 308
doubles
  in battle
    Hannibal (10) as protection for Hannibal (9)?, 45
Dream of Scipio
  Aemilianus' dream
    fictional work by Cicero, 415
  by Cicero, 417
dreams, 239, 240–3. *See* epiphanies
  interpretation of, 240
  of Hannibal
    Juno's warning, 213, 232
  of Marcius Septimius, 241
  of Scipio, 47
  of Scipio Aemilianus
    Cicero's 'Dream of Scipio', 240
  types of
    episode or epiphany, 240
dress, 25
drill, formation, 122, 209
Ducarius, 94

earth, 141
earthquakes, 198
  at Trasimene, 94
Ebro
  river, 68
  treaty, 69, 72, 81
Edeco, 121
Edessa, 292
education
  Roman, 55
Egypt, Ptolemaic
  and Carthage, 288
  and Cyrene, 288
  evidence for, 304
  Memphis
    dream interpreter, 240
  Ptolemies not very active city founders, 292
  strong interest in Crete, 372
  Syrian wars against Seleucids, 301
  unstable in 190s BCE, 303
ekphrasis
  as description of work of art, 276
  Moschion's
    description of Syracosia, 276
Elaea
  Scipio detained at, 329, 332
elephants, 11, 64, 85
  Africa as elephant country, 213
  African, 12
    Bush and Forest, 26
  at Magnesia, 335
  at Metaurus, 190
  at Zama, 218, 358
  Indian, 12, 26
  Lucretius on, 411
  successful Seleucid use of at Panion (201), 331
  Surus, 87
Elissa. *See* Dido
Elizabeth (biblical), 42
elogium, 13, 53, 113
  of Cornelia II, 44
  of Scipio, inscribed, 13
emotions
  decapitation and, 191
  Hannibal's

emotions (cont.)
    on leaving Italy, 213, 225
    tears
        at Carthage after Zama, 221
Emporium, 86
    Scipio lands at, 118
Ennius, 12, 30, 76
    as 'Calabrian Muse', 237
    celebrated Scipio, 13, 30, 237
    for scansion of name Hannibal, 412
    hinted at Scipio's epiphany of Neptune?, 239
    Metaurus probably not named by, 205
    on battle of the Great Plains, 211
    on Geminus at Cannae, 102
    on Hannibal as perjuror?, 410
    on Hannibal's crossing of Alps, 408
    on Hannibal's cruelty?, 408
    on Juno's reconciliation with Rome, 193
    on Salinator's triumph, 193
    on Scipio's heroic status, 237
    on Scipio's res gestae, 420
    on untruthful seers, 228
    personal friend of Scipio, 237, 285
    probably compared Scipio and Hercules, 235
    soliloquy by Antiochus III, 311
    translated Sacred Record of Euhemerus, 238
    tria corda (three hearts)
        as Greek, Latin, and Oscan, 237, 285
    triumph of Nobilior as closure of Annals?, 247
enslaved people, 56, 61, 62, 209, 381
    and Gracchan reforms, 404
    and Hannibal's death, 381
    as accompanying Roman embassies, 299
    at New Carthage, 121
    at Scipio's villa, 394
    on estates in Italy, 402
entrails, inspection of
    as form of divination, 227
Epaminondas, 31
    and tactical reserves, 357
Epeios, 21
Ephesus, 28
    Hannibal and Scipio meet at, 28, 35
    Hannibal meets Antiochus at, 302
    harbour Coressus
        common (dis)embarKation point, 302
Epicydes, 75, 163
    as Hannibal's agent at Syracuse, 146
Epidamnus, 142
epigrammatists. *See* Alcaeus of Messene, Antiphilos, Archimelos, Nossis
epigraphy. *See* inscriptions
epiphanies, 240–2
    at Hannibal's march on Rome, 150
    at New Carthage, 120
    cloudburst after Ilipa, 127
    Juno to Hannibal, 213, 232
    Marcius Septimius visited by Publius and Gnaeus Scipio, 241
    of Neptune, 120, 239
    Rediculus, 232
    to Hannibal in Iberia, 233, 242, 365, 398
    types of, 240
epistulae,
    letters sent by Publius and Lucius Scipio, 160
epitaphs, 13–16
Eratosthenes, 288
    on death of Demosthenes, 379
Eretria
    cult for Flamininus, 420
Erythrae (Ionia)
    exiles who 'fled to the Medes', 298
Eryx, 67, 96
ethnics, 72–7
    of known Carthaginian philosophers, 287
Etruria, 92
    battle in
        Polybius' designation for Trasimene, 202
    Capua originally Etruscan, 279
    coin from depicting mahout, 26
    disaffected from Rome, 208, 362
    diviners from, 185, 186
    Etruscan piracy, 62
    Etruscan treaties with Carthage
        mentioned by Aristotle, 93
    gold tablet from (Pyrgi), 93
    Horatius and Etruscans, 96
    Lucius Scipio's (doubtful) mission to, 390
    Romans neither Greeks nor Etruscans, 292
    rural poor in, 401
    supplies sent to by Flaminius and Geminus, 91
    triumphs
        Etruscan in origin?, 246
Euboea, 60
Eudamidas, 38, 283
Eudamus the Rhodian
    replaces Pausistratus, 324
Euhemerus of Messene, 420
    influence on Ennius, 238
    Sacred Record translated by Ennius, 238
Eumenes II
    helps Romans to defeat Polyxenidas at sea off Corycus, 323
    pushes Antiochus III to war against Rome, 314
    troops of, at Magnesia, 335
    wars with Prusias I of Bithynia, 375
Eumenes of Cardia, 277
Euphorion of Chalcis
    as Seleucid librarian, 304

# Index 479

Euripides, 277
  in Armenian rock inscription, 374
Europa, 289
Eurymedon river
  Cimon's victory at (466), 325
Eusebius
  on Salinator, 184
Eustathius, 110
Eutropius
  on Metaurus 'and Sena', 204
exempla, 31
extortion trials
  at Rome
    development of, 385

Fabius Buteo, Marcus, 84
Fabius Labeo, Quintus (praetor 189)
  visits Crete, 370
Fabius Maximus, Quintus (the 'Delayer'), 3, 33, 71, 84, 96, 165, 176
  and human sacrifice at Rome, 228
  death, 208
  ordered evacuation of unfortified towns, 399
  pontifex (216), 228
  recaptures Tarentum (209), 153
  speech attacking Scipio, 125
  strategy of, 97
Fabius Maximus, Quintus (son of the Delayer)
  recaptures Arpi, 146
Fabius Maximus Rullianus, Quintus (cos. 295)
  vows temple to Jupiter Victor, 198
Fabius Pictor, Quintus, 29, 66
  history written in Greek, 285
  mission to Delphi, 285
  works of, in Tauromenium library catalogue, 278
Fabricius Luscinus, Gaius, 54
face of battle
  modern approach to study of warfare, 338
factions
  at Carthage?, 172
Falernian field, 98
fama
  rumour
    power of at Carthage, 310, 314
fasti
  explained, 176
fatalis dux
  Scipio as predestined leader, 106
Festus
  on Graccuris, 294
*fides*, 161
films
  about Hannibal and Scipio, 372, 415

flaming twigs stratagem, 37, 99, 359, 376
  evidence of for logistics, 354
Flamininus. *See* Quinctius
Flaminius, Gaius, 70, 91
  as forerunner of the Gracchi, 173
  as tribune (232)
    agrarian law, 92, 402
  defeated and killed at Trasimene, 94
  vows allegedly not made by, 199
Flavinius, Marcus
  centurion invented in 1960s, 343
fleet
  Carthaginian, 65
Florus (historian)
  comparison between Hannibal and Pontius Telesinus, 413
focalization, 125
focussing devices, 105
  everyone else … but x alone, 322
Fonteius, Tiberius, 116
food
  Roman need for in Iberia, 115
fora
  assize towns, eponymous, 294
foraging and foragers
  normal soldiers as foragers, 354
*fornix*. *See* monumental arch
Fortuna
  and Sulla, 222
fortune, 236
  as theme in speeches before Zama, 216
  favourite Polybian concept (as *tyche*), 299
foundations, of cities, 49, 60, 68, 131
  Iberian
    by Barcids, 291–5
freedom
  Hannibal offers to Italians, 94, 365
freedom of the Greeks
  Hannibal as champion of?, 274
  proclaimed by Flamininus, 71, 249, 250, 307
  Scipio and, 250, 274
Frentani, 97
Frontinus. *See* Julius
Fulvius Centumalus, Gnaeus (cos. 229), 54, 70
Fulvius Centumalus, Gnaeus (cos. 211), 140
  loses second battle of Herdonea, 150, 153
Fulvius Flaccus, Gnaeus (praetor 212)
  loses first battle of Herdonea, 150
Fulvius Flaccus, Quintus (cos. 179)
  fulfils vows made in Celtiberian war, 200
Fulvius Flaccus, Quintus (cos. 212), 150
  savage treatment of surrendered Capuans, 151
Furius Purpurio, Lucius (cos. 196)
  vows temples to Jupiter, 200

Gades, 11, 85
    Mago excluded from, 136
Galen, 35
Gaul, 142
Gauls. *See* Celts
    Antiochus I's victory over, 305
Gellius, Aulus, 30, 56
    on Scipio tearing up account book, 389
    on Scipio's predictive powers, 231
    reports Hannibal's sarcasm to Antiochus before Magnesia, 326
Gelon, 62
Genius
    of the Carthaginians, 141
*gens*, 46
    Cornelia, 133, 179, 424
geographical knowledge, 93
Gereonium, 100
    as granary, 354
gerousia
    at Carthage, 64
Geryon
    cattle of, 87, 234
Gisgo (5), father of Hasdrubal (8), 46
Gisgo (6)
    Hannibal jokes with, 109, 367
Gisgo (7), 59, 172
gladiators, 88
gods
    assimilation of Greek and Punic, 226
    listed in treaty between Hannibal and Philip V, 226
Gorgo and Praxinoe, 293
    in Theocritus 15,
        proud of Corinthian descent, 276
Gortyn
    Hannibal at, 264
Gortyn (Crete)
    Hannibal at, 369
Gracchi. *See* Sempronius Gracchus, Tiberius (tribune 133) and Gaius
Gracchi, Gracchan attempts at reform, 402
    forerunners of Gracchi, 403
    multiple causes of, 403
    recruitment problems and, 403
Graccuris, 132
    eponymous Iberian foundation by Tiberius Gracchus senior, 294–5
grain
    Syracosia contained, 276
granaries
    Gereonium, Placentia, Cannae as, 354
Great Plains
    battle, 126, 211, 358
Greek language, 10, 215

groups
    at Rome?, 176
Grumentum
    skirmish between Hannibal and Nero, 187
Guadalquivir, 130
Guadiana, 130
gymnasia
    perceived centres of pederasty, 277
    Roman attitudes to, 277
    Sicilian
        paramilitary function, 277
    Syracosia contains one, 276
    Trajan on, 277
Gytheum
    cult for Flamininus, 420

Hadrian, 36
    ambiguous relationship with Italica, 129
Hadrumetum, 214
    Hannibal flees to after Zama, 220
Hagnon (Athenian)
    as hero?, 419
hair
    of Scipio. *See* Cornelius Scipio Africanus, Publius
Hamae, 193
Hamilcar (1), 62, 235
    cult for, 228, 236, 428
        Motya statue and?, 290
    had Syracusan mother, 75
    sacrifices during entire battle of Himera (?), 225, 227
Hamilcar (9), 41, 50
Hamilcar (12)
    at Locri, 168
Handel
    opera about Scipio, 423
Hannah (biblical), 42
Hannibal (6), 74, 75
Hannibal (7), 41
Hannibal (9)
    absent from Thermopylae narrative (191), 322
    Alexander the Acarnanian advises Antiochus to send him back to Africa, 318
    alleged slaughter at Juno sanctuary, 167, 213, 225
    alleged visit to Cyrene (193), 315
    allegedly wins sea battle for Prusias, 361, 375
    and Hercules, 12, 226, 234, 408
    and his Tyrian agent Ariston, 310–14
    and logistics
        situation harder than Scipio's and achievement greater, 353
    apologizes for manhandling Gisgo (7), 60, 66, 220, 244, 266, 268, 390, 435

Armenian stay, 373–4
as connoisseur of art?, 223
as his own diviner, 227, 232, 241
as popularis?, 175
at Avernus, 228
at court of Artaxias of Armenia, 369
attends and hates lecture on generalship by Phormio, 281
belief in incarnation, 229
birth year, 2
childhood and family, 50–3
city foundations of, 377–9
Cleopatra compared to. *See* Cleopatra
comparison with Sertorius, 414
consults oracle at Ammon?, 316
cruelty of (alleged), 400, 408
defeated at sea by Rhodians, 325
defeats (minor) listed, 421
discusses generalship with Scipio at Ephesus, 260, 337, 380
elected 'praetor' (sufete), 269
emotions on leaving Italy, 213, 225
fails at Naples, 139, 275
films about, 372, 415
final years at Prusias I's Bithynia, 374–7
financial abilities already displayed in Italian campaign, 355
flees to court of Antiochus III, 298–302
grave
  traditions about, 382
greed of
  Polybius' explanation, 400
had ? only 12,000 men on leaving Italy, 356
his end
  traditions about, 379–82
humour, sense of. *See* jokes, Hannibal
impiety of
  breach of treaties, 410
inscribed bronze tablet, 10, 11–13, 16–20
isolation of, 107–10
jokes with Gisgo (6), 367, 432
knowledge of Latin
  wrongly doubted, 279
legacy at Carthage, 405–7
letter to Rhodians, 19, 281
love affair at Salapia, 151, 279
marches on Rome (211), 150
meets Scipio at Ephesus (193)?, 259–65
meets Scipio before Zama, 215–17
mother, 41
name
  afterlife of, 414
  scansion of, 412
need for maritime city, 138, 360

no cult of, 236, 239, 428
no libations attested on sailing for Africa, 225
not attested as making battle vows, 226
not formally a priest, 232
oath sworn as child, 51, 315
offers freedom to Italians, 94, 365
on Crete (Gortyn), 369
one-eyed, 27, 87
persecution of opposed by Scipio, 253
Pontius Telesinus fright evokes thoughts of, 413
private castle (African)
  as evidence for his personal wealth, 299
promise of Carthaginian citizenship to allies, 408
reason for limited role at Seleucid court, 307
non-Greek outsider, 327
reasons for avoiding sieges in Italy, 361
reasons for placing Alexander first among generals, 337
reformer at Carthage after Zama, 267–71
rejects miraculous parentage (in Lucian), 232
role as adviser to Antiochus assessed, 327
sarcastic remark to Antiochus before Magnesia campaign?, 326
speech of advice to Antiochus at Demetrias
  urges alliance with Philip, 320
statues of, 28
strategy at Zama, 219
suffers rare defeat at Nola, 141
surrender of
  demanded at Apamea (189), 326, 336
tactical preferences, 347
the 'Hannibalic legend', 223, 232
town house at Carthage demolished, 301
treaty with Philip V, 21, 141–5, 226
tries to relieve Capua, 149
under-rated by Vegetius, 348
unwounded (allegedly), 339
war aims, 137, 362
wife Imilce?, 43, 52
wigs of, 27, 91, 360
wins then loses Syracuse, 146
wrongly represented as perjuror, 222
Hannibal (10)
  the 'single-combat-man'
    suggested cannibalism to Hannibal (9), 354
    supposedly author of Hannibal (9)'s cruelties, 45, 360, 400, 433
Hannibal ad portas, 188, 232, 413
  Hannibal at gates proverbial for danger, 150
Hanno (3), 12, 61
  mentions seers on naval expedition, 228
Hanno (18), 60, 82, 172
  recalled to Carthage, 170

# 482  Index

Hanno (21), 11, 86
Hanno (22), 50, 102
Hanno (26), 126
Hanno (28), 21
   defeated by Scipio and Masinissa, 210
Hanno (31) 'the Mullet', 45
haruspices, 186
Hasdrubal (5), 60, 69
Hasdrubal (6), 39, 41, 163, 182
   commits 'suicide by Roman' at Metaurus, 190, 340
   decapitation of, 95, 190
   defeated on Ebro, 115
   letter to Hannibal in 207, 187
Hasdrubal (8), 116, 126, 210
   denominated as son of Gisgo (5), 46
Hasdrubal (13)
   Carthaginian philosopher. *See* Clitomachus
*hastati*, 349, 358
   as front line of Roman infantry, 211
Hebe, Greek goddess of youth
   temple vowed by Salinator after Metaurus, dedicated by Lucullus, 192
Hegesianax
   audience with Roman legati, 307
   denied Aeneas' voyage to Italy, 305
   honoured at Aetolian-controlled Delphi, 305
   on Seleucid embassy to Rome (193), 305
   Seleucid historian and diplomat, 304
Heircte, 67
Helen, 149
hellenization
   contested term, 290
helpful animal motif, 378
   not same as ox-hide trick, 378
Hera, 12, 85
   as 'present' in treaty with Philip V, 141
Heraclea on the Black Sea, 23
Heraclea under Latmos, 22, 161
Heracles/Herakles, 49, 87
   founder of Fabian gens, 330
Heraclides
   envoy of Antiochus III, 250
Heraclides of Byzantium
   as envoy of Antiochus to Scipio, 331
Hercules, 11, 85, 238
   as 'present' in treaty with Philip V, 141
   temple of (near Rome), 150
   twelve labours of, 87
Herdonea
   first battle of, 150
   population moved by Hannibal, 153, 365, 410
   second battle of, 150, 153
Herennius Siculus
   seer, friend of Gaius Gracchus, 227

hermaphrodite
   intersex infant at Frusino, 185
Hermes, 229
Herodian
   on Caracalla's statues to Sulla and Hannibal, 383
Herodotus, 20, 88, 322
   focussing devices in, 105
   on Cleomenes' sacrifice of bull to Poseidon, 239
   on Demaratus, 42
   on dream epiphany experienced by Hipparchus, 241
   on Scyles' Greek mother, 297
   postpones contents of letters, 156
heroes heroines and hero cults, 237, 246
   Brasidas at Amphipolis, 343
   Herakles' double aspect, 235
   snake at Liternum hints at Scipio as hero, 393
heroes, heroines, hero cults
   alleged for Hamilcar (1), 228
heron, treacherous, 120
Hesiod
   in Armenian rock inscription, 373
Hesychius
   alleged author of Life of Aristotle, 282
Hiero II
   building activity at Syracuse, 275
   death, 146
   sends military help to Rome, 91
Hieronymus
   grandson of Hiero II, 146
Hieronymus of Cardia, 342
   account of early Rome, 276
   and 'spear-won territory', 308
   on Seleucus I's romantic recovery of Babylon, 306
   portrait of Antigonus 'the One-eyed', 305
Himera
   battle (480), 62
Himilco (1), 61
Hippocrates, 75, 163
   as Hannibal's agent at Syracuse, 146
Hippocrates, Spartan
   sends 'laconic' message, 156
Hipponium
   became Vibo Valentia, 295
   Locrian colony
      probably shared revolt from Rome, 366
Hirpini
   abandoned Hannibal, 153
   went over to Hannibal, 138
Hispalis
   near Seville, 126

Historia Augusta
  on Italica, 131
history
  defined by Aristotle, 259
Hodius, 287
Homer, 20, 31, 42, 265, 322
  army doctors in, 352
  Diomedes in, 141
  focussing devices in, 105
  Lucian makes Hannibal claim ignorance of, 280
  Odyssey, 42
    translated by Livius Andronicus, 284
  on epiphany of Athena, 241
  on generalship, 343
  on guile, 359
  on kingship, 319
  on night-fighting, 94
hoplites
  heavy-armed Greek infantry, 343
  phalanx of
    superseded at Rome by manipular army, 350
Horace, 15
  imitates Ennius on the Great Plains, 211
  on Ennius, 237
  on Hannibal's 'rapid flight' after Zama textually problematic, 339
  on Metaurus, 189, 193, 204, 364, 412
  on Tarentum, 149
Horatius, 74, 96
Hostilius Mancinus, Lucius, 99
Hundred
  at Carthage, 65
hyperbaton
  dislocated word-order
    of Pindar, 280

Iamblichus
  on Pythagorean philosophers at Carthage, 287
Iberia, 2, 11 *See* Baecula, Ilipa
  and Scipio's war aims, 137
  Barcid city foundations in, 293
  Carthaginian treatment of, 345, 408
  cause of Roman recruitment problems, 403
  chieftains in, 23
  debate about (193), 258
  Gracchus (father of Gracchi) in, 44
  Hamilcar (9) in, 68
  Hannibal as commander in, 79–85
  Hannibal's offer of, 217
  Hannibal succeeds to command in, 51
  Hannibal's wife from, 43
  Hasdrubal (5) in, 69
  Hercules' crossing to Italy from, 234
  importance for Roman careers, 44, 434
  logistical problems presented by, 353
  loss of by Carthage
    effects felt after Zama, 270
  Marcius Septimius takes command in, 116
  military service in unpopular, 401
  mints, 27
  not fully subdued at start of third century, 421
  Scipio Aemilianus' army reforms in, 352
  Scipio given command in (210), 14, 117
  Scipionic diplomacy with communities of, 118, 345, 346
  Scipio's father and uncle killed in, 44, 48
  senate regularly sends supplies to, 352
  silver mines, 365, 403
  sword named after, 357
  troops from in Hannibal's army
    at Cannae, 356
  troops from in Hasdrubal's army at Metaurus, 190
Ilergetai, 11
Ilipa, 14, 122, 207, 349
  battle, 126–7
  casualties at, 127
  Scipio improves on at battle of Great Plains, 211
  site disputed, 126
Illyrian war
  first, 71
Ilourgeia
  savage treatment of by Scipio, 128, 423
Imilce, 43
imperator
  as title, 124
imperialism, 7, 62, 66
  peripheral. *See* peripheral
  Roman, denounced by Hannibal, 88
imperium, 14
  as 'dominion', 137
  Gnaeus' delegated by brother Publius?, 159
  of Minucius, 100
  proconsular, conferred on Scipio, 117
incubation, 240
indemnity
  and booty
    legal unclarity, 389
  Carthaginian
    after Zama, 220
indutiae
  truce, 229
inferred motivation, 63
inscriptions, 28
  Aetolian league in fifth century, 316
  Aetolian–Roman treaty (212), 145
  at Croton

inscriptions (cont.)
   Hannibal's bilingual record at Juno
      sanctuary, 12, 212
   attest Athenian diplomacy with Carthage
      (406), 63
   attest Carthaginians at Athens, 288
   attest contact between Carthage and
      Thebes, 288
   attest Greek–Punic code-switching, 287
   Augustus' Res gestae, 245
   Baatbal's genealogy, 231
   Chyretiae
      Flamininus' letter to, 161, 362
   elogium of Cornelia II, 44
   elogium of Scipio, 13, 418
   elogium of Scipio Barbatus, 53
   Erythraeans who have fled to 'the Medes', 298
   Etruscan king's bilingual dedication to
      Astarte, 93
   from Armenia
      rock inscriptions about Greek literature, 373
   from Athens
      proxeny decree for Tyrians, 288
   from Bahariya oasis (Egypt)
      dedication by Alexander to father
        Ammon, 232
   from Chios
      Romulus and Remus, 71
   from Colophon
      letters from Scipios, 23
   from Crete
      honours to Scipio brothers and others (189),
        264, 371
   from Delos
      dedications by Scipios, 22, 263
      friendship and kinship with Rome, 263
      honours for Bouzos of Canusium, 68,
        104, 355
      honours to Scipio, 263
      Scipio honoured for virtue and piety, 419
   from Delphi
      Gelon's victory celebrated, 62
      honours to Hegesianax, 305
      honours to Muttines, 148
   from Eretria
      cult for Flamininus, 420
   from Greece
      honours for Flamininus, 419
   from Gytheum
      cult for Flamininus, 420
   from Heraclea under Latmos
      letters from Scipios, 22
   from Italica
      meagre, 132
   from Malta, 289
   from Memphis (Egypt)
      Cretan dream interpreter, 240
   from Pyrgi
      bilingual gold tablet, 93
   from Sicily
      attesting gymnasia, 277
   from Sidon (Phoenicia)
      prince celebrates victory at Nemean
        games, 288
   from Syrian Antioch
      proves 195 as date of Hannibal's flight, 301
   from Tauromenium
      library catalogue, 278
   in Piraeus and Athens museums
      none for Carthaginians, 288
   Lampsacus' kinship with Rome, 308
   Lindian Chronicle, 241
   Macedonian, 305
   modern collections, 28
   Mummius, disputed dedication by, 132
   on warfare between Gortyn and Cnossus
      (Crete), 370
   Ptolemaic, 304
   Punic
      from Ibiza, 357
      from Malta, 289
   Rhodian 'foreign judges' attested by, 309
   Seleucid, 306
intelligence, military. *See* spy network,
   Hannibal's
intercessio. *See* veto
intermarriage, 75, 146
   Ariston as product of?, 310
   Carthaginians with Greeks, 62, 287
interpreters, 98, 128, 279
   Acilius as, 260
   at Zama, 215
   none mentioned in Hannibal's dealings with
      Antiochus, 281
   presumed use of by Hannibal to some army
      units, 347
intersignification, 53, 329
inuidia
   unpopularity
      of Nero and Salinator as censors (204), 196
invented tradition, 195
   about Italica, 134
   origin of concept, 131
inviolability
   of sanctuaries, 23, 161, 163
   personal, of tribunes, 390
Iolaus, 141
Ipsus
   Antigonus 'the One-eyed' defeated and killed
      by Seleucus I (301), 332

Isère, 87
Isthmian festival and games, 71
  Flamininus' proclamation at, 249
Italica
  home city of Trajan and Hadrian, 131
  location at Santiponce, 128
  not founded by Scipio, 128–35, 171, 291
Italy
  as a mere 'geographical expression', 365
  attitudes to Hannibal and Rome, 362–6
  Carthaginian allies in, 142
  colonization in (197–4), 255
  devastation of
    how bad and how lasting?, 398–401
  eponymous assize towns (fora) in, 294
  Greek cities of, 274
  Hannibal offers freedom to Italians, 94, 365
  Hercules crosses from Iberia to, 234
  protected from ferocious Gauls by Rome, 364
Itanos (Crete)
  Ptolemaic garrison at, 372
*iumenta*. *See* pack animals
*ius Lati*. *See* Latin right
*Iuuentas*, Greek Hebe
  temple vowed by Salinator at Metaurus, 192

Jacob (biblical)
  ladder, 229
Jason (mythical figure)
  and fire-breathing bulls, 100
  pours libations from ship Argo, 224
jealousy, *phthonos*, 155
Jesus
  called 'King of the Jews' in sign fixed on cross, 296
John (gospel of)
  on sign attached to cross of Jesus, 296
John the Baptist, 42
joint commands
  at Carthage, 108
jokes
  by Hannibal, 21, 109, 210, 326
  by Scipio, 21, 210, 254
Judaism
  Toynbee's attitude to, 396
judges
  at Carthage, 65
  Hannibal seeks to end life tenure of, 270
Jugurtha
  paraded in triumph, then executed, 247
Julius Caesar, 9
  as rex, 125
  on Sulla, 280
Julius Frontinus, Sextus, 30
  on Maharbal stratagem, 112

praises Hannibal's choice of camp at Numistro, 153, 338
story about 'Scipio Africanus' as not pugnacious
probably means Aemilianus, 340
Julius Obsequens
  collected Livy's prodigy lists, 284
Junius Silanus, Marcus, 118
Juno, 11, 193
  dissuades Hannibal from marching on Rome, 233
  favoured Carthage until 207, 184
  hymn to, by Livius Andronicus, 184
  Lacinia, 11, 12, 16, 85, 167, 232
  Moneta, 197, 200
  perennially angry, 233
  reconciled to Rome after Metaurus, 12, 193, 233, 295, 406
Junonia
  as theophoric name of intended colony, 295
Jupiter, 42, 231
  Optimus Maximus, 226, 230
    and triumphs, 246
  Purpurio vows temples to, 200
  role in provoking the war, 233
  Scipio Nasica vows and holds games to, 200
  Scipio sacrifices to on sailing for Africa, 224
  Stator, Romulus' vow to, 197
  triumphs, 14
  Victor, Rullianus vows temple to, 198
Justin, 30
  on audits of Carthaginian generals, 170
  on Carthaginian constitution, 65
  on Hannibal's naval victory for Prusias, 375
  on Hannibal's precocity, 79
  on Hannibal's wanderings, 370
  used good sources, 170
Juvenal
  compares Hannibal to Alexander, 86
  eighth Satire and prosopography, 176
  on Hannibal as 'supreme general', 411
  on Hannibal's crossing of Pyrenees and Alps, 85
  on Hannibal's end, 369, 379

Kerkouane, 63
kingship
  Roman attitudes to, 23, 122, 124, 212
  expressed by the Scipios, 332
Koine
  as educated Hellenistic Greek, 162
Kronos
  and Baal, 228

Lactantius
  quoted Ennius, 237

Laelius Sapiens, Gaius (friend of Aemilianus), 110
Laelius, Gaius (friend of Africanus), 219
   as confidant of Scipio, 110
   at New Carthage, 120
   awards crown to Digitius, 278
   consul 190 with Lucius Scipio, 323
   sent to raid Africa, 208
Lake Nemi
   Caligula's floating palaces on, 277
Lamprias catalogue, 32
Lampsacus
   Antiochus offers to abandon claim to, 331
   envoys from at Lysimachia conference, 309
   kinship link with Rome, 307
   resisted Antiochus III (192), 305
Laodice
   queen of Antiochus III, 301
   statue on Delos, 264
Larinum, 100
latifundia
   large land-holdings and Gracchan reforms, 402
Latin language, 19
   Hannibal's knowledge of, 98, 279
Latin right
   entitled Italian magistrates to Roman citizenship, 362
law, Carthaginian, 65
legates, 15, 54, 116, 161
   as diplomats, 207, 215
   as staff officers, 136, 164, 258, 328
   ten, as commissioners, 307
legends
   about Scipio and Hannibal. *See* Cornelius Scipio Africanus, Publius and Hannibal (9)
legions, 92, 101
   in Bruttium, 209
   number in 207, 186
   numbers in second Punic war, 356
   Scipio's in Sicily, 208
Leocritus, 287
Leontini, 148
Lepti Minus or Minor, 214
letters
   who composed?, 160
Leuctra, battle of, 33, 357
Leuke Akra, 68, 293
lex Calpurnia
   and extortion trials, 385
libations, 230, 239
   liquid sacrifices
      before sea journeys, 224
Liber-Triumpus, 230
libraries
   attached to gymnasia

Tauromenium, 278
   Syracosia contains one, 276
Libyphoenicians
   explained, 73
   Muttines as, 338
Licinius Crassus (cos.70)
   decapitated after Carrhae, 191
Licinius Crassus Dives, Publius (cos. 205), 118, 176
   given Bruttium as prouincia, 208
Licinius Tegula, Publius, 185
Liguria, 142
Lilybaeum, 88, 221
Lindian Chronicle
   on epiphanies, 241
Liternum, 15, 20, 392
litterae
   meaning of
      language or literature?, 280, 296
Livius Andronicus, 193
   and family of Salinator, 184
   Cicero on career of, 203
   created Latin literature, 284
   hymn to Juno, 184
   translation of Homer's Odyssey, 284
Livius Salinator, Gaius (cos. 188)
   commands fleet against Antiochus (191), 322
Livius Salinator, Marcus (cos. 208)
   probably not decemuir, 184
Livius Salinator, Marcus (decemuir), 185, 196
Livius Salinator, Marcus (victor at Metaurus), 70, 90, 108, 126, 153
   as censor (204) contracts for temple to Iuventas, 192
   career and grievances, 183–5
   legate to Carthage, 84
   moves against Mago (6), 208
   probably not decemuir, 196
   vows temple to Hebe on day of Metaurus, 192
Livy, 5, 16, 29, 213
   accepted story of Hannibal's meeting with Scipio, 260
   and caution theme, 90
   and Horace, 194
   character sketch of Hannibal influenced by Sallust, 52
   claims that Italian senates favoured Rome, the plebs Carthage, 362
   compared to Polybius on Cannae, 101
   compared to Polybius on speeches before Zama, 216
   implies Metaurus a tipping point, 182
   Locri affair topical in his lifetime, 167
   main source for Roman Republican religion, 222

obituary of Scipio, 244
on causes of second Punic war, 81
on Hannibal's bravery, 340
on Hannibal's death
   role of Flamininus, 381
on Hannibal's emotions at departure from
   Italy, 213
on prodigies, 91
on Sena as camp site, 204
on the trials of the Scipios, 387
portents
   change in coverage of, 284
postpones contents of letters, 156
silent on Hannibal's wanderings between
   Antiochus period and 183, 370
speeches in, 31, 159
treatment of Salinator's vow of temple at
   Metaurus, 192, 197
uses asyndeton about Salinator, 183
Locri, 58
besieged by Crispinus, 153
class struggle at, 363
Hannibal wins over in 215, 139
Hannibal's and Scipio's treatment compared,
   163–71
helped by Sparta at battle of Sagra river, 164
Italian city named after Greek founding
   area, 292
man management at
   Hannibal and Scipio compared, 4, 366
Scipio puts Pleminius in charge of, 136
unusually sophisticated city, 164
women prominent at, 164
logistics, 351–6, 435
lot
   as showing will of gods, 251
Lucan, 52
   on Pompey's decapitation, 191
Lucania, 138
Lucanians, 104
   some abandon Hannibal, 153
Lucian, 4, 265, 422
   makes Hannibal assert ignorance of
     Homer, 280
   makes Hannibal reject claim to divinity, 232
Lucretius
   on elephants, 411
   on Hannibal (by implication), 411, 413
   on Scipiadae, 48, 422
Lucretius, Spurius (praetor 205), 208
ludi Romani
   games in Circus Maximus, 113
Luke (gospel of)
   on sign attached to cross of Jesus, 296
lustrum condere

ritual lustration
   carried out by sensors at end of term, 251
Lycophron, 28
   on Anius of Delos, 263
   on Balearic slingers, 357
   on Malta, 152, 289
   on Menelaus in Italy, 149
   on Naples, 139
   on the Apulian Dasii, 363
Lycurgus (Spartan lawgiver), 236
Lysander
   on oaths, 36
   tactics at Aegospotami, 357
Lysias, envoy of Antiochus III, 307
Lysimachia, 320
   Roman–Seleucid conference at (196), 308
Lysimachus
   defeated by Seleucus I (281), 308
Lysippus (sculptor), 223

Macedonia
   as consular allotment, 250
Macedonian legion
   at Zama, 143, 219, 248
Macedonian war
   first, 143, 248
   second, 143
     not opposed by Scipio, 248, 257
Machanidas, 122
Machaon, 352
Macrobius
   source of Ennius fragment about Scipio, 239
   wrote commentary on 'Dream of Scipio', 417
magazines
   as storage depots, 354
magister
   at Secular Games, 196
magistrates
   at Carthage, 65
   wider ancient senses of, 12
Magnesia, 3
   alternative designation of battle, 192
   battle, 22
     analysis of, 335
     numbers at, 333
     terms imposed after, 335
   location under Mt Sipylus, 333
Mago (6), 41, 90, 116, 163, 207,
   215
   at Gades and Balearics, 136
   death of, 136
   false exile story about (193), 316
   receives instructions from Carthage, 157
Mago (7)
   swears treaty with Philip V, 141

Mago (10) 'the Samnite', 45, 72, 74
  at Locri, 168
Mago (12), 119
Mago (15) 'the Bruttian', 75
Maharbal, 90, 96
  as theophoric name from Baal, 49
  criticizes Hannibal, 105, 137
    and gets away with it, 367
    not in Polybius, 262
  disappears from record after Cannae, 163
  more than one bearer?, 111–12
  overruled by Hannibal after Trasimene, 94
  stratagem in Frontinus, 37
Malchus, 65
Malta
  locus of Carthaginian–Greek contacts, 289
  Longus captures, 88, 152, 289
Mamertini, 66
Mandonius, 121
mandrake
  stratagems using, 112
maniples, manipular army, 211
  at Cannae, 103
  at Zama, 219
  when introduced, 349
Manlius Torquatus, Titus
  dictator (208), 183
  ransom speech, 21, 258
Manlius Vulso, Gnaeus (cos. 189)
  on crucifixion of generals at Carthage, 384
  res gestae of, 19
Manlius Vulso, Lucius (praetor 218), 84
  vows temple to Concord during mutiny, 198
man management
  Hannibal and Scipio compared, 366
manpower
  Carthaginian, 115
  Roman and Italian losses in second Punic war, 401
Mantinea, battle (207), 122
maps, 31, 92
Marathon, 242
  battle, 22, 103
Marcius Ralla, Quintus
  dedicates in 192 temples vowed by Furius Purpurio, 200
  dedicates Tuditanus' temple to Fortuna (194), 198
Marcius Septimius, Lucius, 59
  asks senate for supplies, 156
  takes command in Iberia, 116
Marcius, Gaius
  Iberian from Italica, 132
maritime city
  Hannibal's need for, 139

maritime supremacy
  Roman, 360
Marius, Gaius, 46
  abolished property qualification for military service, 429
  and Syrian seer Martha, 227
Marrucini, 97
Mars, 66, 230
  month of March sacred to, 331
  temple dedicated by Cincinnatus, 198
Martha
  seer of Marius, 227
Marullinus, Aelius, 132
Masinissa, 25, 50, 116, 123, 172, 378
  at Zama, 219
  Carthaginian complaints against (195), 313
  despicable treatment of Sophoniba, 212
  enters the story, 123
  joins Scipio with cavalry in 204, 210
  visited by Scipio Aemilianus (dream), 415
Massilia, 75, 85
Masters of the Horse, 90, 96
Mausoleum at Halicarnassus
  compared to Scipio's monumental arch, 329
Mazaetullus, 50
medicines and medical staff
  as part of logistics, 352
Medma
  Locrian colony
    probably shared revolt from Rome, 366
meetings between Hannibal and Scipio
  at Ephesus (193), 259–65, 337
  before Zama, 215
Melqart, 12, 85, 87, 227, 234, 289
  Hamilcar (1) confused with?, 228
  on Siculo-Greek coinage?, 289
  patron god of Tyre, 49
Memnon (historian), 23
men on the spot, 147
Menelaus, 239
  in south Italy, 149
Menippus
  erects statues on Delos, 264
  massacre by, 264, 314, 320
mercenaries, 106
  Mamertines, 66
  sent by Philip V to Zama?, 219
merism
  indicates a totality, 225
Messapians
  as threat to Tarentum, 149
Messina (Sicily), 177
  Scipio, 136
Metaurus, 15
  battle, 12, 15, 90, 95

booty from, 190, 192, 207
casualties, 190
personification, 203, 212
river, 15
topography, 189
triumphs for, 201
metics (registered foreigners)
  at Athens
    philosophers as, 282
Metilius, Marcus (tribune 217)
  on visual effects of Hannibal's devastation, 400
Midas
  drank bull's blood, 380
Miltiades (Carthaginian philosopher), 287
Minnio
  prods Antiochus to war, 318
Minucius, Marcus, 174
Minucius Augurinus, Gaius (tribune 187)
  forensic attack on Lucius Scipio, 389
Minucius Augurinus, Gaius (tribune 184), 180
Minucius Rufus, Marcus
  as Master of the Horse (217), 90, 96
  imperium made equal with Fabius', 100
  on visual effects of Hannibal's devastation, 400
Minucius Rufus, Quintus (cos. 197)
  ouatio, 202
misdirection
  tragic, 416
monumental arch
  Scipio's, 329, 414
moon, 141
Mopsii
  at Compsa, 138
Moschion
  source for the Syracosia, 276
Motya
  statue of charioteer
    and cult of Hamilcar (1)?, 289
    booty or not?, 289
Mozart
  set the 'Dream of Scipio' to music, 417
mules
  logistically important, 353
  mentioned only once in surviving text of Polybius, 353
  of Marius, 353, 422
Mummius, Lucius, 19
  dedication at Italica (?), 132
mutiny
  against Alexander, 342, 351
  against Antiochus III, 309
  Scipio's harsh suppression of, 128
  Vulso makes vow during (218), 198

Muttines or Muttones the Libyphoenician
  defects to Rome, 147, 338
Myonnesus
  sea battle, 200, 325
Myrkanos
  swears treaty with Philip V, 141
Myth of Er. *See* Plato

Nabis (Spartan king), 318
  Damocritus sent to, 318, 362
Naevius (poet), 56, 420
Naevius, Marcus (tribune 184), 180
  accuser of Scipio in 184, 391
names, personal, 41
  and prosopography, 45–7
Naples, 60
  Hannibal attempts to win, 139
  Hannibal fails at, 139, 275, 361
  not barbarized, 296
  Rome's oldest naval ally, 139
Naravas, 50
Naupactus
  Aetolian league meets at (193), 317
naval warfare
  few naval battles in second Punic war, 360
Naxos in Sicily, 60, 129
Nemean festival and games, 71
  Diognetus at, 288
Nepos, 30
  first to name Zama, 194, 218
  on demolition of Hannibal's town house, 301, 424
  on Hannibal at Gortyn, 370
  on Hannibal's Greek, 279, 296
  on Hannibal's naval victory for Prusias, 375
  on Hannibal's oath, 51
  on Romans' role in Hannibal's death, 380
  says Hannibal sailed to Cyrene (193), 315
Neptune
  and Scipio, 120
  more than one Punic 'equivalent', 227
  Scipio sacrifices to on sailing for Africa, 224
Nero. *See* Claudius
Nero Claudius Drusus, brother of emperor Tiberius, 194
  and Metaurus, 204
neutrality
  of Delos, 264
New Carthage, 2, 14, 60, 239
  as supply depot, 119
  compared to Italica, 133
  foundation of by Hasdrubal (5), 69
  name, 293
  Scipio captures, 119–23
  symbolic value of, 119

Nicander (Aetolian envoy)
  later career, 318
  on Hannibal, 320
  sent to Philip V, 318
Nicias, 156
  has favourite seer, 227
nicknames, 74
night-fighting, 94
Nobas, 75
nod
  of Jupiter and Scipio, 258
Nola
  Hannibal suffers rare defeat at, 141
  political oscillation at, 364
nomen, 46
Nossis (Locrian epigrammatist), 164
nostalgia
  colonial
    affected naming of cities, 292
    Timaeus' for Sicily, 275
Numantia, 38
Numidians, 11, 64
  at Cannae
    pretended deserters, 103
  at Trebia
    ambush, 90
  at Zama, 219
  kill Scipio's father, 116

oaths
  breaking of
    by Scipio, 358
  cynical attitudes to, 36
  in treaty between Hannibal and Philip V, 226
  Scipio's after Cannae, 106
  sworn by Hannibal as child, 51, 68, 315
Octavian. *See* Augustus
Octavius, Gnaeus (praetor 205), 215
Odysseus, 42
  as ancient military role model, 359
Olbia (happy, prosperous)
  name as example of onomastic optimism, 295
oligarchies
  always resist reform, 270
Olympiads, 10
Olympian festival and games, 71
Olympias, 55
omens
  bad
    for Hannibal on crossing to Africa, 213
  good
    for Scipio on crossing to Africa, 210
one-eyed man
  Hannibal as, 27, 87
onomastic evidence. *See* names, personal

Ophellas, 72
Oppian law (215)
  debate on repeal of, 255
optimates, 175
optimism
  onomastic: 295
oracles
  Ammon
    Hannibal allegedly consults, 228, 316, 382
  at Delphi, 145
    Dorieus and, 159
  of the dead
    Hannibal's sacrifices at, 228
  promises success to Scipios in Africa, 225
Orcades, 79
Orosius
  alleges terminal illness of Scipio, 393
Orpheus, 233
ouatio, 246
  Claudius Centho, 202
  Minucius Rufus in 197, 202
  not same as modern 'ovation', 201
Ovid
  on 'great Scipio', 422
  on Metaurus, 186, 195, 205
ox-hide trick
  by Dido, 377
  not Greek, 377

pack animals
  Nero's army provided with on march up Italy, 355
  used for carrying weapons, 356
Padus, 88
Paestum, 121
  as 'city of Poseidon' and of Digitius, 278
  relevant to divine help at New Carthage, 278
Pagasai. *See* Demetrias
Palinurus, 224
pallium, 56
  Greek tunic
    Scipio wears at Syracuse, 275
  young Scipio allegedly half-wearing, 278
Pamphylia
  Alexander at, 239
  Hannibal's sea battle off, 325
Panion
  Seleucid victory over Ptolemaic Egypt at (201), 331
Panormus
  ship-building by Scipio at, 208
papyri
  documentary
    from Ptolemaic Egypt, 304

parallels between Hannibal and Scipio
  about apologies, 390
  advisers before Magnesia, 3, 274
    parallel drawn by Livy, 323, 406
  as historians, 20
  both had trouble with 'quaestors', 269
  both learned from family deaths in battle to stay alive, 344
  both suspected of stealing booty?, 267
  brought down by domestic enemies, 3
  deaths, 3, 380
  did not aim at monarchical position, 428
  did not found eponymous cities, 428
  fictional same-sex stories told about both, 52
  financial, 252
  Hercules as model, 234
  literary, detected by modern scholars, 407
  neither received cult, 427
  not great successes as politicians, 431
  oaths or vows taken in youth, 226
  omens during crossings to Africa, 214
  overseas commands, 3, 155, 429, 434
  religious, 242
  stories told after Cannae, 105
  upholders of Greek freedom?, 274
Parmenio and Pythodorus
  envoys from Lampsacus at Lysimachia conference, 309
Parthians
  decapitate Crassus, 191
Parthini, 142
past presumptive, 7, 70
patronyms
  denomination by, 46
Pausistratus the Rhodian
  fleet commander
    death of, 324
pederasty
  fictional story about summoning of boy Hannibal, 52
  gymnasia perceived to be associated with, 277
Pella
  Syrian, 292
Pelopidas, 33
Pergamum
  great altar
    celebrated Pergamene victories over Prusias?, 377
  rulers of. See Eumenes II, Attalus II
Pericles, 46
periochae, 70
  Italica mentioned, 132
  periocha 41,
    on Graccuris, 294
  peripheral imperialism, 86, 158

perjury
  by Scipio?, 211, 229
Persephone
  cult at Locri, 164
  Sicilian cult of, 290
Perseus (king of Macedon), 25, 54
personification
  of Africa on coin, 225
  of Metaurus as 'witness', 203, 212
Petillii cousins
  and attacks on the Scipios (187), 389
Petillius, Quintus (tribune 187), 180
Petrarch
  drew on 'Dream of Scipio' in his Africa, 417
phalanx
  Greek infantry formation. See hoplites
Pharus, 142
Phaselis, 121
Philadelphus. See Ptolemy II
philhellenism
  ambiguity of, 249
Philip II of Macedon, 25, 36, 37, 49
  as founder of eponymous cities, 292
  lost eye at Methone siege, 339
  talent-spots Eumenes of Cardia at gymnasium, 277
Philip of Megalopolis
  alleged agent of Antiochus III, 321
Philip V of Macedon, 20, 25, 79, 207
  accused of neglecting to bury dead after defeat at Cynoscephalae, 321
  Hannibal's letter to, 119
  Hannibal's treaty with, 83
  succeeded to throne (221), 305
  why preferred Rome to Antiochus, 321
Philippi, 49
Philippopolis, 49
Philistus (Sicilian historian)
  works of in Tauromenium library catalogue, 278
Philopoemen, 3, 4,
    262
  death
    compared to Hannibal's, 380
  military training by, 122
philosophers at Carthage. See Carthage, philosophy and philosophers
Phoenice, Peace of, 143, 374. See treaties
Phoenician trenches, 220
Phoenicians, 12, 93
Phormio (Athenian admiral), 118
Phormio (Athenian philosopher), 35, 265
  Aristotelian, 282
Picenum, 97
Pietas. See Piety

piety
    of Hannibal towards dead Romans, 95
    Glabrio family and temple to, 200
Pindar, 1, 15, 216
    house at Thebes spared by Alexander, 223
    imitated by Horace on Metaurus victory, 193
    too difficult for Hannibal?, 280
piracy, 62, 324
    Aetolian, 316
Piraeus, 277
pistis, 161
Pithekoussai, 61
Placentia, 88
    Hasdrubal besieges, 186
Plato
    on seers, 228
    Republic
        Myth of Er emulated by Cicero in 'Dream of Scipio', 417
Plautus (comic playwright), 263
Pleminius, Quintus, 58
    as scoundrel, 151
    at Locri, 136, 163–71, 177, 366, 385
    fate of, various versions, 166
Pliny the Elder, 25
    claims Hannibal spared temple at Saguntum, 222
    on Gnaeus Scipio's funeral mound, 116
    on Hannibal's love affair, 151
    on Italica, 131
    on Libyssa, 382
    on Pomponia (by implication), 42
    on Prusa as foundation by Hannibal, 377
    on Scipio's olive tree at Liternum, 393
    on statues of Hannibal at Rome, 150
    says Cato learned soldiering from Hannibal and Scipio, 421
Pliny the Younger
    on gymnasia, 277
plunder. See booty
Plutarch, 1, 3, 30, 109
    lost Lives of Scipio, 31–4
    on death of Demosthenes, 379
    on discussion between Hannibal and Scipio on generalship, 261
    on Hannibal in Armenia, 369
        Life of Lucullus fuller than Strabo, 373
    on Hannibal's death, 379
    on Pyrrhus' 'integrated' generalship, 343
    on the two Catos, 386
    sceptical about superhuman status of mortals, 238
Podalirius, 352
poison
    Hannibal's death by, 379

politeia
    wider than constitution, 107
Polyaenus, 30, 37
    on Hannibal's belief in incarnation, 229
    on mandrake stratagem, 112
Polybius, 3, 29
    Aetolian breach with Rome as 'spark' lighting Rome's war with Aetolians, 317
    and caution theme, 90
    and ethnics, 73, 74, 77
    and Scipio Aemilianus, 100
    and 'those around', 110
    and tyche, 299
    anecdotes to illustrate Scipio's character, 254
    bias of, 100
    book 6,
        Roman religion discussed in missing section, 230
    book 6 of, 63, 107, 173
    capable of dramatic narrative, 298
    compared to Livy on Cannae, 101
    compared to Livy on speeches before Zama, 216
    confuses Marcus Atilius Regulus with Marcus Minucius, 102
    did not narrate trials of Scipios sequentially, 387
    does not record prodigies, 91
    events not mentioned by
        could still have happened, 262
    fragment described Hannibal's subterfuge at Gortyn?, 371
    interested in Locri, 164
    Italica not mentioned by, 130
    less informative than Livy about Roman religion, 222
    little after Zama about Carthage in surviving text, 220
    Metaurus not named by, 204
    mules mentioned once only in surviving text of, 353
    on causation, 80
    on cohorts, 350
    on deaths of Marcellus, Hasdrubal (6), and Hamilcar (9), 340
    on effects of second Punic war on Italian cities, 399
    on fear and respect for Rome, 98, 364
    on Hannibal's cruelty, 400, 408
    on Hannibal's 'greed'
        explicable by 'force of circumstances', 400
    on Hannibal's impiety, 410
    on Scipio
        sought fame in aristocratic state, 266
    on Scipio and dreams or omens, 242

on Scipio and self-preservation, 341
on Scipio's awareness of father's mistakes, 344
on Scipio's religious attitudes, 114
on Scipio's trial (184), 391
on the tribunate of the plebs, 174
praises dishonest success by Scipio, 210
quotes Xenophon to describe Scipio's 'workshop of war', 350
rightly stresses Hannibal's logistical achievement, 353
speeches in, 20, 31, 158
word for 'rumour' a favourite of, 310
Polyrrhenia (on Crete)
   honours to Hispallus, 264
polysemic interpretations, 49, 422
Polyxenidas the Rhodian
   defeated at sea by Romans and Eumenes II off Corycus, 323
   sent by Antiochus to bring forces from Asia, 321
*pompai. See* processions
Pomponia, 41, 178, 235, 236
   piety of, 113, 222
Pomponius Matho (praetor 217), 54, 90, 96
Pomponius Matho, Manius (cos. 233), 41, 67
Pomponius Matho, Marcus (cos.231), 41
Pomponius Matho, Marcus (praetor 204), 42, 165, 178
pontifices, 184
Pontius Pilate
   fixes sign on the cross, 296
Pontius Telesinus
   compared to Hannibal, 413
Popilius Laenas, Gaius (cos. 172)
   arrogant treatment of Antiochus IV, 84
Popillius Laenas, Gaius (cos. 172), 378
populares, 175
Porcius Cato, Marcus (the Elder), 36, 44, 87, 180
   and indemnity imposed on Antiochus at Apamea, 336
   as censor co-appoints colleague Flaccus *princeps senatus*, 251
   commands warships on crossing to Africa, 209
   drops a Libyan fig, 271
   hated Scipio, 386
   military tribune at Thermopylae (191), 322
   on Scipio
      Cicero's evidence, 421
   on Scipio's auctoritas, 259
   part in Scipio's disgrace, 386
   quaestor, 209
   sends supplies home from Iberia because 'the war will feed itself', 352
   severity of censorship (184), 386
Porcius Cato, Marcus (the Younger)
   paired with Phocion by Plutarch, 386
Porcius Licinus, Lucius
   dedicates temple to Venus Erycina, 200
Porcius Licinus, Lucius (praetor 207)
   at Metaurus, 189
portraits of Hannibal and Scipio, 24–8
Poseidon
   as 'present' in treaty with Philip V, 141
   Romanized as Neptune, 120
Posidonius
   on Fabius and Marcellus, 33
Postumius Albinus, Lucius (cos. 229), 54, 70
praenomen, 46
praetorium
   as meeting of Roman officers, 109
praetors, 44
   as Carthaginian sufetes, 269
Praetuttii, 97
prayers
   Ajax to Zeus, 94, 359
   Roman
      at Trasimene, 199
      Scipio's for safe return from Africa, 223
   Scipio's on sailing for Africa, 224
Priam, 123
priests and priesthoods, 14
   Carthaginian
      some priests women, 231
   Roman, 175, *See* Salian priests
      decemuiri, 184
      usually for life, 230
   Sicilian
      for Persephone and Demeter, 290
princeps senatus, 15
   censors could appoint one of selves as, 251
   had right to speak first in debates, 251
   Scipio as, 249
principes, 358
   as 'chief men' at Locri, 363
   as second line of Roman infantry, 211, 220
   at Zama, 219
processions
   as features of Greek public life, 245
   triumphs as, 14, 230
proconsul, 14
prodigies, 91
   Livy's coverage of, 284
   reported in 207, 185
prolepsis, 81, 89, 138
proletarii
   defined, 401
propraetor, 117
prorogatio, 14
Proserpina. *See* Persephone

proskunesis
  as obeisance, 121
prosopography, 45–7
  and Hamilcar (12) problem, 168
  and Roman Republican politics, 175–80
  Busa, 105
  revival of?, 426
prouincia, 67
  origins of system, 155
proxenos
  Scipio at Delos, 263
proxeny
  Athenian, for Tyrians, 288
  defined, 263
Prusa
  as 'Bursa', 377
  Hannibal's role in foundation, 375, 377
Prusias I of Bithynia, 23, 35, 328
  Hannibal at court of, 369
  letters to, by Publius and Lucius Scipio, 332
Ptolemais
  new name of Barke, 72
Ptolemies, Ptolemaic Egypt. See Egypt, Ptolemaic
Ptolemy I, 306
  as historian, 34, 344
Ptolemy II, 54
  and Theocritus, 276
Ptolemy IV
  loses Seleucia in Pieria, 307
Ptolemy V, 309
  incorrect rumour of death, 309
Ptolemy VI Philometor, 44
Punic co-jurors
  to treaty between Hannibal and Philip V, 162
Punic deception, 128, 211, 358
Punic language, 10, 19, 28, 60, 98, 141
Punic war
  second, 2
Punic wars
  third
    Carthage destroyed, 405
*Punica fraus*. See Punic deception
Puteoli
  Hannibal's attempt on, 141
Pyrenees, 11, 85, 126
Pyrgi, 93
Pyrrhus, 54, 66, 91, 98
  exemplifies 'integrated ideal' of generalship, 343
  helps Tarentum. See
  rated second by Hannibal for generalship, 337
Pythian festival and games, 71

quadriremes, 11

quaestors
  Carthaginian, 64
    Hannibal has trouble with quaestor at Carthage, 269
    on Hannibal's army staff, 270, 355
  Roman
    Cato as, 209
    number of, 64
    recalcitrant quaestor refuses to open treasury for Scipio, 254
Quinctius Cincinnatus, Gaius
  dedicates temple to Mars, 198
Quinctius Crispinus, Titus (cos. 208), 153, 183
  begins siege of Locri, 153
  wounded and killed, 153
Quinctius Flamininus, Lucius (cos. 192)
  organizes a beheading, 191
Quinctius Flamininus, Titus, 3, 4, 71
  and Scipio, 248–51
  asked by Antiochus for formal alliance with Rome, 309
  career resists analysis in terms of groups, 179, 248
  continuation of command, 257
  cultic honours to, 249
  defeats Philip V at Cynoscephalae, 143
  favoured propertied classes after Cynoscephalae, 362
  land commissioner (201), 249
  letters sent by, 161
  part played in Hanniba's death, 380
  sent to impose peace between Pergmaum and Bithynia, 375
quinqueremes, 11, 91

ransom
  Hannibal's offer after Cannae, 106
Raphia
  ends fourth Syrian war, 307
recruitment
  and Gracchan reforms, 403
Rediculus, 232, 233
  god of Return, 151
religion
  Carthaginian, 61, 290
  cognitive, 229
  measures at Rome after Trasimene, 96
  Roman
    Greek elements in, 284
    Livy more help than Polybius, 222
*repetundae*. See extortion trials
res gestae, 19
reserves, tactical
  Epaminondas and, 357

rex
    unacceptable royal title at Rome, 124
Rhegium
    Locrian exiles at, 363
    not barbarized, 296
rhetoric
    of speeches before Zama, 216
Rhoda (Iberian place), 76
Rhode, 62
Rhodes, 75
    Rhodian naval defeat of Hannibal, 321, 325
    Rhodians as 'foreign judges', 309
    Roman friendship with, 62, 71
Rhone, 85
ring-composition
    defined, 313
rituals
    Carthaginian
        Hannibal's violent sacrifice of lamb, 225
    Roman
        expiatory, 91
        Scipio's on departure for Africa, 223
        tripudium, 227
river god
    Metaurus as, 203
Rome
    and Delphi, 71, 145, 285
    and Troy, 291
    army
        hastati, principes, and triarii, 211
        manipular, 211
    as democracy?, 173
    decision for war with Antiochus after Delium massacre, 320
    favoured propertied classes, 362
    foundation of, 60
    Hannibal marches on (211), 150
    imperial but republican power, 346
    imperialism of, 7
    not defenceless, 105, 150
    religion at
        Greek elements in, 283
    Servian wall, 97
Romulus
    and Remus, 236
        coins from Italica, 133
        on Chios inscription, 71
    as founder of Rome
        story combined with Aeneas legend, 291
    vow to Jupiter Stator, 197
Rostra, 13
roving anecdotes, 99, 228, 359, 376 *See* anecdotes, roving
    Hannibal a favourite subject of, 413

sacrifices
    before battle, divinatory, 227
    Carthaginian
        Hamilcar's to Baal, 51
        Flaminius' unlucky, 92
        Hannibal's at Cercina, 300
        Hannibal's of a lamb, 225
        human, at Rome, 71, 228
            included a Greek (228), 284
        neglected by Flaminius, 91
        not usually done by magistrates in person, 225
        of children at Carthage, 72, 228
        performed by commanders, 232
        Scipios, on sailing for Africa, 120, 224
*sacrosanctitas*. *See* inviolability
Sagra river
    battle (Archaic), 164
Saguntum, 11, 69, 72, 158, 172, 233
    appeal to Rome, 82
    as cause of war, 80
    Hannibal's attack on as his own initiative?, 82
    not recaptured by Rome until 212, 115
    siege of, 107
Salaeca, 21
Salapia
    Hannibal has love affair at, 151
Salian priests, 14, 25
    Scipio as, 230
Salinator. *See* Livius
Sallust, 26
    influenced Livy's sketch of Hannibal, 52
    source for Sertorius' divinatory doe, 227
salutatio
    morning greeting at Rome
        Carthaginian equivalent, 300
Samnites, 138
    and Roman manipular army, 350
Samnium, 98
Samson (biblical), 37
Samuel (biblical), 42
Sardinia, 54, 67, 91, 93
    unjustly seized by Rome, 81
satraps
    natural hosts for exiles, 298
    Seleucid
        of Armenia, 373
Saturnia
    as theophoric place name, 295
schools, 55
Scione
    welcome to Brasidas, 245
Scipiadae, 48
scipio
    as rod or staff, 49, 212
    as thunderbolt, 72

Scipio. *See* Cornelius
Scyles
    taught Greek by mother, 297
sea power, 75
sea routes in western Mediterranean, 155
Secular Games, 196
    sanctioned by Sibylline Books, 185
seers, 108
    Carthaginian, 228
    favourite
      of Tolmides and Nicias, 227
    on campaign, 232
    on naval expedition of Hanno (3), 228
    Plato on, 228
    Scipio Aemilianus expels from Iberian army, 352
Seleucid dynasty, 304–7
Seleucus I
    defeated Lysimachus at Corupedium (281), 308, 332
    helped to power by Ptolemy I, 306
Seleucus IV, 309
    Hannibal's advice about, 320
    succeeds Antiochus III (187), 301
Seleucus Romance
    hypothetical work reasserting Seleucid primacy in city foundations, 304
self-preservation by generals
    attitudes to, 339–44
sella curulis, 212
    ivory chair for curule magistrates, 113
Semitic influences
    on treaty between Hannibal and Scipio, 144
Sempronius Gracchus, Gaius, 44
    and extortion trials, 385
    and seer Herennius Siculus, 227
    attempts to found colony Junonia, 295, 406
    head of, after death, 191
Sempronius Gracchus, Tiberius (cos. 238), 81
Sempronius Gracchus, Tiberius (cos. 215), 146
Sempronius Gracchus, Tiberius, father of the Gracchi, 44, 132
    and Cato, 390
    as founder of eponymous city Graccuris in Iberia, 294
    mission to Philip V, 330
    prevents imprisonment of Lucius Scipio, 180
    triumuir who founded Saturnia, 295
    uses tribunician veto to help Lucius Scipio, 389
Sempronius Gracchus, Tiberius (tribune 133), 44
    worried about rural poor in Etruria, 401
Sempronius Longus, Tiberius (cos. 218), 84, 88
    blamed for Trebia defeat, 89
    captures Malta, 152, 289
Sempronius Sophus, Publius (cos. 296)

    vows temple to Tellus, 198
Sempronius Tuditanus, Gaius (cos. 204)
    forces in Greece, 208
Sempronius Tuditanus, Publius (cos. 204), 143, 213
    military tribune at Cannae, 104
    on lot as will of gods, 251
    vows temple to Fortuna, 198
Sena, 15
    alternative name for Metaurus battle, 188, 203
senate, Carthaginian, 59, 79
    senators in treaty with Philip V, 141
senate, Roman, 15, 24, 66, 86
    censors revised membership of, 251
    number of meetings (201–190), 257
    provides supplies, 353
    responsible for supplies, 115
    underestimated Hannibal, 15, 100
Seneca the Elder, 54
    mentioned Scipio, 422
Seneca the Younger, 13
    on Hannibal, 414
    on Scipio's villa, 392
senex
    Livy makes Hannibal self-identify as before Zama, 216
seniores
    senior senators (in debate about Iberia), 258
Sentinum
    battle, 198
Septimius Severus (Roman emperor)
    and Hannibal's tomb, 383
Sergius Catiline, Lucius (praetor 68)
    debt proposals, 404
serpents, 42
Sertorius, 54
    comparison with Hannibal (Plutarch and Appian), 414
    one-eyed, 87
Sertorius, Quintus, 345
    and pet divinatory doe, 227
Servilius Caepio, Gnaeus (cos. 203), 178
    on embassy to Carthage (195), 299
Servilius Caepio, Quintus
    at Arausio, 108
Servilius Geminus, Gaius (cos. 203), 178
Servilius Geminus, Gnaeus (cos. 217), 91, 102
Servilius Pulex Geminus, Marcus (cos. 202), 178
Servius (commentator on Virgil), 48
Sibyl
    inspired by Apollo, 185
Sibylline Books, 96, 185
    consulted in 207?, 185
Sibylline oracles, 22
Sicily, 88, 91

as locus of Carthaginian–Greek contacts, 289
  gymnasia at, 277
  Scipio given as province, 207
Sidicines, 104
Sidon
  Agenor of, 288
sieges
  did not bring Hannibal and Scipio into direct
    conflict, 361
  Hannibal not equipped for, 105, 356, 361
  of Capua, 149
  of Locri, 153
  of Placentia, 186
  of Rome not practicable, 150
  of Saguntum, 82
  of Syracuse, 146
  of Utica, 212
Silanus, Junius, 126
Silenus of Caleacte, 233
Silius Italicus, 28, 31
  and 'Roman Hannibal', 407
  closes epic with Scipio's triumph, 247
  makes Juno send Hannibal to urge Hannibal
    to fight, 233
  names Scipio's mother Pomponia, 42
    Pomponia talks to Scipio in
      underworld, 235
  on Barce wife of Xanthippus, 76
  on Hannibal's oath, 51
  on Hasdrubal's decapitation, 191
  on personal name Barcas, 76
  picks up Livy on Hercules as Hannibal's role
    model, 234
  Virgil's Turnus as Hannibal, 150
Simonides of Magnesia
  celebrated Antiochus I's victory over
    Gauls, 305
  Seleucid poet, 304
Sisyphus, 74
slaves. *See* enslaved people
slingers
  Balearic
    in Hannibal's army, 356
Smyrna, 307
  Antiochus offers to abandon claim to, 331
  envoys from at Lysimachia conference, 309
  resisted Antiochus III (192), 305
snakes, 240
  and miraculous births, 55, 235
  kept guard over Scipio's spirit at Liternum, 393
  poisonous, 35
  tall story about Hannibal's use of to win sea-
    battle, 375
Somnium Scipionis. *See* Dream of Scipio
Somnus (sleep god), 233

Sophocles, 73
Sophoniba, 211
  despicably treated by Scipio and Masinissa, 212
Sosylus of Sparta, 11, 28, 279, 297
  as Hannibal's teacher, 280
Spain. *See* Iberia
Sparta
  adventurers from, in south Italy, 149
  advisers at, 328
  Agesilaus as friend of Xenophon, 9
  Aristotle compares Carthage to, 285
  Brasidas, 38, 343
  Cleomenes I makes bull sacrifice, 239
  Cyrene 'granddaughter' of, 286
  defeat at Leuctra, 33
  Demaratus, 42
  Dercylidas, 74
  Dorieus
    and Delphic oracle, 159
  double kingship compared to Roman
    consulship, 64
  fear of Athens, 80
  Gytheum inscription, 420
  jealousy towards Brasidas at, 155
  kings called Eudamidas, 38, 283
  laconic messages, 156
  lend Dioscuri to Otalian Locri, 164
  Locri the 'Sparta of the West', 164
  Lycurgus, 236
  Lysander
    at Aegospotami, 357
    on oaths, 36
  Machanidas
    defeated by Philopoemen, 122
  Menelaus, 149
  Nabis
    and Antiochus III, 318
  Pausanias (Regent), 66
  Sosylus, 11, 28
  Tarentum founded from, 148
  Thera founded from, 286
  Thermopylae (480), 322
  Tyrtaeus, 280
  Vegetius on Hannibal's teacher from
    (Sosylus?), 281
  women at, 164
  Xanthippus, 76
speech
  direct and indirect, 158, 216
speeches
  exchange between Scipio and Fabius, 208
  Hannibal's at Ephesus to Antiochus
    quoted, 322
  in ancient historians, 20
  in literary sources, 31

speeches (cont.)
  of Locrians at Rome, 165
Spoletium, 97
spy network
  Hannibal's, 37, 92, 100, 213, 357
squalor
  as forensic technique, 183
stasis
  absent at Carthage, 65
  at Compsa, 138
statues. *See* Motya (charioteer)
  at Corinth
    Scipio declines statue, 419
  Caracalla's to Hannibal and Sulla, 383
  of Hannibal at Rome, 28, 414
  of Scipio, 238
  Seleucid, on Delos, 264
  statuette owned by Alexander, Hannibal, and Sulla, 223
Stephanus of Byzantium, 18
  lists nine Olbias, 295
  Metaurus not listed by, 205
  on Barke, 74
  on Capua, 140
  on Italica, 131
  on Rhode, 76
  on Ticinus, 205
Stobaeus, 35
Stoic
  philosopher on the good general, 283
Stoics, 36, 38
Strabo
  and 'those around', 110
  does not mention Italica, 131
  on 'barbarization' of Italy (by Rome), 296
  on Hannibal in Armenia, 369, 373
  on Metaurus, 205
strategy
  Hannibal discusses, 109
Sucro, 128
Suda
  Byzantine lexicon, 387
Suessula, 140
Suetonius
  on oracle about the Scipios, 225
*sufete*, 10, 170
  Hannibal elected as, 269
Sulla. *See* Cornelius
Sulpicius Galba Maximus, Publius (cos. 211 and 200), 314
  commander against Philip in second Macedonian war, 249
  dictator 203, 178
  on diplomatic mission to Asia Minor (194–3), 260

sun, 141
supplication
  Locrians at Rome, 165
  Romans at Trasimene, 199
supplies, 101, 115
  Alexander's arrangements for, 351
  food provided for Nero's army by Italian towns, 188
  normally sent from Italy to Roman commanders in Iberia, 352
  problems of supply
    early Greek poets and historians aware of, 352
surrender
  not same as capture, 424
Surus (elephant), 26, 87
swords
  Iberian, 122, 350, 357
Sychaeus, 76
Symmachus
  explains Roman success against Hannibal religiously, 351
synedroi, 144, 162
  as Carthaginian advisers, 109
Syphax, 14, 160, 221, 345
  and Scipio's triumph, 247
  Scipio's first attempt to win over, 127
Syracosia (giant ship)
  sent by Hiero II to Ptolemy II, 276
Syracuse
  as Scipio's base, 209
  cultural and literary capital, 275
  foundation of, 61
  Scipio at, 25
  Scipio's military display at, 122, 256
  theatres, 275
  won then lost by Hannibal, 146
Syria, 301
Syrian wars, 301
  fifth, 301
    mixed results for Antiochus III, 307
  fourth
    ended badly for Antiochus III at Raphia, 307

tactics, 109
  at Cannae, 103
  Hannibal and Scipio compared, 357
Tader, 116
Tagus, 119
Tagus (river), 80
Tanit, 12, 141
Taras. *See* Tarentum
Tarentum
  Hannibal takes most of, 148

home city of Livius Andronicus, 184, 284
  not barbarized, 296
  sources of prosperity, 149
Tarraco, 86
  Scipio at, 118
  Scipio returns to, 123
Taurini, 87
Teanum, 99
tears, 221
Telesia, 98
Tellus, earth god
  Sophus vows temple to, 198
temenos
  as religious precinct
    to Cineas at Ai Khanum, 292
temple medicine, 240
Ten Thousand (Xenophon's army). *See* Xenophon
Terentius Culleo, Quintus (praetor 187)
  on embassy to Carthage (195), 299
Terentius Varro, Gaius
  as demagogue, 92, 100
  at Capua, 140
  commanded Roman left wing at Cannae, 102
  defeated by Hannibal at Cannae, 101
  elected consul for 216, 100
  thanked for not despairing of the republic after Cannae, 107, 365, 384
*testis*. *See* witness
Teutones, 108
Thapsus (Africa), 299
Tharros (Sardinia)
  traders from, 93
Thebes
  Cadmus founded, 288
  destroyed (335), 223
  foundation legend, 378
  Pelopidas and Epaminondas, 33
Themistocles
  at Ephesus, 302
  drank bull's blood, 380
  flight of, 298
Theocritus, 304
  hopes for patronage of Hiero II, 276
theophoric
  names of city foundations
    Junonia, Saturnia, 295
theophoric names, 49, 111
Theophrastus, 68
  name changed from Tyrtamos, 285
Theoxena
  tragic story of, 298
Thera, 73
  founded from Sparta, 286
Theramenes, 74

Thermopylae (battle of, 191), 322
  Glabrio vows temple to Piety, 200
  Glabrio's son fulfils father's vow made on day of, 200
Thermopylae (battle of, 480), 322
Thessaly
  Demetrias as important harbour of, 314
  kinship with Armenia, 292
Thoas (Aetolian)
  speech of complaint against Rome (193), 317
  speech to Antiochus quoted, 319
  surrender demanded at Apamea, 326
Thrace
  European
    claimed by Antiochus III, 307
Thucydides, 1, 20, 63, 342
  and speeches, 24
  doesn't tell us what anyone looked like, 24
  echoed by Livy on Hannibal's flight, 298
  IR and, 342
  on appointments of generals, 118
  on Brasidas, 107, 155
  on causation, 80
  on Cleon, 101
  on libations before sea journeys, 224
  on Nicias, 156
  on night-fighting, 94
  on Sicilian cities, 60
  on supply problems, 352
  postpones contents of letters, 156
  too difficult for Hannibal?, 280
  treats Cleon as coward, 343
Thurii (Italian)
  became Copia ('Abundance'), 295
Thyestes, 239
Thyrrheum, 145
Tiber, 96
Tiberius (Roman emperor)
  and Metaurus, 204
Tiberius, emperor, 30, 194
Ticinus, 2, 11
  battle, 59, 88–90
  Stephanus of Byzantium on, 205
Timaeus of Tauromenium, 11, 60, 87
  nostalgic for Syracuse, 275
  on Dido, 60
  source of Diodorus for Sicilian cults, 290
timocratic
  Roman assemblies as, 173
tipping points, 182
Tolmides, 227
Tomyris, Scythian queen, 191
Toynbee, Arnold
  Hannibal's legacy
    reception of, 395–8

Toynbee, Arnold (cont.)
  on Judaism, 396
trade, 62, 93, 104
  Bouzos as trader, 68
  Carthage and, 137
  part of sneer against Varro, 101
training, 127
  Vegetius on, 351
training, military
  Scipio's at New Carthage, 122, 350
Trajan
  on gymnasia, 277
Trasimene, 11
  battle, 29, 52, 54, 90–6
  lake, 94
treasury
  Scipio demands opening of, 254
treaties
  at end of first Punic war, 67
  between Capua and Hannibal, 140
  between Carthaginians and Etruscans, 93
  between Hannibal and Philip V, 21, 141–5, 226, 248
  between Romans and Aetolians, 145, 317
  between Romans and Hiero II, 147
  between Rome and Carthage (before 261), 62, 138
  between Rome and Carthage after Zama, 220
  between Rome and Naples, 139
  Ebro, 69, 72, 81, 349
  guaranteed by oaths to the gods, 226, 229
  Peace of Phoenice
    ended first Macedonian war, 317
Trebia, 11, 80
  battle, 90
Trebius, 138
tria nomina, 46
triarii, 358
  at Zama, 219
  third line of Roman infantry, 211
Tribes, 14, 46
tribunes
  military, 14, 106, 109
    Cato at Thermopylae, 322
  of the people or plebs, 14, 113
  Polybius book 6 on, 173
tripudium
  sacred chickens, Roman, 227
triremes, 11
Triton, 141, 236
triumphs
  booty and, 247
  by Scipio family in first Punic war, 53
  conventions for award of, 246
  denied to Scipio in 206, 135, 177

derivation of word, 246
disputes about, 180, 257, 386, 431
Etruscan origin?, 246
explained, 14
few in second Punic war, 245
for Metaurus victory, 193
Hannibal avoids being led in one, 247, 369
hunger for, 403
joint, between Nero and Salinator, 201
no Carthaginian parallel, 230, 245
of Aemilianus, 415
of Cato, 386
of Flamininus, 247
of Labeo, 371
of Manius Pomponius, 81
of Salinator, Ennius on, 193, 205
of Scipio (201), 135, 245–8
of Scipio Nasica, 258
on the fasti, 176
what they looked like, 247
Troy, 96
  Capys as Trojan, 139
  Hegesianax and, 305
  Hercules' sack of, 234
  Romans self-identified as Trojans, 292
truces
  indutiae, 210
  Scipio violates, 210
Tunis
  Scipio seizes, 212
Turdetanians, 129
*turris.* See castle
*tyche.* See fortune
type-scenes, 42
Tyre, 12, 26, 49, 60, 291
  Athenian proxeny decree for Tyrians, 288
  Carthaginian sacred envoys at (332), 300
  Hannibal pretends to be on mission to, 300
  home city of Ariston, 310
  Seleucid when Hannibal arrives at, 301
Tyrtaeus
  read by Hannibal?, 281
Tzetzes
  Chiliades
    inaccuracies, 377, 383

Umbria, 97, 187
underworld, 43
*uolones.* See volunteers
uota
  ambiguous between vows and prayers, 199
Utica, 142
  Scipio besieges, 212

Vaccaei, 79

Valerius Antias, 13, 56
  on beheading by Lucius Flamininus, 191
  on trials of Scipios, 387
Valerius Flaccus, Lucius (cos. 195, censor 184)
  appointed princeps senatus by self and Cato as censors, 252
Valerius Flaccus, Publius
  intercepts Hannibal's treaty with Philip V, 141
Valerius Laevinus, Marcus (cos. 210)
  succeeds Marcellus in Sicily, 148
Valerius Maximus, 30
  on Nero's triumph, 202
  on visit to Scipio of admiring brigands, 394
Varro (scholar), 60, 402
  on etymology of 'triumph', 246
Vegetius, 30, 39, 342
  ascribes eventual Roman success in second Punic war to training, 350
  on causes of Roman initial failures against Hannibal, 348
  on elephants at Zama?, 219
  on military training, 122
  on Sosylus as Hannibal's teacher, 281
Velleius Paterculus
  comparison between Hannibal and Pontius Telesinus, 413
Venus
  Erycina, 67, 96, 200
    Roman adoption of cult, 290
  protector of Pompey and Caesar, 222
Venusia, 153
  colony at, 249
Vestals, 231
veterans
  Scipio's from African campaign
    given land in Apulia and Samnium, 249
veto
  tribunician
    used by Gracchus to protect Lucius Scipio, 389
via Aemilia, 189
via Flaminia, 189
Vibo Valentia
  name conveys strength and valour, 295
Villius Tappulus, Publius (cos. 199), 314, 327
  on diplomatic mission to Asia Minor (194–193), 260
  tries to turn Antiochus against Hannibal, 315
Villius, Lucius, 113
Vindelici, 194
Vipsanius Agrippa, Marcus, 245
Virgil
  Aeneid, 42
  conversation in *Aeneid* 6 between Aeneas and Anchises, 235

hints at Hannibal without naming him, 412
ignores Metaurus, 195
makes Dido foresee Hannibal, 76, 412
on Barce (nurse), 76, 412
on Carthage as 'Bursa', 377
on Dido, 51
on Jupiter's nod, 258
on libations by Anchises and Aeneas, 224
on Priam's decapitation, 191
on Scipiadae, 48, 422
on Turnus, 150
Viriathus, 132
volunteers, 209
vows
  always bring favourable outcomes to battles, 199
  Hannibal's to Melqart, 85, 226
  not attested before defeats, 199
  temple to Iuventas vowed by Salinator, 192
  vows by commanders before or during battles, 197–201

warships. *See* quinqueremes
weaponry
  as branch of logistics, 356
weapons
  Hannibal's men recycle captured, 356
  manufacture of, 122
    by Scipio at New Carthage, 350
wigs
  Hannibal's, 27, 91, 188, 339, 344
witness
  Metaurus as, 203, 212
women
  at Sparta, 164
  Busa as benefactor, 104
  priests at Carthage, 231
  role at Locri, 164
  Scyles' Greek mother, 297
  tragic story of Theoxena, 298
women, naming of, 41
wonder
  as Homeric notion, 123
Wooden Horse
  as ambush, 359
wounds
  Hannibal 'never wounded', 339
  Scipio
    how often wounded?, 341

Xenophanes
  ambassador of Philip V, 141
Xenophon, 9, 342, 344
  compared to Marcius Septimius, 116

Xenophon (cont.)
   Greek of easy enough for Hannibal?, 280
   his Ten Thousand anticipate Roman
      manipular army, 350
   on Agesilaus, 9
   on decapitation of Cyrus the Younger, 191
   on 'laconic' Spartan message, 156
   on 'workshop of war'
      quoted by Polybius, 350
Xerxes (Persian king), 37, 322
Xerxes king of Armenia, 353

Zacynthus, 81
Zama, 2, 358
   battle, 218–20
   casualties at, 220
   name not used before Nepos, 15, 194, 218
   numbers at, 218
   terms offered after, 220
   topography, 218
Zeus, 141
   Ammon
      Hannibal consults?, 316

For EU product safety concerns, contact us at Calle de José Abascal, 56–1°, 28003 Madrid, Spain or eugpsr@cambridge.org.

www.ingramcontent.com/pod-product-compliance
Lightning Source LLC
LaVergne TN
LVHW011007250326
834688LV00004B/122